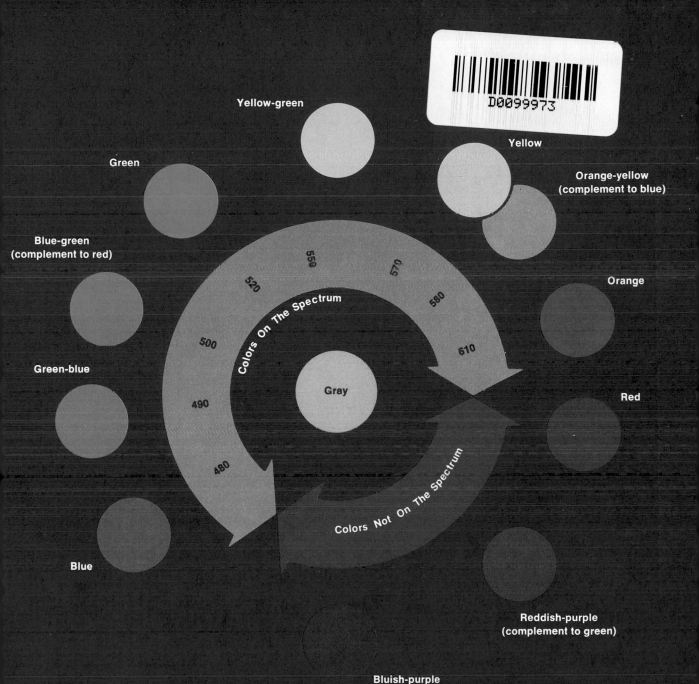

Yellow-green

Green

Yellow

**Orange-yellow
(complement to blue)**

**Blue-green
(complement to red)**

Orange

Colors On The Spectrum

559

570

520

580

500

610

Green-blue

490

Gray

Red

480

Colors Not On The Spectrum

Blue

**Reddish-purple
(complement to green)**

Bluish-purple

A color circle   This illustration depicts various hues placed in order around a color circle. Complementary colors appear on the circle opposite each other and, if mixed in the proper proportions, will yield the neutral gray at the center. Wave lengths of the spectral colors are noted around the circle in nanometers. The nonspectral colors of reds, purples, and violets are inserted in their proper order so as to be opposite their complements, for example, reddish purple lies opposite green.

BEGINNING PSYCHOLOGY

THE DORSEY SERIES IN PSYCHOLOGY
Consulting Editor
GERALD C. DAVISON
*State University of New York
at Stony Brook*

Beginning psychology

revised edition

Perry London

Professor of Psychology and Psychiatry
University of Southern California, Los Angeles
Lecturer in Psychiatry
Harvard University

1978

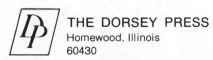

THE DORSEY PRESS
Homewood, Illinois
60430

Irwin-Dorsey Limited
Georgetown, Ontario
L7G 4B3

© THE DORSEY PRESS, 1975 and 1978

ISBN 0-256-02057-4
Library of Congress Catalog Card No. 77–085776
Printed in the United States of America
1 2 3 4 5 6 7 8 9 0 K 5 4 3 2 1 0 9 8

Credits for fine art and photographs are listed at the
end of this book.

I have always been
deeply involved with women.
This book is dedicated, with love,
to five of them with whom
I have been joined the longest
and most romantically:
Hamzee,
Mivie,
Ig,
Irz,
Debby.

Preface

Some things, like violins, people, and textbooks, improve with exercise and perish from disuse. The uses to which thousands of people have put this book, accordingly, and the feedback given me about the first edition, have improved it very much. Like a much played violin, it sounds better than it did, its words more resonant, sharper, and more clearly spoken. Like a person, learning from experience, it knows more than it did, has more information, is more up to date. Its goals have not changed, nor its means of reaching them but, in this edition, they are sought more knowledgeably (if not pedantically) than before —the book is a little longer than it was, and the bibliography a lot longer. The whimsy level is the same as in the first edition, the confidence in its conclusions a little less, though not yet overwhelming in humility. As before, here are some things I have tried to do in it:

To introduce psychology inspirationally, so students will want to learn more of it.

To clarify, on opening, how science is epistemology, and what that means for research method and statistical analysis.

To show psychology as part of evolution, in which humanity fulfills its animal heritage and transcends it without abandoning it.

To make basic areas, like learning and sensation, seem as important as they are.

To speak to students' grave personal concerns—with two long chapters on things like love and work, and one on psychology's role in civilization.

I have tried to do all this in clear, sharp language, especially to state some of psychology's fancy theories in plain words without sacrificing too much precision or detail. Many friends, relatives, and colleagues tried to help, and the hundreds of errors in facts, concepts, and statements which you do *not* find in the book are gone largely by their good offices. The ones that remain are mine.

For the first edition, helpful professional

critiques were graciously given by William Crano, Michigan State University; Anita Fisher, College of San Mateo; Howard Hunt, Columbia University; Marc Marcus, Skyline College; George T. Martin, Jr., Mount San Antonio College; Allen Parducci, University of California, Los Angeles; Stuart Taylor, Kent State University; David Rosenhan, Stanford University; and Leslie M. Cooper, University of Utah. Lois and Arnold Peyser, the late Leonard Freeman and Rose Freeman, Russell and Jo Stoneham, Thomas H. Davies, Miriam Dena London, Judith Gail London, and Sheila E. Lammas, gave valuable comments on Chapters 16 and 17 in particular. Vivian London, sometimes assisted by Susan Eden London, selected most of the illustrations. Avraham Avihai, then acting associate dean of the College for Overseas Study of the Hebrew University of Jerusalem, arranged for me to teach the introductory course based on an early draft of this book in 1971–72 to a brilliant collection of students from some three dozen different American universities.

In preparing the second edition, I received invaluable reviews and feedback on student responses from Richard Klene, Thomas Hardaway, Ronald Siry, Purcell Taylor, and G. J. Zieleniewski, all of University College, University of Cincinnati, and Sidney Birnback, Robert E. Fleer, Anne S. Maganzini, and Robert Pellack, all of Bergen Community College. Lawrence Messe', Michigan State University, Gerald Davison, New York State University at Stonybrook, Robert Hogan, Johns Hopkins University, George T. Martin, Mt. San Antonio College, and Daniel Hawthorne and Lynden Nelson, both of California State Polytechnic University, San Luis Obispo, rendered detailed critiques of the entire manuscript. Felice Gordis, California State University at Fullerton, Hiram Fitzgerald, Michigan State University, and Barbara Newman and Philip Newman, criticized new Chapter 13, Developmental Psychology. Linda Sherman, University of Oregon, helped prepare Chapter 13. Carole de Pould, University of Southern California, helped research Chapter 16. Geoffrey T. Fong, Stanford University, helped prepare Chapters 20, 21, and 22. Wayne F. Peate, Dartmouth University Medical School, helped prepare Chapter 18. Ralph Kolstoe, University of North Dakota, helped by critiquing drafts of the statistical appendix. Miriam Dena London, Yale University, found and checked sources, found and removed errors, and helped prepare new material for the entire manuscript. Holly Harrington selected the illustrations for this edition. Joanna Ross, University of Southern California, critiqued parts of the manuscript, in addition to preparing supplements to the text. Sheila Lammas edited parts, in addition to typing it. Debra London gave valuable clerical assistance and moral support.

To all the people above, and many more unnamed here, I am deeply grateful.

January 1978   PERRY LONDON

To the student

This book is an introduction to psychology, not an encyclopedia of it. It is full of facts, but they are meant to tell you what psychology is about, not to make you an expert in any of its branches. That is not its purpose.

These are its purposes: First, to *interest* you in psychology, perhaps enough so you will study it more, maybe enough to make you think of a career in psychology or some field related to it. Second, its purpose is to help you see how human beings are all alike, and how they differ, so that you will grow in understanding of the human condition, in compassion for people, and in commitment to the brotherhood of mankind. Third, the book intends to help you grow in understanding of yourself, to help you be more sensitive to your private inner world, and to make you wiser in negotiating with the thoughts and impulses and feelings that whirl around the windmills of your mind.

All these goals are difficult to meet. We have tried to meet them by making the book clear and sharp, wasting no words, and trying to capture your attention, tease your curiosity, engage your intellect, and now and then arouse your feelings.

The book was written carefully, with love and, sometimes, pain. It is meant to be read carefully, and with joy. The pain and love may get to you if the book does. The care is something you must bring along.

January 1978   PERRY LONDON

GRAMMATICAL NOTE

Some conventions of English grammar do not yet acknowledge women's equality with men — such as the practice of using masculine singular pronouns for neuter meanings ("A person should watch *his* grammar"). I wanted to change this without always resorting to second person or third person plural or clumsy singular constructions ("You should watch *your* grammar"; "people should watch *their* grammar"; "one should watch *his* or *her* grammar"). So I persuaded the Dorsey Press to let me use "their" as both singular and plural, the way it is often used colloquially ("A person should watch *their* grammar"). I am sorry if this offends grammatical purists, but I think this aspect of the language needs changing badly enough to risk their displeasure. Whether or not you think it a mistake, in any case, know that it is not an accident.

P.L.

Contents

BEGINNING PSYCHOLOGY

The business of psychology

1

1

The business of psychology

Everyone is interested in psychology because everyone is interested in themselves. You do not need to know much about the subject to know that much of it applies to you personally. You are not alone. Psychology is the most popular course in American colleges and universities (some other countries, too) and becoming more popular. Some people study it with casual curiosity about themselves and the working of their minds, others with burning interest in solving their problems. I began reading about it while in high school, hoping to find answers to my concerns about sex, popularity, self-control, hypnosis, and whether my head was really a mess or not—then found it so interesting that I decided to become a psychologist, not quite sure what psychology was and not knowing that studying it would not answer all my personal questions. I am glad I did, and maybe you will be too, though it will not answer all of your questions either.

This chapter will discuss what psychology is about, where it came from, how it became a business of its own (actually many of them), and how its elegant and complicated scientific work is conducted. This chapter is background for the rest of the book, which will introduce you to the main topics of professional and scientific psychology.

Definitions: Literal and scientific

The term "psychology" comes from two Greek words: "psyche," which means soul, mind, or spirit; and "logos," meaning study or discuss. Basically, "psychology" means "study of the mind," just like you thought it did. But that definition is not very precise. For one thing, the term *mind,* on close examination, is pretty vague. For another, even when you use the term *mind* more or less precisely, it turns out that psychology studies a lot more than the mind—it studies mental, physical, and emotional aspects of life.

There used to be a lot of argument about the

Psyche—beloved of Cupid in Greek mythology—whose name, Greek for "mind" or "soul," is the root of "psychology."

Psyche, Prud'hon

definition. Some scholars said that psychology should be considered "the science of mental life," with the study of mental functions as its main object. Others, called behaviorists, said that since there was no such thing physically as a mind, which could be identified, dissected, or studied, but there was such a thing as **behavior** which you could observe, measure, and record, it should be called "the science of behavior." They won, and that is how most people define psychology today.

If you take definitions very seriously, however, this one may also be troubling because the term "behavior" is not unique to psychology.

Astronomers study the behavior of stars, chemists and physicists, the behavior of atoms and molecules, and so forth. Psychology could be called "the science of *human* behavior," but sociology and anthropology also could be; besides, psychologists study animal as well as human behavior. Some scholars, accordingly, call psychology the science of "the behavior of *organisms,*" but the most widely accepted convention is to call sociology, anthropology, economics, and psychology all "behavioral sciences" (sometimes "social sciences"), and to call psychology in particular "the study of behavior," and not to worry about the fine points involved. If you know what you are talking about specifically when you speak of psychology in general, the definition does not matter much. All sciences work in much the same way, by systematically collecting facts and trying to make sense of them, and as long as you can agree on how to go about it and what the facts are, it is not important to have an exact definition of the science (Kuhn 1962). Until very recently, there was no such agreement within psychology. Early in this century, there was a great tumult about definitions, with many different schools of thought arguing about what psychology was and how it should be studied (Boring 1957). Their differences arose from the different enterprises which converged in the new discipline of psychology.

The multiple parenting of modern psychology Psychology is a 20th century business—before that, almost no one called themselves psychologists or called it a subject. The first college course that included that name was given at Harvard in 1875 (Miller 1962). But the roots of the discipline had long been laid in the *humanities,* and the branches started to grow out of *physics, medicine,* and *education* in the last half of the 19th century (Murphy and Kovach 1972; Lowry 1971).

For 20 centuries or so before that, psychology was always a branch of philosophy. So were biology, physics, and chemistry. But they were parts of *natural* philosophy, while human behavior was not yet seen as part of the natural order of the universe which could be approached and investigated like anything else. To this day, in fact, psychology and the social sciences are parts of the humanities departments of many universities, together with philosophy, literature, and languages, rather than in scientific divisions.

Psychology as a field of formal scientific study grew out of physics. The grandfathers of modern psychology were two famous German physicists, Gustav Fechner (1801–77) and Hermann von Helmholtz (1820–94). They did not get into the psychology business just because they were interested in human behavior, but also because some important problems of physics demanded it. Some properties of physical phenomena such as light and sound could only be measured if you knew something of the human characteristics which enable people to see light or hear sound. As soon as you begin to examine those human traits, you find enormous variations in people's vision and hearing—and some common rules which govern them. So studying the physics of sound led to studying the psychology of hearing. The first laboratory of scientific psychology, therefore, which Wilhelm Wundt (1832–1920), the official father of psychology, founded in 1879, was for the study of *psychophysics,* that is, the psychological properties of physical events (Blumenthal 1975; Boring 1957). Fechner, incidentally, was also a physician, a philosopher, and a mystic: Helmholtz was also a physiologist: and Wundt, in addition to books on medicine, physiology, and psychology, published four books of philosophy (Watson 1963). Clearly, the disciplines were not separate in the minds of the people who practiced them.

For about a generation, psychology was more or less officially identical with psychophysics, but medicine and physiology were also deeply concerned with it. Since the end of the 18th century, some scholars, such as Franz Joseph Gall and Johann Spurzeim, had been trying to understand character by studying the shapes and contours of people's heads (Gall 1800, Sills 1968). Although this particular connection between physiology and behavior (it was called *phrenology*) proved false, it gave rise to more and more sophisticated efforts in the same direction. It also gave rise to a related science, physical anthropology.

More important, discoveries in medicine were proving that some mental disorders were the results of damage to the brain and nervous system caused by alcoholism, syphilis, and some other things.

Edward L. Thorndike

Alfred Binet

Ivan Pavlov

A gallery of some of the progenitors of modern psychology

Psychiatry came into existence as an "official" discipline, meaning textbooks were written on it and courses given in it, in 1845 (Griesinger 1845). At first, it was concerned only with physiological causes of mental disorders. Before the end of the 19th century, however, a growing body of doctors in Europe and the United States realized that it was necessary to study *behavior* itself rather than physiology in order to understand many psychiatric problems. American psychiatrists such as Adolph Meyer saw the role of interpersonal relationships as important sources of emotional disorders (Goldenson 1970), and Sigmund Freud's writing on consciousness, thinking, and imagining, as well as neurosis, were a great influence on this field. From these beginnings came what is now called "the psychology of adjustment."

While this was going on in medicine, *education* was starting to change from a seat-of-the-pants enterprise to a subject of formal study. This change fed the study of psychology in two important ways. First, people began to tackle some *practical* problems of education by developing psychological tests that could be used in the schools. Second, they began to scientifically study *learning.* In 1895, Alfred

Binet and Theophile Simon began to develop a test to distinguish Paris school children who would need special help from those who could get along without it. This work created intelligence testing and psychological testing. At the same time, Edward L. Thorndike, at Columbia University Teachers College was doing ingenious experiments on how learning takes place (1905; 1913). The publication of his early conclusions in 1898 soon led Ivan Pavlov, the Russian Nobel Prize winning physiologist, to his famous learning experiments with dogs and bells, which was later to be called "classical conditioning" (Babkin 1949; Pavlov 1911).[1]

Before the close of the 19th century, psychology was well on its way to being an independent business. In 1890, William James, America's greatest philosopher, published a two-volume text, *Principles of Psychology,* perhaps to this day the best psychology book ever written. (A year earlier, he had had his title at Harvard changed from Professor of Philosophy to Professor of Psychology). Six years later Lightner Witmer founded the first

[1] Pavlov was already famous at the turn of the century and already experimenting on dogs, but his early interest was the physiology of digestion, for which he won the Nobel Prize in 1903.

psycho-educational clinic at the University of Pennsylvania (APA 1947). In 1900, Sigmund Freud launched psychoanalysis with the publication of his greatest work, *The Interpretation of Dreams,* and five years after that Binet and Simon published the first important test of intelligence (Cronbach 1970).

Psychology has always been an international business, as you can see from the names and nationalities of its pioneers. But since late in the last century, it has thrived more in the United States than in any other country. Psychoanalysis was treated largely with indifference and contempt when it first appeared in Europe, for example, but Freud and his major students were invited to lecture at Clark University, one of America's most distinguished psychology departments, only eight years after

The other self. Sigmund Freud contemplates a bust of himself sculpted for his 75th birthday by O. Nemon, center, and presented to him in 1931 in the garden of his village home near Vienna.

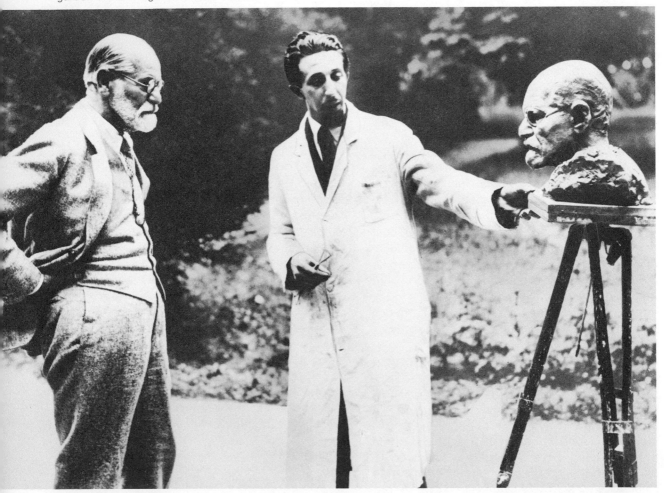

The Interpretation of Dreams was published. Similarly, although the Binet test was a French invention, its translation and revision by Lewis Terman at Stanford University in 1916 became the authoritative version of the test from then on (Terman 1916). Called the Stanford-Binet, its subsequent revisions (Terman and Merrill 1937; 1960) have been retranslated into many other languages, and America since then has been the chief source of psychological tests used almost everywhere. It is also the chief market for tests invented elsewhere, like the Rorschach inkblots, invented by a Swiss psychiatrist, Hermann Rorschach (orig. pub. in 1919). Finally, although Pavlov and his Russian students are famous for the development of classical conditioning (discovered independently by Pavlov, but observed earlier by an American named E. B. Twitmeyer in 1902), and Soviet scientists still are prominent in it, more studies of learning since that time have been produced in American laboratories than anywhere else.

Why has America provided such a favorable climate for the growth of psychology? No one knows for sure. It probably has something to do with the fact that the United States is such a wealthy society that it could afford the apparent luxury of an enterprise which did not make any direct economic contribution. People do not get interested ordinarily in their psychological condition until their basic physical needs are taken care of. Also related to affluence, more Americans have the opportunity for higher education than people in other countries do, and psychology is generally of greater interest to people with advanced education than to those with less. Finally, the American myth, or dream, is that human problems can be solved and human beings improved if we are only inventive enough and industrious enough, something less widely believed in other parts of the world. Since psychology is an enterprise that seeks to *improve* people by changing their behavior, it may be viewed more sympathetically by Americans than by people who do not believe human nature is so changeable to begin with.

Whatever the reasons, Americans have supported psychology more extensively than have any other people, though they have not necessarily been more inventive or ingenious in discovering new facts about human behavior or methods for using them. This probably will continue to be so for years to come because interest in psychology increases all the time in this country. If this is "the American century" (Flanders 1950), as some claim, then perhaps it makes sense—because psychology is certainly the child of this century.

WHAT PSYCHOLOGY IS ABOUT

According to the American Psychological Association, psychology is "a science, an art, and a means of promoting human welfare." In translation, that means that psychology is both a scholarly and an applied discipline. The scholarly and scientific branches aim to understand human behavior; the applied ones try to solve practical people-problems. There are so many different problems that need psychology that, today, psychologists are employed in every branch of government, education, industry, military, and medical institutions.

Topics, titles, and training Applied psychology depends on advances in the scientific branches of the field. So, even if you are mainly interested in application, to understand it well, you need to know something about such academic and scientific areas as the biological basis of behavior, sensation and perception, learning and thinking, motivation and emotion, personality and social psychology, personal adjustment, and behavior disorders.

These topics are studied in different subdisciplines or areas of specialization. You may have noticed how people will call themselves "experimental," "clinical," "social," or other kinds of psychologists. There are so many different specialty areas that the American Psychological Association is divided into more than 30 professional interest groups, and one or two new ones are hatched every year or so. But every area can be grouped, more or less, as either *academic* or *applied* depending on whether it has immediate practical uses.

The common academic divisions of psychology are: *experimental, social,* and *developmental.* Experimental psychology takes in both the biological and psychological foundations of behavior. The biological foundations include: *behavior genetics,* that is, the effects of heredity on behavior; *physiological psychology,* the effects of the body on behavior; and *comparative psychology,* which studies animal behavior.

Psychological foundations of behavior include the study of *sensation,* how our senses work; *perception,* how we interpret sensory information; *motivation,* how we are aroused to satisfy our needs; and *learning.* Learning has been so much the most studied branch of scientific psychology to date, that the study of *conditioning,* its most elementary forms, *memory, skills,* and *complex learning* such as language all have become separate subdisciplines. Much of the research on learning has been done on animals, partly because they are interesting, but also because you can do things with them that you would not think of doing with humans.

Social psychology and *developmental psychology* are also branches of scientific psychology. They are mostly but not entirely concerned with human behavior rather than with animals, and with learned behavior rather than its biological basis. *Social psychology* studies how people *interact* with each other, especially the *effects of groups* and *individuals* on each other, and how *attitudes and opinions* are formed and modified. *Personality* is the study of how we acquire, maintain, and change our enduring behavior traits. *Developmental psy-*chology studies the processes of growth, development, and change as they occur through the entire life cycle, from conception to death.

The main applied branches of psychology are: *clinical and counseling* psychology, *school* psychology, *personnel and guidance* psychology, and *industrial and organizational* psychology. *Clinical and counseling psychology* are concerned mainly with helping people handle personal problems and behavior disorders. These may range from mild adjustment problems to incapacitating disorders requiring hospitalization. *Personnel and guidance psychology* deals mainly with problems of vocational choice, aptitudes, and interests. *School psychology* combines all these methods in the setting of schools. *Industrial psychology* deals with some personnel and guidance problems, but it is also concerned with job efficiency, with worker morale and productivity, with the relations between people in work settings, and with the ways people behave in large organizations.

Some newer branches of applied psychology are becoming important, such as *community psychology,* the attempt to apply psychology to social problems; and *engineering psychology* or *human factors,* which improves the design and operation of machinery so its use by human beings is safer and more efficient. Other more recent applications are *consumer psychology* (Jacoby 1975) and *environmental psychology* (Proshansky, Ittelson, and Rivlin, 1976). As knowledge expands in future years, more areas of application will develop.

After going through all the titles and topics, you may still be hungry for an exact statement of what psychology is about and what a psychologist does, and you may still be asking, "is there anything unique about the field or about its workers that make it or them unmistakable?" The answer to both questions is "no." All the biological and behavioral sciences are too advanced, in this day and age, for there to be anything absolutely *unique* about any of them. What distinguishes them from each other is differences in focus, or emphasis, rather than rigid boundaries of subject matter. Psychology differs from the rest of biology in its concern with behavior rather than with the structures and functions of the body; it differs from other social sciences by its emphasis on individual behavior and how it is learned, motivated, and changed, rather than on the behavior of groups or the influence of cultural and economic conditions on behavior. But lots of psychologists specialize in the biological aspects of behavior and lots in the social aspects, and plenty of physiologists and sociologists in turn study the behavioral aspects of biological and social phenomena. The value of their work has nothing to do with how they classify it. Psychology is a "behavior" science with one foot in biology and the other in social science.

There is also nothing completely unique about what psychologists do, but typically they are more trained than many other professionals in research methods and in the construction and use of tests, and usually they have studied more than most about learning, motivation, perception, and some of the other topics listed

Healing—clinical treatment individually and in groups—is only one of a great variety of jobs psychologists perform.

Christ Healing the Sick, Rembrandt van Rijn

earlier. Some specialists in psychology, such as clinical psychologists, must be licensed or certified by the state to practice or call themselves clinical psychologists, but most other kinds of specialists need no special permission to do their work, just jobs. There have been plenty of them. In 1974, only 1.1 percent of psychologists were unemployed, and annual salaries averaged over $26,000 (U.S. Bureau of the Census 1976). A great variety of work is available to psychologists, and many students are attracted to this profession because of it. Almost 25 percent of psychologists are teachers, about the same percentage make their main livings in clinical or counseling practice, and about 16 percent are engaged in full-time research (APA 1968).

The size of the profession has been growing steadily also throughout the 20th century, as indicated by membership in the American Psychological Association, which was founded in 1892. From 1925 through 1976, for instance, its membership rose from less than 1,000 to almost 45,000 (McKinney 1976). In fact, Fillmore Sanford, who was then Executive Secretary of the APA, testified before a subcommittee of the U.S. Congress in 1955:

> "If the present rate of growth continues we will have, by simple arithmetic, 60 million members a hundred years from now; and in 200 years, if we continue to grow, membership in the Association will coincide exactly with membership in the human race (1955, p. 221)."

If you are interested in making a career of psychology, you had better plan on going to graduate school, regardless of which specialty interests you most. Almost no one gets a job as a psychologist anymore with only a bachelor's degree. For most jobs, a master's degree in psychology or a closely related field, such as education, is a minimum requirement. And for most *good* jobs, a doctor's degree (Ph.D. or Ed.D or Psy.D.) is increasingly required (Peterson 1976). In 1975, 2,749 doctorates were conferred in psychology, almost a third of them to women (U.S. Bureau of the Census 1976). Getting one usually takes three or four years of full-time graduate education (Boneau *et al.* 1970). At the end of that time, you still won't be worth much as a psychologist—because you only get expert at a craft by doing it, not by studying it—but you will know an awful lot about the endless complexities, snares, and delusions that make it hard to get dependable facts about human behavior and to find dependable ways of improving it. And your education in those things has to begin now because the complexities start to snare you at the very beginning of studying psychology.

SCIENTIFIC METHOD: EPISTEMOLOGY, EMPIRICISM, AND LOGIC

All methods of getting knowledge are pretty much the same, and so are all the problems of how to be sure that what you think you know about anything is really so. Some subjects present special problems of inquiry, however, either because they are complicated or because the things you want to know about them are obscure and hard to uncover. In psychology, both problems apply. The subject matter is very complex and the things you want to study are hard to observe because the instruments for observing them are often inefficient and the people making the observations are often inaccurate.

Lines, curves, and pretzels: The complexity of psychological events

Psychology is a complex subject because in order to see why people behave as they do, you need to know a lot about many different aspects of them—physical characteristics, personal history, and about the situation in which the action occurs. And each of these aspects in turn may involve many more things.

Physical characteristics can include both visible things, like size, age, and skin color, and internal physiological events, like the emotional arousal the person is feeling, or their state of alertness, or digestion. The personal history in question can go way back to their relationships with parents and siblings, or their history of successes and failures in school, or at work, or in love life or imagination, or all these things and more. And the context in which a person is acting may have one or two or ten relevant elements, ranging from the behavior of the other people involved to the effect of the weather on mood. All of these may be important, and all of them are *variable* from person to person and from situation to situation. The first factor, therefore, that makes psychology a difficult and complex study is that it deals with many, many *variables.*

The second thing that complicates psychology is that the variables are not all equally visible and observable, and they do not all contribute equally to the behavior they affect. This means that they are sometimes hard *to identify* or isolate in the first place and then hard *to measure* or evaluate in the second place. For scientific purposes, these amount to a single problem, that of how to observe, measure, and record—because you can only be sure you have identified or isolated a fact when you have some means of observing and recording it. Until then, its existence is only a *hypothesis,* that is, an educated guess. It is especially hard to turn hypotheses from guesses into facts in psychology because it has few dependable instruments for measuring its many complex variables.

Measurement error In principle, the problem of measurement and evaluation is the same in all the sciences. In fact, psychology and the social sciences have a harder time of it than do physics, chemistry, and biology because most of the instruments they use are not very efficient and the people using them are all too human, meaning that they are prone to error. These things combine to make psychology the victim of endless **errors of measurement.**

The instruments for measuring the physical universe are **scales, rulers,** and **clocks,** because the events of the physical world can be understood pretty thoroughly in terms of such variables as mass, volume, distance, and time. Even the most elegant variations of the basic instruments are devices for quantifying the measurement of these variables; they are all, finally, fancy scales, or rulers, or clocks, or combinations of them.

Some branches of psychology also use scales, rulers, and clocks for measuring and indeed, these are the very branches that began

We measure the physical world with hardware.

Daylight Saving Time, Pierre Roy

scientific psychology. The psychophysics of sensation, or of reaction time could be studied with such equipment, and though the variability of human beings might make you distrust their observations, at least the instruments themselves could be relied upon. The most interesting problems of psychology could not be explored this way, however, and William James, protesting against the sterility of 19th century scientific psychology, as he saw it, and the trivial-seeming problems it attacked, contemptuously called this stuff "brass instrument" psychology.

The hardware of physics will not help you learn much about the inner working of people's minds, it is true. But what kind of instrument *do* you use to measure what a person is feeling? Or how strongly someone is feeling it? We use figures of speech all the time to the effect that

such measures are possible, but how do you really "weigh an opinion," "evaluate an attitude," or "measure a sentiment?"

When you look at it logically, there are only a few ways to do it:

1. You can ask people about their own feelings.
2. You can ask other people about them.
3. You can watch the way they act and draw your own conclusions about how they feel.

As soon as you start doing any of these things, however, you run into trouble. You find that some people are rotten judges of anyone else, and most people are variable in how trustworthy and how accurate their judgements are from one time and place to another. And if you are a very sensitive observer, you may notice that your own judgements are not always so hot either! They vary with your mood, your interest,

Who is that fellow with William James?

14

your alertness, and your emotional involvement in the thing you are judging.

The best clock in the world will not do you much good, of course, if you don't know how to tell time. And even if you do know how, you may not be able to tell it accurately enough for some purposes. The more precisely you need to know the time, the more cautious you have to be about whom you ask for it and whether or not you believe them. People differ enormously in their powers of observation and in their memories of what they have seen—and the more exact they need to be, the more gross even small differences between them will appear.

As far as the value of the information goes, it makes no difference whether the **source of the error** in a measurement comes from the changeability of the people you are observing, or from the **bias** which distorts the observer's judgement—the information is still **unreliable.** You cannot depend upon the results of your observation, and therefore, to use the technical term, you cannot be sure how **significant** your findings are. And unless you can find a way to do so, they are useless. All scientific knowledge, theoretical or applied, depends on the dependability of information, so the first aim of all scientific methods is acquiring dependable information. This problem is not limited to science, but concerns the whole nature of knowledge and how it is obtained, called **epistemology.** The goal of science is the understanding of physical reality, and the methods of science are "sophisticated common sense" ways of getting it. Scientific method consists of several ways for gathering facts, called the **empirical** method, and some logical rules for evaluating their dependability, called **statistical analysis.**

Epistemology: How do you know?

You know perfectly well how you know anything—through your head, that is, your consciousness. And you know how knowledge of the outside world gets into your head—through your senses. Whether it comes to your senses directly, by your own observation, or vicariously, by your reading, hearing, or seeing pictures of what someone else observed, doesn't make any difference. You are still getting the knowledge through your senses. It is all quite subjective.

You may think that there is such a thing as objective knowledge, but there is not. There may be objective events, or facts, but there is no objective way to know about them. All you can ever know about anything is what your own head tells you, however disappointing that may be.[2]

Fortunately, your own head tells you a number of things about the world which is identical with what other people's heads tell them; so it is possible to get your views of reality substantiated by other people. All of you may be wrong, of course, but you all are made to feel more comfortable anyhow, and more convinced that your "knowledge" is objectively accurate, by the fact that you agree. This agreement is called "consensus," and the process of arriving at it is called "consensual validation."

Consensual validation is the main means by which people can compare their private perceptions of reality and use the results of the comparison as a basis for action. Our private perceptions may, of course, be contrary to the facts—the experience of anyone looking across the Great Plains, for instance, must tell them that the world is flat—and when that is the case, consensual validation will lead us to a false knowledge and erroneous action. It was probably a great comfort to folks who stayed home and laughed at Columbus or chopped wood for burning witches at the stake that everyone around agreed with them. Even so, trying to validate our perceptions from other people serves the valuable purpose of conserving our energies and forcing us to evaluate and check our ideas before we act them out foolishly or self-destructively. Objective reality is not really subject to consensus, by any means, as you

---

[2] You may think this proposition is crazy, or wrong, instead of merely disappointing. If so, you are mistaken.

must realize if you think about all the nonsense that people agree on—but purely personal impressions of reality, like dreams and delusions, are even more likely than consensual ones to be false. It is much easier, for instance, to get people to agree with you that this paragraph is difficult, boring, and unintelligible—even if you are wrong—than to get them to confirm your belief that studying it will turn your brain to jelly—even if you are right. The virtue of consensual validation is that it disposes you towards **conservative** errors. It is thus **economical** or **parsimonious.** Conservatism, economy, and parsimony are the essence of scientific method.

Since almost every manufactured object in the world is new, invented only in this century and as a direct result of science, it may seem strange to hear that scientific method is conservative. But it is. The aim of science is to **increase knowledge,** but the method by which it works is designed **to reduce error.** To that end, scientific method deals only with things that are subject to consensual validation and handles them only in ways which serve to maximize consensus. Science deals only with facts and the relationships between them. A fact, for scientific purposes, is any event, idea, or experience that can be defined in ways that anyone can understand and agree to. It doesn't matter if they *do* agree, only that they *can.* You don't need to run a referundum, just to define your terms in ways that permit other people to examine, discuss, and manipulate events exactly as you do, so that they may confirm or invalidate your statements about them from their own experience. *Publicity* and *replicability*—saying what you mean so that other people can see for themselves whether what you say is so, is the sum total of what scientists call "the empirical method."

Empiricism: Trying things out

When we say that something is "sensible," or that it "makes sense," we usually mean that

Consensual validation can lead us down a wrong street. Galileo flew in the face of what *everybody* "knew" was true: he insisted the earth revolved around the sun, not the reverse.

it is *plausible,* or *believable,* not that it is necessarily *factual.* Saying that something is "common sense" means that people can easily agree to its plausibility. The empirical method of science deals with *literally* sensible things, that is, with information that is available to the senses (and therefore subject to con**sensual** validation), and studies it to discover and prove the true facts about it. "Empirical" means practical or experimental, which means "trying things out." "Discover" means "reveal." "Prove" means test.[3]

There are two ways to get such sensible information. The first is to go out and look for it in its natural habitat, called the **observation,** or *field,* or *survey* method. The second is to try to bring the information home to you, so that you can study it under more comfortable or

_____
[3] Now maybe you see why "the exception proves the rule."

more exact conditions; this is called the *experimental* method.

In *field observations,* researchers have no direct control over the variables that interest them. They observe and measure behavior in a natural setting without arranging the situation to their own design. In social psychology or anthropology, for instance, where such field studies are very common, they may actually be hidden from the people under observation. The mapping of social relationships in factories, offices, or behind the bushes in the park are examples of field studies. This kind of research is known as the *ethological method* because ethology is "the naturalistic study of whole patterns of animal behavior" (Wilson 1975). We usually think of observation as peculiar to the social sciences rather than to the physical sciences, but astronomy depends almost entirely on observational methods.

A number of different observational methods are used in psychology and the social sciences, and some of the most sophisticated research in these disciplines is done with such devices as questionnaires, interviews, rating scales, and personality tests, which you will hear more about later (Chapter 12). Opinion polls such as Gallup, and TV program ratings, all work by similar methods. The essence of them is that they try to observe the facts without changing them.

There are two things wrong with the field approach (over and above what we said earlier about measurement error, which applies to all approaches). First, it is very hard to know whether the observations you are making in one

The science of astronomy used mainly observational methods.

Nikolaus Copernicus

field situation are applicable to others. Second, it is sometimes impossible to observe the field without interfering in it.

If you cannot be certain that the field situation you are studying is *representative* of all the conditions in which the behavior that interests you occurs, then you cannot draw very general conclusions from your observation. And if you cannot observe the field without interfering with it, then you cannot be sure that the things you watched represent what actually happens in the natural order of things. Suppose, for instance, you were investigating social behavior from behind the bushes in the park and one of the subjects of your study saw you—or even your camera! These problems are so troublesome to scientists that they try to avoid them, whenever possible, by substituting *deliberate* interference for *accidental* interference, and by rigidly *controlling* almost everything that happens instead of permitting nature to run its habitual course. This effort constitutes the experimental method.

An *experiment,* technically, is an attempt to find out precisely what is going on in nature by controlling everything surrounding the one thing you want to observe; then you can understand how it operates. The ideal experiment is often a series of separate experiments in which you control different aspects of the situation one at a time, so you can see which one has the greatest influence on it. The things that you control are called *independent variables;* the thing you are trying to learn about is called the *dependent variable.*[4]

The purpose of having a *laboratory* is to be able to create a controlled environment in which you can manipulate conditions any way you please, introducing this or that variable in one situation and removing it in another, as you will. The laboratory is an artificial environment, so

to speak, that gives you maximum control over the variables that interest you.

The essence of the experimental method is the manipulation, however, not the setting. In *field experimentation,* researchers also manipulate situations, but in the *natural* environment itself, not in the laboratory, so they can get a better idea of how it operates in real life. If they want to study panic, for example, they may try yelling "Fire!" in a crowded theater, and then observe what happens. The control of variables in the field is more difficult than in a laboratory, of course, but the field has the advantage of being more natural.

Experimentation, as you know, is the method of investigation par excellence in physics and chemistry, and is responsible for the great advances of those sciences over the past several centuries. In the history of every science, however, observation must precede experimentation because you can't start controlling the different variables in a situation until you have some idea of what they are and how they may work. You get that idea, or *hypothesis,* from careful observation.

Sampling error Even if you know what you want to study, it is not so easy to be careful enough, because any specific observation, you recall, may misrepresent the field you want to learn about. The problem of what details to observe, which is called *sampling,* is the same in all empirical research, whether field studies or experiments. The bloopers that result from doing it badly are called *sampling errors.*

One way to make sure that the sampling error is small, so that your observations will lead to correct conclusions about the general thing you are studying, is to make the sample random. It also helps make the sampling error small to make the sample big. L. L. Thurstone, one of the pioneer students of psychological measurement, used to quip: "All Indians walk single file—at least the one I saw did." The smaller the sample from which you draw conclusions, the more likely the conclusions will be wrong.

---

[4] There are good reasons for this somewhat puzzling terminology, but they are not important here. The reason you need to know the terms is that they are very widely used in experimental reports. You will run into them often.

Suppose, for instance, you wanted to study the romantic impact of popular singers on pre-teen girls, a well-known phenomenon, at least since Frank Sinatra became famous in World War II. From casual observation, you notice some girls drool, scream, faint, writhe, convulse, and stop chewing gum while a crooner is singing. So you decide to systematize your observations, draw general scientific conclusions, and write a learned paper on the subject. Now, whom do you observe? If you watch only one girl frothing over one crooner, it's like the Indian walking single file. If you watch a whole bunch of girls, thus increasing the sample size, your conclusion has a *far better chance* of being right, and you can reach it with a much *higher level of confidence* (note that cautious language—it is important). Even so, you will not know whether the girls are collapsing only over this particular singer or whether they would do the same for another one. You could be more certain if you observed two groups of girls with two different crooners. And you would be more certain still if you could switch girls and crooners around and watch the same effect occur.

At the last step, where you switch girls and singers, you have turned your research from a field observation, where you just watch what is going on, into an experiment, where you manipulate and control it. One of the chief advantages of experiments over field surveys is that they try to make *comparisons* between groups instead of simply observing them. There is one further kind of comparison we might logically make in this experiment (note that it really is a bunch of experiments). We might still ask whether the girls would swoon only to crooners —perhaps junior high school girls are so constructed that they will swoon over anything that sings, or talks, or bats its eyelashes. To test it, we might add another group of girls and have them listen to me sing or watch my Uncle Louis bat his eyelashes. Again, if we could switch the groups of girls around so that each group

would be exposed to both the singers, and to my singing, and to Uncle Louis, we might be able to draw some very clear conclusions indeed. The groups that attend to me and Uncle Louis are called **control groups,** and the groups that listen to the singers are called **experimental groups.**[5] They are both **comparison groups.**

All of this is common sense. All good empirical research is. But complications sometimes occur which cannot be unraveled with **unaided** common sense, though they must finally be understood in commonsensical terms anyway. When that happens, the tool we use to help unravel them is called *statistics.*

Statistics: Fine descriptions and fancy guesswork

What comes now is still common sense, so hold on.

When we go tally up the results of our crooner-swooner experiment, it turns out that the hypothesis was correct—teenage girls do swoon when crooned at, by and large. But not every one of them acted in exactly the same way: nine out of ten swooned to one crooner, eight out of ten did to the other, none of them swooned to my singing, and one of them barfed when Uncle Louis did his eyelash thing. What do we do with these *data?*[6] How can we interpret these results and express meaningful conclusions drawn from them? It is clear that the hypothesis is correct, but not entirely correct. How can we communicate that?

We may wish to summarize our results in a purely verbal way, as I have done above, by saying that the hypothesis is correct *by and*

---

[5] As with independent and dependent variables, the terminology exists for a good reason, but it is unimportant here. You need to recognize it but not to understand any more than I just told you.

[6] "Data" means the information gathered in empirical research. It is a plural form only. Most people, including professors, use it incorrectly as a singular. You may show off with this datum.

Figure 1.1 One kind of statistical chart.

Source: *The Wall Street Journal,* published June 24, 1974

large. But such a statement offers little help to someone who wants to repeat the experiment and see if they can *replicate* the result themself —it does not tell them exactly what to expect because there is no way for them to know how large a "by and large" is. The easiest way to express the result exactly is with some kind of **numerical** statement: "85 percent of all girls listening to crooners swooned, and none of those listening to noncrooners did" or "an average of 8.5 girls out of ten swooned to crooners, while none did to other performers."

Descriptive statistics Any such numerical statement is a **statistical description** of the results. And any numerical method of summarizing information, like **percentages, averages, graphs,** even **scores** on tests, are examples of **descriptive statistics.** You use them all the time in conversation, read them in base-

ball scores, hear them on the news, and are generally familiar with them in a hundred-and-one different contexts of everyday life. Some of the ones used most frequently, like **averages, medians,** and **modes,** are based on very simple concepts; others, such as **standard deviation, variance,** and **correlation,** are based on more sophisticated mathematical notions. There is no need to define most of them here, before you actually run into them. What you need to understand about them is basically that they are means of **summary description,** conveniences for portraying data efficiently.

Correlation is the one descriptive statistic that requires a little more discussion here because it is used almost constantly (you have come across it many times before now) and because it is very easy to misinterpret. A **correlation coefficient** (coefficient means number) is a

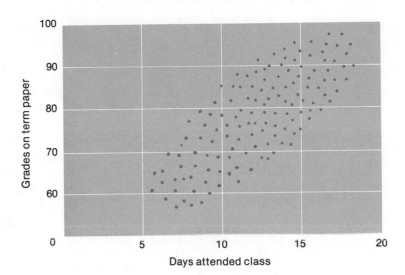

Figure 1.2 A correlation scatter plot.

numerical expression of the relationship between two events. More precisely, it expresses the relationship between the *rates of change* in each of two *variable* events, but that usually means the same thing I just said. A correlation is ordinarily stated as a decimal fraction between −1.00 and +1.00, with 0.00 meaning that there is no relation between the things at all. A + sign, or a positive correlation, means that they change in the same direction; as one gets bigger, the other does too. A − sign, or negative correlation, means they change in opposite directions; as one gets bigger, the other gets smaller. The closer the correlation coefficient is to 1.00, the greater the degree of relationship. This will make more sense with an illustration.

If we looked into the legendary relationship between attending class and getting high grades, a positive correlation would mean that the more you attend class, the higher your grades are; the less you attend class, the lower your grades. A negative correlation would mean that the relationships are just the opposite; the more you attend class, the lower your grades; the less you attend, the higher your grades.

There are two things you must be very wary of in reading correlations. First, **correlation** is not the same as *causation;* even a very high correlation gives no clue as to what caused what. Attending class *may* cause some people to get high grades, but getting high grades, on the other hand, or the expectation of them, may cause certain types of students to attend class more. Yet again, professors may favor some students, for no good reason, and this favoritism may cause both effects, impelling the students to attend class and the professor to give them undeservedly high grades. There is no way to know from the correlation.

The second caution you must exercise with correlation is that the number itself is deceptive. You might think, reasonably enough, that a correlation of .80 indicates twice as big a relationship as a correlation of .40. It does not; the relationship is more like four times as big. Without belaboring the reason, the rule-of-thumb to follow is this: To see approximately how much the variables really correspond to each other, **square** the correlation coefficient. A correlation of .50 means that 25 percent of the variation in one event corresponds to the variation in the other (.50 × .50 = .25); a correlation of .70 means that there is a 49 percent correspondence. The actual degree of correspondence, you notice, is always smaller than the correlation looks; for correlations as high as + or −.50, it is less than one quarter of the possible total. And for correlations between 0.00 and + or −.50, it is very low indeed. Incidentally, when there is no + or − sign indicated, it means the correlation is positive.

The actual size of a correlation, or of any other descriptive statistic, is less important than its *dependability,* or *significance.* It is not very meaningful to know the size of a relationship you have observed unless you can generalize from it to comparable situations and relationships that you have not yet studied. The best *description* in the world of what you already studied is still only *history;* the ability to *predict* from it, that is, to understand correctly what you have not yet seen is what makes it *science.* The branch of statistics that contributes to this knowledge is called *inferential statistics.*

Statistical inference An *inference* is a logical guess at something you don't know based on something you do know. If I *see* you nodding as you read this, I *infer* that you are being bored to sleep by it; if I *hear* you retching, I *infer* that you are nauseated. The inference is never a statement of observed fact, only of deduced probability. I cannot be *certain* how you feel just by guessing it from your action. We all recognize this in everyday speech in expressions like, "chances are, you feel . . ." or "in all probability, she wants. . . ."

Statistical inference is just like any other inference, but it is derived from some very fancy mathematics and expressed in a variety of numerical forms. You don't need to know any of the mathematics or very much about the methods or symbols involved to interpret statistical inferences. You only need a smattering of the reasoning behind them, called *probability theory,* and an explanation of how they are expressed, called *significance testing.*

There are many different methods of statistical analysis used for making inferences; the ones most commonly seen in psychological reports, *t-test, analysis of variance,* and *Chi-square test* (ch is pronounced "k"), are used for making inferences about the differences between groups. All statistical inferences, whether about differences between groups or about the dependability of correlations, take the form of *tests of significance,* and the results of these tests are always expressed by the symbol: *p* = something-or-other, always a fraction between 0.00 and 1.00. The letter *p* stands for probability. All significance tests are used for the same thing: to predict the probability that you would get the same result again if you repeated your study in exactly the same way.[7] It is in that sense that significance tests show you how "dependable" your results are. If you are testing the significance of the difference between groups, the test tells you the probability that you will find no difference between them if you repeat the experiment. If you are testing the significance of a correlation coefficient, it tells you whether repeating the study is likely to give you a correlation significantly different from zero.

A more familiar, and still accurate way to look at it is to view the situation as a gambling problem. You found such-and-such a difference between two groups. What are the odds that you will find it again if you repeat the study? With what level of confidence can you place the same bet on the same outcome? That is what significance tests help you to guess.

Statistical inference is not merely analogous to gambling—it is the essence of what smart gamblers do. They bet that the dice will roll out seven, or eleven, or whatever, on the basis

---

[7] As usual, I have simplified and, in this instance, technically misstated the case. In fact, significance tests are *used* as I have indicated, but what they literally show is the probability that you would get the same result from repeating your study in the same way if the hypothesis were actually wrong and the results you got were an accident.

of probability theory, the mathematics of luck. Gambling theory got its mathematical basis in 1716 from the work of Abraham de Moivre, a French Huguenot mathematician living in England, who was hired by professional gamblers to figure out betting schemes that would improve their "chances" (the French word for "luck") at the gaming tables of London. He discovered the binomial distribution (you learned it in high school algebra), the basis for most good gambling and most statistical inference in science (Weaver 1963).

You don't need to understand the mathematics of probability to understand statistical inference, but it is useful to understand the nature of mathematics. Mathematics is *pure logic,* expressed in the form of numbers and of some shorthand symbols for the rules by which they can be manipulated (+ means add the numbers, × means multiply them, and so forth). Numbers, the data of mathematics, are the inventions of reason; they are not physical entities with mass, volume, or energy, so they do not exist in a physical sense. They literally are not "sensible"; knowledge of them does not depend on the way they look, feel, sound, or taste—they are not sense data, and therefore they are not subject to consensual validation.

As a practical matter, that means that mathematical knowledge, unlike scientific knowledge, is *absolutely* dependable, subject to *reason* alone. You don't need to do an experiment to prove that two plus two is four and you can't possibly invent a research that would prove it is not. Two plus two is four because we have *defined* the numbers and the rules for combining them in ways that absolutely make it so. As Bertrand Russell put it, "Thus mathematics may be defined as the subject in which we never know what we are talking about, nor whether what we are saying is true (1921, p. 75)." He meant that mathematics is not subject to sensory, empirical, or scientific knowledge.

But the opposite is true of sensory data; empirical information *is* quantifiable. You cannot *taste* numbers, but you certainly can *count* apples, *gauge* distances, *score* tests, and assign numerical values to anything in the real world. Once you do that, you can manipulate those values arithmetically, like any other numbers.

In statistical inference, we quantify the facts we have observed and compare them to the abstractions of mathematical probability theory, always asking the same question: If everything in the world happened by accident, at random

Figure 1.3 The binomial distribution.

(the basic assumption of probability theory), then what were the chances of this accident (the facts I observed) occurring?

The question is asked that way because science is looking for the *lawful* relationships between facts, and scientific method, as we said before, works by the conservative principle of eliminating *accidental, random, lawless* events that only appear to be related. Probability theory provides a basis for deciding what to believe about the facts that have been observed—if the probability of this fact occurring by accident was very low in a world where everything occurs by accident (the world of mathematical probability), then I will take the chance of believing it happened lawfully, not at random, in the real world.[8]

The business of matching quantified observations of reality to the mathematical world we create in our heads is really a gambling game. The fact that it works well enough to win money, send people to the moon, and publish psychological experiments does not change its character as a game. It is a mathematical substitute for replication and consensual validation, but not a decisive one. If a test of statistical significance indicates that your result had only one chance in a thousand of occurring by accident, *it may still have been an accident.* There is no way you can ever know for sure.

So we have come full circle, and it still turns out that there is no way to know anything except in your head and no way to be sure that any generalization from what you have seen to what you have not is correct. Statistical inference increases your **confidence,** but not your **knowledge.** Replicating the experiment increases your knowledge, but not by too much.

---

[8] The convention in psychology experiments is to consider a result dependable if it is "significant at the 5 percent level or less," meaning that there was 5 percent or less chance of its occurring accidentally (usually expressed as $p < .05$). When a report says, incorrectly, "the results were not significant," it really means they were not significant *at that level* and the experimenter therefore does not consider them dependable.

If it comes out the same way the second time, there is still no assurance that it will come out that way again. When all is said and done, it is a gambler's universe. Science is the most honest and accurate method that exists for getting knowledge, but the knowledge you get from it is not **absolutely** dependable.

All this is not new. It was definitively written more than two centuries ago by a British philosopher, David Hume, in *A Treatise of Human Nature: Book I: Of the Understanding,* published in 1739. Hume's argument, that knowledge is limited to your experience, was not very important to chemists or physicists in his day because the variables they dealt with were so simple that it was easy to replicate experiments and usually unnecessary to use any statistics at all, either to describe or interpret their results. One molecule was much like another, for the purposes of that day, and one scientist could easily verify another's work in his own laboratory.

One person is *not* very much like another, and Hume's argument is very important for psychologists and social scientists to understand. The enormous variability of human behavior makes it enormously difficult to establish clear facts about it.

The result of all the problems in understanding behavior is that psychologists have become terribly sophisticated scientists, not because they have wanted necessarily to devote themselves to studying scientific method, statistics, and logic, but because they have had little choice. The worlds they explore are subtle and begrudge giving up dependable or useful information, so psychologists have had to become subtle, sophisticated and very critical of the facts that their research **appears** to unearth.

PSYCHOLOGY AND THE QUALITY OF LIFE

Most psychologists do not make a living doing research, but all of them receive fairly intensive training in it. This happens, in part, because the facts of human behavior are elusive, as we have seen. But it also happens because the practical problems which psychologists deal with are almost always of great importance in people's lives. Is segregated schooling more or less damaging to children psychologically than the upheaval which busing may create? Will preschool programs like Headstart make it easier for socially deprived children to develop reading skills or not? Are children more damaged by their parents' divorcing or by the tension of seeing parental conflict? Are psychedelic drugs harmful to

Headstart.

Segregated schooling may be
psychologically damaging to some
children: the controversy over busing
may also be.

personality? Does early sex experience harm
later marital adjustment? Does counseling or
psychotherapy help it?

These and a thousand other questions people
try to answer in their personal, or social, or
political lives, are all questions about the
quality of life. And the quality of life itself,
in the final analysis, is summed up by how you
are and how you feel about yourself, the conditions of your existence and your experience
with it. So there are only two questions: "What

things are good or bad for your physical
survival and functioning?" and "What things
are good or bad for your feelings of well being
and fulfillment?"

Our own experience, how we feel—about ourselves, about the world around us, about life,
matters more to us than the objective conditions
of survival. The process of evolution has made
us this way for good reasons, but reasons aside,
it is part of the deepest fabric of everyone's
being. For all of us, as one student put it:

"Nothing is what it is—it's only the way you feel it is." The objective conditions of life are *"prior but less important"* (Bryson 1953); our basic needs for physical safety and security, in other words, have to be taken care of before we can be concerned with more refined problems of education, career, love, and religion. Without satisfying those elementary needs, no one has the leisure to examine their more abstract concerns or the energy to pursue their fulfillment. And the process of satisfying them itself contributes to the feeling of well being when it is successful—a full stomach, good health, and confidence that one can go to sleep in safety, all help to make us feel that life is hopeful. Once that is so, we can concern ourselves with making it meaningful.

As a science, psychology is concerned with discovering the facts of human behavior. As an art, it is concerned with applying them to the improvement of human welfare, especially those aspects of it related to the way people experience life.

The business of psychology is bettering the quality of life. Ultimately, this makes it an important study in everyone's life.

SUMMARY

1   The definition of "psychology," which literally means study of the mind or soul, was once in great dispute. Today it is generally defined as the study of *behavior,* and recognized as overlapping with social, behavioral, and biological sciences.

2   Psychology was a branch of philosophy until the end of the 19th century. Then it started becoming a separate discipline, with roots in philosophy, physiology, medicine, education, and physics. In 1879, Wilhelm Wundt opened the first psychophysical laboratory in Germany. In 1889, William James changed his title at Harvard University from professor of philosophy to professor of psychology. In 1895, Alfred Binet began the work in Paris which gave rise to intelligence testing. And the roots of psychoanalysis and the psychology of learning were all established by the turn of the century. The origins of professional psychology are international, but it has always thrived most in the United States.

3   Psychology today is divided up into many *academic* and *applied* specialties. Three major academic groupings are: (1) *experimental psychology,* dealing with biological and psychological foundations of behavior; (2) *social psychology,* dealing with group interactions, attitudes and opinions, and personality; and (3) *developmental psychology,* dealing with the processes of growth and development through the whole life cycle. The main applied branches of psychology are: (1) *clinical and counseling,* (2) *personnel and guidance,* (3) *school psychology,* (4) *industrial psychology,* (5) *community psychology,* and (6) *engineering psychology.* But these do not represent the whole field; the American Psychological Association is divided into more than 30 special interest divisions.

4   There is nothing unique about what psychologists do for a living, but they generally have very extensive training in research methods, including the construction of tests. Increasingly, a Ph.D., Ed.D., or Psy.D. is the required professional degree for psychologists, and most states have laws for certifying or licensing people who want to practice psychology.

5   Psychology is difficult to study because it deals with many *variables* that are not

equally observable nor equally influential on behavior. This makes them hard to *measure,* which makes it hard to test *hypotheses,* the educated guesses of science.

6 *Measurement error* results partly from the variability of the things being observed and partly from the *bias* which distorts the judgment of different observers. In either case, it reduces the *reliability* or *significance* of observations.

7 Scientific research depends on the *consensual validation* of observations, meaning that they are not accepted until many people have agreed on their reliability. In the *empirical method* of science, this means observations must be *replicated* in order to be accepted.

8 There are two empirical methods. The first is *observation, field,* or *survey* research, which means observations and measurements in the natural environment or in situations where the behavior under study is not interfered with. The second method is *experimentation,* which means controlling all the circumstances surrounding the one thing you want to study, so you can see how it operates under different conditions.

9 It is necessary to make random observations in order to reduce *sampling error,* which is the mistaken conclusion one might reach from making observations of some specific behavior which is not *representative* of the general behavior you are interested in.

10 *Statistics* are mathematical methods of aiding common sense by (1) providing concise *descriptions* or summaries of observations and by (2) helping to draw logical *inferences* about the *probability* that the observations made were accidental. Scores, averages, percentages, and correlations are all descriptive statistics. *Tests of significance,* such as the t-test, analysis of variance, and Chi-square test are inferential statistics, used to predict the probability of future events based on past information. Statistical inference increases *confidence* in our observations, but not firm knowledge. In 1739, the British philosopher David Hume, stated the problem clearly—knowledge is limited to the individual's past experience.

The biological basis of behavior: One—heredity and evolution

2

2

The biological basis of behavior: One—heredity and evolution

Why do people shrink at the sight of a snake? Is it because they have been *taught* to fear snakes—or because an inborn biological mechanism triggers fear in them without any previous introduction? When you order trespassers off your property—or away from your locker—are you simply defending possessions that you have learned are valuable, or are you obeying a "territorial imperative," an instinct deep within you that automatically arouses your defenses when your territory is invaded? When little boys start playing cops and robbers while little girls the same age play demurely with dolls, are the children simply reacting to what society has taught them about their different sex roles, or are they obeying *genetic orders* that make little boys aggressive and little girls maternal? Are bonds of friendship and camaraderie among men more "natural" than those among women? Does "nature" smile on the Elks Club but frown on the League of Women Voters?

Some of these questions may sound silly, but all of them have been seriously investigated in modern times by psychologists, sociologists, anthropologists, and ethnologists. And philosophers, theologians, scientists, lawyers, teachers, and crack-pots, among others, have been musing on similar themes since the beginning of civilization. Stated seriously, the question is: Are some states of mind, or some traits of character, or some kinds of behavior more "natural" to humans than others, and if so, are they therefore better?

One of the oldest and deepest misgivings that has haunted thinkers is the suspicion that civilized humans are breaking rules of nature which are prerequisites for "the good life." In Biblical times, this idea was expressed in the story of the expulsion from the Garden of Eden. When Adam and Eve ate of the tree of knowledge, they lost their innocence, became self-conscious, that is, *unnatural*—and therefore were doomed. The belief has remained an important part of some religious creeds to this day. The same theme was expressed in the secular

To some, a return to the land symbolizes a more "natural," and therefore better, way of life.

The Song of the Lark, Jules Breton

writings of the 18th century French philosopher, Jean Jacques Rousseau (1712–78). Civilized living corrupted people, he thought, so that they did not develop the virtues which come from growing up in the "natural" state of the "noble savage." If Europeans could only live like the American Indians, they would return to the paths of natural human behavior and all would be well (Rousseau 1761, 1762; de Chateaubriand 1768–1848, 1952).

Believers in the "natural order of things" have not all been of the sweet innocence school, of course. Toward the end of the 19th century, another group of thinkers used Darwin's theory of evolution as a basis to proclaim that Europeans *were* behaving perfectly naturally by fighting ceaseless wars! They were following the "law of the jungle" which ensures the "survival of the fittest" (Huxley 1969). And barely a generation ago, the Nazis justified their monstrous slaughter of millions by pseudo-biological theorizing about the "natural" superiority of the "Aryan race" over other people. Today, less blood-thirsty speculators, spiritual descendants of Rousseau, maybe, are insisting that living in crowded cities is unnatural—and some people do move to the country hoping that there they can "get in tune" with the "rhythm of nature."

Whether nature has a "rhythm," as far as human behavior is concerned, and whether it is worth getting "in tune" with, are the main problems of this chapter.

Nature versus nurture

We are circling around a huge question: **What is the nature of human nature?** This divides up into many individual problems:

Is there such a thing as *human nature,* that is, an innate (inborn) biologically-determined pattern of human instincts? Does the human race, as a whole, have a common biological nature? Do individuals have traits which are precisely established by the genetic material they receive from their parents? What part does one's environment, upbringing, and social experience play in shaping human nature? If heredity and environment both shape human behavior, which factor looms larger? And how large is large? How can you tell how much and in what ways each contributes? If human behavior has a **biological** basis, how do we separate it from the **cultural** determinants of behavior? Is the distinction between heredity and environment really meaningful?

Before we examine these questions in detail, we need to put the term "human nature" in perspective. It should be used with caution for two reasons. First, the word "nature" implies that humanity has some kind of essence, that there is some basic principle of "humanness" that lies above and beyond the observable facts

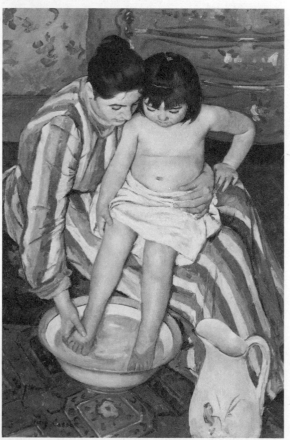

The Bath, Mary Cassatt

This little girl receives many things from her mother: her dark hair and plump form, good habits, and love.

Hitler found millions of supporters for his vile theories of racial superiority.

of human anatomy and physiology and behavior. Science cannot deal with such an idea because science measures and interprets only observable events and the inferences that can be drawn from them. For scientific purposes, *behavior* is a more useful term than nature be-

cause it deals with activities taking place in the physical world and subject to observation.

A second reason for being cautious with the term "human nature" is political. Arguments about human nature have commonly been used to justify the enslavement or murder of helpless people by their "natural" superiors. As you know, the Nazis used such arguments to rationalize wiping out Jews, Gypsies, Poles, and others. Similar arguments are often used to justify racial discrimination and religious prejudice: "Black people have *natural* rhythm; Jews are *naturally* smart and tricky," and so forth. You could use human nature just as well to argue *for* the *kinship* of humanity, of course, and the Declaration of Independence did exactly that: "We hold these truths to be self-evident, that all men are created equal, that **they are endowed by their Creator** [italics added] with certain inalienable rights . . ." means that it is part of human nature to be equal and therefore to be entitled to "life, liberty, and the pursuit of happiness." But the "human nature" position seems more often used against brotherhood than for it. So be on guard when you hear it used at all.

All questions about "human nature" are variations on a long-standing debate among scientists and thinkers about how much of human behavior is inborn, or *innate* to our natures, and how much of it is acquired as a result of learning, or *nurtured* in us by experience. The *nature-nurture controversy* as it is called, has raged on inconclusively, partly because the issues involved have not been clearly distinguished nor the terms tightly defined, and partly because the evidence is insufficient, and to some extent, contradictory.

For many reasons, a lot of good scholars have argued intensely for the forces of *nurture.* Human behavior seemed so flexible to them, in view of the vast variations among different cultures, that many investigators flatly denied that people had inborn instincts at all (Mead 1935). But most scholars would not take an uncompromising pronurture position today, whether or not they believe in instincts, because it is so clear that many aspects of behavior, such as intelligence, temperament, and other things may be partly determined by heredity (Bodmer and Cavalli-Sforza 1970; Heston 1970.) This does

not completely wipe out the controversy, however, because even inherited characteristics are profoundly shaped by cultural influences. And cultural characteristics in turn may be determined in part by our hereditary animal attributes, as is suggested especially by studies of apes and monkeys (the primates), our closest cousins on this planet (Keesing and Keesing 1971; Montagu 1965). While different cultures embody wildly diverse languages, customs, economics, social structures, and religious beliefs, they are all variations of a few commonly held themes, some of which have their counterpart in the behavior of apes and monkeys (Mason and Lott 1976; Morris 1968). Every human society, for example, has some kind of *family* structure (a thing which gorillas and baboons share with us), though what one culture considers bedding of strangers another may regard as incest. And every human society has some form of religion (unlike our primate kin), though the number of gods worshiped may vary from hundreds (as among the Hindus) to none at all (a common belief among Buddhists and atheists). The argument does not have a final turning point.

The nature-nurture problem is often stated in a way that makes you think of heredity and environment as *opposing* forces. But they are not (Dobzhansky 1957). Both for individuals and the cultures they live in, biology sets the limits on behavior (birds fly because of their wing structure; you do not because of yours), but it does not dictate many specific activities. Culture does that. Everyone needs food and water and shelter from cold and heat, and opportunities to sleep, mate, and just fool around. But whether we enjoy eating grasshoppers or yogurt, sleeping on feather beds or floor mats, mating with uncles or aunts or total strangers, and fooling around by playing chess or headhunting, depends on what the environment gives us as we are reared, not on what we bring to it when we are born.

In the final analysis, the nature-nurture problem is not a *controversy* at all because biological organisms and functions do not develop in a vacuum but in some kind of environment—and because the environment influences a specific biochemical organism, not a random blob of protoplasm. Apes cannot grow up to be Einsteins, no matter how well they are taught—and you need a lot of teaching in order not to act like an ape, no matter how great your hereditary intellectual potential may be! But even with the needless controversy dismissed, the question still remains: How much of our *specific patterns* of needs and activities is dictated by our biological nature, and how much by our life experience? For this question, all the honest answers are complicated, or puzzling, because they come out somewhat different as you approach the question from different angles of inquiry. We shall look at only three: the organizational hierarchy of behavior, the variety of cultures, and the method of twin studies.

THE ORGANIZATION OF BEHAVIOR: REFLEX, INSTINCT, AND TEMPLATE

The naturist case seems to get special force from the fact that behavior almost never occurs at random, without *organization.* Just as cells are structured into organs, and organs into systems, and systems into organisms, the behavior of organisms also seems to have a "natural" structure, and it is reasonable to suppose that the structure of behavior, like that of the body, is predetermined by genetic forces. The lowest level of organized behavior, called a *reflex,* certainly is inborn. But even at the highest level, some people believe, entire ethnic or cultural groups have inborn behavioral dispositions called the "collective unconscious" (Jung 1956). Whether a "collective unconscious" really exists is unknown, but no one doubts that reflexes exist, and that they are part of the unlearned *behavioral repertoire* of humans and beasts alike (Lorenz 1958).

A reflex is the unlearned, fixed, specific reaction of muscles or glands to the stimulation of a specific group of nerves (Lashley 1938). When the lips of a newborn baby are touched, by nipple or finger or whatever, its cheeks start to suck reflexively. When a flashlight shines into your eye, the pupil contracts reflexively. When the doctor taps your kneecap, your leg jerks up reflexively.

The reflex, you will note, is an organized action of only one part of the body. When the whole animal does something, the action is more likely to be called an "instinct."

It is over instinct that controversy about human heredity begins. An *instinct* is an activity pattern of the whole animal which is triggered by a single stimulus, apparently without any learning having taken place. It is as if the whole program of movements for fighting, or nest building, or sex, at least in lower organisms, were genetically "built in" so that they could appear full blown when the need arose (Fraenkel and Gunn 1940). Even when some sense organs or muscle groups are destroyed, the instinctive behavior persists, the animal using whatever faculties it has left—to fight, to copulate, or whatever. It is instinct which brings moths to seek light, birds to migrate in the autumn, and salmon to swim upstream to spawn before they die (Hesler and Larsen, 1955; Pengelley and Asmundsen 1971). None of these are *learned* behavior in the sense that the animal had to have previous experience doing them in order to do them right. None of them are *intelligent* in the sense that the animal thinks it over before doing them. In fact, the results may be far from intelligent—moths fly into flame, not knowing it isn't sunlight, and salmon swim blithely into the traps of waiting fishermen. The hallmark of instinct is its *automatic* character and its *sameness,* that of intelligence is *delay* and *flexibility.*

The important thing about instinctive behavior is that it can have the same *complexity* that intelligent behavior does, but apparently

The mating dance of the albatross is not learned; it is just "there" instinctively at maturity.

does not require the same accretion of experience to get it. Complexity seems somehow to be programmed into the animal's nervous system. The big question is: Are such complex programs genetically fixed in the brain and nervous system of humans beings as well?

Even within ethological circles, the whole idea of instinct is subject to a lot of doubt. Many activities of many animals once thought to be instinctively programmed turn out to depend on cues in the environment which dictate specific fragments of the overall behavior sequence, so that the marvelous "whole pattern" that casual observers see is really just a series of individual stimuli and responses, not an internal program at all (Beach 1955). Even so, the question remains, do humans possess any of the **fixed action patterns** that some animals do? Can any of our complex behavior be explained as the inevitable result of our innate neural wiring? In general, the answer almost universally agreed on is "no." If we have any instincts, they

are **diffuse** to the point that they affect only the most **general** dispositions, *not* any specific behavior patterns. These general dispositions, also of doubtful existence, are sometimes called **templates.**

A **template** is a much less specific determinant of behavior than an instinct; it is a kind of biological guide of some general types of activity and experience. No one is really certain whether templates of human behavior exist or not. Claude Levi-Strauss, a French anthropologist, finds evidence for templates in such facts as that, in all cultures, people categorize their thoughts into **pairs of opposites:** raw–cooked, sacred–profane, strong–weak, and so forth. Pairing-into-opposites might be a template for human thinking patterns everywhere (Levi-Strauss 1969). Opposites like dominance–submission or mine–yours might be more important concepts or have different meanings in one culture than another, but the rule which says: "organize the content of your thinking into opposites" would be constant across all of them. A template sets a kind of basic behavior disposition or theme that applies to all cultures, regardless of the variations each plays upon it.

The concept of the template is a gentler statement of an older idea about the genetic basis of culture, called the *archetype.* The theory was made famous by Freud's student, and later antagonist, the Swiss psychiatrist Carl Jung. He said that ancient tribal memories are programmed into the brain and nervous system of human beings, and that these memories are reflected in the common dream symbolisms of normal people, the hallucinations of the emotionally troubled, and the symbols and religious emblems of farflung cultures around the world which have never had direct contact with each other (Jung 1933). There is no way of testing this theory scientifically; so it is generally not noticed as part of the nature-nurture problem. But if there are common genetic determinants of thematic behavior among human beings, then there probably are common memories buried among the same little gene molecules that determine the behavior patterns, and you should know that these theories go together.

Reflexes are quite rigid and do not respond to learning; instincts are slightly more flexible; but templates are still more flexible behavioral themes that can be elaborated into a myriad of melodies. Whether templates are biological, or merely similar approaches to common problems, is not known. But they are a way of explaining important common features in the organization of human behavior everywhere, in which learning has some effect, on the one hand, without the universal common element having to be completely coincidental, on the other. At the highest and most complex levels of human organization, of course, no one is silly enough to suggest that behavior is genetically determined. Even the most rabid racists (all racists are "nature lovers" in the nature-nurture argument) do not believe that whites have a skyscraper-building gene, Orientals a pagoda-instinct, and black Africans a mud-hut reflex. But they would say, and everyone would have to agree in principle, that just as human capacities differ genetically from those of *other species,* it is possible that there are genetically determined differences in capacity *within the human species* itself. Such intra-species differences certainly exist with respect to some diseases—childhood autism is more common among Jews than Gentiles (Rimland 1964), as is Tay-Sachs disease, and sickle cell anemia more among American blacks than whites (Goldsby 1971). Whether the same things could be true of behavior traits like intelligence, temperament, aggressiveness, sexuality, or maternal tendencies is the subject of endless dispute and serious trouble. We will stumble over that problem again and again in this book.

Cultural variety: The allspice of human life

The hypothesis that biological templates or a racial unconscious produce common behavior patterns among different cultures is an attempt to square the enormous diversity of human cultures with instinct theory. Most anthropologists, however, don't believe it. If anything, the great variety of cultures and the astounding number of different adaptations they have made to common human problems presents at least as strong a case for the "nurture" position as the data for reflexes and instincts does for the "nature" side. There are endless examples. Depending on which tribe he belonged to, a male child born in New Guinea could grow up to become a fierce warrior or a peace-loving farmer; a gentle father who spends hours with his babies or a sadistic brute who terrorizes his brood; an elegant lazybones who passes every day perfecting his toilette or a fair-minded soul who pitches in and trades off chores with his wife. The same New Guinean child, moreover, adopted by New Yorkers, could grow up with equal ease to become a theatre-going, subway-

The Day of the God, Paul Gauguin
Different cultures teach their members different roles.

riding, office-working, therapist-paying big-city sophisticate (Mead 1935).

The same variety occurs in something as basic as food and eating. In the Middle Ages, serfs arose at dawn and worked for six hours in the fields before eating a single morsel (Davis 1928). In modern Sweden, most people have six small meals a day. On Christopher Columbus' third voyage, he met Central Americans who lived on nothing but pineapple wine and sardines (Morison 1942). Although human teeth suit us to be omnivores (eaters of both meat and vegetables), the Hindus are solely vegetarian. Still more remarkable, some people, passively resisting tyrannical governments, have starved themselves to death.

Or take sex and marriage. In western society alone the "rules" governing sexual behavior have changed frequently. At the beginning of Shakespeare's play, Juliet is berated for not having married yet—she is all of 14! By the 19th century, the marrying age for girls had risen to late adolescence, but the ideal age for a gentleman to settle down was 35. For some, sex was banned altogether; the Catholic Church established a large community of priests and nuns sworn to chastity. And today, the marrying age for most American males is around 23.5 and for females just over 21 (U.S. Bureau of the Census, 1976).

All over the world, sexual codes vary enormously. In the Solomon Islands of the Pacific, the Kwaio insisted on premarital chastity for girls and killed both partners if the taboo was broken. In the Trobriand Islands, however, girls were encouraged to be sexually promiscuous at age six or eight, and only in their mid-teens did couples begin to pair off. The Muria of India place adolescents of both sexes in coeducational dormitories. In some dormitories no couple is permitted to sleep together for more than two nights running; a senior boy and girl *assign* bedmates. Yet curiously, the marriage rules specify that a boy must marry a girl from a different dormitory—someone he has scarcely seen, much less made love to (Keesing and Keesing 1971). Malinowski gives excellent descriptions of sexual practices in preliterate cultures (1929).

It makes no difference what the domain of behavior is—if there are different ways for human beings to do something, there will be different sets of humans doing it differently—and often insisting that theirs is the best, if not the only right way. Students of culture have long looked for some kind of rule or norm of behavior which was really common across all human societies—the closest they have come up with is that all cultures have some kind of incest tabu. But even there, the definition of incest varies so much that calling it a common tabu is saying no more than that every society has rules

The great variety of adaptations to common human problems makes a case for the "nurture" position.

Buckwheat Harvest, Jean Francois Millet

for sexual conduct and family life—and that is a long way from templates.

Clearly, human beings have more flexibility than any other animals. They are better able to adjust to new and complex situations and to learn from past mistakes. They also have a genius for social adaptations to their environment, that is, for creating different cultures. All this, taken together, makes most students of human culture insist that culture, not biology, determines how people behave. But here, as with instincts, the evidence is not compelling, only interesting. The variety of human behavior says nothing about the underlying determinants of it. To find them, we need a more direct approach than either ethologists or anthropologists can offer. Such an approach comes from the work of behavior geneticists.

Twin studies: Climbing the family tree

The important question about the role of biology in determining human behavior is: "How much of a specific *individual's* behavior is shaped by heredity?" For that, we must look away from instinct studies and from cultural studies and try going directly into heredity. One good way to do this with lower animals is to study *pedigrees,* or family trees. It does not work well with humans, however, because the subjects live as long as the scientists who study them, marry whomever they please, and suit themselves about having children, regardless of its scientific consequences. A more practical way, which has produced some fascinating results, is to study *human twins.*

The neat thing about twins is that they contain relatively controlled amounts of heredity-environment mixtures compared to other siblings. Brothers and sisters share similar environments when they are raised at home; fraternal twins (conceived at the same time but from different egg-sperm combos and, therefore, of different genetic makeup) share even more similar environments, starting with conception; and identical twins (one-egg) have both similar environments and the same genetic makeup. So when we examine any behavioral trait among siblings, we should expect identical twins to be most alike, compared to the others, if heredity is the critical factor; and fraternal twins and siblings should be about equally alike, compared to them, if environment is what counts most.

It does not work so neatly, of course, because no two creatures ever share *exactly* the same environment—breathe the same air, eat the same food, experience the same sensations. Even so, it is a fair approximation. Pairs of identical twins have occasionally been split up at birth. A poor family, for instance, may keep one child and put the other up for adoption. Since the child is often adopted by a rich or middle-class couple, the twins are reared quite differently. This has made it possible to study the effect of different environments with heredity held constant. One study of 53 identical twins raised apart showed that their ability to perform on intelligence tests was strikingly similar (an .86 correlation). Not only did the twins have similar scores on general intelligence scales but also on tests of specific intellectual abilities. Their interests and personality, however, were not particularly alike; in fact, they are never identical even when the twins are raised together (Lindzey *et al.* 1971, p. 49). In another study, a Danish psychologist examined the personalities of a few identical twins raised apart and found little resemblance in their religious or social views, in their friends, or in the people they married—but he *did* find startling similarities in their gestures, smiles and laughter, tone of voice, and even in the psychosomatic diseases they complained of (a psychosomatic disease is an emotionally induced physical ailment; ulcers and asthma, for instance, can both be brought on by stress and worry) (Jules-Nielsen 1965).

Such twin studies help to identify the relative contribution of hereditary or experiential factors in behavior more clearly than instinct or cultural

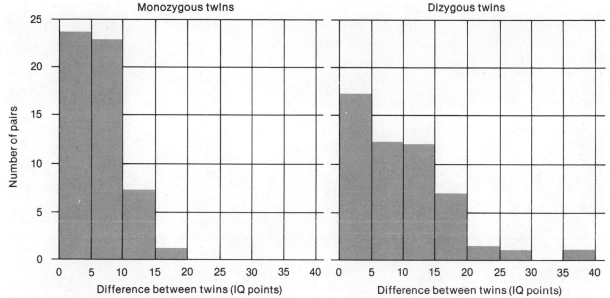

Monozygous twins   Dizygous twins

Experiment of nature based on IQ data collected by Horatio H. Newman of the University of Chicago gives a rough measurement of the relative influence of heredity and environment on intelligence. Chart at left shows IQ differences between the members of 50 pairs of monozygous twins, that is, twins who developed from the same egg and have identical genotypes. IQ differences between members of these pairs tend to be low: 24 pairs (or almost half of the sample) show a difference of from zero to five points. Only one pair shows a difference of between 15 and 20 points. The mean difference between the members of each pair is 5.9 points. Since the genotypes in each pair are identical it appears that the environmental effect tends to be small. The second chart shows IQ differences between 45 pairs of dizygous twins, that is, twins with different genotypes who developed from separate eggs. In this case the mean difference in IQ between the members of these pairs is about ten points. Thus a fairly large difference appears to be attributable to heredity. Such a comparison does not separate the effects of heredity and environment precisely. Members of monozygous pairs have very similar environments, whereas genotypes of dizygous twins are less different on the average by a factor of two than those of unrelated individuals. Comparison thus underestimates effect of heredity but also minimizes environmental influence.

studies did, but they too do not give any final answer to the question of which contributes what to behavior. Heredity and environment are both more complicated than one thinks when the question first arises.

To the question: "How much of an individual's behavior is innate and how much learned?" the answer seems to be that, beyond a few simple reflexes *all* of human behavior is learned *but within the limits set by heredity.* For example, a human infant at about nine months usually begins to fear strangers. Now baby monkeys and apes (our closest relatives in the animal world) also begin to fear strangers at a corres-

Los Proverbios, Francisco Jóse de Goya
Heredity sets the limits. If we had wings, we might learn to fly.

ponding point in their development, and therefore we might conclude that such timidity is innate. But both monkeys and human babies must first **learn** to recognize **familiar** faces before they can recognize and then fear strangers. To take another example, baby monkeys and baby humans both have temper tantrums, outbursts in which the child, not being able to get what it wants, explodes with rage. The fact that other animal species closely related to us have such tantrums suggests that tantrums too are innate, but once again, the child must first *learn* what it wants before it can experience frustration. Fear of strangers and temper tantrums look like innate behavior because they occur so early and

without previous instruction, but the situations in which they are relevant must be *learned*. Donald Hebb, from whom these examples have been taken, once wrote that we cannot separate learned and unlearned behavior, since this would be like asking "how much of the area of a field is due to its length, how much to its width." Both heredity and learning shape every piece of behavior (Hebb 1968).

BECOMING HUMAN: SENSITIVE PERIODS AND THEIR IMPRINTS

If we were to make a single generalization in this connection, it would be that the higher the species in the phylogenetic scale of animals, the greater is the role of learning in complex behavior and the more inseparable are the relative contributions of heredity and environment to that behavior. Take something as basic as sexual performance, for instance. If monkeys are isolated at birth and raised apart from other monkeys, they cannot copulate properly. Female monkeys raised in isolation without mothers violently resist adult sexual encounters and, even when they do become pregnant, turn out to be utterly devoid of maternal feelings towards their offspring (Harlow 1962). Just the opposite seems to be true of rats; a sexually experienced male may perform the right acts of copulation, more or less, even if his genitals are removed; and the female will build her nest all right, once she gets pregnant, even if she has never seen another female do it. These instinctive acts look like "fancy reflexes." But in primates and humans the sexual urge, however innate, has to be channelled and released entirely by experience. So does most everything else. Now let us see what that means.

When experience speaks: Maturation and learning

We have been speaking of both heredity and experience as if they are each monolithic, that is, all of a piece. But neither one is a single event or thing and both change constantly in the way they are expressed in living creatures. Most of our hereditary side is expressed in our physical structure and the physiological processes that are constantly changing us. Most of our experience is reflected in the things we learn. But we cannot learn anything without our bodies taking part. And the things we learn, the speed with which we learn them, and our changing ability to retain them, all depend on the interactions between our experiences and the phase of physical growth and development we are in. The process of physical growth and development is called *maturation;* it is essentially a product of heredity. And it is the platform on which learning occurs, in humans and lower animals both.

Sensitive periods There are different points in the maturation of every species called *sensitive periods,* when certain kinds of learning become possible. These periods are not evenly spaced, and do not last indefinitely. Before that time, it is too early; afterwards, it may be too late. It is as if the door to certain kinds of experience is opened for a moment of time, and the infant animal must catch what it can from that moment or possibly lose it forever.

The most dramatic instance of such an event occurs in birds, and is called *imprinting* (Lorenz 1952; 1970; Ramsay and Hess 1954). Certain species of chicks are able to follow their parents about almost as soon as they are hatched. Sometime in the first 36 hours after birth, there is a period during which they will attach themselves permanently to whomever it is that they happen to be following—mother, a man, or even a blue ball (Hess 1956). Once the attachment occurs, they tend to follow that object around forever. Greylag geese, for instance, who have been cared for only by humans during that period, will make sexual advances only to humans when they mature. The fable of the *ugly duckling* undoubtedly got its start from the reality of some hapless swan chick attaching itself to a brood of ducks during this period.

It was once believed that the period involved was absolutely *critical,* meaning that once the attachment was learned, it was firm and irreversible. That is not quite the case. In fact, the depth of the attachment depends largely on how much effort the chick put into following grownups around in the first place. So the time involved is now recognized as a *sensitive period* instead of a *critical period.* But sensitive or critical, the point is the same. Learning occurs most rapidly, and experience *imprints* its mark most deeply, when the animal has matured to the point of greatest sensitiveness to it.

Another example of such imprinting at a critical moment explains how a chaffinch learns its song. If the male bird never hears an adult of its species sing its full song, he will learn to sing only a few notes of it. But if he hears the full song during the period when he is sensitive to imprinting, he will master it after only two or three trial runs (Thorpe 1954).

Something like imprinting occurs in higher animals too; it takes longer to develop, but the effects are just as great. When sheep, goats, guinea pigs, dogs, and chimpanzees are raised exclusively by humans out of contact with other sheep, goats, *et cetera*, they tend to see themselves as human, it seems, and to lack interest in their own species. Quite often, they will approach their human keepers sexually when they are old enough and reject the affections of their own kind (Hebb 1968; Mowrer 1950).

In most respects, it seems clear that **early experience** is more critical than any other for learning behavior patterns that will determine much of what happens to an animal through the rest of its life. There is a large literature on the effects of understimulation and overstimulation on animals who are raised in different kinds of infantile environments (McGill 1965; Held 1965; Levine *et al.* 1967]. Its general conclusion is that this is the most important time in an animal's life.

There may not be **sensitive periods** in the lives of human infants that are anything like those of lower animals; certainly there is nothing known in humans that is comparable to imprinting in birds. Most theories of child develop-

A bird must hear its song at the right time if it is to be imprinted.

Wood Thrush

ment, however, do agree that children go through *developmental stages* in which they are particularly sensitive to certain kinds of learning. Sigmund Freud (1905) and Jean Piaget (Flavell 1963) have proposed such theories, and Jerome Kagan, an American psychologist, has actually used the term *critical periods* to describe the stages of his child development theory (Kagan 1968).

Whether or not humans have sensitive periods like those which some animals have, maturation is certainly as important for us as for other species. Children cannot learn to run until they have learned to walk, nor to walk before crawling, nor to crawl before their neural apparatus permits the necessary coordination of muscles. Once they are maturationally ready, *then* they have to learn! You have probably heard of *"reading readiness."* But if you think about it, there must also be some such thing as roller skating readiness, violin and piano playing readiness, mathematical learning readiness, and language-learning readiness. And I am naming just those things because they have all been subjects of dispute among parents, teachers, and scientists—who still agree that these things cannot be taught before a child is "ready," meaning biologically, maturationally ready. But nobody knows when that is.

Whatever kinds of sensitive periods human children have, it is virtually certain they would drag out over a longer time than those of other animals—the rule, apparently, is that the more an animal's behavior is shaped by learning, the more extended its infancy, that is, its period of most intensive learning (Mussen 1970).

Surely this is so with language learning, the most extensive, and specifically human, of all our capacities. One prominent theory of language says that we are genetically programmed to be able to learn it. But children are not maturationally advanced enough to begin using language until almost a year old, though they can recognize some speech sounds be-

tween two and six months (Eimas 1971; Moffitt 1971), and their language ability speeds up rapidly once they start talking. As everyone who has watched them also knows, small children can learn foreign languages much more easily than adults can; they can learn a whole batch of them at once. And though they forget them in a few years of disuse, they can relearn them later with remarkable speed. Language learning is learning, all right, but the things that underlie it in the brain and nervous system are the products of biological experience, not of learning.

Finally, there are some children who never learn human language when they should and apparently cannot learn it later—these are the *feral* children that have either been raised in the wilderness by animals or have been isolated by cruel or crazy parents so that they never experienced the sounds of human language. When they have been found and trained, they would pick up many of the habits of civilization—but never learned language well. Maybe they were mentally retarded in the first place, before they were lost to human company—or perhaps they were not in the right place at the right time, during the *sensitive period* for language learning (Bettleheim 1959; Itard 1962).

When all is said and done, learning and heredity always *interact* to shape behavior. Monkeys, birds, and human beings are all *genetically programmed* to perform certain ways, but they can do so only if the right *environmental influences* are present. Without them the behavior will not appear. Babies are genetically programmed to talk, but they will never say anything meaningful unless they hear conversation. A chick is programmed genetically to follow the mother hen, but it will follow Dr. Lorenz, or you, or whomever, and maybe fall in love with them to boot, if they were there and the mother hen was not when the chick was ready to fulfill its genetic destiny. A feral child was meant genetically

Le Gourmet, Pablo Picasso

This child is big enough to stand on two feet and eat with a spoon. But if she had been raised with wild animals, she wouldn't learn to do this.

to speak but could not because the child was raised to be an animal, not a human. The interaction of genetics and experience is too close, in most respects, to sort them out.

But if that is so, and no one knows where genetic capacity stops and learning begins, then perhaps, just as you can downgrade human performance, regardless of capacity, by raising human children to be animals—you can upgrade apes, and discover their capacity, by raising chimps as children. Considering their smaller brains and different bodies, how much could apes be taught to act like human beings if they lived in human environments? Could we teach an ape to talk? Some people have tried to find out.

Teaching a chimp to talk

All evidence indicates that language is the exclusive property of humans, but not everyone agrees as to why this is true. Some say it is biology—our ability to communicate through symbols depends on our superior brain with its complex circuits and fancy neural equipment for associating ideas (Blumenthal 1970). They argue that language is genetically programmed so that children come into the world able to pick up the sounds and grammar of any language after very little exposure to it (Chomsky and Halle 1968; Lenneberg 1969; Wahler 1969; Bandura 1969; Bloom 1970).

The argument makes sense; in fact, compari-

Teaching a chimp to talk. Do you think they teach him to clean his teeth, too?

sons of all the world's languages show few differences in their basic structures. Despite their variations, all languages are more alike than not in fundamental ways.

Opponents of the idea that language is innate point out that while the human brain is larger than the ape brain, it is similar in make-up. They argue that speech depends less on neural wiring than on imitation of adult family members (Mowrer 1958; Skinner 1959). So, if a baby chimp were raised exactly like a human baby, would it start babbling "mama" before long?

The question is crucial, since language is what makes humans human. The great apes build crude shelters, if not skyscrapers, create rudimentary social alliances, if not country clubs, and make simple tools, if not laser beams and rockets. What they cannot do is manipulate symbols—so far.

Language is the most universal form of symbolic manipulation among human beings. It has allowed us to store information about the world into arbitrary units of speech and writing. This accumulation of information permits a culture to develop and knowledge to be passed on so that each generation can build on the experiences of the previous one. Whereas apes are doomed to live now as they always have lived, human beings are able—through language and the culture it makes possible—to transform every aspect of their existence. The radical changes wrought by science and technology depend on manipulating symbols. And computers, the pride and terror of our civilization, are really enormously swift symbol manipulating boxes.

So you can see what all the fuss is about—and why many people were surprised at the news in 1969 that a chimp named Washoe was learning to talk. Actually, not "talk" since the chimp's vocal apparatus is less well developed than ours, but rather to use American sign language (the hand symbols used by deaf people).

Now, no one gets excited when a parrot talks, because parrots do not know what words "mean"—that is, they cannot create new combinations of words to fit new situations. Parrots simply "parrot." Washoe, however, learned the sign language symbol for *flower* and applied it not only to real flowers but to *pictures* of flowers. When Washoe wanted to go past a gate into a garden, he combined (all on his own) the symbols for *flower* and *open.* When he heard an unseen dog barking, he combined the symbols for *listen* and *dog* (Brown 1970; Gardner 1969; Premack, 1970).

Neoteny Don't get worried. You will not have to "rap" with every chimp you meet or let your sister marry one. Teaching Washoe was a long and painful process and his stock of words never exceeded a hundred items, more or less. What the experiment has shown is that an ape's ability to learn is much more like a human being's than we had suspected (Fleming 1974; Rumbaugh, *et al.* 1973). *Baby* chimps, incidentally, are every bit as good at learning as human infants. The difference between the two species is that *adult* chimps are much less able to learn than adult human beings. We go on learning fast, the chimp stops. This fact has led some scientists to suggest that perhaps human beings are in a state of arrested infancy

relative to other primates (Clark 1959; Montagu 1965).

This theory, called *neoteny,* comes from the observation that humans, at any stage of life, have many characteristics resembling those of *baby* apes, such as a flatness of face, the large volume of the brain relative to the spinal cord's and whole body's weight, and the relative hairlessness of the body. Perhaps the evolutionary step from ape to human occurred because, somehow, some apes were able to retain their infantile facility to learn. Indeed, human beings retain some capacity to learn right up to senility, though beyond early childhood, it grows slower and slower with age.

EVOLUTION: THE LONG VIEW OF THE NATURE-NURTURE STORY

Up to now, we have talked as if it was obvious what heredity means. But it is only obvious in a very narrow sense, as the structural determinants of an individual's behavior. Viewed this way, the distinction between heredity and experience seems easy to understand, even if it is hard to separate them empirically. But a broader view of heredity says it is not merely the inborn structure of the individual but the accumulation and transmission of those structures down the generations. Then, an entirely new perspective opens up on the nature-nurture question. It comes from understanding the meaning of *evolution.*

Evolution is the genetic process by which species change and by which one species emerges from another. In 1859 Charles Darwin first presented clear evidence for his theory to the world—one of the most revolutionary ideas in history. For centuries, people had observed the similarities between different species, but Darwin was the first scientist to document in detail how each species might have arisen out of an earlier one. He hypothesized that three

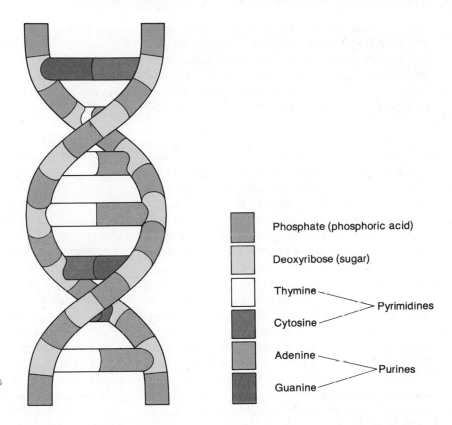

Figure 2.1 The double helix is the molecule of DNA. It carries the blue print of our genetic makeup.

Phosphate (phosphoric acid)

Deoxyribose (sugar)

Thymine ⟶
                    ⟶ Pyrimidines
Cytosine ⟶

Adenine ⟶
                    ⟶ Purines
Guanine ⟶

principles were at work: *Heredity, random variation,* and *natural selection* (Darwin, orig. pub. in 1859). The details actually governing their operation differ somewhat from Darwin's ideas about them, but their fundamental meaning is unchanged. Taken together, these principles offer a new way of looking at the interaction of heredity and environment.

Heredity here simply means the tendency of like to beget like—the law of nature that dictates that children will resemble parents due to what we now know to be the self-replicating genetic material in the egg and sperm, i.e., DNA, the *coding* molecules, which cause cells to duplicate themselves exactly.

Random variation refers to the bewildering abundance of living forms that occurs within every species. No child ever exactly resembles either parent, or even an exact composite of both parents. The number of different genetic combinations which each parent carries in its array of sperm or eggs is so gigantic, that the chances of any individual ever being born an exact natural duplicate[1] of any other, from the beginning of life on earth until its yet unknown end, are almost infinitely small. And the number of new combinations of the species is doubled each time an offspring gives birth. Of the genes the child actually does receive from its parents, moreover, some are active

---

[1] By "natural duplicate," I mean as a product of the parents' sexual union, with sperm, egg, embryo, and fetus, permitted to grow, unite, and split at will. There are other ways aborning, called "genetic engineering."

determinants of its characteristics and some are not. Those that are not are merely passed along with no effect on the child's appearance or behavior. Brown-eyed parents, for instance, may bear a blue-eyed baby; the genes for blue eyes were passed along in their bodies, from their parents, without affecting the eye color of either of them.

Variation in the species occurs not only through new combinations of old genes but also by the creation of new genes. This is called *mutation.* A mutation is a radical change in the structure of a gene which produces a new characteristic, sometimes even a new species. A few mutations occur in every several million births. Most mutations are *maladaptive,* that is, harmful; for instance, a maladaptive mutation might cause a child to be born with three eyes or no arms. *Mutants* usually do not live long and are often sterile if they do. If they do live, moreover, they have a hard time competing with the normal members of the species for food. They are weeded out by *natural selection* or "the survival of the fittest," the third principle of evolution, according to Darwin. But on very rare occasions, a lucky mutation occurs, and the whole contest for survival in that species takes a new turn.

Natural selection

All living things compete for food and water and space—and in the long run, all of them lose the struggle for survival. Meanwhile, some have natural advantages over others, in size, in speed, in ability to bear thirst or hunger for long periods, and so forth. Some creatures crowd out the competition by becoming bigger, fiercer, and more intelligent. Their superior size, aggressiveness, and cleverness allow them to take food from their inferiors—or to make food of their inferiors. Other animals succeed by developing the capacity of getting food in new, unoccupied *ecological niches,* that is, positions in the balance of organisms

and environment where other animals have not previously staked a claim. Developing the necessary capabilities, in evolutionary terms, means living long enough to bear progeny whose ability to survive in that environment enables them to live long enough to have progeny—and on and on. The process is a cruel one. The only criterion of fitness for survival is surviving. Whoever is left, wins—for a while, until conditions change unfavorably or until some new species, even better equipped for your environment than you are, comes in to push you out. Changing climate wiped out the dinosaurs; predatory men all but wiped out the bison. From the standpoint of evolution, it is all the same.

It is important that you understand this process because it explains how we got to be the lords of the planet that we are—by accident—and because it will help you to understand that this kind of accident will not occur again, nor the process of evolution on this planet ever again proceed in a "natural" course, meaning one in which we *respond* to the environment, as all earth's creatures have done until now. Humanity actively changes the environment; we do not just adapt to it.

When a lucky mutation occurs, a new trait develops which permits an animal to adapt better to the environment than its brothers and cousins can. The environment then exerts what is called *selective pressure* favoring the propagation of the new mutant. In plain language, it means this one's offspring live, the others' die. Eventually, the favorable mutation, once a freak or *sport* among its kin, becomes the dominant member of its species or, if it has changed enough, becomes the ancestor of a new species. One selective pressure favored some animals becoming larger—the larger an animal is, the harder it is to eat it and the more likely, therefore, that it will live to propagate more of its own kind. Being big also improves their chances of survival—up to a point. Bigger size also needs bigger food supplies, which

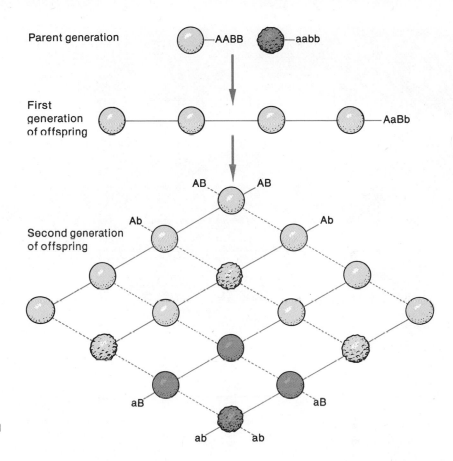

Parent generation

First generation of offspring

Second generation of offspring

Figure 2.2 Gregor Mendel's exhaustive studies of pea plants in the 1800s established the laws of genetics.

may require more speed or endurance or brains to get—or lucky new mutations, which permit the species to occupy new territory. When mutant fish became amphibians, for example, they were able to lumber up to dry land and feed on insects, which previously had not been harried by predators. Similarly, when mutant reptiles became birds, they were able to fly to treetops, an *ecological niche* that had previously been unoccupied. These mutations were adaptive and survived. There is no such thing as a perfect adaptation, though, because circumstances keep changing, making new demands on animals, and mutations are not dependable ways to meet them. What you have perhaps been taught to think of as "nature's balance" is *never in balance.* New

species come and go all the time, as the environments they live in constantly change. Just ask the dinosaurs and ferns, whose oily remains are pumped up from the Arabian desert, about the lush swamps in which they once thrived.

But even though no adaptation is perfect, clearly some are better than others at any time in evolutionary history. And though new forms or evolution may not be long-range improvements over the old ones, there still seems to be some direction to the evolution of animals over millions of years. The earliest organisms were probably single-celled and evolved into larger and faster creatures with specialized cells as they engaged in ever more complex actions to get food. Some of these cell groups

Lioness with gazelle she killed. Some lose the struggle for survival earlier than others.

turned into receptors (the sensory organs) for recording impressions of the environment— eyes to spot food, ears to detect enemies, and so on. Other cells became effectors (glands and muscles). Muscles allowed the animal to move; glands gave it internal controls over growth and intake of food and water, and over emotions, like fear or rage. Yet a third category of cells became the nervous system, coordinating the information from the receptors with the activities of the effectors.

As the *complexity* of animals increases, so does their *adaptability.* An animal with sense organs has tremendous advantages over animals without them. A creature with an internal heating and cooling system can survive much greater changes in climate than one dependent on the sun for warmth. An animal with a brain can respond adaptively to far more changing conditions than one without. Mammals have many advantages, in complexity, over other animals; primates over other mammals; humans over other primates. It is mostly differ-ences of brain and nerve that made this so.

The evolutionary history of humanity is linked to the experience of our early primate ancestors, perhaps 25 to 70 million years ago, because during that period, primates took to the trees in the broad forests that made up most of the habitable world. This was an ecological niche never occupied before (birds lived higher up, and did not compete directly for food, in most respects). Filling it dictated the evolution of body structures and behavior patterns which eventually made it possible for the prehuman descendants of those primates to descend from the trees and live first, in open woodlands (Simon · 1977), and then on the beaches when climatic changes made the interior too hot. There, the evolution of brain and body continued to advance, so that later still, when humans headed inland once again to forage in the savannahs, the dry grassy plains that replaced the forests everywhere, they were tool-bearing animals who knew the uses of weapons and of shelters (Morgan 1972; Pfeiffer 1969). In the

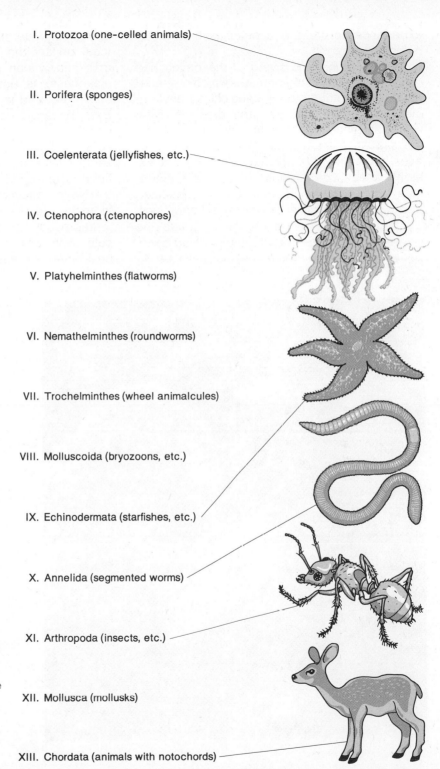

I. Protozoa (one-celled animals)

II. Porifera (sponges)

III. Coelenterata (jellyfishes, etc.)

IV. Ctenophora (ctenophores)

V. Platyhelminthes (flatworms)

VI. Nemathelminthes (roundworms)

VII. Trochelminthes (wheel animalcules)

VIII. Molluscoida (bryozoons, etc.)

IX. Echinodermata (starfishes, etc.)

X. Annelida (segmented worms)

XI. Arthropoda (insects, etc.)

XII. Mollusca (mollusks)

XIII. Chordata (animals with notochords)

Figure 2.3 As animals go from one cell to larger numbers of cells, the functions of different cells tend to become more specialized and the behavioral capabilities of the creature accordingly become more complex.

experiences of trees and beaches, the birth of humankind began.

Tree dwelling and living at the beach had dramatic effects on the primates which prepared them for adaptation to all kinds of later environments. Its first, and perhaps greatest effect was that, since tree dwelling and wading into the sea gave them protection from most enemies, primates did not have to evolve many highly specialized organs like fangs and claws; their bodies remained relatively unspecialized and widely useful in a variety of situations.

Second, these living conditions made the sense of smell less important than it had been, because smelling (olfaction) is less useful in trees or water than on land for tracking down food or avoiding enemies. As olfaction diminished, vision grew sharper. *Visual acuity* (keenness) is essential for the delicate precision required to swing from branch to branch. Eyes became more sensitive to color, detail, and texture, and they also became stereoscopic — that is, both eyes were placed on the same plane of the face so that their visual fields overlapped. This gives a better perspective which allows the viewer to gauge position in space precisely.

Improved vision allowed apes to communicate with one another in new ways. They developed a great variety of facial expressions

Grooming, a primitive form of affectionate social communication.

and posturings. Social communication through such means, through touch, in the form of mutual grooming, and through a variety of growls and screeches, tended to encourage grouping into bands of perhaps 10 to 50 members; with that, primate *society* was born (Morris 1969a and 1969b; Clark 1959). Creatures that could screech and growl intelligibly to each other could live together without constant danger of bashing each other's heads in by impulse or mistake.

These processes did not occur in orderly fashion, of course, but by lucky accidents of mutation which happened to let one creature survive and propagate under the circumstances in which it found itself and which killed another, differently mutated one, under those same circumstances with equal indifference. Evolution is not a kindly process, nor an obviously purposeful one. It just worked out all right for us — so far. And while it took millions of years, most of the important changes probably did not occur gradually at all, but rather suddenly, as a chance mutation (itself always a sudden event, viewed from the perspective of history) started making itself felt within a species as soon as the generation which had it started giving birth to lively offspring, while the neighbors' children died.

The most important difference between the primates and lower mammals, in any case, is that in the apes instinctive behavior was replaced more and more by learned behavior. Apes profited from experience, learning to *delay* their reactions to it rather than reacting to it instinctively. Simpler members of the animal kingdom are programmed, by and large, to respond to their environment in strict, unvarying action patterns (Finger and Mook 1971). These creatures are dominated by their senses — they respond to the immediate sights, sounds, smells, and other sensations from their surroundings, and they respond with only a small variety of quite stereotyped actions.

But the higher mammals, and the primates in particular, are wired to behave in a more complex way through *mediating processes* (ideas, thinking). A mediating process is a delaying process; it permits an animal to inhibit its reaction to a new stimulus, recalling past experiences and shaping new responses in accord with them. The same stimulus provokes different responses on different occasions. And some behavior originates entirely from thoughts or ideas, rather than from an immediate sensory stimulus.

In lower animals, the message received through the sense receptors is routed directly to the effectors (muscles and glands). But among the higher mammals, and most of all us, the stimuli registered by the senses first pass through parts of the brain that sort them out, weigh them in the light of past experience, and decide what, if anything, to do before a message is sent down to the muscles. Such processes have a high evolutionary value, since they permit mammals to adjust to *new* situations — new threats and new promises — and to respond with *original* behavior. Memory, learning, and thinking free an animal from fixed action patterns.

But this freedom was not bought in one or even a thousand generations, and *it was not the product of anything we learned;* on the contrary, *it produced our capacity for learning* by gradually changing our hereditary structure in ways which were more and more flexibly adaptive to the environment. As it turned out, the capacities it left us with were so flexible that we could eventually learn to create our own environments!

In any case, if we now return to the question of what heredity is, and repeat that it is the physical structure which species acquire and transmit through the process of evolution, we come to an interesting irony, because *evolution is the process by which experience shapes heredity.* Natural selection is the effect of experience on the random variations which one generation has transmitted to another. It slowly weeds them out, favoring one mutation over another, giving one species preference in the endless competition of living things for life.

So while we are products of learning, all right, and while learning is involved in virtually every human activity above the level of reflexes, *we inherit the ability to learn from experience.* We have indeed come full circle in the nature-nurture problem. They are products of each other.

Perhaps there are biologically coded "memories" of our primate past that continue to haunt us. Perhaps our fear of snakes really is innate. Monkeys who have never seen snakes shrink from them in horror (Hebb 1968); maybe we too are programmed to recoil from serpents. Since we are human, however, we can *learn* to ignore such fears and open up shop with flute and cobra. Perhaps the impulse to order trespassers off your property does obey a genetically laid-down "territorial imperative." Primates *do* have home ranges, and one very popular book claimed that the "instinct" has passed over to humans (Ardrey 1968 and 1970). But maybe not. Monkeys do not stake out rigidly defined "territories" like we do but rather roam across overlapping home ranges. When one band is traveling, it screeches loudly to scare off another band and avoid a collision (Washburn and DeVore, 1961). Fights rarely break out between different bands of apes, unlike humans. Maybe territoriality is a template, but it is not instinctive among human beings.

When a six year old boy starts fighting with his playmates, instead of playing peacefully with dolls, he probably is not revealing an innate male dominance. Certainly the life of hunting tribes (hunting has occupied a large fraction of human existence) favored the natural selection of big, strong males; any fool could tell you that men (i.e., the hunters) are larger than women and stronger in short-term exertions (although women are better able to endure pain, cold, and fatigue). But it is very doubtful that men are "instinctively" dominant over women. If men lord it over women, it is because they have found themselves with a "good thing" going, not because some biological instinct makes them do it. By the same argument we must dismiss the claim that friendship bonds among men are more "natural" than those among women. Such claims seem to be merely pouring the old wine of male chauvinism into new, supposedly "scientific" flasks (Montagu 1968; Tiger 1969; Walster 1970).

Clearly human beings have reflexes, and clearly they have developmental norms as well. But it is not clear that anything exists in between, more general than the former and more specific than the latter. If human beings have instincts, they are too diffuse and vestigial to identify. This does not mean, as you should know by now, that we are any less the products of heredity than other animals. It simply means that the structure we have inherited permits us to adapt so flexibly and so intelligently to stimuli that our behavior is more characterized by its flexibility than by the primitive response structures that limit it.

In large part, that is what psychology is all about; the enormous adaptive flexibility people have, called the ability to learn, or educability. It does not replace our heredity; *it fulfills it.* But in doing so, it overshadows it as well and makes it more important for you to know about the vast number of things we can learn to do than about the few we cannot help doing.

SUMMARY

1   There is a widespread belief that there is some "natural" way of living which would be optimal for humanity. Starting with Adam and Eve living in "purity" in the Garden of

Eden, the idea is expressed in the writings of Jean Jacques Rousseau that the "noble savage" is corrupted by civilization and that children, left alone to express their natural inclinations, or *instincts,* would grow up fine.

2 The debate over whether behavior is determined by inborn characteristics or by learning from experience is called the *nature-nurture controversy.* The "naturist" position is that most human *behavior* is determined by *genetics* playing much the same role in temperament and personality that it does in eye color or height. The "nurturist" position is that most behavior is learned by reward and punishment.

3 In reality, heredity and environment are not opposing forces. Biology sets the limits to human behavior, but permits a wide range of cultural and individual differences for meeting our needs within those limits. The variety of behavior patterns across cultures suggests that most human behavior patterns are learned, not inherited.

4 Behavior occurs at different levels of organization. The lowest level of organized behavior is the *reflex,* an unlearned fixed response of a muscle group or gland to a specific stimulation. Reflex behavior is simple and immediate. *Instinctive* behavior involves a higher level of organization. Here, a whole pattern of unlearned behavior, often quite complex, is triggered by a single stimulus, called a *release mechanism.* Some scholars believe that some human behavior patterns are instinctive, but there is no clear evidence that instincts exist in human beings. *Templates* are a still higher level of organization, referring to a kind of biological behavior program which may be common across cultures. Like instincts, templates are hypothetical.

6 *Twin* studies are often useful in demonstrating the relative influences of hereditary and environmental factors in behavior. Such studies have shown some hereditary influences in intelligence, in some mannerisms, and in some health patterns, but not on interests, preferences, or other aspects of personality.

7 *Imprinting* is a good illustration of the interaction between innate biological processes and learning. When young ducks, and some other species, reach a *sensitive* or *critical period* in their *maturation* (that is, their biologically determined growth), they learn to attach themselves to certain companions, usually their mother, and remain attached to her until adulthood. If the object in front of them at that time is a man, however, they will attach themselves to him with equal devotion. The behavior is learned, but it only gets learned on the animal's inborn maturation schedule. Human beings do not undergo imprinting, though some maturational periods may be more critical than others for certain aspects of human development, such as language learning.

8 There is some dispute about whether language ability is innate or not, though specific languages are always learned. Language ability seems to be unique to human beings, but chimpanzees have been taught to use speech signs meaningfully. A theory, called *neoteny,* argues that human ability differs from that of other animals because we keep our *infantile* capacity to learn rapidly throughout life, whereas this capacity diminishes in other animals as they mature.

9 All human capacities have evolved. The theory of evolution proposed by Charles Darwin in 1859 has three principles. *Heredity* is the idea that children resemble their parents because they are created from the self-replicating genetic material which the parents transmit. *Random variation* says that variety within a species results from random combinations of parental genes in the offspring and by the creation of new genes through *mutation. Natural selection,* or the "survival of the fittest," is the idea that some mutations are more adaptive than others, and the bearers of these mutations will reproduce more successfully than their cousins.

10 The theory of evolution contributes to the nature-nurture discussion by indicating that *our hereditary structure is acquired by experience* through the natural selection of favorable mutations and that *the ability to learn from experience is the most important part of our hereditary structure.*

11 The primate heritage of human beings accounts for many of our characteristics. By living in trees and on beaches, primates did not have to develop specialized organs to fight or burrow with; also, the sense of smell became less valuable and the sense of vision grew sharper. This in turn permitted the development of tools and of precise communications by gesture and expression. All of these contributed to a more refined nervous system with which the higher apes could mediate (process) information in the brain before responding to stimulation. In us, every activity beyond the simple reflex is mediated. The intelligence that a human being inherits, the developmental stages that we pass through, even such basic drives as hunger and sex—all are subject to learning. All can be molded into new behavior. *Homo sapiens* is the animal that can be *educated.*

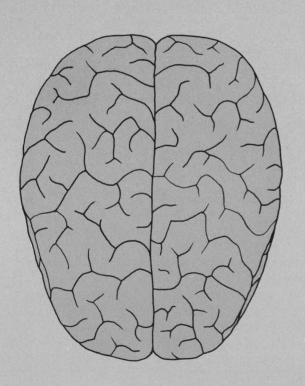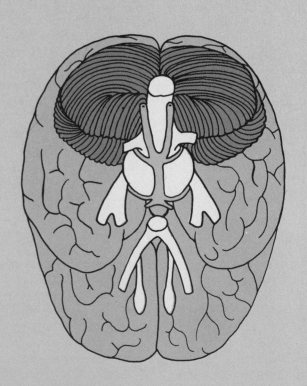

The biological basis of behavior: Two–the brain and nervous systems

3

3

The biological basis of behavior: Two–the brain and nervous systems

Psychology, you recall, means the study of the soul or spirit. Most of that spirit dwells in the brain. All of the processes we will discuss in this book are connected to the structures of the nervous system, especially the brain. Its anatomy and physiology will generally be of little interest to us because we are concerned with the psychological processes that are governed inside the skull, and not with its plumbing. Even so, in any extensive study of psychology you will have to encounter such technical terms as *neural impulse, reflex, excitation, threshold, autonomic response, afferent,* and *efferent neurons,* and many others which convey things you need to know about the machinery underlying behavior to fully grasp the behavior itself.

While psychology is more concerned with behavior than with its physical basis, you cannot completely disregard one and thoroughly understand the other. How much you need to know about the brain and nervous system in order to understand behavior depends partly on the kind of behavior you are studying and partly on the kind of analysis you want to make of it. The more you are concerned with the fundamentals of individual behavior, like sensation or emotion or memory, the more you may need to know about the mechanisms which underly them. If you are concerned more with people's interactions with each other, that is, with the social rather than the biological aspects of psychology, then the less you probably will care about the physical apparatus involved.

But the *level of analysis* is more important than the *kind of behavior* studied in determining how much attention you must pay to neurophysiology. Ultimately, social behavior is as much a product of the physical workings of the brain and nervous system as are vision and emotion. This becomes obvious when someone "runs riot" and commits mayhem because they are suffering from "temporal lobe epilepsy" or some other form of brain damage (Mark and Ervin 1971). Or when neurosurgeons manipulate the social behavior of monkeys, or of humans, by electrically stimulating the right brain tissue (Delgado 1969), turning passive, subservient monkeys into ferocious warriors and "boss" monkeys into snivelling cowards. This does not make it sensible to try reducing everything to brain physiology by a long shot, because it does not mean that you are interested in understanding it in those terms. To drive a car, you need to know plenty about steering and clutching and braking and accelerating (the behavior of the machine), and perhaps even more about traffic and signals and pedestrians (the interaction with the environment), but you don't need to know much about the physics of combustion or the mechanics of transmissions or the hydraulics of brakes (automotive neurophysiology).

In their efforts to make psychology as scientifically rigorous as physics or chemistry, some psychologists once fancied that only a model of the brain could provide the final understanding of behavior that would command the universal respect of scientists. A nerve fiber that can be traced and probed seems, at first glance, more *real* than the impalpable sequences of human behavior; brain tissue seems more certifiably *there* than such airy sprites as thought, emotion, perception, and volition. Today psychology is enough accepted so that the once heavy emphasis upon neurology has been lifted; we need not know exactly where a memory is stored in the brain to study the rate at which it is acquired or retrieved, nor do we have to fathom the psychophysiology of vision to teach someone how to read.

Even so, you need to know something about the brain, not so much as an anatomical structure nor a set of physiological processes, but as the **executive apparatus** of your life. Your brain is the control center of your body and the headquarters of your mind. It is the seat of your consciousness and the arbiter of your existence. It is the latest development in humanity's evolution from a brutal wild animal victimized by its environment to a powerful intelligence that can shape the environment to fit its needs. It is all that makes you know or care that you are alive. It is all that stands between you and death, officially now, because legal determinations of death are now largely measured by the brain's failure to emit electrical discharges on the EEG or electroencephalograph (a Greek word meaning "electric brain writer") rather than by when the heart stops beating. It is all that makes you *yourself* rather than a random blob of wired-up protoplasm. So you should know a little bit about it, like where it is located,[1] what its general shape and structure is, and something of how it works. There is probably no subject in all the biological sciences that will get as much scientific and clinical study, in the long run, as the study of brain tissue and brain processes. There is none more important.

There are three things you will get some perspective on by knowing a little about the brain. First, you will understand more about where humankind came from, for the evolution of the human brain is what distinguishes us most from other animals. Second, you will get some idea of just how complex the executive apparatus of behavior really is, which should help you understand why it is so hard to speak with certainty about the basis of human behavior. Third, you should come to understand that the brain is a piece of soft machinery that can be tinkered with, and that such tinkering can provide powerful controls over behavior, which may be exercised more and more in the future.

THE EVOLUTION OF THE BRAIN: GETTING A SWELLED HEAD

The brain gets more pampering and protection than any other part of your body. The blood supply to the brain is more constant and more dependable than that which a fetus gets from

---

[1] The brain is located in the head.

its mother. When a baby is born, the bones at the top of the skull are not yet joined together. Once they do join, the closed skull, with its thick wall of bone, gives more armor to the brain's tissue than anything else in the body gets. And when that armor is pierced, and some brain tissue gets damaged or destroyed, the enormous *redundancy* (overabundance) of this machine comes into play and new parts sometimes take over the functions which were lost.

All this makes sense considering what the brain does. *We live in our heads;* if they get chopped off, we die more decisively, and less by accident, than with any other part. If you transplant a heart or lung to someone, you *repair* them; if you could transplant a brain, you would *destroy* them. The transplantee lived in the old brain; the new one has another person in it. What might happen in such situations

Brain container.

Stone Head,
Amedeo Modigliani

has been speculated in popular science-fiction writings, such as *I will fear no evil,* by Robert Heinlein (1970). This idea is not entirely an *anthropomorphization* of the brain (giving human characteristics to it, as if it were a person instead of a thing), for everything in us that makes up awareness, sensation, and experience, involves it. We *think* with our brains opening and closing electrical and chemical switches; we *feel* with our glands pouring stimulants and depressants into the blood stream and signalling the brain to interpret their effects; and we *act* in a concert of electrical, chemical, and mechanical negotiations between dozens, or hundreds, or millions of distinct parts and pieces, almost all of which are tied to the brain's commands.

From an evolutionary point of view, the entire brain is simply a swelling at one end of the spinal cord. In lower vertebrates, the mass of the spinal cord is much larger than the mass of the brain. As we move up the ladder of evolution, the brain becomes bigger and the relative mass of the spinal cord becomes much smaller (Meglitsch 1967).

The effect of this shift is to delegate many of the activities formerly handled by the spinal cord to the control of the brain. Reflex actions are governed by the spinal cord and can be modified only a little; if you grip your hands together just before the tendon is tapped for a knee jerk reflex, for instance, the jerk will probably be more pronounced. But that is about as big a variation as ever occurs in reflexes (Weidenweich 1948). More complex human activities—those that are capable of being delayed, learned, or combined with other behavior—are in the province of the brain.

The parts and pieces of the human and primate brain differ in many ways from those of other mammals and lower organisms. Primates still have the primitive brain structures common to all vertebrate animals but have erected new structures with new mental capacities upon this foundation. Basically, the brain consists of three layers: (1) next to the spinal cord, a primitive *brain stem;* (2) behind it, the *cerebellum;* and (3) above it, taking up most of the space in the skull and covering the other structures, the *cerebrum,* or *new brain.* The new brain is the center of all higher mental processes, of perception, memory, reasoning, and volition (making decisions).

As we move up the phylogenetic ladder in our direction, there is a striking increase in the relative size of the entire brain, but even more in the size of the outer surface of the cerebrum, called the *cortex* (meaning bark). In humans, that surface is terribly *convoluted,* that is, covered with folds and wrinkles. Primitive brains are smooth. But the human cortex permits us by its wrinkles to have a vastly enlarged total surface area without necessitating a similarly enlarged skull size. The primitive vertebrate brain is like an inflated beachball encased in the skull box; nature, without much increasing the relative size of the box, has squeezed a brain like a deflated rubber raft into our case.

The expansion of the *cerebrum,* and thus of the total brain size, meant a great increase in mental ability over earlier, smaller-brained species. A gorilla's body, for instance, is about 230 times heavier than its brain, whereas the human body is only about 50 times heavier than our brain. The relative growth of the human brain occurred with remarkable rapidity—far faster than most other large-scale mutations. In the course of only 65,000 generations,[2] the human brain has increased two and one half times. Obviously a strong selective pressure was at work favoring an increase in our mental capacity.

Brain size is not important *within* our own species, however; relative intelligence among people has nothing to do with differences in brain size. The average human brain weighs about 1,350 grams, but the Russian novelist Ivan Turgenev had a brain that weighed about

2,000 grams; the French novelist, Anatole France, had a brain mass of only about 1,110 grams (Montagu 1959, p. 319). Many geniuses have had lightweight brains, and some real dumbbells have been quite top-heavy.

The cortex first appeared as a "pinhead-sized patch of cells on the brain surfaces of the first creatures that came out of the sea and took up life on land." It really became important with the development of mammals, to organize complex behavior. Our earliest primate ancestors, some 65 million years ago, were about the size of rodents. Called prosimians, their brains were "about the size of a walnut on the average, but by this stage of evolution its cortex had spread like a gray tide over the brain's surface and consisted of a thin sheet of millions of nerve cells" (Pfeiffer 1969, p. 27). Gradually, the visual centers at the back of the cortex became more and more important and the smell centers toward the front less so. The centers controlling finger movements also became larger and more specialized; previously there had been a single area controlling the movement of all five fingers at once, but there now developed separate areas to control the separate movements of each one.

These changes in the brain served the needs of animals who had first moved to the trees and required brain structures "designed to coordinate at extremely rapid rates the movements of muscles and sets of muscles involved in . . . climbing, leaping, chasing, and being chased. These structures could take orders from the cortex. . . ." (Pfeiffer 1969, p. 32).

As they became bigger, primates increasingly spent more time on the ground, became meat eaters, and organized in hunting bands. This dangerous, competitive way of life demanded long-range planning and disciplined cooperation, which favored a decrease in the importance of the instantaneous reflex centers of the spinal cord and an increase in the capacity for conscious deliberation which is seated in the higher brain (Campbell 1967).

---

[2] Give or take a few.

Young Woman Mending, Camille Pissarro

A sophisticated brain lets us control each finger separately, and sew.

New nerve pathways developed in consequence—the cerebral expression of new possibilities. . . . The possible routes along which nerve signals may pass from sense organs to muscles increased enormously. The cortex is in part an organ of analysis . . . which lies between stimulus mechanisms and response mechanisms, between experience and action. Its complexity reflected the new complexity of the apes' world.

The ape brain responded to a new way of life and expanded with increased body size. As usual, the cortex expanded most . . . it became wrinkled and folded primarily because the increasing variety of movement, the increasing role of hand-eye coordination, demanded more nerve pathways for the transmission and analysis of information.

The evolving cortex expressed another important trend, a greater and greater stress on inhibition, on the art of not doing things. . . . Choosing a course of action demands the ruling out of many possibilities. It also demands time, deliberation, and delay. Life becomes less automatic and depends to a greater extent than ever before on learning, and learning is an inevitable consequence of complexity in evolution. It became increasingly important among higher species whose environments offered a wider and wider range of choices" (Pfeiffer 1969, p. 35).

And so it has gone, from several million years ago until today. The old parts of the brain have receded in importance and in relative size as more complex needs have demanded a larger cerebral cortex. If evolution were to continue in the same direction, we probably would have a much larger head relative to the rest of our body a million years from now than we do at present. Some science fiction writers have actually pictured us that way (also bald). But evolution is not too likely to go in that direction because our cortical abilities are already so well developed that we can invent tools to do the work that would take millions of years for our brains to evolve capacity for. The most important such tool is the electronic computer, which stretches our computational capacity almost infinitely. By the same token, the technology of transportation extends our legs and mass communication enlarges our senses. We may not evolve a much better brain because the one we have has made it unnecessary.

Let us look briefly now at its machinery.

Neurons and nerves

The brain is the central part of an enormous information processing system. Its basic element, from which the entire structure is put together, is called a *neuron.* Neurons are highly specialized cells with some of the properties of telephone wires, they are biological wires which carry information in the form of tiny electrochemical impulses. There are about 10 billion of them in the human brain.[3] They are generally *insulated,* covered by a fatty tissue called a *myelin sheath.*

Neurons are one-way streets for nerve impulses; they receive messages at one end through short fibers called *dendrites* and pass them to the other end through long fibers called *axons* (Davson 1966). Neurons have type names according to their functions. A neuron that carries information *towards* the spinal cord

or brain (generally meaning that its dendrite is close to a sense organ, its axon further from it) is called *afferent* (Latin for "carrying towards"); one which goes from the brain or cord towards the body (generally meaning the dendrite is close to cord or brain, the axon to a muscle or gland) is called *efferent* (Latin for "carrying out from"). Still other neurons act as connecting wires within the nervous system rather than between a body's organs and the nervous system: they are called interneurons or *associative* or *internuncial* (again Latin for "messengers between") neurons.

Neurons do not actually touch each other or the things they connect; there is a tiny fluid filled gap between them called a *synapse.* When a neuron is *excited* (that is, stimulated) and fires its electrical impulse, tiny vessels in the axon release chemical *transmitters* which generate a new impulse in the next cell. This impulse is called an *action potential.*

A neuron works like a photoflash battery, discharging a pulse of electricity when it gets sparked by some external stimulus. Once it has fired, the neuron must rest before it can fire again. This *absolute refractory period,* when nothing can get the neuron to fire again, is generally very brief—averaging about a thousandth of a second. But it is followed by a *relative refractory period,* when only strong stimulation can get the neuron to fire, and that may last another tenth of a second or more.

Regardless of how strong the stimulus is that excites a neuron, the impulse it fires is always the same strength. A soft sound, for instance, does not make the neuron fire a weak impulse nor a loud sound a strong impulse. If the sound is *too* weak, the neuron will not fire at all; its *absolute threshold* has not been reached. But once the threshold is crossed, the neuron always fires with the same intensity. This is called the *all-or-none* principle. In that respect, the neuron works like a light switch. It makes no difference whether you flick a switch with a fingertip or slam it on with your

---

[3] By actual count. See unpublished doctoral dissertation by Jeremy Glotz, "You can count on your cortex," 1971, U. of Pooh. Dr. Glotz is now employed at the Braille Institute, where he is Chief Example.

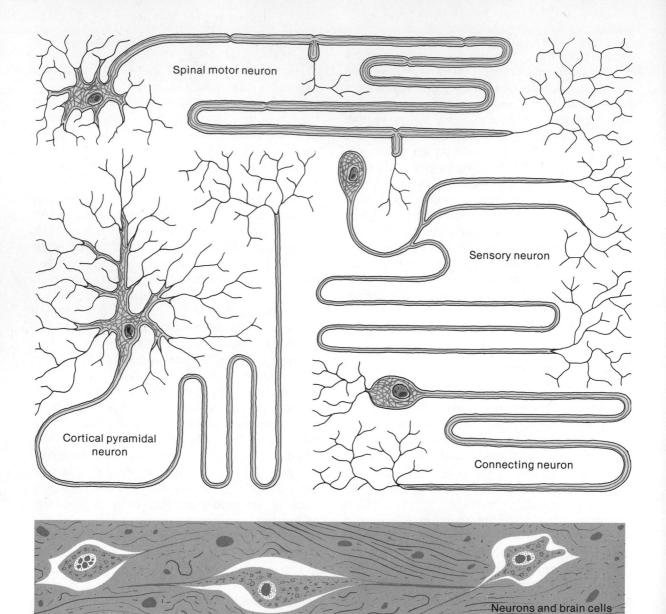

Spinal motor neuron

Sensory neuron

Cortical pyramidal
neuron

Connecting neuron

Neurons and brain cells

Figure 3.1 Neurons come in many varieties but they all have the same
basic structure.

fist, the bulb will always light with the same
intensity.

Of course, we do not *hear* all sounds as
equally loud or soft nor do all sights *look*
equally bright or dim. There are two main rea-

sons for this. First of all, a strong stimulus will
cause the neuron to fire fast and often (but without affecting the strength or speed of each
firing). The greater *intensity* of the stimulus,
in other words, is converted into a greater

frequency of nerve impulses. So even though each firing is *identical,* there are more of them in a given unit of time.

Secondly, a strong stimulus fires more neurons than a weak one. In fact, neurons seldom function singly; they are generally bundled together like copper strands into wires. These bundles are called **nerves** and may consist of many thousands of neurons. The nerve that runs from the ear to the brain, for instance, is made up of about 30,000 individual fibers. The different neurons in a nerve have different thresholds, and a strong stimulus gets more of them into the act. A weak stimulus activates only neurons

Figure 3.2 Complex activities are controlled from a number of brain centers. Here, muscles receive orders to move the arm, while in response to the sound produced, the fingers of the other hand are positioned.

Green Violinist, Marc Chagall

with low thresholds; a strong stimulus activates the neurons with high thresholds as well. In other words, the sound of a Ping-Pong ball might make only a few low-threshold neurons fire, and they would fire at a slow rate; but a cannon blast would fire many neurons, including those with high thresholds, and all of them would fire often (Davson 1966).

Most neurons have thresholds too high for a single weak stimulus to fire them; however, this does not mean that it has no effect at all. These "too-weak" stimuli (called **sub-threshold stimuli**) can each give the cell body a small "push" up towards its threshold (the level at which it will fire). If enough sub-threshold stimuli occur in a short enough period, the little "pushes" can all add up to cause the firing of an impulse. This is called **spatial summation.** It is like the task of lifting a large weight over a wall—one strong man can do it, one weak man cannot. But several weak men pushing in unison can. A single weak stimulus can also push a neuron over the threshold if it fires repeatedly and often enough. This is called **temporal summation.**

The all-or-none principle prevents neurons from being "burned out" by relentless strong stimulation or from being overloaded with information. The neuron is physically designed to process a good deal of information, but in a way that permits it to be **informative,** rather than a jumble of noise. To achieve that end, the number of signals it carries in a given amount of time must be limited.

The bunching of neurons into nerves also vastly increases the amount of information that can be handled by neuronal transmission. We require a lot of neurons and a lot of bundling, which is what we have. The areas of the body in which the nerves are collected in greatest masses, the brain and spinal cord, are, as you would expect, the centers governing the whole business. Thus their title: **the central nervous system.** You need to know a little more about its setup than we have said so far.

THE CENTRAL NERVOUS SYSTEM (CNS)

We have been talking about the central nervous system (CNS) as if the spinal cord were separate from the brain and the parts of the brain from each other. But they are continuous with each other in much the way your hand is continuous with your wrist. In evolutionary terms, remember, the whole brain is a great swelling of the spinal cord, and much of the **brain stem** looks exactly like that, a thickening at the top. The **cerebellum** and **cerebrum** are quite distinct, and so is the upper part of the brain stem, but it is all one system, and to understand its significance, you must keep its continuity in mind as you examine the parts.

In general, the geography of the different parts follows their functions and evolutionary history. The farther south something is, the more primitive and essential to life its functions are; the farther north, the more complex and sophisticated are the things the system can do.[4] By the same token, the older parts of the system are far more specialized and rigid in their functions and the newer, cortical parts far more flexible. Although there is also plenty of **localization** of function in the cortex, meaning that specific areas control specific aspects of behavior, there is an enormous capacity for what is called **mass action**—the ability of millions of unspecialized cells to serve a variety of functions.

For practical purposes, you need to see the CNS as two interlocking systems: The old part, spine, cerebellum, and brain stem, which controls the processes of life and the animal characteristics of people, and which is not easily subject to learning. And the new part, the cere-

---

[4] This does not refer to Southern California, where I live, but to looking at the CNS from a top-to-bottom perspective. The conventional anatomy of the brain, however, calls the cerebrum and top of the brain stem *forebrain*, the middle of the brain stem *midbrain*, the cerebellum and the bottom of the brain stem *hindbrain*. If you get down on your hands and knees in front of a mirror, you will see why.

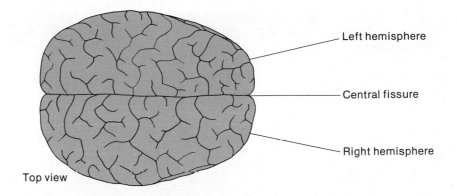

Left hemisphere

Central fissure

Right hemisphere

Top view

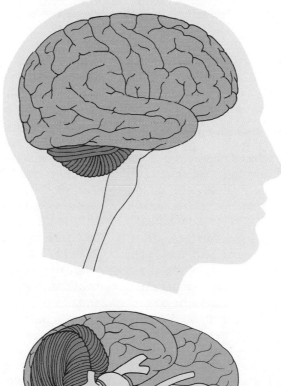

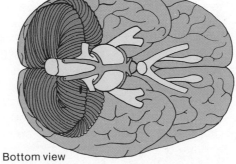

Figure 3.3 The brain.   Bottom view

brum, which controls all the most complex acts of higher animals and which, in people, makes us distinctively human; it is very subject to learning.

We need not say much here about the spinal cord and cerebellum. The spinal cord evidently performs reflex functions only, with all the higher processes like perception and learning seated in the brain. Its "wiring" is very simple. A *sensory* neuron carries an impulse into the cord, an *association* neuron relays it to a *motor* neuron, and the motor neuron in turn sends a message to a muscle or gland for action. The process is a rudimentary one-two-three affair. The cerebellum is largely responsible for maintaining posture, balance, and movement. Also, it has neural connections with all the sensory systems, but no one knows its exact functions. There is more to say about the brain stem, and most of all about the cerebrum.

The brain stem: Vegetation and animation

The most important reflex processes are not those which cause muscle responses, but those which maintain life itself. These are called *vegetative functions,* an apt name because it reflects the basic biological kinship of humanity and celery—they both breathe, they both grow, they both metabolize nutrients, and they both dispose of wastes. Different parts of the brain stem regulate all such activities: respiration, metabolism, and the glands which control some of these things and of emotion. Parts of the stem also control body temperature, the concentration of salt in the blood, heart rate, and blood pressure. If sudden danger throws the body into alarm, or if sudden changes of temperature threaten its survival, parts of the brain stem set processes in motion to prepare the body for self-defense or to return it to a state of equilibrium.

In general, the functions of different parts of the stem follow the geography, or line of evolutionary development, indicated above. Breath-

ing, a pure vegetative function, is controlled by the medulla, at the bottom of the brain, near the spinal cord. Simple animal-like functions, such as controlling internal temperature or blood pressure, are regulated higher up in the brain stem in the **hypothalamus,** just beneath the top part of the brain stem, called the **thalamus** ("hypo" is Greek for under). And structures like the hypothalamus and the groups of organs composing the **limbic system,** also in the upper regions of the brain stem, control many animal activities that require a sequence of performance steps, like hunger, thirst, fighting, making love, and some of the emotional reactions connected with them. People with lesions (cuts or breaks) in a part of the limbic system become incapable of carrying out sequences that they have planned (Scoville and Milner 1957). If one starts off to market to buy things for supper, for instance, the smallest distraction, such as a greeting from a friend or a sudden rainstorm, may make them forget all their intentions.

Two main structures in the brain stem connect its functions with each other and with the cerebrum: the **thalamus,** at the top of the stem, near the cerebrum, and the **reticular formation** (also called **reticular activating system**), towards the bottom of it. The thalamus is called the "great relay station" of the brain because it connects so many activities of the cerebral cortex and the stem, just as its strategic placement between them would suggest. The reticular formation also has innumerable connections with all parts of the cortex and the stem. It seems to be the primary mechanism in vertebrates for regulating *consciousness* and attention. This makes it important in every aspect of learning and thinking, let alone in feeding, fighting, and so forth. No bigger than your little finger, it is a kind of alertness switch. If you are put to sleep by general anesthesia, unconsciousness apparently results from the deactivation of neurons in the reticular formation (Maincastle 1968). Damage to this area makes an animal sleep most of the time. You too.

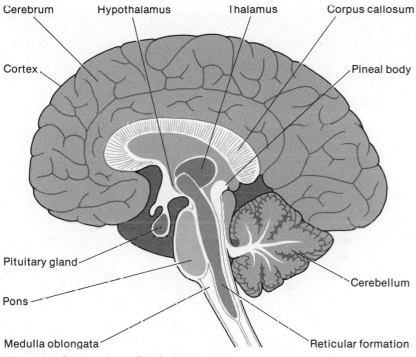

Cerebrum   Hypothalamus   Thalamus   Corpus callosum

Cortex

Pineal body

Pituitary gland

Pons

Medulla oblongata

Cerebellum

Reticular formation

Figure 3.4 Schematic medial view of the brain.

The cerebral cortex: Becoming human

Although even the brain stem of human beings is fancier than that of lower animals, it is the new brain, and particularly its covering, the cerebral cortex, that is our chief glory. Our most distinctively *human* behavior originates in the cerebral cortex. It is the largest as well as the fanciest part of the human brain. Nine billion of the brain's ten billion neurons are in the cortex. It is constructed for maximum flexibility, moreover. Unlike those of the spinal cord, cerebellum, and brain stem, the circuits that run through the cerebrum are to a large extent undetermined at birth. Learning and experience link up new circuits every day and lead to new responses. Even when some cells of the cortex are destroyed, as happens constantly to toddlers, who are always falling on their heads and suffering minor brain concussions, the functions involved can be restored by other

cells that are apparently waiting around unused. If you watch a baby who has hit its head hard enough to hurt but not to be knocked out, you will see it stumble around dazed and klutzy for a while—then its coordination (such as it is) will gradually return and it will become alert. again. This capacity continues throughout life for many functions. It is part of the **redundancy** built into the cortex to secure its executive position in the brain's activity.

Another aspect of the cortex' security system is the fact that there are two cortexes, sort of— actually two hemispheres, a left and a right one, which are largely (but not entirely) capable of doing the same things. In most circumstances, they mirror each other—the activities of the left side of the body are generally controlled by the right hemisphere and those of the right side by the left hemisphere (Sperry 1968). You may have heard of people being paralyzed on one side by a "stroke," technically called a "cere-

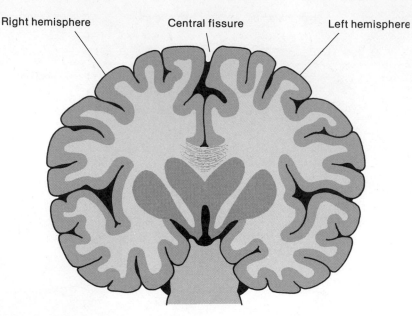

Right hemisphere   Central fissure   Left hemisphere

Figure 3.5 The cortex (dark grey area). Note how much alike the two hemispheres are.

bral hemorrhage." They have suffered a kind of heart attack of the brain, in which a blood vessel burst in one hemisphere and a lot of brain cells died as a result. The hemispheres are not completely redundant or mirrored, of course, which is why some people are left- and others right-handed instead of everyone being ambidextrous. Some aspects of speech, perception, and problem-solving ability are also centered more in one hemisphere than the other. But many functions of one hemisphere are synchronized with the other, largely by the many connecting tissues between them so that damage to the tissues of one will not necessarily destroy the functions it controlled.

There is, in fact, a growing body of evidence which suggests that the two hemispheres of the brain control different aspects of mental function. The left hemisphere may control analytic aspects of thought, like the kinds of reasoning by which you solve problems and do mathematics, and also language. The right hemisphere may control nonanalytic thought of a more intuitive kind, which is used in some

kinds of creativity, in musical and artistic ability, and in holistic perception (Ornstein 1972).

Each hemisphere is divided into four lobes: the frontal lobe, the parietal lobe, the occipital lobe, and the temporal lobe. They are partly separated by large cracks, called *fissures;* the *central fissure* is on top and there is a *lateral fissure* on each side. The different activities controlled by the cortex are spread out over the surface of these different parts.

Most cortical activity involves many of the parts at once. Complicated mental processes like language, memory, reasoning, and perception all require the close interaction of several cortical areas, and translating them into physical movement and other activities involve several more. Information from the sense organs first goes to the different *sensory areas* of the cortex, then gets relayed to the *association areas,* which analyze it, and then gets transmitted to the *motor areas,* from which instructions for action (or inaction) are sent to the body. This may sound just like the sequence in the reflex responses of the spinal cord, but

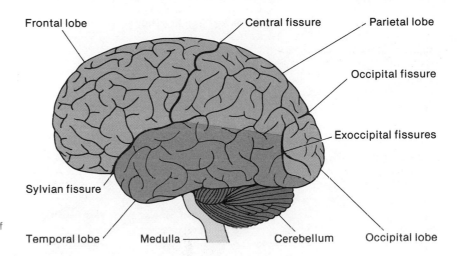

Frontal lobe   Central fissure   Parietal lobe

Occipital fissure

Exoccipital fissures

Sylvian fissure

Figure 3.6 Lobes and fissures of the brain.

Temporal lobe   Medulla   Cerebellum   Occipital lobe

it is a far cry from it. For one thing, reflex stimulation is very simple, while the cortex can process enormously complex messages. For another, information processing in reflexes is always automatic and instantaneous, whereas in cortical activity it can be very lengthy and have any number of outcomes. As Donald Hebb put it, "the distinguishing mark of the higher animal is the capacity to hold an excitation for some time before it has its effect on behavior." In computer talk, you might say that the impulse can be kept alive in the brain on a "circuit loop" until an appropriate decision is made on what to do with it.

Figure 3.7 Motor area of the cortex.

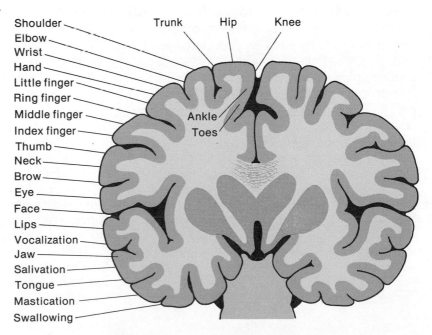

Shoulder   Trunk   Hip   Knee
Elbow
Wrist
Hand
Little finger
Ring finger
Middle finger
Index finger   Ankle
Thumb   Toes
Neck
Brow
Eye
Face
Lips
Vocalization
Jaw
Salivation
Tongue
Mastication
Swallowing

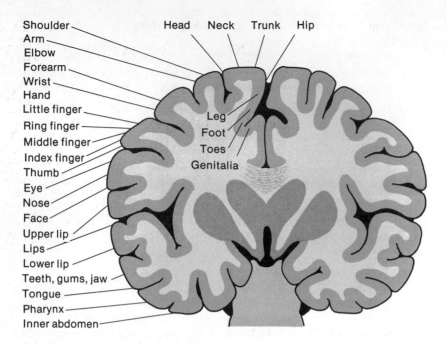

Shoulder
Arm
Elbow
Forearm
Wrist
Hand
Little finger
Ring finger
Middle finger
Index finger
Thumb
Eye
Nose
Face
Upper lip
Lips
Lower lip
Teeth, gums, jaw
Tongue
Pharynx
Inner abdomen

Head   Neck   Trunk   Hip

Leg
Foot
Toes
Genitalia

Figure 3.8 Somatosensory (body-sense) area of the cortex.

The *motor area* of the cortex controls voluntary muscle movements. It is in the frontal lobe, just in front of the central fissure. It covers the area in a sort of upside-down map of the body; roughly speaking, toe movements are controlled by the part near the top of the head, and tongue movements by the part near the bottom. This brain map appears distorted as well as upside-down; on an exact map, the part that controls the legs would be larger than the part that controls the tongue; here it is just the opposite. But the map *is* an accurate representation of the *work* the brain expends on these parts. It takes far more brains to control the tongue than to control the legs.[5] In humans, the tongue must perform extremely varied movements to articulate thousands of speech sounds. Accordingly, it gets a disproportionately large representation in the motor area.

The *speech area* is also in the frontal lobe,

but in the left hemisphere of right-handed people and vice versa. It actually plays only one part in the control of speech; speech is too complex a function to be limited to a single part of the cortex.

The sensory areas of the cortex are spread out much more than the motor areas, and in the parietal, temporal, and occipital lobes rather than the frontal one.

In the parietal lobes (Campbell 1967), just across the central fissure from the motor area, are the brain cells that handle the main skin senses and sense of body position. This area also appears upside down and distorted to reflect the importance of different things. As you might expect, the areas devoted to the lips and fingertips, which are extremely sensitive, are much larger than those devoted to the senses in the feet or trunk of the body.

The mouth and the hands take up a large part of both the motor area and the body-sense area of the human brain. In a dog, only a small amount of cortex represents the forepaws or

---

[5] In fact, some people never make it.

the muzzle; manipulating objects with the fore-paws and the production of articulated sounds (barking) do not play crucial roles in a dog's life. But human beings live in a sea of words and engage in precise, delicate activities with their hands, from playing the piano to cracking safes.

Vision is in the occipital lobe, mainly, though visual perception involves other areas of the brain as well. Apparently, some occipital cells are highly specialized for particular kinds of vision: some cells, for instance, respond only to a horizontal bar of light and others respond only to a vertical bar (Hubel and Wiesel 1965). This suggests that the visual cortex does not wait for visual information to get processed and analyzed only when it is sent along to *association areas,* but rather that it sorts out some of the information as it comes in. The full extent of such sorting is not known, but it is possible that even such perceptual skills as distinguishing between figures in the foreground and the surrounding background may be built into the neural gadgetry of the occipital area.

The *auditory* (hearing) *area* of the brain is in the temporal lobe. The temporal lobe controls some memories as well, in its *association areas.* A Canadian neurosurgeon named Wilder Penfield discovered that stimulating one part of this area produced different kinds of illusions in people's minds, and stimulating another part made them *hear* music that they had long ago listened to, thinking it was being played in the operating room at the time. The people were not crazy; they were just inaccurate. Penfield had accidentally found an area of the brain that controls such perceptions. He called that part of the temporal lobe *the interpretive cortex* (1954).

You may have the impression that the different functions of the cortex are not understood in great detail. This is very true. Most of what it does and how and where it does them are not known. This is most true of the other *association areas.*

Association and integration

The brain functions we have discussed so far use about one quarter of the entire cortical area. The hordes of remaining cells function as *association areas.* These areas integrate and interpret the scattered information the brain receives from all the senses, making them decisively important in learning, memory, and thinking. The abilities to abstract a general principle from a specific situation and to apply old solutions to new problems are skills mediated (processed) by association areas. Also, when we experience ourselves, we always feel *unified,* a single being, not a set of parts. We have an experiential center, a unifying consciousness that enfolds all of our diverse habits, goals, memories, and acts, and gives them meaning. The *meaning* we attribute to what we see and hear, or to the feelings of our bodies, originates in the association areas. They are the interpretive clearinghouse of the brain that we call "mind."

The association areas are used in problem solving, in shifting attention, in interpreting sensory messages, and in the symbolic use of speech. Different sections handle different skills; the association areas in the frontal lobes are used in problem solving. Those in the main sensory areas are used to make shapes, sounds, and tactile sensations meaningful. If association areas in the temporal lobes are damaged, people have trouble recalling words, naming things, or understanding what is said to them. As we saw, electrical stimulation of some association areas can produce feelings, memories, or sensations as vivid as if they were actually happening.

Two amazing attributes of the cortex are that it has enormous information storage capacity and that each bit of information seems to be stored in many different parts of the brain. The billions of neurons in the cortex have trillions of information bits redundantly recorded in them in such a way that damage to half of the brain does not result in the loss of half a person's memories.

No one knows exactly how this storage process works. Memory was once thought of as being like an album of photographs. Looking at your family would be like taking a snapshot of them; it would presumably register a tiny "negative" somewhere in the brain—or so the theory went. Karl H. Pribram of Stanford University, however, has suggested that memory and perception may actually function much like *holography.* In photography the finished picture looks like the original scene; if you rip a picture of your family in half, Mom and Dad will be on the right hand side and Brother Joe and Uncle Willy will be on the left. In holography, however, light from *every* point in a scene is distributed to *every* point on the film. If you ripped a holographic plate to bits, you could still reconstruct the entire picture from any one fragment—Mom, Dad, Brother Joe, and Uncle Willy would all be there. The association areas may contain "holograms" of this sort with each bit of information distributed whole throughout many association cells (Pribram 1971).

THE AUTONOMIC AND GLANDULAR SYSTEMS: THE BRAIN'S JUNIOR EXECUTIVES

Most of the behavior which psychologists study is directly managed by the cerebral cortex, but it does not act alone—not ever. Some controls over drives and emotions are operated by lower centers. Two sets of subordinate operations, managed by the central nervous system, deserve some separate mention. They are the *autonomic nervous system,* and the *endocrine glands.* Both are vital in our emotional lives.

The autonomic nervous system As we have seen with reflexes, not all behavior is voluntary or mediated (processed) by higher centers of awareness and understanding. Many automatic functions are controlled in part by the autonomic nervous system (ANS), centered in the spinal cord. The nerve fibers running from the central nervous system are hooked up directly between the brain and the skeletal muscles. The autonomic nervous system, by contrast, consists of shorter nerve fibers from the spinal cord that link up with other neurons on the way to smooth muscles or glands. Smooth muscles generally control involuntary activities, like digestion and heartbeat; glands are small internal organs that secrete fluids called hormones; they regulate such activities as sexual behavior, crying, sweating, and a host of others. By controlling them, the ANS plays a vital part in *how we feel,* both physically and mentally.

The ANS has two parts to it. The *sympathetic* division has the general role of rousing up excited feelings; the *parasympathetic* serves generally to soothe and subdue them. It is actually more complicated than that. The sympathetic division dominates the body in exciting or alarming situations and, by its action, prepares you for "fight or flight" (Cannon 1928). It causes your heart rate to speed up so blood will be available to the body. It dilates (expands) the blood vessels in skin and muscles so that the blood needed for speed and endurance can be delivered. In constricts (narrows) the blood vessels in the digestive tract, since you do not need to waste blood on digestion while running or fighting for your life. And so forth. It also dilates the pupils of the eyes; increases sweating; and produces sexual ejaculation in the male, which may not be alarming, but certainly is exciting.

The parasympathetic division inhibits the sympathetic division and maintains vital functions when the body is at rest. It offsets the sympathetic nerves by: slowing down the heartbeat; constricting blood vessels in the heart, muscles, and skin; dilating blood vessels in the digestive tract; constricting the pupil; and causing

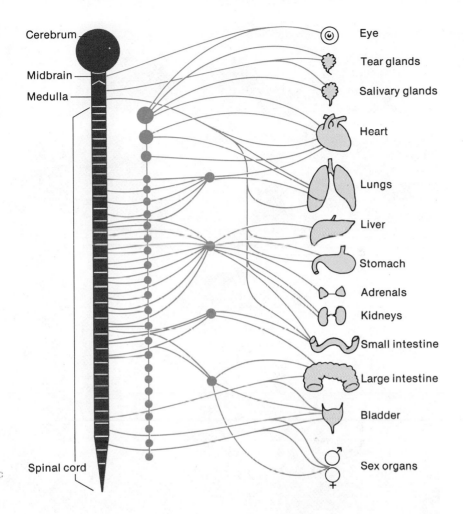

Cerebrum

Midbrain

Medulla

Eye

Tear glands

Salivary glands

Heart

Lungs

Liver

Stomach

Adrenals

Kidneys

Small intestine

Large intestine

Bladder

Sex organs

Spinal cord

Figure 3.9 The autonomic nervous system.

erection in the male genital organ. In most cases, the two systems have equal but opposite effects on the body; occasionally, however, they function cooperatively, as in male sexual performance, where erection and ejaculation must occur in sequence.

The glands Much of the effects of the ANS on behavior comes indirectly by stimulating the glands. Most glands regulate metabolic processes that have few direct effects on behavior. But some of them produce internal changes which arouse strong feelings. In this sense, the glands may be considered regulators of emotion, which is largely the conscious in-

terpretation of the changes they cause in the body. The adrenal medulla, one of the endocrine glands, triggers many of these changes and thus plays an important role in our emotional life. The kinds of feelings we connect to these changes depend on brain processes, but their intensity is largely a product of the autonomic nervous system and the glands.

TINKERING WITH THE MACHINERY: THE FUTURE OF THE BRAIN

If you have derived nothing else from the previous section, I hope two ideas will remain

Electronically controlled cat. When its brain is electrically stimulated, the cat becomes furious.

with you anyway. First, that the physical basis of behavior in the nervous system is very complicated, and second, that no matter how great the complications are, there still *is* a **physical** basis in the brain and nervous system for all kinds of behavior. The ultimate control center for most behavior, and especially for things you would call "psychological," is in the brain. If it were possible to know where all the brain centers are and how they work, it might be possible to control people's moods, their feelings, their emotions, their desires, their fears, their will, and their thoughts, by getting at those centers. It is possible. It is being done. It may be done a lot more in the future as knowledge of these things increases. It is not called "brainwashing," a hokey (and phony) name for extreme attempts at persuasion, but **psychosurgery** and *electrical brain stimulation* (London 1977; Delgado 1969; Peck 1973; Valenstein 1973; Gaylin *et al*. 1975).

Psychosurgery generally works by finding the brain centers which control the behavior of interest, then placing tiny electrical or chemical stimulating devices in those centers. Modern technology of miniaturizing electronic and surgical equipment makes it possible to do this without destroying vital brain tissue. Many of the devices that are "implanted," moreover, can be safely left in the brain for years, and some of them can dependably control the electrical and chemical activity of those centers in different ways.

For the most part, these techniques have only been used in medicine for treating ailments which could not be dealt with in another way, such as some kinds of epileptic seizures. They have also been used successfully, however, to permanently inhibit some people's outbursts of violence which endangered themselves and everyone around them (Mark and Erwin 1971). And they have been used experimentally to

In an experiment by José Delgado, a charging bull was made to stop in its tracks by an electronic receiver implanted in its brain.

Dibersion de España, Francisco Goya

increase sexual desire, to increase the speech rate of a retarded child, and for a number of other purposes.

Experiments in brain stimulation of animals have gone a lot further than any such attempts on people. Some of them have had amazing results, in which animals could be made fearful or ferocious, could be made to eat themselves to death, or to starve to death, to become socially dominant or socially withdrawn, to move around in meaningless fashion, or to do countless other things at the whim of the experimenter.

The potential uses of psychosurgery on people are not yet known, but it may soon be possible to permanently control many kinds of human behavior by this means. Some people think it should be used to wipe out aggressive impulses in people convicted of violent crimes.

Others realize that it could be used also to tranquilize political opponents.

At the present time, brain implantation methods are not so advanced or dependable or easy to use that these things could be done much, even in a totalitarian country. But there is good reason for public concern about the ethics and the practical dangers to freedom from this kind of technology. You should be as concerned as anyone because the methods are improving and will be more and more effective in years to come.

You should also be convinced, perhaps more by the existence of this technology than by anything else you have learned on the subject, that the brain is indeed *the* control center of human behavior.

SUMMARY

1   It is important to know something about the brain and nervous system, even in a beginning overview of psychology, for three reasons:

  a   It provides the most important evolutionary perspective on the difference between humans and animals.

  b   It makes you realize that our *executive apparatus* is a bunch of physical machinery, which can be critical for understanding and changing our behavior.

  c   It gives you some insight into the fact that this executive machinery where *you* live can be tinkered with to control your behavior. And will be.

2   The evolution of increasingly elaborate nervous systems is the main difference between one phylum and another in the animal kingdom. The human *central nervous system* is the most advanced on earth, distinct even from that of other primates by the extensive development of the *cerebrum,* or new brain, which controls the higher mental processes: memory, language, reasoning, and voluntary behavior. Although the human brain is fundamentally the same as that of other vertebrates in its *central core* and *old brain,* our cerebrum is proportionally far larger and has far more surface area than that of any other creature.

3   The development of the human brain represents an evolutionary shift from the reflex activities controlled by the spinal cord to the processes of delay, inhibition, memory, and learning, which characterize the *conscious* control of behavior. The neurophysiological difference between humans and other animals, in other words, is in our greater physical capacity for *consciousness,* that is, for thought.

4   The evolutionary conditions that produced our increased brain power are not known for certain, but many anthropologists believe it was a result of our prehuman ancestors

gradually shifting from tree-dwellings to ground-dwelling, becoming meat eaters, and walking upright. Living on the ground and hunting animals was more dangerous than living in trees and hunting fruit; so greater intelligence was required for survival. Walking upright offered disadvantages of locomotion, but it freed the hands to carry large amounts of food, or infants, and for the extensive use of tools. All these things favored the development of more brain capacity for deliberation and downgraded the importance of reflex reactions.

5   The basic mechanism of the central nervous system is the *neuron,* a specialized cell that transmits information by means of electrical impulses. There are three main kinds of neurons: *afferent,* which take messages (receive stimuli) from the senses to the spinal cord or brain; *efferent,* which take signals from the brain or cord to the muscles and glands; and *association neurons,* which connect nerve cells with each other. All neurons transmit messages in one direction only.

6   A neuron fires an equally strong impulse every time it is excited (the *all-or-none* principle), and must then rest briefly before it can fire again (*refractory period*). A strong stimulus will cause a neuron to fire more often, and will fire more neurons, than a weak stimulus will. Neurons rarely function singly; they are bundled together to make *nerves.*

7   The Central Nervous System (CNS) consists of most of the spinal cord and all of the brain. The *spinal cord, cerebellum,* and *brain stem* control the *vegetative* functions which sustain life, such as respiration, body temperature, and metabolism; the *reflexive* or automatic functions governing animal life, such as digestion, circulation, locomotion, feeding, fighting, and sex, and some of the emotions connected with them. The *cerebrum,* or new brain, controls the higher mental processes. Most spinal cord and brain stem functions are not easily subject to learning; most learning takes place in the cerebral cortex.

8   The *cortex,* or cover of the cerebrum, controls most of the higher functions. It is divided into two halves, or *hemispheres,* each of which consists of four clumps of brain called *lobes.* The human cortex is very *convoluted,* that is, full of folds and wrinkles, which give it a large surface area. This makes humans literally much more brainy than other animals. Sensory, motor, and speech activities are controlled by different areas of the cortex. They are spread out on a kind of upside down map of the body; the actual amount of cortical space for each function is proportional to how important the brain function is, not how big the body part is. The part that controls the legs, for instance, is much smaller than that which controls the tongue.

9   Most of the cells in the cortex are *association neurons,* which integrate the different kinds of information the brain receives from the senses. The association areas are important in learning, remembering, and thinking; their integrative function enables us to break out of rigid response patterns and to develop new solutions to old problems.

10   The brain has enormous storage capacity. Its billions of neurons can store trillions of bits of information. No one knows how the storage process works, but it is highly *redundant,* that is, repetitious, such that material stored in some parts of the brain can be reproduced in others if the first part is damaged or destroyed.

11   Some of the body's regulation of drives and emotions is managed by subordinate systems to the central nervous system, especially by the *autonomic nervous system* (*ANS*) and *the glands.* The autonomic nervous system is a derivative of the spinal cord.

It has two parts, a *sympathetic* division, which serves to arouse and excite, and a *para-sympathetic* division, which tends to soothe and relax. The two divisions generally work antagonistically to each other; when one is active, the other is not. The glands are important in arousing emotions, though the particular feelings we use to describe them depend on cortical, not glandular activity. Both the autonomic nervous system and the glands are controlled by the central nervous system.

Sensation

4

4

Sensation

Psychology as a science begins, historically, with sensation, and your experience of living begins, personally, with the same topic. When you hear psychologists talk of "stimuli and responses," what they mean is "sensations and the things we do because of them." When philosophers talk of "sense data," they are referring to anything which can be experienced by your senses—seen, heard, touched, tasted— as opposed to things that can only be imagined or thought about. Sensation is the name for everything that connects you to the world outside your body and for everything that you are able to know about within your body. The organs of sensation are older, in evolutionary terms, than the brain and nervous system, which evolved in the first place mainly to serve them. If the cerebral cortex of the brain is where you end up a human being, unique among creatures on this planet, the sensory apparatus is where you start off as an animal, and find your kinship with all the beasts of the field.

Kinship is not identity. All living creatures have some kind of sensory apparatus which makes it possible for them to negotiate their existence with the world around them. But in most plants and one-celled animals, there is no **apparatus** to speak of, just a kind of **irritability** or **sensitiveness** to light, heat, or food. Sometimes that irritability is concentrated in one part of the body—*it* senses food, or danger, or whatever, and then moves the animal towards or away from them. In more elaborate organisms, sensitive areas evolved into **sense**(itive) **organs** —**touch** receivers, that could feel pain, heat, cold, or poison; **distance** receivers, that could smell allies, see food, or hear danger; **position** receivers, that could tell the animal whether it was upside-down or right-side-up in the water or in the sky, and balance its movements on the ground. The sense organs tell a creature how to act in response to their experience; its muscles and motor system move it accordingly; the nervous system connects them.

In this respect, the main difference between

an animal with a fancy nervous system like you and a simple one, like fish, earthworms, or amoebae, is that *they* are completely bound to their senses—there is no pause in the transmission of sensory information to their reaction systems, and there are no alternatives to the action they can take on the information they get. Their behavior is **reflexive,** that is, automatic. The brain's cortical apparatus permits yours to be **reflective;** it frees us from the enslavement of lower animals to the dominance of their senses.

But not completely. Which is why you have to read a chapter like this. You are still partly the victim of your senses and the beneficiary of your senses—both ways, very much the product of them. For your experience, no matter how much it is processed and interpreted by the brain, is limited by the capacities of your senses. So you need to know something of those capacities.

In learning about them, however, you cannot just forget about the brain. For we do not see *in* our eyes nor *in* our ears, only *with* them, that is, with their help. We see and hear in the brain. When you dream, you *see*, even though your eyes are closed. A blow on the head will make you *see* stars. Although Beethoven was deaf in his last years, he heard in his head every note he wrote. Someone who has lost a leg may feel pain in their "phantom limb"—but actually, of course, the pain is in their head.

All perceived experience is in the brain, where there are no light waves or sound waves but only coded electrochemical messages from the body's sense receptors. All the senses work differently, but all the messages they send to the brain work the same way, using the same code, like a computer. If you wanted to measure the light in the room you are in, for instance, you would use one instrument; for the sound from a dripping faucet, another; and for the smell of food cooking, a third. But all your measurements, with all your different instruments, would be coded into the same kind of numbers and punched on the same kind of punch cards to be fed into a computer. The computer analyzes all of the data and relates one measurement to another.

The senses are like the measuring instruments and the brain is like that computer. We sense the world via the impulses relayed through the visual and auditory and other afferent nerves. By converting sound waves and light waves into a single code, the brain can relate the impressions from one sense to those from another and get your motor system off its axons and into action at many levels. Thus, the sound of a fire alarm sets you simultaneously to *looking* for an exit, *sniffing* for a smell of fire, and *feeling* about under your desk for your shoes. All of these things occur in concert because nerve impulses from the auditory cortex of the brain, which sorts out signals from the ears, go rapidly to other centers of the brain which set other senses into action. Drugs like LSD, as we shall see in Chapter 11, can sometimes scramble the brain's code so that impulses from the eyes are perceived as sound rather than sights and vice versa.

SENSORY THRESHOLDS: TO SEE OR NOT TO SEE

The senses send their messages to the brain via afferent neurons. Now, the impulse of one neuron does not have enough oomph to make much impression on the brain, which is one reason neurons cluster into nerves in the first place. And since individual neurons have thresholds—lower limits of excitability—so do nerves, and so too, finally, do each of the body's sense organs. Nothing registers on your senses until enough neurons fire to pass these thresholds. Two kinds of threshold are important here. An **absolute** lower limit on sensation, beneath which nothing seems to happen. And a relative threshold, called a **differential** threshold, because it tells how much change there has to be in a sensation for you to notice it.

The Shriek, Edvard Munch

Scrambling: perceiving a sound visually, or vice versa. This is how the sound of a scream might look.

The so-called *absolute threshold* of a sense means the weakest stimulus (sound, sight, smell, taste, touch, and so on) you can *detect* with it. It is the lower limit of your sensitivity to anything. For most people, for instance, the absolute threshold of vision is the light from a candle burning about 30 miles away on a dark clear night. For hearing, it is the tick of a watch held 20 feet away in a silent room, or the sound of half the front leg[1] of a mosquito[2] falling on an eardrum.[3] The absolute threshold for touch is

[1] Left front leg.
[2] A small mosquito.
[3] Either eardrum.

the pressure of the wing of a bee falling on your cheek from a height of one centimeter (Galanter 1962).

If these thresholds were any lower, they would interfere with normal functioning. If your hearing were more acute, you would pick up the sound of the molecules whirling in the air (Uttal 1973). If your vision were much sharper, you would see the chemical changes occuring within your own eyeballs.

Today, absolute thresholds are often called *detection thresholds* because they are not really absolute (Swets 1961). A stimulus so weak that most people detect it only 50 percent of the time under laboratory conditions is defined as the detection threshold. But sensory discriminations vary enormously even in the laboratory, and nobody lives in laboratories. In real life, all of your senses are constantly bombarded by stimuli. If you had to notice all of them all the time—every cough or murmur in the library, the sight of the tip of your nose when you are reading, the constant sound of your pulse in your ears—you would be a wreck.

Attention

The detection threshold of sensations evolved as a biological lower limit on creatures' ability to derive information from the world around them. At that point, stimuli have barely enough energy to get your *attention.* Attending to them makes it possible to evaluate them and respond effectively in ways which will help you cope with the demands of the environment. Attention is thus an important basis of perception and of learning.

But how attention works is not obvious, not simple, and not well understood. Little is known about the physiology of attention in the brain and nervous system (Moray 1969). There seem to be reflexes connected with some senses, which direct their attention in ways which optimize their effects. In the case of vision, for instance, a built-in reflex seems to make you confront whatever you aim to look at with the part of your eye which has the sharpest vision. (Yin and Mountcastle, 1977). But this is not certain. It is even less clear what makes you aim to look at one thing rather than another in the first place, since there are always many things competing at once for your attention.

Attention evidently has several functions, one of which must be to *select* incoming sensory signals which are important to evaluate and another to *filter out* and eliminate "noise," that is, noticeable but unimportant events. Attention seems to involve a sequence in which your brain is first oriented towards some general region or pattern of stimulation and then systematically selects some components of that pattern to attend to and eliminates others (Broadbent 1977).

The attention process not only selects some signals and eliminates others within a sense, but also can change the absolute thresholds of senses. In fact, the threshold level for one sense may drop suddenly when attention is focused on it by a response to a different sense. In experiments on cats, for instance, brain wave responses to the sound of clicks stop after a while because, we say, the cat *adapts* to them. If the cat is *watching* though, and the experimenter pretends to tap his fingers while the clicks are still audible, the brain waves start recording again. He has gotten the cat's attention. But then, if he shows the cat a mouse, the threshold for the clicks immediately rises again. The cat hears them less because its attention has been distracted (Hernandez-Peon, Scherrer, and Jouvet 1956). *Vision* has broken the adaptation to *hearing.* Let us look briefly at adaptation.

Sensory adaptation

Some distracting stimuli are eliminated by a process called *sensory adaptation.* Technically, it means that constant exposure to an unchanging stimulus causes the sensation to disappear. In plainer talk, it means you get so used to something, you stop noticing it. Thus, after you have worn a hat for a while, you stop feeling it. Your touch sense has not gone dead— if someone knocks you in the head, or if your hat slips, you will feel it again. Adaptation is adjustment to a *constant* level of excitation. You do not *decide* to eliminate the sensation; it happens automatically as you get used to it. If you are wearing a strong perfume, you may *want* to keep smelling it, but soon you will be unable to. Fortunately, the process works the same way for obnoxious odors. Whether your nose is being treated to "Evening in Paris" or "Night in South Omaha," it will adapt to the smell as long as the level of stimulation stays the same.

If you think about its function in survival terms, then adaptation can be understood as a corrective for the sensory processes set in motion by attention. Once you have become aware of whatever stimulation needs your attention and have done whatever needs doing about it, you don't want to continue having to pay attention to it, especially if nothing about the stimulus is changing. There are always other things to attend to, and if your attention remains fixed on the same routine event that has seized it previously, you cannot deal with those other things. Adaptation, by reducing your sensitiveness to the constant level of stimulation you have already dealt with, allows you to be *more* sensitive to low intensity changes that take place in the rest of the environment. This is true of all the senses, including even hearing and vision (Corso 1967). Your eyes, for instance, are moving as many as 100 times per second when you think you are actually staring fixedly at something, and you are really only seeing it *between* the movements (Alpern 1971). If an image is stabilized on your visual receptors so that you really do look at it constantly, you soon adapt to it—and it becomes almost invisible (Riggs *et al.* 1953, 1968; Riggs, 1977)!

The sensory processes not only inform you of stimulation, as you can see, but alert you to changes in it. How much change must occur to be worth noticing brings us to the subject of *differential thresholds.*

Differential threshold

The absolute threshold of each sense is the weakest stimulus a person can detect with it. The differential threshold is the smallest *increase* in a stimulus (brightness or loudness or saltiness or whatever) that a person will notice. That increase is called the ***just-noticeable-difference.***

This area of investigation, called ***psychophysics,*** is one of the oldest branches of psychology (Guilford 1954; Green and Swets 1966). One of its important principles is that if a stimulus is already very large, then a change must be very large indeed for you to detect any difference in it. If your finger grew a quarter of an inch longer overnight, you would certainly notice the change, but if your height grew that much, you might not notice. Similarly, the sound of a burp would be deafening at a church service, but added to the roar of a storm, it would go

Figure 4.1a The bigger the difference between two stimuli, the more noticeable it will be.

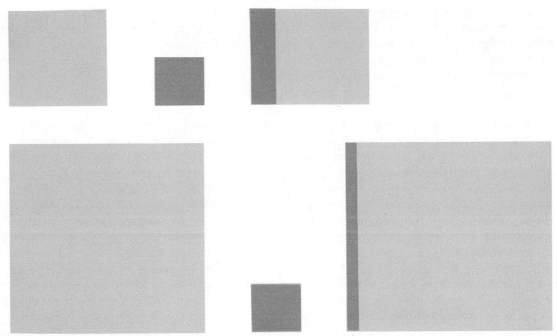

Figure 4.1b The Weber-Fechner Law explains how, if a thin person gains ten pounds, it would make a great difference in appearance, while the same ten pounds might not be apparent added to the body of a fat person.

unnoticed. The precise formula for this relationship, called the Weber-Fechner Law, was one of the earliest discoveries of scientific psychology.

Our senses do not report every change in stimulus energy tit for tat. The sensation of loudness (the sound that you *hear*), for instance, grows more slowly than the actual physical intensity of sound waves. The sound from an electric guitar might be *ten times* more intense than that from an ordinary guitar, but it will *sound* only *twice* as loud to you. The touch sense works in quite a different way. An *electric shock* passing through your fingers may be only *four* times more intense than a previous shock, but you may *feel* it as *100* times greater (Stevens 1957).

In evolutionary terms, the different responsiveness of different senses is very adaptive. For most purposes, we cannot make use of the full blast of very loud sounds. As long as we can distinguish a lion's roar from a turtle dove's coo and tell from it whether we are being asked to dinner as guests or as entrée, we have no need to know exactly how loud the sound is; what we hear is loud enough to comfort or alarm us. With pain, on the other hand, it is probably most adaptive to *overreact* to any increase in painful stimulation, whether it comes from a thorn in the foot or a stab in the back. The difference between a playful nick and a lethal cut is small, in terms of energy, but in terms of survival, it is very great.

The important point of all these general principles of sensation is that the brain is not a passive switchboard flooded with messages from the senses. It actively controls its own sensory input by increasing or reducing the number of messages relayed to it from the senses (Miller 1965). When smells are picked up by the sensory receptors in the nose, for instance, they are conveyed to a sort of way station, the brain's olfactory bulb; it routes them to higher olfactory centers in the brain. But the brain can also order the olfactory bulb to kill some of the messages coming from the nose. Through control of these brain control centers, adepts of hypnotism and yoga can consciously modify sensations. But no one knows how. More of this in Chapter 11.

One psychologist, K. H. Pribram, has hypothesized that the brain's ability to enhance or reduce its own sensory input may produce different personality types. He thinks that a person who cannot reduce sensory input may be incapable of reflection or impulse control but will tend instead to respond to a stimulus through action. People who are capable of input control on the other hand, might *act* less but *feel* more. The "doers" and the "feelers" of the world perhaps have different wiring systems in the brain (Pribram 1968).

Sensory deprivation

The mechanisms for reducing sensation, and for filtering it, are so important that it is easy to forget how important it is to get stimulation in the first place. We recognize this in everyday speech, in approving phrases like "this is a *stimulating* book," or "that's a *sensational* idea," or "he's an *exciting* person." Getting stimulated is terribly important.

There is a good deal of evidence that animals (including us) who do not get sufficient sensory stimulation in infancy and early childhood can never perform some vital functions in adult life. There is some evidence also, though it is more doubtful, that giving small children an enriched environment, in which they have more sensory stimulation than their homes and neighborhoods would ordinarily provide, may make it easier for them to learn the social and intellectual skills they must master in school. Headstart programs are based on this idea. And there is clear evidence, on baby rats at

least, that an enriched sensory environment in infancy produces changes in brain chemistry that may be favorable for learning (Krech and Rosenzweig 1966; Rosenzweig, Bennett, and Diamond 1972).

A number of experiments on adults have tried to find out just how important sensory stimulation is in maintaining adjustment. In some studies, people sat in *sensory isolation chambers* for periods ranging from minutes to days — soundproof, dark, temperature-controlled rooms where they would see and hear nothing. In other studies, people were floated in water to produce weightlessness, their eyes and ears were covered, and their hands were placed in plastic cuffs to reduce touch sensation. Nothing much happened to some people — they slept a lot, they got bored eventually, and they quit the experiment. But others became disoriented and had some frightening episodes, including wild thoughts and some hallucinations (Zubek *et al.* 1961; Zuckerman 1969; Heron 1961). For them, it was no fun. The meaning of these experiments is not always clear because, in some cases, it seems that the experimenters themselves were fearful about what would happen and communicated some of their fears to the subjects. So some people may have gotten upset because the *demand characteristics,* that is, the social expectations of the situation, led them to (Orne 1959). Even so, it is still clear that adults feel a need for stimulation, even if they will not go crazy from lack of it. We are all, in a sense, thrill seekers, even if the thrills are the ordinary sensations of our everyday environment.

Stimulation is not always good for you, however, and a number of recent experimental studies have even demonstrated that sensory deprivation may have positive value for the treatment of some bad habits or emotional problems in which people get *overstimulated,* such as phobias and cigarette smoking (Suedfeld 1975a and b; Suedfeld and Buchanan 1974; Suedfeld and Ikard 1974). More commercially,

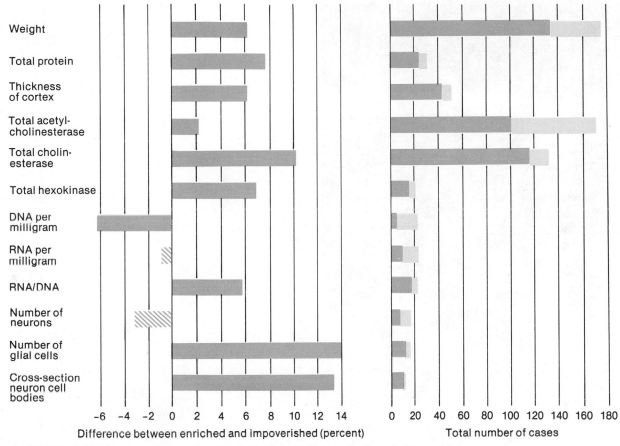

Difference between enriched and impoverished (percent)	Total number of cases

OCCIPITAL CORTEX of rats kept in enriched or impoverished environments from 25 to 105 days showed the effects of the different experiences. The occipital cortex of rats from the enriched environment, compared with that of rats from the impoverished one, was 6.4 percent heavier. This was significant at the .01 level or better, as were most other measures (*dark colored bars*). Only two measures were not significant (*hatched bars*). The dark gray bars on the right show the number of cases in which the rat from the enriched environment exceeded its littermate from the improverished environment in each of the measures that are listed.

if less scientifically, you can buy your own sensory isolation chamber, called a *Samadhi Tank,* for only a thousand dollars or so, and do all kinds of soothing good things to your mind, according to its ads, such as "cleaning up accumulated mental garbage," by lying naked in its warm salt water.

THE INDIVIDUAL SENSES AND HOW THEY GREW

Since ancient times,[4] people have referred to "the five senses," meaning sight, hearing, touch, taste, and smell. But there are a lot more

[4] Until about a week ago, I think.

Touch.

than five senses, any way you count them, though the exact number depends on how you define each separate sense (Kling and Riggs 1971). Most are near the surface of the body, the best place from which to communicate between it and the outside world; a few are internal. We will study them individually a bit, and look at how they evolved, how they are built, and how they work. Doing so will demonstrate, more clearly than any argument could, how little it is possible to understand sensation *by itself,* independent of the executive faculties of the sensing organism, that is, the "brainy" attributes you possess which make possible the integration and interpretation of sense data in your head. For with all that is known about sensation, and it is a lot, its unsolved mysteries are still more prominent than its known mechanics.

Cutaneous receptors: The skin senses

The entire surface of the body is the sensory apparatus of an amoeba—and while you have more specialized gear for some kinds of reception, the human body too is sensitive over its entire surface. Our largest sense organ is ***the skin.***

Just under the surface of the skin are ***cutaneous receptors*** (from Latin *cutis,* meaning "skin"). They convey four distinct senses: pressure (touch), heat, cold, and pain. Each type of stimulation is sensed at different spots under the skin (Field *et al.* 1959).

Responsiveness to pressure is one of the most primitive of all senses. Even the lowest forms of life become irritable when they contact foreign objects. In lower mammals, specialized tactile (touch sensitive) hairs called *vibrissae* report pressure; a cat's whiskers are a good example. Vibrissae are extremely sensitive because the skin they grow from is richly supplied with nerves (Campbell 1967). Sensory hairs are of particular advantage to nocturnal animals. They can feel what they cannot see.

In the evolution of the primates, these primitive sensory hairs were gradually replaced by sensitive pads on the fingertips. The erect posture of most primates freed the hands for feeling. A fingertip could tell more about the size, texture, and temperature of an object than could any whisker. Some monkeys still have facial vibrissae, but the apes that most closely resemble people do not. In human beings, the vibrissae have disappeared altogether, but occasionally a human fetus will have a small, temporary sensory hair near the wrist—a "memory" of the wrist vibrissae found in lower primates.

Although human beings have shed their sensory hairs, most of the sensitive pressure points under the skin are still at the base of hairs. Not all: The underside of the forearm, the lips, the tip of the tongue, and the tips of the balls of fingers and thumb are all highly sensitive areas to touch (Clark 1959).

Just which nerve cells transmit pressure is uncertain, though. There are four different kinds of nerve endings in the skin, and though you might think that one kind is for receiving pressure, one for pain, one for cold, and one for warmth, that is not the way it works. Actually, one kind of skin nerve, called free nerve endings (because they end in little branches instead of having different-shaped things at their ends, as in Figure 4.2), is capable of producing the whole range of skin sensations—warmth, cold, touch, itching, tickling, pain—and maybe erotic feelings (Melzack 1973)! And other skin nerves are responsive to at least two different kinds of stimulation, such as pressure and temperature, or hair movement and temperature change. Two nerves that respond to the same *kinds* of things may still differ from each other in the degree of their responsiveness, moreover; one temperature sensitive nerve will be stimulated by one narrow range of heat or cold, another by a different range. Also, the skin nerves are not distributed evenly over your body. They overlap each other a lot with the result that some areas of the skin have more nerve endings than others, which makes them more sensitive spots. And finally, the skin nerves seem to fire in complicated patterns, so that the sensations you

Figure 4.2 Cutaneous nerve endings

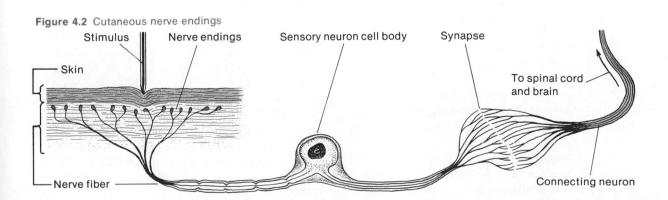

*Creation of Man, Sistine Chapel,
Michelangelo Buonarroti*

Communication through touch:
Michelangelo's "Creation of Adam."

actually feel depend on which nerves interact with which to what extent when a more or less sensitive area is stimulated by which kinds and amounts of energy.

If all that sounds complicated, it is complicated. That very fact helps you understand some puzzling facts about skin sensation. It explains, for instance, why your forehead is more prone to feel cold than to feel warm—it has more nerve endings sensitive to low temperatures than to high ones. It also helps explain the curious phenomenon called *paradoxical thermal* sensation in which a warm stimulus will produce a cold sensation when it is applied to certain spots on the skin, or when a cold and warm stimulus are applied at the same time, you feel a sensation of heat. The same fact of complexity also helps to explain why extreme heat or cold stimulation produces pain, rather than temperature sensation, and why pain is, perhaps, the most puzzling and intriguing of all the senses.

Pain

All the senses have specific organs for conveying their information to the brain, but some senses involve more organs than others, spread over large parts of the body. The skin senses and movement sense are like that. Pain is among these global or all-pervasive senses. Pain receptors are spread all over the body, and it is not even clear what all of them are. This is only one of the characteristics which make pain the most puzzling of all the senses. Another is the fact that there is no single kind of stimulation which causes pain. Light energy is necessary to stimulate vision, sound energy to produce hearing, heat to arouse the temperature sense, and so forth. But each of them, and virtually any other kind of stimulation, can produce pain under the right conditions. In fact, says Ronald Melzack, a leading scholar on pain, "painful stimuli are usually extremes of other natural stimuli (1973 p. 19)."

Pain!

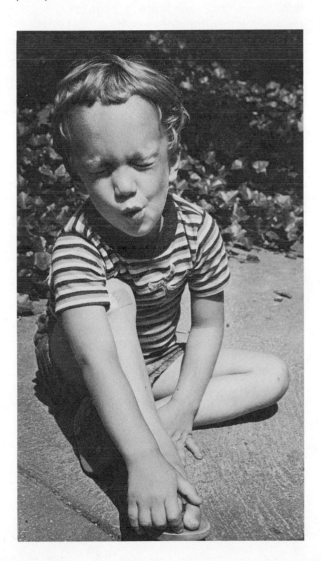

Just as some people are born blind or deaf, a few are born insensitive to pain. They generally do not live very long, because they are so certain to injure themselves seriously that, if they do not die of the injuries directly, they perish from the many infections and illnesses which follow them. But unlike congenitally blind or deaf people, no one can say just what is wrong physiologically with people who are congenitally insensitive to pain. And in at least one case, a young woman who lived to age 29 in this condition began feeling pain for the first time just a month before she died.

Neither the physiology nor the psychology of pain are well understood, and many of the best known facts about them only deepen the mystery of just what the pain sense is and how it works. Physiologically, for instance, spinal or other nerves are sometimes cut surgically to relieve intense pain. But such operations are successful only about half the time, though the severed nerves seem to be the ones that are carrying pain sensations from the affected area to the brain. Another treatment device is an electrical stimulator placed on the surface of the skin around the nerves that might be conducting the pain sensations. The vibrations from this gadget sometimes relieve pain and sometimes not. No one knows how or why, nor even where to place it—except, as its users say, somewhere "between the pain and the brain."

Many kinds of pains are well documented but poorly understood. The most famous, and dramatic, is called *phantom limb pain,* a condition first described in 1552 by Ambroise Paré, a French physician who is sometimes considered the father of modern surgery. Phantom limb pain is a painful condition which people feel *in a limb which has been amputated!* In about 35 percent of surgical amputations, tingling and pain start shortly after the amputation and follow the physical lines of the missing limb. It is so real that, as a result, people may reach out with a handless arm or step on a footless leg, forgetting that the limb is gone. Such pains may last for months or years before disappearing spontaneously. Even more strange, they can sometimes be permanently cured by apparently opposite means—a novocaine injection into the stump, which wears off chemically in a couple of hours—or a salt-water injection into the stump, which causes intense pain for a few minutes!

The psychology of pain is as weird as its physical side. Cultural background, early experience, the meaning of the situation in which pain is stimulated, and the attention you pay to it, all have important roles in pain perception. People everywhere have the same range of thresholds for pain *sensation,* for instance, but your *perception* of something as painful and your *tolerance* for pain are likely to be correlated with your cultural background. In one experiment, American women of Italian descent could not stand as much electric shock as women of Old American or Jewish origin (Sternbach and Tursky 1965). In another, Jewish women increased their pain tolerance when told that they had stood it less than other religious groups; but Protestant women, told the same thing, did not change (Lambert, Libman, and Poser 1960). You are probably familiar with the fact that, in some societies, warriors are taught to bear pain bravely without expression. In one district of India, though, male children are taught this so well that as adults they are less sensitive to pain than other people, and surgery is often done on them without anesthetics!

No one knows why it is that such social learning affects one's responsiveness to pain, but it is known in this connection that early experience affects other animals as well as people. Scottish terrier puppies, for instance, who were raised from infancy in complete isolation from other dogs never learned to respond to painful stimulation. At maturity, to everyone's surprise, they would stick their noses into a flame repeatedly and casually tolerate having pins stuck into them (Melzack and Scott 1957).

Beagles raised the same way respond a little more normally (Lessac 1965), showing that there are differences between species. Even so, the idea that "a burnt child dreads the fire" may not be true unless that burnt child has other people around to tell them that fire is dreadful!

Evidently, we learn that some kinds of stimulation are painful from watching the reactions of other people to them. The *meaning* of pain it seems, determines the *feeling* of it. That would help explain why in World War II only one out of three soldiers wounded in combat wanted morphine when they were taken to field hospitals. They said they felt little or no pain. Their main response to their situation, in fact, was relief, even euphoria, that they were alive and out of the battle. Four out of five civilians suffering similar wounds from surgery, reported severe pain and wanted morphine for it (Beecher 1959). It also explains why Pavlov was able to train dogs to respond to severe electric shock, intense pressure, or heat as if to a bell — that is, as signals of food. Once the shocks had acquired this meaning, the dogs stopped showing any signs of pain to them. The context can dictate the meaning of the stimulus, and how the stimulus makes you feel depends on that meaning — which is why you feel quite differently about a pat on the back and a slap in the face, even if the one is hard and the other light.

Meaning also depends on attention, of course, and so does pain perception. You have probably injured yourself, as most athletes and many soldiers have, while your attention was so completely absorbed in something else that you did not even notice you were bleeding or felt pain until later. Indeed, there was no pain until later, when you actually felt it. And once you feel pain, it makes no difference whether or not you can identify the stimulus, the pain is still real. For the sensory input that goes into pain is not simply a matter of outside stimuli acting on pain nerves in skin or muscles, but on the complex processing of sensory information which goes on at many levels of the nervous system. As Ronald Melzack and Patrick Wall argue, in the most important pain theory extant, pain is an interaction "between stimulus patterns, the cells of different spinal cord systems, and brain activities." They have pointed out the important role in pain perception played by the higher centers of the brain — and have concluded that "virtually the whole brain is the 'pain center' . . ." (Melzack and Wall 1965). Some details of their theory have been found incorrect since it was published in 1965, but its central theme, reflected in this statement, is still considered valid (Liebeskind and Paul 1977). It means, among other things, that there is no such thing as "psychological" or "psychosomatic" pain, in which you merely *think* something is hurting you and nothing really does. Physicians sometimes dismiss people's complaints of aches and pains for which the source is not obvious by saying, "It's all in your head." They are largely right about where the pain is, but wrong to think it is, therefore, unreal.

The mysteries surrounding the pain sense extend even to its biological functions. To some extent, pain functions as a warning signal that we are being injured and a stimulus to move away from the source of danger, which gives it a high evolutionary value in insuring survival. On the other hand, many of the most serious illnesses attack without warning, and the pain that goes with them not only comes too late to warn us of anything but also can interfere with our ability to heal. It is impossible to survive without this complex sense, but it is one that easily runs wild and can make life a torment.

Movement and body balance: Kinesthesia

Have you ever awakened with your arm asleep? You have to look around or feel in the dark in order to find exactly where your arm is. Your kinesthetic sense is impaired, and though you still receive touch sensations from your limbs, you do not know their location.

Kinesthesia is the sense of movement. It is probably one of the oldest senses, and certainly one of the most important ones. Also, it is one of the senses you are least likely to know you have until you get into trouble for lack of its working. Without kinesthetic sensibility, no efficient sequence of movements would be possible. You would have to look at your feet as you walked in order to know where they were, if you could walk at all, which, in fact, you could not because locomotion requires a series of tiny adjustments in the carriage of your body—all conducted by kinesthetic nerve receptors. Locomotion ability is one of the main things that differentiate animals from plants; so kinesthesia is among our elementary animal attributes.[5]

The cutaneous receptors pick up information from the surface of the skin. *Kinesthetic* receptors report on the movement of joints and muscles *within* the body (*kine* is from the Greek word meaning "to move" as in "cinema," moving picture); kinesthetic receptors are essential for coordinating muscles and for maintaining balance. There are kinesthetic nerve endings in tendons and muscles and in more than 100 body joints. When you move, the stretching and contracting of the muscles and the movement of the joints activates them.

All the kinesthetic receptors operate by gauging the direction and angle of every muscle movement. Driving a car, playing golf, kicking a ball, knocking down little old ladies rushing for the bus—all depend on kinesthesis. People with highly developed kinesthetic senses can close their eyes, hold their hands two or three feet apart, and then bring them together so that the tip of each finger touches the other exactly on target (Mountcastle 1968).

The position sense

The body has another set of receptors to maintain balance—the *vestibular* sense. It is located in the inner ear, but has nothing to do with hearing.

The vestibular sense may well be the first in evolutionary history for which a specific organ developed. The cutaneous and kinesthetic senses rely on nerve endings distributed throughout the entire body. But the vestibular sense depends on five structures in the inner ear; three semicircular canals signal when the body is being rotated; and two adjoining sacs report on movements up and down, on acceleration in a straight line and on changes in gravitational force.

These structures are analogous to one of the earliest known sense organs—the statocyst. The statocyst, which is found in jellyfish (a very ancient animal), is a pouch that usually contains a grain of limestone. When a wave tilts the jellyfish, the pebble shifts and stimulates tiny bristles lining the walls of the pouch. These bristles send a signal to the nervous system instructing the animal to right itself (Romer 1962; Milne and Milne 1962). Essentially the human vestibular sense is only a refinement of the statocyst.[6] The semicircular canals are filled with a fluid that shifts with every change in the body's position. The fluid ripples against receptor hairs, which signal the body's position to the brain.

It is not movement which activates the vestibular sense, however, but *changes* in movement, specifically changes in acceleration (speed) rather than direction. These changes make the fluid move in the canals with the force of gravity, and our sense of position changes according to their movement. When movement speeds up or slows down suddenly, the fluid sloshes around, and dizziness (vertigo) results. Sea-

---

[5] Augmenting, thereby, the distinction between you and celery.

[6] Some people, likewise, are only refinements of the jellyfish.

The vestibular sense maintains our balance.

Be Careful with This Step, Francisco Goya

sickness and car sickness are both caused by vestibular malfunctioning (Wendt 1951). When speed changes very gradually, however, the fluid may shift position so slowly that the vestibular receptors are not activated at all, even if direction changes completely. Pilots flying airplanes in the dark or in clouds, where there are no outside visual references to tell them what position they are in, may not notice their plane gently turning or banking at all. As a result, they become disoriented in space and sometimes find themselves flying upside-down—or dead.

The chemical receptors: Taste and smell

Taste (gustation) and smell (olfaction) are both senses that detect the chemical ingredients in a stimulus. Taste buds are located on the *outside* surfaces of many kinds of fish, but in all mammals they are placed on the tongue, the palate, the floor of the mouth, and the insides of the cheek. In humans, they are mostly on the tongue, in and around little bumps, hills, and ridges called papillae. As food dissolves (only liquid molecules get tasted), it contacts the taste buds and activates taste sensation.

Taste.

Since the taste buds are unprotected from contact with all kinds of corrosive juices and sharp substances[7], they are damaged and destroyed a lot (which is why smokers taste less than non-smokers). Through most of life, taste buds also regenerate a lot (Uttal 1973). Old people have less taste sense than youngsters because, past middle age, fewer buds regenerate.

Taste is not a very refined sense; most of what people describe as the "taste" of meat or marmalade actually is a response to temperature, texture, and more than anything else, smell. Take those effects away, and only four primary taste sensations remain: *salty, sweet,* *sour,* and *bitter.* Some taste buds sense all four sensations, while others react only to one or two (Zotterman and Schade 1967). The different taste sensations do not each depend on a specialized receptor of its own (Tucker and Smith 1969), though some receptors are more sensitive to one taste than to another.

Having a sense of taste does not serve any life-saving purpose nowadays, but it probably had a vital evolutionary function at one time. Sweet tastes, for instance, tend to identify natural carbohydrates; some minerals necessary for survival taste salty (such as salt); and sour and bitter tastes are often natural indicators of poison or food spoilage. Add to this the powerful repulsive effects of putrid

[7] Did you ever watch what people put in their mouths?

odors, and you can see that taste-smell ability may once have contributed greatly to survival by helping our hominid ancestors to tell good and bad food apart, thereby finding nutrients and avoiding poisons. A fair number must have died, also, from the exceptions to such rules.

Most actual *food preferences* are learned, of course, but the natural *taste* inclination of humans, rats, and horses (not cats), among other species, is to prefer sweets to anything else. You have heard, doubtless, how some pregnant women develop sudden cravings for certain foods. Such **specific hungers,** or un-learned taste preferences, may express real bodily needs. Rats with a sodium deficiency in their diets, for instance, show an unlearned desire for sodium: no trial and error process is required to guide them to it (Rozin 1967). The same is true for cows at salt licks. For human beings, it is unclear whether babies will supply their own nutritional needs from their "natural" taste preferences without instruction. If nature has to teach them nutrition, they may die from learning.

The condition of your body may also affect your taste and smell senses themselves, some-times peculiarly. People with certain glandular deficiencies may actually become *more* sensi-tive to tastes and smells (sometimes to sounds also) which are from 120 to 10 thousand times weaker than those most of us can detect (Henkin 1970). More commonly, a number of ailments, ranging from a mysterious flu-like attack to head injuries, brain tumors, and totally unknown causes, may diminish or destroy taste-smell sense or, perhaps worse, cause a peculiar perversion of these senses in which foods you once liked taste rancid and putrid, or in which you walk around with a constant bad taste in your mouth (Henkin, Schechter, Hoye and Mat-tern 1971). Such conditions are professionally disastrous for wine tasters, restaurauteurs, and perfumers, but it is dangerous for anyone to be unable to distinguish fresh from spoiled food. Anyway, it is miserable to lose the plea-sures of good tastes and smells, even when it is not dangerous. Over a half million people in the United States alone suffer from these problems, which are poorly understood, and the National Institutes of Health now have a Taste and Smell Clinic to study and treat them (Lamberg 1975).

Most senses monitor activities happening inside or close to the body. Smell (the olfactory sense), like vision and hearing, is a **distance** receptor; it informs an animal of events that are far away. Insects and all of the vertebrates have olfactory senses. Most vertebrates, in fact, have smell senses far more acute than ours. A spawning salmon, for instance, can *smell* the difference between its home stream and others (Tucker and Smith 1969; Veda *et al.* 1967). When a dog sniffs a fireplug, it is identifying the urine odor of another *specific* dog. Dogs apparently urinate in order to stake out territorial claims.[8] Each animal has its own personal odor, and a dog can tell by sniffing whether it is trespassing on another dog's turf. Smell is so important to some mammals that if an opossum, for instance, is *looking* at a friendly animal while smelling an enemy, it will behave as though it were in the enemy's presence. To most vertebrates, smells are far more dependable than sights.

How olfaction works is almost completely unknown. In all vertebrates, including humans, the olfactory system is basically the same. Only a gas can produce an odor. Odorous sub-stances in the air are sensed by receptor cells in the upper part of the nasal cavity. There are several million such cells, and each one has about a thousand hairs. How the hairs function, how odors are distinguished one from another, and how the information is coded and passed on to the brain—are still unknown (Heimer 1971). Among the more than 30 theories of odor which are current, the most popular is a variation of one proposed over 2,000 years ago by the Roman poet-philosopher Lucretius. It says that

---

[8] In addition to, not instead of, relieving themselves.

the main determinant of odor is the shape of the molecules of smellable substances, that is, of gases that are soluble in water and fat. Experiments on this theory have indicated that there are seven *primary* odors, from which all others derive: *Camphoraceous* (as in mothballs); *musky* (as in some perfumes); *floral* (as in flowers); *pepperminty* (as in guess what); *ethereal* (as in airplane glue or ether); *pungent* (as in vinegar); and *putrid* (as in rotten eggs) (Amoore Johnston, and Rubin 1964). Despite the popularity of this theory, "the safest conclusion, . . . to be drawn at the present time is that there is no theory of olfactory primary sensory action that is universally accepted (Uttal 1973)."

In the course of evolution, smell has become a less and less important sense for the primates. In fish, the olfactory center takes up about one third of the whole brain; in a dog, about one fourth; but in monkeys, apes, and humans, the smell center is only a small fraction of the total brain area. Since most primates are vegetarians, smell sense was not needed for hunting. Since they lived in trees and on beaches, it was not needed to track other animals over the ground. More important, having a smaller nose and a free upper lip (most lower mammals keep a stiff upper lip) allowed primates to develop a wide repertory of facial expressions—which are essential to their sophisticated social behavior. Finally, improvements in hearing and, even more, in vision may have made a refined smell sense less useful (Clark 1959). In humans, however, some people believe that it is the loss of smell as a determinant in sexual behavior which is most significant in recent evolutionary history. The sexual heat of the estrus cycle is signaled by smell in many mammals. Since human sexuality is not seasonal, a keen smell sense was not needed to turn it on (Campbell 1967). It may have worked just the opposite way, of course—since the smell sense was not doing much anyhow, human sexuality became inde-

The Flower Vendor, Diego Rivera

If you were physically near this flower vendor, the perfume of his wares would blend with the body bouquet of a hard working man.

pendent of the estrus cycles and odors which had made it seasonal. There's no telling.

Finally, though we may not use our smell sense very much, it still works very well indeed. Many odors so light that they can only be identified and distinguished tediously by the finest laboratory instruments, can be detected and sorted out almost instantly by the human nose. You may not need to smell much, but it's nice to know you can.

Hearing

Audition, the sense of hearing, is a relative latecomer in evolution terms. Not in complexity or importance. It is as delicate a sense as smell and infinitely more useful. It is also a major social sense, unlike smell, because it is the sense which makes speech possible. And since language is the most distinct of all human capacities, we may say, therefore, that it is the sense which does most to civilize us.

Except for certain insects, no invertebrate can hear. Certain species of fish can pick up sound waves via an air bladder in the stomach that vibrates when sound waves hit it and a bone linkage from it to an inner ear, which codes the vibrations and sends them to the brain (Stevens *et al.* 1965). Some amphibians, such as frogs, have an eardrum—a major step towards the more advanced ears of mammals. And as you keep going up the evolutionary ladder, to reptiles, then birds, the auditory structure keeps improving—so a bird's ear has both a complex inner ear, or *cochlea,* and an eardrum. The cochlea, like the vestibular sense organs next to it, is a fluid-filled tube lined with tiny hairs. A bone carries vibrations from the eardrum into the cochlea; these vibrations set up waves in the fluid that brush up against the little hairs. The hairs then send impulses to the brain.

The human ear is basically the same, but more elaborate. The fleshy outer part scoops up sound waves and directs them down an inch-long canal to the *eardrum,* or *tympanic mem-brane.* The canal resonates and amplifies the sound, doubling the pressure of the sound waves on the eardrum, which starts vibrating. The vibrations go from there to the middle ear, about the size of a sugar cube, which has three small bones called the hammer, the anvil, and the stirrup. The vibrations from the eardrum vibrate the hammer, which vibrates the anvil, which vibrates the stirrup, which amplifies the pressure from the eardrum another 22 times. The stirrup pushes against the opening of the inner ear (cochlea), which is rolled up like a snail's shell and is full of fluid; the stirrup's vibrations make waves in the fluid, which push another membrane up and down inside the cochlea. Touching this membrane are little hairs, the auditory receptors, which connect to the auditory nerve and thence to the brain (Mountcastle 1968; Thurlow 1971; Tobias 1970). If that sounds complicated, it barely begins to describe the process. And none of it, so far, begins to tell you how amazingly efficient hearing is, why it is worthwhile having two ears[9], or why you should turn down your radio, electric guitar, or discotheque.

The middle-ear bones, incidentally, derived through evolution from the gills of the fish. You, as an embryo, had gills like the mature fish. But in the womb, the gills become reorganized into throat and facial muscles, into bones in the middle ear, and occasionally into muscles above the ear. If you can wiggle your ears, you have this last kind of transformed gill arch (Clark 1959).

Considering the physical apparatus involved, you could best describe hearing as a *vibratory* sense. Most of the vibrations that end up as sounds in your head get there through the air around you in the form of waves of pressure. Sound waves travel through air at about 750 miles per hour, not awfully fast—the reason you can hear the echo of your voice in caves or narrow valleys, for instance, is that it takes a

---

[9] In case you were thinking of dropping one.

while for the sound to travel from you to the nearest solid ground facing you, bounce off it, and travel back. Sound waves have to pass through some kind of medium (there is no sound in outer space because there are no pressure waves in a vacuum), but hearing does not depend on sound waves only. Part of your hearing ability results from the fact that bone conducts the necessary vibrations very nicely, the harder the bone, the better the conduction. Your skull is the hardest bone in your body, and many sounds are conducted by it directly to the inner ear without needing to be amplified by the eardrum. Some of the sound of your own voice, speaking or singing, is carried to you by bone conduction, and when you hum with closed lips, most of the sound you hear gets to you that way. Stop your ears with your fingers, and your humming will sound louder because you cut out interfering sounds from the air and because you get better reception of the low pitched vibrations from your throat which get lost when they have to travel to you through air. The reason your voice sounds thin and maybe squeaky on a tape recording, by the way, is because when you hear yourself speaking, you are hearing both air-conducted sound *waves* and the bone-conducted sound *vibrations.* But the tape recorder, like anyone else that listens, hears only the sound waves; so what gets played back to you is your-voice-as-others-hear-it.

Although sound waves all pass through the air at the same speed, the vibrations producing them occur at different speeds, ranging from one or two times per second to many thousand per second. This rate, called the *wave frequency,* dictates the *tone* or *pitch* of the sound. The ordinary human ear can detect tones as low as about 20 wave cycles per second (cps or Hz for short) and as high as about 20,000, depending on things like age and size: Kids may hear tones as high as 40,000 cps, but this ability drops steadily from about age 40

on as the tissues of the inner ear lose their elasticity. It also depends somewhat on the size of the inner ear, however, which in turn depends somewhat on the size of your head– so men can generally hear some lower tones than women (because they have bigger heads), and women can hear some higher tones than men. Everyone's ears are less sensitive to very low tones than high ones, however, in part as a matter of physical necessity. Otherwise, you would hear all the low pitched sounds of your own body. Stick your fingers back in your ears, in fact, and you will. The low, irregular tone you hear is produced by the contractions of the muscles of your arm and finger (Von Bekesy 1957).

Sound waves also vary in size, that is, in the distance from the top to the bottom of each wave. This is called amplitude ("ample" means "of large size"), and it is the main factor in *volume*—larger sound waves sound louder. If you hit the A key harder or softer on a piano, it vibrates 440 times per second in either case, but the sound waves are larger or smaller in size and, accordingly, in volume.

Loudness is measured in *decibels* (abbreviated (*db*), a form of amplitude scale. Ordinary conversation occurs at about 60 decibels; whispering about 25db; rock music about 125 db, and a jet plane about 150db. A sound of 85db is generally considered the beginning of the danger zone, beyond which loud sounds will produce nerve damage, and 130db is the point at which sound starts to feel painful. Your ears are incredibly sensitive; the eardrum sometimes vibrates at amplitudes of one-billionth of a centimeter (1/10th the diameter of a hydrogen atom), and the inner ear membrane at amplitudes 100 times smaller (Von Bekesy 1957). Nerve deafness generally comes on very slowly, after years of overexposure to loud noise. And there is no cure for it. Many teenagers today have the same hearing ability as 60-year-olds because of modern noise

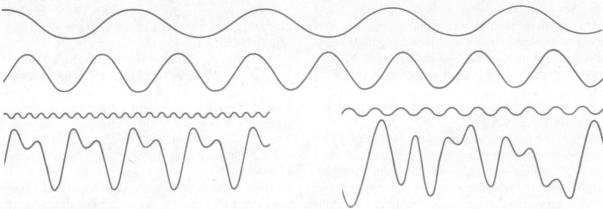

Figure 4.3 Wave forms

pollution. So, stay out of small discotheques with large hard rock ensembles, and turn your radio down!

Localizing sound: The cocktail-party problem   In addition to its decorative value, having your ears far apart on your head serves a valuable purpose—it enables you to tell where sound is coming from. If you are trying to understand one voice against a background of other voices, what acoustical engineers call the "cocktail-party problem," you have got to be able to identify its location. Having two ears at a distance from each other makes this possible largely because the sound reaches one ear faster than the other and at a higher amplitude. Your brain automatically calculates the differences (one ten-thousandth of a second difference in the time the sound reaches each ear is enough to locate it) and navigates your attention towards the source of the sound. This problem was investigated almost two hundred years ago by a great Italian physicist, Giovanni Venturi. His findings, published four times in three languages (twice in German; once in French; once in English), were essentially unnoticed for a century (Rosenzweig 1961). Nobody listened.

As with the other senses, the brain is the ultimate controller of hearing. The auditory cortex was discovered by Sir David Ferrier in 1870. He also found that the hearing of each ear is controlled by the auditory cortex on the *opposite* side of the brain.

Hearing as a social sense   Since speech is our main means of social communication, hearing is a major social sense. We get most of our social feedback from watching other people's faces and from hearing what they say to and about us. When deafness cuts off that information, it seems to affect people more sharply, even, than when blindness strikes them. People adapt well to blindness, but with deafness they tend to become depressed and sometimes paranoid (because they are unsure what people are saying). Since hearing declines steadily with age, old people are especially prone to these psychological problems, adding to the burden already placed upon them by a society which values youth and vigor as much as ours does.

Vision

The ears and the eyes are humanity's social sense organs, much as the nose is the dog's, because language and facial expressions are our chief means of social communication. Language is a more recent and a more subtle code, but it is also easier to fake than facial expression and bodily posture. Their wordless language must be sincere if human relationships are to proceed smoothly; maybe that is why control of facial expression is usually placed beyond our conscious reach, below the level of awareness (Bateson 1968).

Nearly all animals are sensitive to light. The lowest organisms do not have eyes, but their whole bodies are light-sensitive. An amoeba, for instance, will shrink from brightness. Some lower organisms have a pigment spot on their bodies that is especially sensitive to light. Such spots are not eyes, but they identify the presence, direction, and intensity of light. Crustaceans, such as lobsters, and insects, have compound eyes such that each eye consists of many small eyes. The brain composes a mosaic, presumably, from all the small bits of information sent by each eye (Bernhard 1966; Munn 1965).

A number of animals, including goldfish and bees, can see colors, but *color vision* is generally poor below the primate level. Primates, you recall, were the first creatures to have *stereoscopic vision,* which occurs when the visual fields of both eyes overlap so that they both see the same thing (Mueller and Mueller 1966).

Light travels in waves, like sound, but they are electromagnetic waves, like those of X rays and radio, not vibratory waves. Contrary to sound waves, in fact, light travels unobstructed through a vacuum and at the fastest speed of anything in the universe—186,000 miles per second.

Vision and hearing, the social senses.

Wavelength in measuring light, parallels *frequency* in measuring sound. It is the distance from the top of one wave to the top of the next (which, for light, is simply an easier measure to get than frequency is.) Color, technically called *hue*, depends on wavelengths, which are so tiny that they are measured in billionths of a meter (called *nanometers*). The range of wavelengths is called the *color spectrum*, and all the colors which the human eye can see take up only a small fraction of it, called the *visible spectrum.* Violet and blue colors, at one end of the visible spectrum, have very short wavelengths (400–500 nanometers), reds, at the other end, have relatively long ones (750 nanometers). Wavelengths are very precise indicators of color; if someone told you they had shined a light of a particular wavelength, you would know exactly what color was involved and could reproduce it exactly. Pure light, or white light, consists of *all* the visible wavelengths mixed together. When wavelengths of one color mix with those of another, the pure colors are *desaturated*, that is, weakened; the mixture of different color wavelengths is what produces the thousands of hues the human eye can see.

Amplitude in light waves is the same kind of thing as amplitude in sound waves; just as sound wave amplitude indicates loudness, light wave amplitude indicates the *brightness* or *intensity* of light.[10]

The eye The eye is, essentially, an instrument that collects light rays, much in the fashion of a color-television camera. The human eye is not the most complex or highly developed in the animal kingdom, but it is quite good enough to serve the human brain, which is. Interestingly, looking both at lower phyla and at the fossils of prehistoric creatures, it becomes

clear that "complicated eyes often go with simple brains (Gregory 1973, p. 27)."

Even so, the human eye is an incredibly specialized and refined instrument. Some of its most important tissues, like the cornea and the lens, are virtually isolated from the rest of the body by having no blood supply (they are nourished from the fluids surrounding them). And the light sensitive receptors of the retina, which collects the visual images from the lens on the back surface of your eye, "are as sensitive as it is possible for any light detector to be" —they can be stimulated by a single *quantum* of light, "the smallest amount of radiant energy which can exist (Gregory 1973, p. 19)."

At the front of your eyeball bulges out a tough, transparent membrane called the *cornea* (which means "horny" in Latin), and behind it, a watery fluid, which is constantly being used up and replenished about every four hours. Light waves slow down and bend when they pass through any transparent medium, which makes possible the formation of images. The density and convex shape of the cornea and fluid behind it causes light to bend inwards towards the *pupil,* an opening in the center of your eyeball. The size of the pupil changes with the expansions and contractions of the *iris* muscle surrounding it (the colored part of your eye); this regulates the amount of light which gets through the pupil to the *lens.* More important, it concentrates the light rays on the best part of the lens, its center, and improves the focus of the lens for viewing nearby objects.

The function of the lens is to focus the images formed by the cornea and to project them onto the *retina,* a light-sensitive, curved "movie screen" at the back of the eye, where the light receptors are. In a camera, or a fish, the lens focuses on nearby or distant objects by moving forward or back; in humans, it does so by changing its shape through the action of a muscle which tightens to let it focus on near objects and relaxes to focus it on far ones. Unfor-

---

[10] This statement oversimplifies a somewhat more complex reality, both for sound and light wave amplitudes. So do most statements about most things. As worded, it is close enough to accurate for our purposes in this chapter.

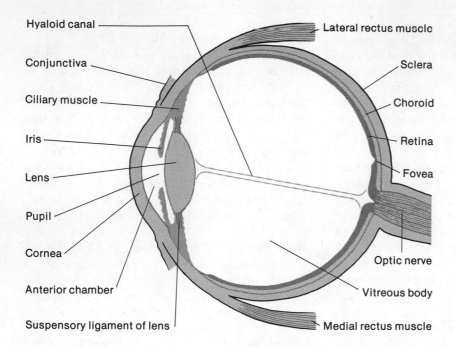

Hyaloid canal

Conjunctiva

Ciliary muscle

Iris

Lens

Pupil

Cornea

Anterior chamber

Suspensory ligament of lens

Lateral rectus muscle

Sclera

Choroid

Retina

Fovea

Optic nerve

Vitreous body

Medial rectus muscle

Figure 4.4 Anatomical drawing of the eye

tunately, the lens keeps growing all your life from its center outward and, as the old cells die, they harden. By middle age, the lens often becomes too stiff to bend, and near vision becomes very difficult without artificial lenses.

Calling the retina a movie screen is pretty literally true. The great astronomer Kepler figured out in 1604 that it was a screen on which the image from the lens formed, and in 1625 Scheiner proved it experimentally by cutting away the coating from the back of an ox's eye; it revealed the retina as a semi-transparent film on which he could see a small, upside-down image (Gregory 1973, p. 45).

The retina contains all the *photoreceptor* cells (from Greek, *photos*-light) that convert light energy into electromagnetic impulses that are then carried by the optic nerve to the brain. Unlike other sense organs, however, the retina is considered an outgrowth of the brain itself, "a specialized part of the surface of the brain which has budded out and become sensitive to light . . . (Gregory 1973, p. 46)." The retina is

thickly packed with receptor cells, maybe 125 million or more. Most of these (maybe 120 million) are called *rods,* the rest *cones.* The cones function in daylight conditions, and they are the color receptors of the visual system. Most of them are concentrated in a small pit in the center of the retina called the *fovea,* where they are arranged in a single layer. There are no blood vessels and no other tissue in the fovea; so light comes into direct contact with the cone cells (the fovea has no rods). Also, the cells of the fovea have more intimate connections with the optic nerve than do any other cells of the retina, and visual acuity, that is, the sharpness of our vision, is therefore greatest at the fovea. This means that you can generally see things most clearly by getting them in the exact center of your visual field (Clark 1959; Palyak 1957).

Almost all the retinal cells outside the fovea are rods. They function when there is little illumination, and they are blind to colors; they can see only shades of gray and also are responsive to movement. Rods are not as effective as cones in transmitting detailed images, which is why night scenes appear fuzzier than day scenes. But since the rods are more sensitive at low levels of lighting and concentrated on the side of the retina, you can see things best at night by looking at them out of the corner of your eye. Astronomers and aircraft spotters use their peripheral vision when searching for objects in the dark (Adler 1953).

The optic nerve, which connects the retina to the brain, hooks up to the eyeball at a point not far from the fovea. At that point, interestingly, there are no visual receptors at all. You ordinarily do not notice any such gap in your visual field, because you are used to filling in that space mentally with the surrounding things you do see—but it is a true blind spot, in which your mind may see, but your eyes do not.

The human eye can distinguish *thousands* of different hues (colors), but the eye could not have a different cone for each hue. Evidently, there are three different kinds of cone cells, each most sensitive to the wavelength of a different color—one responds most to red, one to green, and one to blue. But there are other cells, both in the optic nerve and in the brain, which are responsible for mixing the impulses from the cones in ways which allow you to perceive the variety of colors you do. This process is not entirely understood, and no current theory which tries to explain it is universally accepted.

Color blindness Not everyone sees colors. Some people are born partially or totally *color blind*. Color blindness is an inherited disability, far more common among males than females. About 5 to 7 percent of males and about one tenth of one percent of females are born unable to see one or more primary colors. The most common kind is red-green blindness, in which the world of colors looks all blue and yellow to you. Its opposite, blue-yellow blindness, is more rare. And total color blindness, in which you see *only* black and white, is very rare indeed. Most scientists think that some inherited deficiency in the cones is responsible for color blindness, but no one knows for sure.

SUMMARY

1   Sensation is the oldest topic in psychology, and the most elementary side of individual experience. The sensory processes are the primary means of any living creature for relating to the world around it.

2   All living things have sensation, but having specific *organs* of sensation is typical of animals as they go higher and higher on the phylogenetic scale of evolution. The nervous system originated as a means of connecting the information provided by the sensory appraratus to the response capacities of muscles and glands.

3   The different senses can communicate information to each other and to our motor apparatus because all incoming signals are coded in the brain by the same means, much as the readings from different instruments are prepared for computer analysis by the same kind of coding and keypunching. The brain does not directly receive light waves, sound waves, gas molecules, or other sensory stimuli. All sense receptors send electrical impulses to the brain.

4   A sense organ will register stimulation only when the absolute threshold of its nerves is crossed. The absolute threshold of a sense is the weakest stimulus that most people can detect 50 percent of the time. It is not really absolute, and today is often referred to as the *detection threshold*.

5 The brain does not passively receive signals from the senses; it can also control which signals it gets by such mechanisms as *attention* and *adaptation*. Attention is a filtering mechanism, which focuses a sense on one kind of stimulation, selecting it and avoiding distraction from others. Adaptation is a process in which attention to any stimulus gradually declines if the level of stimulation stays the same.

6 Senses also have *differential thresholds,* which means different degrees of change in stimulation which must occur before the person can sense it. The unit is called the just-noticeable-difference. The Weber-Fechner Law is a formula for stating how big a change in stimulation must be, relative to the original stimulus, in order to be noticed.

7 All animals need a fairly large amount of sensory stimulation in order to develop normally. Insufficient stimulation in infancy may harm the ability of adults to function effectively, while enriched sensory experience in childhood makes it easier to learn later on. In experiments on *sensory deprivation,* some people are upset by the prolonged absence of stimulation. There is some evidence, however, that sensory deprivation may be useful in treating some psychological problems connected with *over*stimulation, such as cigarette smoking.

8 The skin, or cutaneous, receptors are just under the surface of the skin. There are four different kinds of nerve endings in the skin, but there is not a single kind of nerve for each of the main skin senses: pressure (touch), temperature, and pain. Some nerves will produce all the skin sensations, from warmth or cold to itching, tickling, and pain—others respond to fewer kinds of stimulation and under different conditions. Also, skin nerves are not distributed evenly over your body, and they often fire in complicated patterns.

9 Pain is among the most complicated senses. It is largely a skin sense, but pain can be produced by extreme amounts of virtually any kind of stimulation. A few people are born insensitive to pain, but they usually do not live long. Much of our response to pain is learned, and how much we feel pain in response to intense stimulation depends largely on the prior experiences we have had with such stimuli, how much attention we are paying to them, and what they mean to us. Relatively little is known about the physiology or psychology of pain, but it is clear that the true pain center is the brain, not any specific nerves—and the brain is quite skilled at blocking out pain messages under many circumstances.

10 *Kinesthesia* is the sense of movement, probably one of the oldest senses and certainly one of the most important. There are more than 100 different body joints which house kinesthetic nerve endings. This sense allows you to move efficiently. Without it, you would have to look at your feet as you walked to know where they were. It coordinates muscular activities of your body and helps maintain posture.

11 The *vestibular,* or position sense, depends on structures in the ear. The semicircular canals there are filled with fluid, which shifts with every change in the body's position, activating receptor hairs which signal the body's position to the brain. Actually, it is changes in acceleration rather than direction of movement which produce this effect—sudden changes cause the fluid to slosh, produce dizziness, and very slow ones may cause it to shift so slowly that you do not notice that any changes in position are occurring at all. This fact can produce dangerous spatial disorientation in airplane pilots.

12 *Taste* and *smell* are called the chemical senses. There are four basic tastes—salty, sweet, sour, and bitter. As with the skin senses, some taste *buds* (clusters of taste receptors) respond to all four sensations, others to only one or two. Only liquids get tasted, so substances must dissolve for the taste receptors to be activated. Taste is not a very refined sense; most of what we experience as the "taste" of things is really a response to smell.

13   Only gases can be smelled. Smell receptors are several million cells in the upper part of the nasal cavity, each with about a thousand hairs in it, the workings of which are almost completely unknown. The most popular theory of odor is a variation of an ancient theory, which says that odor depends mostly on the shape of the molecules of smellable substances. Experiments on this theory have turned up seven primary odors.

14   Hearing can be considered a *vibratory* sense because it depends on the vibrations of waves in your inner ear. Most of the waves get there through air, but some of them pass through your skull (including part of the sound of your own voice). Sound waves vary in size, or *amplitude,* which determines volume (the bigger, the louder), and in number, that is, *frequency* per second, which determines pitch (the faster, the higher). Most humans can hear sounds from about 20 to about 20,000 waves per second. Hearing gets worse with age, especially after about age 40.

15   The human ear has three main sections: the outer, middle, and inner ear. The canal running through the outer ear amplifies sound waves. The eardrum converts them into vibrations, which are further amplified by three small bones in the middle ear and transmitted to the inner ear, where they set up waves in the cochlea. Hairs lining the walls of the cochlea register each wave and convert the information into an electrical impulse that goes to the brain.

16   Vision depends on light waves, which are electromagnetic waves like X rays or radio waves, not vibratory waves, like sound waves. *Wavelength,* in light measurement, is like frequency in sound—in vision, it determines *color. Amplitude* in light waves determines *brightness.*

17   The eye is an instrument for collecting light rays. The *cornea,* a tough transparent membrane at the front of your eye, bends light waves and sends them through a hole, called the *pupil,* which concentrates them on the *lens.* The lens in turn focuses the image formed by the cornea and projects it onto the *retina,* a curved movie screen at the back of the eye where the visual receptors are. They convert it to electromagnetic impulses which are then carried by the optic nerve to the brain. Unlike other sense organs, the retina is considered a specialized outgrowth of the brain itself. It has two kinds of photoreceptor cells—*cones,* for fine detail vision and for color vision, and *rods,* for night vision and for black and white perception.

Perception

5

5
Perception

Perception concerns the *interpretation of experience.* Broadly speaking, that is the essence of psychology. Physics is about the nature of reality; psychology is about the perception of reality. Philosophy studies the nature of truth; psychology studies the perception of truth. Social science concerns people's relations to each other; psychology adds to it their perceptions of their relations. Within psychology itself, people's most basic experiences are those conveyed by their senses. So the most basic aspects of perception concern the interpretation of sensation. That is what this chapter is about.

SENSATION, PERCEPTION, CONCEPTION: THE DEFINITION PROBLEM

Maybe it is already clear to you from the last chapter that the senses do not give us a full story of events — that the eye, ear, or sense of touch cannot simply pick out the relevant sensations that impinge on us and add them together. If we had to rely on uninterpreted sensory data alone, the world would seem like a hopeless jumble. If we took our vast sensory input just as it comes, for instance, we would think that a tall man standing 20 feet away was short, and at 40 feet we would think him a midget. Similarly, every time you hear a familiar word, or melody, it is pronounced or played differently — on different pitches, with different intonations, and at varying loudness — but you always recognize these different reproductions of the word or tune anyway; you have grasped their unity and continuity in your experience. That grasp, or recognition, or understanding, is what defines perception.

More or less. The word *perception* comes from a Latin root which means "to take," or "grasp," or "seize." It is used in everyday language to mean recognition, awareness, or understanding. But in scientific use, it has no exact meaning, though it refers to some very

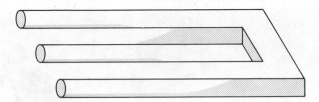

The impossible magnet.

specific processes. Many of them fall somewhere between sensation and thinking.

There is no completely satisfying way to define perception, and there is no very firm way to distinguish it from sensation (Dember 1960). If you viewed your nervous system as an information processing machine, however, one useful way to think of perception would be that it is the part of the system that takes signals which have been received in a relatively raw form and refines them into more useful information.

This processing begins in the sense organs, of course. The detection thresholds and the difference threshholds we talked about in Chapter 4 are such processing devices because they keep you from getting some signals and allow you to get others. But most of the information processing that most scholars call perception takes place in the brain, not in the sense organs, and that difference is one rough way to distinguish between sensation and perception.

It is very rough indeed. The distinction between sensation and perception can be very arbitrary. So can be the distinction between perception and thinking. Some things that we call perception in this chapter could just as well have been discussed under sensation—and indeed, *are* treated under sensation by some scholars. Others might be dealt with under thinking or imagination, which we have delayed until Chapter 9. It is not important to decide which things ought to go under which heading. It *is* important to know what the concepts mean in general and to know what you are talking about when you discuss the specific processes they involve.

We spoke of pain, for instance, in Chapter 4 as a skin sense. But no *sense* illustrates *perception* better, that is, the importance of interpretation to the experience of sensation. For most purposes, pain sensation and pain perception are inseparable, and we could as well have put pain in this chapter as in the last one. That is true of all the senses, and of most of the events that we commonly refer to as *sensation.* The scientific convention is to consider something sensation when the process you are discussing depends conspicuously on the sense organs involved and to call it perception when the brain is managing the show and the sense organs are not. But bear in mind that the distinction is largely a convenient fiction for discussion purposes—you must understand both brain and sensory process to understand how we grasp experience. A similar, but more subtle thing, is true, when we try to distinguish very sharply between perception and imagery, an elementary form of thinking. We will not belabor that right now, but notice that one of the things that makes you aware of yourself as having "a mind" is your perception that things going on in your head do not always mesh with your ordinary sense experience. Whenever you do not "know what to make of" your sensory experience, meaning how to interpret it, you are confronting the distinction between *concepts, percepts,* and *sensations.* That happens to you, inevitably, when you look at an impossible figure, like the one at the top of this page, or at any of several drawings by Maurits Escher, like the one at the top of the next page.

The *sense data,* that is, the actual lines and spaces which you *see,* do not correspond to

Waterfall, M. C. Escher

What the eye can see and what the mind will believe can be two different things!

the understanding you normally have about how such things "ought to look." So, you say, they "look funny," or they do not "make sense," that is, your physical sensations and your mental images or expectations do not fit. Such *perceptual anomalies,* or *illusions,* as they are popularly called, make some people uncomfortable because they seem so odd. But there are many perceptual patterns equally odd with which you are perfectly comfortable precisely *because* you are so accustomed to their being a certain way. Your **eye** shows you seven lines in the figure at the top of page 123, for instance; your **mind** shows you three pairs of lines and one extra line. In the figure at the bottom of page 123, your eye sees seven brackets. But

your mind, if you start looking from the left, sees three incomplete squares and half of a fourth; and if you start from the right, it sees three designs of narrow pillars or building columns and half of a fourth one. The distinction between what you actually see and what you are able to make of what you see is the difference between sensation and perception; that between what you seem to see and what it "looks like" is sometimes the difference between perception and thought.

THE EVOLUTION OF SENSE PERCEPTION

Perception is one step removed from the realities of sensation. But sensation is itself re-

122

A perceptual pattern.

moved from the realities of the physical world. David Hume (1964, orig. pub. in 1739), you recall, pointed out that the upper limit on knowledge is personal experience, so that all knowledge is ultimately subjective. Some philosophers, called *Idealists,* went further to argue that there may not be any physical reality beyond our individual subjective perceptions (Berkeley 1709). Most of us, neither philosophers nor scientists, tend to take for granted that our senses directly convey accurate impressions of reality to us. In thinking so, we might rightly be considered *naive realists.*

It is a mistake to get carried away by such stark, raving realism. For one thing, there is plenty of perceived experience that is not subject to consensual validation, such as dreams, or hallucinations, or prophetic visions. For another, sense experience itself is *always* an interpretation, and never a mere reflection, of the events outside your head. Sense receptors may be stimulated directly by physical events, but the brain's interpretation of them is never a mere copy of the external world. Light waves may occur in wavelengths and amplitudes, but the brain perceives them as color and brightness. Its perceptions may *correspond* to the physical events, but they do not copy them.

Even so, physical events do limit what we commonly perceive. Maybe in a dream time can run backwards and one person can merge into another; but in the world of conscious ex-

perience, we are generally more hidebound in our perceptions. In fact, we tend to view wildly unconventional perceptions as hallucinations or illusions. We limit most of our perceptual efforts to the personal experiences in which we have most confidence, our sensations. The limits to perception that most of us recognize, therefore, are the limits of our sensory capabilities. Those are largely defined by the thresholds and refractory periods of the sensory neurons, which differ for different senses. Two sounds, for instance, must be separated by at least 10 milliseconds (ten thousandths of a second) of silence for a human being to hear them as separate sounds instead of a single buzz. The eye, however, needs a longer interval between separate sights, 100 milliseconds.

For all senses, and for all sensing creatures, the biological limits are products of our evolutionary needs. As the folk saying puts it, "Different strokes for different folks." Hunting animals, such as owls and cats and us, usually have steroscopic (three-dimensional) vision. Their eyes both face in the same direction so that their two visual fields overlap, and the brain (not the eyes) integrates the two images to give them depth perception. This allows them to judge distance very accurately, and thus, to "jump" their prey. Vegetarian animals, however, that simply browse for food, such as cows, horses, or deer, have eyes facing more in different directions. They do not need the hunter's

The distinction between what your eyes see and what your mind "sees" is the difference between sensation and perception.

judgment of exact location, but they do need a lookout across a wide visual field to spot the approach of predators.

Different species also hear at different ranges, according to their needs. We can hear sound waves from about 20 to about 20,000 cycles per second; this range takes in the sounds most important to people. Bats, however, navigate by *sonar,* emitting high-pitched squeaks and listening to the bounced-back echoes; so they need to hear supersonic waves between 10,000 and 120,000 cycles per second.

Perception apparently evolved as a kind of filtering process, aimed at programming the reactive patterns of each species to the kinds of sense data it needed to survive. In every species, the activities of the perceptual system are directed by the capacities of the sense organs,

but they are not limited by those capacities in any simple or easily predictable way. In humans, part of the perceptual system may represent an evolutionary bridge between sensation and thinking. You *sense* what your organs are built to sense; you *think* what you can conceive or imagine; you *perceive* something in between what your mind can articulate and what your organs sense. Such perceptual processes are more concrete and biological and automatic than thinking, and are also more variable and educable and creative than sensing. Some of them are apparently innate, genetically fixed and built into your brain to meet primitive survival needs. Others seem to be learned, educated, and civilized to meet the needs of your local environment. The question of which is which brings us back to the nature-nurture

Perception is the bridge between sensation and thought. Vision alone tells you the child is coming out of nowhere—but you know better.

business once again, now focusing on the dominant themes of perception, *vision* and *movement.*

Vision and movement: The foci of perception

In the course of successful evolution, the structures and processes which are most important to survival are the ones which develop most fully. In human beings, as in many other species, the visual and kinesthetic aspects of perception are therefore the most elaborate. Vision and movement are our dominant senses because they are the ones most important for staying alive; spotting danger, and food, and moving away from it fast, or grabbing it quickly, are vital abilities. It is less important to sense stationary objects because they do not require fast reactions. The eyes of lower animals, in fact, do not respond to stimuli which are not moving. And the edge of the human retina, likewise, the most primitive part of our visual apparatus, responds *only* to movement; you can see the motion of something waved on the side of your visual field, but you cannot identify what it is. *"All eyes,"* according to British psychologist R. L. Gregory, *"are primarily detectors of*

When we perceive movement, are we really noting the step-by-step position of the moving object, like frames in a movie, and interpreting this as motion?

Nude Descending a Staircase,
Marcel Duchamp

movement" (1973, p. 92). In that case, it should make good sense that some important perceptual processes depend on the interactions of visual and movement senses. And it should also make sense that most studies of perception, therefore, are about the *organization* and *stabilization* of the visual world, that is, the study of visual patterns and how they change.

LEARNING AND PERCEPTION

Philosophers were speculating about whether perception is learned or innate at least as far back as Classical Greece, a long time before scientists got into the act. Then, as now, the issue was, how much of our perceptual ability comes ready made at birth and how much of it depends on learning and experience? We have met the same question before under instinct, and we will come upon it again in connection with language, intelligence, personality, and social behavior. Among European philosophers, the *rationalist* view, that *ideas* (percepts) are inborn, was argued by Descartes and other 17th Century philosophers on the Continent. At the same time, Thomas Hobbes, in England, began what was to become the British *empirical* tradition, whose most famous representatives, John Locke, George Berkeley, and David Hume, subsequently argued that perception is essentially learned. The most famous statement of this idea was made by John Locke in 1691 in his *Essay Concerning Human Understanding.* It said that the mind of a newborn baby is a *"tabula rasa,"* i.e. an "empty slate" on which experience is inscribed by the "association of ideas." It is not; today's scientific views are agreed that much of the apparatus of perception is ready for operation at birth and that some of the contents of what you perceive are also predetermined.

The philosophers who argued these matters over the centuries were not all armchair speculators. Nineteenth century physicists, philoso-

phers, and early psychologists, in particular (often the same people wearing all those hats; see Chapter 1), took positions on the question, basing their views largely on data they had accumulated about sensory physiology. The argument got its greatest modern impetus from the theories and experiments of the *Gestalt* psychologists, a group of Germans who began working under Max Wertheimer around 1911, and whose controversial ideas have since influenced social psychology, personality, and psychopathology as well as perception.

Gestalt is one of those difficult-to-translate German words[1] which means "form," or "configuration," or "good figure." The main idea of the Gestalt psychologists was that the brain is constructed so that perception will work by a number of built-in *organizing principles.* We are born, they claimed, with a natural tendency to organize experience in meaningful ways so that, without any special experience, we will know how to perceive figures apart from their backgrounds, to see groupings of things rather than to perceive them in isolation (as in the figures of lines and brackets a couple pages back), and so forth. A lot of experimentation since then has shown them to be largely right. They did not realize, however, just how intricate the physiological apparatus of perception is and how much of its proper operation requires that experience be added to our inborn perceptual tendencies.

The physical apparatus of perception The senses are finely tuned to give you information as soon as your attention is turned in the right direction. The machinery which turns it there is the first part of the perceptual apparatus. Some of it resides in the sense organs themselves. Stimulating the extreme edge of the retina, for instance, may produce no awareness, even of movement, but it may trigger a reflex which turns

---

[1] As opposed to *geschlitsubereitenzetsenkeithandlenzich,* which is one of those impossible-to-translate German words.

your eye to bring the stimulating object into the central line of vision, where your fovea can concentrate on it (the fovea, you remember, is the part with the greatest visual acuity). A visual stimulus above the absolute threshold has even stronger *alerting* effects, in the brain as well as the eye. It will cause you to turn your head in the right direction, will dilate the pupils of your eyes, and will set the lens muscles working to focus on the image—all reflexively. This alerting process is called the *orienting response*. It is also seen in jolts of increased activity in the electrical rhythms of the brain, signifying the arousal of attention. There are changes in blood vessels and glands also, as the autonomic nervous system gets into the act. The same process that prepares you to *perceive,* starts getting you ready to *respond.*

When visual images pass from the eye through the optic nerve into the visual cortex in the occipital lobe of the brain, highly specialized cells process different parts of the image. Experiments on cats and monkeys have shown that some cells there respond only to horizontal images, others to vertical ones, and still others to other angles; there are also cells there which are particularly responsive to the direction a moving stimulus is travelling in (Hubel and Wiesel 1962). Other experiments suggest that the same kinds of mechanisms occur in human beings (Sekuler and Levinson 1977).

The presence of such mechanisms means that you are programmed from before birth so that you can process sensory information of certain kinds. But that does not mean those perceptual processes will operate automatically. Whether they are able to function depends partly on your having the experiences which enable them to develop.

Adding vision to the senses A classical way of putting the question of the role of experience in perception has been to ask, "What would happen to someone who was born and raised blind if they were suddenly able to see? Their sense of touch would allow them to tell one object from another. Would their new visual sense allow them to make the same distinction or not?" The British philosopher William Molyneux raised the question to John Locke, who figured that the newly sighted person would not be able to tell things apart visually (1690). Later, George Berkeley, considering the same problem in his own *New Theory of Vision,* came to the same conclusion, that as "objects of vision" the things would involve "new sets of ideas . . . which can by no sort make themselves perceived by touch (1609)." All these empiricist philosophers agreed, as one would expect, that you need experience in infancy or childhood for good visual perception to take place.

They were right. There have been, according to R. L. Gregory, some 60 recorded cases between 1020 and modern times of people born blind or whose sight was lost early in life and restored later on. The best documented case was one that he himself studied, together with Jean Wallace, of a man who went blind at ten months and regained his vision when he was 52 years old. In most such cases, including the one Gregory saw (called S. B.), people had difficulty at first in naming the simplest objects by sight, even though they were very familiar with them through other senses; and sometimes they needed long training before they could make much use of vision at all. There were even worse effects in some cases; people got depressed, apparently feeling more burdened than benefited by this new sense, which they could never quite trust or get under control. S. B., like others, reverted after a while to living in darkness, his depressions became general, and he died within three years. These cases suggest that the lack of early experience with vision does permanent damage to the perceptual system, and there are a number of animal studies in the same vein. But they are far from conclusive. For one thing, a lot of things could go wrong between babyhood and adulthood; so there is no way of knowing for sure if the perceptual system failed to develop in the first place or if something screwed it up. Second, and more important, in some cases people did see well almost immediately! The conclusion Gregory comes to is that these cases do not, after all, tell us much about normal perceptual development in infancy. Adults, with their vast experience from other senses, are just too different from babies, with their lack of experience from any (Gregory 1973, p. 198)!

Vision in the newborn The way to find out how much babies must learn how to see, evidently, is to watch the babies. Several ingenious scholars have done so, and the results of their studies show that some aspects of perception surely are either inborn or develop very early.

Robert L. Fanz began by studying baby chickens and found conclusive evidence that they are innately able to perceive shape and size, showing a strong preference for things that are most likely to be edible. He then devised an apparatus for following the eye movements of baby chimpanzees and found that they too showed definite preferences indicating an inborn ability to distinguish between some objects. Finally, he expanded the studies to human infants and found not only that they show distinct pattern preferences (see chart opposite) practically from birth (despite their poor visual acuity), but that they show stronger preferences for the pattern of a human face than for anything else. Fanz worked with babies aged from four days to six months old, and found the same results for all age levels; so the preferences, if not innate, represent something close to love at first sight (1961)!

Form preference is not the only ability that is seen so early. The ability to distinguish foreground from background occurs as soon as a baby can see properly, and babies almost immediately can distinguish motion as well as constancy of a visual object—Mama is always Mama, even if she is seen at varying distances and angles (Fanz 1963). Both human infants and the offspring of lower species can gauge distance fairly well as soon as they can see (Fanz 1957; Zimmerman 1962). There is also some evidence that they may have an innate tendency towards depth perception.

More dramatically than any other such research, however, the "cliff avoiding" experiments of Eleanor Gibson have shown that depth perception is acquired very early, if not inborn. She built a table with a hole in the middle of it and then covered the hole with glass. The glass was treated so that it would not reflect light—so the hole appeared to be uncovered. The baby's mother stood on one side of the table and the baby was placed on the other. Then the mother called for it to come to her. The baby would crawl up to the edge of the visual "cliff" and then go no further. This shows that crawling babies already have depth sense (Gibson and Walk 1960). A more recent experiment shows that babies even younger can perceive depth. A baby was "rewarded" with a game of peek-a-boo when a cube was held a yard from its eyes and it turned its head to the left. After the baby learned this trick, it was shown the same cube and a larger cube, from ten feet away. Even a ten week old baby could single out the "peek-a-boo" cube, no matter where it was placed. The larger cube was ignored. Not only could the infant sort out the objects in the distance (depth perception), but it already had the perceptual equipment for understanding how the same cube, no matter where it was placed, always remained the same size (size constancy) (Bower 1966). The visual cliff experiments, incidentally, have also been done with babies of other species, generally with about the same results.

THE PERCEPTUAL SYSTEMS: ORGANIZATION, STABILIZATION, AND ILLUSION

More important than whether perception is inborn or learned is that it is *organized* along principles which are not all obvious from knowing about our sensory apparatus. It is this fact which, in the long run, separates thinking and imagination from sensory processes. Some organizing processes seem designed to permit *rapid* interpretations of sensory data so that one can act quickly on minimum information. These we shall call *patterning* processes. Others seem designed to foster dependable interpretations of sense data under different environmental conditions so that one can disregard irrelevant information. These we shall call *stabilizing* processes. Both of them inter-

act to interpret the world—and sometimes misinterpret it, to produce *illusions.* The rest of the chapter describes these processes and the relationships among them. To "get it," it is useful to have in mind an overall picture of what perception is and what it is for.

The evolutionary aim of all perceptual systems is to help animals accommodate to an ever-*changing* world. The fact of change means that nothing happens *by itself.* Things happen *in contexts, against a background* of other things, *in relation* to them. To understand what is going on, you must have some *dependable* way of

Interest in form was proved by infant's reactions to various pairs of patterns (left) presented together. (The small and large plain squares were used alternatively.) The more complex pairs received the most attention, and within each of these pairs differential interest was based on pattern differences. These results are for 22 infants in ten weekly tests.

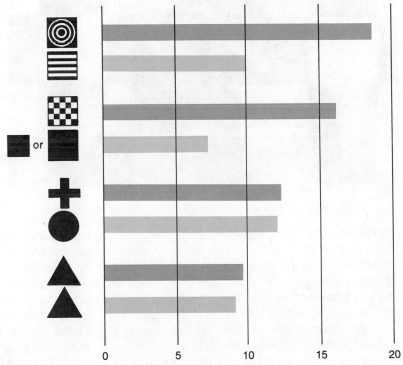

Average seconds of fixation in one-minute test

Source: From R. L. Fanz, The Origin of Form Perception. Copyright © May 1961 by Scientific American, Inc. All rights reserved.

Visual cliff.

apprehending and *organizing* those contexts and relationships so that you can act in response to them. The whole business is a problem of movement. You move and the world moves; both movements can be dangerous or full of opportunity. Perceptual processes try to harmonize them so that danger can be averted and opportunity exploited.

They work, in general, by putting the pieces of sense data together, organizing them. Some of these organizations are innate, others learned early on; all depend on the same stimulating principles, such as intensity, contrast, and movement, for their activation. There are two main kinds of organizations. One is *patterning,* which gives you a shorthand for putting large amounts of information together quickly and getting the "big picture" of what is "going on" in the world, that is, how it moves. We shall speak of *figure-ground relations* and *grouping* here. The other could be called *stereotyping* or *stabilizing* or "constancing." It works to make the world stop moving, so to speak, to let you have standard, stable, and dependable ways of interpreting events so that you can respond dependably to them. In large part, the constancies compensate for limitations of your sensory apparatus which, operating unchecked, would misinform you about what is happening and perhaps let you get killed in the process. Your perceptions of *location* and *distance,* of *size, shape, color,* and *brightness* are all affected by constancy principles. Some of these are determined by known machinery of your brain and nervous system, others by *perceptual sets,* that is, learned dispositions to see things in certain ways.

A fascinating byproduct of the successful operation of the perceptual systems is the experience of *illusions,* which represent the normal operation of perceptual mechanisms in situations where the information you end up with is uninterpretable or incorrect. Some of these, such as *illusions of motion,* are more or less automatic outcomes of the way your sensory apparatus works. Others, which we shall call *static illusions,* are more commonly byproducts of the perceptual sets and stereotypes which experience has taught us.

The contrast principle

Some things demand more attention than others. A bright color is noticed before a muted one, and a loud noise more than a soft one. The folk saying that "The squeaking wheel gets the grease," meaning that people who complain get attention, is true of all perceptual processes, not just interpersonal ones. Stimuli which stand out attract attention.

Standing out does not depend just on the intensity of a stimulus, however, but on how it stands out *in context,* that is, in the situation where it occurs. It is a matter of *contrast* between the stimulus and its surroundings. If the contrast between stimulus and background is great enough, you will perceive that something is going on; if not, not. If you look back at the previous chapter now, you will see that this

proposition is just a restatement of the Weber-Fechner law which describes differential thresholds of sensation. The principle of contrast also applies to absolute detection thresholds—there has to be a certain amount of contrast between stimulus energy and "the random background of the neural noise present in the brain for you to sense that anything at all is happening (Gregory 1973, p. 89)."

The point, which cannot be overstated, is that, in a changing world, nothing happens by itself; things happen in relation to other things, and your perception of what is happening depends largely on your sensing the differences between them.

In vision, it is contrast between the dark and light parts of an image that determines your responsiveness to it, perhaps innately. If an infant is shown a black triangle against a white background, its eyes will dwell on the three corners of the figure because the contrast between black and white is sharpest there (Salapatek and Kessen 1966). Babies automatically focus on faces rather than other parts of the human body, in part, probably because the face has sharper contrasts of shadow and light and more sharply contrasting contours than other parts. A more important reason babies focus on faces may be that the eyes in faces are generally moving. This means that the scene is *changing* all the time, and *change arrests attention by preventing adaptation.* You quickly get used to the murmur of conversation in a restaurant and then ignore it; but if the room suddenly goes silent, you immediately look around to see what is the matter. A constant stimulus level soon fades out, but when it changes, it surges back into perception.

Contrast between light and dark parts of an image is the governing principle for both movement and pattern perception, but it takes less contrast for you to tell that something is moving than to tell exactly what it is. There may be two separate channels in the nervous system for recognizing movement and pattern and, in evolutionary terms, the recognition of movement is more primitive and more important.

> Often during the evolution of our species it must have been much more important to respond to the direction in which some poorly defined form moved than to appreciate the details of that form. Any pedestrian who has dodged traffic in a large city appreciates this fact. . . . (Sekuler & Levinson, 1977, p. 73).

And the continued movement of your eye, remember, is needed to prevent adaptation to visual images, even when contrast is great enough to make them clear. So even the perception of stable forms depends, finally, on movement within the perceiver system, i.e., you. That principle underlies Gestalt psychology and the discoveries it has made about patterning processes.

The main idea of *Gestalt* psychology can be summed up in the notion that the whole context of perception is important in determining what you see, over and above the individual elements in it. In that sense, it is true that "the whole is more than the sum of its parts." The phenomena which make this clearest are those of figure-ground organization and of grouping.

Figure-ground organization One of the main effects of our disposition to respond to contrast is that we automatically see things *in relation* to each other, that is, in contexts. This means that, when we look at anything, we see some things stand out against a background of other things that are less prominent. This is called *figure-ground organization.* It operates with two as well as three-dimensional objects. Thus we say that words are "on" the page; the black print seems to stand "against" a white background. When you are focusing on an object, the background elements may be indistinct, and you may even be unaware at any given moment of their presence. But it is easy to shift your attention, and when that happens, you find that the background becomes more distinct and the object previously in the foreground now becomes less clear. What you *cannot* do, try as you might, is see any stationary image as foreground without seeing a background, or bring a background into focus without losing focus on the foreground.

Which things are foreground and which background is not up to the things, but up to you. Another important principle discovered by Gestalt psychologists is that some aspects of organization are imposed by the perceiver and vary with individual differences among people, even though the tendency to organize is itself innate. The particular dispositions you have to see one thing as foreground and another as background, for instance, depend on your expectations, interests, motives, and experience. Their product is called your *perceptual set.* Shifting perceptions back and forth is called "alternation of perceptual set." Mostly, you can do it at will. Sometimes you cannot help it.

There are some situations where the different visual elements have equal attention-getting power. When that happens, your perceptual set will start to alternate spontaneously between them, and you will see first one, then the other, as figure and as background. Reversible figures, like the goblet faces, the ugly old lady-pretty young woman, the Necker cube, and many of the most fascinating drawings of Maurits Escher, have these properties (Teuber 1974). The goblet drawing can be seen as a white goblet on a black background *or* as the profiles of two facing people on a white background. Notice that you can perceive either the goblet or the profiles, but not both at once. When one is figure, the other must be background, and vice versa. The same is true of the fish-water/geese-sky of Escher's drawing, and of the old lady-young woman picture on page 134. Which figure you see first probably depends on your perceptual set. Most people see the vase before the profiles; I see the pretty young woman before the ugly old one. The Necker Cube is a little different; here, one interpretation is seen just as readily as the other.

An ambiguous figure.

Necker Cube.

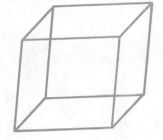

We see the figure and ground alternately—but not at once. In the middle area of the picture we see birds *or* fishes, as they change places before resolving their ambiguity upwards or downwards.

Sky and Water, M. C. Escher

Ugly and old or pretty and young? What you see depends upon how you perceive.

Grouping and patterning Perception is organized in more refined ways than just by figure and background. A whole figure can look very different from the way its parts look when they stand alone. For one thing, the parts may seem to be separate or grouped together, depending on things like how close together they are (called *proximity*) and how much they resemble one another (called *similarity*). The lines and brackets on p. 123 illustrate proximity; so do the dots below. You see them as four *groups* of 3, rather than as 12 dots, because of the spacing differences between them.

Another basic grouping principle is *similarity.* If you stare at the bathroom floor, you will invariably start to pick out patterns in the tile. You will perceive the white tiles as forming lines that are crisscrossed by the lines of the black tiles. A row of *alternating* black and white tiles probably may not look like a line to you. The brain tends to make wholes (lines, in this case) out of units that share striking similarities of color, spacing, brightness, and size.

Continuity is a third grouping principle, in which your eye tends to follow continuous contours and to disregard abruptly changing ones. Because of it, you see a wavy line on top of a rectangular line in the figure rather than seeing several sets of separate figures connected to each other.

Closure is another grouping principle, related to continuity. If you look at an incomplete circle, you automatically fill in the missing piece mentally, rather than perceive the figure as the letter **C** or some other open figure. Most

• • •   • • •   • • •   • • •   Grouping.

In this arrangement, horizontal rows of colored squares result from the principle of proximity, vertical columns from the principle of similarity.

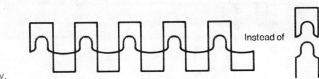

Instead of

Continuity.

cartoonists, and some modern painters such as Paul Klee (see his cartoon birds in the drawing on p. 136, use this principle to draw stylized partial figures from which you deduce the whole picture they suggest. They did not invent the method. Prehistoric cave drawings sometimes used stick figures; they were also the basis of Egyptian hieroglyphic writing; and you, some years ago, drew no other kind.

Notice, with all the grouping principles, that the patterns of dots and such which you see are *permitted* but not *demanded* by the stimuli themselves. They *are* demanded, it seems, by

the mental processes of the perceiver. Some grouping tendencies seem to be innate, at least in lower animals; others are learned and vary with people's perceptual sets. All of them, according to Gestalt theory, serve the principle of Pregnanz.[2] The word implies the idea of "good" form; the principle is that the mind strives to see patterns in a simple, stable, regular, symmetrical, unified way. The scientific status of the Pregnance principle is in doubt, but the grouping principles from which it is

_____
[2] In English, Pregnance.

Twittering Machine, Paul Klee

Stylized, partial figures are used in some modern paintings and most cartoon drawings to suggest much more than is shown.

derived *do* operate in perception (Gregory 1973, p. 145).

Common fate A final Gestalt principle connects figure-ground, grouping, and patterning principles with movement. It says that individual objects are likely to be perceived as a single whole if they move together, whether or not they are connected. If you watch a gaggle of geese in flight, for instance,[3] you will notice the entirety rather than the individual birds. If the animals in the batch were a motley assortment of geese, ducks, penguins, Peter Pan, and Dumbo, you would still see the whole array as one entity, even though you could identify the individuals in it.

Nature and military folks take advantage of these principles in camouflaging such things as butterflies, chameleons, jungle uniforms, and vehicles. Patterns of protective coloration and design are painted on them to make them blend into the local scenery (see Figure 5.1). As long as they are stationary, the proximity, similarity, and continuity of these elements with the natural background makes them seem to be part of it, thus disguising the object. When it starts to move, however, it is seen right away as a unitary figure, distinctly different than its background.

---

[3] Or an exaltation of larks, or a host of angels.

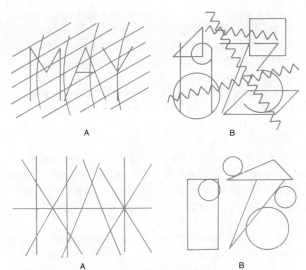

A   B

A   B

Source: Mussen et al. *Psychology: An introduction*, Lexington, Mass.: D. C. Heath and Company, 1973. Reprinted by permission of the publisher.

Figure 5.1 An illustration of unsuccessful (top) and successful (bottom) camouflage.

Movement perception

When something breaks out of camouflage by moving, you can perceive the movement well before you can tell what is moving. The perception of images and patterns is subordinate to the perception of movement in your nervous system. When things move at very slow speeds, say slower than the minute hand on a watch, you perceive no movement at all (Howard 1975). In survival terms, there is no need to; anything moving that slow will get no chance to eat you. At high speeds, though, you will still see blurred streaks of motion long after you can no longer make out a definite image. Sense thresholds serve survival needs.

The amount and complexity of movement perception systems in eye and brain also serve those needs. We have mentioned the movement-detection cells in the brain and on the edge of the retina and the saccadic eye movements which stabilize images by their short fixations. In general, however, there are two connected systems that direct your perception of movement. One, which Gregory calls the *image/retina* system, makes you perceive movement when your eyes are stationary and a moving object crosses your field of vision (the image crosses your retina, firing the receptors). The other, which he calls the *eye/head* system, lets you perceive movement when your eye is actually following a moving target (and the image stays in one place on your retina). Under some circumstances, the normal operation of these systems makes you see illusions. Some of them can be dangerous; all can be interesting.

Autokinetic effect If you[4] were to light a cigarette and leave it at one end of a completely dark room, and then watch the glowing tip from the other end,[5] in a few seconds you would see it start to move in odd ways.[6] It will shimmy, swoop around in different directions, and meander slowly back and forth. This is called the *autokinetic* (self-moving) effect. You cannot prevent it. Even though you know the light is stationary, you will still see it moving. The

---

[4] Or anyone else, for that matter.
[5] Of the room, not the cigarette.
[6] The glowing tip, not the room.

autokinetic effect sometimes bedevils pilots at night, who mistakenly think distant beacons are moving lights. To avoid such mistakes, experienced pilots line up a beacon with a spot on their windshield.

No one knows for sure what causes the autokinetic effect, but the best explanation seems to be that it results from the brain sending signals to the eye/head system to try to keep your eyes fixated on the light. Your eye muscles tire quickly, making the eyes wander very slightly, and the brain's commands to fixate back on the target produce the illusory movement (Gregory, 1973, p. 103).

Induced movement   The autokinetic effect happens only in a situation where your eye has no frame of reference for telling whether something is moving or not. But true motion is relative, and you can measure it only with reference to something else. Bishop Berkeley noticed that over three centuries ago, and Dr. Einstein based his theory on it. So, over and above the visual systems which track movement, your brain has to make a decision about what is moving and what is not. Sometimes it gets help from your kinesthetic senses, as we shall see. But when it has only vision to go on, it tends to operate in a frame of reference which assumes that *small things move against large backgrounds.* In the evolutionary world of hunters and hunted, that is more often true than not, so it is not a bad idea to have the notion programmed into your brain. Having it there gives you a more stable view of the world. But it also means that when you get into a situation where the big object or the visual field moves and the small one stands still, you are *induced* to see the small one moving and to think the big one is stationary. You are still using the big one, in other words, as a frame of reference. That is why, if you watch clouds blowing across the moonlit sky, it will look as if the moon is moving and the clouds are still. The same thing happens when you watch the train on the next track sliding past and think your train is moving; the other train is part of the larger visual field; so you think it is standing still. Not so; you are.

Movement aftereffect   The autokinetic effect happens from the *eye/head* system's troubles dealing with a *stationary* object which has no background. Movement aftereffects are illusions resulting from the *image/retina* system's trouble dealing with certain kinds of *moving* objects. The trouble comes when they stop moving (or you stop looking at them, which is the same thing), in the afterimage which you see. The "waterfall effect" has been known since ancient times. If you look steadily at the center of a phonograph turntable while it is rotating, then stop it suddenly, it will seem to rotate backwards for several seconds. The ancients, lacking phonographs, got the same odd effect by watching moving water for a while, then turning their eyes to some stationary object. The object would appear to move in the direction opposite to the water.

The most dramatic instance of this business is the *spiral aftereffect,* which should perhaps more properly be called the spiral during-and-aftereffect. When you rotate the spiral clockwise, it seems to expand as it moves. Then, when you stop the rotation, it seems to shrink. Vice versa when you first rotate, then stop it in the opposite direction; it shrinks first, then expands. Also, it looks like it is *simultaneously getting bigger*

Archimedes spiral

or smaller and still remaining the same size! Don't ask me why. It is known that these effects result from the adaptation of the image/retina system to the movement, but no one knows whether that adaptation occurs in the eye or the brain, nor just how it works.

Apparent movement The movement illusions which probably affect your life most, and most pleasantly, are the ones that make movies possible. Like aftereffects, they are properties of the image/retina system. The illusion is that, when you watch motion pictures, it looks as if you are seeing continuous movement. You are not. In reality, you are looking at still pictures, shown one at a time, but fast—24 per second for sound movies. Each picture shows action a tiny bit different from the last, and your brain treats the whole thing as if it were a display of continuous motion. This illusion depends on two facts, the *persistence of vision* and *visual closure* (also called *phi phenomenon*).

Visual persistence refers to the fact that your vision cannot switch off as fast as the light that stimulates it. If a light flashes on and off rapidly, it will look to you like it is flickering until, depending on its brightness, it gets up to 30 to 50 flashes per second. Then the *flicks* will *fuse* into what seems to be a continuous, steady light. In the early days of motion pictures, the slow projection rate really made them "flicks." Nowadays, the projectors have a shutter which flashes each picture three times so that there are 72 flicks per second from the 24 still-picture frames. This is higher than the *critical flicker fusion* point; so it looks to you like one continuous light.

Visual closure, or *phi,* then works to make the action seem continuous. Phi is the tendency of your visual movement detectors to fill in the blank spaces between two lights sitting side by side. When one is switched on right after the other is switched off, it looks to you like there is a single light moving from one place to another. The principle works to fill in the visual spaces for adjacent objects, seen one after another in slightly different actions each time; it looks to you like you are watching movement. The same principle makes the neon lights on billboards and bar signs look like they are moving.

Stroboscopic motion Flickering lights can do worse things than interfere with your enjoyment of the movies. Slow light flashes, looked at steadily, cause the electrical rhythms of the brain to synchronize with them, that is, to occur at the same rate. This can sometimes produce seizures in people with a tendency to epilepsy. What is worse, it can happen to them when they are driving along a road where the sunlight flashes through a row of well spaced trees, or from staring at the whirling blades of a propellor or electric fan that has a light flashing through it. Called stroboscopic motion ("strobos" means "whirling round" in Greek), it can produce a variety of odd illusions of color and motion even in normal people, and some unpleasant effects, such as nausea and headaches. Strobe lights are popular in discotheques, where they fit right in with the general sensory bedlam. No one knows just what causes strobe effects, but it probably involves disturbances of the brain's visual systems.

From change to constancy: Movement and distance

All the movement illusions we have discussed so far, except *induced movement,* depend on the sense apparatus directly. In induced movement, however, a *decision* is involved rather than a mere sensing process, and it is even a decision which you can articulate and think about: "Which train is moving, mine or the other one?" The decision is based on a hypothesis about what the sensation means, not on a reflexive response to the neural upset. The perceptual processes involved in such decisions are all attempts *to stabilize* the world of moving, changing objects rather than just *to follow* the movements. They do this by

"Vega," Victor Vasarely

The illusion of movement in space, which you will see if you study this picture for a moment, is basic to all op art.

perceptual constancy principles, interpretive rules for judging what is going on, for making comparisons "between the object as it is perceived and the object as it is understood to actually exist (Dember, 1975, p. 43)." The process uses interpretations of motion, contour, and texture to judge location, distance, depth, size, and shape—the whole set of perceptual schemes we require in order to feel that we have some dependable understanding of the world.

Distance Most dangers, and most opportunities, are only important when close up. The further you are away from them, the less important it is to know how fast things are moving, exactly where they are, or what their

size, shape, and color is. Accordingly, most perceptual schemes for both movement and constancy perception break down when you are too far from the object of interest to judge its distance accurately. The clues you ordinarily use to judge depth, like the angle at which the images converge from each eye, no longer work. This produces interesting illusions, like the one you get while driving on a moonlit night, that the moon seems to be travelling along with you but never gets left behind. All the other constancies break down as well. Early in our evolution, it would not have mattered. When we could only move slowly, and for short distances at a time, and by the power of our own bodies alone, far distance judgments were not needed, and everything you did need to know about where things were and where they were going could be told by the interaction of visual and kinesthetic cues. (The induced movement illusion, for instance, never occurs when you are moving under your own steam, because the information from your kinesthetic sense that you are moving makes it unnecessary to rely on visual cues.) But now that we move fast, and sit still doing it, the breakdown of constancies can be dangerous. Our intellectual abilities have outdistanced our perceptual ones. Even so, most of our perceptual lives are lived close enough to our bodies and under sufficiently routine conditions for the constancies to be useful, and we use them so routinely that we are generally unaware of them.

Location constancy   In 1897, a psychologist named George Stratton at the University of California blindfolded his left eye for eight days.[7] Over his right eye, he placed a special lens that turned his visual field upside down and shifted right to left and left to right. Now his perceptual world was completely inverted and reversed.

At first, Stratton was very disoriented, as were the people who saw him stumbling around the campus. His coordination was severely disrupted. When he reached to his right for something, it was really to his left. By the third day, however, Stratton was making progress, and by the end of the eight days he had adjusted very well to his strange world. Things again began to seem where they should be—sort of. Stratton did many more experiments in which he used different kinds of lenses and mirrors to displace the visual location of things, and many other experimenters have followed up his work since with a variety of displacement and distortion goggles, lenses, and the like, and for auditory as well as visual perception. In all of the

studies done on human beings, adaptation occurred within a few days, that is, people got used to the odd positions in which things appeared to be and learned to correctly coordinate their sense of touch and movement to the new situation.

Lower animals are less flexible than human beings in adjusting to such shifts. E. H. Hess hooded newly hatched chickens with goggles which displaced objects seven degrees to the right (or left). When a hooded chick saw a kernel, it would peck seven degrees to one side or the other of it. *The chicks never adjusted to the distortion* (Hess 1956). Monkeys do better than chickens, but not nearly as well as people. Human ability to compensate perceptually for new conditions is far greater than that of other species.

There is some evidence, moreover, that to whatever extent the ability is learned, it depends on feedback from kinesthetic and touch senses as well as on the sense of vision. Animals that are kept either physically passive, or in the dark from infancy on, are virtually blind perceptually when they are first given the opportunity to see. It takes them quite a while to recover from such states; and, if they have been deprived of light for too long a time, they may suffer permanent damage to the visual system (Held and Hein 1963; Riesen 1950).

Size and shape constancy   It is sometimes as important to know how big things are and what shape they take as to know their location and distance from you. The judgments of each, in fact, sometimes depend on the other. The ability to see constant size and shape in objects is largely preprogrammed. A young baby, you recall, can already perceive a familiar cube as constant in size even when it is moved some distance away. It can also distinguish some forms quite dependably, even if they are presented at different visual angles (Bower 1966).

Both size and shape constancies serve important survival needs. They compensate for the fact that the actual size and shape of images

---

[7] In California, we started doing funny things a long time ago.

on your retina changes drastically with movement. The image on the retina doubles in size when its distance from you is cut in half. Its shape on the retina, moreover, changes with the angle from which you are viewing it. If someone enters a room through a door 20 feet away from you, the image of the person in your eye is literally twice as small when they enter the room as when they have walked half way across it. The shape of the door, moreover, as far as your retinal image is concerned, is rectangular before it opens, becomes trapezoidal as it opens, and becomes a thinner and thinner trapezoid until it is visually nothing but a straight line, as it moves to the perpendicular of your line of sight. If it keeps opening further, it becomes a trapezoid again, expanding in the other direction. But all that you perceive, of course, is a door opening and a person entering. The person is the same size at either end of the room, and the door looks like a door throughout. Your brain has kept their size and shape constant and, by compensating for the changes their movement has produced, has allowed you to make a dependable (and correct) interpretation of what the things are and what is happening to them.

Both shape and size constancy were described accurately in 1637 by Descartes, who realized that they depended on "our knowledge, or opinion," about "the way we see the distance and position of their parts," not on "the pictures in the back of the eye."

Some of our size constancy judgments are based on experiences we have had with *perspective,* that is, the *point of view* from which we have learned to judge distance and depth. Looking at parallel rows of trees, or tracks, or telephone poles going off into the distance, for instance, we are accustomed to seeing them look smaller when they are very much further away from us and accustomed to the sight of the parallel lines seeming to converge as they move off in the distance. Such observations of horizontal distance are called linear perspective. Many other experiences with distance and depth cues, to aerial perspective, texture, color, and shadow, also help develop judgments of size. Distant objects look hazier and more softly colored, for instance, than near ones. The surface textures of things look smoother from far away than from up close.

Binocular parallax and *motion parallax* are also primary perspective cues to depth and distance. Binocular parallax refers to the fact that the distance between your two eyes gives you slightly different perspectives on where a thing is; combining them stereoscopically, as we have seen, produces a third dimension of perspective which locates it more precisely, giving you a sense of its depth. In motion parallax, you judge distance by apparent differences in speed; if you move your head to the left while keeping your eyes fixed on a distant point, for instance, things which are close to you seem to move to the right farther and faster than things which are farther away.

Brightness and color constancy Brightness and color constancies provide some perspective cues to distance also, but they are probably more important in *pattern recognition,* that is, the identification of objects, than of location. Like the other constancies, they reflect the brain's interpretation of events in situations where the sensory inputs vary. If you *know* that something is bright in normal sunlight, for instance, like a bracelet or a silver plated suit of armor, and that something else is dull, such as a grey velvet bicycle, the bracelet will keep on looking bright and the bike dull even when the bike is actually reflecting more light. If a spotlight were trained on the bike and the bracelet were in shadows, a light meter would show a greater brightness reading when held against the bike than against the bracelet, of course—but your brain will ignore the *sensory report* and stick with its own preconceptions.

As every photographer knows, color also varies enormously with the time of day. One evening, you photograph your new white car to send a picture home, and it comes out pink. In the sunset, the white paint was reflecting the glow of the sky. Your sensory apparatus saw pink, as the camera did; your mind saw white, as you always did. Similarly, in sensory terms, the world is more or less monochromatic just before sunrise—black and white with shades of grey. In the early morning, things take on a red or orange quality because the colder blue hues are filtered out by the air. *Shadows,* however, are bluish. At high noon, colors are very bright and shadows very black, but everything appears harsh and characterless.

The color photographer must take all of these sensory variations and perceptual constancies into account at once. An eyewitness will automatically compensate perceptually for the sun's position. But someone viewing a photograph will see things as the camera saw them.

Constancy illusions

You do not have to take a course in psychology to learn the cues to distance and, accordingly, to size (or shape). They are products of experience which occurs early enough and often enough so that your use of them is intuitive and automatic. You combine the cues and make the judgments without thinking consciously about it. Your perceptions of size, shape, depth, and distance depend on the interactions of these cues. In situations where your observations correspond with your habitual interpretations of the most *salient,* that is the most noticeable, cues, your perceptions will be correct. Where your interpretations of the cues fails to correspond to the realities of the situation you are observing, however, you will be deceived and will perceive visual distortions. When that happens, it is your judgment, not your senses, which is at fault. Your perceptual distortions of depth perspective and distance perspective create some remarkable illusions.

Some of the simplest size illusions are fairly straightforward matters of context. That is why, even though the illusion effect is quite strong, you can easily understand that the two center circles in the figure below are the same size and the one on the left only looks bigger because it occurs in the context of relatively smaller circles.

Muller-Lyer illusion No such simple explanation is apparent for the Muller-Lyer, or *arrow illusion,* you see on p. 144. The figure with the outgoing fins looks longer than the one with the arrows pointing inward; some people estimate the difference between them to be as much as 20 percent (Figure A.). Animals see the same things here people do. And the image is just as powerful when the center lines are missing as when they are there (Figure B.). Yet, if you measure the distance between the center points of the arrows in Figure A and Figure B alike, you will find that they are identical. Many explanations have been offered for the Muller-

Size contrast.

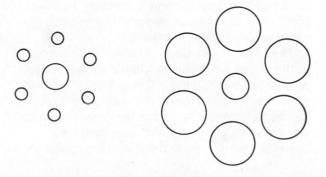

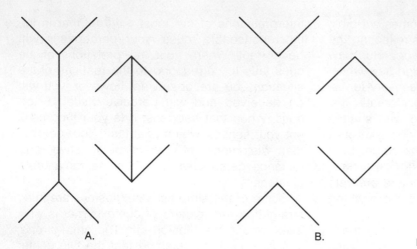

A.   B.

Muller-Lyer illusion.

Lyer illusion, but none of the theories have been flawless. R. L. Gregory has offered the most plausible, perhaps. He says that this one, like most visual distortion illusions, is based on our normal use of the size-constancy principle in our perception of corners to judge distance. We are used to the corners of walls on the inside of buildings, that is, the walls of the rooms we sit in, having out-pointing arrows at the ceiling and floor. Corners of outside buildings, on the other hand, have in-pointing arrows at roof and ground. Since inside corners are normally close to us and outside corners far away, we see the inner corners as bigger than the outer ones through our ordinary use of distance perspective. In the arrow illusion, the perspective principle continues to operate by force of habit in our perception of corners, even though there are no walls or buildings present to justify it. Not all the data support this theory, however, and plenty of research suggests other possible explanations (Weintraub 1975).

The Ponzo illusion A clearer illustration of the same principle is visible in the Ponzo, or railroad-track illusion on p. 146. The two horizontal lines between the tracks are exactly the same length. The upper tie looks bigger to you because of misplaced size-constancy in a scene in which your mind is dominated by distance perspective. The converging tracks and other cues of distance make you think the upper cross-tie is further away, and so your mind enlarges it; the lower tie seems nearer; and so your mind diminishes it. Notice that distance perception dominates size perception and, in this case, screws it up. If you had no distance perspective cues, the two lines would immediately appear the same size.

The Ames illusion Most visual distortion illusions are of this nature. They tend to be flat, two-dimensional figures, where constancy follows apparent distance and is distorted by it. But the figure does not have to be flat, and constancy will still bow to distance. The Distorted Room of Adelbert Ames, an American painter turned psychologist, uses perspective cues to take advantage of shape constancy and create distortions of size perception. The far wall of the room is sloped way back at one side, but distance perspective cues are used to make it look rectangular to anyone looking at it head on (p. 147). What happens is that when you put something into the far corner of the room, it seems to shrink in size. The image you see is smaller than you expect for the distance you mistakenly think it is from you. If you put a baby in the near corner and a grownup in the far one, the baby looks like a giant and the grownup

The arrow illusion. Since the inside corners of a room are usually closer and the outside corners far away, the inside corners with out-pointing arrows seem to be bigger than the outside corners with in-pointing arrows. By force of habit, according to R. L. Gregory, this principle continues to operate in our perception of corners or arrows.

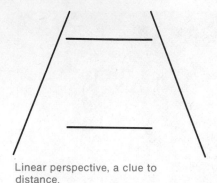

Linear perspective, a clue to distance.

like a dwarf. Apparently it never occurs to us to think that the room is the wrong shape rather than that the people are the wrong size. We are that accustomed to rectangular rooms, and that

dominated by perspective cues to distance in our evaluations of what we see.

Perceptual set

We rarely think about how much Western civilization turns around right angles and flat surfaces, but the list of such things in our cultures is almost endless. Rooms, buildings, boxes, windows, street corners, books, pages, and pictures are but a few. In the same way, long parallel lines are constantly converging off in the distance of our common experience— streets, railways, pipelines, canals, flower beds, and even the "amber waves of grain" of "America the Beautiful," are all laid out in rows. The experience of linear perspective, and what it

The Ponzo illusion.

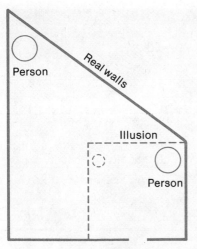

Peephole

This diagram shows the construction
of an Ames room. To a viewer
situated in a particular location,
the room appears to be rectangular.

does to our perception of constancies, therefore, is part of the perceptual set of our culture. People living in other environments, without a lot of books and pictures and right angles and long parallel lines, are not very subject to these illusions at all. The Zulus of South Africa, for instance, live in what is called a "circular culture"—their houses are round, with round doors, they plant their fields in curves, and they have few possessions with corners or straight lines. They do not see most of our illusions because, having been raised in so different a perceptual environment, their **expectations** are different (Allport and Pettigrew 1957; Segal *et al.* 1963).

Perceptual set is a matter of personal experience as well as cultural conditioning. Look at the line drawings in Figure 5.2, for instance, that gradually merge from one figure to another. If you show just the first drawing to someone, they will see it as Santa Claus. So too with the next several. But if you start with the drawing of an ogre and *then* show the next couple

drawings, they will probably perceive them as ogres, too. Depending on the viewer's previous experience of one figure, their perception of the other will vary (London 1958).

Selectivity is determined by distant personal experience as well as by present cues. Each of us has a "perceptual style" or "set" based on our own history. Thus, while milling around in the same crowd, the guitarist will notice who is carrying musical instruments; the man on the make will watch the prettiest girls; the junkie will note whose sleeves may be hiding puncture marks; and the alcoholic will see only the flashing bar sign in the distance.

Experiments using rapid-fire, or **tachistoscopic,**[8] stimulus presentations have produced a lot of information about **set.** In general, subjects in these studies have to identify words flashed on a screen or pronounced quickly through earphones. Such tests show first, that people perceive most readily words that are connected with their own interests (Postman et al. 1948). A preacher grasps the word **sacred** faster than the word **football,** and an athlete responds in the opposite way. Second, the more *often* people are exposed to a word, even a nonsense word, the more readily they perceive it. This second finding may explain the first—a preacher is **used** to the word **sacred.** Third, when people are told to **expect** a word on the screen or over the earphones and then no word comes, the subjects are nonetheless certain one *has* appeared. They usually think it was some word common in the ordinary American vocabulary. Finally, people are very prone to suggestion. If they are told to expect words related to transportation, for instance, and then are shown **bomt,** they often think they have seen **boat.** Similarly, people who have been told to expect words about war, and are shown **bomt,** think they have seen **bomb** (Goldiamond and Hawkins 1958).

---

[8] "Tachistoscope" comes from Greek words meaning "fast view."

Encounter, M. C. Escher
How would you like to shake hands with your fantasies?

Time perception

Like all things perceptual, our notion of *duration,* of how long something lasts, is an activity of the brain and not an exact replica of physical time. Much of our "time sense" is imposed on us by the *biological rhythms* of existence, however, and all of those, ultimately, are related to the physical rhythms of "spaceship earth." The fact that the earth revolves on its axis once every 24 hours, and around the sun every year, rhythmically alternating cycles of light and dark, of heat and cold, and of wind and weather ac-

cordingly, dictated an evolutionary development of plants and animals that makes large parts of their biology and of their behavior rhythmic — by seasons, by days and nights (called "diurnal" and "nocturnal" or "circadian" rhythms), by hours and minutes. You never thought of birds flying south in autumn, bears hibernating in winter, or bats coming out at night as matters of time perception, perhaps, but so they are. The same is true, in the same way, of cats, hamsters, and monkeys going into sexual heat in "estrus" — and you, in the slower rhythms of maturation, doing so in adolescence (Luce 1973).

Figure 5.2 Perceptual set depends on previous experience.

One of humanity's remarkable evolutionary gifts has been our ability to free ourselves from the natural rhythms of existence and to manipulate our own responses to the passage of time. It is part of the general flexibility of human evolution, that goes with being able to live almost anywhere on the planet, eat almost anything, and reproduce (at least copulate) almost any time. There are limits, of course—the taming of fire and the invention of artificial lighting conquered night, but did not change the human need for sleep. This, and many subtler functions, are governed by "biological clocks." Their mechanisms are understood for some physiological functions but not much in connection with consciousness, sleep, and the perception of time. Most people have had the experience of awakening exactly on time for an important appointment, or of estimating the passage of time accurately without looking at a watch or getting clues from changes in sun and shadows. Everyone has been surprised at times to discover they have drastically *mis*perceived the passage of time—two hours have seemed like five minutes and vice versa.

Some people think that heart rate or metabolic rate must influence time perception. Certainly, depressant drugs like quinine, which slow metabolic processes, make time slow down, and stimulants like caffeine make it speed up. A state of high arousal, like tension or anxiety, may also produce a faster subjective time rate; anxious people overestimate the passage of time, while depressed people find time heavy on their hands. Time perception can also be altered by psychological techniques such as hypnosis (Zimbardo *et al.* 1973).

The meaning of a situation obviously affects time perception too. Boring experiences seem to drag on, interesting ones to pass quickly. A meaningless sentence made up of nonsense syllables such as "glorp farb mik blip dax cockamamie" seems to take longer to hear than a normal, meaningful sentence[9] (Miller and Selfridge 1950). This may be due to the fact that the nonsense sentence is confusing, while the normal sentence is not. Or it may be, as one

[9] It takes longer still to hear nonsense sentences made up of words—as in meaningless lectures or speeches which seem to last forever.

theory says, that our sense of time is influenced by the number of changes, of separate items that we perceive. If so, perhaps the nonsense sentence seems to take longer because it is made up of so many disconnected units; real words flow into larger units of meaning; so we listen to a few phrases, not a lot of individual words. There is other evidence, however, suggesting that the more complicated a task, the *less* time it seems to take. Thus taking down dictation, which involves both listening and writing, seems to take up less time than merely listening.

Our mental perception of time is generally less reliable than our body rhythms. When Michel Siffre lived in a completely dark cave for 58 days, he estimated that his stay had lasted only 33 days. In sensory deprivation studies, subjects also greatly underestimate time. Perhaps their "biological clocks" are off because they have so little bodily activity—no one knows for sure. Nevertheless, despite the fact that the cave-dweller's time perception was so far off, his time-linked body processes were not. During his stay of 58 days, he slept 57 times (Siffre 1963). He later expanded on this experiment by staying for six months in the Midnight Cave near Del Rio, Texas, but with somewhat different results. For one thing, unbeknownst to him, he was soon living on a 26-hour cycle, though he thought he was on a 24-hour one. For another, by the time he had completed the 151 cycles which eventuated from this time distortion, he was a psychological wreck—and it is not clear that the results of his experience can be generalized to

Translating from one sense dimension to another, we can have a strong visual image of an auditory experience.

Echo of a Scream, David Alfaro Siqueiros

an understanding of either time perception or sensory isolation (Siffre 1975). It is clear, on the other hand, that our bodies tend to follow their familiar rhythms even when our environment changes radically. This is why jet travellers to different time zones need several days, sometimes, to readjust their waking and sleeping periods to the time change.

SUMMARY

1   Without perception, our sense experience would be a mess. Perception is the name for all the processes by which we "make sense" of the senses, that is, make sense data intelligible. The perceptual ability of all other animals is far less intricate or flexible than ours. Our greater perceptual acuity is facilitated by our more highly developed brain, especially the human cerebral cortex, where perceptual processes are centered.

2   There is no completely satisfactory definition of perception, and the boundaries which distinguish perception from sensation, on the one hand, and from thinking, on the other, are unclear. The common distinction made is to consider something sensation when the process involved depends conspicuously on the sense organs and to call it perception when the brain is managing the show and the sense organs are not. This distinction is really a mere convenience for discussion.

3   The nature of perception occupied philosophers long before psychology existed as a separate discipline. *Realistic* schools of philosophy argued that our perceptions interpret objective reality. *Idealistic* philosophers claimed that we cannot be sure that any reality exists outside our own heads, since we are limited only to the knowledge our percepts can give us.

4   The accuracy of perception in representing external reality (if there is one) is limited by the sensory apparatus on which perception depends. The thresholds of different senses make it impossible to accurately perceive sounds, sights, and so forth outside those thresholds.

5   In human beings, as in some other species, the visual and kinesthetic aspects of perception have evolved as the most elaborate because vision and movement are the dominant senses involved in staying alive. Many important perceptual processes, accordingly, depend on the interaction of visual and movement senses, and most studies of perception concern the *organization* and *stabilization* of the visual world.

6   There is some controversy over which perceptual skills are learned and which are innate. The existing evidence tends to support the position of *Gestalt* psychologists, that certain ways of organizing perception are inborn. The opposing position taken by *Empiricists,* that experience is an unformed mosaic of sensations that get organized as the child *learns* to perceive, is too extreme. Even so, learning has a great influence on perception. Every new perception is modified by previous experience.

7   Some stimuli demand more attention than others. The intensity of a stimulus, such as the brightness of colors or the loudness of sounds, is one factor in how much attention it gets. How much any stimulus stands out depends on the context in which it occurs, that is, on the contrast between the stimulus and its surroundings. Contrast between light and shadow, movement and background, and high and low intensity of stimulation are all factors in drawing attention. Your perception of what is happening, in a changing world,

depends largely on your sensing the differences between events. This is a restatement, in effect, of the Weber-Fechner law.

8 Perception also *organizes* our experience. We perceive things in the foreground of vision as *figure,* for instance, and perceive the surroundings as *background.* Grouping and *patterning* of things on the basis of *proximity, similarity,* and *closure,* the filling in of visual gaps, makes us perceive individual elements as parts of wholes rather than as isolated things. *Camouflage* takes advantage of these principles to conceal objects from easy detection in their environment.

9 There are apparently two visual systems involved in the perception of movement. Their operation demonstrates the interpretive character of perception for, far from always giving a true report of the world, movement perception sometimes misapprehends completely what is going on, creating some remarkable illusions, such as:

a *Autokinetic effect,* in which a fixed point of light in a dark room seems to shift.
b *Induced movement,* in which you always see small things moving against a larger background, as when you watch clouds blowing across the moonlit sky and it looks like the moon is moving.
c *Apparent movement,* used in the movies, in which a series of successive still images give the impression of continuous movement.
d *Movement aftereffects,* in which you continue to see an afterimage of motion in objects which have actually stopped moving.

10 We also have elaborate perceptual facilities for stabilizing our perceptions of the world so that we can appreciate the sameness of familiar objects when they are seen under unfamiliar circumstances—at unusual distances from us, under different lighting conditions, and so forth. Principles of constancy permit us to perceive the correct size, shape, brightness, and color of familiar things, even when the information the sense organs receive about each of them differs under different circumstances. Constancies break down under extreme conditions, and their normal operation also creates some familiar illusions.

11 The internal factors which determine what we select to perceive are past experiences, current interests and expectations, familiarity with the stimulus, susceptibility to suggestion. Taken together, these dispositions constitute our *perceptual style* or *set.*

12 Little is known about time perception. In general, anxiety or high arousal seems to make time fly, while depression or low arousal makes it crawl. Most of the time, we *estimate* rather than *experience* the passage of time—and sometimes our estimations are far off. Reducing bodily activity or sensory input makes us underestimate the passage of time.

Learning

6

6

Learning

When you form a mental image of human beings, you see bureaucrats in business suits, or college kids in sweaters and jeans, or men and women in other sorts of clothes at leisure or at work—but you see human beings, not animals, not even fancy primates. When you hear about human destructiveness, or aggressiveness, or callousness as to how we are destroying the ecological balance of the planet, or the social balance of civilization, by littering, overpopulating, and making war, you may fancy that we would all be better off by stripping ourselves of culture and going back to "nature," wherever that is. Maybe you picture doing this by somehow getting rid of the business suit, maybe even the tennis dress, and still keeping your humanity. The simple life, communing with nature, tilling your little plot of "pot," seems most appealing as we smart under the constraints of our technological, urban culture.

It is not. Life was never simple, and not as easy without clothes as with them. Back to nature may mean back to dirt, more death and disease than you ever dreamed of, and more knowledge of brutality and misery in a week than you may experience in a lifetime of urban imprisonment—but even then, you would not be free of culture. Humanity did not first mutate into standing on two feet, then talk, and *then,* with nothing left to busy it, invent culture. If anything, culture invented humanity, forcing an intelligent, socially oriented primate into evolutionary molds that bred it for more flexibility and intelligence until it became *Homo sapiens.* Culture is heredity's partner in molding the shape and capacities of our bodies. Human evolution was determined not only by the selective pressures of the environment but also by the demands of our cultural development.

For most of human history, for instance, we have been hunters and gatherers. Hunting often involved killing big animals, which demands several things of the hunters. They must make weapons, since no one ever killed an elephant in a fist fight. They must band together, plan their attack, stalk the game quietly, and fight it bravely. All of these actions take skill, and all skills must be learned. Even crude tools require many manufacturing skills—as anthropologists learned when they tried to recreate them (Clark 1959)!

Chimpanzees can learn to make a simple tool out of reeds to fish termites out of holes; most primates live in loosely structured social groups; and a sort of emotional "language" of facial expressions and sounds is important in all primate behavior (Morris 1969). Human beings do share some forms of social organization and mental capabilities with other animals. But the most meaningful social scream of the baboon is a far cry from the dialogues of humanity, and a chimpanzee fishing for a snack of termites is a far cry from a human reaching out to blast off a spaceship. Even when other primates have the coordination to make tools, they still lack the patience, the foresight, and the memory needed to manufacture them. And though monkeys and apes sometimes cooperate in hunting or foraging, they show little long-range planning, little division of labor, and only occasional food-sharing. The earliest human hunters could do all three things. They inherited the ability to learn them.

These three skills greatly influenced human evolution in favor of progeny with good learning ability. As anthropologist Clifford Geertz has written:

Humans are the best tool makers but not the only ones.

All these various abilities . . . are, of course, dependent in turn upon nervous system development. And so the introduction of tool manufacture and hunting must have acted to shift selection pressures so as to favor the rapid growth of the forebrain, as, in all likelihood, did the advances in social organization, communication, and moral regulation, . . . to overlap between cultural and biological change (Geertz 1964).

Humanity emerged through a strong evolutionary pressure favoring flexibility. The rigid patterns of other animals were discarded in favor of a plasticity of behavior that could be shaped and reshaped by learning (Montagu 1965). Learning made our hominid (human-like) ancestors uniquely adaptable. The pooling of their learning so it could be shared and transmitted made them human.

Culture—the body of common learning transmitted by a group from one generation to another—came to dictate our evolutionary development as much as the natural environment did. In fact, it let humans control their environment. By manufacturing clothes and learning how to make fire, people could live in polar regions, for which our anatomy is unsuited; by building boats, they conquered the water, although they had neither flippers nor gills; by making containers for water and food, people could survive in arid, burning deserts. Physiology is destiny for all other animals, who are confined by their biological limitations to their ecological niches, but human-kind has spread all over the globe and now is invading outer space.

Culture and biological evolution emerged together and produced each other in a continuous complex interaction. Cultural adaptations have largely replaced biological mutations among human beings as the chief means of adjusting to new situations. This becomes more true as science advances, giving culture increasing control of biological functioning and reproduction as well as of the external environment. They are inseparable in human development.

> A cultureless human being would probably turn out to be, not an intrinsically talented though unfulfilled ape, but a wholly mindless and consequently unworkable monstrosity. Like the cabbage it so resembles, the *Homo sapiens* brain, having arisen within the framework of human culture, would not be viable outside of it (Geertz 1962).

The change from hunter to farmer to mechanic to bureaucrat has taken barely one percent or so of human evolution, and it has been made without the long evolutionary overhaul of the human body and brain. Most of the change was produced culturally, not biologically, by increasing knowledge and the means of transmitting it, not by improving genes or the means of transmitting them.

That enormous increase in knowledge, oddly enough, did not require human beings to evolve totally different means than other animals have of learning things. With the partial exception of language, the basic processes by which people learn are largely the same as those of lower animals, especially of vertebrates (Rosenzweig and Teiman 1968). As usual, the closer you come to people on the phylogenetic scale, the more behavior processes of other animals resemble our own. Members of the lower phyla don't learn much or remember it well, but even the lowly flatworm has been taught some simple movements. A few scholars claim that protozoa have also shown some learning, but if so, it is of little use to these one-celled creatures and does not "stick" long (McConnell 1962). The most basic kind of learning is involved here. Usually called *classical conditioning* or *Pavolvian conditioning,* it represents the first step upward in the great shift from helpless reflex action to intelligent voluntary thought. Another basic learning process, called *instrumental* or *operant conditioning,* can be considered a fancier kind of learning, in evolutionary terms, because it is not seen below the level of the vertebrates, and because it appears after classical conditioning in the development of the individual. Actually, it is just as critical in human learning as classical conditioning.

Learning by observation and imitation, or vicarious learning, is still more refined, unseen below the level of mammals and relatively unimportant until we get up to the primates. Finally, the learning of language is virtually the exclusive property of human beings—and at once so important and so poorly understood that we will study it alone in Chapter 10.

CONDITIONING

You may already know about Pavlov's drooling dogs, maybe too about Thorndike's angry alley cats. But conditioning is too important to almost every aspect of human learning to leave it out. It is the basis of all habits, all skills, and in some people's opinion, all learning. Some scholars think that conditioning is the basis for psychosomatic illness, voodoo death, religious conversion, brainwashing, hypnosis, and psychotherapy. During the Korean War, news about Chinese treatment of American prisoners gave rise to stories of how conditioning was used to destroy the morale of our soldiers (Griffin 1965). The fact that much of the technical literature on conditioning was in Russian reinforced this idea.

Actually, little complex behavior can be controlled by conditioning methods. Neither classical nor instrumental conditioning are very good for washing out brains or turning people to robots. Instrumental methods are used to control voluntary behavior and work by strictly voluntary means; classical methods are used to control involuntary activity and cannot be used at present to produce very complex behavior changes at all.

Even so, conditioning plays a vital role in learning language, imagination, emotion, motivation, habits, and skills. People can be conditioned to blush over meaningless phrases; to hallucinate to signals; to feel fear, revulsion, embarrassment, or arousal upon demand; to feel cold when they are being warmed or warm when being chilled; to become ill when lights are flashed; to feel like urinating with an empty bladder or to not feel the need with a full one; to narrow or enlarge blood vessels or the pupils of the eyes; to learn mannerisms they had never known before; and to break free of lifelong habit patterns they thought could never be undone.

Instrumental conditioning was first described by E. L. Thorndike in 1898 and *classical conditioning* by Ivan Pavlov in 1904. There are several important differences between them. Perhaps the main one, in structural terms, is that *classical conditioning* is the training of sensory processes and *instrumental conditioning* is the training of motor processes. In classical conditioning, in other words, you teach someone to connect a familiar response to new stimuli; in instrumental conditioning, you learn to make a new response to familiar stimuli.

The main practical difference is that by classical conditioning you can learn to control *internal, involuntary behavior* like emotion, mood, or sensation, and the functioning of glands and of smooth muscles in the stomach, blood vessels, and heart; instrumental conditioning, on the other hand, teaches control of voluntary behavior, including social and intellectual skills and *voluntary muscle* activity. Both methods can be used to influence thinking and attitudes. They may also be used in combination with each other and with drugs, surgery, and electronic gadgetry. Those combinations may make conditioning useful to teach all kinds of attitudes, skills, or emotional tendencies.

Classical conditioning: Training involuntary behavior

You probably learned in high school about the famous experiments of Ivan Pavlov at the turn of the century. Pavlov was a Russian physiologist, who won the Nobel Prize in 1904 for his work on digestion. In the course of that work, some problems in his laboratory gave rise to the most famous experiments ever done in psychology. Pavlov's assistants would put meat powder in a dog's mouth in order to stimulate salivation, which they would then measure. In one experiment, they noticed that the dog was salivating before it actually got the meat powder, as soon as it saw the experimenter. Later, it began salivating even earlier, when it heard the experimenter's footsteps. Pavlov puzzled over this for a while, then began to study it systematically. He would station the dog in a harness facing a window, ring a bell behind it, and then deliver meat powder to the hungry animal. It began to salivate. He repeated the procedure several times. After a few repetitions, the dog began to salivate as soon as the bell rang, *before* any food appeared. The bell alone could cause the dog to drool.

This simple experiment established an important learning principle. When a dog expects food, it automatically salivates. Salivation is a *reflex*—an involuntary and inflexible response to an unchanging stimulus. Pavlov discovered that a reflex could be partly modified, in that the old response could be "turned on" by a new stimulus. A bell does not naturally cause salivating; but if it is *associated* with the appearance of meat, it soon can stimulate the salivation response. For this reason, classical conditioning is also called *stimulus substitution.*

An American named Twitmeyer had made the same discovery, also by accident, while studying the knee-jerk reflex in humans. But when he reported his findings to the American Psychological Association in 1904, people shrugged their shoulders indifferently. He was discouraged, went home, and dropped the subject. A year later, Pavlov reported the finding, not knowing of Twitmeyer.

Pavlov called the meat powder the *unconditional stimulus* because it works *absolutely*—it gets a response under all conditions. Saliva-tion to food he called the *unconditional response* for the same reason. The bell, by contrast, was called the *conditional stimulus* because the dog's initial reaction is conditional to (depends on) its connection with the meat powder. He called the dog's salivation in response to the bell the *conditional response* for the same reason. The several trials in which he connected the bell and meat powder to produce the conditional response Pavlov named *reinforcement,* meaning strengthening. Once the conditional response has been learned, Pavlov found, reinforcement trials had to occur periodically for it to be retained. If food did *not* follow the bell for several trials, the bell alone would stop eliciting salivation; the conditional response had been *extinguished.* Curiously, extinction does not permanently destroy the conditioned response. After some rest, a new trial will bring it out again, and it will last a few more trials, even without reinforcement. This is called *spontaneous recovery.*

The important principle to grasp is that classical conditioning is actually a special form of instruction in the use of *signals,* by means of which one learns to expect forthcoming events by attending to forecasting signs, somewhat like learning to expect thunder when you see lightning. The difference between classical conditioning and other kinds of signal learning, however, is that the events being forecast are all automatic processes in the body, and the signs which foretell them are all arbitrary. The signals in classical conditioning are parts of a *code;* they have no intrinsic meaning of their own. There is nothing special about a bell that signals forthcoming meat powder, or that has any *intrinsic* connection with dinner time. The signal could just as easily have been a chime, a light or the boom-boom-bom-bah of Beethoven's Fifth Symphony. It was the arbitrary association with meat that turned the bell into a meaningful *sign* that food was coming. For this reason, classical conditioning is also sometimes called *sign-learning.*

Our automatic reaction to traffic signals is conditioned. The signs themselves are completely arbitrary.

Basic training in becoming human: The uses of classical conditioning The principle by which classical conditioning works is the arbitrary linking of new stimuli to old ones, but the results of those linkings are not arbitrary. Much of our emotions are learned by classical conditioning; so is much of language learning and of the activity of some internal organs.

The basis for *love,* for instance, may start from the association a baby makes between the appearance of mother and the feeling of warmth and comfort that generally follows. Emotions such as fear, unhappily, are often learned in similar ways, usually by accident; a child who is barked at, chased, or bitten by a dog soon learns to fear dogs, just as children who have been burned dread fires, and so forth. A single painful experience with a harmful or frightening object may condition its victim to feel fear every time it faces the object in the future.

Several such experiences may have even worse results. Recent research has shown that general feelings of helplessness, depression, and psychosomatic illness can all be learned by classical conditioning — and can be learned by lower animals as well as humans. In these experiments, dogs were first given painful electric shocks from which they could not escape. Later on, when they were not restrained, they were given more shocks. But, as a result of the earlier experience, they no longer showed any tendency even to try to escape. They had *learned* that they were helpless (Seligman 1968).

Painful conditioning can be used to benefit people also, under some conditions. Called ***aversive conditioning*** treatments, they have been used with varying degrees of success for alcoholism (Blake 1967), stuttering (Goldiamond 1965), and sexual deviance (Marks and Gelder 1967), among other things. More of this in Chapter 19.

Generalization It may take only one scary encounter with a dog to make a child fear all dogs, even if they are far away, even if they do not bark, and even if they are caged and harmless. The child may fear *pictures* of amiable, colorful, well-intentioned doggies, despite knowing that the picture is harmless. The principle in operation here is called *generalization;* it applies to all learning. In the conditioning of emotions, its "downside" is that, having been frightened by one doggie, you are frightened by all doggies without further bad experiences. On the other hand, having learned to feel love for mother, you also become capable of loving other people without a whole new training program for each one.

Though most emotional conditioning occurs by the accidents of everyday life, there is no basic difference between emotions conditioned accidentally or intentionally. Anyone who wants to make children fear the fire can easily do so by sticking their finger in it or, less cruelly, by frightening them when their attention is fixed on a flame. The same principle applies to adults, though it may take a little more work. Millions of people saw the victim in Alfred Hitchcock's terrifying movie *Psycho* suddenly stabbed to death while she was showering in a motel room, and have been unable to take a peaceable shower since, when they are alone. They have generalized from the fictional situation to the real one.

The second level of emotional conditioning is called *semantic generalization,* which means making conditioned responses to *words* when these responses have previously been made only to objects or to other words. Thus, the child conditioned to fear dogs may also learn to fear the word "dog."

The most powerful conditioning connects words to emotions, but words can be attached to other physical processes as well. Gregory Razran, of New York's Queen's College, conditioned people to *salivate* to words like "style" or "urn" just as Pavlov's dog did to the bell; then he got them to transfer their salivation response to synonyms like "fashion" and "vase" (1939). Such a generalized response is usually weaker than the original one, and your intellect may play an important role in producing it. The point is that it is possible deliberately to

give words emotional connotations totally unrelated to their simple meanings.

Throughout history, demagogues have used the emotional power of words in this way without knowing anything about classical conditioning or semantic generalization. Love of god, of country, of tribe, of party, or of principle; fear, distrust, and contempt for strangers, minorities, majorities, races, religions, garter snakes, and spinach—all have been taught, in every human society, by classical conditioning, in which words take on emotional meanings from the feelings surrounding their use. Hate peddlers, warmongers, evangelists, and politicians "on the make" all use the same technique for the same purpose: to arouse the emotions they want to the words they use (Brown 1963).

Demagoguery is not the only means for attaching emotional connotations to words. Teachers and parents condition children's attitudes all the time by coupling words like "Negro," "Jew," "Catholic," or "cop" with sneers, scowls, or gestures of contempt. The descriptive or derogatory meanings we give these terms depends on the experiences we have had with them, not on their intrinsic properties; ugly meanings come from the ugly intentions and intonations of adult usage.

The classical conditioning of words, like all classical conditioning, is *irrational.* In the "rational" use of language, the entire message comes from the *denotations* of the words—that is, from their unemotional meaning. In irrational language, the message to be communicated is an emotion, and the word is only a signal for it. Ironically, the beginnings of language learning are all irrational; classical conditioning plays an important role in it because the process of association is the means by which *verbal signals* of any kind come to have *meaning* of any kind, emotional or otherwise. We shall see how this works in more detail in Chapter 9.

Emotions and salivation are only two of the

These words get their emotional *connotations* conditioned in us by the nasty feeling accompanying their use.

many physiological processes that can be conditioned to words and thus controlled by them. The opening of blood vessels or contractions of the stomach can also be controlled by a process called *interoceptive conditioning.* In one experiment, people were told that their stomachs were being warmed though nothing was actually being done to them, and they reacted physiologically with stomach muscle dilations; told that their stomachs were being cooled, they reacted with stomach contractions. In other experiments, people were trained to react physiologically in one way to a series of blue lights flashed in a certain order; then they were taught the same reaction pattern to red lights flashed in a different sequence. Lights of both colors were then presented in random sequence—and the subjects became ill, sometimes vomiting, having sensory distortions, and complaining of headaches. Other experiments on other visceral functions have shown similar results (Razran 1961).

There are laboratory demonstrations connecting *psychosomatic illness,* diarrhea, yawning, and much more with a great variety of verbal and other conditional stimulation.

Conditioning can involve virtually every organ of the body and any expression of mood and emotion (Hovland 1937). As we shall see in Chapter 19 (Treatment and Control), classical conditioning provides a model for treatment as well as for disorders. It has been used pretty successfully for relieving anxiety and changing sexual impulses, and has also been used (not always successfully) to treat alcoholism, smoking, drug use, and overeating. Maybe conditioning methods can someday be used to inhibit aggressive impulses too, but the "treatments" of *Clockwork Orange* (1972) are still a long way from reality, and even in the movie, they miscarried.

Classical conditioning has been combined with hypnosis to produce a dramatic *sensory* phenomenon called "conditioned hallucination." Originated by Osake Naruse, of the University of Kyoto, it works as follows: While a hypnotized subject watches a screen, the experimenter sounds a bell or flashes a light, then flashes an image on the screen at low illumination for a fraction of a second. He gives the subject a pad of paper, has them draw the image several times, then suggests amnesia for the whole experience and brings them out of hypnosis. Later, he tells the awakened subjects to watch the screen; he sounds the bell, projecting nothing, and asks subjects to draw what they "see." People do, as if an image were being freshly shown (1962). There are no practical applications of this phenomenon yet.

There is really nothing unusual in the fact that people react emotionally to words or that their bodies respond to their perceptions. These are familiar events of everyday life. By understanding the principles of classical conditioning, it becomes possible to invent a technology for producing these reactions at will, by social machinery deliberately designed to manufacture them.

The Nazis did just that, with their **propaganda machinery,** especially through their youth groups. So did the Russian Communists, and so, to some extent, do all the "true believers" described by Eric Hoffer (1951), such as the early Wesleyan Methodists, Russian and Chinese brain-washers, and religious and political zealots from ancient times to the present, who have been described by such writers as William James (1901), George Orwell (1948), and Aldous Huxley (1932). The method of all these movements has been, first of all, to destroy the old loyalties and values that their victims believed in; this means "extinguishing old conditioned patterns" of *personal meaning.* Once that is done, they may try to replace them with new loyalties and beliefs, or, having crippled their victims for further resistance, leave well enough alone. The early Nazi concentration camp managers, as described in Bruno Bettleheim's *The Informed Heart* (1960), and the subtler Chinese, in the Korean War prisoner camps, were often content merely to weaken the prisoners' ability to resist. Training youth to be loyal to the Nazi or Soviet state, however, like inducing religious conversion or eliciting confessions of witchcraft, required that the breaking down of resistance be followed by a program of positive indoctrination. This has succeeded millions of times in religious con-

versions, especially in what are called the "Dionysian" rituals of primitive tribes (Benedict 1934) and evangelical churches. And nobody knows how many innocents accused of witchcraft or of betraying "the revolution" in Russia and other places confessed to awful and untrue crimes with absolute sincerity in their own guilt. Arthur Koestler gives a powerful fictional description of one such person in *Darkness at Noon* (1941); and *Battle for the Mind* (1961), by the British psychiatrist William Sargant, reviews many such phenomena and explains them in terms of "Pavlovian psychophysiology," i.e., classical conditioning.

The techniques of breaking down beliefs, both in propaganda campaigns and in getting confessions, are much the same as those in the experiment where subjects become ill—conditioned signals are alternated so rapidly you cannot respond meaningfully. In propaganda, for example, the Nazis argued that the Jews were capitalists and Communists, democrats and tyrants, racist and mongrel, all at once, until the confusion of messages broke down the meanings of all these terms, leaving only one emotion-laden idea: *Jews are bad!* George Orwell's Big Brother, in 1984, destroys ordinary meanings totally with propaganda slogans like "war is peace" and "slavery is freedom." Where the intention is to break down personal beliefs, as is necessary to get sincere false confessions, anxiety and exhaustion are added to the rapid, meaningless stimulation until victims are ready to give up life itself for rest or sleep; by then, they will agree to anything. If the method works, they have now become highly suggestible, and will accept new ideas.

At that point in "thought reform," as the Chinese call it, classical conditioning must be supplemented by the tools of instrumental conditioning to yield a more refined effect than either method could produce alone. The combined method still does not work very well; the "new" ideas are not accepted by most people, or not accepted for long, as shown by studies of American prisoners during the Korean War. Even so, the resistance-breaking part of the process does tend to work and is still a common tool of many governments.

The combination of classical and instrumental conditioning methods is more effective on other behavior than on the manipulation of beliefs and attitudes because instrumental conditioning adds to the classical conditioning of meaning, a technology for teaching habits and skills.

Learning as an Instrument

Instrumental conditioning means learning behavior that serves a purpose, solves a problem, answers a question, or provides relief or pleasure. In the instrumental learning situation, the stimulus is always a "problem" in the sense that it arouses you; you then try to reduce the arousal by gratifying yourself if the stimulus is pleasurable or by escaping if it is painful. You usually try out several different responses; the one that turns out most useful in providing the relief or, to use the jargon of the trade, *which is most instrumental to the resolution of the problem,* becomes habitual, i.e., gets learned.

In the original instrumental-learning experiment, in 1898, E. L. Thorndike caged Harlem alley cats one at a time in Columbia University Teachers College's Dodge Hall. The freedom loving alley cats were infuriated and made violent efforts to break out of the cage, most of which were useless. Eventually, by a process of

Parents use both positive reinforcement and, here, punishment, in shaping their children's behavior.

Fatherly Discipline, Honoré Daumier

trial-and-error (another name for instrumental conditioning), the cat would accidentally hit the latch, the cage door would spring open, and it was temporarily free. Thorndike would then put it right back in the cage, and the whole business would start over again. Gradually the cat would learn to press the latch deliberately, solving the problem. *All habits are learned this way.* A habit starts as a means of solving some problem, and instrumental learning is always *solution learning.*

The mechanics of instrumental and classical conditioning differ in two ways. In classical conditioning, a *reflex* (salivation) gets connected to an *arbitrary new stimulus* (the bell) by *first* having its reinforcement (meat powder) paired with the new stimulus; the behavior gets controlled by its *antecedents.* In instrumental conditioning, a *voluntary act* gets connected with a *trouble-making, arousing stimulus* by the rewarding discovery, *after* the act has occurred, that it resolved the trouble; the behavior

Who hasn't dreamed of a utopian society where "the lion lies down with the lamb"? One version is based on operant conditioning.

The Peaceable Kingdom, Edward Hicks

gets controlled by its *consequences.* These differences go back to the fact that classical conditioning is *sensory* learning and instrumental conditioning is *motor* learning. In the former, you learn to perceive new *stimuli* as being significant; in the latter, you learn to perceive new *responses* as significant.

The best known form of instrumental conditioning is called *operant conditioning* or *behavior shaping.* It is used for teaching skills rather than for solving problems of the alley cat type. Behavior shaping comes from the work of B. F. Skinner, who has guided its application to psychotherapy, teaching, and the general reformation of society (1953).

Two simple principles form the basis for behavior shaping. First, the familiar principle of *reinforcement,* which says that an animal will learn to repeat an act for which it is rewarded and to avoid one for which it is ignored or punished. The second principle is that of learning by *successive approximation;* it says that complicated behavior patterns, especially *skillful* ones, are learned gradually, in small steps that come closer and closer to an optimal level of performance.

In theory, virtually any skill can be taught by behavior shaping, if only it can be applied with enough ingenuity. It is widely used in training programs in residential institutions, such as prisons and hospitals, but it is also used in halfway houses and in schools — and in a variety of programs for the mentally retarded, for chronic psychotics, for delinquents and criminals, and for teaching ordinary children. One of its most popular applications is in the manipulation of "pay schedules" in a "token economy."

Token economies A token, as you know, is a piece of plastic or metal used as a substitute for money, like a poker chip, or a subway token. A token economy is a place, such as a hospital ward, which is operated like a business, with tokens used for money. On admission to a token-economy hospital ward, for instance, patients may be given a few free tokens. From then on, they must earn them as pay for doing chores or rewards for good behavior. Their behavior is shaped this way partly because they learn to repeat acts which earn rewards, no matter what the rewards are. More important, tokens are made into *valuable* rewards by the fact that necessities as well as luxuries must be paid for by them. In a token-economy ward, patients may have to pay to eat, to go to bed, to shower, to sleep, even to use the toilet. Training such habits of normal social intercourse may teach psychotic or retarded people skills needed to function outside a hospital (Ayllon and Azrin 1965; Kazdin and Bootzin 1972; Kazdin 1975; Craighead, Kazdin, and Mahoney 1976).

The use of behavior shaping for practical problems is sometimes called *operant technology* and the person who does it a *behavioral engineer.* The limits of its value are uncertain. Skinner believes that its proper use can create a utopian society of productive, competent, and happy people. In one collection of essays, *Contingencies of Reinforcement: A Theoretical Analysis,* he proposed that psychologists should program all of society to work by positively reinforcing rational, constructive behavior and by extinguishing hostile, destructive behavior. Our genetic endowment should be controlled by biologists, Skinner says, and our cultural evolution should be controlled by psychologists. "To refuse to do either of these things," he writes, "is to leave further changes in our culture to accident, and accident is the tyrant really to be feared. . . . The very misuse of personal control to which we object so violently is the product of accidents which have made the weak subject to the strong, the dull to the sharp, the well-intentioned to the selfish. We can do better than that (Skinner 1969)." In a more recent book, *Beyond Freedom and Dignity* (1971), Skinner argues that scientists in general are better equipped than others to plan the organization of society. Many people, including many scientists, do not agree.

Walden Two: The model society To illustrate

how society could "do better than that," Skinner wrote a novel called *Walden Two* about a utopian community where every aspect of life is carefully engineered (1948). The community's planners decide that self-control is the most important ethical virtue; they then proceed to train the children in self-control through a graded series of frustrating situations. As one character explains, "It's possible to build a tolerance to painful or distasteful stimuli, or to frustration, or to situations which arouse fear, anger, or rage. Society and nature throw these annoyances at the individual with no regard for the development of tolerances. Some achieve tolerances, most fail."

Accordingly, until age six, when their ethical training is completed, the children of Walden Two are subjected to more and more annoying situations. They must stoically endure more and more painful shocks, or drink cocoa with less and less sugar in it until they can swallow a bitter concoction without a bitter face. Hungry children must stand and contemplate supper for five minutes before digging in. At first, the children spontaneously invent compensations, like clowning and singing, to while away the time. Later, however, all such devices are banned and silence is enforced. Each child must endure the frustration privately.

In school, the children are not "taught" any subjects. "We help them in every way short of teaching them," explains an adult character. "We give them new techniques of acquiring knowledge and thinking. We give them an excellent survey of the methods and techniques of thinking, taken from logic, statistics, scientific method, psychology, and mathematics. That's all the 'college education' they need. They get the rest by themselves in our libraries and laboratories." No artificial motivations are built into the children, no desire for a diploma or parental approval or an A. They are motivated simply by "natural" curiosity.

Walden Two is still a dream for society at large, but partisans of the idea have been pro- moting a live Walden Two community in the United States, and there is a Walden Two Society, which publishes information about such communities. The utopian ideal of a society whose members are motivated by incentives rather than by fear of punishment may be more active now than at any previous time in American history. The largest of the several communes that now exist, Twin Oaks Community, in Louisa, Virginia, publishes a bimonthly journal, *Communities: A Journal of Cooperative Living.* And many serious scholars study the applications of operant technology to the social and political life of our society (Wheeler 1973).

Biofeedback

When classical and instrumental con- ditioning are combined, people's learning ability can be sharply increased, especially when information about their own behavior is "fed" back to them. One Russian experimenter, M. I. Lisina, for example, tried to condition people to tighten or relax the tiny muscles which control the narrowing and widening of blood vessels by electric shocks. She did not succeed until her experimental subjects observed the recordings of their own responses; then, know- ing what the experimenter wanted, they were conditioned very quickly. Another Russian, E. S. Ayrapetyants, did an even more interesting experiment on bladder control. He put liquid into people's bladders, recorded their bladder swelling and other functions related to the need to urinate, then showed them the instrument readings. Some of the readings were faked, showing little swelling when there was really a lot; but people reported, in such cases, that they did not need to urinate, and their other physiological responses corresponded to the reports. Joe Kamiya, at the University of Cali- fornia Medical Center in San Francisco, has been demonstrating for years that people can be taught to control some of their own brain

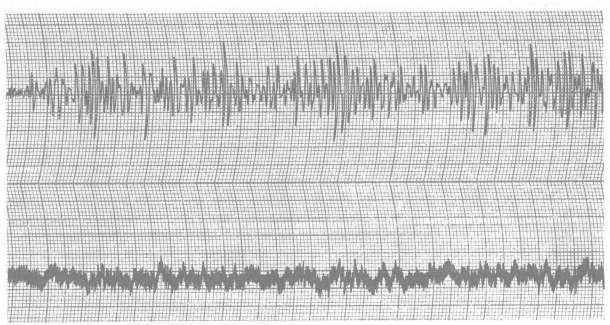

Researchers find that if you "see" your brain wave, you can control it.

waves by hearing a buzzer sound whenever the desired pattern is occuring. Eventually, they learn to associate their subjective mental state with the buzzing so that, by reproducing that mental state, they can reproduce the brain-wave pattern without the buzzer.

All the experiments above involve body processes which we usually think of as involuntary. Evidently, some body functions become voluntary in direct proportion to the amount of information feedback we get from each previous response of our bodies before our next response occurs; in such cases, what you can *will to do* depends on what you *know about what you are doing* (Miller 1969).

This whole domain of learning has recently started to become popular under the name *biofeedback.* It is called that because it involves *information* about an internal *physiological* process, like heart rate, blood pressure, or electrical activity of the brain. All biofeedback methods work in essentially the same way as

the Russian experiments above. You are given an external record of the physiological event, as it takes place. You see an ongoing record of your heartbeat, or hear a buzzer synchronized to your brain wave, or watch a counter rise and fall with your blood pressure. Once this internal process is externalized this way and made available to your senses, you learn to correlate the behavior of the gauge you are watching with your own mental state. After a while, you find that by manipulating your thoughts and mood, you can manipulate the gauge accordingly—and with it, the internal process changes too.

The possibility of gaining control over all kinds of internal body processes through biofeedback has created a new psychotherapeutic industry for treating psychosomatic conditions (Brown 1974). Biofeedback has been used for relaxation training, relieving headaches, lowering blood pressure, and many other conditions (e.g. Alexander 1975). But

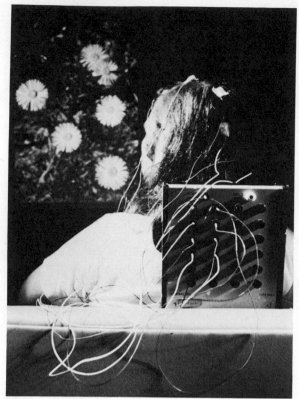

Biofeedback. Slides of a flower and a nude are projected before a young man whose brain is in the alpha state, a state associated with relaxation. The alpha state continues as the flowers appear, but his brain wave pattern becomes less "relaxed" upon seeing the nude.

experimental results have been mixed so far. Some report success with biofeedback (Small and Hull 1975), and some do not (Blanchard and Young 1973).

Latent learning: What you know and what you show

So far it sounds like learning is a pretty straightforward thing. Both in classical and instrumental conditioning, it seems, you learn something by connecting it with something you need and getting rewarded for making the connection. Bells go with meat when you are hungry, and so you salivate to them; pressing a latch goes with freedom when you are trapped,

and so you make a habit of it. But neither the motives for learning nor its rewards turn out so simple. Creatures often learn things for no other reason, it seems, than curiosity, and no other reward than their own amusement. A bored monkey will play with a puzzle for hours and learn how to solve it, apparently out of simple curiosity or a desire for amusement (Harlow and Harlow 1962). And learning sometimes will occur with no obvious reinforcement at all. Subjects may not *display* what they have learned unless they are rewarded, but they may be privately learning nonetheless. If two sets of rats are run through a maze, for instance, and only one group receives food at the end of it, then the rewarded rats *perform* more accurately

170

than the unrewarded rats on later trials; they make fewer mistakes and get to the feed box more quickly. But if the unrewarded rats are then given food, they show that they have been learning about the maze all along, and have just not translated it into performance until the introduction of the reward (Tolman and Honzik 1930). This process is called *latent learning.* The discrepancy between what you show and what you know is not easy to evaluate. The problem comes up in trying to judge the meaningfulness of such measures as I.Q. tests, where there is an unknown distance between performance and ability. It is even more important in language learning, where there is a big difference between language *performance* and language *competence.* You understand far more than you can speak. So does everyone.

OBSERVATION AND INSIGHT

Imitation: The sincerest flattery

The most important kind of learning that occurs without obvious reinforcement is *imitation,* often called *observational learning* or *vicarious learning* (vicarious means "substitute") because the person you are imitating presumably *is* getting reinforcement for having learned what you are copying from them. Bandura and Walters have written: "There is considerable evidence that learning may occur through observation of the behavior of others even when the observer does not reproduce the model's response during acquisition and therefore receives no reinforcement" (1963).

Imitative learning is affected by reinforcement, however. Children imitate models who are rewarded more than models who are punished for what they do. "In addition, models who are rewarding, prestigeful, or competent, who possess high status, and who have control over rewarding resources are more readily imitated than are models who lack these quali-

ties" (Bandura and Walters 1963). Once an act is learned by imitation, moreover, it has to be rewarded occasionally to be maintained. Otherwise, it tends to be forgotten. Like anything learned.

Learning by imitation is vital to personality development because children imitate their parents' attitudes and anxieties and styles of interpersonal relationships as well as their superficial behavior traits. As they grow older, they also imitate their siblings and schoolmates. And in adolescence, they tend to imitate "heroic" figures of their own sex and romantic objects of the opposite sex. More of this in Chapter 13.

Insight and cognition

Insight is another kind of learning which, like imitation, occurs without obvious reinforcement and in a single trial—or without any trials at all. Insight occurs when you stare at a problem for hours without understanding it, and suddenly, in an instant, it becomes completely clear. This has been called the "aha!" experience.

Less dramatic insights occur all the time in the ordinary thought processes that give purpose, integration, and organization to much of human behavior. "Figuring things out" is an undramatic way of "gaining insight."

Like imitation, insight is not a uniquely human way of learning. Chimpanzees share this ability with us. In a classic experiment, Wolfgang Kohler confined a hungry chimp in a cage with a stick 6 feet long. Another stick, 12 feet long, lay just outside the cage, and a piece of fruit lay in plain view 12 feet outside the cage. For a while the animal paced back and forth, completely frustrated. Then, suddenly, it stopped, reached out with the shorter stick for the longer stick and pulled it to the cage. Now armed with the longer stick, it maneuvered the fruit into its hands. The sudden burst of insight did not depend on previous trials nor upon gradually

Learning by imitation.

more difficult tasks. It was a complete and novel learning experience (Kohler 1925).

In general, a simple, orderly presentation of a problem increases the chances of finding an insightful solution. Insightful solutions are easily remembered, moreover, and you can apply the principle to other problems. Once the chimp found out how to use a short stick to get a long one, it understood without further training how to use a short wire to reach for a long one. Similarly, once we learn what an adjective is in English, we can apply the knowledge to adjectives in French or any other language. What we have learned is not a specific habit—that one stick can fetch another, or that *pretty* modifies face—but rather a *general principle* of spatial or grammatical relationships (Birch 1945; Harlow 1949).

Even rats, learning the twists and turns of a maze, seem to master more than a pure motor habit. They evidently develop some mental impression of the maze, called a *cognitive map,* because if the maze is flooded, they can *swim* their way to the food just as they *ran* to it. Swimming uses different motor responses than running, but the rat switches easily from one to the other. So even habit learning may involve some cognitive activity (Macfarlane 1930).

It is not known just how insight comes about, except that it appears dramatically after pondering over a problem. That could mean that there has been a lot of internal trial-and-error thinking leading up to the moment of discovery. If so, then insight would be an intellectual version of instrumental conditioning. Thinking things over would be the trial-and-error process; the discovery itself would be the equivalent of hitting the latch that opens the door to freedom; and maybe the satisfaction of solving the problem is so great that it alone makes insightful solutions memorable without more practice. If so, it is still odd that the right answer only has to be discovered *once* for the whole system to work. In instrumental conditioning, the right latch must be pressed many times. To master the solution, you have to practice!

Practice

Most learning takes practice. Classical conditioning generally has to have several trials of bell and meat to be sure the signal is learned; instrumental conditioning has to have many repetitions of correct movement and rewarding consequence. Most imitation is imperfectly done at first, most instructions are poorly understood or hard to follow for a while.

Most ideas, however neatly figured out, take some more thinking over to be memorized. Any fool knows that.

Of all the learning that requires practice, the best understood in this connection is **skill** learning. Riding a bicycle, playing a musical instrument, playing tennis, skating, or any other complex **sensory-motor** skill takes lots of practice. The right movements have to be learned in the right places, and the wrong ones eliminated, one by one, until the whole sequence is mastered. From the discussion so far, you would think that skill learning is accomplished by operant conditioning (step-by-step approximations) combined with imitation. And so it is. But the kinds of practice which are most reinforcing, interestingly, are not entirely obvious. They have been studied experimentally mainly with tasks involving fine

Practice makes perfect, they say.

Dancers Practicing at the Bar, Edgar Degas

eye-hand coordination unfamiliar in people's day to day experience—like having to follow a small metal disk on a revolving turntable with a pen held in one hand (Digman 1958), or trying to trace a drawing you are looking at it in a mirror (Lorge 1930).

Such experiments show two things about practice. One is that people learn a skill more quickly if practice sessions are spaced out rather than bunched together. Fifteen hours of practice massed in a single session are less effective than 15 hours parcelled out over 15 days. Second, people often change learning habits in midstream. If you are learning to type, for instance, you may work letter by letter at first, but after a bit, you learn to type the more common words as whole units. As long as you are using only the letter method, you will show steady progress; but when you begin to memorize whole words, your typing speed will show a slight dip. You are caught between two habits. Since typing words is more efficient than typing letters, eventually your learning progress will recover and dramatically advance. Virtually any kind of skill learning shows dips and plateaus as you proceed. Progress in learning is never steady.

Two other principles are vital in practicing. First, it helps to know how you are doing while learning is in progress, that is, to get feedback. If you are learning to bowl, for instance, you learn more quickly if you can watch the ball roll down the alley toward the pins than if someone simply told you "do it more to the right"; the verbal message is less instructive than seeing for yourself. Constant **feedback** of results speeds learning, particularly towards the end of a learning process (Ammons 1956; Brown 1949). The second principle is that some skills can be best learned by breaking them down into small parts, while others should be learned as wholes. If you have to memorize a speech from *Hamlet,* for instance, you might best concentrate only on the hard parts and ignore the ones that come easily. This piecemeal

approach requires an extra learning step—putting all the parts together. The value of part or whole learning also depends on the learner; in general, more intelligent and older people do better with the whole method (Peckstein 1918).

Overlearning Finally, there is another peculiarity about skill learning. It is **best done when overdone,** that is, you learn a skill best when you master it so completely that you can perform the steps in it **without thinking consciously about them at all.** It makes no difference whether the skill involved is a motor performance, like playing the piano, or driving a car, or even walking—or whether it is an intellectual, cognitive skill like learning a foreign language. You have mastered it most thoroughly when you can perform without deliberation. The technical term for that process is **overlearning,** but it is a misnomer. No skill is really well learned until it has been completely overlearned.

You have observed this in yourself and others many times. But perhaps you have never stopped to notice how ironical, or odd it is, that in order **to learn** a skill, you must be terribly conscious of what you are doing—while in order **to know** it, you must be able to perform with no thought at all of the individual movements. Think about driving a car—when you learn to do it, you must pay attention to the steering, the interaction of the clutch and the gearshift and accelerator and brakes, letting go the ignition switch when the motor catches, stopping on a hill and starting up without stalling, and on and on. Once you have mastered those things, and "know how to drive," you do them all without thinking. You *can* think of them as you do them if you want to, but you don't need to. They are a part of you.

And once they are part of you, they tend to last indefinitely. If you stopped driving for 20 years, having once done it well, you would relearn very quickly. If you learned a language in childhood, stopped using it for 20 years,

Overlearning means mastering a skill to the point where its performance seems effortless.

Lady at the Piano, Pierre Auguste Renoir

and studied it again, you would relearn faster than people starting for the first time, even if they had "talent" for languages and you did not. If, after finishing this book, you read nothing for the next 20 years, you will still know how to read.[1]

Attention, expectation, and reinforcement: The payoff in learning

You must be conscious in order to learn, by and large, and once you have learned something well, it tends to stick. There may be no such thing as sleep learning, and you should

not buy fancy machines and put loudspeakers under your pillow to study for exams. You may learn a little while you are drowsy, but not much; and nothing at all while you are deep asleep. If you want to learn a lot, do like your mother and your piano teacher said, pay attention. It is about the same in learning an elegant skill, or studying for exams, or associating bells and meat powder in the simplest classical conditioning situation. Your ability to learn depends a lot on your ability to attend.

If you look carefully at the idea of reinforcement now, you will see that it uses the term too loosely to think of reinforcement as *reward*. *Reinforcement* really means anything that *strengthens* (reinforces) the new connections between things you are paying attention to — in

---

[1] In fact, even if you don't finish this book.

classical conditioning, the connections between a new stimulus and an old one; in instrumental conditioning, between a new stimulus and a new response, and so forth. It does make sense to say that something is reinforcing if it is rewarding. But there is more to it than that. Actually, *things are reinforcing, and therefore promote learning, if they make a situation memorable,* that is, *if they make your attention fix on something regardless of whether they are rewarding or punishing or neither.* Now we can summarize some things about learning which will pull all this together and make it easy to remember.

The reason you need to reinforce most learning with *practice,* apparently, is that attention has to focus on most things for a fairly long time in order for them to register enduringly in the brain. The reason *feedback* is reinforcing is because it helps to fix attention on the correct connections you want to learn.

There are two kinds of learning which require only one trial: *insight learning* and *traumatic learning.* We have spoken of insight. Traumatic learning is where something terribly frightening gets connected with some neutral event, and from that time on, the neutral thing frightens you by itself. This is called *phobia;* we mentioned it under emotional conditioning, and we will speak more of it in Chapter 18. Terribly *exciting* events are like traumatic ones, though psychology books don't talk much about them. They tend to be remembered forever, for the same reason. *Shocking* occurrences sometimes make such a profound impression that they register permanently.

The reason rewards and punishments reinforce learning, apparently, is because they make it more memorable, that is, they capture your attention and interest more. *Intermittent* rewards and punishments are much more reinforcing than steady ones, perhaps because you habituate to steady ones and therefore your attention declines (go back to Chapter 4, do not pass Go until you understand that stuff on adaptation and attention). *Variable intermittent* rewards and punishments, which occur too irregularly for you to know when they are coming, are the most reinforcing of all because they are the hardest to habituate to. Therefore, your expectations and interest and attention stay high.

If you watch little old ladies at the slot machines in Las Vegas, you will see them stay glued to the machine for hours on end, clutching their little cups full of quarters. They do not win enough money often enough to feel satisfied, and they do not lose consistently enough to give up. Since they cannot tell *when* there will be a payoff, their expectations stay high, and they keep trying.

The same principles explain why everyone's head is full of irrelevant garbage that they remember endlessly for no apparent reason. Either they were paying attention to those irrelevant things at the time something very arousing happened, or they unknowingly rehearsed them a lot, like the TV commercials that float idly through your mind. Either experience would reinforce the connections and file them in your head.

What all this says is that *the reason you learn things is because they are interesting,* meaning that you are paying attention to them when something happens to fix your interest in them indelibly. If educators understood that principle, and tried to teach children (adults too) by getting them interested, I don't know what our educational system would look like. But it would surely be different from what it is now. Anyway, that is the only way anyone ever learns anything. Anyone! Anything!

When things get learned, they tend to remain learned or to be forgotten according to how much they register on the brain. No one knows exactly what that means, but it must involve the same general process in the spontaneous recovery of conditioned responses and in relearning how to ride a bicycle after 20 years.

The physiology of learning is a mystery. But

The Gulf Stream, Winslow Homer
When survival is at stake, we learn to discriminate very subtle signals of impending danger.

there has to be one, somewhere in the brain. Discovering it will be one of the next great enterprises in understanding humanity's greatest talent.

SUMMARY

1 Culture is part of our evolutionary endowment. Human cultural and biological evolution emerged together in a complex interaction. As early humanlike animals formed into groups, their way of living created a selective pressure in favor of fine coordination, foresight, and such social skills as cooperation and language. Gradually, culture has become a more important influence on people than the natural environment, and cultural adaptation has largely replaced biological evolution among human beings.

2 Human beings share many of the same learning processes found in lower animals. *Classical conditioning* builds upon *reflex* reactions, such as salivation or the constriction of blood vessels. In classical conditioning, a new stimulus gets substituted arbitrarily for the normal one; the response to it is strengthened through *reinforcement* (reward or punishment) and disappears (is *extinguished*) when it is no longer reinforced. The new stimulus becomes a sign or signal that the old stimulus will soon appear. For this reason, classical conditioning is called *sign learning.*

3 Classical conditioning is the basis for emotional learning. Love, hate, and fear, can all be learned by the respective association of new stimuli, such as mother, or enemy, with natural feelings of satisfaction, anger, and anxiety. Such feelings *generalize* rapidly from the situations in which they first occur to other situations like them. Emotions may be conditioned to words as well as people, which is the basis for demogoguery and most propaganda. Psychosomatic ailments and controls may be learned by conditioning different stimuli to physiological processes; this is called *interoceptive conditioning.*

4 *Instrumental conditioning* is the learning of new responses which solve problems or bring relief to the individual. It works on voluntary behavior by a process of *trial-and-error,* in which a useful response is reinforced and therefore becomes more frequent, while other responses are gradually eliminated. Instrumental conditioning is also called *solution learning* or *habit learning.*

5 The most common kind of instrumental learning is *operant conditioning* or *behavior shaping.* It is the basis for skill learning. It works by *successive approximation,* that is, rewarding small steps in learning as they come closer and closer to the desired performance. Operant conditioning is widely used in mental hospitals, in the form of *token economies,* where patients learn social skills by earning tokens for performing correctly. The discoverer of operant conditioning, B. F. Skinner, believes that it can be the chief instrument of social change to create a utopian society.

6 Learning ability increases sharply when people are given information about their own performance, called *feedback.* Some ordinarily involuntary physiological processes can be brought under voluntary control by this means, commonly called *biofeedback.* Brain waves, heart rate, and some other functions have been controlled in this way.

7 Learning sometimes occurs unobserved, when no reinforcements are given at all, and appears at a later time, when it is reinforced. This phenomenon, called *latent learning,* has been observed in animals, and it happens to people especially in the learning of language, where the performance they demonstrate is always less than the competence they have achieved.

8 A great deal of learning occurs by observation and *imitation,* in which you learn something by watching a model do it and then trying it yourself. The process is called *vicarious,* or "substitute" learning, because the model generally gets reinforced for learning, which is what interests the imitator in copying it. Observational learning is particularly important in the development of complex skills and of personality.

9 *Insight* is a dramatic form of learning in which the solution to a problem is suddenly "figured out." It occurs in chimpanzees as well as human beings, and possibly in other species. Insightful learning is easily remembered once it occurs, and easily generalized to other problems from the one it originally solved. Insight may occur through a kind of mental trial-and-error procedure, but this is not proved.

10 *Practice* is important in skill learning. For most purposes, practice helps more when it is *distributed* over many short sessions than when it is *massed* into a few long ones.

Feedback also helps speed learning. Some skills are better acquired piecemeal, and others are mastered better in large units.

11 *Overlearning* means mastering a skill so well that it can be performed without conscious attention to its details. Overlearning produces the most highly skilled performances and the least loss of ability with disuse. Skills like driving a car, playing the piano, and riding a bicycle, are generally overlearned, and can be resumed easily after long disuse.

12 You must be paying *attention* for learning to occur. *Reinforcement* is the process of strengthening learning. Anything is reinforcing which makes you pay attention more carefully and makes what you are attending to more memorable. Some learning occurs in only one trial because it is so strongly reinforced. This is also the reason that you learn best when reinforcement occurs variably rather than steadily, and when you cannot predict its exact occurrence. Your expectations are uncertain; so you do not get used to the situation and your attention stays high.

13 Little is known of the physiology of learning. Things remain learned, evidently, because of the kind of impression they register on the brain when they are first learned and then practiced, but nothing is known about the biochemical process.

Motivation

7

7

Motivation

Motivation deals with the question of why anybody does anything—why they eat, sleep, avoid pain, seek sex and love and power and security and money. What starts them looking for these things, makes them keep striving, or stops them when they have enough? These are hard questions. Sometimes it is not clear that there are reasons, and often the reasons cannot be known.

Motivation concerns the "whys" of behavior, but the answer to all questions of motivation is "what" or "how" things happen, not why.[1] When you ask why someone wants to make money, you are asking *what* motivates them, *what* leads them to this striving, or *what* goal will money satisfy that makes them want it in the first place. Another way of asking the same question is: *how* do they come to want money, *how* does the process work by which they are led to this desire, or *how* does its achievement serve their purposes? To put it fancy, you are really asking about the **antecedents** and **consequences** of their behavior (the "whats") and the **process** or **sequence** of events involved (the "hows"). Put back in simple terms, motivation means **causes** and **goals.**

The term "motivation" comes from the Latin word for movement, a pretty comprehensive word to convey the idea that motivation is a pretty comprehensive subject—it is what arouses, energizes, or moves us to action in the first place, and keeps the action going, *directing* or *integrating it,* in the second.

Motives are inferred So far, it sounds like **motive** and **stimulus** mean the same thing. They almost do, but not quite. A stimulus is *anything* that arouses you; a motive is any **internal** thing that arouses you, anything in your body. So all motives are stimuli, but external stimuli are not motives. This makes big trouble scientifically—if they are internal,

---

[1] In fact, the scientific answer to all questions of anything is "what" or "how."

motives can only be inferred; you cannot "see" a motive.

Inferring motivation from behavior is not easy, however. If a person scratches their head, for instance, it may be because they have an itch, or because they are puzzled—or it may just be a random movement with no special motive behind it. You cannot tell from observing the single act.

The same problem applies to all motivation, even the most basic kinds. If someone eats, it may be to reduce hunger, but it might also be to calm their nerves, or console them for loneliness, or divert them from boredom. And when you get into even more complicated behavior, like voting preferences, or dating, or career seeking, it gets even harder. You can ask people what is going on inside them that motivates their overt behavior, but their answers do not always help—people are not always aware of their motives, and sometimes they lie. And with other animals, we cannot even ask.

So pinpointing motives is not easy. We must infer them from observed acts. A single act may represent different motives. Some motives are unconscious. People sometimes lie; and animals can't talk.

The taxonomy of motives

We all take for granted that there are different kinds of motivation. By and large, we assume that the motive for eating is hunger. And by and large, we take for granted that the motive for writing poetry is different from the motive for eating. Obviously, it is not the same thing to want a square meal, or to want a sexual liaison, or to want a million dollars. Some motives seem simpler than others, some more important, some more urgent.

Thirst is a motive experienced by all living things. The primary need for water is powerful enough to have driven whole nations to war.

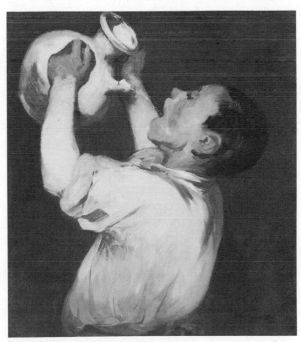

Boy with Pitcher, Edouard Manet

The scientific conventions for classifying motives are about the same as your intuitive ones—and have about the same faults when they are examined carefully. Motives are commonly divided into three groups: biological motives, social motives, and things in between—or primary motives, secondary motives, and motives whose status depends on how you look at them. Some motives are biological in the sense that they are aroused by tissue needs in the body ("need" means lack; so does "want") and are primary in the sense that your survival depends on them. The behavioral expression of such motives can be pretty urgent; so the psychological term often used for them is *drive*—they drive you to action. Other motives are secondary in survival terms, because you can live without satisfying them, and they are not biological in the sense of being aroused by specific apparatus in the body. Most important motives of that kind are social in the sense that they were learned in a social context or that they serve some special purpose—like wanting wealth, prestige, or power. And a third class of motives is neither fish nor fowl—like the curiosity motive, which is not social, has no specific physical mechanism in the body known to produce it, and is still very real and very powerful. Another kind of motive in this group is both fish *and* fowl—like sex, which involves very specific physical mechanisms, but is also very social, is unnecessary to *your* survival as a person, and is vital to *our* survival as a group.

There are other ways of classifying motives also, in terms of concepts like *arousal* or *activation* or *incentive* or *cognition*. And there are varying conventions for the terminology used for different motives; for instance, some people use the term **need** or **drive** to refer only to biological motives, and the term **motive** to refer mainly to social motives. Those distinctions are not very important. It makes sense to distinguish the three kinds of motivations indicated: First, the things you die from not getting, which are, in that sense, clearly primary motives;

second, the things that are plainly social, like prestige and publicity; and third, motives that don't fall clearly in one or the other place, but are still strong, like sex, curiosity, or the need to play.

No motives are really pure, of course. The most social motives are rooted in physiology, because you don't go anywhere without taking your body along, and the purest of survival motives are powerfully expressed or inhibited in socially determined forms. Hunger is a physiological motive, on the face of it, because you have a stomach for handling it; and sex, because you have genitals; while making money is not because it lacks an organ. But since the real source of control for all of these is in the brain, that distinction is not all pure. A professional crap shooter could as well say his arm is his money-making organ—and be just as wrong; his brain is. There is a physiology to social motives, about which relatively little is known, and a sociology, or at least a learning history, to physiological motives, which has to do with why you like ice cream better than sugared chicken fat and broiled steak better than creamed cat colon. You cannot fully understand motivation, when all is said and done, without dipping into physiology at one end and sociology at the other. Most of psychology is like that.

THE PHYSIOLOGY OF MOTIVATION

Saying that motivation is an internal stimulus to action does not say where it comes from internally. Take hunger. Does it originate in the stomach? In the brain? Do we know we are hungry because our stomachs are grumbling or because we glance at a clock? And are we really hungry or do we just think we are, or is there any difference? To know, we have to see the chains of events in the body when someone goes without food for several hours and ends up saying they are hungry—and the chains of subsequent events that allow them eventually to say they are not hungry any more. Why do they not just keep eating forever, once they start in? You can ask the same questions about virtually every internal process that leads a person into action. And in every case, you will get a very complex answer, to the effect that any number of organs and body systems are involved, all masterminded by the brain in a kind of physiological symphony that puts you in motion and through the paces that meet the need, and then, in an equally complex series of unseen bodily orchestrations, settles you back down to the relatively inactive state you were in before it all started. I am not emphasizing complexity in order to make it sound hard, but because the complexity of the process and the variability of the action you go through is what makes motivation more than a merely *reflex* action. Hunger, thirst, sex, and virtually any other motive is not aroused by a single, simple internal event, and it is not satisfied by a constant, unchanging series of responsive acts. It is an extension of the processes by which the body maintains its metabolic and chemical activities in good order, called **homeostasis.**

Homeostasis: Keeping the delicate balance

If you ever stop to ask yourself precisely what is *you* and what is your environment, you meet some interesting puzzles. It is easy enough to say that your eyes are part of you and this book part of the environment, but what about the air you breathe? And what about the passages it goes through? Are they part of you or part of it (Murphy 1947)? They are both, of course. Your internal environment is so immediately responsible for life and health that you automatically (and reasonably) treat it as part of yourself. Homeostasis is the process of "maintaining a constant internal environment" which means keeping your metabolic processes functioning as nearly as possible in their optimum ways. Most body processes, like tem-

perature, the amount of sugar and other chemicals in the bloodstream, the amount of oxygen available to the cells, and so forth, can only vary within narrow limits without seriously damaging the body's functioning. If they vary too much, too quickly, all kinds of disabilities, and death, result. Life really does hang in a delicate balance. Its chemical maintenance is called homeostasis (from Greek words meaning "standing steady" or "steady state"). The concept was first expressed by a French physiologist, Claude Bernard, more than a century ago, but the term was coined by an American physiologist, W. B. Cannon, in 1939, in a book called *The wisdom of the body*. It has been the basis of motivation theory ever since.

Homeostatic mechanisms are automatically thrown into action when a metabolic process changes beyond a certain point, just as your room thermostat turns the heater or air conditioning on when the room temperature rises or drops beyond a certain point. If the amount of oxygen in your bloodstream drops, for instance, as it would when you fly from sea level to a high place like Denver or Mexico City, or the amount needed rises, as it does when you run, then homeostatic mechanisms will make you breathe faster. The same kind of thing happens when you get overheated, or chilled, or have too much or too little of some kind of food. In all these cases, there is a kind of optimum level of functioning at any time, an equilibrium in the body. When it is disturbed, homeostatic mechanisms work to restore that equilibrium.

Most homeostatic mechanisms function reflexively, without arousing the total organism. It is only when they fail to work smoothly or involve so many different organs and activities that *all* of you gets into the act that the homeostatic process becomes motivational. Then, the body's need to restore equilibrium can only be met by some global act of the whole person. Body cells need nutrients, for instance, mostly supplied by food. In their absence, homeostatic disequilibrium results and we feel aroused by hunger. To satisfy it, and restore the homeostatic balance of cell nutrients, we have to go through the complex activity of eating. There are many physiological activities underlying hunger, and they make up the homeostatic mechanisms; the *feelings* and the *acts* we do to satisfy hunger make up the motivation.

The homeostatic principle seems to underlie most motivation—a condition of disequilibrium arises in the body which we experience as *tension, irritation,* or *need,* and we do things which reduce that tension and restore equilibrium. Motivation, in that elementary sense, is the search for peace and quiet.

Homeostatic activities are based on tissue *needs.* The psychological consequences of these needs are called *drives.* Most tissue needs have corresponding drives, but there is no perfect correspondence between them. Some needs, like the need for certain vitamins, do not have any psychological drives accompanying them; we may be unaware that we have some vitamin deficiency. Further, a drive does not necessarily get stronger as a need gets stronger. We may feel a great deal of hunger (drive) at meal time, but if we do not eat, the "hunger pangs" subside after a while even though we still need food. The drive is less intense, but the physiological imbalance remains. You *have* needs, but you *feel* drives.

Measuring drives The correlation between tissue needs and feeling driven is so poor that we have to measure them independently of each other. Your body, for instance, needs about 2,000 calories of food per day to maintain itself, but the amount of hunger you feel, and the things you are hungry for, are not related in a precise way to your caloric needs.

Even so, the obvious way to measure a drive is to *deprive* someone of something they need and see how their reactions differ for short and long periods of deprivation. There are several things you would expect to happen as drive

changes with deprivation. First, the level of activity should change, presumably increasing as deprivation grows longer and drive therefore grows stronger. So you would expect a rat in a cage or a student in a classroom to get more and more active as they grow hungrier, perhaps to become more nervous and irritable also. Second, and a corollary of increased activity, you might expect performance speed to increase. In a rat, that would mean that it runs through a maze faster than it did before. In you, it means that you cross campus more quickly to get to the kitchen or dining room. A third, and subtler index of drive would be to see what kind of obstacles you are willing to overcome to get what you want. A hungry person would take more risks to get food than one who is full; a thirsty rat should be more willing to cross an electrified grid than one who has just had a drink. Finally, we can get a subtle index of the relative strength of a drive or of a particular means of satisfying it by seeing which of two alternatives is preferred. If you have deprived someone of food and drink both, and then permit them to get either one, but not the other, will they choose the food or the drink?

All of the above measures are useful, but they only work roughly, both on people and animals. For some drives, like hunger, deprivation tends to increase activity for a while, but after a point, it decreases it. A hungry person may actively seek food; a starving one is likely to become lethargic and passive after a while. For other drives, like sex, *satisfaction* of the drive tends to increase it over time, while deprivation tends to reduce it—unless a period of deprivation comes after a pattern of satisfaction has already been established, in which case it briefly increases activity. The short-term relationship of deprivation and drive varies a lot with lower animals, and even more with people, whose intellects and emotions get into the act and complicate it even more. The homeostatic model of motivation may be accurate, but it does not work in a simple way. The question it raises is whether there is any general scheme that applies to all motivated behavior, or whether different kinds of motivation work by different principles. More things hinge on this question than you may realize.

The motivation of motivation

The "deprivation model" of motivation is an obvious one, but is it the only one? Hunger and thirst and the like are ultimately based on de-ficiencies in the body of nutrients and fluids, and it is correct to say that the aim of the hunger motive is to reduce the need for food, even though time of deprivation is not a perfect way to measure such drives. Some other motives do not fit a deprivation scheme in the same way, however. The need to avoid pain, for instance, does not arise from a lack of painless-ness in the body. Or does it? If you look at the actual sensations you experience during hunger, they are quite uncomfortable. Indeed, it

Millions of people live constantly on the edge of starvation. The lethargy of quiet desperation is their common state.

is no accident that we speak of hunger "pangs" (meaning sharp, short pains). In fact, if you start examining the basis of any motive, you may find that you can interpret it in much the same way, namely, that the motive aims to satisfy some longing, physical, or mental. So here we are, back at the homeostatic ranch, with all motivation seeming to aim at tension reduction. Are there other kinds of motives?

Probably not, though this has been a subject of serious controversy for ages. Probably all motives have, as their general object, the reduction of tension, though the channels in which they work to reach this goal differ widely for different motives and, at times, appear to arouse more tension than they reduce.

Most motives involve a sequence of activity in which you first discover that you are aroused, then take **preparatory action** to satisfy your need by finding some **incentive** towards which to aim. An incentive is a potential reward, or reinforcer, or need reducer. Then you go into a **consummatory** phase, in which you get the incentive. This is fancy talk to indicate simply that the motive is not satisfied in a single act, but in a whole chain of them. Therein arise the complexities that make people wonder whether there may be different kinds of motives.

Even with something as simple as hunger, for instance, positive incentives may actually increase drive states. The smell of freshly cooked food may make someone hungry all over again after having recently eaten. Or the effects of different **channels** in which we have learned to satisfy motives may be so powerful that they have a motive value of their own— which is what is happening to you when you are quite full from eating and then find that you want a certain piece of pastry or a favorite dessert.

The peculiarities of true deficiency motives like hunger are not nearly as dramatic as the operation of the **curiosity drive** or **exploratory drive.** These are areas of motivation which have unspecified physiological (need) cor-

relates. Many animals, including us, seem to have drives to explore their environments and to manipulate objects. In some experiments, animals will learn how to open doors simply to see what is on the other side. Deprivation seems to be irrelevant to these drives, and "rewards" such as looking through a doorway do not seem to fit the idea of rewards implied by the deficiency model.

In fact, they may fit it well enough, but the deficiency involved is probably one which we take so much for granted that we never think of it as a need—namely, the need for stimulation.[2] Satisfaction of that need may be what leads us into exploratory activity. Some people try to distinguish such motives from deficiency motives by the fact that they are **approach motives,** while deficiency motives are **avoidance motives.** In other words, you explore in order to find out something; but you eat in order to avoid hunger. Approach motives like curiosity are channelled by positive incentives, while avoidance motives like pain are channelled by negative incentives.

Some people find special charm in the distinction between approach and avoidance motives because they feel that the former are the basis of more exalted things, like love, altruism, and creativity. Exalted or not, the basis for approach motives still seems to be the same as for avoidance motives—to reduce a state of tension by filling a need. The fact that the need gets stronger, in some cases, as you come closer to satisfying it, as in sex, only makes the gratification at the end more glamorous. The end itself remains the same.

If you think about it carefully, you will realize that motives do not really reside in body tissues anyway, but in brain centers. In some motives, deficiencies in body tissues arouse those brain centers, and the centers then stimulate you into motivated action. But some motives apparently arise from the brain itself, without the de-

_____
[2] See Chapter 4 on sensory deprivation.

ficiency proddings of muscle cells or blood cells or glandular secretions. Curiosity motives must be of this kind, as must all social motives — and the reason we think there is something marvellously different about them from hunger and thirst is that we forget that the deficiency motives also really come from the brain, not just from the body.

The brain centers involved actually control most of the behavior connected with that motive, as we saw briefly in Chapter 3. A number of experiments have found many motivation centers in the brain, including *pleasure* and *pain* centers (London 1969; Delgado 1969; Olds and Milner 1954). Electric current passed through tiny electrodes in these areas produces rapid and continual approach behavior for pleasure centers and avoidance behavior for pain centers, completely independent of the animals' other needs. Rats were first trained to bar-press in order to receive electrical stimulation. Then, when the current was directed to a pain center, the rats quickly learned to turn it off. When a pleasure center was stimulated, they pressed the bar until they virtually dropped from exhaustion. The same thing has been found with many other motives, and in people as well as animals, including the pleasure center, according to some claims (Heath 1968).

The hierarchy of motives

There is not much point in trying to classify motives according to their general importance, because the perspective on what is primary or secondary is not absolute. Even survival is not a good criterion for evaluating motivation, because it really concerns tissue needs, not the feelings that arise from them. For most purposes, it makes more sense to classify motives in a many-dimensional way, according to the space they occupy in the routines of living — the intensity of feelings they arouse in us when they are not met, and the amount of time we spend on satisfying them. Often, these differ

sharply from our routine awareness of what matters most and least in our lives, but if you think about it, you can see that a fairly common hierarchy of motives exist among people.

Sleep is the paramount drive, for instance, and among the least understood. It takes up almost a third of everyone's total life, in infancy occupies most of it, in fact, and it is a need that, at any time of life, can be abused but not denied. Prisoners fall asleep in the midst of torture, soldiers fall asleep on the march, college students fall asleep while desperately cramming for exams. The need is so basic that there is no sense talking of it as something you die without — there is no way, it seems, to keep anyone awake long enough to kill them from it. They just fall asleep.

Thirst and *hunger* are probably next in order of importance. They are far better understood than sleep, as we shall see, because the conditions that arouse them are not entirely limited to the brain, and the results of their not being satisfied are fairly quick and obvious. They take up a lot of everyone's life space because they must be indulged so often and because the need for them is felt so urgently.

The *need for stimulation* may be third in line, but its true position in the hierarchy is ambiguous because it is so hard to measure the effects of stimulus deprivation. You may need stimulation about as badly as you need oxygen, but oxygen shortage will have serious effects in a matter of seconds, while stimulus deprivation is a slow-acting thing. Sleep needs may be the homeostatic counterpart of stimulation needs; their main function may be to cut off external stimulation. Experiments on the effects of "enriched" and "deprived" sensory environments of baby rats have shown differences in the brain tissues of the two groups. Lack of sufficient stimulation in infancy may damage the biochemical development of the brain so that some kinds of abilities cannot later develop. Hanging things in baby's cribs and giving them baubles to play with may be good for them.

*Madonna and Child with Infant St. John,
Jacopo Pontormo*

Mothering—a life-or-death need for
all babies and some mothers.

The **need for affection,** or *parenting,* or whatever you call it, is also very basic, but also occupies an uncertain place in the hierarchy of importance. If you don't get enough parenting in infancy, then you may be damaged emotionally, and perhaps intellectually. But the exact ingredients of parenting are uncertain, and it is also unclear how long or how much you have to get them. Baby monkeys that don't get adequate parenting grow up socially incompetent and sexually inert. In humans, babies that don't get enough of it early enough may grow up disturbed—but that is not certain.

Sex is probably next in importance, though it is peculiar in two respects. First, it is not important to the survival of the individual, as all the other basic needs seem to be. Second, the sexual motive clearly has a biological basis, but equally clearly, all of its expression seems to depend very strongly on learning, at least in human beings. "Doing what comes naturally," as the song puts, is not doing *anything* automatically. In some respects, sex, like affection, is more a social than a biological motive. Like affection, in any case, it bridges the distinction between them. As far as the space they take up in our lives is concerned, these two motives are completely interdependent. The sexual side of the affection motive, so to speak, starts to express itself in adolescence, and keeps express-

Experimental condition	Present age	Behavior				
		None	Low	Almost normal	Probably normal	Normal
Raised in isolation: (Total)						
Cage-raised for 2 years	4 years	P D S				
Cage-raised for 6 months	14 months	D S	P			
Cage-raised for 80 days	10½ months			P D S		
(Partial)						
Cage-raised for 6 months	5 to 8 years		P S	D		
Surrogate-raised for 6 months	3 to 5 years		P S	D		
Raised with mother:						
Normal mother; no play with peers	1 year	S	P			D
Motherless mother; play in playpen	14 months			D	S	P
Normal mother; play in playpen	2 years					P D P
Raised with peers:						
Four raised in one cage; play in playroom	1 year				P	D P
Surrogate-raised; play in playpen	2 years				S	P D
Surrogate-raised; play in playroom	21 months					P D P

P Play   D Defense   S Sex

Results of experiments are summarized. The monkey's capacity to develop normally appears to be determined by the seventh month of life. Animals isolated for six months are aberrant in every respect. Play with peers seems even more necessary than mothering to the development of effective social relations.

Source: From H. F. Harlow and M. K. Harlow, Social Deprivation in Monkeys. Copyright © November 1962 by Scientific American, Inc. All rights reserved.

ing itself throughout adulthood. In the best relationships, sex is never completely independent of affection.

The true **secondary,** or **social,** or **cognitive** motives, as most of them turn out to be, are like sex and affectional motives in that they take little life space at the beginning and they become more and more important and preoccupying as we learn them better and better. By adulthood, they are the main motivations of almost everyone—certainly of everyone whose basic needs for food, shelter, sleep, and affection are being met. If you ask yourself, or almost anyone you know, what their *long-range* motives are, they will turn out to be things like *career, family, achievement* plans. No one will say to you, "What I really want out of life is a good meal—or a good night's sleep—or a good sexual encounter," unless they are sorely lacking those things right now. People are more likely to speak of their wish to be a doctor, lawyer, banker, teacher, pilot, to have a family, to make such and such contribution to humanity, or to their country, or religion, to be rich, or powerful, or beloved. As the sense of time develops with memory and language ability in childhood, we become aware of ourselves more and more in terms of **goals,** rather than **wants.** Eventually, this leads to a concern with the most distant of motivational purposes, the idea of **self-actualization.**

Self-actualization or **higher-order motives** are an extension of secondary motives. They are learned, like all secondary motives, but they differ by the fact that we see them as representing our positive purposes rather than fulfilling some deficiency in our existence. In order to have strong motives of this kind, which Abraham Maslow and others have called **growth motives,** people must have a sense of positive **self-esteem.** The growth motives fulfill that sense of self-esteem by making them become the kind of persons they want to be.

The hierarchy of motivation is not an important practical issue, though it is academically interesting. In fact, all strong motivation is important in your personal experience, whether it is a short-term need, like eating or sleeping, or a complex bio-social event, like sex or affection, or a purely learned and civilized desire, like for achievement or fulfillment. So we shall look at some details of these different kinds of motives now, without pretending that one kind is worth more attention than another, but only noting the different complexities that are involved in each category.

HUNGER

Hunger is a good physiological motive to examine for several reasons: (1) It has been more studied than any other one; (2) It is about as complicated as any motive gets, illustrating the ins and outs of a primary drive in humans as well as anything would; and (3) You have a lot of personal experience with it, and if you are a member of the heavier 50 percent of the American population, you have some trouble controlling this motive well enough to keep your weight in check and your figure in proportion.

We will look at hunger in the following order. What is it that makes you hungry? What do you do about it, that is, what are the consequences in action that hunger has? And what makes you stop, or fail to, when your body's need for food has been satisfied?

The physiology of hunger

Most of us associate hunger with feelings of pain or emptiness in our stomachs, just as we connect the feeling of satiation with the sensation of our stomachs being full. Hunger is a good deal more complicated than that, but as far as it goes, this description is accurate. When the stomach is empty for some time, its muscles start to produce rhythmic contractions; and when it is full, and gets stretched or distended, those movements are replaced by the churning of digestion and hunger disappears. This discovery, by Walter Cannon (1934), had a fluke in it, however; he put a balloon in his subject's stomach and measured the contractions by the changes in the balloon's inflation. It turns out that the balloon in the stomach itself produced the pattern of contractions that Cannon observed. Still, everyone who has observed their own sensations of extreme hunger has noticed that stomach "pangs" signal it. They do not do so all by themselves, though. Later experiments on humans who had no stomachs and on animals whose stomachs had been removed or whose sensory nerves between the stomach and brain had been cut found that hunger still occurred (Tsang 1938). Once the pattern of eating has been established, it does not need stomach contractions to keep it going. While they do signal hunger, all right, they are not alone in doing so. This is an important fact to remember, you will find, when trying to control excessive eating.

Blood chemistry is another important factor in signaling hunger to the brain. When the amount of sugar (glucose) in the blood drops too low, for instance, and that of some other chemicals, such as certain fatty acids, gets too high (Klein et al. 1960), you feel sensations of hunger. Many people, possibly including you, walk around with a very mild version of a disorder called *hypoglycemia,* which is a deficiency of blood sugar which makes you feel weak or faint. In extreme cases, or if people have had excessive doses of insulin, the condition causes unconsciousness, and it can kill you. Anyway, blood sugar level is raised by eating, and experiments have shown that the stomach contractions of hunger could be reduced merely by transfusing blood from a recently fed animal to a famished one (Bash 1939).

In any case, the variety of physical and chemical events in the body that stimulate hunger have to be translated by the brain before they become a hunger *drive.* Much of that translation seems to occur in and around the *hypothalamus,* which, you recall, is a kind

The hunger drive in human experience becomes mixed with so many social and private psychological motives that by the time you sit down to eat you are satisfying a whole network of needs.

Welcome Home, Jack Levine

of connecting area between the cortex and the old brain (See Chapter 3). The exact role of the hypothalamus is not certain. When it is stimulated electrically, eating, drinking, and other activity start, sometimes quite dramatically, as when an already well fed rat will continue to stuff itself more (Coons et al. 1965). But a single point in the hypothalamus may actually arouse several different acts, like eating, drinking, exploring, and copulating (Caggiula 1970; Valenstein et al. 1968a and b), and the hypothalamus may really only be a connection center for other control points (Grossman 1968) or some kind of booster center for completing motivated behavior which has already been learned (Valenstein et al. 1971). It is not certain right now.

What is certain, on the other hand, is that hunger is aroused by bodily sensations of discomfort, primarily resulting from deprivation, that get transmitted to the brain's arousing and control centers, and then further transmitted to the cortex, where they are translated into the form of consciousness that we call *drive.* That term covers a multitude of events, however, depending on the individual and the situation. In a baby, it is probably felt as a general discomfort, which gets relieved in whatsoever manner, the baby only slowly coming to recognize distinct activities like eating and drinking, and distinct sensations, like taste in the mouth or fullness in the belly. Specific hungers, such as for water rather than food, is partly regulated by built-in chemical processes which give rise to a craving sensation, called "deficiency craving"; it applies to other substances as well, such as the need for salt and, in experiments with lower animals, some vitamins and minerals. In a classic experiment with human infants, moreover, C. M. Davis let three infants select their own foods from a wide assortment of things over periods of six months to one year, and found that all three did right well in balancing their diets (Davis 1928). This study is, to this day, a source of endless comfort to the

"naturalist" view of human behavior, and of nutrition.

It should not be. For while babies may be "natural," parents are not, nor are there any "natural" cafeterias around in which baby can balance its diet uninfluenced by television commercials, cereal boxtops, and the endless array of beautifully packaged tooth-rotting yummies lying around our processed, non-organic civilization. With hunger, as with most every other need, drive, or motive high enough above the reflex state to be left in consciousness, *learning* is almost all.

What that means, as a practical matter, is that people's specific hungers are mostly *learned,* and if, from a nutritional point of view, the wrong things get learned, then the chemical hungers of the body can be overridden and become inoperative. With respect to the kinds of hungers which create such nutritional problems as obesity in our society, the wisdom of the body does not stand a chance! The physiology of hunger does little more than set the stage for the conditioning processes by which you learn to eat. What sets you to seeking food, determines what you eat, and lets you stop (if it does), is, to all intents and purposes, the psychology of hunger.

The psychology of hunger

Stop someone on the street and ask them what makes people eat, and they will doubtless say "hunger,"[3] meaning food deprivation. But in your own and everyone else's experience, that is only partly true. Hunger is one thing that motivates eating, but not the only one. Haven't you ever finished a filling meal and then gotten turned on an hour later by the prospect of an ice cream sundae or some other gooey? Or haven't you sat down to a meal with no appetite at all, then discovered you were really hungry *after* you started eating? And at least a couple

---

[3] They will doubtless *think* you are crazy.

times a year (to put it very kindly), like Thanksgiving and Christmas, haven't you felt full by the end of the second course, but kept on bravely eating yourself into a near stupor? Most people have. Such special events complicate the discussion because the usual measure of *hunger motivation* is *eating action,* and food deprivation is the usual way of connecting them. (Now you can see why it is so hard to infer motivation from behavior.) These events also complicate people's lives, because in our food-rich culture, they produce overeating in almost half the population, with all the problems of overweight and poor health resulting from it. At least three different kinds of problems and mechanisms seem to be involved: (1) the *signal source;* (2) the *crackerjack effect;* and (3) the *addiction syndrome.* Understanding them can be a big help in controlling the tendency to overeat.

Signal source: How you know you're hungry Regardless of what is going on chemically in your bloodstream or stomach or hypothalamus, you do not feel like eating until something suggests it to your mind, that is, to consciousness. For some people, the main source of that suggestion is the signals that collect internally from food deprivation—stomach contractions, blood sugar changes, and so on. For others, especially for people who overeat, the main signal source seems to be external—the clock, which tells them it is time to eat; billboards and magazine pictures of yummies that stimulate hunger; or even the sight of food left on the plate after they are already full. There is a good deal of evidence, in fact, that people who overeat tend to disregard internal cues to hunger more than slender people do, while they also tend to respond more than slender people to external cues that they have learned to associate with eating (Schachter and Gross 1968; Nisbett 1968; Goldman et al. 1968; Stunkard 1969).

It seems pretty clear that we are all naturally disposed to "eat for calories" to begin with, which means that our early experience of hunger depends on the internal chemical results of food deprivation. Somehow, we learn to shift from *internal* to *external* eating cues as we develop, with the result that, in extreme cases, people lose the ability to distinguish physiological hunger and then take on eating habits which are so unrelated to their body's needs that they store a lot of excess fat.

In evolutionary terms, this is a good thing. An animal that could not store fat by gorging itself when food was plentiful would starve in a hurry when it was not. And since primitive people, as hunters and foragers, had to survive an undependable food supply, evolving the ability to convert excess food into body fat undoubtedly helped them survive situations where they could not get food. People who had more of this ability may have had better survival chances than the rest, and passed that ability down to us in two forms: (1) a tendency to slow metabolism, that is, for the body to use food with great efficiency, thus saving calories, and (2) an appetite control mechanism which permits us to keep eating long beyond the point where the body's short-term need for nutrition is satisfied (Gwinnup 1970).

The trouble is, that phase of evolution is over—humans are no more foragers or hunters, the food supply is dependable for more than a few hours or days at a time, and all this ability to use external cues to eating and disregard internal ones to stopping accomplishes practically is to make us fatter than we ought to be. Some of the mechanisms involved, moreover, have the scientific effect of complicating any simple homeostatic theory of motivation. The greatest of these complexities is produced by the "crackerjack" effect.

The crackerjack effect: "Tastes like more" From a simple homeostatic point of view, if hunger is a state of internal disequilibrium, eating would have the effect of reducing it and restoring calm. In that case, it figures, putting food in your mouth should start to reduce hunger right away. It does not, of course. If anything, the taste of food is one of the greatest stimuli there is to eating. That is one reason undoubtedly, why some people find it much easier to diet by fasting than by only partially reducing caloric intake. In the long run, of course, the food does reduce the hunger—and in the short run, its stimulating effect on appetite, which works largely by increasing salivation, guarantees that you will not eat too little before stopping. This crackerjack effect, technically, is called *incentive motivation:* it works for sex and some social needs, like affection, as well as hunger.

Turning off For most people, of course, stopping too soon is not a problem, no more than insensitiveness to food stimuli which would start them eating in the first place. No one knows the precise physiology of satiation any better than that of hunger. It makes sense to think that hunger should terminate, and we should stop eating, when the body's cells receive the nutrients they need. But this could not be the case because most nutrients are not received by the cells for some time *after* eating, and even at our piggiest, we rarely eat continuously for very long. There must be some process or mechanism which *anticipates* the satisfaction of the hunger need. Three such mechanisms have been investigated: blood chemistry, taste receptors in the mouth, and distention (stretching) of the stomach. All three are related to satiation, since all send messages to a part of the hypothalamus called the satiation center. When the satiation center in a rat's hypothalamus is destroyed, the animal simply continues to eat; when the satiation center is stimulated, it stops eating. So there must be cues from the mouth or stomach or blood that signal the brain to feel full and stop eating—and that do not signal fast enough for many people. But what the cues are, or how they are aroused, is not known. Their failure to operate, in the extreme, produces *cravings* to start and inability to stop in time. This potent combination of hunger motives run wild is called *addiction.*

Addictions There are differences between one kind of addiction and another, as you will see in Chapter 11, but it is useful to realize that *all* addictions are hungers and that all uncontrollable hungers are addictions. The difference between drug or alcohol addiction, on the one hand, and food addiction, on the other, is simply that the former do not originate inside your body, as homeostatic needs, while the latter do. Psychologically, the origins of an addiction make no difference at all to someone who is craving their particular "monkey." If anything, the problem of food addiction is more problematic than alcohol or drugs because there is no way you can go "cold turkey," i.e., withdraw completely from the addicting stuff, and survive. In some cases of extreme obesity, people are hospitalized and put on lengthy fasts—but that is only a temporary palliative to get weight off them quickly. It does nothing to cure the cravings that create the problem.

Dieting

If you see how little is really understood of the ins and outs of hunger motivation, then you should not be surprised to learn that little is known about how to curb it or get it back under control either. Despite the several billions of pages, dollars, claims, and tears expended yearly on diet books, programs, ballyhoo, and efforts, there is no single method of dieting that has been shown to work for everyone or to produce permanent effects for anyone. It is well known that, if you want to lose weight, you must use up or put out more calories than you take in, but no one can say how that is best done. This is why there are countless arguments for countless different kinds of diets—high carbohydrates, low carbohydrates, high protein, low protein, all the fat you can eat, no fat at all, nutritional balance, nutritional imbalance, count calories, don't count them, fast, eat all the time —there is no end to it. Most diet programs emphasize *food* and the nutritional consequences of one or another plan for what you eat. Most people with an overweight problem, however, find that their problem revolves more around *eating* than around food, and that it is the motivational more than the nutritional aspects of the subject that confound their efforts. You can take some practical hints that may help you diet from the things that have been discovered about the psychology of eating. The suggestions which follow here are taken from LIFESTYLE Programs, Inc., a Los Angeles weight-reduction training center.

Internal and external cues   The first major step might be to observe yourself and discover what your own internal and external cues to eating are. The object would be to teach yourself to recognize and rely on more internal cues than you have been doing.

If you are an external cue eater, you may actually have forgotten what the internal sensations of true hunger are like, especially if you grew up in a home where you were told to clean your plate ("children in India are starving, so you. . . ."), or where you were rewarded with edible goodies ("practice your bassoon 15 more minutes, darling, and I'll give you a big dish of gooey"), or where you were solaced in that way ("stop crying, sweetheart, here's some yummy whomba pie to make you feel better"). Where food was made into a generalized reinforcer in childhood, people grow up using it as a response to all kinds of emotional states. If you are like that, you may discover that you feel like eating whenever you are depressed, angry, sad, or happy, whether or not you are actually hungry. Hunger hurts in the stomach, not the heart. If you can learn to notice that your stomach is full when some other hunger grabs at you, you can then avoid food.

The second thing you can do to become an internal-cue eater is to start observing your own metabolic processes when you are truly hungry. You will find that there are some foods that satisfy you more quickly than others. Much of the controversy about what kinds of food are best

for dieting would probably disappear if more attention were paid to the different metabolic needs of different people. Differences in thyroid metabolism, or in carbohydrate metabolism, may make one kind of diet more useful for one person and a different kind for another. You can experiment with yourself in this connection, and probably do so best with your doctor's help.

If you can teach yourself to eat slowly, moreover, you will find that your caloric intake drops because your blood-sugar level rises and you feel full before you have eaten a whole lot. Combining slow eating with the foods that work best and fastest for you can be a big help. Also, if you are the kind of person who tends to let themselves get ravenous and then wolf down big meals almost without tasting the food, you can help yourself a lot by eating very often, nibbling at small quantities all the time. There are other things you can do to give your body a chance to catch up with its hunger pangs before you eat too much. Try setting down your utensils after you have taken a bite, and don't pick them up again until you have swallowed what's in your mouth. Many overeaters are in constant motion at the dinner table, preparing to shovel in the next mouthful when they have hardly begun tasting this one.

Along with sensitizing yourself to internal cues, you can do something effective about your tendency to be stimulated by external cues. For one thing, you can keep foods away from you that you don't think you should be eating — keep them out of your room, out of your kitchen, out of access. That way, you avoid tempting external stimulation. Another thing you can do is to deliberately choose to have around you a few of the foods you like best in the world! This is a way of capitalizing on external stimuli. By allowing yourself a few things that you like best, it is easier to resist many things that you should not have and do not really crave as much.

Finally, you can maximize your chances for success by giving yourself a great deal of *feedback* about how you are doing and what you are trying to accomplish—weigh yourself regularly, keep records of your food intake, weigh and measure what you eat, get a full length mirror to observe yourself in so you can check visually on how you are doing, use refrigerator warning signs and other such gimmicks to remind yourself to keep away from food you do not want to indulge in. Everything you do to make yourself more aware of the control you are trying to establish over your eating habits, will actually serve the process of gaining that control. If you are trying to diet, it is probably your eating habits, not your hunger motivation, that needs to be controlled.

We have used hunger as a model of physiologically based primary motives. It is high up on the hierarchy of such drives, both in terms of how strongly it is felt and how dire the consequences are if it goes unsatisfied for too long. Even so, there is no way to speak of the hunger *motive* in terms of purely physiological mechanisms, nor even in terms of the body's pure survival needs. "Hunger" refers essentially to the *feeling* of hunger and, as we have seen, that feeling is only partly related, and even then in very complicated ways, to the deprivation of nutrients in the body's tissues.

So it goes with every "primary" need. Thirst, sleep, stimulation, and, in large part, the need for the special kinds of care, attention, and contact that we lump together as "parenting" or "affection" are all like hunger. They are aroused by deprivation, ultimately, and in some physiological sequence which is partly understood— but the stimulus conditions of their arousal and satisfaction alike are complicated, and the physical mechanisms involved are far from completely understood. They are homeostatic processes, all right, but not in the neat and tidy way that such processes as temperature regulation and metabolism are homeostatic. They do not have to be learned to be *felt,* but the ways they are expressed almost all depend on how we have learned to handle them.

In important ways, the opposite will apply to "secondary" or social motives, as we shall see. But before going into them, we will take a look at the area which bridges the primary and secondary motives, showing the complexity of this subject as nothing else can and providing the most interesting and puzzling problems and perspectives of perhaps any human motive.

SEX

Of all motivated behavior, sex has probably been the most controversial, from a social point of view, and certainly the most entertaining. It has also been controversial and intriguing as a scientific problem, with much debate and doubt about the physiological character of sexual needs and about the relative effects of physiology and education on sexual expression. This motive demonstrates the slightly cockeyed aspects of classifying motives as "primary" or "secondary."

Sex is not a primary need in the sense that you die from the lack of it. And while it is true that the species would die from a total lack of it, and that someone therefore has to do it (at least as a matter of civic duty), it would abuse the whole concept of primary drive, based as it is on tissue needs, to confuse the requirements of species survival with those of individual survival. But sex is not a secondary motive either, not in the sense of depending entirely on learning or of being entirely derived from primary motives. It has a basic physiology of its own, far more visible than is the physiology of hunger or thirst and as chock full of genes and hormones and biochemistry of body and brain as are the hardiest appetites for food and drink.

In humans, on the other hand, that physiological apparatus gains no function until very extensive learning has taken place, far more than is needed for channeling hunger and thirst into preferences and habits. And while human sexuality is not *derived* from any primary motive, it tends to be linked pretty closely with parenting or affection, a more basic motive which, left unsatisfied in early life, may damage a person sexually in adulthood.

Sex has some of the attributes of a deficiency motive in that sexual feeling becomes very powerful as a form of tension, and orgasm provides such a massive relief from the tension that it thereby becomes the greatest of physical pleasures. On the other hand, having learned how delicious the sequence of tension and release can be, the sexual motive becomes an *incentive motive* rather than a deprivation one—that is, you come to seek sexual arousal in order to go through the sequence. Not having learned that, you aren't likely to go in much for the whole business.

Here is the crackerjack effect with a vengeance! Despite its physical basis, sexual behavior in humans is so much a learned motive that if you do not encourage it, or at least create the learning conditions in which it will flourish, then it does not become an awfully strong motive —sex simply isn't that primary. But once you do learn sexual behavior, your incentive to perform it increases the desire for it. The most basic motive in sex then becomes the performance of the act itself. Sex, in other words, is habit-forming, developing and strengthened through the reinforcement its pleasurable feelings provide. Let us look at how it works.

The psychophysiology of sex The machinery for sexual behavior depends, like hunger, on both hormonal and brain mechanisms, the hormones, in this case, being supplied primarily by the special sexual organs of male and female respectively. Both sexes, incidentally, produce some male *and* female hormones, though ordinarily in different quantities. Perhaps the most interesting thing about sexual physiology, though, unlike that of other basic motives, is that it does not come into significant play, or have much effect on behavior, until the years of pubescence, which is pretty far along in life as far as most important kinds of social learning go. That fact has two interesting

implications. One is that the greatest impact of sexual physiological development is on *establishing* patterns of sexual behavior, but not on keeping them going. If you do not develop the usual hormonal secretions and such that produce mature sexual apparatus, in other words, you will not become capable of adult sexual arousal and activity. But once you have developed them, on the other hand, the behavior patterns can remain intact even if the sexual organs which produce the hormones do not. Thus, if you castrate a male before maturity, he will not mature sexually. But if you do so afterwards, he will continue to have sexual feelings and be capable of sexual acts (though his interest may decline somewhat). So—some of those stories about the goings on of eunuchs in the Sheikh's harem must be true!

Of course, this phenomenon occurs only in primates and humans, but not in lower organisms. Castrate a rat, for instance, and you will stop his sexuality cold. The same changes in dependency on the physiology of sex apply to females as to males as you climb the phylogenetic ladder. Females of lower species are dominated in their sexual behavior by the *estrus,* or fertility cycle, which depends on the interaction between some hormones produced by the ovaries and others from the pituitary gland. Estrus, or sexual heat, occurs only during ovulation from lower organisms, and the female is only receptive to sexual activity at that time. As evolution becomes more complex, the fertility cycle has less and less control of female sexual behavior until, finally, in humans it has virtually none at all. Like their male counterparts, human females are more or less ready for sexual activity at any time, in any season, dictated by the psychology more than the physiology of sex.

The second thing that makes it so important that sexual development comes along so late in growth is that **sex-role behavior** is pretty firmly fixed long before it can be expressed in **sexual behavior. Sex-role** or **sex-typed** behavior means activity which is linked to a per-

A lady taking tea.

son's gender—little girls learning to play with dolls, little boys preferring baseball to tiddly-winks, and so forth (more on this in Chapter 14). Sex-role learning sets the stage for directing children's attention towards the opposite sex when their capacity for sex relations matures. Clearly, it is *learning,* not instinct, sex organs, or the internal physiology of sex which plays the major part in determining a child's preferences, revulsions, and responses in adult sexual arousal. There are cases where children some-times learn the roles of the opposite sex so well that they come to feel they belong to it. These people, called **transsexuals,** may become so unhappy with their biological sex that they un-dergo surgery to change it (Laub and Gandy 1973). Even more than with hunger, and despite the complex physiology involved, the study of sexual conduct is clearly a study in the psychol-ogy of sex.

The psychology of sex Just as the capacity for arousal is limited by season and chemical circumstance in lower animals, the sex acts which follow the arousal are also rigidly stereo-typed. The colors of plumage and body parts, or the sweet smells of readiness, or the appointed mating call, cue males and females of a species to each other, arousing each according to its kind and season. So too, the acts of sexual inter-course which follow differ from one kind to another, but within each are rather firmly fixed. Some animals copulate for hours, some for seconds, some with endless mates or repetitions from moment to moment, some with barely one act ending the possibility of encounter from then on, with this or any other mate, until the time is ripe again.

None of this is so with human sex. Its keynote, if any, is an endless variety of situations and possibilities for arousal and consummation, which is part of the reason for the greater inter-est sexual behavior has among human beings than among other species and is also one rea-son that sex is a greater area of potential problems than are most other motives—variety is its greatest virtue and its greatest vice.

Human beings can be aroused sexually by virtually any stimulus. Like their animal cousins, they are susceptible to the lure of grooming and smells and colors—note how you dress, and preen, and comb, and brush, and perfume for a date—but they respond as well to a great variety of sensual and symbolic stimuli, to touches, pictures, memories, a look, a wisp of thought, a sense of tenderness, or joy, or grief—or, perhaps less commonly, but by the same process of conditioning, to fetishes, like articles of clothing or a lock of hair, a chain of daisies, a worn out rubber glove, or what you will. There is literally no end to it.

There are important differences between cultures in the kinds of stimulation that are predominantly considered arousing or repulsive—being fat is attractive in one place, being slender in another, being short or tall or what have you in still another. What is provocative and appealing in one place is repulsive or immoral in another.

For years, it was thought that males were more easily aroused by symbolic stimuli, like fantasies and pictures, than were females, and that females were aroused more by touch (Money 1965). But this notion may have reflected the long-time sexual suppression of women by Victorian standards more than any true difference between the sexes. More recent evidence suggests that not only are females "turned on" by dirty movies, but perhaps even more than males (Mann, Sidman, and Starr 1971).

As with arousal, the pattern of consummation and copulation is as highly varied among humans as it is rigid among other species. The main centers of sexual feeling are in the genital organs, of course, which makes orgasm the main object of sexual stimulation for both males and females. Mostly, it is achieved by sexual intercourse—but this in itself may be done in a great variety of positions which produce different amounts of pleasure to the different partners as much by virtue of the psychological interest in-

volved as from the physical sensations. In fact, the relatively greater length of the penis in humans than in other animals, the more forward positioning of the vagina, and the greater flexibility of the human body which has evolved with our upright postures and opposable thumbs, all contrive to make such variety of positions possible. In addition, the variety of types of sexual partners available to human beings is greater than to other species—so things like homosexual behavior are seen less among animals below the primates, and interspecies intercourse is an even rarer result of chance imprinting and conditioning. Finally, humans use self-stimulation in many different ways as a means of sexual gratification, again setting them apart from other species both by their ingenuity and the degree of their lust.

The degree of sexual activity in the course of life is, like its initiation, partly determined physiologically. The peak intensity among males seems to be in the late teens and early twenties, and among females to be a few years later, perhaps for cultural rather than strictly physical reasons. Even here, however, psychological factors tend to be more significant than purely physiological ones. There is a gradual decline in sexual activity with age, especially with poor health and fatigue, but both men and women tend to remain very active sexually deep into old age if they are positively stimulated and their attitudes towards themselves and their sexuality remain favorable.

Sexual motivation, to sum it up, is complex and potent, involving any number of stimulating physical events from brain or skin or other sense which interact with hormones, spinal reflexes, and hypothalamus, to name too few, in an elaborate process which is finally orchestrated by the brain, experienced in consciousness, and consummated in one or many of the endless list of sexual acts. Which acts come out is so unpredictable from the physiology of sex, even to the extent it is understood, that much of our understanding of sexual motivation can disregard it altogether. This is even more true of most other human motives, whose physiology is so subtle, both in origins and effects, that its existence is obscured entirely in most examinations of them. What is generally apparent is that they are not life and death matters, except as we have learned to see them that way, and that the learning which creates them is mostly taught to us by other people, not just by circumstance. They can be considered *secondary* to our *immediate* survival, and they are *social* in their source or their objective.

THE SOCIAL MOTIVES

When most people talk about *motivation,* they are referring to the secondary drives or social motives. Why do bright children do poorly in school? They are poorly "motivated." Why do poor Black children drop out? They lack "motivation." Why don't you think he stole the mixenblixen? He had no "motive." All these questions are of a piece—they are talking about motivation in a conventional sense, to mean goals or desires or purposes. The quest for money, fame, prestige, social status, skill, and most other things that people call "ambitions," are all of this kind.

All the secondary motives are social, in that you either learn them from other people, pursue them for other people's sake, or value them, at least partly, because of what they do to make you valuable in other people's eyes. Most of these motives are obviously learned, because most of them are meaningful only in the context of a *culture,* and you have *to learn* the contents of your culture. No one has an innate drive to make money, for instance, because money is an artifact of human cultures, not a product of the natural world. So is almost everything else we seek in life.

Some social motives, on the other hand, are deeply rooted in biology—love between adults, for instance, is partly rooted in sexual instincts.

More important, some very social behavior, such as the "mothering" of young, at least among primates, and the capacity for social behavior that comes from a baby having been mothered, seem to have an instinctual basis rather than to be totally products of learning.

Harry Harlow and his co-workers investigated this question in some important experiments with monkeys by raising them without a mother. The monkeys were kept in isolation and bottle-fed. Gauze pads were put on the cage floor for comfort, and the experimenters were surprised to see that the monkeys became "attached" to the pads. If the pads were removed, the monkeys became upset and clung to them, the way a child clings to its mother, or to a blanket. So, in the next stage of the experiment, they created two kinds of "surrogate" mothers, one from terry cloth and one from wire mesh. Both "mothers" had a bottle built in to look like a breast and give milk, and both had monkey faces at the top of the "body." The monkeys with the cloth mother clung to "her" as if she were real, but the monkeys with the wire mother did not. Monkeys which were fed from the wire mother but had access to the cloth mother would run over to cling to the cloth mother when they were frightened. They never ran to the wire mother for such "support" (Harlow 1953).

When Harlow examined the maternal side of the mother-child relationship, he found that monkeys which had no mother were unable to love, support, and care for their own offspring. He concluded that maternal behavior was an innate characteristic which could be seriously affected by the absence of affectional experiences early in life. (See Table on p. 191).

But whatever innate basis the social motives may have, the way they actually grow is probably by a learned spinoff from primary drives in which they become associated with the satisfaction of the former. Love, for instance, may develop by a process in which the infant becomes classically conditioned to associating feelings of satisfaction with food, warmth, con-

Even a terry-cloth mother can be missed.

tact, and so on. Gradually, it connects these good things with the figure who provides them, mother, and feels that satisfaction towards her. Thus babies learn to love mother, and from that grows the capacity to love other people. At every step along the way, the good feelings have to be reinforced and rewarded. If they are not, then the motive does not get extended very far or become very vital in the child's life. If they are, then the behavior becomes more and more habitual, part of the child's character.

This is true of all social motives. As they are reinforced and become habitual, they become stronger, not weaker, or lead into the pursuit of other motives, just the opposite of primary drives. When you satisfy hunger by eating, you turn it off. When you satisfy love, you magnify it. The reinforcement itself creates new motives and new activities.

This is the thing that makes social motivation so different from the more purely biological motives. Social motivation grows, its basic forms giving rise to derivative motives which become more and more distinctive and independent of each other and of the parent motives from which they arose. And since the derivative motives may be fed from many parent motives, the possibility of reinforcing them from many different sides is a big help in sustaining them for long periods of time.

Let us go back to love as the example. I said it may start off by classically conditioning the baby's feelings of satisfaction with its image of mother as its provider. The motives of dependency and the need for affiliation with other people (Schachter 1959) arise from the same source. Dependency originates in the helplessness of the infant, and its gradual discovery that the presence of other people reduces fear and frustration, as well as soothing its needs for other comforts. These positive feelings persist into adulthood and continue motivating us to seek social contact, even when we are no longer helpless. Anxiety, in particular, stimulates the affiliative tendency in most of us. We need others most when we are fearful. First-born children have somewhat stronger affiliative tendencies than do later-born children, which goes with the fact that they tend to have more need for approval, lower self-esteem, and a greater tendency to be shy than do their younger siblings (Forer 1976; Miller and Zimbardo, 1966). By the time a child reaches adolescence there is a conglomerate of motives and needs — sexual, affiliative, dependent, affectionate — all working in conjunction to support its efforts at social contacts and, ultimately, at the formation of adult love relationships. It is a powerful system.

Social motivation is the source of all **long-range** motivation. Not only does it get impetus from the different primary motives from which it derives, but also, as a child grows, it gets a sense of time and develops a memory, which lets it project wants into the distant future and substitute symbolic reinforcements for real ones by remembering past rewards and using the memory to sustain a sense of future promise. In a child's subjective experience, this is felt as **aspiration** or **ambition.** It is the only thing that lets human beings develop elaborate educational systems and, ultimately, scientific technologies.

The longer the range of a person's motivation, the more difficult it is to sustain the activities needed to achieve their goals. To sustain such motives, you generally need to get a good deal of short-term reinforcement, to have your basic survival needs reasonably well met, and to be able to maintain a **psychological set,** that is, a fairly constant picture of yourself to keep in mind as someone capable of meeting goals. This in turn depends on your **self-esteem,** something we will deal with more in Chapter 15. These requirements apply to the accomplishment of long-range goals, like becoming a doctor or lawyer, learning complex skills like

flying an airplane, and so forth. But there seems to be a more general social motive which develops in childhood, much like the love motive, and which sets the stage for all of a person's later specific long-range aspirations. It is called the **achievement motive.**

Achievement motivation

The need to achieve, as defined by Harvard University's David McClelland and his colleagues, who have done most of the research on it, is the need a person feels within themselves "to compete against an internal standard of excellence" (McClelland et al. 1953). People with a high achievement need tend to work hard and perform well on all kinds of challenging tasks, whether or not they have any special interest in the content or skills involved. Their need is a **general** rather than a **specific** motive to excel in what they do.

Achievement motivation seems to develop in childhood as a result of early independence training administered by a generally warm and accepting mother. At least that seems to be the case with achievement motivation in boys. Marian Winterbottom (1958) found that the mothers of high-achieving boys below the age of seven made about twice as many demands for independent behavior on their children as the mothers of low achievers, and were more likely to use love and affection as rewards for responding to those demands. With girls, the growth of achievement motivation is more complicated and less understood (Heckhausen 1967).

One thing that makes achievement motivation more complicated for females than for males in our society is that women who have strong achievement needs run the risk of being labelled "unfeminine" and thereby being socially unacceptable. Matina Horner found, for instance, that bright Radcliffe women reacted quite negatively in an experiment to a story about a successful woman; she inter-

The Changing West, Thomas Benton
The need to achieve builds buildings and muscles.

preted the reaction as a fear of success in these women (Horner 1969).

The measurement of achievement need is not easy, and the method McClelland and his partners have relied on to study it is an imperfect one. Even so, it has led to some accurate predictions about some aspects of behavior. For example, McClelland (1955) did a follow-up study of male college students 11 years after they were first studied. He found that those with low achievement scores were personnel workers, office managers, appraisers, treasurers, and so on—jobs which involved little or no risk-taking or high individual achievement. Those with high achievement scores, on the other hand, had more jobs in which promotion and salary depended on individual success, as in sales, real estate, and self-owned businesses.

If the conditions that foster high achievement motivation in an individual are general across an entire culture, then the effects should be apparent in the achievements of that culture. McClelland has explored this idea by examining the economic development of different countries. In countries where achievement is highly regarded, he argues, children are encouraged early in life to excel. They become entrepreneurs, investors, scientists, and businessman, and their country consequently progresses.

To measure the level of economic development, McClelland used the production of kilowatt-hours of electricity in relation to a country's population in 46 countries, because the amount of electricity a country uses is directly related to its level of industrialization.

Stag at Sharkey's, George Wesley Bellows

The competitive drive keeps things going in sports, commerce, and other fields.

By comparing electricity production in 1929 with that in 1950, he could get an indication of economic *growth* in each country. For an index of achievement motivation, he took 2nd, 3rd, and 4th grade textbooks of that same period and examined the stories in them for achievement themes. There was some relationship—the countries with the most achievement themes in their 1925 textbooks had the greatest growth in electric power use and hence, supposedly, in economic growth between then and 1950.

The generality of secondary motives If you think about it, you will realize that the problem of studying a motive like achievement is not merely one of measurement—it is also one of figuring out just what it is you are trying to study. It is easy enough to understand that someone is motivated to become a doctor, lawyer, or merchant chief, or that someone is motivated to make a lot of money, or to get political power, and so forth. But does it really make sense to say that someone is motivated to achieve a lot ***in general*** regardless of what content the achievement has? If I am frustrated in my life-long strivings to become a surgeon, for instance, and someone offers me a golden opportunity to become an undertaker, or a sculptor, or a butcher, is it so obvious that I will rush to seize the chance or, having done so, will pursue it with the same zest I had for surgery? Not at all.

Just this problem pervades our efforts to understand much of social motivation and, as we shall see in Chapter 14, much of the study of personality. When we describe primary motives like hunger, we have an approximate idea of the domain to which they apply. Hunger refers to food, to drink, to sensations in stomach or mouth, to appetite and, ultimately, to the nutritional needs of cells on which our survival depends. But what is the domain of love? Sexual behavior, romance, marriage, child bearing, rearing? Are all of those outcomes of the same motive? And what about love of God, of country, of mankind, of beauty, of Raisin Bran? Are all these loves the same? Are we really talking about a single motive? It doesn't seem likely.

You can ask the same question pretty much of any social motive. Altruism, achievement need, dependency, the need to nurture others—all of them can be identified in specific situations which arouse us to help others, to strive for some achievement, and so forth. But the idea that these are general motives which we carry around within us ready to express at the drop of a circumstance is not easily proved.

Altruism

Perhaps the most *social* of all social motives is *altruism* that is "behavior carried out to benefit another without anticipation of rewards from external sources" (Macauley and Berkowitz 1970). It illustrates the problem nicely. Altruistic behavior can range from helping little old ladies across the street, to defending a person under attack, provided that the helper is not thinking of any gain. The reward seems to come from inside them, either by feeling good at having been able to offer assistance, or by feeling good at not having been guilty of *failing* to do the right thing.

The situational determinants of altruism were studied by Latane and Darley (1970), among many others. They found that some helping behavior is more likely to occur only when fewer people are present. Other research on altruism has dealt with the effects of social norms on behavior (Bryan 1970), and the experience of guilt about not being altruistic (Freedman 1970). And some naturalistic observations have been made, such as examining the altruism shown by Christians who rescued Jews from the Nazis in World War II (London 1970). Fellner and Marshall (1970) studied present-day kidney donors. Both investigations looked at people who risked their own lives to prevent the certain deaths of others.

It is clear, from such studies, that people do a lot of altruistic things as occasion demands it. What is not clear is that they have any dependable inner motivation to do them.

But it is too easy to dismiss the subject by saying that they do not. If there were never any general motive involved, and altruism were only aroused by the specific situation in which someone needs help, then why would medical missionaries go off to spend their lives in the jungles of the Amazon or Congo, why would people join religious orders in which they take vows of poverty or celibacy and spend their careers in ministering to the poor, why would people commit themselves to consumerism or ecology or any of the causes people undertake without obvious hope of external reward? Why would the *volunteer* movement be so immense?

Plainly, some people develop and sustain very long-term goals along very broad fronts of their consciousness. A child does not, to begin with, have any purposes in its life. But it gradually develops an image of itself in relation to long-term goals, and increasingly sees the achievement of the goals as the *purpose* of a large part of its existence. To the extent that it then organizes its life around that purpose, it certainly makes sense to say that its motivation is general, not specific to a few situations. Some scholars believe that altruism is such a general motive, with roots that go deeper than the social learning experiences of children, into the genetic characteristics of the species. The biological basis of altruism, they feel, has allowed us to evolve into social beings who are capable of cooperative living and of caring about each other, not just about ourselves (Campbell 1975; Wilson 1975).

Aggression: The antisocial motive

It is hard to classify aggression in the hierarchy of motives; it has some of the characteristics both of physiological and of social motives, but it also differs from other motives in either category. There are not just one, but several different brain centers implicated in the arousal and expression of aggression, and it certainly is, in that sense, a physiological motive (Moyer 1976). There are some cases of uncontrollable aggressive behavior which result from disorders of those centers, and which are sometimes treatable by drugs or surgery. But they are a minority. Aggression of most kinds, and in most people, is largely learned behavior. The circumstances under which it is aroused, moreover, and the ways in which it can be expressed, are so thoroughly governed by social stimulations and social consequences that, for all practical purposes, human aggression can be understood mostly as a social motive (Bandura 1973). In fact, it is only when people become violently aggressive under circumstances which are *not* socially intelligible that we tend to think of their aggression as motivated by something gone wrong in their brains or nervous systems. Then, we speak of them as having "gone berserk," and of their behavior as "meaningless violence." As long as they are bashing people's brains out in response to having been angered by them, called "hostile aggression," or in course of trying to get something from them, called "instrumental aggression," their aggression is all too meaningful—and generally considered social!

Some of the evolutionary functions of aggression are obvious—it evolved as a means of securing food, as a means of defense in situations where flight is impossible, and as a means of getting power over members of one's own

Aggression.

208

species in order to control such resources as sexual mates, choice things to eat, good places to nest, and territory to dominate. In our pre-human ancestors, such capacities would have been largely automated, which explains why there would be multiple brain centers and interconnections to handle the many kinds of aggressive arousal and response that would be required by different situations.

What is *not* obvious in the evolution of human aggression, but is horribly plain in the behavior of human beings, is that we have developed patterns of aggression and cruelty towards members of our own species which are all but unheard of throughout the animal kingdom. Whether they are primarily products of biology or social learning is the source of endless scholarly debate.

In lower animals, aggression is aroused either by the incentive to get something the animal wants, as in hunting or mating, or by the threat to those goals or to its safety. When animals aggress against members of their own species, typically, a fair amount of posturing, gesturing, and threatening generally precedes any actual fighting and makes it unnecessary; someone backs down. On the relatively rare occasions when fighting does take place, moreover, the loser or weaker adversary can generally "call off" its opponent by indicating submission in any of several ways. Among cockroaches, for instance, the loser will gesture "salaam." Among some species of monkeys, submission is indicated (in both sexes) by exposing one's hind parts to being sexually mounted. Among wolves, the vanquished exposes its neck to the victor. Inevitably, this ends the contest. The dominant animal takes what it wants and lets the loser go.

Human aggression is virtually unique in two important ways: First, it can be stimulated without anger and without wanting anything which the victim has. The goal may be nothing more than the pleasure it gives the aggressor to watch the victim suffer or to have others watch the demonstration of power. The victim need not be threatening or frustrating the aggressor in any way, nor even be someone the aggressor has ever met. Second, and more important, showing signs of submission, far from calling off the aggressor, may actually result in more severe and merciless punishment. Cruelty, torture, and "lust-murder," as senseless killing is sometimes called, are all peculiar to the human race. Where do they come from?

Some students think that they originate in an instinctive aggressive drive which evolution has buried within us. Elaine Morgan believes, in fact, that an aggressive instinct, stronger in males than females, evolved as an accidental byproduct of some very unhostile sexual advances of our prehominid grandfathers (Morgan 1973). Whether or not her theory is correct, it is true that aggressive behavior is more common among males than among females, from childhood on (see Chapter 14). Freud, along with many other personality theorists, believe that aggressive drives, along with sexual ones, are among our most primitive instinctual tendencies. So do a lot of people.

Whatever its biological *basis*, however, there is a mountain of evidence that aggressive *behavior* is learned, that it is learned from many sources, and that the most important ones for teaching and for maintaining it are all social. Frustration is one important source of the irritable feelings which can lead to aggression, and punishment is another. But neither of them is likely to produce aggressive reactions (they will produce bad feelings) unless children have seen other people react aggressively to such situations and get rewarded for it. Modelling is the most important basis for teaching aggression, and imitation the main means by which it is learned. Once it has been learned, moreover, it is most likely to be sustained in situations where the aggressor is socially reinforced for acting aggressively, or in situations where the aggressor would ordinarily be ashamed to act that way, where the cloak of anonymity provides cover for the hostile behavior (Bandura 1973). Since social situations stimulate the channeling of irritability into aggression so easily, the public concern with television violence is not an idle one. The bulk of the evidence *does* indicate that television violence is potentially an important device for teaching children to be violent, especially if the children are already emotionally vulnerable to such things.

Ironically, the same principles of social learning are responsible for the teaching and maintenance of altruistic behavior. But more innocent human beings probably have been senselessly tortured and savagely slaughtered in this century than in the whole history of the world until now! So it may be more important for us to learn how to curb aggression than how to foster altruism.

Self-Actualization: The purpose of purpose

It is a far cry from feeling hungry and going to the refrigerator a minute later to feeling a need to serve humanity and going to college, medical school, internship, residency, and so on for 10 or 12 years. In the former case, we speak of motivation as **needs** and **drives;** in the latter, as **goals** and **purposes.** Just as tissue needs create the feeling we call drive, so personal goals create the sense we call purpose in our lives. It is clear enough what the mechanisms are that sustain specific goals—they are the short-term reinforcements we get in their pursuit coupled with the long-range image we keep in mind to sustain that pursuit when the reinforcements dry up for a while. But why is it, as goals get fulfilled, that we keep going, keep doing the things we have striven to be able to do?

The late Abraham Maslow, basing his theory on earlier work of others, said that the reason is because we all have a very general motive that eventually becomes the paramount motive of our lives—it is the motive towards **growth** or **self-actualization,** that is, to develop oneself to the

fullest (1954, 1959, 1968). This motive, in his view, is at the upper end of a hierarchy of human motives which must be satisfied in ascending order before it can be felt and acted on. The lowest must be satisfied before the next higher one can be attended to, and it must be satisfied before the third one up can be dealt with, and so forth. He calls most primary and secondary motivation **D-** or **deficiency-motives,** and places them at the lower end of the hierarchy. The growth motives, called **B-** or **being-motives,** go at the upper end. Physiological needs for food, air, water, and such, must be met first, followed by needs for safety, love, belongingness, and esteem, in that order. If a person experiences deprivations in some of these, they must satisfy the deficiency motives before they can work up to being-motives. If you are hungry, frightened and alone, for instance, you must satisfy these needs (for food, safety and belongingness) in that order. Self-actualization, a B-motive, does not function as a state of deprivation. Only when a person has satisfied all their D-motives can they *grow* psychologically toward self-actualization.

We will speak of Maslow's theory in more detail in Chapter 14. Unfortunately, he does not say anything about how the actualization motive actually develops, only that it does. This, and some other flaws in Maslow's writing, have led some scholars to argue that his theory is invalid.

Maybe it is. But certainly there is no doubt that some people, motivated by some kind of purpose, and reinforced in its pursuit by something or other, are indeed capable of pursuing far distant goals relentlessly, sometimes without even a glimmer of hope that these goals can be accomplished in their own lifetime. It is this ability, among others, that gives humans the unique capacity to create and sustain cultures and to construct the links in a chain of activities which carries us and our descendants over untold generations in the direction of far distant goals. Whatever the motivational mechanisms involved may be, it is clear that they exist, and make it possible for us to see ourselves, *correctly,* as creatures of purpose.

If the motivational mechanisms involved are in doubt, the operational ones are not. Thought and language and memory provide the machinery humans use to forge the links of culture that constitute that chain. So, after one more digression to look at a special aspect of motivation, *emotion,* we examine them.

SUMMARY

1 Motivation is the internal stimulation of goal directed behavior. Motives arouse, direct, and integrate purposeful activity. Since motives are internal processes, they cannot be observed directly, but must be inferred.

2 Motives are generally classified as primary, meaning physiological, and secondary, meaning socially learned or expressed. Primary motives, also called needs or drives, are those whose fulfillment is necessary for survival, like hunger. Secondary motives, such as the drive for status or power, constitute our main life goals. A third class of motives, such as the sex drive, does not fall clearly into either category, but is vital *both* biologically and socially. In all motivation, both physiology and social learning determine how motives are gratified.

3 Physiological needs are based on a *homeostatic* imbalance in some body process such as temperature, breathing, or blood chemistry. *Homeostasis* means the maintenance of a constant internal environment; it refers to the mechanisms which automatically correct large variations in physiological activities and return them to usual levels of functioning. When a homeostatic imbalance is so great that the whole body is aroused to corrective action, we say the behavior involved is *motivated.* The psychological consequences of tissue needs are called drives. You have a physiological *need* for food, but you feel a hunger *drive.* The tension of a drive is reduced by meeting the need which aroused it, thus restoring the body to its previous state.

4 It is hard to measure drives accurately, since they are internal states. One means of doing so is to *deprive* someone of something they need and measure how their reactions change with the amount of time they have been deprived. In animals, general level of activity, willingness to overcome obstacles to get what they want, and preferences for one goal over another are all useful indices of drive level. In human beings, it is also possible to measure intellectual and emotional reactions to deprivation. All measures of drive are tricky, however, because the conditions arousing different drives are so variable and because the responses studied are influenced by other things than the drive in question.

5 Drives can be ranked in terms of the intensity of feelings involved, and the amount of time spent on satisfying them. In this hierarchy, sleep may be the paramount drive, with hunger (and thirst) a little less strong; needs for stimulation, affection, and sex fall just below that; needs for social status, prestige, and a good self-image come next; and finally, come the higher-order needs by which we define our life goals. Most educated people consider the less consuming needs more important because their more basic needs are usually so well met that they forget about them. Poor people, especially unskilled, overworked, or unemployed laborers with many children, accents, or dark skins remember the basic needs very well!

6 Hunger motives are physiologically based needs. Hunger for food is not as strong as hunger for water (thirst is a hunger); both are aroused, satisfied, and turned off by very complex interactions between *deprivation* (having been without them for a while), homeostatic signalling mechanisms in brain, stomach, mouth, and glands, the act of eating, and the further action of homeostats which turn off eating and end the cells' need for nutrients. Addiction to drugs or alcohol is a form of hunger which is adopted by the body's chemistry over many weeks, rather than native to it. Once it "takes" however, the hunger of addiction works just like that of food or water.

7 Sexual drives are midway between basic physiological needs and social motives. They are not necessary to individual survival, but the tensions they arouse are very strong. Every aspect of their expression is dictated by social learning, from choice of sex partner and sex position to choice of sex play. People learn which stimuli are sexual invitations, which methods and places of satisfaction are acceptable, and with whom. Once a situation is *defined* as sexual, the physiological processes involve hormonal changes, hypothalamic activity, and spinal reflexes. Sexual activity in lower animals is little affected by social factors. The main arousers are the initial stimuli and hormonal changes.

8 The biggest difference between social and physiological motives is that the physiological mechanisms underlying the social motives are unknown. For that reason, the study of social motives is almost entirely concerned with *how* they are learned. Most scholars agree that drives for money, esteem, and affection, are largely acquired through socialization, but they disagree over whether they have an innate component. Harlow's work with monkeys provided strong evidence for innate affectional and maternal motives. Freud's psychoanalytic theory argued for innate sexual and aggressive instincts.

9 Basic social motives, such as dependency needs, affiliation needs, and aggressiveness, are formulated in very early childhood through the socialization process. Other secondary motives, such as altruistic motives and the need for achievement, are also probably rooted in early experience, but they are not actually seen until the elementary school years. Achievement need illustrates a cognitive motive, which results in planned, purposeful behavior of far-reaching consequences. People with a high need to achieve have been shown to have (1) greater persistence than others with challenging tasks, (2) jobs that place a premium on risk-taking and individual effort, and (3) mothers who expected early task independence and who rewarded success with affection. The presence of an "achievement ethic" in a country, moreover, has been tentatively correlated with economic growth.

10 Complex cognitive motives, such as long-range goals, may be aspects of a general "growth motive" which Abraham Maslow named "self-actualization." These motives can only be satisfied, he argues after "deficiency" or tension-producing motives, are satisfied. The development of self-actualization motives is not described in Maslow's work.

11 Aggression is a physiological motive in the sense that there are several brain centers involved in arousing and sustaining it, but it is a social motive in the sense that most forms of aggressive behavior are socially learned and directed at social objects. The evolutionary function of aggression was vital to human survival, as a means of securing food, defending life against predators, and securing resources. What is peculiar about human aggression, however, is the fact that it can be stimulated more easily (at least with less conspicuous provocation) among humans than among other species and that it often continues far beyond the point where its victim submits to the aggressor. Some scholars consequently believe that humans have an instinctive tendency to become aggressive. Most aggressive behavior is plainly learned, however, especially by children imitating the aggressive behavior of adult and peer models.

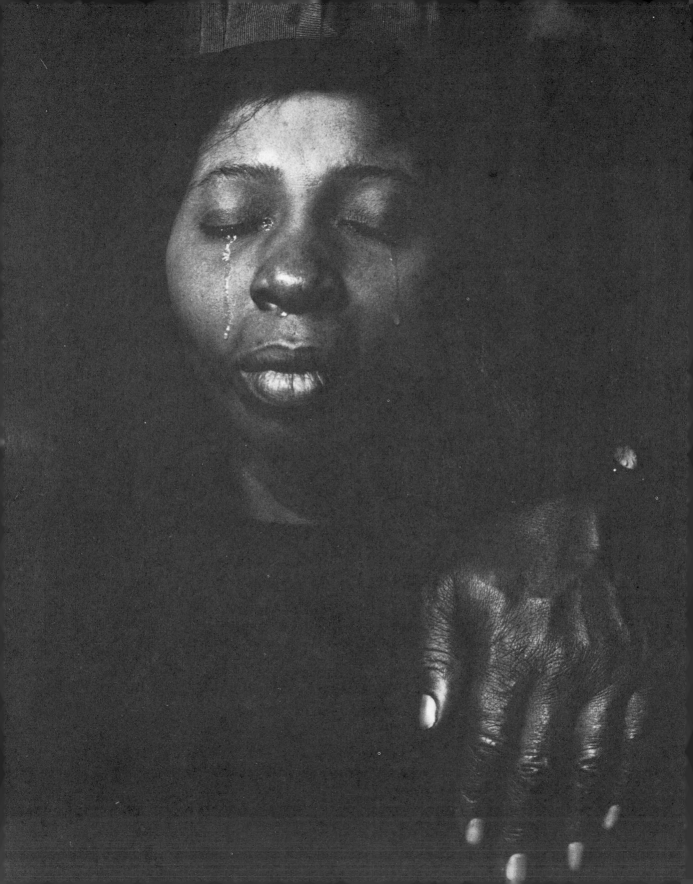

Emotion

8

8

Emotion

Many of the facts of human behavior, and of motivation, would probably be the same if we did not have emotions, but none of them would be as interesting. Emotion is the fuel that fires the human spirit, that gives passion and urgency to what we do. Some people think that our emotions are the most "human" things about us, and that they are the best things about us. They are wrong in the first claim (language is the most uniquely human attribute), and I don't know about the second. Maybe emotions are not the best things about people, but they are the things that make us most eagerly interested in the world and in ourselves. They are the booster mechanisms which arouse us from ordinary consciousness to passionate concern.

The lowest creatures on the evolutionary ladder presumably have no emotions at all, but as species get closer and closer to our own, their emotionality increases. The *general* level of human emotionality differs from individual to individual, and is most likely determined in part by a person's genetic makeup, but all human beings are highly emotional animals. Either some evolutionary pressures have selected emotionality as a useful aspect of behavior (Darwin 1872), or it is an unfortunate side effect of belonging to the phylogenetic upper class.

Most scholars believe the former. Donald Hebb proposes that the evolutionary value of emotion comes from its connection with **arousal** in the central nervous system. Arousal has its chief evolutionary value, he suggests, because

> . . . all conditioned reflexes and mediating processes cease when activity in the arousal system ceases. All the mammal's learned behavior, that is, and all thought processes or consciousness, depends on the arousal system deep in the brain stem. (Hebb 1968)

But arousal also is important because of its booster effect on motivation. All emotions, Hebb says, are "special states of motivation, and closely related to arousal." This has important implications both for personal and social survival. "Anger, for example, is a temporary heightening of arousal accompanied by a tendency to attack. Fear is a temporary heightening of arousal accompanied by a tendency to withdraw or flee."

The evolutionary social virtues of emotion, as well as heroic emotions, are seen in many mammals. Chimpanzees demonstrate tenderness and altruistic signs of concern for one another. Even if two chimps loathe one another, they will share their food or rush to protect a companion from attack. Adult porpoises will support a stunned adult until it can swim again. Hebb sees altruism as a "motivational consequence of complex mediating processes" (1968).

The social value of emotion in evolution has received a lot more attention, in fact, than has its role in individual survival. David A. Hamburg proposes that emotions have had the function of strengthening social bonds to create cohesive groups of early humans. Emotions insure that these bonds will be as strong as possible by making them intensely pleasurable and their disruption equally painful. Just as the all-important function of reproduction is insured by the fact that sexual feeling is intensely pleasant, the equally important function of group cohesion has been made emotionally rewarding. When social bonds are broken, the individual is made miserable, not only by dark moods, but also by profound physical consequences, such as malfunction of blood circulation and of food and water metabolism. Hamburg concludes:

> We are positively bound deeply by a few relations. Threat to these relations is equivalent to an attack on life itself. From the standpoint of the species, these are the critical relations for survival. The physiology of emotion ensures the fundamental acts of survival: the desire for sex, the extraordinary interest in the infant, the day-to-day reinforcement of interindividual (group) bonds (Hamburg 1963).

Interest in caring for infants is an especially critical social function of emotion. Anthropologist Daniel G. Freedman lists the many aspects of this activity which emotion promotes:

> ... the desire for physical proximity, the appearance of mutual watching, mutual smiling, cooing, mutual laughter and play; protection of the young when they cry or become tearful may also be viewed as means by which attachment is increased as may the very act of time spent together. By the time imitation and the first use of words start late in the first year, social bonds are normally very strong and the child is an integral part of the lives of those about him (Freedman 1968).

It is easy, when all is said and done, to put this evolutionary package together and see what emotions have done for human survival. Our capacity for *anxiety* stimulates *flight;* our *anger* promotes attack; our *tenderness* supports nurturant, mothering, and protective behavior. An animal whose two feet carry it more slowly than the four-footed predator can run must be ready to flee with little warning. Hunters who have no claws and whose teeth are short and whose skin is thin must be easily provoked to anger if they are to fight ferociously. A parent whose offspring are helpless and inept for a long, long time must be able to love them dearly if they are to care for them through thick and thin until they can manage by themselves. Emotion served humanity in all these ways. It gave substance to our intelligence, permitting it to work effectively, by giving a sharp edge to our intentions, sustaining them and us through all the cruel exigencies of nature and of history.

So much for history. Now let us look at just what this vital aspect of motivation is and how it functions in our lives today—for better and for worse.

THE DEFINITION OF EMOTION

We commonly use the term emotion as though everyone knew what it meant. But the defini-

Anxiety, Edvard Munch

Anxiety.

tion of emotion is not easy or obvious. Everybody agrees that hate is an emotion—but what about interest? And if interest is not an emotion, is enthusiasm? How about enthusiasm raised to a fever pitch? Love is always considered an emotion, but are love of God, love of mother, sweetheart, candy, and the United States all the same emotion? George Mandler has suggested that **emotion** is not a single thing at all, but rather a "chapter-heading term," a broad umbrella stretched over many related concepts (Mandler 1962). Other scholars would like to drop the term altogether and to discuss emotions under motivation, possibly as one aspect of primary drive. On the whole, emotion *is* part of motivation, so it is not a bad idea.

The conventional description of emotion puts three different aspects to it: (1) a **feeling** aspect, or private experience of emotion—the sadness you feel, the hatred your nurse, the joy you are bursting with; (2) a **behavioral** aspect,

consisting of expressions that can be observed by others, like smiles, frowns, slumped shoulders, or elated activity; and (3) a **physiological** aspect, such as changes in body temperature, blushing, blanching, sweating, weeping, glandular activity, or shifts in brain-wave patterns. Now, primary motives also have three such aspects. You **feel** hunger, for instance, you **behave** in ways that express that feeling, like looking for food, and your body goes through all kinds of **physiological** turmoil in the process. Thus far, emotion does look like any other primary drive.

The difference between emotion and other primary motives is that the objects of emotion have to be learned in the first place and that there is no obvious consummatory behavior that reduces the tension of emotion in the second place. In plain language, this means first, that you do not develop a specific emotion except in connection with some object of it. The experience of hunger, on the contrary, is built into your body and relieved by supplying it with nutrients, whether or not *you* know they are there. But you do not experience love or anger or grief to begin with unless there is some object to love or hate or miss in your conscious experience. And once an emotion does get fixed in your consciousness, it is consciousness itself, rather than tissue needs, which arouses it. The second difference is that when other primary drives are aroused, their tension is relieved by some definite acts—it is clear what it feels like to be hungry, or thirsty, or sleepy, or sexy, and

clear what things can be done to relieve those feelings, and clear what it feels like after they are relieved. But with emotions, the feelings may be very strong, but there is no single definite means of relieving them, and their expression may, as with secondary motives, actually strengthen the feelings rather than reduce them! If you express love for someone, you may then feel it *more* strongly, not less. If you vent your anger, you don't necessarily "get it out of your system" at all. And there is no fixed way to express love or vent anger or dispel grief. The feelings are strongly and easily aroused, but

Sorrow.

The Pieta, Michelangelo

most of the time, they are dispelled and diffused by time and fatigue and shifting your attention to other things, not by any straightforward kind of "tension reduction."

What this means is that emotions have a combination of flexibility, intensity, and pervasiveness about them that sets them apart from garden variety primary drives—they tend to be aroused in the first place by learned symbols rather than body tissues, they get attached to virtually anything, it takes very little to sustain them, and they can be expressed in unlimited ways. In effect, this makes them into what you might call **all-purpose primary drives,** one of whose main functions becomes that of supporting or boosting or intensifying other motives.

Measuring emotions The flexible character of emotion makes it hard to measure in some respects, but the fact that emotion is a rather massive kind of arousal, not a subtle one, and the fact that it is a generally conscious event compensate somewhat for the difficulties.

Each of the components of emotion becomes somewhat vague upon examination. Private experiences such as feelings are hard to describe to others and harder still to measure. Moreover, they can be falsified or inaccurately reported or ambiguous—a word like *melancholy* may mean one thing to me and another to you. Behavioral expressions of emotion also may differ greatly from culture to culture and from person to person (Ekman et al. 1969). Even if a smile, for instance, were a reliable index of emotion, not all smiles express happiness, nor is all happiness expressed by a smile, no more than all sadness is accompanied by weeping and gnashing of teeth. Even when physiological changes indicate that an emotion is being felt, it is rarely clear *which* emotion. The same stomach contractions and discharges of adrenalin accompany both fear and anxiety, for instance (Cannon 1929). And some physiological changes may or may not be connected with emotion at all. The contraction of small muscles just beneath the skin that gives human

beings goose-bumps and stiffens the bristles of animals *may* occur when a person is spooked— or simply standing in a cool wind (Skinner 1953).

Despite all these qualifications, it is still fairly precise to say that emotions are **subjective feelings** and attitudes accompanied by **physiological states of arousal.** Love, hate, anger, fear, grief, and humor are the feelings that accompany emotional arousal in the autonomic nervous system and the brain (Schachter and Singer 1962). Emotional arousal is not a subtle event, moreover; most of the physiological changes in emotion are distinctively *large,* so large in fact that they are always perceived **consciously.** Also, emotional arousal is most often **involuntary;** and as a result, we generally consider emotional reactions as the opposite of rational thoughts.

The physiological aspects of emotion have received a good deal more attention than behavioral or feeling aspects. Part of the reason is that they are relatively gross and dependable. But a more important reason is that virtually every organ and body process is affected by emotional arousal. Perhaps the most common single thing measured has been people's galvanic skin response (GSR) to various emotion-arousing stimuli. GSR is a measure of the resistance of the skin to conducting electrical current, and is roughly indicated by the secretion of sweat; in general, the skin's resistance to electricity drops in response to emotional arousal. The so-called lie detector test is actually a measure of GSR (Fenz 1964). Presumably, guilty people will get upset when asked incriminating questions, and the GSR will then "give the lie" to their response by dropping sharply. Heartbeat also responds strongly to emotion; fear, rage, anxiety, and love all cause your heartbeat to accelerate—and in extreme cases may cause a heart attack (Friedman and Rosenman 1960). Blood pressure also is raised by emotional arousal (Hokanson and Burgess, 1962a, 1962b).

The stomach also reacts to emotional stress. Emotional states affect the flow of gastric juices and the rippling of smooth muscles lining the stomach (Weiss 1968). Conflicting emotion, in particular, unresolved over long periods of time, can bring on an ulcer. How much you urinate, the temperature of your skin, muscular tension and tremor, electrical acitivy in your brain, even the outbreak of psychosomatic diseases—all can be physiological indices of emotional arousal.

It is possible to some extent to tell emotions apart on the basis of physiological changes, but not easily. Two common hormones, for instance, epinephrine and norepinephrine, are *both* produced more when you are under stress. The difference is that they increase at different rates for anger and fear, which are physiologically similar, but not identical (Brady 1967). Both emotions cause a decrease in face and hand temperature, a quicker heartbeat, and a rise in systolic blood pressure. But they also differ significantly. Anger produces more muscle tension and a rise in diastolic blood pressure, whereas fear produces a rise in the rate of breathing (Ax 1953).

The behavioral expression of emotion has been studied least among its three aspects. Animal ethologists are trying now to find the origins of smiles, grimaces, sneers, and frowns in the expressions of subhuman primates (Morris 1969).

One thing that is clear about emotional behavior, in humans as well as primates, is that it is

Melancholy.

generally *involuntary,* in the sense that, if you are shy or embarrassed, for instance, you *naturally* blush, your heart beat speeds up, and so on, whether you like it or not. You have not *chosen* to feel the emotion in the first place, and you cannot voluntarily banish it—at first. But here too, as with so many aspects of human behavior, it is possible to intervene in the natural process through acts of consciousness which mediate between your physiological state of arousal and your overt expression of it. Through careful training and practice, you can learn to control many of the behavioral manifestations of your emotions in situations where you want to "keep cool." Doing so will actually reduce the visceral (autonomic nervous system) aspects of your emotion as well, even if you cannot completely squash those butterflies in your stomach

or make your mouth less dry. Behavioral psychotherapy is largely based upon the fact that people can learn emotional controls (See Chapter 19).

In some ways, it would seem that the third aspect of emotion, *feelings,* or *private experience,* should be the best understood. If there is anything we know about ourselves, it is the way we feel. But in fact, feelings have been studied more by poets and philosophers than they have been by psychologists and behavior scientists. The reason is not so much because the latter are unfeeling clods as it is because feelings are less clear and simple than they might seem. There is no easily predicted correspondence, from one person to another, between the stimuli that arouse emotion and the feelings that result from them. The very same stimulus may promote

Both positive and negative emotions can be expressed visibly in behavior.

joy in your friend and rage in you (Schachter and Singer 1962). There is no direct, inevitable, invariable link between the stimulus and your response. This means that *emotions are interpretive.*

INTERPRETING EMOTION

Motivation, you remember, refers to an *internal* stimulus to action. But the stimulus to that stimulus can sometimes be external, as in the case of people who get hungry from looking at their watch and noticing it is lunchtime. The same thing is true of emotion. You feel emotion in your head, but the stimulus to that mental experience may come from anywhere. Much of the scientific dispute about the nature of emotion revolves around that question, as we shall see. Anyhow, emotion may be aroused in you by some external situation—the sight of a loved one, the frightening screech of automobile brakes, the sound of the national anthem. But you may get emotionally aroused by internal events also, and not just by the physical activities of your autonomic nervous system, which are the immediate chemical source of emotion, but even by memories. You must have had the experience of remembering too late what you should have said in a humiliating conversation weeks before, and finding yourself getting angry and embarrassed all over again. When that happens, the emotion is reenacted, complete with all its physiological components. The same thing happens when you get sexually aroused or grieved by your own thoughts.

The content of your emotional arousal, when it does occur, has nothing to do with where the stimulus came from. In fact, the way you are affected has no necessary connection with what the stimulus is. Emotional stimuli simply do not have fixed meanings which will arouse precisely this or that emotion. If teacher writes on Johnny's report card that he is a reliable, hardworking, and unimaginative child, she may thrill one parent and depress another. If someone says "He's

no genius, but he certainly has character," you can't be sure whether the person being judged would feel insulted or complimented. There is no telling from the stimulating statement itself. Even at the level of physiological arousal, the same thing is true. A stimulant drug that makes your heart beat fast, your palms sweat, and your breathing rapid might seem like a source of pure bliss to you in one situation and of abject terror in another.

The *feeling* aspect of emotion is interpretive; you have to attach some private or personal meaning to it, perhaps even a verbal label, if you are to experience it clearly. Children sometimes discover this, to their surprise, as they pass into adolescence. The same boy who once was contemptuous of moony love songs and silly love poetry finds himself mystified around a girl by feelings he, at first, cannot fathom in himself. He longs to see her, can't breath when he's around her, doesn't sleep well, daydreams about her, and so on. When it suddenly comes to him that he is "in love," all the song lyrics make sense and all his mystifying feelings are clear. Having labeled his vague, disturbing reactions as love, he can now understand his feelings.

At virtually any age or time of life, it is helpful to people trying to understand their feelings if they can learn names for their emotions. Until we know words like *irked, perplexed, frustrated, stymied, vexed,* and so on, we probably cannot discriminate among the niceties of such closely-related feelings. Having words for their feelings can help free children from a gray, private world of inarticulated sentiment into a bright, social world of well delineated feelings. And the same principle has been suggested by some scholars as one of the most helpful factors in doing psychotherapy with adults (Dollard and Miller 1950).

B. F. Skinner proposes that labeling is the second part of a two-stage operation in which emotions are learned (1969). In the first part, the sensation exists in a kind of undefined way because we are not aware of the stimulus until we have some label for it. If a small child has a toothache, for instance, it would feel pain and discomfort, but would not identify it as a toothache unless it heard the label from someone else. **Awareness,** according to Skinner, would come only when the child interacts with others who teach it how to label feelings. In this view, the private experience of emotion is derived from the public one.

Which is only another way of saying that emotions are learned, mostly socially. High or low **general emotionality** is inherited in us as it is in other species, but **specific** emotions have to be acquired. A newborn baby shows only gross excitement when aroused. Early in infancy, you can distinguish reactions of distress and delight (Bridges 1932). Later, anger, fear, joy, and affection can be separately identified. Emotions increase in number and variety as a child grows older. Specific emotions, like specific motives, are probably learned through conditioning. Let us see how.

THE GROWTH OF EMOTION

Classical conditioning, you recall, is the assignment of meaning to arbitrary signals. The flash of light or the ringing of a bell is not an **intrinsic** stimulus to salivation. But if it precedes food often enough, a dog will learn to salivate to the light alone. It has assigned a meaning to a hitherto neutral event in the environment.

Emotional learning occurs by classical conditioning. Human infants start life with a very small repertory of emotional responses to a very small number of stimuli. As their generalized capacity for distress and delight gets more refined, they begin to show **fear** to three kinds of stimuli: **pain, startling** things such as loud noises, and **sudden loss of support,** such as falling. Pleasure reactions, such as smiling and cooing, are similarly shown to just a few stimuli, such as stroking and sucking.

A baby, however, does not remain fearful of only pain, noises, and falling. These reactions get paired with all kinds of harmless, irrelevant stimuli which then become capable of arousing the same fear reactions. For instance, if a loud noise (the unconditioned stimulus) suddenly sounds while the child is looking at a rabbit (the conditioned stimulus), it may subsequently fear the rabbit as much as the noise, even though it did nothing frightening (Watson and Rayner 1920). The unpleasant emotions originally set off by painful or startling stimulation become extended to many other conditioned stimuli. You may recall from Chapter 6, that the process described here is that by which a **phobia** develops. Many phobias are conditioned fearful emotions.

In the same way, the few events that produce pleasure in an infant soon become extended through conditioning to a large repertoire. The unconditioned pleasure response to suckling soon becomes generalized to food, to mother, to all kinds of oral activity like babbling and cooing and, in the adult, to cooking, kissing, sipping cocktails, and smoking.

Stimulus generalization We noted earlier that emotions are always felt consciously. But the events that trigger the feeling are sometimes mysterious to us. We may become elated when we smell fresh cut grass, or angry when we hear a mother softly scold her little son, without the foggiest idea why we are responding so strongly.

The reason is that our emotional repertoire is broadened through stimulus generalization without our being constantly aware of it. As you recall from Chapter 6, stimulus generalization means making the same response to a new situation that you did to an old one that was similar to it. This may happen because the new situation is generally like the one to which you customarily respond or because it has some special elements which are so reminiscent of the old one that you respond to them. In the case of emotional responses, this means that

A newborn baby's emotions are undifferentiated.

Baby in Red Chair, artist unknown (American)

some element in a new situation brings out the same emotions in you that another situation did, even if you don't remember the other one. So—the smell of grass may be linked in your distant past with a wonderful event of some summer day and the mother's scolding of her son may be associated with an unpleasant childhood moment when you were scolded publicly and humiliated by it. The original experience stimulating the emotional reaction may have been forgotten, but the emotion itself is all too conscious and vivid.

The capacity for stimulus generalization saves enormous wear and tear on the machinery of learning. What it does with respect to emotions is save you the trouble of having to learn every emotion all over again each time you get into a situation conducive to emotional responses. Having learned to love mother, for instance, you know how to love. After that, you only need *some* of the same love-producing stimulation from others in order to relate lovingly to them. Otherwise, each new relationship would take an awfully long time to develop, and you would be restricted to very few of them in the course of your lifetime.

The downside of stimulus generalization is that it works the same way for bad feelings as

Longing.

for good ones. When you dislike someone without knowing why, that may be the reason.

THEORIES OF EMOTION: WHERE MIND AND BODY MEET

The physiological difference between emotions and other motives which make the former especially interesting is that emotions involve the action of the autonomic nervous system (ANS). Emotional arousal is generally related to arousal of its sympathetic division, while calm and quiet states are dominated by the parasympathetic division. The importance of the ANS in emotional arousal, together with its geography (it is located in the body, coming from the spinal cord) and its control over the function of internal organs, has caused emotional responses to be labeled "visceral reactions." But there has been a long-running debate about the extent to which this aspect of behavior is, indeed, visceral, that is, physiologically determined, and the extent to which the physiological reactions involved may be consequences rather than antecedents of our feelings. The question of the connections between the physiology and psychology of emotion, ultimately, is the question of the relation between the events of the body and those of the mind. Many theories have tried to answer it.

The James-Lange theory

One of the most interesting is the James-Lange theory, separately thought up at about the same time by the American psychologist William James (1884) and by the Danish physician C. G. Lange.

For centuries, philosophers had known that physiological changes played *some* part in the production of emotion, but had assumed that emotional thoughts preceded and caused physiological discharges. It was generally believed that an external stimulus triggered certain conscious feelings that in turn produced physiological reactions. James and Lange proposed, however, that the stimulus directly produced physiological changes and that *these changes* in turn produced the experience of emotion. James claimed "that we feel sorry because we cry, angry because we strike, afraid because we tremble, and not that we cry, strike, or tremble because we are sorry, angry, or fearful, as the case may be." They turned the traditional idea upside down by suggesting that felt experience *follows* visceral discharge; as James put it, "our feeling of the (bodily) changes *is* the emotion." Previously anyone would have described fright, for instance, by saying that an individual first evaluated a stimulus as alarming and then felt their stomach muscles contract. James insisted that prior conditioning or association is sufficient for a menacing stimulus to produce visceral arousal without being mediated by the conscious mind. In fact, he argued, our felt emotions are simply an extra bonus, a side effect, or what he called *epiphenomena.*

Cannon's objections

The James-Lange theory went unchallenged for many years. Then W. B. Cannon raised some important objections in 1929:

1. The viscera cannot be the sole cause of felt emotion, because even when surgery separates the viscera from the central nervous system, emotional feeling is still present.
2. Visceral changes do not differ from one emotion to another, as would be expected if the James-Lange theory were correct. The same inhibition of gastric juices that accompanies fear also accompanies anxiety.
3. Few sensations from the vicera are fed to the brain; visceral sensations that do reach the brain are too vague and diffuse to form the basis for differentiating emotion.
4. Changes in the viscera occur rather slowly, about two seconds after they are stimulated. Yet our felt emotions well up and change much more rapidly.
5. When visceral changes are artificially induced by drugs, emotional changes do not result.

Denying the James-Lange theory, Cannon and an associate, P. A. Bard, proposed that the true seat of emotions is the hypothalamus, which serves as a clearinghouse of messages between the brain and the body and, you recall, plays an important role in the control of sleep, hunger, thirst, body temperature, sexual behavior—and to some extent the emotions (Bard 1928; Cannon 1927). According to the Cannon-Bard theory, external stimuli cause the hypothalamus to arouse the autonomic nervous system which, in turn, causes the physiological changes of emotion. Cannon and Bard agreed with James and Lange that we "are sad because we cry" —but they thought that what makes us cry are not the viscera but the hypothalamus. The Cannon-Bard theory is called a "neurological" explanation of emotion because it puts the main center of emotional arousal in the head rather than the guts. The source of visceral emotional activity, as of feelings, says this theory, is the central nervous system's response to emotional stimulation.

The Schachter-Singer theory

Both the James-Lange and the Cannon-Bard theories presume that a crucial physical mechanism, either in the body or the brain, translates the arousing stimulus into the felt emotion. In 1962, Stanley Schachter and Jerome Singer made a vital new discovery about the nature of emotion. They found that, regardless of what physiological changes contribute to emotion, our conscious experience of emotion depends very much on what we *think* and how we *interact* with other people when emotionally aroused, that is, on the "Cognitive, social, and physiological determinants of emotional state taken together" (Schachter and Singer 1962).

In the Schachter-Singer experiments, a subject was asked to participate in a study of "vision" (actually, the study was about emotions). He was given an injection of the powerful stimulant epinephrine (adrenalin), but he was told only that the injection would produce a slight headache and numbness of the feet. Then he was asked to wait for 20 minutes until the drug had its effect so his "vision could be analyzed." During this waiting period, he sat beside a stooge who had secretly been instructed by the experimenters to behave in a madcap, euphoric way. The stooge ran around, shooting baskets with wads of paper, playing with an improvised hula-hoop, and flying paper airplanes—and asked the subject to join in the fun. As the epinephrine began to have its effect, arousing the subject's autonomic system and producing flushing, rapid heartbeat, and tremors, he could no longer resist the stooge's invitation and soon was participating euphorically in the sport.

A second subject was also injected with

The Laughing Audience, William Hogarth

An experimental group injected with epinephrine howled with laughter at a slapstick film which left a tranquilized audience bored.

epinephrine, but he was told exactly how the hormone would affect him. When he went into the waiting room, the stooge began the same antics as before. This second subject, however, refused the stooge's invitation to join in. All of the same bodily changes occurred in him as in the first subject, but he did not become euphoric.

This experiment was repeated with many subjects. In every case, the subjects who had been *mis*informed about the injection were strongly affected by the stooge's behavior, while the well-informed subjects all dismissed the stooge as a nut and refused to participate in his high jinks.

Schachter and Singer then did a variant of the experiment. Subjects were again injected with epinephrine. Some were informed and some were misinformed about its true effects. During the waiting period, however, they were put with an angry stooge. He was bitter, aggressive, and insulting. Those subjects who were informed about the drug ignored him; those who were misinformed became angry themselves.

In a third experiment, three groups of subjects watched a slapstick movie. Before the movie, Group I received an injection of epinephrine, Group II an injection of a tranquilizer, and Group III an injection of salt water, which has no effects on mood. No one got special information about the injections. As expected, Group I howled with laughter at the movie, Group II was bored by it, and Group III was somewhere in between (Schachter and Wheeler 1962).

The juke-box theory All of these experiments show that physiological arousal causes *some* strong emotion, but does not determine *which* emotion gets worked up. An aroused subject cooped up with a happy stooge will become elated. But subjects with an angry stooge will become furious. The physiological effect of the hormone is the same in both cases, but the emotions produced are opposites.

A second principle these experiments demonstrate is that emotions, at least to some degree, are **socially contagious.** Happiness spawns happiness; rage infects others with rage.

A third principle, perhaps the most important, is that *knowing* the cause of physiological changes in oneself can reduce emotionality. The informed subjects interpreted their rapid heartbeat and tremor as the expected effects of the hormone, and experienced no change in feelings. Understanding their physiological symptoms, they had increased control over them. The misinformed subjects, by contrast, were victims of the interaction between their sensations and the emotions generated by the social situation.

Schachter and Singer have compared this last principle to the operation of a juke box. A juke box works in two stages: first, you insert the dime, and then you select the song. Similarly, in emotion, a stimulus activates you physiologically (the dime), but you yourself *interpret* these events (select a song) as one emotion or another. As George Mandler has put it, "We do not have to produce different visceral states in order to induce emotions as different as anger and happiness; these different emotions can arise out of the same physiological background" (1962).

These experiments shed light on both the James-Lange theory and the Cannon-Bard theory. James' position that emotions are *nothing but* the perception of visceral reactions is wrong, though the experiments do seem to show that visceral events are *necessary* prerequisites of emotional experience. Presumably you must have *some* sort of visceral activity in order to feel an emotion, though it alone does not determine *which* emotion you will feel, or whether you may feel *any emotion at all*. What you are *told* about your visceral reactions is a very important determinant of what you feel.

The experiments also cast doubt on Cannon's idea that the hypothalamus is the seat of emotion and that visceral states are simply side effects. Epinephrine is a product of the adrenal gland, directly activated in the body by the autonomic nervous system. In other words, your gut is at least as important as your hypothalamus in arousing your emotions.

The precise relationship between arousal and the *affect* (feeling) you attach to it, however, may not be quite as straightforward as Schachter and Singer have proposed. One study which tried to create physiological arousal by hypnosis instead of by epinephrine injections found that people whose arousal was inexplicable to themselves felt bad, regardless of the confederate's mood (Maslach 1977). Another study used epinephrine in an effort to replicate Schachter and Singer's euphoric condition precisely, but it failed to obtain the same results (Marshall 1976). So the information given the subject about what is happening to them may not be enough by itself to dictate how they will feel when aroused. Since Schachter and Singer began these studies, in any case, more recent experiments have continued to examine the role of thinking in emotion. One study on how humor is affected by cognition established that children prefer cartoons at the upper limit of their comprehension. When children are most challenged intellectually, they respond most to the humor of a joke (if they "get it" at all) (Zigler et al. 1967).

Another study has shown that among those people who parachute out of planes for sport, beginners have the most subjective fear and the most physiological arousal just before the jump. Experienced jumpers, on the other hand, get nervous a few minutes before the jump but then calm down as the time approaches. Whereas *some* arousal helps a parachutist perform, a *very high* level is inefficient. A "pro" has learned to ignore many of the danger signals which provoke anxiety, to concentrate on a few, and to plan throughout. This skill at interpreting internal cues leads to a reduction of fear and better performance. Learning to ignore warning bells is called "cognitive desensitization" (Epstein 1967). It is one of many techniques that have been developed for deal-ing with the most pervasive and most troubling of all emotions—anxiety.

ANXIETY

More effort has probably been spent on the study of anxiety than on any other aspect of human emotion, but there is still no complete agreement on just what anxiety is. It is an emotion, of course, which motivates a lot of behavior aimed at freeing oneself of its grip. Broadly speaking, anxiety means *fear,* but it is most commonly used to mean a vague, apprehensive kind of fear in which people feel generally wretched, often without quite knowing why, rather than the easy-to-understand fear which has a specific object attached to it. Anxiety is generally broader than fear.

When people feel anxious, they commonly have subjective feelings of worry, tension, and apprehension, and unpleasant physical sensations as well; nervousness, dizziness, sweating, shortness of breath, mild nausea, and a sinking feeling in the pit of the stomach are common anxiety signs. All of them are signs of high arousal in the sympathetic division of the Autonomic Nervous System as well. In very severe anxiety, diarrhea, stomach upset, and heart palpitations can occur, indicating very extreme arousal. If such states occur often enough and last long enough, they can cause serious illness, such as ulcers—and may contribute to diseases associated with aging, like heart conditions.

The physiological component of anxiety is largely a high degree of *activation* or *arousal,* itself an indication of how awake and alert you are. As arousal rises from sleepy and comatose states to greater and greater alertness, it gradually turns into a state which you can recognize in yourself as *tension;* if it still continues to rise, your tension will turn into general *nervousness;* the nervousness gets worse, if arousal keeps going up, until you may feel frantic. If any kind of worry accompanies your rising tension state, moreover, you will feel anxious, probably with some of the physical symptoms mentioned. It is an extremely uncomfortable condition which, fortunately, blows over after a while. Your body cannot stay energized indefinitely, and high anxiety is a high energy-wasting condition.

Anxiety tends to be learned, like other emotions, by classical conditioning. Some people are conditioned to respond anxiously to a wide variety of situations which would not be very stressful to most of us. So many situations make them anxious that anxiety-proneness becomes a personality *trait* in them. For most of us, anxiety *states* are more transient products of stressful situations to which we have learned to respond anxiously, and we tend to return to more relaxed feelings quickly (Spielberger 1972).

It is not difficult to understand the evolutionary origins of anxiety. The ability to flee is one of the most vital traits animals need to survive, and anxiety, reflecting a high state of arousal, mobilizes the animal to be ready to flee. Since danger can come from many sources, a *general signal* of danger is more useful than a *specific* one. This means, in evolutionary terms, that it is more useful to have an alerting system that makes you generally fearful, with no particular object of your fears, than to have one which makes you afraid only of specific things. In the latter case, you would have to do a lot more learning and generalizing in order to have broadly efficient fear-provoking cues than in the former. This also makes it intelligible that the arousal of anxiety should correspond to *overall* arousal of the sympathetic parts of the Autonomic Nervous System. The sympathetic division, you recall, dominates excited states, the parasym-

Anxiety.

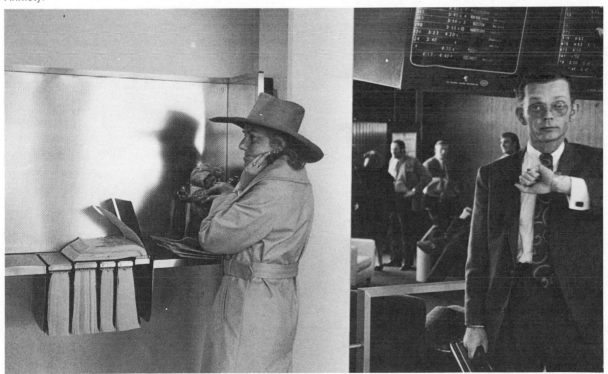

pathetic dominates relaxed ones. Sympathetic arousal prepares you for what Cannon called the "fight or flight" reaction. Anxiety alerts you to the idea that you are going to use that arousal for flight.

The vital evolutionary function of anxiety also makes it intelligible that, as individuals today, we can be more easily conditioned to become anxious, perhaps, than we can be trained in any other emotion. The basis for anxiety-learning lies in the ease with which all kinds of *aversive* or *avoidance-responses* may be learned by classical conditioning. There is some evidence, though it is controversial, that aversion is the most primitive kind of learning in the animal kingdom, found perhaps, in species as low as the flatworms (Ungar 1970). There is also some evidence, also controversial, that the human fetus can learn a simple aversive response while still in the uterus (Spelt 1948). With such a head start, it would be small wonder that we could learn anxiety easily once we hit the open air.

Unfortunately, in that respect, times have changed a lot in the past few million years, and the capacity for anxiety which may have saved our ancestors' lives repeatedly does not serve us so well today. We are as prone to become anxious as they were, but the circumstances that make us anxious are more varied in the first place and less life-threatening in the second. As a result, we are frightened by a greater variety of things, including threats to our good opinions of ourselves as well as threats of external dangers. In addition, it is not often that we can get rid of anxiety by responding to our mobilized machinery with physical flight—and we then become like automobiles whose engines are racing fast while sitting idle. We get worn out, physically and mentally.

We also get a remarkable variety of physical and mental disorders in the course of wearing out. Since many of these are direct or indirect results of anxiety, a great deal of theory and experimentation on personality development and behavior disorders has been based on theories of anxiety.

Freud was the first modern scholar to formulate a theory of anxiety. He believed that, in childhood, anxiety is first experiences as a response to danger signals from the outside world. Later, the child begins to respond to internal sources of anxiety, and this produces neurotic anxiety, which may, in turn, give rise to a variety of defense mechanisms and emotional disorders in abortive attempts to calm down inside (see Chapters 15 and 16). Other theorists disagree with Freud's formulation, but almost without exception, they agree that anxiety, and attempts to deal with it, lies at the core of many emotional disorders (Fischer 1970; Strongman 1973). The variety of treatment methods called psychotherapy are largely efforts to help people get rid of their anxieties or learn to handle them without too much distress. Two of the three most widely prescribed drugs in the world are for relieving anxiety (the third is for pain). And much of the self-help literature which is most popular, on meditation, yoga, relaxation, and the like, is aimed at helping people cope with anxiety. No emotion is more prominent in our lives; none is more in need of control.

THE CONTROL OF EMOTION

Emotionality has been a valuable asset in the evolution of mankind because it allowed the species to survive long enough to develop *rationality.* We have become thinking animals much more recently than feeling ones, or, to put it more precisely, we have learned to exploit our intellectual faculties for *improving* life a lot more recently than we learned to use our emotional faculties for *preserving* it. The task, in fact, is still a long way from finished, and the question is often raised whether our emotions do not actually prevent us from functioning rationally in our own best interests. The question is especially important in modern times because our intellectual development has proceeded far enough to build a technological civilization which enables us to blow ourselves to pieces if we cannot manage our emotional existence better than we have been doing.

Emotions have been especially adaptive, from an evolutionary point of view, for the development of what is called *prosocial behavior,* that is, behavior which serves the interests of the species, like affection, altruism, and cooperation. But there are three kinds of emotion, at least, whose unlimited expression creates grave problems in modern times, however valuable it may have been eons ago:

1. *Anxiety* is an emotion of questionable value because it makes it difficult to think rationally or perform effectively in many areas.
2. *Anger* is a doubtful emotion because it sometimes promotes uncivil, aggressive, hostile, and antisocial behavior.
3. Powerful *pleasure-seeking* or *impulse gratification* emotions, unchecked, are dangerous because they may impel people to ride roughshod over others in their eagerness to get what they want.

This is not to say we would be better off if we did not experience or express these emotions at all. People who are *emotionally inhibited* tend to lead sad, lackluster lives. Their lack of anger or impulsiveness tends to be part of a general pattern in which they also lack joy, tenderness, and zest for living. In fact, most people who are very inhibited emotionally are inclined to suffer from an *excess* of anxiety, at the same time they are spared excesses of more passionate emotions.

From a social point of view, however, the inability to *express* strong emotions spontaneously is a less dangerous condition that the inability to *inhibit* them. The latter condition can be tragic for the individual and des-

perate for society. For the sake of both, it is important to control.

Direct control of emotion: ESB As we saw in Chapter 3, the most direct form of behavior control comes from the manipulation of brain centers, generally by surgical procedures in which tiny radio transmitter-receivers are implanted in strategic locations in the brain. This makes it possible to directly stimulate the brain, and thereby to arouse or reduce a wide spectrum of human emotion, including anxiety, fear, hostility, pleasure, loneliness, and erotic ardor (Olds and Milner 1954; Delgado et al. 1954).

Direct stimulation of the brain provides the one situation in which an *interpretation* of stimuli is not necessary for emotional arousal. But even electrical stimulation of the brain (ESB) conforms to individual quirks, training, and preferences to some extent. In one of his experiments on monkeys, for instance, Jose Delgado learned that when a dominant male monkey is aroused to rage through ESB, he does not strike out at random, but more often attacks a male whom he has long disliked, and avoids attacking his favorite female lover (1970). In such complex situations, ESB seems to work as drugs do. It increases the disposition to a certain kind of action (attack or lovemaking), but does not dictate who will be the victim, object, or beneficiary of the act.

Delgado does not believe:

> that a robot-like control of human beings is possible, because our personality depends on the functioning of millions of nerve cells. The brain is made up of so many factors that its duplication by brain manipulation is not feasible (1965).

Indirect control of emotion: Stimulus control The routine control of emotion, in any case, does not require such elaborate gadgetry. In fact, the very nature of emotion facilitates suppression. There is a time lag between our reception of a stimulus, its interpretation, and emotional reaction. People can learn not to be aroused quickly by potentially emotional stimuli and they can devise ways to prevent full reaction to them. Cognitive desensitization is one kind of emotional learning for inhibiting anxiety. Several more such techniques constitute the main repertory of behavioral psychotherapy (See Chapter 19). Teaching delay of impulse gratification, by methods ranging from toilet training to the self-restraint disciplines which Skinner recommends in *Walden Two* (See Chapter 6), also helps produce emotional control. So do many of the ordinary games played by middle-class children, in which they learn to play "by the rules." Teaching this sort of self-control to children is one of the central tasks of civilized society.

We often think of emotionality and rationality as if they were opposite qualities of human behavior. In fact, they are complementary qualities, which have to be integrated harmoniously if we are to function effectively and feel good in most life situations. Rationality is the thing in us that makes intelligent decisions. Emotion is what powers them. Up to this point, we have been most concerned with the power or motive source of our behavior. In evolutionary terms, it comes first. Now we shall look at the most human qualities which it supports—thinking, language, and imagination.

SUMMARY

1 Emotion is the physiological activity that boosts motivation by investing it with *feelings*. Emotion has had a great evolutionary value by intensifying motivated activity: *Anxiety* stimulates flight; *anger* promotes attack; *tenderness* supports nurturant, affectionate, and protective behavior. The tender emotions have been particularly important in making humans into *social* animals, thus promoting the evolution of language and the other abilities which define our humanity.

2 Emotion is hard to define, but it involves three kinds of reaction: (1) private experiences—your subjective feelings; (2) behavioral expressions—like smiles, tears, and frowns; and (3) physiological events—changes in the brain and body during emotional reaction. All emotions are states of physiological *arousal* accompanied by subjective *feelings*. Emotions differ from other primary motives in that they have to be learned and there is no obvious act that reduces the tension of emotions. They function as general-purpose primary drives.

3 Emotion is hard to measure because of its flexibility. Feelings are difficult to describe reliably. Behavioral expressions have multiple meanings in different situations and among different individuals and cultures. Physiological changes are often identical among different emotions.

4 The changes involved in emotional arousal are distinctively large, so that emotions are always perceived *consciously*. They are also experienced as *involuntary* reactions, over which people feel they have little control. Emotions can be aroused either by stimulation of the senses or by the internal stimulation of memory. When you remember an embarrassing moment, for instance, you may repeat the mental and physical reactions of embarrassment that you felt at the time.

5 Emotions have no intrinsic meaning. Their meaning depends entirely on the interpretation you give them. That interpretation in turn depends on the situation in which you find yourself when emotionally aroused and the label you learned for that event.

6   A baby expresses emotional reaction only as distress or delight. As the capacity for feelings gets more refined, the infant begins to show fear to three kinds of stimuli: (1) pain; (2) startling stimulation, such as loud noises; and (3) sudden loss of support, such as falling. It also starts to show pleasure reactions, such as smiling and cooing. Specific emotion then gets learned by classical conditioning. The infant reactions get paired with new stimuli which can then arouse the same reactions. Just as Pavlov's dog learned to salivate to a flashing light by its association to food, so a baby learns to feel good towards mother by associating her with being fed, held, or changed.

7   The events that trigger emotions are sometimes unknown to us. This happens because emotions spread through stimulus generalization without our always being aware of it. *Stimulus generalization* means making the same response to a new situation that you did to an old one that was similar to it. In emotional learning, this happens when a new situation arouses the same emotions in you that a previous situation did, even if you do not remember it.

8   Different theories try to connect the physiology and psychology of emotion. The most common belief has long been that the sequence of emotional reactions is: first, we feel sad, then have a sinking feeling at the pit of our stomach, and finally weep. But the James-Lange theory argued that our stomach sinks first, then we cry, and only third do we feel sad. This theory emphasizes the primary importance of the viscera in causing emotion.

The Cannon-Bard theory agreed that we feel sad because we cry, but proposed that it is not the viscera that cause us to cry in the first place, but the hypothalamus, a part of the forebrain, that triggers emotional behavior.

The more recent Schachter-Singer theory has drawn a subtler picture of how emotions develop. It says that the viscera produce emotionality *in general,* but the same visceral activity may cause emotions as different as anger and elation, depending largely upon the mood of the other people around us. Moreover, if we know in advance that we will be aroused by a drug, we will not interpret our feeling as emotion at all.

9   Anxiety is the most pervasively upsetting of all emotions, perhaps the one most easily learned in infancy, and the one which does most long-range damage to people's health. It is a general, often vague feeling of fearfulness, produced in high states of central nervous system arousal, which is often accompanied by such physical symptoms as sweating, dizziness, or nausea. In evolutionary terms, anxiety was probably our most important survival mechanism because it mobilized our hominid ancestors for flight from dangerous situations. Today, however, since it is still very easily aroused and we are rarely able to flee physically, the powerful activity of the sympathetic part of the autonomic nervous system which is involved may produce physical damage over many years, such as ulcers. Personality theorists also believe that anxiety plays an important role in the creation of maladaptive psychological defenses and perhaps also in the development of serious emotional disorders.

10   The control of emotion, especially of the uncivil acts that may come from emotions like anger, hostility, or despair, is a subject of great social concern. The most direct means of controlling emotion is probably via control of brain centers by electrical stimulation (ESB), but this method is impractical to use on most people, unnecessary for many, and unethical for some. The best potential for managing emotions is probably by education. Since emotions are interpretive and since there is a delay between the arousal of emotion and the attachment of feelings to it, educational methods are the most promising means of teaching children emotional control.

Thinking, language, and imagination

9

9

Thinking, language, and imagination

If you think about it, you know that **thinking** is the big people thing. People have known this for thousands of years. The Delphic oracle of ancient Greece had KNOW THYSELF written on its threshold as the greatest thing one could strive for. The great 17th century philosopher and mathematician René Descartes postulated, "I think; therefore, I am" as the starting point of all his philosophy. And when people needed a biological species name for human kind, they chose *Homo sapiens,*[1] meaning "knowing," or "wise man." It is the classiest thing about us.

Thinking differs psychologically from everything else we experience about ourselves because it *seems* to be incorporeal, that is, to have no physical substance. Everything else we sense or perceive has some relationship to the physical world. We see, hear, taste, and touch *things,* palpable entities, parts of the real world. Even when we *feel* strongly, though the event takes place internally, we experience physical sensations. Not so with thought. We only think we think.

Probably the main reason people started believing they had incorporeal souls, along with believing that people's ghosts could stay around after their bodies had departed,[2] was because they had never been able to find any physical substance in the very thing about a person that made them **them,** and their spirit recognizable—**thoughts,** reflected and represented by their words.

You don't have to believe in ghosts to realize that it is hard to figure out precisely what thinking is, or where it comes from, or how many different ways it can be expressed. In general, it is clear that **thinking** means doing things in your head, and that the things include **reasoning, wishing, talking,** and **imagining.** Those

---

[1] From a Latin word, *sapere,* which means "to taste," here meaning to taste knowledge.

[2] Ghost means "spirit," not "spook"; incorporeal means bodiless, without flesh.

reduce in turn to **verbal thinking** and **image thinking;** in effect, thinking means making words or pictures in your head.

Thinking is connected with other kinds of experience too, like feeling, and sensing, and perceiving, but it is not identical with them. When you think of a feeling, you are really **imagining** it or **labeling** (talking about) it. The same is true when you are aware of your sensations or perceptions. Well, almost true. Actually, you cannot always separate **imaging** from sensation and perception (see Chapter 5). And you cannot always separate **reasoning** from learning by conditioning or insight.

To the extent that you cannot make those separations, you must concede that thinking is not an exclusively human activity. Other animals sense and perceive and learn and solve problems, and for all we know, their heads may be full of dreams and other images as well, which enable them to remember things and to act intelligently. Animals **think,** broadly speaking, but they do not think as well or as much as we do. The main difference, on the face of it, is that they do not have **language** to think with. This not only prevents them from telling us what they think, it also limits the amount and kinds of thinking they can do. From an evolutionary point of view, therefore, nonlanguage thinking is more primitive than language thinking. So we shall look at it first.

Nonlanguage thinking consists mostly of **imaging.** But both operant and classical conditioning involve thinking also, in some sense — they require your attention, they involve learning and they solve problems by changing your expectations (classical conditioning) or your reactions (operant conditioning), and they are controlled in the cortex of your brain — that is, in the parts where thinking happens. Imaging and language are a higher order of thinking than conditioning in the sense that they do not depend on **external stimulation** and that they can be done entirely through the activity within your head, not requiring the apparent participation of glands or muscles. This gives them a tremendous amount of adaptive economy, which reaches its peak, in certain respects, in the invention of mathematics and of computers to do it. But the more fundamental processes which underly this kind of thinking also partake of it. **Insight** learning, in fact, which primates do fairly well, requires a lot of thinking, with the delay between meeting the problem and solving it apparently taken up by the animal's puzzling out what to do in its head.

Language is the fanciest kind of thinking, and most of our discussion will concern it. It will end up with an irony too, in that logic and mathematics (they are the same thing) turn out to be the fanciest kind of language, in some ways — and the fastest and most intricate logical and mathematical manipulations are done by computers, not by us.

That too, fits the evolutionary scheme of things. The development of thinking is a continuous one from lower species through humans to the machines we invent to stretch our brains and hurry evolution.

IMAGERY: PICTURES IN YOUR HEAD

Images are the stuff that dreams are made of, pictures in your head. An image is not the same as a percept. When you are **imagining** the sunrise, you are not **looking** at it. The difference between an image and a percept is whether you think the thing you are picturing is there or not. If you do and it is, you are **perceiving** it; if you do and it is not, you are **hallucinating** it; if you do not and it is not, you are **imagining** it. The technical difference between a percept and an image, as we are discussing them, is that a percept implies the **presence** of some sensory stimulus, while an image involves the **memory** of a percept, without any stimulus being present. The distinction, however, is not really as simple as this description implies. Suppose, for instance, you stare hard at a bright light for a minute, then turn away and close your eyes. You will *see* an afterimage of the light, that is, the image will remain before your eyes after you have turned away. As you may also recall from Chapter 3, if you get hit on the head and see stars, you are really *seeing* them—the optic nerve is activated. Even when the senses are not involved directly in your imaginings, as in these two cases, imagery is still linked to perception somewhat, because in general, the things you image are things that you have actually seen or extensions and variations on them. Imagery is a creative process, as we shall see, but your mind does not create its images from whole cloth, not even in hallucinations (Siegel, 1977).

Still, you can pretty much define an **image** as a mental picture for which there is no external stimulus apparent. Images occur in every sense modality—you can imagine sights or sounds or tastes or textures. Most images tend to be less *vivid* in your mind than most percepts, which is one way you distinguish them. They also tend to be more **labile,** or volatile, going in and out of mind with relative ease, and often independently of any apparent choice on your part. But there are enormous differences in how vividly different people tend to image things, and people also vary greatly in **imagery dominance**—that is, in the kinds of imagery that they tend most to experience. Visual imagery is the most common kind for most people, but there are some people who have no visual imagery at all. Auditory, touch, taste-smell, and movement imagery are dominant in anything from 2 percent to 24 percent of people whom Morris Leibovitz, Leslie Cooper, Joseph T. Hart, and I tested in one large study—but visual imagery dominated the other kinds for 33 percent to 54 percent of our subjects, depending on what

Imagery

kind of scoring was used in our imagery test (Leibovitz, et al. 1972).

If you think about your own thinking, most of it is not a voluntary process. It can be, as when you choose to attend to something or concentrate on something. But most thoughts, most of the time, just wander in and out of your head as if they were on their own.

The same thing is true of most imagery. You can choose images, of course, conjure them up, and manipulate them. But most of the time you don't. They just come and go as assorted stimuli, in and out of your head, impose on you. Those stimuli grow out of the **context** in which you are operating and sometimes dictate the direction your imagery will take. A thirsty wanderer in a desert has images, if not mirages, of cool drinks, air conditioned theatres, swimming pools, and ice cubes, not of antique furniture, carpeting, and medieval tapestries. In that sense, imagery tends to be somewhat reality-bound — stimulus bound, anyway.

It does not start that way. Infants probably start forming mental images very soon after they become capable of focusing their eyes and their attention — and thus of forming percepts. Their first images are probably vague impressions related in a vague way to the sensations of discomfort and relief they experience in connection with their basic needs. As the infant's perceptual ability develops, its imaging ability must also, though no one can say at what rate. At this time, though, its images are *autistic,* that is, reflecting its own wishes and desires, not a realistic memory of anything. Freud called this primitive mode of thinking the **primary process.** It is motivated by the infant's needs for comfort and not by its perceptions of the world. It has no valid perceptions of external reality yet. Those will come, says Freud, only as it starts discovering that it and the world are separate things and begins to negotiate with it on that basis. In doing so, it begins **secondary-process** thinking, that is, realistic thinking, aimed at problem solving and the

satisfaction of needs, not merely at the creation of wish-fulfilling fantasies. In secondary-process thinking, it learns to use language communicatively and to think rationally; in conscious life, imagery becomes less personal and more a representation of memory. The wild wish-fulfillment fantasies of the primary process get shuffled back into a corner of the mind, to appear again, somewhat misshapen, mostly in the form of dreams, but not in waking fantasies.

There are different ways of describing this developmental sequence, but essentially it comes out the same way with respect to thinking. Imagery develops before language does, and it functions in a more primitive, concrete way, referring primarily to the personal experience of the imager. According to a theory developed by Jean Piaget (1929) and elaborated by J. S. Bruner (1966), the course of thinking starts even before imaging does. The infant first relates to its environment and learns through its movements, which Bruner calls "muscular speech" — by kicking its mattress, by pawing a toy dangling in its crib, by rolling over, or by lifting its head. Its comprehension of its world is defined by the actions it performs in it. In this stage, it can represent to itself only those things that are in its immediate environment. It must be looking at the toy or touching it in order to think about it at all.

Later, the child learns to make pictures in its head of things that it has previously seen — that is imagery. This system is more abstract and flexible than the muscular system because the child can carry around in its head a visual shorthand of all the things it has seen and can evoke an image of a chair even when none is around. Finally, it acquires a still more serviceable system of representation, language. Since language symbols are *arbitrary,* that is, words do not resemble the things they refer to, and since language is *productive,* that is, grammatical rules enable us to create new, unique sentences, a linguistic system can code more

<table>

	Percentage of First Choice Responses in Each Modality (N = 126)					
Item	*See*	*Hear*	*Touch*	*Taste-smell*	*Movement*	*Discard*
Applause	13	73*	2	0	10	2
A shriek	2	90	1	0	6	1
Bacon and eggs	17	4	0	76	0	3
Breathing	4	19	6	1	69	1
Cigar smoking	12	0	2	86	0	0
Clay	27	0	65	2	5	1
Coughing	4	56	5	0	34	1
Dizziness	7	0	18	0	71	4
Fire	67	7	14	10	1	1
Floating	12	0	18	0	66	4
Fog	75	1	15	8	0	1
Fresh paint	17	0	8	73	1	1
Fur	20	1	77	1	1	0
God Bless America	7	69	6	0	4	14
Gasoline	8	0	1	90	0	1
hot chocolate	17	0	9	73	0	1
Itching	7	1	62	1	28	1
Lightning	88	7	0	0	1	4
Mothballs	18	0	1	79	0	2
Nausea	5	1	20	20	42	12
New-mown hay	21	1	1	72	0	5
Ocean	52	25	3	14	4	2
Onions frying	13	10	1	74	0	2
Perfume	8	0	2	86	0	4
Pole-vaulting	63	0	2	1	33	1
Rainbow	95	0	0	0	1	4
Ringing	3	93	3	0	0	1
Rose garden	53	1	2	40	0	4
Sand	33	1	64	2	0	0
Showering	11	17	59	3	8	2
Skating	27	6	3	0	60	4
Slime	24	1	64	6	4	1
Sneezing	6	26	17	2	48	1
Snoring	4	85	1	0	6	4
Sunset	92	2	1	0	2	3
The American flag	86	0	5	1	3	5
Toothache	7	0	72	2	29	13
Typing	11	32	27	0	29	1
Walking	14	3	2	0	79	2
Wet	17	0	73	3	1	6

* The modal response for each item is underlined.

Source: Morris P. Leibovitz, Perry London, Leslie M. Cooper, and Joseph T. Hart, "Dominance in Mental Imagery," *Educational and Psychological Measurement,* 1972, pp. 679–703.

Figure 9.1 Vision is the main source of imagery, but some ideas evoke other kinds of images in people's minds.

bits of information than imagery can and these bits can be strung together in long sequences. Imagery is not abstract in this way and the preverbal child is always stuck with a picture of a particular red dog or red shoe or red barn.

Camera in the mind: Eidetic imagery As language develops, it dominates the child's thinking more and more so that it tends to make relatively less use of imagery as it grows older. This process evidently continues throughout life, though language never replaces imagery entirely. In one study where teenagers and old people were both asked to make mental associations in response to concrete nouns, the young people thought of pictures 77 percent of the time, more than twice as often as the old folks did; the old people responded to words more with words, though they used images fairly often too, 34 percent of the time (Hulicka and Grossman 1967).

In childhood, however, when imagery is still the dominant mode of thinking, it also tends to have a vividness and sharpness which it loses with age. The most dramatic phenomenon of this kind is called "eidetic" imagery, from a Greek word meaning "that which is seen," because the person experiences this kind of imagery more as if they were actually looking at something than as if they were merely remembering it. They will describe it in the present tense, often while staring at a blank wall or page, as if the image were being projected on it. The image tends to last a long time (unlike an afterimage, which disappears in a

In our imagination, we can see pictures of things that never were and never will be. The mind can conjure up, for example, a fur-lined teacup. Imagine!

Object (fur-lined cup, saucer, and spoon), Meret Oppenheim

few seconds), and is generally seen in technicolor (Richardson 1969).

Eidetic imagery is not a very common thing, occurring in only 6 to 12 percent of children past six or seven years, and therefore old enough to be tested reliably (Richardson 1969); and there are some adults who still have the ability. But in general, it declines with age, as language takes over. Scholars speculate that it is very common in much younger children.

No one knows anything about the biochemistry of eidetic imagery. It is easier to guess at its evolutionary and developmental function. The late Gordon Allport thought that its role might be to permit the young child to develop **memory,** that is, to learn what is going on around them by holding an image in mind long enough to study it out. As language ability develops, with the enormous amount of information it permits to be stored in memory with relatively little effort, the need for such vivid imagery would diminish, and the practical ability to produce it would probably atrophy from lack of practice even if the physiological ability remained. After all, you cannot communicate images very well, certainly not as well as words. They are too personal and too concrete. Whether there is anything you can do with them besides having them, and maybe enjoying them, is something we will look at a little later.

Photographic memory In very rare instances, strong eidetic imagery may be retained into adulthood, when it is referred to popularly, and with wistful jealousy, as "photographic memory." There really is such a thing, but it is generally nothing to be jealous of. It has no connection with intelligence—some severe mental retardates have it (they are called "idiot savants"). Normal people who have it, moreover, find it a very mixed blessing. Having your memory cluttered with photographic images is very useful for relooking up a number in the phone book when you don't have a phone book at hand, but cluttering your head with such generally useless images makes it hard to concentrate on other things. This is a real complaint of photographic imagers. By and large, you can do more thinking, and better, with words, than with pictorial images, no matter how well you remember them.

LANGUAGE

The evolutionary gap between humans and other animals is so small, in so many ways, that it is hard to appreciate the enormous biological distance that language puts between *Homo sapiens* and other species and the enormous equality of abilities it implies within our own species. But no other species can talk or communicate with its members in anything close to human language, even if it has vocal cords like ours, even if it has an elaborate social organization, and even if some of its members have mastered some human words (Brown, 1973).[3] Conversely, all human beings have *human* language, regardless of how isolated any tribe or society may be from other tribes and cultures, or how primitive the conditions of its survival may be, or how savage, barbarous, or self-destructive its rites and customs may seem to us. And all human languages are just about equally complicated and difficult to learn and equally capable of unlimited communication, regardless of the different sizes of their vocabularies, the idiosyncrasies of their grammar, and the different things they are used to communicate about in different cultures. There are vast differences between the intellectual accomplishments of different cultures and of different individuals, but any fool can learn to talk, almost, and most fools everywhere have indeed done so, and about as well as you or I. What is more, they do so without having any idea of how difficult and complex the job of learning a language is, or how smart they have to be to do it.

---

[3] Dolphin and whale whistles are partial exceptions, as are chimps using sign language—but only partial.

Other animals have communication codes, but ours is vastly different in vital ways from those of other species (Sebeek 1968): the elements of human language are *arbitrary* (which is why there are many different languages within the species), on the one hand, and yet they follow strict rules of **sequence** and **context** which make them easily intelligible to anyone who has learned the local conventions for what they are and how they go together, on the other. All human languages consist of a **lexicon,** a bunch of **words,** that is, *sounds* which *symbolize* (stand for) something, and a **syntax,** or **grammar,** or **diction,** that is, *rules* for putting the words together in meaningful ways.[4] These are put together to make a system of **semantics,** that is, meanings (Lenneberg 1967).

Words are arbitrary in the sense that there is generally no connection between the sound of a word and its meaning—the only thing that gives it meaning is **social convention,** that is, the fact that people agree that "house" is something you live in, "chair" something you sit on, and "mud" something you make pies of. Words are not modeled *physically* on the things they stand for, though some words first got their conventional meanings because people voiced sounds which they thought imitated sounds in nature—"whoosh" sounds like air escaping, "crash" sounds like something falling with a harsh noise, "bang" sounds like an explosion, and "splat" sounds like Batman smiting the foes of justice hip and thigh. Or so it seems to people who already know what the words mean! Someone from China would be mystified by these words until you told them what they mean in English and that they are supposed to sound like the natural events. The attempt to create

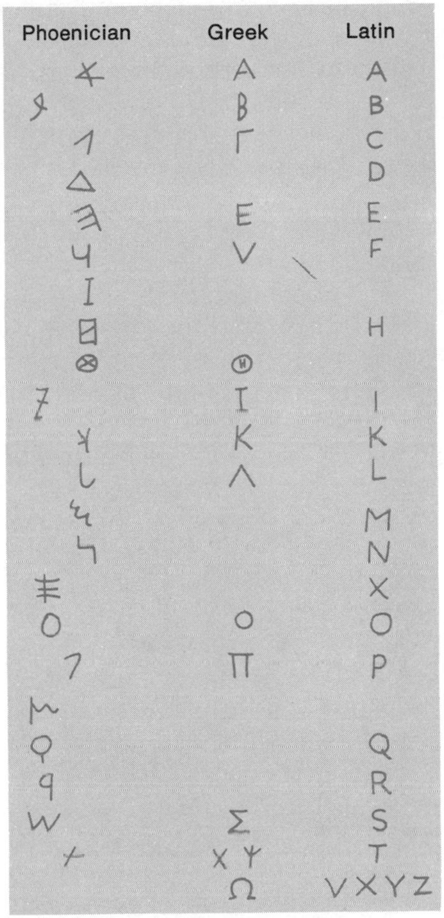

Figure 9.2 The evolution of our alphabet.

such concrete associations of sound and meaning in poetry is called "onomatopoeia"; you probably learned about it in high school English. Primitive written language, such as the **hieroglyphics** of ancient Egypt, did base its symbols on the physical appearance of things (Chomsky 1957), because writing grew out of drawing and was originally a shorthand way of drawing pictures. It often got transformed, not just abbreviated, though, so that picture writing gave way to alphabetical writing, in which the written symbols represent *sounds* (not words)

---

[4] All these terms, and a lot more omitted here, have special technical meanings in linguistics, but the differences between them are not important here. For our purposes, what you need to understand is that a language is a bunch of *symbols* and a bunch of *rules* for combining them meaningfully.

which have to be combined in the right order to tell what words they represent.

Syntax and *grammar* are arbitrary and lawful in the same way that words are—they have no intrinsic meaning, that is, there are no universal rules by which languages combine words into phrases or sentences. But a fairly definite set of local rules, legitimized by *consensus* (social convention), exists for word combinations in every language.

The rules of language permit words to be used in a great variety of ways that multiply infinitely the number of different meanings they can have; they do this in ways that tend to reduce the ambiguities of word combinations so that the message that gets communicated to the listener is the same as what the speaker intended to send. This works somewhat differently for spoken language and written language.

Although most rules for combining words in spoken and written language are about the same, there is more variety and flexibility possible in spoken language, and the rules do not need to be adhered to so closely for communication to be clear. The reason is that the meaning of spoken language is "helped along" by the speaker's use of gestures, facial expressions, and shifts of inflection, intonation, and emphasis which carry part of its meaning to the listener, regardless of the word order. In listening, moreover, we all have a remarkable ability to recreate coherent sentences in our minds out of incomplete and garbled sounds, which differ enormously among different speakers. "Voiceprints," in fact, are as uniquely individual as fingerprints are—but interpreting the sound of different voices and the mumbled and fragmented fashion in which most spoken sentences are recited is no trouble for most of us. Usually, we do it without even concentrating.

Written language depends more on the formal conventions of syntax and grammar because it lacks the face-to-face contact which helps spoken communication along. In some languages, such as English, the order in which words are placed in a sentence is the main determinant of their meaning; in others, it is the way words are **inflected** (used in different forms) which matters.

The important thing to remember is that the rules of language and the amazing human ability to understand it permit vast novelty of expression. We all create new sentences every day that we have never heard before, and some of which have never been said by anyone else before. We decipher the meaning of sentences almost instantly and can readily distinguish between similar seeming sentences that are radically different grammatically, such as:

They are buying glasses.
They are drinking glasses.
They are eating lettuce.
They are eating companions.

We do not imagine that "they" are imbibing glass in the second sentence, nor do we suspect that "they" are cannibals in the fourth sentence.

A three- or four-year-old child is a master linguist and grammarian, though it never heard the words *linguistics* and *grammar.* Simply listening to speech around them, children have been able, all unknowingly, (1) to put together a mental dictionary of several hundred words; (2) to learn how each of these words is pronounced; and (3) to know what *part of speech* each word is—that is, which slots in a sentence it can be dropped into. They speak grammatically, as does everyone else, without having learned it in school, because that is the only way they get understood. The natural process of learning their native language is one in which they get reinforced for using it well. The purpose of training in *grammar school,* therefore, should presumably be to help children communicate better, since that is what grammar is really about, rather than merely to learn the formal

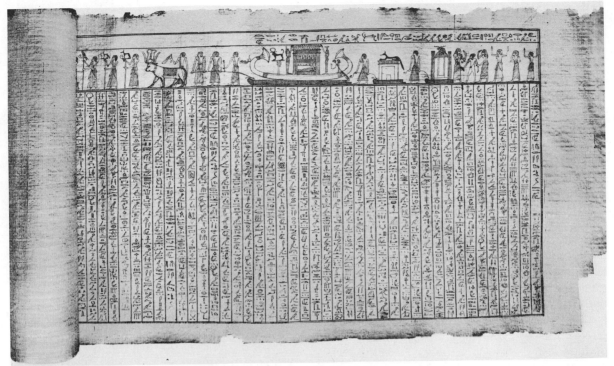

Figure 9.3 The Milbank papyrus, a hieroglyphic papyrus of the Ptolemaic period (ca. 332 B.C.). Hieroglyphics, a condensed form of picture writing, preceded the phonetic alphabets we use today.

rules of grammar for their own sake. That is, of course, what educators say the training is for.

Some people, however, especially members of ethnic minority groups, feel there is a hidden political purpose to grade-school English classes, which is to make minority group children lose their cultural identity with their own groups by absorbing the dominant language practices of middle-class white people and abandoning the pronunciation and sentence structure common in their own group. Whether or not this is so, it is true that some aspects of grammar teaching have no practical value and represent meaningless conventions rather than meaningful contributions to usage. Such rules as "don't use a preposition at the end of a sen-

tence" are meaningless; as Winston Churchill is said to have commented: "This is a rule up with which I will not put."

In every complex society, socioeconomic and political status has always been connected to language use. The rules of street language and poor folk's language have always differed noticeably from those of high society, government, and diplomacy. In both cases, however, there *are* definite rules of language, both written and spoken, and those rules provide the context in which words can be interpreted and made meaningful. ***Context provides meaning.*** This will prove to be true with images too, as it becomes clear that words *are* images, and that all thinking, if not all problem solving, is done in images.

THE ORIGINS OF LANGUAGE

There is a mystery about the origins of language that is all the more intriguing because it seems so impenetrable, on the one hand, and because language is such a vast and vital and constant part of our experience, on the other. The evolutionary history of language is unknown, its chemistry and neurophysiology are barely guessed at, and even the learning of language in small children is the subject of more debate and guesswork than of knowledge. Something is known about the transmission of already developed languages across cultures, which produces new dialects and new languages. Even more is known about the structure and organization of languages, so that a scientific discipline of *linguistics* flourishes, analyzes natural languages, and invents new ones by computers and other means. But the further you go back towards the origins of language, the less there is that can be said with confidence.

The neurophysiology of language

So much of human life is thought, and so much of thought is language, you would think the brain must be full of machinery for running it; it would be, presumably, in the front of the new brain, or cortex, where the most advanced evolutionary functions are managed. The location is right, but the machinery is mostly camouflaged and under wraps, because the role the brain plays in language is hardly known at all. Language functions seem to develop in the temporal and frontal lobes of the brain, and they seem to work hardest during a *sensitive period* between about the ages of one and a half and four years, when the basic words and rules of language are mastered. But no one knows what has to have matured in the structure of the brain for this apparently critical period to begin: "there is no specific evidence that a particular brain weight or specific biochemical or electrophysiological changes are necessary conditions for language" (Herriot 1970, p. 129). What is more, while the brain functions involved have mostly been localized in the *left hemisphere* by puberty, with separate areas controlling *motor* aspects (speech) and *receptive* language (understanding), it is not certain that they start off there. A small child will suffer *aphasia* (language disorder) from a brain injury that damages *either* left or right hemisphere. Generally, it is not permanent or complete, and speech will recover, even if one hemisphere is destroyed. A young enough child, in fact, may learn to speak without any problems even if one hemisphere is destroyed. The brain mechanisms involved in acquiring speech, whatever they are, are very *plastic* (Clark and Clark 1977).

With the neurophysiology of language unknown, the physical evolution of the brain's thinking and speech mechanisms is also unknown, of course. There is no doubt that language is a *brain* function; so it is likewise sure that having a fancy brain helped early hominids learn to speak. Once that started happening, though, natural selection would likely have favored the talkative (which may be why they are so common today), who could communicate better with each other and therefore manage their lives better than their speechless kin— which means that language would have helped to produce fancier brains in the species as well as being the beneficiary of them.

Without knowing what the biochemistry or neurophysiology of language is, there is no way to be sure what role those things may play in the acquisition of language. There probably is some kind of chemical time limit, or critical period, for language learning, indicated by the fact that *feral* children and *autistic* children never do learn language well and that normal children never learn it better than when they are little.

Feral children, you recall, are children who have grown up wild, either abandoned by parents and nurtured by animals and accident, as happens sometimes in places like India, or bound and hidden in a closet by cruel or insane grownups who do not want to be bothered with them, as happens sometimes in American cities. When these children are recovered, long past infancy, they do not have language. And while they may pick up some rudiments of it with painfully careful training, they never really speak adequately (Bettleheim 1959). The reason might be that they have passed the *sensitive period* for language mastery.

Autistic children are similar to feral children in some respects, though their early history is generally better known. Childhood autism (or childhood schizophrenia) is a condition in which a previously bright child becomes psychotic, with some symptoms like those of adult schizophrenia but, more important here, with a general loss of conventional language usage. One of the main efforts in treating this condition is trying to teach (or reteach) conventional speech to the child, who either does not talk at all or uses mostly autistic language with little communicative meaning. These efforts have had only limited success in almost all cases (Rimland 1964). Since childhood autism generally develops in the first five years of life, perhaps the reason language never recovers completely with treatment is because the critical period for it has gone by (Lovaas 1967).

Normal children, on the other hand, have an almost incredible facility for learning languages in the first few years of life. Children of vastly different levels of intelligence almost automatically become competent users of virtually any language. A two-year-old can master Chinese, Hebrew, and English simultaneously without even knowing it is hard to do. This ability apparently diminishes with age so that an adolescent or adult has a much harder time learning foreign languages than a small child. When children learn a new language, moreover, they become proficient in its native inflection and pronunciation; when adults learn it, they almost never seem to get the sounds just right, and always continue speaking it, no matter how fluent they become, with a noticeable "foreign accent." Finally, when a small child learns a language, then moves to a place where some other language is spoken, and forgets the first one, they will relearn it much more quickly in adulthood than they could learn it from scratch, even if they forgot every word they had learned in childhood.

All these facts seem to support the notion that there is a sensitive period in childhood during which language-learning ability reaches its maturational peak, when it is possible to learn the principles of all language, and of many individual languages, with greater ease than at any other time of life. A large vocabulary and the ability to talk in complicated sentences all come later, but the fundamentals are grasped fastest and best in those tender years. After that, all tongues besides your own may seem "foreign," and learning them is a struggle.

Nature-nurture almost revisited: The Chomsky-Skinner controversy

If the maturational or sensitive period notion is right, then there must be some innate factor involved in language ability. Noam Chomsky and some other scholars think there is; Chomsky believes that the human brain is genetically programmed to create and understand language so that an innate linguistic capability exists which prepares a child to be competent in all languages (1968). This ability ripens in the second year or so of life and stays in bloom for a couple years more, gradually fading in later childhood and adolescence to the point where language learning takes the same kind of effort as learning history or mathematics or chemistry.

If competence in all languages is genetically programmed, then all languages must be basically similar. Chomsky argues that there is a "universal grammar" governing the "deep structure" (basic characteristics) of all natural languages, that is, a universal set of rules for producing all meanings, sounds, and grammar. A small child is able to learn the complex structure of its own language, or of several different languages if exposed to them, because a "general theory" of language is built into its brain, that is, a program for understanding how language works.

But that is all unproved speculation, and there is a big argument about whether language learning is really an innate ability. The alternative view is that language is initially learned like many other things, by conditioning. In that case, it would make no difference whether languages all had the same basic structure or not because your actually learning them would depend entirely on being exposed to the stimulation of words, sounds, and grammar, and being reinforced for using them. The chief advocate of this theory is B. F. Skinner, who thinks that operant conditioning accounts for virtually all of language learning. Most scholars do not agree with him. A conditioning theory of language would not explain any of the sensitive period phenomena we just discussed. It might say, on the contrary, that language learning would become easier with age, if you were exposed to it a lot, because the use of language would generalize and reinforcements for it increase. Also, it would not easily explain *novelty* in language, that is, how children learn to invent totally new phrases, sentences, and ideas to which they have had no direct associations or rewards. Finally, it would not explain why everyone's linguistic **competence** is better than their **performance,** that is, why all of us understand all kinds of complex sentences and ideas we hear or read without ever being able to compose such things in our own speech and writing. Our linguistic performance is only a small sample of our linguistic competence. A strict reinforcement theory of language would say that competence is a direct result of performance, in language learning as in ice skating, so there should not be a great gap between them. But in language there is.

The argument is not entirely one-sided though, because even if children are endowed with a "prewired" system that makes language learning swift and sure, *language still has to be learned,* and the learning itself makes heavy use of both classical and operant conditioning, and of imitation. Even linguists who think language is innate agree that only the **predisposition** to acquire language is genetic; to be realized, the disposition must be activated through experience. That experience involves an interaction between maturation and learning.

The sequence of language learning

At birth a baby makes indiscriminate cries, grunts, and breathing noises. Within a month, it makes different sounds for discomfort and contentment. About three months later, it starts to babble and coo. Around the ninth month, it begins to imitate sounds made by other people, and soon after it can imitate distinct syllables and even simple words; by the age of 18 months, it can say several words (McCarthy 1946). Then,

I CANNOT ALWAYS ARTICULATE
THE CONCEPTS I FORMULATE.

I CANNOT ALWAYS
EXPRESS MY IDEAS.

Figure 9.4 Linguistic competence is greater than performance. You can *understand* the fancy first sentence all right, but you would probably *make up* something closer to the second one.

By five or six, much of what children say is indistinguishable from adult speech.

no longer imitating, but now inventing, it starts stringing words together to form short, telegraphic sentences that do not yet amount to much, like "see boy." Typically, they omit auxiliary verbs (*do, have, will*), articles (*the, a*), and determiners (*this, that*), and often use unconventional grammar, like "you bye-bye go." Around two or two and a half years, although still using very short sentences, children start to say some "little" words like auxiliary verbs and pronouns (*he, she*); soon after, they start using them in many contexts, adding more and more detail to their utterances until, by age five or six, much of what they say is indistinguishable from adult speech. At that point, a child's language has become very much like an adult's (Berko 1958). It has learned the fundamentals, doing so by a process which seems to follow the same course in every language (Clark and Clark 1977).

The different learning processes involved operate simultaneously almost from the beginning. At the very first, however, *imitation* is the

tool for language acquisition, coupled first with classical conditioning, then with operant conditioning. The babbling and cooing period prepares the infant for imitating sounds. Maturing control of its vocal muscles permits it to produce more and more varied sounds and to reproduce many of them over and over. Sensing its own muscle movements and hearing the sounds they produce, the child learns the close correlation between the muscle contractions and the resultant noises.

It is then able to imitate. It learns to pattern its own vocal responses after the adult speech it hears around it, and thus slowly acquires the *phonology,* i.e., the intonation and pronunciation pattern of its native language. As soon as imitation begins, and the infant parrots adult sounds, classical conditioning comes into play. It is the process by which imitative sounds begin to have meaning.

An infant imitates sounds long before it could know what they mean. Its first "speech" is no different than the sort of "speech" made by a

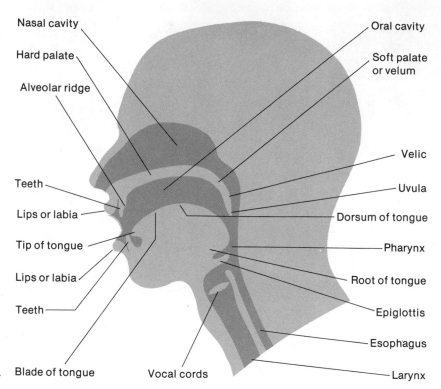

Nasal cavity

Hard palate

Alveolar ridge

Teeth

Lips or labia

Tip of tongue

Lips or labia

Teeth

Blade of tongue

Vocal cords

Oral cavity

Soft palate or velum

Velic

Uvula

Dorsum of tongue

Pharynx

Root of tongue

Epiglottis

Esophagus

Larynx

Figure 9.5 Diagrammatic view of the oral cavity, showing the organs involved in speech sounds.

parrot or mynah bird. Just as a talking bird is rewarded with food or affectionate tickles under the chin for saying "Polly," so a baby is rewarded by milk, attention, handling, and warmth for its first attempts at reproducing human speech.

The uses of magical thinking: Mowrer's autism theory It is easy to see how, by classical conditioning, the infant associates the sound of "bottle" with the sight of it or with the taste of milk. Like Pavlov's dog with the bell, our infant would soon start to perk up at the sound of "bottle" alone, without actually seeing the thing. That explains how the word would start to have meaning. But what makes the child start to *imitate,* that is, *to say the word itself,* instead of just responding to it? For that matter, what makes Polly Parrot do it?

No one knows. But O. H. Mowrer (1950) has advanced an ingenious theory to account for

this phenomenon in birds, people, and seeing-eye dogs. Mowrer suggests that the infant starts to say "bottle" because, in associating the sound with the bottle, it *fails to understand* that they are not the same. It has no ability to distinguish reality from its own perceptions, in this *autistic,* or *primary process* phase of development, and since the sound of "bottle" has always been followed by milk in the past, it thinks that it will be now, too. It therefore makes the sound, says Mowrer, in a magical effort to relieve its hunger. It is not really calling mother to give it the bottle, but calling the magic word from which bottle, milk, and comfort should automatically result. Even a dumb bird like a parrot can learn to do that, says Mowrer, because at this point, the word is merely an automatic fantasied need-reducing mechanism. And the reason the infant's magical effort does not extinguish, and it keeps on imitating sounds, is because mother *does* treat them as calls to mother, brings the bottle, which reinforces the fantasy, and applauds baby for having said a word, which reinforces it still more. By the time the infant wises up enough to realize that saying words will not magically make its wishes come true, it is too late to forget them. It has already learned to speak and is getting other kicks from it. By now, operant conditioning has taken a firm hold on language learning.

Rewarding baby talk: Operant conditioning of language When a child utters sounds that parents want to hear, mostly meaning sounds that they imagine to approximate words, they respond with pleasure and excitement, which positively reinforces it. As it uses speech-like sounds more, its parents approve the ones that approach correct meaning and pronunciation. Irrelevant or incorrect responses get extinguished by being ignored. A great deal of verbal behavior gets shaped this way. Even when children first begin to use words by association, they *continue* to use words they have already chanced upon and improve their mastery of them by operant conditioning (Rheingold et al. 1959). To some extent, the growth of more elaborate speech patterns also occurs by operant conditioning, with each new usage requiring reinforcement for its mastery. In general, though, a child accrues vocabulary much more slowly than grammatical rules, suggesting that there is more than just reinforcement involved. Children use words more freely than do adults, and kids do not find a sentence like "The stove sweats" particularly strange, which is why children's fantasy stories exhibit this sort of semantic flexibility.

There is no stage of language learning, from here on, in which operant conditioning is *not* involved, from learning to talk in complex sentences to using or avoiding contractions or slang to writing poetry or psychology books or dirty words on bathroom walls. In other words, there is no aspect of language use which is unaffected by being rewarded or ignored or punished. Insofar as language is a communicative skill, it could hardly be more subject to the principles of reinforcement.

At the same time, there is a great deal of language use which cannot be explained *only* in terms of reinforcement theory. Most sentences that most people say are probably new. Most creative use of language could not have been predicted from any knowledge of the reinforcement history of the creator's language patterns. And most thought, which is the thing language is used most for, depends on **concepts,** which grow and flourish, once planted, without benefit of any known reward.

The social history of language

The origins of individual language are unknown, but a good deal is known about how existing languages change, and enough is known about the total anatomy of language to easily make up **artificial** languages to replace **natural** ones. Getting people to use them is another story.

Universal languages It has long been popular, among good-hearted, if naive students of human affairs, to think that a lot of the misunderstanding, conflict, and antagonism among our species would disappear if we all "spoke the same language," literally. René Descartes, it seems, first proposed that universal languages should be invented for everyone to speak. Since then, about 600 such languages have been devised, but only three seem to have gotten anywhere: **interlingua,** a written language used for scientific communication; **Volapük,**[5] now extinct, and **Esperanto** (Pei 1967). Of these, Esperanto is by far the most prominent.

Esperanto, meaning "hopeful," was the pen name of Ludovic Zamenhoff, a doctor from Bialystok, Poland[6], who published his new

[5] Yes, Volapük!

[6] Bialystok, now part of Russia, is also the alleged birthplace of the "Bialystoker," a breakfast roll with onions.

language in 1887. It uses the Roman alphabet, but omits the letters q, w, x, and y. Most of its words are common ones in the leading languages of Europe. Its pronunciation is perfectly regular, with all words accented on the next to last syllable. Its grammatical rules have no exceptions; all nouns, for instance, end in "o." It is easy to learn and use. About 8 million people speak Esperanto, there are thousands of books translated into it, and about 100 newspapers and magazines are published in Esperanto in around 30 countries (Richards 1967).

Still, Esperanto is a failure, on balance, as all the made-up languages before it have been. As for preventing strife and promoting human understanding, the biggest problems are probably not linguistic to begin with: the American Civil War, all of whose antagonists spoke the same language, was the bloodiest conflict in history, and civil wars are typically far more ferocious and bloodthirsty than others. As for general convenience, it seems that most people do not want to have to learn a universal language, or any language at all, for that matter. Their own language seems natural to them. It *is*, though that very fact makes it difficult and "foreign" to others.

Natural language A natural language is one which grows up without anyone planning it, by being spoken rather than being composed. Like anything which grows, natural languages are *always* changing, and nothing about them is absolutely regular and precise. Grammatical rules have exceptions, spelling is not always what the spoken words sound like, and the vocabulary in the dictionaries can never quite keep up with the new words and phrases that are born on the street. Natural language is full of **idioms,** peculiarities of expression and meaning which make sense to the users of the language but seem strange to people who are just learning it.

Natural language changes constantly, because language is a flexible instrument and people are flexible and inventive creatures, whose needs and interests change. Spoken language always changes faster than written

Figure 9.6 Examples of cognate words in different languages.

English	Swedish	Danish	Dutch	German
arm	arm	Arm	arm	der Arm
book	bok	Bog	boek	das Buch
bread	bröd (n)	Brød	brood	das Brot
fish	fisk	Fisk	visch	der Fisch
ice	is	Is	ijs	das Eis
life	liv (n)	Liv	leven	das Leben
oven	ugn	Ovn	oven	der Ofen
smith	smed	Smed	smid	der Schmied
stone	sten	Sten	steen	der Stein

English	French	Spanish	Portuguese	Italian
flower	la fleur	la flor	a flor	il fiore
fountain	la fontaine	la fuente	a fonte	la fontana
language	la langue	la lengua	a língua	la lingua
marriage	le mariage	el matrimonio	o matrimónio	il matrimonio
memory	la memoire	la memoria	a memoria	la memoria
mustard	la moutarde	la mostaza	a mostarda	la mostarda
painter	le peintre	el pintor	o pintor	il pittore
salmon	le saumon	el salmón	o salmão	il salmone
surprise	la surprise	la sorpresa	a surpresa	la sorpresa

language because it is more flexible to begin with; writing freezes language into permanent form by the fact that it is structured. It tends to reflect high fashion speech of its own day, which may be obsolete tomorrow. That is why English spelling, for instance, seems to be so cockeyed—words like "night," "cough," and "Worcestershire sauce" are still written in ways that reflect pronunciations which have long since disappeared. It is also why the poetry of Goeffrey Chaucer may sound like a foreign language to you. The more widespread knowledge of written language is, however, and the better and faster the communication of spoken language is, the more **standardized** language use becomes. You can read the Declaration of Independence as easily today as you could two centuries ago because standards of speech and writing in English have changed little in the interim. Radio and television are doing the same thing today for standardizing pronunciation.

In any case, the criterion of use and of change is *fashion,* nothing else. It is true that some constructions are clearer communications than others, but that is no guarantee that they will be "correct" by the only standards that matter in language—namely, how people speak.

The way people speak changes gradually in different ways. Some **slang** and other kinds of new or specialized terminology called **argot,** or **jargon,** become so popular that it gets absorbed into fashionably "correct" usage —for instance, "feedback" or "input," common words today, were strictly technical terms a generation ago. Also, fashions change, sometimes for no obvious reasons—"you" was exclusively a term of formal, polite address in spoken English five centuries ago, as **"usted"** is in Spanish today.[7] Words drop out of use, or change their meaning over time, and grammatical practices shift unexplainably—you

___
[7] That is why Quakers (Society of Friends) say "thee" and "thou", these were the familiar forms, used for friends and family.

still say "bedeviled" and "beguiled;" but not "beshiten" or "besotten." You use "fond" to mean "devoted" today, where it meant "foolish" a couple of centuries back. And so forth, without end. Living language changes.

The propagation of language

There are two variants of this process which produce such dramatic changes in language, over several generations or centuries, that the product constitutes a new language altogether. These are **geographic isolation** and **foreign invasion.**

Isolation For most of human history, geographic isolation has been the chief means of creating new natural languages. When a group of people migrates to an isolated place, the natural changes that occur in its language are not influenced by the changes occurring in the parent group from which it came. So the form the changes take differs more and more from the original; first, it becomes a **dialect,** that is, a recognizable variant of the original. As it continues changing, though, the original language does too—until eventually they are both **cognate** languages, that is, language cousins, both based on the same historical mother tongue.

This process among languages is the equivalent of asexual reproduction among living species. As with reproduction, it is the most primitive way for a new language to develop. Anyway, **families** of languages grow up this way. Thus, the hundreds of dialects of the Indian subcontinent are mostly related to each other and traceable back to early Indo-European mother tongues, one of which is frozen in the written form of **Sanskrit.** And so may hundreds of African languages be traced back to **Bantu,** which in turn is part of a huge family of languages called the **Niger-Congo** family (Long 1971).

Invasion Foreign invasion is a faster and more dramatic means of creating new languages. It parallels sexual reproduction because it comes from the merger of two mature languages with each other. As with reproduction, the outcome is generally a richer product than would otherwise result. Languages which grow in isolation tend to be narrower and less expressive than languages born of mixing cultures. Since the mixing process is rarely a placid one, moreover, and generally involves a lot of rape, murder, pillage, and commercial exploitation, foreign invasion is the way new languages grow among advanced, civilized societies.

Virtually all modern languages have developed by a combination of isolation and invasion. French, Portugese, Spanish, Italian and Romanian, for instance, are all called *Romance* languages because they are variants of Latin, sired by Roman conquests. The Romans invaded each of the areas where those languages are now spoken, and colonized them with veterans of the Imperial Legions. They con-

When the Romans carried off the Sabine women, the Latin language made strides.

The Rape of the Sabine Women, Nicholas Poussin

sorted with the local folks, communicating at first by a *pidgin* or *patois* of Latin and the local tongue, i.e., a *trade language* which makes commerce and seduction possible. The pidgin was mostly Latin, of course, because conquerors always do most of the talking and the people they enslave do most of the listening. As veterans settled in, though, increasingly they married local girls, and each party tended to become more fluent in the other's tongue, meaning that the girl learned Latin and the man learned a little of her language. To the children of these unions, the hodgepodge of their parents was *itself* a mother tongue, which we would now call a *creole* language. The process did not take just one generation, of course, but hundreds of years. In the first few generations after the conquest, the prestige speech was simply Latin, infiltrated more and more by new words and odd pronunciation. As communication gradually collapsed across the Roman Empire, however, and the isolation of the colonies from Rome increased, the dialect evolved into a separate tongue. The more isolated the colony was from contact with any other cultures, the more its dialect continued to resemble the Latin of the Empire — so modern Romanian is much more like ancient Latin than French is.

English was born in much the same way. The Romans conquered the Celts of Britannia, and Latin dominated Celtic, which gradually disappeared (except in Scotland and Ireland, beyond the reach of the Romans, where modern Gaelic still preserves much of the ancient tongue). As the Empire collapsed, Roman Britain was invaded so many times by nearby Germanic neighbors, Jutes (Danes), and Angles and Saxons, over the next few centuries, that the people knew themselves as *Saxons* and their tongue as *English* a thousand years ago, and Latin remained a living language only in the Church. Then came the Norman conquest of 1066, and the whole thing started over, with Norman French now imposing itself on the very Teutonic native English. In this case, however, French did not dominate English, partly because the Normans and English hated each other for a long time and therefore did not intermarry quickly. French was the language of the nobility and the court, and English of the people, who were largely serfs. But the Norman conquerors soon settled in England and ruled Normandy from there, instead of vice versa, so their connections with their English subjects grew and with their French cousins waned, while English remained the dominant *vernacular* (popular language). Since Latin was the language of the church and, therefore, of most learning anyway, French never had a chance on that score either, so it never became widely spoken. The common people learned some French, but the nobles learned more English. Scholars consorted in Latin, and plain folks in bed and marketplace. A few learnéd treatises and many modern Englishmen resulted, speaking a language whose lexicon is mostly of Latin parentage and whose grammar is largely Germanic.

The proportions of native language and invading tongue which go into the language blend depend on how numerous and ruthless the invaders are, how long they stay, and what ways they mingle with the native people. The more they impose themselves, the more their language will dominate the mix. But in any case, the sequence of development always goes from two languages to pidgin to creole to forgetting there ever was a different mother tongue. *All languages,* in other words, *are creoles!*

The politics of language If you understand that all languages are really creoles, then you will understand also that no language is basically superior to any other, no more than any tribe or nation or race is inherently superior to any other. You can then face the fact that language is just as much a political weapon and a socio-economic tool in people's lives as are wealth or social station. The tongues people speak, and the way they speak them, have al-

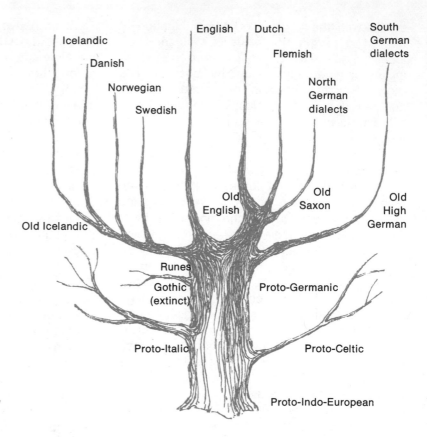

Figure 9.7 A diagram of the family tree of Germanic languages.

Icelandic
Danish
Norwegian
Swedish
English
Dutch
Flemish
South German dialects
North German dialects
Old English
Old Saxon
Old High German
Old Icelandic
Runes
Gothic (extinct)
Proto-Germanic
Proto-Italic
Proto-Celtic
Proto-Indo-European

ways marked their social positions almost everywhere and often indicated the limits of the mobility they could have within society. They still do.

A *pidgin* develops, for instance, primarily to meet the needs of the intruding group, not of the natives on whom it is used. The foreign tongue dominates the pidgin to the extent that the intruders dominate the relationship. The more the native population needs to please them, the more it learns of their language; and if the prestige and opportunity associated with the invader's language is great enough, they learn it well, so that the pidgin or creole which results is far more a dialect of the invader language than a rich blend of the two. It becomes like the horse-and-rabbit stew whose proportions are one horse to one rabbit. A few languages have be-

come *lingua francas,* or international commercial languages, in this way, the path of language generally following the march of empires. So Greek became a lingua franca after Alexander the Great, Latin under the Romans, and Spanish, French, and English when the discoverers of the New World began carving empires out of the whole world.

Americans are more familiar with the status aspects of language in the effects of accent and pronunciation than in the competition of different tongues. English is so much the dominant language of this country that first generation immigrants to the United States almost always start to learn it, and their children are often embarrassed that they speak it with a foreign accent. Even among native-born Americans, however, there is a widespread association in

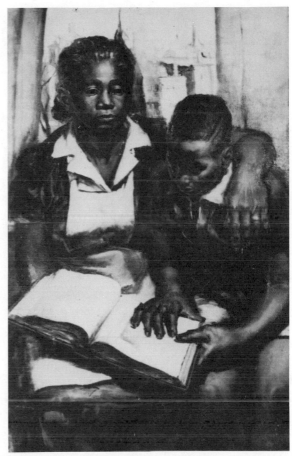

The language you learn at your mother's knee stays with you.

Mother and Child, John Wilson

people's minds between pronunciation and status. British accents, for instance, are generally considered more "cultured," that is, classier and more elegant, than native American accents. Among the latter, the educated accents of the East Coast,[8] which sound closer to British accents than those of Middle America, are considered prestigious, while the twangs of the Middle West are considered provincial and "hickish." Television and population shifts westward have been changing this. But until

---

[8] As taught in classy private schools, as opposed to standard Bronx, Brooklyn, Dorchester, or Roxbury.

recently, nothing much has affected the position or prestige of America's lowliest language community, the forms and accents of black English.

For most of the three and a half centuries that black people have lived in this country, their patterns of English speech have been considered incompetent. Until recently, it never occurred to people that they had spoken real languages in the countries from which they were sold into slavery, or that the ways that they spoke English would reflect first the pidginization, and then the creolization, of their native tongues with English. To most Americans, the black community had no history. To this day, the accents and

stone fox	fine woman
bear	opposite of fox
work out!	do your thing
bowdacious	a bold act
hawk	hurting weather
smoking	fast
tomorrow	never
to burn	to do well
shine me on	avoid, snub
pushed	upset
box	radio
bad sides	good records
raggidy	ugly
tighten up	get it together
over	success
hammer man	person with authority over you

List compiled from *Black Language,* by Malachi Andrews and Paul T. Owens, Berkeley: Seymour-Smith Publishers, 1973.

Figure 9.8 English, black and white.

grammatical usage of black English is more widely viewed as a symptom of poverty, ignorance, or stupidity, than as a legitimate dialect of one tenth of the American people. Since black English is not considered "good" English, the public schools strive to get it out of the heads of black children. This has caused some argument and consternation (Garcia 1972).

If black English is a legitimate dialect of American English, then teaching children that it is "bad" English denies them a part of their cultural heritage and damages their self image, which is unfair and hard on the children, who enter school speaking and understanding it just fine. But to teach it as a legitimate dialect, perhaps even to write textbooks in black English, as some people have been doing and advocating, is to perpetuate a pattern of speech that has long since been identified, among many blacks as well as whites, with poverty, ignorance, and stupidity! The answer may be to teach children that black English is a legitimate dialect of American English, but to teach them to become expert in using the dominant modes of speaking. The trend of any homogeneous

society, where people dress alike, share common kinds of jobs, interests, and family and community patterns, is to speak alike as well. In American society, it may be the price of equality.

LANGUAGE AND THOUGHT

One of the conventional arguments used in defense of teaching conventional grammar in school is that the rules of language, as handed down to us, promote clear thinking. This is also the argument used a couple of generations ago to defend the mandatory teaching of Latin ("grammar" used to mean Latin). It is not entirely true, but it is a plausible argument, because most of our thinking is done with language. The question is, "how much?" Specifically, (1) to what extent does language determine thinking? (2) to what extent does thinking require language? (3) how much and what kind of thinking can you do without language?

Language and reality The most critical of these questions is whether the language we use may actually determine the way we perceive reality instead of merely reflecting our interpretation of it. Does language, in other words, *express* our thoughts or *shape* them? Most scholars think the former, but Benjamin Lee Whorf, following the earlier work of Edward Sapir, has argued that the language a person speaks shapes many of their perceptions and therefore their thoughts (1956). Eskimos have many different terms for snow, he points out, because snow conditions are so important in their lives; but *because* they have these many terms, they are able to perceive the differences with an ease which escapes us urban temperate zone dwellers. Opponents of this view agree that the linguistic differences exist, all right, but believe that our different perceptions are dictated only by the differences in the situations, not in the languages. Children and skiers and airplane pilots and meteorologists have all the words and the percepts they need for their own interactions with snow and would pick up more if they needed them. The common view is that language merely *reflects* our perceptions of reality.

Neither position has been proved, however, and the issue is too important to dismiss lightly. If having or not having words for things seriously affects my perception of them, then it stands to reason that I will perceive things best, that is, with the greatest refinement of detail, if I am given more words to label them with. That is precisely the argument some psychotherapists make with respect to the labeling of emotions, you recall (See Chapter 8); and if it is valid, then it may apply to other kinds of learning, too. If refinements of language can refine people's social, political, and esthetic perceptions, then the main job of education should clearly be the teaching of language skills, because refinement of perception is the tool to refined choices and skills in many things.

Thinking and speech Whether or not language dictates perception, it certainly colors and refines thinking, so much so, in fact, that thinking was once considered identical with language (Sokolov 1967), a form of **implicit** (meaning "silent") speech. Early in this century, John B. Watson observed that the vocal cords make small contractions when persons are thinking to themselves, just as the cords would do on a larger scale if they were voicing the same sounds out loud. This caused Watson to conclude that all thoughts are words and that all thinking is really silent speech. It isn't proved. In experiments where subjects were injected with curare, causing temporary paralysis of all muscles, they were still able to think normally (Smith et al. 1947). It is true that muscle movements of the voice box frequently accompany thought, but they may not be essential for it.

You do not really need experiments with curare, dramatic as they are, to realize that this is true. Everyone thinks at a faster rate than they can possibly speak, even to themselves. And while it is hard to observe that fact objectively, it is easy to observe that some people can *read*

several thousand words a minute (nobody can speak faster than about 500) with excellent comprehension—and reading is a form of thinking. Finally, we have all had the experience of clearly understanding a concept but groping for the word that stands for it. If the concept *is* the word, then we would never have that problem. Undoubtedly *covert* (hidden) verbal activity often accompanies thinking, but it probably serves mainly as an aid for things like focusing our attention on one subject, digging thoughts up from memory, and dealing with abstract concepts. Young deaf children who have not yet acquired language are able to make sophisticated discriminations among concepts through other symbolic means than words. Language serves many useful functions within the total cognitive enterprise, all right, but it is not exactly the same thing as thought (Flavell and Hill 1969).

It is not exactly the same thing as speech either, of course, though we have been using *speech* and *language* as if they were interchangeable. Language is the total symbolic system of communication, which includes speech, writing, and the symbols of mathematics and logic. It is clear that *speech* and *writing* are not identical with thinking; the question remains whether other symbols may be.

Thinking without language The most elementary and the most advanced kinds of thinking may be the only ones that occur without language. Elementary thinking takes the form of imagery and, in some sense, of the behavior involved in emotional and muscle learning, that is, in classical and operant conditioning. We are used to thinking of these activities as non-thinking events because we define thinking as a process where all the stimuli and responses are inside the head. But in reality, it is not so easy to separate internal and external processes so rigidly, and clearly, some aspects of conditioning are very conscious, without in any way being linguistic events. A pigeon trained through operant conditioning to peck at triangles, eventually learns to *recognize* them, but probably has not mastered the *concept* of triangularity; through trial-and-error, it has solved the problem of getting fed, and it remembers the solution. Problem solving through operant conditioning is not always such a deliberate and accurate process; it is sometimes a superstitious one, as when a baseball player, who hits a home run after tugging at his cap, may come to imagine superstitiously that there was some cause and effect relationship between the tug and the hit (Skinner 1948). But do not knock it—superstition itself, is a statement of expectation—and imaging and expectation are the beginnings of thought.

No one doubts that **insight** is a form of thinking, and since rats, monkeys, and preverbal children are all capable of it, thinking is plainly not an exclusively language art. Insight among these little folk depends on imagery. This may also be true of the very sophisticated insights involved in mathematical and scientific discoveries. Some famous mathematicians, including Einstein, reported that their discoveries generally occur in the form of **intuitions,** that is, sudden massive "understandings" of what it is they are about, often in the form of mental pictures of the relationships between the things they are studying. Here too, thought takes the form of pictorial images, not words. But the pictures are not merely those of objects, but of relationships. They are pictures of **ideas,** in other words, and it is their capacity to represent complicated ideas, rather than concrete things alone, that changes their stature from the lowest to the highest form of thinking. When a word or image passes from representing a thing to representing an idea, it is called a **concept.** The manipulation of concepts is the most elegant act of thought.

Concepts: The idea of ideas

A child's earliest words, you recall, are not even names; they are just utterances that be-

come names, and thus words, only as they get connected with an image of some thing in its head. As long as the word names a single thing, though, it is a mere conditioned stimulus, conjuring up an image of "Daddy," "bottle," or whatever, without having any mental stature of its own. A concept is a word with "class," literally, one which has "branched out" to represent not just a single thing, but several different things which have the same property. The ability to form concepts grows gradually, with age and with language use, but age is probably more important, provided the child has had enough experience with language in the first few years of life to have mastered the fundamental rules. Then, its concept-forming ability increases steadily through puberty and early adolescence (Flavell and Hill 1967). It starts with words all naming single objects, and next advances to where a word represents a whole class of objects—so "chair" comes to mean anything you sit on rather than a specific chair, a multiple image rather than a single one. From there, it goes to a higher level of **abstraction,** that is, independence of any concrete image at all, in which a word can refer to a class of **nonobjects,** of properties, or attributes, like "red" or "tall" that can describe things which have nothing else in common. Finally, it becomes able to deal with concepts which refer to neither objects nor attributes, but only to **relationships.** At this level, all words are "general," that is, they mean only what they are defined to mean, which is to express the relationships stipulated by their creators, who are, in effect, inventing their own language for the occasion. The technical name of such inventions is **mathematics** or **logic** (See Chapter 1).

There are two important things to understand here. First, the more general a word becomes, the more it becomes an image in its own right, an increasingly flexible, shifting image. The concept "dog" for instance, calls up more imagery in your mind than does the thought of your own dog. And the concept of "speckled" calls up even more imagery than does "dog" because it can include dogs, cats, measles, and poppy-seed cookies. Second, and more important, all concepts serve an **abbreviating,** shorthand function, and the more general a concept is, the more information it can abbreviate. For most purposes of thinking and remembering, this makes words more useful than images, but it does not make verbal thinking **replace** imaging, any more than the use of images replaces conditioning just because it lets insight substitute for trial and error learning. As each new process develops, it does things that the more primitive process could not accomplish; far from discarding the earlier process, however, it may build on it.

Words and pictures Imagery sometimes assists verbal thinking, for instance, because, as Allen Paivio (1971) says, it "is specialized for dealing with concrete tasks. The verbal system, on the other hand, is at once sequential and abstract. . . ." He states that imagery is better than verbal thinking for conceptualizing **concrete** things and **simultaneous** events; we use verbal thinking more for contemplating **abstractions** and **sequences** of events. We can **picture** through imagery, for instance, all of the things going on at once in a three-ring circus much more easily than we can describe them in words. But we also use imagery sometimes to picture sequences or to make abstract concepts concrete in our minds. You might respond to the word *liberty* by picturing the Statue of Liberty or the sentence "Gross national wealth has reached an all-time high" by picturing mercury rising in a thermometer. In general, though, our understanding of abstract words mostly depends upon other words; thus we generally associate words like *equality,* not with pictures, but with other words such as *fairness, democracy,* and *justice.*

Paivio's point is that we constantly use images *in conjunction with* words when we think. The systems interact so that a word like *cat* may evoke both verbal and visual associa-tion; upon hearing "cat," we might think the words *feline, cuddly, milk,* while at the same time summoning up a mental picture of a cat. The picture itself, moreover, is not necessarily that of a particular cat; such images can be highly schematic. Mental images are not fixed and static but are like an artist's loose pencil sketch that can be elaborated, erased, or transformed according to the demands of the moment.

Creativity The interweaving of each advance in thinking ability with the mode of thought that preceded it is an automatic process. But the ability to shift back and forth skillfully from one mode to the other is probably trainable in people and probably valuable to learn. Shifting between imagery and language, for instance, seems to be particularly important in a lot of creative activity. The creative person uses imagery to portray situations to themself clearly and to make rapid associations between one context and another. Language, on the other hand, organizes their ideas and gives them focus and direction (Paivio 1971). Imagery evokes; language organizes. Imagery provides content; language lends form to that content. As Harold Rugg has put it, the creative act requires "a well filled storehouse of imagery to guarantee richness and freedom of association," but also demands "ordered key concepts to guarantee organization of thought" (1963). Thus a creative person might be able to relate their knowledge about music in an original way to knowledge about physics or the sewer system of Paris; their competence in using imagery enables them to "see" meaningful patterns among unrelated things. And these patterns get combined and organized through their competence in language.

THINKING MACHINES

We have concentrated on how people think, and not on the nature of thinking; on how language works, and not on the nature of language. Those things take us beyond psychology and into the realms of logic, mathematics, and for practical folks, maybe electrical engineering. For there is nothing *intrinsically human* about thought or language, however much we glory in our mastery of them, little in them that, by itself, will make us act humanely. This is important to understand technically to appreciate the fact that a **computer** really is a ***thinking machine;*** it is important to understand in moral terms to appreciate the fact that *you* are *more* than that. Learning to think accurately, or compute, or reason, all of which mean the same thing, gives you knowledge. But wisdom for figuring out how to act on that knowledge in your own best interests, you must get elsewhere, in consultation with your motives and emotions.

The most general form of thinking, you recall, is that in which symbols and the rules for manipulating them are defined by the people using them. That is the essence of mathematics. A language is also a bunch of symbols—words, and rules for manipulating them—grammar, syntax, and such. The difference between natural language and mathematics is simply that ordinary language is sloppy; words often have ambiguous meanings, and the rules are often inexact. There is one way of using natural language, however, in which the sloppiness goes and precision reigns—it is called ***logic.***

The difference between logical reasoning

Creativity.

and ordinary discourse (the word "logic" literally means "discourse") is that, in logic, the rules of argument are rigidly laid out in advance, and nothing may be introduced in argument which does not follow those rules. An argument is "logical" or "rational" to the degree that it sticks to the agreed-upon rules of argument. The principle is exactly the same in math; that is why there are right and wrong answers to math problems.

So the only difference between mathematics and logic is a difference in symbols, since the rules for following rules are the same. In mathematics, the symbols are very general; in logic, they are words with specific meanings. But they need not be; the more general the symbols you use in logic, the more it becomes mathematics; the more specific the meanings you apply to the symbols of mathematics, the more likely you will call it "logic." It is all the same; reasoning is reasoning; mathematical reasoning and logical reasoning are of a piece. Both are language, highly purified, into the most **abstract,** that is, imageless thought.

Mathematics is pure reason. So computers are reasoning machines. Do they have language? Yes, they have nothing but language, the purest of languages, unaffected by emotions, or the multitude of images which human sensory faculties produce. Can computers think? Of course they think—there is no more thoughtful thinking than mathematics. Can computers talk? Sure, usually in writing; that is how you find out what they are thinking. Can they remember? Certainly, a lot. Are they intelligent?

Depends what you mean by intelligent. If you mean able to do mathematics, solve problems, and things like that, yes, they are intelligent. If by intelligence you mean the kind of flexible problem-solving ability that people have, then computers are pretty stupid. They have speed and organization, but far less flexibility than us. A computer never "gets" a question that isn't phrased just right, and it does not respond with partial information, or with doubt (Nievergelt and Farrar 1973). If you ask, on the other hand, can they create? Yes, they can; computer poetry isn't much, and computer drama is pretty bad, but computer chess playing is very impressive. Then are they human? No, computers are not human. Only people are.

A computer is a thinking machine; it does nothing else. A person is a thinking animal. Animals do not think as rationally as does hardware built for that purpose, and you therefore cannot think as fast or precisely as a computer, but you can think about a much bigger variety of things. The fact that you can **feel,** moreover, clouds your thinking, subjects you to pains which a totally rational thing like a computer apparently does not endure, and makes you orient your life towards feeling good. Thinking is humanity's most elegant accomplishment, but it is still only a tool for the pursuit of experience. We invented computers to do some of our thinking for us, to help us get free to entertain ourselves—with doing, dreaming, feeling, and with thinking, too. All those things, pooled, are living. Thinking alone is not.

SUMMARY

1 Thinking includes reasoning, wishing, talking and imagining, which reduce to verbal thinking and image thinking. In effect, thinking means making words or pictures in your head. Verbal thinking seems to be the exclusive property of human beings, but imaging occurs in lower species as well. In some respects, learning by conditioning can be considered a primitive form of thinking.

2 Images are mental pictures; in general, an image (hallucinations, dreams, and day-dreams are all images) differs from a percept by lacking an immediate external stimulus. This distinction is not precise, however, since after-images and "seeing stars" from getting hit on the head, are direct results of external stimulation.

3 Images occur in every sense modality; you can imagine sound, sight, taste, textures, and movement. Images generally are less vivid than percepts; they also tend to be more volatile, going in and out of the mind with relative ease. People differ enormously in the vividness of their imagery, and in *imagery dominance*—the kind of imagery they experience most. Visual imagery is most common for most people.

4 The images of infants probably start forming soon after their eyes focus. These early images are *autistic,* that is, they reflect the infant's own wishes and desires, rather than representing realistic memories of anything. Freud called this primitive mode of thinking the *primary process;* realistic imaging and thinking he called *secondary process.* Language is an outgrowth of secondary process thinking.

5 Imagery dominates thinking in early childhood and tends to have a vividness then which it loses with age. The sharpest imagery is called *eidetic imagery,* or photographic memory, in which a person imagines something as if actually looking at it. Eidetic imagery is not very common in children and is even rarer in adults. Evidently, it declines with age, as language takes over.

6 All human societies possess languages with the same general characteristics, capable of virtually unlimited communication. All human languages consist of a *lexicon,* a bunch of words or sounds which symbolize something; and *syntax* or *grammar* or *diction,* rules for putting the words together into a system of *semantics,* or meanings. The elements of language are arbitrary, meaning that there is no physical correspondence between the sounds of words and their meanings. The only thing that gives meaning to words and the rules for combining them is *social convention.*

7 The rules of language permit words to be used in a great variety of ways; these rules multiply infinitely the number of different meanings words can have and reduce the ambiguities of word combinations so that the message the listener receives is the same as that which the speaker intended to send. The rules of spoken language are more flexible than those of written language because the meaning of spoken language is helped along by gestures, facial expressions, and shifts of inflection and emphasis. The enormous ability of people to understand and use language from early childhood with little formal training suggests that there may be some genetic basis for this process.

8 Little is known about the neurophysiological origins of language. It seems to develop in the temporal and frontal lobes of the cerebral cortex, and there seems to be a critical period which is optimum for language learning (between about one and a half and four years of age). If parts of the brain controlling language are damaged at a very early age, other parts can generally take over their functions. Also *feral* (wild) children and *autistic* (psychotic) children never develop normal language ability, probably because they have not learned language during the critical years. Normal children, however, become competent in language almost automatically, and can learn several languages fluently, more or less regardless of their intelligence. This ability seems to diminish with age. All these facts suggest that the *maturational factor* in language is very great.

9 Noam Chomsky and some other scholars believe there is an innate factor in language ability, such that the human brain is genetically programmed to create and understand language. Chomsky argues that all languages are basically similar, with a "universal grammar" governing the "deep structure" that is, the basic characteristics of all natural languages. The opposing view, argued chiefly by B. F. Skinner, is that language is learned entirely by conditioning, that is, by being exposed to the stimulation of words, sounds, and grammar, and being reinforced for using them correctly.

10 Language has to be learned, whether there is an innate predisposition for learning it or not. A newborn baby starts making differential sounds for discomfort and contentment by the time it is a month or two old. Around 9 months, it starts imitating sounds, and by 18 months it can say several words and combine them into two-word sentences. By two and a half years, the child uses auxiliary words and has a grammar very much like an adult.

11 *Imitation* is the first tool for language acquisition. Babbling and cooing prepares the infant for imitating sounds; it then patterns its own vocal responses after adult speech, imitating sounds long before it knows what they mean. O. H. Mowrer believes that an autistic process stimulates the child to utter these first words; the infant imagines that mother, bottle, and comfort will magically present themselves. It is reinforced and rewarded for making the sounds, and therefore, remembers and repeats them. In this way, operant conditioning builds the child's further language skills.

12 A number of efforts to invent universal languages have been made over the past three and a half centuries, but the only two artificial languages now widely known are *interlingua*, a written language for scientific communication, and *Esperanto*, a hybrid of European languages invented at the end of the 19th century.

13 A *natural language* is one which grows up without anyone planning it, by being spoken rather than being composed. Natural languages are always changing, as people's habits, needs, and interests change. Spoken language changes faster than written language because it is more flexible to begin with. Changes in slang produce many permanent changes in any living language.

14 New languages develop largely as a result of *geographic isolation* and *foreign invasion*. When a group of people becomes isolated from the parent group whose language it speaks, natural changes in usage first turn it into a *dialect,* that is, a recognizable variant of the original language. As it continues changing, however, so does the original language, and both gradually become *cognates,* that is, language cousins. Families of languages grow up in this way. Foreign invasion creates new languages faster and more dramatically. When one group of people conquers or trades with a society speaking a different language, a *pidgin* or *patois,* that is, a trade language arises; it is a blend of the two languages involved. As contact continues, the hybrid language becomes the mother tongue of newborn generations; it evolves into a *creole,* a new language based on both of the earlier ones. Virtually all living languages are creoles because virtually all human societies have been invading, murdering, and marrying each other since time immemorial.

15 Language use has important political and socioeconomic aspects. In America, British-sounding accents are generally considered more cultured than native American accents, and the accents of well-educated Easterners are generally considered classier than those of the Middle West. The forms and accents of black English are signs of low status throughout this country. Many public schools try to "cure" children of speaking black English without recognizing its important historical roots in the many languages of Africa.

16 Most scholars believe that language use reflects our perception of reality, but some think that it actually shapes our perceptions and thoughts. The leading advocate of that position is Benjamin Lee Whorf. Some psychotherapists implicitly support Whorf's position by arguing that labeling emotions increases our control over them.

17 It was once widely believed that thinking is identical with language, a notion bolstered by the observation that people often make slight movements of speech muscles while they are thinking. Such movements are not essential to thought, however. Some thought takes the form of *insight* or *intuition,* that is, sudden understanding of relationships, often in the form of mental pictures.

18 A *name* is a word which represents a single thing. A *concept* is a word which represents several things having a single property. The ability to form concepts grows gradually, depending largely on maturation, through early adolescence. Concept formation starts with naming, advances to words which represent a whole class of *objects* (e.g., chair), then to words which refer to *nonobjects,* that is, properties or attributes (e.g., red or tall), or *abstractions,* ideas which have no concrete image at all. The highest level of abstraction is that of "general" words, or symbols which mean only what they are defined to mean, i.e., the symbols of mathematics and logic.

19 As concepts become more abstract, the images associated with them become increasingly flexible. The concept "dog" for instance, calls up more imagery than does the thought of your own dog, and the concept "speckled" calls up more imagery than "dog," because it can include dogs, measles, and poppyseed cookies. All concepts serve an abbreviating function; the more abstract a concept is, the more information it can abbreviate.

20 Developmentally, thinking in images is more advanced than muscle learning, and thinking in language is more advanced than imagery, but each new mode of thinking interacts with the previous one rather than replacing it altogether.

21 There is nothing intrinsically human about thought or language, and in their most sophisticated forms, a computer is able to use them efficiently. A computer is a true thinking machine, because it is able to reason, that is, to carry out mathematical and logical operations. In that sense, computers are also intelligent. They are not human, however, unlike most people.

Memory

10

10

Memory

Talking and thinking and imagining would not be worth much without memory. Neither would home or family. Nor personality. Nor learning. Nor intelligence. Nor almost anything else in your life. In large part, you *are* what you remember because your sense of self depends on your perception of your own history.

The evolutionary advances of one animal phylum over another, as you go up the phylogenetic ladder from protozoa to *homo sapiens* can be described in terms of increasing physiological complexity and increasing psychological flexibility or adaptability. The flexibility consists mainly of the ability to learn, especially **problem solving, thinking,** and **remembering.** Language is a big deal in this process because it extends the range and flexibility of thinking by vastly increasing the amount of thought that can be remembered. Culture is important here because it permits memories to be stored outside the genes so that humans can have mountains of information at hand without having a brain the size of a public library. And human beings, in turn, become a big deal because they have such enormous capacities for manipulating information into so many memorable forms, and such ingenious methods for storing it and retrieving it. **Memory means the storage and retrieval of information.** The process by which that is done on a phonograph record, book, or magnetic tape, is well understood. How it is done in the human brain is not. Nor is very much known about the behavioral processes by which information is stored, retrieved, or lost. That is the subject of this chapter.

We deal with memory after thinking and language more or less for the same reason we put emotion after motivation—it is a special event which gives power to the thing it supports. Memory is the receptacle in which thought and language are poured, the crucible in which they are mixed and melted and reshaped, and the well from which they are drawn out again to use them in our lives. There is no way of knowing if our *physical* capacity for storing information, that is, for memory, is any better or worse than faithful dog Fido's. What makes memory significant is that the information we store there is the stuff of our dreams and plans and poems. As you would expect, almost all the study of memory has been preoccupied with **verbal memory,** and only a little with the kinds of memory we share with such other creatures as monkeys, dogs, and small children.

Memory, like emotion, is one of the oldest topics of formal study in psychology. The first scientific work on it was written by H. Ebbinghaus, a German psychologist, in 1885. Ebbinghaus reasoned that you could not get a pure measure of memory if you studied the memorization of meaningful material, because the very fact that it was meaningful meant that people were already familiar with it, and therefore already had memories of it. So he invented **nonsense syllables**—meaningless combinations of wordlike letters, such as **bix, poz, rel,** and so forth. He would put these into lists and, using himself as the subject, study the list until he could repeat it twice in correct order. The method was so good that it is still widely used today.

Unlike emotion, on the other hand, there is no question at all about where memory happens physically; it happens in your brain, just like thinking. Just *where,* and *how,* is not so clear. The precise chemistry of memory is not known, nor are the precise locations in the brain that process and store different kinds of memories, like long- and short-term memories, or sense memories, like visual, auditory, or taste, touch, and smell—or fictitious or distorted "memories" of things that never happened.

The psychology of memory is as full of puzzles as its anatomy and chemistry. Why are some things remembered only briefly and others for years? What determines which things get remembered and which ones forgotten? What makes both processes fragmentary so that you do not remember all of almost anything or forget quite as much as you thought you did, and sometimes have things sticking at the tip of your tongue, or back of your mind, suspended between memory and oblivion?

Even the *definition* of memory is not as obvious as you might think, once you try to be precise about it. Memorizing poetry is memory, all right, but what about mastering motor skills? Are the gradually improving movements in operant conditioning instances of "muscle memory?" And if that is the case, then would salivating to a flashing light or blushing to a dirty word in classical conditioning be instances of "glandular memory?" How about the transfer of training from one skill to another, as say, from ice hockey to field hockey or from tennis to squash? Or maybe even the chemical transfer of ability from one organism to another—as when worms who have learned to crawl through a maze are chopped up and fed to untrained worms, who then can do the same? If we incorporate all these things into our definition of memory, then we have included just about *all* of learning! But if we do not, then we are omitting some aspects of remembering.

In fact, students of learning have not tried generally to separate memory from learning. "Learning," says Jack A. Adams, "is a relatively stable tendency to react, and the storage and retrieval of this persistent internal state is the topic of memory. Learning and memory are two sides of the same behavioral coin (1976, p.6)." Just as learning is thought to be permanent, many students of memory, including Freud and William James, feel that memory is permanent, whether or not you can remember any given thing at any given time you are trying to (Adams 1967.) Most learning theorists agree, and as we shall see, there is some physiological evidence, in the surgical work of Wilder Penfield, supporting this idea.

Not much is known about the developmental processes or biochemistry underlying memory. Maybe there is a genetic basis for memory, as there may be for intelligence. Eidetic imagery, which we discussed in the last chapter, is a kind of memory ability, and it must have some

The Persistence of Memory, Salvador Dali
The persistence of memory.

chemical basis. And the superior ability of children to learn languages implies some kind of special memory ability related to maturation. But no one knows how closely specific memory skills, like the ability to memorize poetry, learn new words, or remember lists of nonsense syllables, is tied to other developmental curves. Maybe it goes about like the so-called intelligence test curve, increasing faster and faster through the first few years of life, increasing more slowly from five or six through adolescence and early adulthood, holding steady through the early thirties, and slowly declining into middle and old age. Memory ability may not be *identical* with learning ability, but it is closely related.

Whatever the basis of memory may be, the processes involved can be grouped into two broad classes: *information storage,* that is, the ways memories are acquired, and *information retrieval,* the ways memories are recovered or lost. We shall look at them in that order.

INFORMATION STORAGE: THE WAREHOUSE IN YOUR HEAD

If you were to remember any sizable fraction of the events that cross your senses daily, you

Concentration.

would be too stupefied to think and too paralyzed to act. The evolutionary function of memory is to make behavior more efficient by storing *useful* impressions, not simply recording everything in sight. Memory is a warehouse, not a garbage dump. Most of the impressions that bombard your senses are unimportant to you, and therefore meaningless and uneconomical for your brain to store memories of. *How* you choose among sense impressions, *where* they get put in the brain once they are chosen, and in *what* form, are the problems of memory storage.

Attention You cannot remember what you haven't noticed. So, the first principle of memory storage, as of sensation and perception, is that you must be paying *attention* for any sense impressions to occur. Even then, most impressions are recorded only momentarily; a little of that initial sensory-information-store passes into memory storage, and a little of that storage stays for a still longer time (Norman 1969). Attention is necessary for most any memory, it seems, but some events impress themselves more deeply

Figure 10.1 How long does it take you to memorize this list? How much of it do you remember an hour from now? Tomorrow? Next week?

BLAX
ORPA
KOJE
PUDE
PILC
TAYS
PERO
KOOB
GINT
OSAR

and swiftly than others, and are remembered better and longer accordingly, though you may have been paying equal attention to them. Some things, in other words, "capture attention" rather than just receive it, and are remembered forever after; others require a constant investment of rehearsal and review and willful concentration to make a lasting mark upon your mind. Exactly what determines the difference is unknown; Robert Livingston, of the University of California at San Diego, calls it a "now-print" mechanism that tells the brain that what is happening is worth remembering. But the nature of that mechanism is unknown.

The geography of memory However material is selected for storage, it gets stored in the brain. But just where in the brain is another story. There is lots of room in there for lots of memories, probably more room than could ever be used in the lifetime of any person, but the physical location of memory in the brain has escaped discovery to this day. Karl Lashley tried to discover the location of *engrams,* or memory traces, through surgical experiments, and concluded that the whole associative network of the cortex, with its billions of cells, could be involved (see Chapter 3). That would mean there is no single area of the cortex where memory is neatly contained.

But there are two areas of the brain that definitely do have something to do with the control of memory, even if they are not themselves storage centers. These areas are the *temporal lobes* of the cortex and the *hippocampus* of the old brain.

Wilder Penfield, a Canadian neurosurgeon, performed over 1,000 brain operations for the treatment of epilepsy. The techniques he used left the patient conscious during the operation, and so Penfield would stimulate different parts of the cortex electrically and ask the patients to report their subjective experiences. In an early case, he found that stimulating the temporal lobe caused the patient to recreate the memory of a childhood experience (it happened, in that

case, to be related to the symptoms of his epilepsy). This result led Penfield to some important discoveries in later surgery.

He found, for instance, that stimulation of *sensory* or *motor areas of the cortex* produces all kinds of meaningless sights, sounds, and movements, but not specific images. But when the *temporal lobe* is stimulated, meaningful experiences and memories are reported, often with great realism, sometimes as if they were actually recurring while the patient lay on the operating table reporting them. Penfield found this phenomenon over and over again. At first, it made him think that the temporal lobe is the seat of memory, but that could not be so because if it is surgically removed, a person's memories still remain intact. So, he designated it the *interpretive cortex,* because it seems to integrate the different impressions of the senses into meaningful experiences. Penfield also believes that the temporal lobes contain the brain's recording apparatus for memory storage, so that

> whenever a normal individual is paying conscious attention to something, he is simultaneously recording it in the temporal cortex of each hemisphere (Penfield 1951, pp. 23–24, as cited by Adams 1967).

In his view, this record is permanent, even though ordinary tests of memory will not reproduce most of it.

Removing the temporal lobes may not damage a person's memory, but destroying the *hippocampus* will produce a tremendous impairment in memory ability from then on. While overall IQ remains as high as ever following this operation, people become unable to learn new things requiring even simple memories. In a fairly typical case, for instance, a 29-year-old man

> retained little if anything of events subsequent to operation, although his IQ rating is actually slightly higher than before. Ten months before I examined him, his family had moved from their old house to one a few blocks away on the same

street. He still has not learned the new address, though remembering the old one perfectly, nor can he be trusted to find his way home alone. He does not know where objects constantly in use are kept; for example, his mother still has to tell him where to find the lawn-mower, even though he may have been using it only the day before (Milner 1959, p. 49, as cited by Adams 1967).

Now, the memory deficit created by destroying the hippocampus is not total; a victim of this operation can keep new information in mind for a short time by concentrating intensely and repeating it over and over again. But then it slips quickly and quietly away. It is not that people cannot remember anything at all, but that they cannot remember it *for long*. This supports the notion, now widely believed among memory researchers, that there are at least two different kinds of storage process—short-term memory and long-term memory.

Short- and long-term memory

Short-term memory is "telephone" memory, the sort that permits a person to retain a telephone number just long enough to dial it. The short-term memory system cannot handle very much information at once, five to nine items for most people. And it is severely affected by interruptions and other interference (Adams 1976). If someone asks you for a match while you are dialing a phone number you just looked up, you may have to look it up again.

Long-term memory differs from short-term memory in several respects. First of all, the amount of information you can store in long-term memory is virtually unlimited. Nobody has ever filled their memory up, much less overloaded it. Secondly, almost any information can be inserted into short-term memory with ease, but it is much harder for an item to qualify for long-term memory. Once a memory is inscribed in long-term storage, however, it probably has a permanent place there, whether or not a person

can recall it (Keppel and Underwood 1962). Third, information is organized for storage differently in each system. Short-term memories are coded in images or words, whereas long-term memories are organized by concepts and meanings (Lloyd 1960). When short-term memory gets confused, we mix up words that *sound* alike, not words that have the same meaning. We mistakenly remember *horse* instead of *hearse,* but not *horse* instead of *steed.* When retrieving a word from long-term memory, we might mistakenly recall a synonym (*steed* instead of *horse, house* instead of *home*), but we are not likely to confuse words merely because they sound alike. In long-term memory, we remember what a sentence *meant,* if not exactly what it *said.*

Most impressions apparently pass through short-term storage before they get into long-term storage, but that is not altogether clear. Remember, some things get remembered indefinitely in a one-shot exposure to them. It may depend on how *powerful* and *meaningful* the impressions are to begin with. Evidently, meaningless events are not retained for long; they are the stuff of short-term memory. They get into long-term storage by being shaped into units which "make sense," and are then stored in terms of their meaning. If they make dramatic, powerful impressions to begin with, they go directly into long-term memory. So—memories of what someone was doing when they heard about the assassination of President Kennedy are hurled into long-term storage the first time round; the same sometimes happens with the traumatic events that cause phobias. Less dramatic happenings require various amounts of time, rehearsal, and reorganization before they can be, more or less literally, "pounded into your head." The "Zeigarnik effect" illustrates an event of medium power to get remembered, while the drudgery of most memorization tasks represents the lowest level of memorability, requiring the most effort to register in long-term storage.

The Zeigarnik effect: Medium memorability

It is common for skilled conductors to memorize all of the scores in a symphony orchestra.

If you have ever left off some important thing you were doing because of an unexpected interruption, then you know what the **Zeigarnik effect** is. It is the feeling of preoccupation people have with uncompleted tasks that makes them remember them. Zeigarnik discovered in her formal experiment on memory that people tended to remember *interrupted tasks* which they were not allowed to complete much better than they could remember **tasks they had finished,** when they were questioned about both a few hours later (Zeigarnik 1927). The effect tended to disappear a day or so later, probably because none of the tasks were very memorable in themselves. But the point seems to be, as far as we are concerned here, that getting interrupted before they could get **closure,** that is, a sense of having finished up with a task, aroused the subjects mentally, drawing their attention to the unfinished business more forcibly than it had been drawn, and thus *making* the task more memorable. This same phenomenon may be what makes some fishermen dwell on the one that got away rather than the several they

Although the poet Gertrude Stein sat for this portrait many long hours, in the end Picasso erased the head, went on vacation, and later painted it from memory. Miss Stein loved it. Her friends thought she did not look like it; Picasso said, "She will."

Gertrude Stein, Pablo Picasso

caught, some lovers pine for the one affair they never consummated instead of basking in the many they did, and some businessmen bewail the one deal they didn't make, forgetting the ones they did. Unfinished business becomes memorable by the tension it provokes, diverting attention from better things.

Most things that have to be memorized, of course, have too little drama and tension associated with them to make a powerful impression and become memorable by themselves. Shopping lists, historical dates, the capitals of the states, the bones of the body, the number of sharps and flats in each of the major and minor keys—many of the dull facts of final-exam cramming and of life in a technological civilization, all have to be memorized, and stored long enough to be retrieved, or regurgitated, on demand. For these, nature has provided a couple of helpful means, and human ingenuity has exploited them to invent a couple more. The rest is drudgery.

Codes, chunks, and clusters: Making things memorable Things get into long-term memory by making a profound impression, but they have to make at least a mild one to get into short-term memory first. And most things must go through the short-term process before they can get long-term storage. The basic mechanism permitting short-term impressions is attention; when you pay attention to something for a tenth of a second or more, you can absorb up to nine items of information (like numbers, letters, and so on) and recall them correctly if you are tested immediately. For most people, the average number of items is closer to five, and if they are given less than a tenth of a second's exposure to them, it will be even fewer because they don't have time to "fill the short-term memory to capacity (Adams 1967)." The absorption capacity of short-term memory is called *memory span.* It seems to set an absolute, perhaps chemically determined limit, on how much you can remember of any given occasion. This would drastically curtail our ability to learn much of anything were it not for the fact that the mind has its own rules for defining an occasion and counting the pieces of information in it. The processes involved can probably best be labeled *coding.*

The basic coding process in memory is an extension of the perceptual *grouping and patterning* tendencies which are probably innate in humans and other animals (see Chapter 5). It is called *chunking,* which means organizing percepts into units or chunks so that, for instance, you perceive whole words instead of individual letters (Miller 1956). This increases short-term storage capacity because it condenses a large number of items into a small number of packages, each of which is a storable unit. So, while you cannot store more than five or seven or nine chunks, each one may contain a lot of information.

Y O U M U S T R E M E M B E R T H I S

is 19 items of information presented this way, for instance, and therefore far too much to memorize quickly. But presented differently,

YOU MUST REMEMBER THIS

is only 4 chunks, each of which is instantly and easily remembered as a word. And in the context of the song from which it comes,

YOU MUST REMEMBER THIS,
A KISS IS JUST A KISS,

may impress you, not as 10 words, but as two phrases, each of which is a single chunk, and both of which are therefore easily remembered.

Chunking, like a lot of perceptual grouping, occurs *automatically,* for the most part, not by deliberation. The units that make up chunks are mostly learned, but once learned, the act of chunking is inevitable. Once you know words, in fact, it is very hard for you to see them as separate letters or hear them as separate *phonemes* (speech sounds). Subjectively, chunking is not experienced as part of *memory,* but as *perception.* You experience it as memory only when asked to recall what you saw or heard, but it got into memory storage in the first place as chunks of percepts. That is important because chunking provides the basis for increasingly elaborate and deliberate strategies for committing things to memory. These include *associative* or *grouping* methods, some of which code information into memorable packages of items which are *conceptually* related, that is, which "make sense" together; others are simply conscious extensions of chunking which code information into *perceptually* related units. All of them are *mediating processes,* which make information memorable by imposing a memorable structure on it. The intentional use of mediating processes for remembering things is called *mnemonics.*

Virtually all verbal memory involves mediating processes. If you give someone pairs of terms in which they must recall one member when they hear the other, they will use their lifelong experience with language to invent connections among the different items which make them easier to recall, noting which ones sound alike, or rhyme with each other, or how they follow in relative alphabetical order, or which ones can be clustered together as animal, vegetable, or mineral, or which familiar images or ideas might make two otherwise unrelated members of a pair seem sensible together, like connecting CRACKER—TELEPHONE by thinking of Alexander Graham Bell. People differ greatly in their specific choice of these "associative aids" to memory, or "natural language mediators," as they are also called, but everyone uses them in one form or another; it is an automatic outgrowth of all our earlier experience of learning and using language. It is so natural to people that true *rote learning,* in which something gets remembered only by repetition, hardly exists (Adams 1967, 1976).

Mnemonics and mnemonists There are some people who specialize, either accidentally or deliberately, in memorizing things; they are called mnemonists. Some of them make a profession of their ability, giving performances, like magicians, or training courses, like college professors—and even holding conventions, where they impress each other with their memory skills (Bower 1973). It is not always easy to discover just what these people do to master their remarkable memories, and sometimes they themselves do not know how they came upon their ability. The processes they actually use for memorizing may differ also. In two of the most famous cases that have been studied, one of the mnemonists made extensive use of visual imagery (Luria 1968); the other, though he occasionally used imagery, relied mostly on verbal tricks for memorizing (Hunt and Love 1972). Some mnemonists are highly specialized in the kinds of things they memorize. Chess masters, for instance, can often carry on several games at once, glancing at the pieces on each chessboard for as little as five seconds or, in some cases, never seeing the boards at all, but just hearing about the positions of the pieces. The ability to grasp many configurations so easily is closely related to overall skill at chess playing ability (Chase and Simon 1973; Klatzky 1975). It does not mean that chess players have remarkable memories in other areas.

Mnemonics tries to make things memorable both by conceptual and perceptual associations. Organizing lists by *rhymes* is a good *perceptual* scheme—"Thirty days hath September, April, June, and November. . . ." A popular *conceptual* mnemonic device for memorizing numbers is to find a catch word whose letters each correspond to one digit. To memorize a telephone number like 4262537, for instance, you might come up with the word G-A-M-B-L-E-R. Numbers are particularly hard to memorize be-

cause they are abstract and we have few associations to them in ordinary life; an interesting word is easier to recall because it can summon up rich associations. The same device works pretty well for memorizing lists of unrelated terms, like the names of different anatomical structures or chemical compounds. Each letter in the mnemonic term is the first letter of the word that has to be remembered. Increasingly, in our technological world, people invent mnemonic terms, called **acronyms,** to coin new words for things, and they often get widely accepted in the language. *Radar,* for instance, is an acronym for "radio detecting and ranging," and a *laser* is "light amplification by stimulated emission of radiation." Most people forget what mnemonic was intended by the acronym, if they ever knew it, but the word sticks in the language, and it saves a mouthful.

There is nothing new in modern mnemonics. Mnemonics is an ancient art, and was especially valuable in cultures where there was plenty to remember and hardly anyone around to write it down or read it back if it got written. Poetry may have been invented as a mnemonic device—the rhythms of singing, of metered speech, and of lines and stanzas made the details of stories easier to remember so that bards and minstrels could tell them at great length. And long before verse was rhymed, *acrostic* poetry (and prayer) was popular—arrangements in which the first or last letter in each line, when taken in order, would spell out the author's name, or the alphabet, or some other *key word.* The key word was a mnemonic for people who had to memorize the stuff, but could not read it. Some of the Psalms, for instance, in the original Hebrew, start each line in succession with the appropriate letter of the alphabet, making it easier to remember them in recitation or prayer.

Another ancient mnemonic device used a visual technique in which you would form an image of each thing you want to remember and mentally place it in a different room of a house or building you know well. Then, when you wish to recall an item, you mentally stroll through the house, looking into every room. The Roman senator Cicero used this technique to memorize the outline of his eloquent and seemingly endless speeches, which would sometimes last for hours. Professional memory experts, such as nightclub entertainers, still use it today.

Mnemonics uses more sophisticated storage methods than chunking or automatic mediating processes because they are conscious and deliberate in the first place and because they make things memorable (a) by condensing and abbreviating them, (b) by making them tuneful or catchy, and (c) by making them meaningful. The abbreviation process works like chunking, registering things in short-term memory, but probably by itself does not give the memory much staying power. How long do you remember the list of bones *after* the final exam? How long, for that matter, do you remember the acronym you used to remember it? A jingle or rhyme, on the other hand, may have more staying power because its sensory appeal is greater and because it makes some sense in its own right. The sense it makes gives the mnemonic device most of its power. These are the same

Look at this painting for one minute, then see how many objects in it you can remember. What memory tricks did you use?

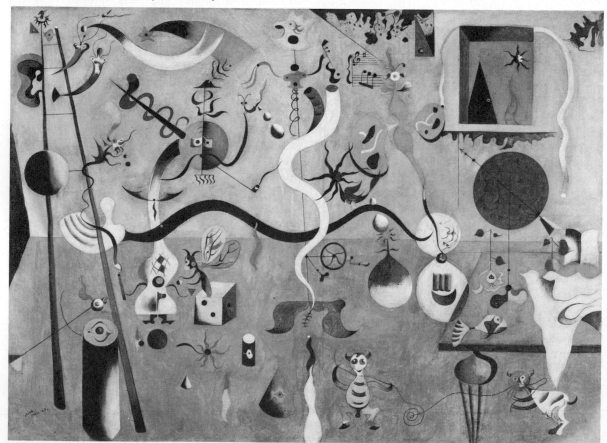

Carnival of Harlequin, Joan Miro

things that characterize long-term memory, where, you recall, storage occurs in terms of the *semantic* properties, that is, the meaningfulness of events. Mnemonics is made up of devices for producing long-term memory, as most efforts to remember anything in the real world are likely to be. Their success is a function of how meaningful an impression they make. And this, in general, seems to be the determinant of transfer from short-term to long-term storage. The more a mediating process in short-term memory makes the material to be learned meaningful, the more enduringly memorable it becomes. Material which is meaningless cannot arouse you very much to learn it. So it cannot make much of an impression.

There is another way to make an impression, however, besides making sense. That is, to make noise. If material does not become memorable by virtue of its interest or its meaning, it still can do so, to some extent, by virtue of its presence. If a stimulus is forced upon your consciousness often enough, exposure can substitute enough for interest and for meaning for you to notice and remember it.

Practice Practice makes perfect in memorizing as in anything else. That pretty much sums it up. No matter how boring, meaningless, disconnected, or abstract the information to be learned, no matter whether it is pictures or numbers or words or movements, whether it is to be learned in serial order or any which way, practice makes the learning occur faster and last longer; it makes the material memorable and keeps the memory fresh.

Any kind of practice, moreover, helps. *Rehearsal,* that is, repetition and review of the material, is effective in *overt* form, such as reciting it aloud, and in *covert* form, studying it silently. And too much practice is better than enough practice, that is, continuing to practice *beyond* the point where you have mastered the material will make you remember it longer. This is called *overlearning* because it refers to someone's continuing to rehearse after they have already met the criterion for successful learning. Overlearning is the key to mastery of almost any skill, mental or physical. You know you have overlearned something when you can do it, not just correctly, but automatically, without having to think through the motions one by one (see Chapter 6).

The fact that practice facilitates memory is not big news, and so it is surprising to discover that no one really knows how. In a general way, it "performs a 'stamping in' function in which the response becomes increasingly resistant to forgetting processes" (Adams 1967, p. 138). But this may happen because practice increases the number of associations between the material to be learned and other things which are already meaningful—which would make it simply a special case of deepening impressions by increasing their meaningfulness. Or practice may work because it permits persons to find internal reinforcements for remembering which they could not find from just one exposure to the material. Or it may work because exposure time alone makes an impression by cumulating the amount of attention paid to the information to be learned.

Regardless which mechanisms account for it, one of the main effects of practice is that it tends to transfer material from short-term to long-term memory, just as coding processes which increase meaning do. Apparently these processes can work either separately or in combination to produce long-term memories. You remember your true love's phone number forever, having heard it only once, because your chance meeting at the hog-calling contest was fraught with meaning for you. The telephone weather lady's number isn't, so you don't remember it until you have called it many times, and even then, you probably won't start remembering it until you have occasion to call it *often* enough. The practice exposures have to be close enough together to make some cumulative impression. If your meetings with your true love start depending on the weather, though, you likely will remember the weather lady's number forever with little more practice. Now she matters, and practice merges with importance to make the memory indelible.

INFORMATION RETRIEVAL: REMEMBERING

To this point, we have been talking mainly about how to get information into memory storage. Now we shall be concerned with how to get it out, called *retrieval.* This divides into two main topics: *remembering,* the ways in which some memories are recovered, and *forgetting,* how others are lost.

Remembering: Recognition and recall

Every effort at retrieving material stored in memory is an act either of recognition or of recall, and tests of memory, accordingly, use one of these two methods. *Recall* is "the capability for repeating a response," while *recognition* is "the capability for identifying the criterion events from among alternative, new events" (Adams 1967). Your ability to recall is being tested, in other words, when you have to remember something "out of the blue" that you have supposedly learned, without any clues or hints to its content. In a recognition test, the thing you have to remember is sitting there among the different alternatives, and you have to identify it. The processes seem very different, subjectively, regardless of what kind of information is being remembered. If you look at a drawing of a cat, for instance, you can tell immediately whether the ears are placed correctly; you *recognize* its accuracy with ease. But if someone asked you to draw ears on the cat, you would have much more difficulty. You may have seen a cat's ears countless times, but recalling just where they go on its head is a troublesome task for most people.

Recognition In most situations, recognition is a much easier task than recall, sometimes as much as three times easier (Adams 1976). The reason may be that in recall we have very little to go on. We have to search through our entire storage of memories for the one we need. With recognition, on the other hand, we are given much more prompting. We have the drawing of the cat in front of us and our only job is to tell whether its ears are on straight. The drawing provides a host of cues from which we can evaluate the ears in relation to the rest of the anatomy. We only have to decide which of a few possibilities seem correct without having to search our memory in detail (Shepard 1967).

The amount of remembering produced by the recognition method, under some conditions, vastly exceeds anything obtained with recall. In some experiments of R. N. Shepard and his colleagues (1967), subjects first studied a deck of 540 cards, each of which had one word printed on it. Then they were given a new deck of 60 cards; each had two words on it, one from the original deck and one new word. They were able to identify the words from the first deck correctly on about 90 percent of the cards. In similar experiments using sentences and pictures instead of words, with the original batch containing 612 stimuli and the test deck having 68 pairs, people averaged 88 percent correct recognition of the sentences and 98 percent for pictures! Retention diminishes with time, of course, but it can take quite a while; Shepard found that picture recognition remained 92 percent accurate after a week and was still 57 percent accurate after 120 days.

Recognition is not always easier than recall, however. If you must choose the correct response from among a very large number of alternatives, the recognition method does not make memory easier. And if the alternatives are hard to tell apart from each other, then it will be hard to tell the old stimulus from the new ones. You have experienced this yourself in taking multiple-choice tests and matching tests. If the choices are very much alike, or if there are a very large number of items to match, then these recognition tests are no easier to manage than a test which asked you to call things directly out of memory. Another instance where recall is easier than recognition for some people is *spelling.* Many people can tell you the correct spelling of a word almost without thinking, but then cannot recognize for sure that it is correct when they see it. Spelling may be a case of motor memory, however, and the differences we have been talking about in recognition and recall are mostly things involving verbal memory.

In fact, there has been considerably less research on recognition than there has been on recall, and less is known about it. It is possible that recognition and recall are different kinds of retrieval processes, operating by different mechanisms on different aspects of memory. Adams feels that the preliminary evidence supports this notion, and that research on it would provide crucial information on the nature of learning as well as on memory (1967, 1976). At this point, however, the question is unanswered.

Recall Recall may not be any more complex than recognition, but it looks that way because it has been studied more. For one thing, there may be different processes involved in recalling different kinds of things, such as imagery, motor memory, and verbal memory. For another, personal episodes in particular seem to be remembered in somewhat different ways from other things; their recall occurs piecemeal, and it is *productive* as well as *reproductive,* i.e., full of distortions. Recall also occurs in vague uncertainties, for which we seem to possess some mechanism that can evaluate their accuracy.

Much of recall is, of course, verbal, as when you draw words from memory to speak or write. Nonverbal images may be useful in recall, according to Paivio, depending on the nature of the material being learned (see Chapter 9). According to what he calls the *dual-coding hypothesis,* verbal and imagery coding are both used to store some verbal information in the first place, and things which are easily imaged can be recalled more easily by imagery than by words (Paivio 1971). The "imageability" of words has been rated on a scale he invented (Paivio, Yuille, and Madigan 1968). Other experimental results support the idea that imagery can be a powerful device in recall (Bower, 1970; Bower and Winzenz 1970).

Eidetic imagery, which we discussed in the last chapter, is also a form of recall, but unlike memory for other imagery, it probably is not learned. Little is known about the recall of images in general, but Penfield's surgical work suggests that the brain has the capacity to store complex images of the kind that the eidetic imager produces voluntarily (Adams 1967).

Motor recall is particularly interesting because the retention of motor skills works very differently from that of verbal memory. *Continuous* motor tasks, like driving a car, riding a bicycle, ice skating, or, in the laboratory, "tracking" tasks, are retained almost indefinitely and can be recalled, sometimes after years of disuse, with almost immediate precision. Once you learn to ride a bike or drive a car, the skill will stay with you even if you don't practice it. *Discrete* motor skills, on the other hand, such as pulling switches or pushing buttons in response to signal lights and such, are forgotten with about the same speed as verbal memory. Their recall becomes very difficult after fairly short periods of disuse. These peculiarities of motor memory, relative to verbal recall, are not well understood, and may be very important in understanding the nature of forgetting. The study of memory has concentrated on verbal memory, and theory accordingly has been based almost entirely on results in that area.

Redintegration: The archaeology of personal memory The laboratory study of recall is limited chiefly to impersonal events. But there is a kind of recall common to everyone's personal experience in which you reconstruct or *reintegrate* a past event in full detail starting out with only one small recollection. These *re-dintegrative* memories, as they are called, are almost always drawn from personal experiences; they are not usually intellectual memories, as of school subjects, but rather recollections of such personal events as the first dance we ever went to, a childhood birthday party, or a first love affair. Unfortunately, redintegrative memory tends to be more vivid than it is reliable; such recollections are often distorted, even when people are ready to swear by them (Rieff 1959). You can prove this for yourself by arranging to have someone unexpectedly run into the classroom, wearing a welder's helmet and pink corduroys, write a dirty word on the blackboard, erase it, pirouette, do three deep knee-bends, point their fingers like a pistol, say "bang," and flee the room. Immediately afterwards, if you ask everyone to describe what happened, you will get some surprising results. One person may insist it was a man and that he wore a jumpsuit, brandished a real pistol, and wrote *mother* on the blackboard. The local avant-gardist may claim with equal certainty that the stranger was a woman in drag who held a crucifix in her hand and wrote *Mao* on the blackboard. And other reports will differ from these, perhaps reflecting the personality of each per-

Nostalgia—yearning for a remembered past—sometimes idealizes the thing remembered.

Christina's World, Andrew Wyeth

ceiver. In organizing redintegrative memories, we often create scenarios that conform to our personal view of the world.

We are also likely to be influenced a lot by our own stereotypes and by what other people tell us we should have seen or not seen, which creates a terrible problem in situations where eyewitnesses must testify about what happened in crimes or accidents (Buckhout 1974). Leading questions can lead small but significant minorities of witnesses to see things that were not there in the first place or to fail to see what was there. People unwittingly amend their memories with the passage of time, and it is these amended versions which are reconstructed when they testify (Loftus 1975).

When *amnesia* causes people to lose large parts of their memory, it is the redintegrative memories that are most often lost. The amnesia victim can still speak their own language, hail a taxi as usual, and behave at a party like everyone else because these are relatively impersonal habits, reinforced daily throughout life. The names of their third grade teacher, or of the city where they were born, or of their first spouse, are harder to retrieve. This is the stuff of which their *personal* life is made.

Redintegrative memories are reconstructed very much like archaeologists reconstruct the details of a primitive village from four potsherds, an arrowhead, and a fossilized turd—compiled imaginatively from the combination of the items at hand and the storehouse of information they have about other details of this culture or of others like it. You do the same thing, combining the few details you remember with a host of other information about your own history. Some of it is false, of course, but there is no immediate way to check on the workings of your imagination. The few cues you start with are put together in whatever context your current perception of your own past dictates. The result is a mixture of fact and fiction, as our recollections of our own lives always are.

Almost remembering: Searching memory

Redintegrative memory is a way of searching memory, using the single detail with which you start as a kind of address from which to locate the whole family of personal memories that should be associated with it. There are some kinds of internal mechanisms that permit us to engage in some fancy search strategies for recalling other kinds of material, and that help us evaluate, when we think we have found them, whether or not they are accurate. Four such mechanisms are known. Adams names the first two *omission behavior* and *error rejection* (Adams 1967, pp. 282–84); the others are known as the *tip-of-the-tongue* phenomenon (Brown and McNeill 1966) and the *feeling-of-knowing* experience (Hart 1965).

Omission behavior simply means not reporting a response you sort of recall; usually people withhold such responses because they are unsure that their recollection is correct, and usually they are wrong not to take the chance. If you have taken the SAT or some other of those classy multiple choice tests, you doubtless were given instructions to guess at any answers you had some idea of, even if you were unsure. The instructions are based on the fact that a large proportion of such guesses actually are correct answers. Your memory for such things is generally better than your confidence in it.

Error rejection is dismissing our own wrong answers before we get any outside information telling us they are wrong. We all do it all the time—mispronouncing words, saying the wrong word, and immediately correcting ourselves: "No! I mean . . ." Since there is no external corrective or reinforcement operating here to tell us we are wrong, some internal memory searching process, which has access to the correct memory, must be doing the job.

Tip-of-the-tongue phenomena are related to error rejection; you don't have enough cues at hand to recall the stored information, but there are enough to know that you have stored it and to initiate the search. In the tip-of-the-tongue experience you cannot recall the information immediately, but you have the clear feeling that you know it and that it will come to mind soon. You start thinking of words, and you narrow down the search and retrieve words that are similar to the ones you want or reminiscent of them. You reject these, generally recognizing whether or not they are close to the correct response—and eventually it comes out.

The *feeling-of-knowing* is a kind of reliability test for memory searching strategies. Hart gave subjects a recall test for a list of questions and verbal *paired associates*[1] he had given them to memorize. He then had them judge whether they had a feeling of knowing the correct answers to the questions they had missed. It turned out that this feeling actually did predict their choice of the correct responses to those items on a subsequent multiple-choice test (1965). The feeling of knowing, in other words, was a reflection of a memory searching strategy operating throughout the recall and test period.

Relearning Even when recall and recognition fail to recover a memory completely, it may not be lost entirely or forever. As indicated earlier in the chapter, there is some good reason to think that memory, at least any memory that has entered long-term storage, is indelible, whether or not it is immediately recoverable. One test for this permanence is speed of *relearning* material which has been mastered at an earlier time and then forgotten. In general, material once learned is relearned more quickly than it was learned in the first place. The more meaningful the material and the better it had been learned the first time, of course, the more true this is. The best example of this event in everyday life is language relearning, described in the previous chapter. Children who move to a foreign country when they are quite young may completely forget their native tongue. If

they then start studying it in college, they will pick it up much more quickly than someone who is exposed to the language for the first time (Burtt 1941).

Forgetting: Decay versus interference

It is nice to think that everything you ever learn may be permanently etched in your brain, but it would be more credible scientifically and more comfortable personally if you could extract things from the top of your head with more confidence that they are in it to begin with. As it is, we all *forget* things, and we all forget a lot more things than we would like. Why does this happen?

There are two general theories of forgetting, which have evolved since memory research began: *trace decay theory,* which says that some memories just fade away, and *interference theory,* which says that some memories get blocked by events which prevent their recall, even though they remain intact in the brain. The important difference between them is that memories lost by decay are lost forever, while those forgotten because of interference are potentially recoverable. The difference could have very practical implications, ultimately, for things like the development of a "memory pill."

Trace decay theory The decay theory says that a memory will fade away if it is not retrieved from time to time and entertained consciously.[2] The theory assumes that memory involves some kind of chemicals in the brain which, like radioactive substances, disintegrate with the passage of time (Gomulicki 1953). The bulk of evidence contradicts the idea that decay results from mere disuse. Personal memories from the distant past that have not been periodically retrieved are often still available. Continuous

---

[1] A list of linked word pairs, such as book-knob, flower-paper, and so on. You have to memorize the whole list; then memory is tested by saying one word of each pair, and seeing if you can recall the other.

[2] Memory traces are entertained by singing, dancing, thinking, and musing; they do not, however, enjoy spectator sports or watching television.

motor skills are often retained almost whole even if not practiced for years. The great French novelist, Marcel Proust, generated a 5,000 page book, *Remembrance of Things Past,* from a series of long-lost childhood memories that were suddenly evoked in vivid detail by the taste of a certain cookie he used to eat as a child (that's redintegration). Sometimes very old people recall in detail events from childhood that they had not thought of for years. Similarly, people in states of delirium occasionally speak a foreign language unused and forgotten since childhood. Memories have not necessarily decayed physically just because they are unavailable. If anything, the restoration of long-lost memories after years of disuse suggests that they have been blocked by the interference of other learning. Interference could, of course, cause the physical erosion of memory traces, as time alone is thought to do in trace decay theory, but there is no evidence at all to this effect (Adams 1967, p. 27). If interference is what causes forgetting, it apparently does so by *inhibiting* memories, not by *erasing* them.

A classic experiment by Jenkins and Dallenbach (1924) explored this question by testing the recall of nonsense syllables after varying intervals of several hours in which the subjects were sometimes awake and sometimes asleep. If time alone determined how much forgetting would occur, it should have made no difference what they were doing in the hours between

A potpourri of images remembered from childhood can often be recalled with great clarity and precision.

I and the Village, Marc Chagall

learning the lists and having to recall them. In fact, both of their subjects remembered more than twice as many syllables after *sleeping* intervals than after *waking* ones. Obviously, their memories had been subjected to less interference. Variations of the experiment have subsequently confirmed these findings, and at least one study, using subjects who spent the interval after learning in a sensory isolation chamber, showed a tiny improvement in memory for a prose passage over the amount they had remembered on first hearing it (Grissom et al. 1962, as cited by Adams p. 185).

These experiments are very suggestive, but they are not conclusive proof that there is nothing to trace decay theory. Once things are inserted into long-term memory, they may become permanent; but there *was* some loss of memory in the Jenkins-Dallenbach study even when subjects were asleep, and there is no way to be certain that it was the interference of dreams and such rather than the time alone which caused the loss. By the same token, who knows whether the remembrance of things long past is complete and accurate? And unused motor skills are retained *almost* whole, not whole. Maybe the "almost" reflects the ravages of time. Interference theory explains more of long-term memory loss than does trace decay, but not all of it. Trace decay theory cannot be completely dismissed as an explanation for some short-term forgetting either. Although short-term verbal forgetting seems clearly to depend on interference (Waugh and Norman 1965), short-term motor forgetting seems to depend on trace decay alone (Adams and Dijkstra 1966).

Still, far more forgetting, long- and short-term both, is explained by interference theory than by the notion that time alone wipes memory away. And most research on forgetting, therefore, has studied the mechanisms by which interference works.

Inhibition: Retroactive, proactive, and repressive Have you ever noticed on waking up in the morning that if you lie still in bed for a while, you often remember your dreams, and as soon as you get up and start doing things, the details slip away? The press of stimuli on your senses and of thoughts on your mind has interfered with them and dismissed them from consciousness. Most forgetting seems to work like that, by *blocking* or *inhibiting* memories.

There is a constant competition among events in your mind for a place in consciousness, it seems, and the interaction between these competing thoughts and memories causes some of them to obscure others at times when you want to recall them. You experience this, subjectively, not as conflict, but as forgetting.

Sometimes you forget things because they compete with things you *subsequently* learn — the new things you learn make you forget the things you learned at first. This is called *retroactive inhibition* (Postman and Riley 1959). If you memorize something and are tested on it hours later, you will remember more if you have not had to learn anything during the interval. If you went to sleep after learning it, your success in recall the next morning will be even greater than if you merely stayed up and studied nothing, since you are even less subject to learning new things asleep than awake.

At other times, you forget things which are competing with things you have *previously* learned; the original learning makes it harder to learn new material. This is called *proactive* inhibition. The more lists of words you have learned in the past, for instance, the less likely you are to retain a new list. Proactive inhibition is strongest when the material to be learned is nonsensical, and weakest when it is meaningful. If you have been memorizing lists of nonsense syllables, you will have trouble learning yet another one. But if you have memorized a speech from *Hamlet* and then have to learn another soliloquy, it will not be any harder.

Retroactive and *proactive* mean "backwards" and "forwards," but they do not actually refer to a time process in forgetting, but to the interaction of memories that have been stored at different times. Retroactive inhibition means forgetting the things you originally learned because they compete with what you learned more recently. Proactive inhibition means forgetting things you have just recently learned because they compete with things you learned earlier. The processes work somewhat differently for short- and long-term memory and for verbal and motor memory, but they seem to be the fundamental kinds of interference in both.

Repression is another story. It is a special kind of inhibition, in which things are forgotten because they are too anxiety-provoking to bear remembering. Repression is a central concept in Sigmund Freud's psychoanalytic theory of personality and neurosis (*see* Chapters 15 and 18). Freud claimed that many emotional disorders develop as a result of people's unsuccessful efforts to repress painful memories. Neuroses often involve the forgetting of some disturbing memories, and much of psychotherapy is aimed at restoring them to consciousness.

Repression is apparently a type of retroactive inhibition, but it occurs only for personal memories which are frightening, especially those which threaten our view of ourselves. Since all memory is permanent, in Freud's view, everyone experiences some repression because everyone learns some anxiety-provoking things about themselves. When repressed memories are freed, as often happens in psychotherapy, they may return with great drama and a storm of emotion. It is the most dramatic demonstration of the interference theory of forgetting.

The chemistry of memory

As we said earlier, everybody forgets things, and everybody forgets more things than they would like. So it is no wonder that people have been dreaming for a long time of finding something easier than practice and rehearsal and concentration to improve their memories. One hope has been for a memory pill. The chances of finding one depend on finding the chemical nature of memory.

The chemical basis of memory has eluded discovery for a long time, but there has to be one, and some research has explored the idea that chemical changes in the brain connected with memory are chemically reproducible. James McConnell, at the University of Michigan, developed an ingenious behavioral approach to this problem. First, he trained flatworms to solve simple mazes. Then he chopped them up and fed them to naive, uneducated worms—and the uneducated cannibals apparently ate an "education!" Although the cannibals had never been previously exposed to the mazes, they were able to solve them as rapidly as if they *had* received previous training. This was the first important series of *memory-transfer* experiments, demonstrating that some chemical changes in memory can be transmitted directly. Some studies have been unsuccessful in replicating these results, however, and for years McConnell's research group has published *The Worm Runner's Digest,* a delightful technical journal for keeping score on work in this area (Best 1954).

Some studies of chemical memory transfer have been made of higher organisms as well. Allan Jacobson and his colleagues at the University of California at Los Angeles have improved the memories of rats and hamsters with a brain-extract porridge from other rats and hamsters who had previously learned some simple response patterns by conventional training. George Ungar of the Baylor University College of Medicine at Houston, Texas, instilled fear of darkness in uneducated rats by giving them injections of material extracted from the brains of rats who had been trained to fear the dark. The acquired fear usually lasted no more than ten days, but the extent of fear absorbed chemically depended both on the length of training given to the educated rats and on the amount of brain material injected into the uneducated rats. The extract from rats trained for eight days was far more potent than that from rats trained for only two days. Similarly, animals given three-tenths of a gram of brain extract were only mildly afraid of the dark, whereas those given a gram were quite frightened (Ungar, 1970).

There is much disagreement in the scientific world about such results, however, since many scientists fail to reproduce them. Even so, the late David Krech and his colleagues at the University of California at Berkeley have shown definite changes in brain anatomy resulting from "environmental enrichment." The plausibility of a chemical basis for memory is great, and research continues on various compounds that may facilitate it. The partial success of these experiments has led some experimenters to believe that some day a "memory pill" may be discovered that will facilitate human learning and the retention of knowledge.

The most popular current notion is that memory is physically embodied in the brain's supply of RNA (ribonucleic acid), one of the nucleic acids which control the transmission of genetic information. Several experiments have tried to improve memory by administration of RNA, and at least one commercial product, called Cylert, was touted a few years ago as a possible "memory pill," based on its initial effects on rats; its initial results on human beings have been mixed. The growing body of research on memory drugs typically yields ambiguous results, so many scientists remain highly skeptical about the possibility of an injection or pill that could impart to human beings a set of memories or intellectual skills. As Seymour Kety of Massachusetts General Hospital has put it, "Drugs function at the level of emotion, not cognition. I don't see how you could make one that would teach French" (*Newsweek* 1971). Rats and flatworms may learn how to solve a maze or to fear the dark by ingesting the right chemicals, but their nervous organization is much simpler than that of human beings. The search for chemical aids to human memory may be a futile enterprise, or at least a long time coming. James McGaugh of the University of California at Irvine has shown that some memory drugs work only on the most stupid animals, not on beasts that are smart to begin with. Even such a limited result would be very valuable, however, if it could be applied to human beings. At present, in any case, no true memory pill exists and nobody should hold their breath waiting for one. Certain current drugs do aid memory at times, but only by indirect means, as hypnosis does. A tranquilizer may make it easier for someone to concentrate, and thus to remember what they are reading, by removing the distracting effects of anxiety. An energizer may have a similarly beneficial effect on memory by arousing a person enough so they can pay attention. Direct memory pills today, however, are no better than the garlic pills which grandmother used to make her smarter or the glutamic acid pills used for the same purpose in the 1940s (the same ingredients are available commercially as Accent in the United States)—and they will not even flavor or tenderize meat. But the basis for seeking a memory pill is sound, and as knowledge of the chemistry and physiology of memory grows over the next several years, the prospect of such an invention grows more real (London 1977).

SUMMARY

1   Memory means the storage and retrieval of information. Memory is commonly viewed as a learned capability for responding. Operant conditioning may thus be considered a primitive case of *muscle memory,* and classical conditioning as a primitive kind of

glandular memory. Human memory abilities are much greater than those of lower organisms because we can code and store information in the form of language, but neither the biochemistry nor the development of human memory are well understood.

2　You must be paying *attention* for any sense impressions to be memorized. Even then, most impressions are recorded only briefly, and only part of them get remembered. Memory storage takes place in the brain but it is not clear just where. The temporal lobes of the cerebral cortex are apparently responsible for recording information to be stored, and for interpreting it when it is recalled. The hippocampus of the old brain seems to control the transfer of impressions from short- to long-term memory, because long-term memories are no longer stored if the hippocampus is destroyed.

3　Short-term and long-term memory are apparently different storage processes. Short-term memory is "telephone" memory, the sort that permits you to remember a telephone number just long enough to dial it. It differs from long-term memory in three main ways: (1) Only five to nine items can be processed at once in short-term memory, while long-term memory has virtually unlimited capacity; (2) Almost any information can go into short-term memory but it is much harder to qualify for long-term memory; and (3) Short-term memory is stored in images or words, and is disturbed by *acoustic* similarities (words which sound like the ones to be remembered). Long-term memory is stored in concepts and meanings, and gets disturbed by *semantic* similarity (concepts whose meanings are similar to those to be remembered).

4　Information is *coded* into short-term memory in the form of *chunks,* that is, perceptual units. Chunks are *mediated* by learning into large enough sizes to handle considerable information at once. Total *memory span* is nine or less chunks at once, but a lot of information can be pooled into a single chunk. That is why we can remember whole words of far more than nine letters, and whole phrases of far more than nine words.

5　Information goes into long-term memory only if it makes a powerful enough impression to get past short-term memory. Very dramatic events may be permanently remembered the first time they occur. Material which is not very meaningful, on the other hand, must be mediated into groups or concepts which "make sense" in order to be permanently remembered.

6　The deliberate use of mediating processes for remembering things is called *mnemonics.* Mnemonics tries to make things memorable, both by conceptual and perceptual organization. Organizing lists into rhymes is a form of perceptual organization. A series of numbers remembered by finding a word which can represent it, or by acrostics, is a type of conceptual organization. An acrostic is an arrangement in which the first or last letters of words or lines of poetry, when taken in order, would spell out some key word, or easily remembered list, such as the letters of the alphabet. Mnemonics is an ancient art widely used for memorizing poetry and prayers before literacy was common.

7　*Practice* is important in memory storage; it improves memorability of all kinds of information and both kinds of storage. *Overt rehearsal,* such as reciting and reviewing material aloud, and *covert rehearsal,* studying it silently, both help. *Overlearning,* that is, practicing beyond the point where you have first mastered the material, also improves memory. You have overlearned something when you can repeat it automatically, without having to think the motions through one by one. Practice helps to transfer information from short- to long-term memory.

8 Remembering (information retrieval) occurs by *recognition* or *recall*. Recall is the ability to repeat a response, while recognition is the ability to choose correctly among alternatives. Recognition is usually easier than recall, but it is harder if you must choose from among very many alternatives, or if the choices are very much alike. Much less is known about recognition than about recall; they may be fundamentally different retrieval processes which reflect different aspects of memory.

9 Different recall processes are involved in imagery, motor memory, and verbal memory. Eidetic imagery is probably not learned at all. Memory for continuous motor tasks is retained for long periods, while memory for discreet motor skills disappears at about the same rate as verbal memory. *Redintegration* is a special kind of recall in which past events are reconstructed from single small details. It occurs mostly for personal experiences, and is quite subject to distortion.

10 We use several kinds of search strategies for recalling previously learned events and for judging whether our recollections are accurate. *Omission behavior* means not reporting a memory because you are unsure your recollection is correct. Such guesses are more likely to be right than wrong. *Error rejection* is dismissing your own wrong answers before getting outside information that they are wrong. Some internal process which has access to the correct memory must be making this decision. *Tip-of-the-tongue* is related to error rejection. Here, you cannot recall something, but you feel that you know it and that it will soon come to mind. In this process, the search narrows down to words similar to the one you want. You generally reject these, recognizing how close they are to the correct response, which finally comes out. The *feeling of knowing* is a fourth search strategy. When people feel they know the correct answers to items they have forgotten, they actually do tend to choose correct responses on a subsequent recognition test.

11 *Relearning* is the recovery from long-term storage of memories which seem to have been forgotten altogether. In general, material once learned is relearned more quickly than it was learned in the first place. The more meaningful the material and the more it was overlearned the first time, the faster relearning takes place.

12 There are two main theories of why forgetting occurs. The *trace decay theory* says that some memories simply fade away with time. *Interference theory* says that some memories get blocked by events which prevent their recall, even though they remain intact in your brain. Most evidence supports interference theory, but does not prove conclusively that trace decay theory is completely wrong. Some forgetting does occur with the passage of time, and the forgetting of short-term *motor* memories apparently can only be explained by trace decay.

13 Most forgetting is explained by interference theory, especially by the notion that forgetting occurs by the *blocking* or *inhibition* of memories. Most forgetting results from the interaction of competing memories which obscure each other when you want to recall them. Forgetting things which compete with subsequent learning is called *retroactive inhibition;* the new things you learn make you forget the things you learned at first. Forgetting things which compete with previous learning is called *proactive inhibition;* the original learning makes it harder to learn new material. *Repression* is a special kind of inhibition, in which personal experiences are forgotten because they are too anxiety-provoking to bear remembering.

14   People have been dreaming for a long time of finding some kind of pill to improve memory. The chemical basis of memory has been studied a good deal, and while there is considerable evidence that it will be understood soon, the evidence also suggests that a memory-improving drug may not be found in the near future.

Consciousness
11

11

Consciousness

It is common to think of **consciousness** as a light switch—either on or off—and ourselves as either "conscious" or "unconscious." But everyone experiences many different states and degrees of consciousness for which everyday language has a whole vocabulary of different terms. Some of them refer to the *amount* of energy or alertness we seem to feel—excited, calm, sleepy, frenzied, groggy, poised, dull, aroused, comatose. Others tell more about the quality of consciousness than the amount of it—pensive, ecstatic, drunk, stoned, hypnotized, turned on. All of us are all of these at different times because consciousness is a continuous thing, shifting constantly in amount and quality, ranging between coma, the lowest possible state of arousal above death, and frenzy, the highest state of excitement. For the most part, sleep represents the low point of normal arousal and ecstasy (if it is pleasant) or frenzy (if it is unpleasant) the high point.

The quality of consciousness is expressed chiefly in the kind of orientation we experience. In normal wakefulness, we can alternate from a sharp focus upon a specific task to daydreaming, from deliberate concentration, or meditation, to automatic absorptions that overcome us, like anxiety. A state of moderate arousal and sharply focused orientation towards external stimuli is optimal for learning. In normal sleep our level of arousal also fluctuates, and mental experience fluctuates with it.

Different states of consciousness have been recognized throughout history as having different significance in people's lives. In some cultures and religious systems, the achievement of uncommon states has been regarded as virtuous, even saintly, and something worth great effort, suffering, and self-discipline to achieve. In Asia, **Yogi adepts** and **Zen masters** are highly revered for their ability to control their consciousness by respectively manipulating their *breathing* or their *attention*. Among the American Plains Indians, and many other peoples throughout the world, long sieges of fasting or self-punishment are used to produce "sacred dreams," that is, prophetic visions to guide people in choosing careers, wives, hunting policy, or their own names. In the American Southwest, as in many other societies, such *drugs* as *peyote* or *alcohol* have long been the royal road to exalted states of consciousness and the religious experience they brought about. There is virtually no society in the world that has not discovered some kind of fermenting or distilling process to make alcoholic beverages—and the motive for drinking them is the effect, not the taste.

In Western countries, especially where Protestants predominate, there has been a general abhorrence of altered states of consciousness induced by alcohol in particular but also by drugs. Psychological methods like hypnosis have been frowned on, but not reviled completely, perhaps because they have been so widely associated with legitimate medical uses. Yoga and meditation have not been well known outside of Asia, and there have been no popular counterparts to them in the West, though Jewish mystical and Chassidic sects practiced variant forms of meditation for many centuries.

The most popular experience of altered consciousness in "straight" Protestant societies has been ecstatic religious conversions. Some conversion experiences gave rise to some important denominations, starting with St. Paul, but more recently, The Society of Friends (the Quakers), and the Methodists. One of the best descriptions ever written of such events is *The Varieties of Religious Experience* by William James (1902).

Scientific interest in *altered* or unusual *states of consciousness* has been greater than interest in the nature of consciousness itself until very recently. For this reason, there is a much older literature on hypnosis than on sleep, and since the 1960s, when the popularity of psychedelic drugs became so great that everyone began getting interested in them, the literature on it has proliferated faster than on everything else on consciousness put together.

Much the same thing has happened with meditation and Yoga as with psychedelic drugs, apparently for the same reason (Ornstein 1972). They have become popular in recent years, partly because, like drugs, they appear to promise beneficial alterations of consciousness, and partly because, unlike drugs, they do so without harmful side effects.[1] Their popularity is limited, in this connection, by the fact that it takes a great deal of disciplined effort to master them, while the mental effects of drugs are easier to come by, but people generally do not think much about that when they first get into these things.

This chapter tells about the different aspects of consciousness which are commonly regarded as different "states," especially about their induction and their effects on behavior. It includes *sleep* and *dreams; hypnosis;* the various forms of *"turning on"* or of *intoxication* involved in drug and alcohol use; and deliberate meditative states related to "nirvana hunting," such as *Yoga* and *Zen.*

SLEEP

Considering how much of our lives are immersed in sleep, it is amazing that so little is known about it. It is among the most fundamental and primary biological drives because it cannot be denied for long. A person can die of starvation or thirst, but there is no direct way to sleep-deprive someone to death because there is no way to keep them awake long enough for them to die from it. One of the most horrible forms of torture is keeping someone awake for unduly long periods. The main technique of "brainwashing" used to get confessions of all kinds of crimes in the Communist purge trials between

---

[1] Such as getting arrested or poisoned.

Sleep.

1920 and 1953 was a combination of sleep deprivation with endless interrogation. Cramming for final exams or suffering from insomnia should give you an idea in miniature of what it is like.

Despite its great importance, the exact *biological* function of sleep is still unknown. Newborn infants do almost nothing else — they sleep about 22 hours per day for the first several days of life. Some new brain cells are still being created during this period, and some scholars think that sleep contributes something to this process (Altman and Das 1966). In general, sleep seems to be needed to maintain some brain functions and to repair some kinds of wear and tear which the body sustains during the day. But precisely how is mostly unclear.

Infants need less and less sleep as they grow, but the need for sleep at any time from childhood until old age never seems to get much less than seven or eight hours per night, a third of our entire lives. People's total sleep needs apparently start to decline again as they pass into middle age, but they often begin repeating the once familiar patterns of infancy and early childhood — requiring periodic short naps every few hours.

There is tremendous variation in the total amount of sleep different people need at any time of life and in whether sleep is most restful for them in small, short snatches or in the great clumps of time imposed on us all by the culture, which has our lives segmented pretty neatly into work hours, leisure hours, and sleep hours. Evidently, most people are most rested by sleeping in fairly large blocks of time, and mostly at night — it makes sense that our internal sleep clocks would have evolved patterns which follow the diurnal rhythms of the solar day. But many warm weather societies add "siesta" to sleeping at night, also based on an important environmental event, the excessive heat of midday. And the general control which technology is gradually giving us over the environment—in the forms of incandescent lighting, air conditioning, a minimum of working hours, and late shows on television—may make it more possible than ever before in history for people to sleep according to the dictates of their personal internal rhythms and requirements. Everyone's arousal level varies throughout the day in cyclic manner, called circadian rhythms. The pattern of your sleeping varies, depending on where you are in your circadian cycle when you first fall asleep (Kleitman 1963). Your personal sleep needs, accordingly, may vary a good deal from day to day.

People also vary greatly in how long it takes them to fall asleep, how deeply they slumber, and how long it takes them to be fully alert once they wake up. The facts about these things are also not well known, nor are their meanings well understood. If you have trouble falling asleep easily, or if you sleep very deeply, or lightly, or if you take a long time waking up, and are accordingly grumpy and rotten to be around, or if you wake up like lightning and are cheerful and delightful to be with—almost all the most interesting things about people's sleep habits and patterns are not understood.

Even so, the field is not a total blank. Some things are known about the *psychological* functions of sleep, and more is being learned all the time about its measurement, both physiologically and behaviorally.

The current view of the main biological function of sleep is that it tries to conserve energy during the low energy point in an animal's circadian cycle (Webb 1971). The psychological function of sleep, in any case, seems to be just what you think it is—to make you feel refreshed. Sleep relaxes tensions, restores an even mood, that is, makes you feel more calm and good-natured, gives a sense of mental alertness which improves both intellectual problem solving and skilled psychomotor performance, and in that sense, sleep restores your intelligence. Great *fatigue* has devastating effects on most people, tending to make them depressed, irritable, anxious, stupid, and physically uncoordinated. Sleep undoes much of that damage.

The beneficial psychological effects may be far reaching—at the end of the 19th century, some of Europe's most distinguished psychiatrists were experimenting with a "sleep treatment" for neurotic disorders. And fatigue effects can be very serious prolonged disturbances in sleep patterns can be symptoms of serious emotional problems, and insomnia or even laboratory-induced "sleep fasts" always produce minor trouble, such as irritability and depression (Gilbert and Patrick 1896). Although the treatment was quite plausible, it has not been pursued much in this century in Western Europe or the United States, but Soviet psychiatrists are said to be continuing to study its possibilities.

Insomnia, the inability to fall asleep or stay asleep long enough to feel rested, is one of the most awful ailments of everyday life. Many people get temporary insomnia because of unusual circumstances, such as going to bed in a strange place for the first time or trying to fall asleep after a terribly stimulating conversation or before a very exciting trip. Chronic insomnia, where you cannot sleep night after night, is an extreme, and common, version of the same problem.

Insomnia may result from too much arousal. Sleep is a state of low arousal; to fall asleep, the central and autonomic nervous systems must both quiet down enough so we can lose consciousness. Being terribly worked up prevents that from happening, whether you are aroused for pleasant reasons or because of unshakable tensions. Anxiety is a common source of insomnia among college students. This is one reason you should avoid heavy exercise just before going to bed—your large muscles relax from it, but your body is energized and alerted overall.

There is no sure cure for insomnia. Sedative drugs will help many people sleep, but at the risk of some side effects and dangers from barbiturates like *phenobarbitol* or *seconal.* Milder drugs like aspirin or antihistamines work fine for some people. Sex does for others. Recently, relaxation training, a behavior therapy method, has been used with some success in some cases (Borkovek, Steinmark and Nau 1973; Budzynski 1973). For still others, nothing works, and they must simply wait out the agonies of sleepless fatigue as best they can.

One of the worst agonies of insomnia is that *trying to fall asleep* only makes it harder to succeed. The idea of "counting sheep" is aimed at distracting insomniacs from the thoughts preoccupying them including thoughts about how to make themselves fall asleep! Indeed, they would fall asleep if they could discipline themselves to *let their mind wander*—just the opposite of the discipline needed to learn efficiently! Practicing meditation or hypnosis can help develop that ability. For most people, sleep comes naturally whenever they are tired and lie down because they have been conditioned by experience to respond to fatigue by lying down and relaxing their minds. It is a skill which everyone knew at one time, but which insomniacs have to relearn.

Measuring sleep patterns Since sleep is not a simple, uniform state any more than being awake is, its measurement is also not a simple, uniform thing. There are three ways of measuring sleep: (1) by a person's subjective reports; (2) through changes in brain-wave patterns; and (3) from changes in the tension or relaxation of muscles, called *muscle tone.*

In terms of brain-wave patterns, four distinct stages of sleep have been discovered. They differ from each other mostly by showing slower brain-wave activity as sleep becomes deeper. After first falling asleep, we drop fairly soon into the deepest sleep, and then fluctuate back and forth between the different stages all night. Exactly what happens to us mentally during deep sleep is unknown, but there is some evidence that *sleep walking* and the worst nightmares occur in deep sleep (Jacobsen and Kales 1967).

The most important distinction in sleep patterns is that, following deep sleep, a lighter stage develops about an hour and a half after falling asleep. This stage is characterized by *rapid eye movements (REM)* in which the eye muscles become extremely active and the eyeball twitches from side to side. It is called *REM sleep.* Some people claim that they never dream, and others say that they dream constantly; both are probably wrong (Williams et al. 1964). Everyone apparently spends a total of about one hour out of every four in REM sleep, and dreams occur, it seems, whenever there is REM sleep. REM sleep becomes more frequent toward morning, but no one ever spends *all* their time in this stage.

The brain seems to be very active during REM sleep, as shown by increased blood circulation and a rise in body temperature. Conversely, the muscles lose all firmness and become quite slack—so much so that loss of muscle tone is as good an indication of REM sleep as the eye movements themselves. *Some* muscles, however, do a great deal of spontaneous twitching, particularly those associated with walking (Dement 1965). The old wives' tale that when a dog twitches its paws, it is dreaming of chasing a cat, may not be so farfetched after all.

Other strange reactions are related to REM sleep. Males usually get erections during it, and cats that have been deprived of REM sleep become sexually aggressive, hostile, and hungry. Schizophrenics do not seem to require as much REM sleep as do normal people; perhaps since some schizophrenics hallucinate frequently, they discharge the same kinds of brain activity during waking hours that normal people need to do only during REM sleep (Vogel and Traub 1969).

Several experiments have tested what happens to normal people deprived of REM sleep (and therefore of dreaming) for several nights in a row by being awakened whenever their muscle tone or brain-wave pattern shows they are starting to dream. They will make up for their lost REM periods as soon as they are permitted to do so by sleeping a lot. Beyond a certain limit, however, no additional REM deprivation takes place; people need no more REM sleep after 70 days than after 30 days of REM deprivation. A second less certain finding is that the longer people are prevented from dreaming, the more irritable and anxious they become, the more weight they gain, the more stress they show and the more trouble they have concentrating. The uncertainty of this conclusion results from the fact that it is hard to do REM-deprivation studies lasting longer than 12 nights because it gets harder and harder to awaken subjects out of REM sleep. People start to hallucinate, lose their sense of reality, and become apathetic and agitated. Severe alcoholics sometimes have hallucinations, called the "DTs" (delirium tremens), and there is a theory that alcohol suppresses REM sleep so that the dream functions are transferred into walking periods. Perhaps we *must* dream, if not when asleep, then when awake. But why?

The function of dreams

In *The Interpretation of Dreams* (1900), Sigmund Freud proposed that the main function of dreaming is to keep us asleep. Everyone has dreamt sometime that the buzz of an alarm clock is some wonderful message telling us we do not have to get up. Similarly, when it is cold or we have a full bladder, we sometimes dream that we are fetching another blanket or urinating.[2] More important, says Freud's theory,

in dreams we resolve problems that are so disturbing they might otherwise awaken us, often disguising the problem within the dream by converting it into symbolic terms which may seem nonsensical when we recall them.

Freud called dreams "the guardians of sleep" and also "the royal road to the unconscious." To interpret a dream, according to Freud's theory, we must first discover the "daily residue" of things troubling a person before going to sleep; these are the problems their dreams have attempted to work out. Their real content, called the *latent content,* is hidden under the symbolic cover of the dream they report, called the *manifest content,* that is, the outward story. Freud hypothesized that the dreamer uses three different methods to disguise the latent content: (1) *condensation,* that is the collapsing, accordion-fashion, of several different themes into a single word or image; (2) *displacement,* a process in which one object stands for another related object, for instance dreaming of a finger as a substitute for the penis, and (3) *symbolization,* in which one object, like a snake, stands arbitrarily for something totally unrelated, like a mother-in-law.

Freud's dream theory is probably true in large part, but most students do not accept the idea that the main function of dreams is to preserve sleep. They reason that if REM is a good measure of dreaming, then babies and lower mammals do more dreaming than adults do, but they certainly do not have more problems on their waking minds to make so much dreaming necessary. Also, it is impossible to measure scientifically how accurate Freud's notion is of the symbolization process in dreaming. Psychoanalysts use the Freudian method of *free association* with considerable success in analyzing patients' dreams, but disagree about what different dream symbolism means. Carl Jung and Erich Fromm, for instance, give very different explanations of dream symbolism than Freud did (Fromm 1951; Jung 1969a and 1969b). An objective scale has been de-

---

[2] In the case of little kids, they are not always dreaming.

The Sleeping Gypsy, Henri Rousseau
Dreams . . . the guardians of sleep?

veloped for studying the manifest content of dreams. It shows typically different contents for male and female dreams, reflecting stereotypic differences between the sexes in our culture (Hall and Van de Castle 1966).

Of course, it is always possible that dreams serve no practical purpose at all, but are merely a side effect of the fact that your brain stays on while you are asleep. No one knows.

HYPNOSIS

Hypnosis has been known and used, in one or another form, since very ancient times. It began to gain scientific recognition (condemna-

tion, to be precise) during the American Revolution, when Benjamin Franklin helped a French Royal Commission put down "animal magnetism" or "mesmerism," as it was then called, and dismantle the booming business of Franz Anton Mesmer, generally considered the father of modern hypnosis. Mesmerism was renamed "neurohypnotism" by England's James Braid because of its superficial resemblance to sleep. It was variously used and rejected by an assortment of European hospitals, surgeons, and psychiatrists through the 19th century, and was first adopted and then abandoned by Freud at the end of the century in favor of the psychoanalytic method he had deduced from it.

Despite a long history and huge case literature, there is less real knowledge about hypnosis than there are great claims for its power over human behavior. Current work on hypnosis in the United States is still done by a very few individuals and laboratories; Russian scientists have had a more consistent interest in it than Americans have, but they do not seem to have learned as much about it. But while Americans have done better in some respects, many crucial scientific questions about hypnosis remain unanswered.

Even so, hypnotic lore continues to grow. More claims have probably been made for the power of hypnosis to manipulate people than for any other technique in history. There is hardly any human behavior untouched by somebody's claim that it could be changed significantly, for better or for worse, by hypnosis.

The scariest, and generally most fictitious stories about hypnotic behavior control claim that hypnosis can turn people into automatons, subject to the will of the hypnotist, who can force the victim to do absurd, dangerous, or criminal acts. Worse than that, victims cannot help being hypnotized; it can be done against their will or without their knowledge, can be done to individuals or to masses, over radio or television, and can even be done without the physical presence of the hypnotist. Finally, the hypnotic trance can be perpetuated or renewed periodically by signals or posthypnotic suggestions which will make its victims hypnotize themselves. Such notions are not only the stuff of plays and novels. Many educated people, to this day, believe that the monk Rasputin controlled the last Czarina of Russia by hypnosis, and there have been court trials for murder and seduction in which the criminal

Some people can be transported, via music, to a state of consciousness resembling hypnosis.

The Musicians, Michelangelo da Caravaggio

acts were ostensibly committed under the irresistible sway of hypnotic suggestions.

Less extravagant claims for hypnosis say that it can be used to control thinking, emotions, attitudes, motivation, physiological processes, physical performance capacities, and all sorts of mental and physical ailments. According to these claims, it can be used to increase memory or recover lost memories or produce amnesia; to speed up learning; to provoke dreams and hallucinations; to make people lose consciousness of their surroundings; to reduce resistance to interrogations; to induce emotional states; to change attitudes toward race, religion, or politics; to increase motivation, making people capable of abnormal feats of strength, endurance, or coordination; to increase resistance to heat or cold or fatigue or pain; to change heart rate, blood pressure, or the electrical activity of skin or brain; to raise heat blisters on the skin; to anesthetize people so that major operations can be performed without chemicals; to remove warts; to cure asthma; and much, much more. There is some real evidence in support of such claims!

All these things have actually been done with hypnosis and described in the clinical literature; a few have been verified by experiments. There are cases of athletes hypnotized before contests to improve their performance; there are laboratory studies substantiating such procedures; and such upright, serious organizations as the National Institutes of Health and the USAF Aerospace Medical Laboratories, support research on hypnosis as a medical, educational, and military tool. Still, the power of hypnosis is overrated. The variety of hypnotic effects is remarkable, but they are also remarkably undependable from one subject to another. They can rarely be produced without the consent and cooperation of the subject; and when they do occur, they are not always the result of hypnosis itself, but may be a byproduct of the situation. Mass hypnosis is certainly possible, as anybody knows who has watched

stage hypnotists perform; it can be done over radio or television—but not everybody will be hypnotized, even if they want to be; almost no one will be hypnotized unless they are paying attention and cooperating with the hypnotic suggestions; and even then, no one is likely to become a robot or to be helplessly irresponsible for what they do. Hypnosis has some potent effects, but they are not come by cheaply, easily, or dependably.

Hypnotic control of cognition Learning, memory, and imagination can all be affected by hypnosis. It can aid learning by improving concentration and by relieving anxiety, which inhibits concentration and learning ability. Sometimes a technique called "time distortion" is used to speed up mental rehearsal; the subjects imagine living through hours, days, or months in what the clock marks as a few seconds, or minutes, and can practice music, foreign languages, or other skills in their minds.

Hypnotized people often undergo unusual tricks of memory, called "amnesia" (loss of memory) and "hypermnesia" (increased memory). Amnesia sometimes occurs spontaneously after a hypnotic session, but it is more often suggested by the hypnotist. Posthypnotic suggestions commonly include the suggestion to forget that they were given. In psychotherapy, the ability to request amnesia enables the hypnotist to elicit disturbing ideas during the session and to put them "under wraps" again afterward.

Hypermnesia does not seem to occur spontaneously; it is used to aid learning and to help people recover lost memories. Police and lawyers have used hypnotic hypermnesia to get witnesses to recall crimes or accidents, especially in cases where the witness is suffering some kind of traumatic loss of memory.

Hypnosis generally has a relaxing effect on people, which tends to lower their psychological defenses. One reason that learning and memory sometimes improve in this state may be that tension and anxiety do not have their usual distracting influence. The combination of lowered defenses and hypermnesia sometimes makes hypnosis useful for the interrogation of spies or prisoners.

Many people can have vivid hallucinations when hypnotized and can project themselves so completely into a suggested scene that they believe they are part of it. This capacity is used to produce "age regression," in which the subject re-experiences some event of earlier life, often with intense repressed emotions from the past. Hallucinations may also be induced by having subjects imagine watching a movie screen while a scene from their life unfolds on it; they can just observe and report what they watch rather than tax their memory and emotions to recollect. Or the hypnotist can suggest that upon some such signal as the snapping of fingers, the count of five, or the tap of a pencil, the subjects will find themselves growing smaller and younger until they are only "x" years old, in their childhood house, maybe attending their birthday party, wetting their pants, or lusting after their mothers. Stage hypnotists use this method to get people to act roles in public that they are ordinarily too embarrassed to play.

Hypnotic control of emotion and motivation Dramatic emotional changes also occur in hypnosis. People laugh at no obvious jokes, grieve over no apparent deaths, are furious at no visible enemy, or fearful of no apparent danger, or sexually aroused by no evident partner—all upon demand. Stage hypnotists put people through such emotional paces to entertain their audiences; psychotherapists do it to enlighten their patients. Emotional outbursts sometimes occur spontaneously in hypnosis, but more often they are elicited by hypnotists. People have been aroused to murderous fury or extreme sexual excitement during hypnosis. Some experiments have induced antisocial behavior in hypnosis in which people have thrown acid in somebody's face, picked up live poisonous snakes, and other

pleasantries, on instruction. Some brilliant studies by Martin T. Orne and his colleagues suggest that this kind of behavior is not a direct outcome of hypnosis but rather of the implicit expectation experimental subjects have that the scientists who get them into these things will protect them against harm, even if their instructions seem not to (Orne 1971). Whether or not Dr. Orne is correct, hypnosis *is* the kind of situation in which people sometimes obey crazy or dangerous suggestions.

Hypnosis can also be a tool for raising motivation. People's normal desire to do well can be increased if they are exhorted to do well while hypnotized. At Stanford's Laboratory of Hypnosis Research, Robert Slotnick, Robert Liebert, and Ernest R. Hilgard found that hypnotic exhortations were even more effective if experimental subjects were emotionally committed to the experiment (1965), a result confirmed by Kenneth Schaeffler and myself at the University of Southern California (1969).

Hypnotic control of performance and physiology Military planners and trainers of athletes are most interested in hypnosis for its positive effects on strength, endurance, coordination, and attention. Aerospace scientists are interested in it for stress resistance, to help pilots or astronauts function in the face of equipment failures which might subject them to extreme heat, cold, pain, or fear. At Wright-Patterson Air Force Base in Ohio, college students were trained hypnotically to resist extreme heat for up to an hour, while continuously working at a "vigilance" task, by devoting part of their consciousness to more comfortable things. One student, after leaving the "hot box," where physiological recordings showed that he was slowly being "cooked" by the 140 degree heat, said that he thought about his summer as a life guard and felt comfortable throughout the session. Michael Ogle, I. P. Unikel, and I found a similar result in a heat-stress study at the University of Illinois (London et al. 1968b).

Merely feeling good while one slowly roasts

or freezes to death is not a good resistance to stress, however; there is some evidence that hypnosis affects body functions as well as subjective feelings. There have been studies showing that hypnosis helps diminish the effects of freezing temperatures on heartbeat and shivering, among other things (Kissen, Reifler, and Thaler 1969). Ronald McDevitt and I found the same thing using autohypnosis. Still others have reported or evaluated other physiological effects of hypnosis and concluded that it can, indeed, produce such effects as skin blisters (Paul 1963), altered blood flow, skin-temperature changes, and more (Hilgard 1975). It has also been used successfully to treat some psycho-physiological problems, such as warts, migraine headaches, and asthma (Bowers 1976).

Perhaps the most interesting use of hypnosis is for the relief of pain in medicine and dentistry. This is actually one of the oldest medical uses of hypnosis; hundreds of major surgeries under hypnotic anesthesia were reported in 1850 by James Esdaille, a British Army surgeon in India (Esdaille 1957). Its scientific investigation has only recently become popular, however, and relatively little still is known about how or why it works. One of the most curious facts so far learned about hypnotic anesthesia is that physiological indicators of pain remain present even when subjective reports of it are absent (Hilgard and Hilgard 1975). The hypnotically anesthetized subject *feels* no pain, in other words, but the autonomic nervous system recordings say they should be feeling it!

Hypnosis in psychotherapy   Hypnosis has had a mixed history as a psychotherapeutic tool. Most psychoanalysts have had nothing to do with it since Freud observed that symptoms removed by authoritarian means, which he thought were involved in hypnosis, later returned or were replaced by other, sometimes worse, symptoms. A few psychoanalysts, however, have written favorably of its therapeutic value. Hypnoanalysis, so called, is psycho-analysis that uses hypnosis to facilitate the analytic process.

The most important uses of hypnosis in psychotherapy are for lowering mental defenses, which gives people access to their hidden thoughts and feelings, and for raising the capacity to have powerful imagery. Lowering defenses helps people to free associate, to talk, to dredge up memories, and to disclose their inner selves. Evoking imagery enables the therapist to help patients uncover hidden material as if it were being experienced for the first time, rehearse new situations as if they were real, and as if patients were strangers observing themselves—and to cover up the whole mess at the end of the session should it look like too great a burden for the patient to consciously handle. With hypnotic suggestions, the therapist can get patients to write "automatically," with no conscious plan; to distort time; to have images flash in and out of mind, or make emotions rise, play out, and disappear. Patients sometimes come to understand the dynamics of their own physical symptoms and explain their unconscious causes as if they always knew what troubled them and only lacked the opportunity to tell—or to transfer symptoms to another part of the body where they would be less troublesome. One hypnotherapist I knew persuaded a man with a dangerous bladder retention problem to urinate as he needed, but to develop a twitch in his "pinky," just to have a physical symptom for his hidden mental woe. In another case, a psychiatrist reported how he persuaded a schizophrenic girl, obsessed with ghostly shadows following her, to deposit all of the ghosts in his coat closet between therapy sessions, and the rest of the time to go about like everybody else. There are innumerable reports like these, many of them well documented. Even the Royal Commission that "did in" Mesmer two centuries ago admitted that his cures were real, and criticized them only because they were achieved "merely" by suggestion.

No one knows why most hypnotic effects occur. Some of them probably are byproducts of relaxation, or of the expectations which subjects or patients have of scientists or doctors. In such cases, hypnosis itself is irrelevant to what happens; any impressive interpersonal situation or any mumbo jumbo like the hypnotic induction might produce the same effects. For such things, we ought to study the persuasiveness of hypnotists rather than the potency of hypnosis. Some hypnotists, indeed, claim that hypnotic effects are a result of their skill, but there is no clear evidence that hypnotic effects depend on such skill.

What they do depend on is evidently so subtle, complicated, and poorly understood as to make hypnosis a very undependable instrument, despite its great value in some cases. Learning, memory, and emotion are dramatically manipulable in some people by hypnosis; but methods which have profound effects on one person have no effect on another. One subject is totally amnesic; another remembers everything, including the suggestion to forget; a third remembers some things, but not others; a fourth remembers what they were supposed to forget and forgets everything else. And so it goes.

Hypnotic susceptibility One of the main factors in responsiveness to hypnosis is the susceptibility of the subject to being hypnotized in the first place. Susceptibility does not mean willingness or gullibility, but the ability to follow unconventional instructions to have uncommon subjective experiences.[3] Almost everyone can be hypnotized to some extent, children much more easily and deeply, on the whole, than adults (Cooper and London 1966; London 1976). The ability to be hypnotized does not depend much on sex, intelligence, or personality traits—but it is a very stable characteristic of individuals, much like IQ, and a

number of standardized scales exist for measuring it objectively in children and adults.

To be hypnotized, you must give up the critical faculties with which you would normally view the suggestions someone gives you. This enables you to accept logical contradictions, immerse yourself in unreal or bizzare roles, shift quickly from one mood to another and perceive your own body in unusual ways. Almost nobody can be hypnotized unwillingly, but occasionally, a person may be hypnotized unknowingly, without realizing what is going on.

Nobody really knows what hypnotic susceptibility is or, for that matter, what hypnosis is. The scientific convention is to call it "an altered state of awareness," but that does not tell much.

Until recently, there was no evidence that hypnosis had any physiological side; it seemed to be a purely behavioral event. For this reason, some theories said that hypnotic behavior was really an attempt by subjects to take behavioral roles of whatever kind the hypnotist wished—a sort of unconscious dramatic acting (Sarbin and Coe 1972). Other theories argued that hypnosis was a "state" of altered consciousness to which "acting" of any kind was irrelevant. Though there is no sure proof for either case, several experiments have shown that there is a definite physiological correlate of hypnotic susceptibility in people's brain wave patterns. People who are highly susceptible to hypnosis produce more *large, slow brain waves* under normal waking conditions than low susceptibles do (London et al. 1968a; Galbraith et al. 1970). These brain waves, called *alpha* and *theta waves,* characterize relaxed states. The production of alpha waves, and of hypnotic susceptibility, can be increased by teaching people to adjust their mental states to auditory feedback signals when they are emitting this rhythm. The subjective feelings of people emitting alpha waves and of the same people when they are under hypnosis are very similar (Engstrom et al. 1970).

---

[3] This definition really says that hypnotic susceptibility is the ability to be hypnotized. A more elaborate definition could only make this fact more obvious. I am sorry.

CHILDREN'S HYPNOTIC SUSCEPTIBILITY SCALE
SCORING & OBSERVATION FORM

Child's Name_____

	Year	Month	Day
Date	____	____	____
Birthdate	____	____	____
Age:	____	____	____

Session #_____

Hypnotist_____

Observer_____

Score_____
using (check one):
____ 4-point scale
____ + — scale

Standard scoring procedures call for a four-point scale and it is recommended that performances be recorded in this manner. Those who prefer a simple Pass (+) vs. Fail (−) dichotomy may later reduce scores to such a scale by counting 0 and 1 scores as Fail (−) and 2 and 3 scores as Pass (+).

Try to record time in the left hand margin, but remember that observations of behavior are more important than precise time records. In the blank space under each item, make special note of the child's apparent subjective reaction to the experience, e.g. is he particularly sluggish? alert? sober? amused? How hard does he seem to be trying on the challenge items? Do some of his responses appear to be "unconsciously" determined, e.g. does response to post-hypnotic suggestion seem natural and unstudied or merely compliant?

Check the appropriate response in each item and enter its number on line at right.

PART I

Time | Score

1. POSTURAL SWAY
(Score only on first attempt, i.e., on basis of performance during initial reading of Paragraphs 2, 3, and 4.)
____ (3) Falls.
____ (2) Loses balance and recovers without falling.
____ (1) Sways, but does not lose balance.
____ (0) Little or no swaying, no loss of balance.

2. EYE CLOSURE
____ (3) Eyes close and remain closed before examiner completes Paragraph 5.
____ (2) Eyes close within 10 seconds after completion of Paragraph 5, or close before time limit but occasionally reopen briefly.
____ (1) Becomes drowsy, but eyes do not close within limit.
____ (0) No marked drowsiness, and only closes eyes when specifically told to do so.

3. HAND LOWERING (Left)
____ (3) Hand lowers to resting position within time limit.
____ (2) Hand moves through 30 degree arc or more, but does not lower to rest.
____ (1) Hand lowers through less than 30 degree arc.
____ (0) Hand does not move noticeably.

4. ARM IMMOBILIZATION (Left)
____ (3) Hand rises less than 1" from chair by time limit, or with slow, effortful movement, up to 3".
____ (2) Hand rises from 1" to 3" by time limit, or with slow, effortful movement, up to 4".
____ (1) Hand rises from 3" to 6", relatively easy, smooth, rapid movement.
____ (0) Hand rises more than 6", relatively easy, smooth, or rapid motion.

Figure 11.1 Sample of a scoring sheet (first page only) from the Children's Hypnotic Susceptibility Scale.

DRUG TRIPS

One of the most controversial legal, moral, and medical questions of modern America is the effect of "mind-bending" drugs (Klerman 1974). Since 1955, when modern tranquilizers burst into the American market, mood-changing drugs have been used routinely in mental hospitals—and have become, sometimes with unfortunate effect, a part of the lives of millions of Americans. By 1967, 178 million prescriptions for mood-changing drugs were

Name	Chemical or trade name	Slang name	Classification	Usual dose	Duration of effect	Effects sought	Long-term symptoms
Heroin	Diacetylmorphine	H., Horse, Scat, Junk, Smack, Scag, Stuff, Harry	Narcotic	Varies	4 hrs.	Euphoria, prevent withdrawal discomfort	Addiction, constipation, loss of appetite
Morphine	Morphine Sulphate	White Stuff, M.	Narcotic	15 Milligrams	6 hrs.	Euphoria, prevent withdrawal discomfort	Addiction, constipation, loss of appetite
Codeine	Methylmorphine	Schoolboy	Narcotic	30 Milligrams	4 hrs.	Euphoria, prevent withdrawal discomfort	Addiction, constipation, loss of appetite
Methadone	Dolophine Amidone	Dolly	Narcotic	10 Milligrams	4-6 hrs.	Prevent withdrawal discomfort	Addiction, constipation, loss of appetite
Cocaine	Methylester of Benzoylecgonine	Corrine, Gold Dust, Coke, Bernice, Flake, Star Dust, Snow	Stimulant, local anesthesia	Varies	Varied, brief periods	Excitation, talkativeness	Depression, convulsions
Marijuana	Cannabis Sativa	Pot, Grass, Hashish, Tea, Gage, Reefers	Relaxant, euphoriant; in high doses, hallucinogen	1-2 Cigarettes	4 hrs.	Relaxation; increased euphoria, perceptions, sociability	Usually none
Barbiturates	Phenobarbital, Nembutal, Seconal, Amytal	Barbs, Blue Devils, Candy, Yellow Jackets, Phennies, Peanuts, Blue Heavens	Sedative-hypnotic	50-100 Milligrams	4 hrs.	Anxiety reduction, euphoria	Addiction with severe withdrawal symptoms, possible convulsions, toxic psychosis
Amphetamines	Benzedrine, Dexedrine, Desoxyn, Meth-amphetamine, Methedrine	Bennies, Dexies, Speed, Wake-Ups, Lid Proppers, Hearts, Pep Pills	Sympatho-mimetic	2.5-5 Milligrams	4 hrs.	Alertness, activeness	Loss of appetite, delusions, hallucinations, toxic psychosis
LSD	D-lysergic Acid Diethylamide	Acid, Sugar, Big D, Cubes, Trips	Hallucinogen	100-500 Micrograms	10 hrs.	Insightful experiences, exhilaration, distortion of senses	May intensify existing psychosis, panic reactions
DMT	Dimethyl-triptamine	AMT, Business-man's High	Hallucinogen	1-3 Milligrams	Less than 1 hr.	Insightful experiences, exhilaration, distortion of senses	?
Mescaline	3,4,5-trimethoxy-phenethylamine	Mesc.	Hallucinogen	350 Micrograms	12 hrs.	Insightful experiences, exhilaration, distortion of senses	?
Alcohol	Ethanol Ethyl Alcohol	Booze, Juice, etc.	Sedative-hypnotic	Varies	1-4 hrs.	Sense alteration, anxiety reduction, sociability	Cirrhosis, toxic psychosis, neuro-logic damage, addiction
Tobacco	Nicotiana Tabacum	Fag, Coffin Nail, etc.	Stimulant-sedative	Varies	Varies	Calmness, sociability	Emphysema, lung cancer, mouth and throat cancer, cardiovascular damage, loss of appetite

Figure 11.2 Table of drugs, including alcohol.

being filled yearly, and by 1977, about 270 million, with tranquilizers far outselling stimulants. By now, up to 40 percent of the adult population of the United States uses some chemical compound to ease psychological distress in any one year (Balter and Levine 1971; London 1977).

But tranquilizers are not the drugs that have stirred up all the trouble. Five other kinds of drugs plus alcohol cause the turmoil: (1) *opiates* (from the poppy flower), including *heroin;* (2) *marijuana, THC* (tetrahydrocannabinol) and *hashish;* (3) *LSD* and the hallucinogens; (4) the *energizers* (especially amphetamines); (5) the *sedatives,* (especially barbiturates); and (6) *alcohol,* which has made more trouble in more lives than all the others put together.

Opiates: The geography of Xanadu

Opium has been used since ancient Egyptian times as a sedative and pain-killer. Helen of Troy probably used it as a "sorrow-easing drug." Only in the 19th century did it become an addictive drug for large numbers of people. The invention of the hypodermic needle and the chemical isolation of one opium derivative, morphine, facilitated addiction by allowing concentrated doses to take effect very quickly, producing an easy "high." Morphine and some variants of it are still widely used by doctors as pain-killers.

Another opium derivative, *heroin,* has become a major health problem in the United States. Heroin can be taken either by injection or by sniffing. Injection works fastest because the drug goes directly into the blood stream. Heroin produces a feeling of euphoria and relief from pain and anxiety. Some addicts report that they feel invulnerable, mysterious and inscrutable, immune to the "slings and arrows of outrageous fortune" (Williams 1964). In the Vietnam War, the use of heroin among American soldiers reached epidemic proportions, partly because the drug is cheap and plentiful there and partly, perhaps, because it reduced the anxiety of soldiers in great danger for long periods. It did so, sometimes, at the price of giving them hepatitis or other serious diseases from "dirty needles," and an assortment of social and health problems. The most serious of these, of course, is addiction, more for legal than physiological reasons.

It takes longer to get "hooked" on heroin than most people realize, generally several weeks of frequent usage, one or more times daily. Once hooked, however, the craving for heroin increases steadily, and larger and larger amounts are necessary to produce the same "high." Since the drug is illegal almost everywhere, the growth of this craving can be disastrously costly, forcing addicts into theft, prostitution, or other crimes in order to get money for the drug. It is not known whether heroin use does any physical damage to the users—its greatest damage, if any, is to the pattern of their life, not to their body. The incidence of heroin addiction in the United States reached epidemic proportions in the 1960s and climbed steadily until 1967-69, but has declined sharply since then. So has the crime rate connected with it (McGlothlin 1975).

Withdrawal from heroin is a painful process, but not a dangerous one (unlike addiction to barbiturates, where sudden and total withdrawal can be lethal). Addicts who stop taking heroin go through five or six days of vomiting, sneezing, delusions, and hot and cold flashes— but then are free of the drug's physiological spell, although they may still crave it.

No treatment has had complete success with heroin addiction. The most successful institutions, such as California's *Synanon,* are self-help communities which give addicts a chance to change their life style among a group of people who demand great interpersonal openness and social responsibility of them.

The most widely used current treatment method is another addictive drug called

Withdrawal.

Methadone, a synthetic opiate which is much like heroin except that it is legal to administer. This means that doctors can give heroin addicts decreasing doses of methadone until their craving disappears without making them suffer the anguish of "cold turkey" (total withdrawal). In England, it is legal for doctors to give "maintenance doses" of heroin to confirmed addicts as a means of helping them ease out of the addiction.

Studies of opiates have the considerable advantage over most studies of psychotropic drugs in that their chemical action in the brain is beginning to be well understood. It was recently discovered that the brain manufactures opiate-like substances of its own, called **endorphins,** and that there are specific sites in the brain, called **receptors,** to which these endorphins get attached or **bound.** The more tightly a compound can bind to these receptors,

the more powerful the reaction. Since opiate drugs, such as morphine and heroin, have the right chemical composition, they can bind to the brain receptors to suppress pain or relieve "sorrow" just as the brain's own endorphins would (Snyder 1977). The discovery of the endorphins, incidentally, may help to explain why hypnosis or other psychological states can relieve pain—they may work by stimulating the brain to produce its own anesthetic!

Psychedelic drugs: Expand your mind—or blow it?

The worst thing about any addiction is that it forces addicts into a lifestyle which revolves around their craving. The psychedelic or "mind-expanding" drugs do not force such changes in lifestyle because they are not addictive at all. They do affect people's perceptions of the world, however, and may influence them to re-examine their relationship to it. Some people consider this therapeutic; others fear that it will lead young people to forsake conventional goals and view it as dangerous.

The Indian rope goes up in smoke: Marijuana and hashish Marijuana ("pot" or "grass") is not a narcotic, is not addictive and probably is not detrimental to the user's health. It and **hashish** (called "hash" or "shit") both come from the Indian hemp plant, cannabis, marijuana from the leaves and flowering tops, the stronger hashish from the resin and pollen. *THC,* the major active ingredient, has been synthesized in the laboratory. There is no evidence that the use of marijuana or hashish leads to the use of heroin or other "hard" drugs. Hemp drugs are not physically dangerous, it seems, although some users have had "bad trips," that is, unpleasant or disturbing experiences, on them. Under some circumstances, marijuana may actually be useful medically because it tends to lower blood pressure. Research on the hemp drugs is now being done in the National Institutes of Health in Bethesda, Maryland.

Despite medical commission reports starting in 1894 and reporting over and over again since then that marijuana is not a menace, but just a nuisance, the hemp drugs have had a "bad press," which has caused them to be illegal everywhere in the United States (Julien 1975). At the same time, they have become popular enough so that by 1971 (and since) Gallup polls found more than half the college students in this country admitting to their use at least once (McGlothlin 1975). There has been a corresponding trend in professional and government circles to have possession of marijuana "decriminalized." In 1977, President Carter asked Congress to pass laws for this purpose; a few states, such as California and Oregon, have already started to do so.

The hemp drugs may be either eaten or smoked. When eaten, it takes longer to feel the effect; smoking works in a few minutes. "Trips" usually last two to five hours. The most noticeable drug effects are changes in sensation and perception; sounds and sights seem bolder and sharper. Skin receptors become more sensitive; heat, cold and pressure are felt more acutely. Time seems to pass more slowly. Ordinary objects seem new and strange; their functions seem less important, their forms seem fresh and vivid. Your attention seems less easily distracted, and what you do focus upon seems immensely important. One theory about these effects is that marijuana cuts down the number of mental associations people have to an event; missing some of your customary associations to these familiar things consequently makes them seem strange. Those things you do experience, however, are evoked with great potency.

The apparent focusing effect of cannabis and the altered perception that goes with it makes some people feel that using these drugs stimulates creativity. In most cases, it does not; it just makes you feel good. Almost any kind of creative work, from writing poetry or painting pictures to building bird cages, needs intense concentration; that is not what you get on drug trips.

Two final effects of cannabis drugs are of interest. One is that for some people, they have a strong aphrodisiac effect. The other is, that for many, they are also a great hunger stimulant. No one knows why, just as no one knows how the physiology of the cannabis drugs produces their peculiar mental effects.

LSD: The acid test of psychedelics LSD was discovered in 1943 when a Swiss chemist, Albert Hoffman, accidentally swallowed a minute quantity of a new chemical compound, lysergic acid diethylamide-25. As he stumbled crazily around, Hoffman realized that he had also stumbled upon the most powerful mind-altering drug known to man. LSD is derived from ergot, a fungus that infects rye. It is a white powder, odorless, and essentially taste-less. It dissolves easily in water, but it is used in such minute quantities that there is little need to take it "in" anything. A dose of 100 micro-grams (one ten-thousandth of a gram) can pro-duce dramatic effects lasting 8 to 12 hours or more. LSD-25 is very similar in chemical struc-ture to serotonin, a substance in the brain that may be important in emotional, perceptual, and cognitive functions. Exactly how LSD and the brain's production and distribution of serotonin affects behavior is not yet known. Current re-search seems to indicate that LSD partly blocks the action of serotonin in the brain (Aghajanian, Heigler, and Bennet 1975).

One cannot say with certainty that LSD is harmless. A small number of psychoses, suicides, and murders have apparently been induced by LSD. These amount to only a tiny fraction of the drug trips that people have taken, and some of the horror stories attributed to the drug are doubtless evasions of responsibility for bizarre behavior. Even so, there is no way to be sure. A drug as powerful in minute doses as LSD seems likely to have some uncon-trollable effects on some people, especially in large doses.

LSD has widely varied effects on the mental experiences of users. It alters perception, re-duces verbal thinking, and intensifies sensory experience and imagery. In a more heightened way than marijuana, LSD also causes a suspen-sion of conventional perceptions of space and time and in the perception of the body and the self; these may be extreme enough to amount to hallucinations.

Advocates of LSD claim that it increases the user's creativity and understanding of their personal problems; until the mid-1960s, some psychotherapists used it extensively on their patients. Since then, legal prohibitions ended most LSD-therapy and research in the United States. In Europe, some LSD-therapy is still practiced. The drug is used to reduce mental defenses and to revive inaccessible emotions and memories. Drug sessions alternate with regular hours when the patient pieces together and makes sense of the information they gained under the influence of LSD.

Some champions of LSD treat it like a sacra-ment in a new religion. Timothy Leary, for in-stance, founded the League for Spiritual Dis-covery—L-S-D. In 1966, the *Journal of Religion and Health* published a paper by Walter N. Pahnke and William A. Richards which claimed that LSD could produce a mental experience they called "mystical consciousness," which has nine terrific qualities.[4] There is a formal religion in the United States, the Native Ameri-can Church, which uses *mescaline,* a natural hallucinogenic drug, in its rituals. The League for Spiritual Discovery has no rituals.

The use of hallucinogenic drugs like LSD tends to be self-limiting. For one thing, you develop tolerance to them so fast that if you take a hallucinogenic drug three days in a row, it will have little punch left by the third day. For another, the effects are unpredictable—and not always pleasant. As a result, far fewer people use hallucinogens than use hemp drugs, and they commonly stop using them after a period of experimentation (McGlothlin 1975).

"Uppers": The energizing drugs

The "energizers" are also called "activators," "stimulants," "anti-depressants," and "uppers." The most common ones are caffeine and nicotine, plentiful in coffee and cigarettes. More elegant energizing drugs are often members of the *amphetamine* family; they are more widely sold as aids to reducing diets than as mood-changing compounds. The best known amphetamine is *dexadrine.* It is sold in a great variety of capsules, tablets, and spansules of varying sizes, shapes, and colors, and often combined with sedative or other drugs to reduce

---

[4] Nonmystical consciousness has only four ordinary qualities, which gets very dull.

its potency. Its major effects are to depress appetite and to elevate mood; in some people stimulating feelings of alertness, euphoria, and confidence; and in others, causing irritable excitement, nervousness, and restlessness. Taken in large doses and over long periods of time, it may also stimulate hallucinations. But unlike the true hallucinogens, such as LSD, these are probably indirect, resulting from the fact that "uppers" keep you awake, and anyone who stays awake long enough will inevitably suffer perceptual distortions. The most powerful of these drugs, called *methedrine* ("speed"), does all the same things much more strongly, and seems to produce some paranoid delusions as well. Its effects are so disastrous that the slogan "speed kills" has become widespread among drug users.

There are several other popular energizers, the subjective effects of which are similar to amphetamines but which have different centers of chemical action in the nervous system. *Ritalin* and *Preludin* are brand names of two of the most popular ones.

Perhaps the best possible illustration of how little is understood of the chemical interactions of these drugs with the brain and of the behavioral effects which follow is the fact that energizers, especially *Ritalin,* are used extensively to *calm down* hyperactive children (Safer and Allen 1976). Many psychiatrists believe that these children are suffering from a subtle kind of brain damage which they call *MBD, minimal brain dysfunction.* But there is no firm evidence that they are brain damaged.

The dangers of most energizers have been overrated; so have their benefits. In modest doses, they are useful to relieve depression, anxiety, and fatigue. Tolerance for them occurs fairly quickly. They do have short-term effects as appetite depressants, but once you adapt to them, they do not work. Worse still in that connection, once their effect wears off, you may get depressed and voraciously hungry. People who diet with pills tend to *gain* an average of five pounds a year. Finally, "uppers" do not improve intelligence or test-taking ability, as some naive users and researchers have suggested, but they do produce useful boosts in alertness under some conditions.

"Downers": Sedative drugs

The term "downers" applies to tranquilizers as well as sedatives, but tranquilizers are used pretty exclusively for relieving anxiety, not for "highs," so we will not discuss them here, but in Chapter 19. The sedative or depressant "downers," however, do need some discussion, especially the barbiturates, which can be very dangerous.

Barbiturates have been widely used since before World War I as sedative drugs. They exert a powerful calming effect on the central nervous system, and are most widely prescribed medically for that reason as sleeping pills. The most common ones are phenobarbitol, secobarbitol or seconal, and more recently, quaaludin. The common slang term for all of them among drug users is "goofballs."

Barbiturates are often taken alone for their sedative effect, but are sometimes combined with amphetamines, alcohol, or other drugs for the interesting variations they produce on the "highs" of the other drugs. In large quantities or, combined with drugs such as alcohol, even in small quantities, they may be lethal. Even in modest quantities, they are addicting, and withdrawal from them can produce severe convulsions and death. Also, accidental death from overdose is easier with these than other drugs because you get befuddled from them, and forget how much you took and when. Among all the mind-affecting drugs, barbiturates are the most dangerous.

Alcohol

At least 9 million Americans are alcoholic, by current estimates, or are "problem drinkers"

(Chafetz and Demone 1974). But no one has a precise definition of what alcoholism is or how you "get it." At one extreme, you are certainly a "problem drinker," perhaps a dead one, if you never touch the stuff until once—when you have two martinis and then drive home. At the other, you may sit quietly drinking in a corner for years before you get hallucinations, the "DTs" (delirium tremens), alcoholic psychosis, or cirrhosis of the liver, which finally kills you and confirms the diagnosis.

Alcoholism is one of the biggest public health problems in the United States, but this country is only 7th, worldwide, in absolute alcohol consumption.[5] France is first, with 10 to 12 percent of its population, including children, estimated to be alcoholic. Israel has the lowest consumption in the world, and the Soviet Union, which is known to have a dreadful alcoholism problem, does not report its figures. Within this country, more men are alcoholic than women, but the women are catching up fast. So are the young people, among whom drinking is now almost universal, beginning in high school or earlier (Goldenberg 1977). Alcoholism patterns in the United States also follow ethnic and religious lines. Groups which sanction alcohol use in religious ceremonies, like the Jews, or as part of family meals, like the Italians, have low alcoholism rates, even though they may drink often. In groups where drinking is done privately or in bars, as among Irish Americans, alcoholism rates are higher (Keller and Rosenberg 1971). As our culture grows more homogeneous, however, and we become more like one another, the alcoholism rates tend slowly to equalize.

Some students of alcoholism do not consider it an addiction because it takes a long time to make excessive drinking into a lifestyle. Even so, chronic alcoholics suffer from withdrawal symptoms when they try to "go on the wagon," much like heroin addicts. They have

_____
[5] Only!

physical pains, mental depression, a rise in blood pressure and body temperature, and occasional memory loss. These symptoms can continue, moreover, for months after they have completely stopped drinking. *Alcoholics Anonymous,* the one organization which has had relatively good success with alcoholism, considers it a permanent addiction. Participants in AA programs are taught to view themselves as eternal alcoholics, even if they have stopped drinking many years earlier.

Some theorists think that alcoholics are biologically deficient in some still unknown chemical needed for proper metabolism. An inherited tendency towards alcoholism has been tentatively isolated in mice (Rogers 1966)—as well as an enzyme called aldehyde dehydrogenase (ACDH), that seems to be needed for the chemical break-down of alcohol; 300 times more of it is found in drinking than in nondrinking strains of mice (Sheppard et al. 1968).

These findings on animals support the popular belief that alcoholics get drunker than other people on smaller amounts of booze, but there is no proof of that on human beings, and no evidence at all that some people have a genetic disposition towards alcoholism.

Physiologically, alcohol acts differently from the psychedelic drugs and from the energizers alike, though it has some effects like each of them. It is a central nervous system *depressant,* which reduces alertness, induces fatigue, dulls sensation, and causes a general state of torpor—followed by unconsciousness, when taken in large doses. The sequence of psychological events involved is precisely the same in getting drunk and in receiving a general anesthetic—and indeed, alcohol is an anesthetic, much like ether. It reduces pain sensation just as it dulls other sensations. Some people think that alcohol stimulates sexual and aggressive behavior. It does sometimes arouse people sexually or aggressively, but does so because it is a *depressant,*

Alcohol: More available and more dangerous than other drugs.

not a stimulant. It tends to relax *inhibition* in people who are fearful in the assertion of sexual or aggressive feelings so that they become more expressive in these respects. For most people, however, the effect is more to induce sleepiness than lust or anger, and in large quantities, drink is likely first, to cause impotence, and then unconsciousness.

Getting drunk People have been drinking since time immemorial, and sometimes suffering bad effects; so there is an enormous mythology about drunkenness. Like all mythologies, some of it is true, some false, and some maybe. Here are some relevant facts:

How much makes you drunk? It depends on the amount of alcohol, the amount of you, and the speed with which you join them.

The amount of alcohol in a drink is indicated by its "proof," which is double the alcohol content. *Wines* generally range from about 15–40 proof (7.5–20 percent alcohol), *beer* around 12 proof, *liqueurs* and *cordials* from about 40–80 proof, and hard liquors—whiskey, vodka, gin, rum, brandy—from about 70–100 proof. *It is the amount of alcohol, not the kind of drink, that matters most.*

Your body volume determines the rate of absorption in large part. The bigger you are, the more it takes to make you drunk because the more alcohol is absorbed in other places than the brain. *It is true* that you get drunk faster on an empty stomach than a full one because the alcohol is absorbed faster. *It is not true* that you get drunker on mixed drinks—unless they contain more alcohol than straight ones or unless you drink them faster.

Getting drunk, an ancient and still universal means of altering consciousness through drugs.

The Drinkers, Vincent van Gogh

What causes hangovers? Cures them?
Drinking too much. Time. There is some evidence that substances called congeners cause hangovers, and these are contained in different amounts in different kinds of alcoholic beverages, but anyone will get a hangover from too much of any drink. Many people get sick, as well as drunk, from an excess of sweet wine or other sweet drinks, for unknown reasons. *It is not true* that having another drink will relieve a hangover. While hung over, you are still mildly drunk. Having another drink will just make you drunk again, with all the more hangover to follow.

Drink and drugs: Courting the big sleep
Combining alcohol with any of the consciousness-changing drugs can be dangerous. Some people report that a combination of alcohol and the hemp drugs merely enhances the effects of the pot or hash. I do not know any reports of illness or death from that combination, but this does not apply to other combinations of drink and drugs. Alcohol vastly boosts the effect of *energizing* drugs, and can combine with them to produce *toxic psychosis* (going crazy from being poisoned), with hallucinations, uncontrolled, even frenzied behavior, and convulsions—then unconsciousness, if not death.

There are even more drastic effects from combining alcohol with *sedative* drugs, especially with powerful ones like the barbiturates. Many people have killed themselves accidentally by innocently taking sleeping pills and then, getting impatient while waiting for the pills "to take," had several drinks.

Except for its being legal, and therefore easily available, alcohol has few virtues as a road to altered consciousness. In many forms, it tastes lousy. It does not provide a very good "high." It makes you quite dysfunctional rather quickly. And if you have very much of it, you get sick and miserable for many, many hours afterwards, and court some real dangers if you drive or take pills in between.

MEDITATION

Western civilization is characterized in literature and sociology books by great activity and little contemplation, a lot of hustle and bustle, physically and mentally, and little inner peace. The "mysterious orient," on the other hand, has nurtured many philosophers and priests devoted to the cultivation of the inner life by different rituals of self-discipline. One of these especially, *meditation,* has spread to the West and captured the imagination of many people seeking growth in their inner lives.

Meditation has been developed most systematically by Indian Yogins, practitioners of Yoga, and Japanese Zen monks; Zen is a form of Buddhism. In both systems "adepts" strive to achieve a complete experience of their own nature by an intense concentration on *nothing,* in the case of Zen Buddhism, and on complete control of body functions via controlled breathing in the Yoga systems. Concentrating on nothing is very different from not concentrating. On the contrary, it is an extremely hard discipline to achieve because, in the ordinary course of experience, our minds are constantly wandering from one subject to another.

One fascinating finding of brain-wave studies is that both Zen monks and Yogins produce high amounts of alpha brain-wave patterns while meditating. This is particularly remarkable among the Zen monks, since they keep their eyes open and alpha waves are ordinarily produced most when the subject's eyes are closed. The more years spent in Zen training, the more EEG-wave patterns increase amplitude and decrease frequency (become larger and slower), as mastery over Zen techniques progresses.

Loud noises or other distractions, however, will interrupt the emission of alpha waves in Zen monks, but not in Yogins. In fact, in one study two Yogins were able to keep their hands in cold water for long periods without reporting discomfort or interrupting alpha wave patterns; apparently the Yogins were able to block all

Meditation.

sensations coming to their brains from their hands (Kasamatsu and Hirai 1966; Anand et al. 1969).

Some meditation and relaxation methods which require less skill, but give some beneficial effects, have become popular in Western countries. They are harmless, and their use may actually decrease the use of drugs as consciousness-altering methods (Brecher 1972). To do transcendental meditation (nowadays officially called TM), you sit in a comfortable position and repeat a specially chosen word or sound called a *mantra.* Silent concentration on it induces a state of deep relaxation and, according to Maharishi Mahesh Yogi, who founded TM, an expansion of consciousness (Bloomfield, Cain, and Jaffe 1975). Physiologically, the relaxation part does work—TM decreases oxygen consumption, increases blood flow, slows brain waves—all things which reflect lowered autonomic nervous system arousal (Kanellakos and Ferguson 1973). It works the same way, in fact, without the *mantra,* just by concentrating attention on any stimulus as you relax. So do hypnosis and just plain relaxation training (Beary and Benson 1974). The main things to do are: (1) Find a quiet environment, where distractions are few. (2) Sit in a comfortable position, which decreases muscle tone, and close your eyes, which further reduces distraction. (3) Make yourself feel as passive as you can. (4) Focus your attention on something trivial by repeating a sound or word until it is meaningless.

There are some good books, widely available, such as *The Relaxation Response,* by Herbert Benson (1975), which spell out lessons for doing this stuff. If you would like to relax more, get one and try it. It's good for you.

SUMMARY

1 Different states of consciousness are really points along a scale of *arousal*. Sleep can be considered the low point on the normal continuum of arousal and frenzy or ecstasy the high point. States of consciousness can also be described in terms of orientation; it is either turned inside the person or reaching out to the external world, and attention can be either sharply or weakly focused.

2 The exact biological function of sleep is unknown. The current view is that its main function is to conserve energy during the low point in an animal's circadian cycle. The amount of sleep people need declines with age, and their sleep patterns change at different ages. At any age there is great variation in the amount of sleep different people need, and in the ease and speed with which they fall asleep and wake up.

3 Insomnia is a state of overarousal that prevents sleep or awakens people after insufficient sleep. Drugs, hypnosis, and techniques of distraction are all helpful with this condition, but there is no sure cure known for it.

4 Sleep is studied by measuring muscle tone and brain waves. It consists of four different phases. Dreaming occurs during a phase called REM (rapid eye movement), in which the brain is extremely active. About a quarter of all sleeping time consists of REM sleep, in brief, scattered periods, and not in one long stretch. The amount of REM sleep (and therefore dreaming) usually increases towards the end of the sleep cycle.

5 Freud hypothesized that dreams help us to solve problems that might otherwise so trouble us that they would awaken us; he viewed dreams as the "guardians of sleep." Some modern evidence, however, suggests that Freud's theory is an incomplete explanation. No one knows the function of dreams.

6 Hypnosis involves a voluntary relinquishing of normal critical faculties—and hypnotized people have performed some extraordinary feats of cognition, emotion, and changes in physiological processes. Hypnotic effects are undependable, however.

7 Children are more susceptible to hypnosis than adults. People who are highly susceptible to hypnosis produce large, slow brain-waves even when awake and not hypnotized. Hypnotic susceptibility is not related, however, to most personality traits.

8 Drugs produce temporarily altered states of consciousness. The *opiates* are all derived from the common poppy. The common ones, *opium, morphine,* and *heroin,* are all highly addictive, whether they are taken by sniffing or by injection. That means that users crave larger and larger amounts of the drug over time and suffer severe withdrawal symptoms when they cannot get it. Treatment of heroin addiction has been largely unsuccessful.

9 *Psychedelic,* or "consciousness-expanding" drugs, are not addicting, but they are still illegal. *Marijuana* and *hashish* are both derived from the Indian hemp plant, cannabis. They are eaten or smoked. Their effects are an intensification of perception and sensation, a slowing down of time, and the feeling that familiar objects are strangely new and interesting. These drugs are being studied for their possible healthful effects on blood pressure.

10 *LSD* is a powerful drug that may affect the brain's production of serotonin, a substance that seems to affect the emotional, perceptual, and cognitive centers of the brain.

Even in minute doses, LSD causes the most powerful effects of any drug known, in "trips" that may last 12 hours or more. Some reported cases of psychosis caused by LSD may be exaggerated, but the drug is so powerful that it probably could be dangerous to some users.

11   There are many claims that psychedelic drugs increase artistic creativity. They are false in most cases.

12   *Downers,* the tranquilizing and sedative drugs, have a calming effect on the central nervous system. Barbiturates, especially phenobarbitol and secobarbitol, or seconal, are commonly prescribed as sleeping pills. All barbiturates are highly addicting and very dangerous. Withdrawal from barbiturate addiction can cause convulsions and death; so can combinations of barbiturates with other drugs, such as alcohol.

13   *Energizers,* particularly the *amphetamines* (dexadrine, benzadrine, and methadrine) can produce alertness, euphoria, and confidence in the user and can depress appetite, but they can also have ill effects. They are also used to treat hyperactivity, because they have the peculiar property of calming hyperactive children. Both their dangers and their benefits are overrated.

14   *Alcoholism* is the most serious behavior disorder in America. Chronic alcoholism is an addiction, with withdrawal symptoms. Alcohol causes a steady loss of function, even in small amounts, because it depresses the central nervous system. Over a long period, heavy drinking can cause psychotic reactions and cirrhosis of the liver, which is lethal. Alcohol and pills combined can be lethal also. There is some evidence of a genetic disposition towards alcoholism in mice. Not in people.

15   *Meditation* has been largely developed by Oriental mystics, especially Indian Yogins and Japanese Zen Buddhists. The skilled use of meditation produces many physiological and behavioral results like those of hypnosis, including the production of large, slow brain waves and the ability to avoid distractions of pain and discomfort. Meditation is legal, unlike drugs; cheap, unlike alcohol; and undramatic, unlike hypnosis. It cannot hurt you. And *it* might improve creativity.

Individual differences and assessment

12

12

Individual differences and assessment

This chapter introduces what is sometimes known as "soft" psychology: personality, adjustment, the behavior disorders, and psychotherapy. To understand them, you need to know something about the scientific concepts and the practical methods that are used to study them. The concepts go under the general title of "individual differences" and the methods under the heading of "measurement" or "assessment." There are many technical aspects to this subject, as there were to the sections on scientific method in Chapter 1. But keep a cool head. As with scientific method in general, they are simply sophisticated versions of common sense.

INDIVIDUAL DIFFERENCES

You did not need a course in psychology to learn that no two people in the world are *exactly* alike. You have known this about fingerprints since childhood, and if you thought about it, must have deduced that the rest of a person also could not be *identical* with anyone else. This does not mean that we are completely different from each other, of course, because if that were true, there could be no sciences of human behavior at all. In both respects, we are enough like one another to compare, to compete, and to share our lives, to develop common political laws for regulating human beings living together, and to seek common scientific laws for understanding them. At the same time, we differ enough to make us interesting and to make the understanding, prediction, and control of behavior complicated and uncertain. Discovering the subtle similarities and even subtler differences between people has challenged and teased some of the best religious, philosophical, and political thinkers of all ages. It still does today, with all the social and behavioral sciences added to the domain of discovery—and of puzzlement.

The term "individual differences" commonly

has two different meanings. The first is intuitive and imprecise; it reflects the political values of freedom and democracy. The second meaning is technical rather than political; it concerns the genetic, anatomical, physiological, and behavioral similarities and differences between people that make them alike in some respects and unique in others. Most of our attention in this book goes to the technical side of the subject, but not all of it. People justify most of their political ideas about how to treat each other by appeals to the scientific "facts" of individual differences. There is no area of biological or behavioral science where the facts in question have more important political implications.

The politics of individual differences

The meaning of individual differences in American political ideology is stated in the Declaration of Independence, in the idea that people's "inalienable rights" include "life, liberty, and the pursuit of happiness." It gets down to particulars more in the Constitution's **Bill of Rights,** the first Federal laws in the United States which sought to protect individuals from being pushed around by government. And it becomes increasingly specific as more amendments are made and laws passed to enhance the individual freedom of blacks, women, and other groups. But people's right to live their individual lives as they see fit, expressed in Thomas Jefferson's idea that the best government is that which governs least, that is, which leaves people alone, is based in the Declaration on the statement that "all men are created *equal* [italics added]," not that they are different (see Chapter 2). And this in turn comes straight from John Locke's "tabula rasa" theory (see Chapter 5); Locke believed that people are literally equal and that the differences between them as adults get put into them by experience. That is not entirely true, as we now know, but it does not matter. For most purposes, most of us believe that most people are sufficiently "up to" each other in their ability to function in society and in their capacity to bear responsibility for their own actions that we believe their rights to individuality should be honored.

What is important to understand, in this connection, is that the justification or denial of political rights revolves primarily around the *psychological* or *behavioral* differences between people, not around differences in their physical appearance or makeup. Anyone who wants to *deny* the rights of black people, for instance, justifies it by attacking their intelligence, their capacity for responsibility ("they just love dancing and singing and gaiety"), and their motivation ("they're happier this way"), not by attacking their **color.** In the same way, people do not deny civil liberties to children on the grounds that they are short, but that they are irresponsible. And women are not denied equal jobs and salaries because they have breasts, but because their "natural" inclinations are towards home and children.

Even when genetic or physiological differences seem to underlie the political questions—as in the genetic intelligence of blacks, or the instincts of women, or whether Jews and Gypsies are "mongrel races,"[1] as the Nazis said—it is because of the *behavioral* traits implied, not because of the biological characteristics themselves. Nobody cares if the village idiot has a larger brain than the brilliant philosopher. Peoples' rights and privileges are *rationalized* according to the differences in their behavior, actual or expected, not their brain size—even if the rights and privileges are not dealt out that way.

It is the business of government to regulate, of course, and, to some extent, that necessarily means to restrict and control people's individual liberties. In modern times, and in benevolent societies, it also increasingly means that govern-

---

[1] Whatever that means.

1776 · RETOUCHING AN OLD MASTERPIECE · 1915

The Declaration of Independence guarantees equal rights to the tall and
the short, rich and poor, the smart and the slow—political equality despite
physical or psychological differences.

Standardized fashions and contrasting life-styles.

ment has the obligation to help people make the most of their potential abilities by providing them with funds, education, health care, and job opportunities. Today, many responsible leaders look beyond their kindly intuition for systematic information upon which to base such decisions. One of psychology's most important contributions is to provide accurate information about how and why people differ from each other so that discriminatory laws based upon personal prejudices may be shown to be wrong.

The practical restrictions that we place on people's individual differences in behavior are not all governmental, by any means. Most of them are matters of custom, not of law. In virtually every society, for instance, people agree to standardized fashions of dress, discipline, child rearing, education, and the rites of social passage from baptism to burial. Although we are living in a time of great experimentation in individual lifestyles, and probably more so in the United States than anywhere else on earth, it is still unlikely that you will find men walking down the street in ballgowns, parents giving castor oil to control their children's rowdy impulses, college students hiring their own teachers, or funerals conducted in airplanes over the ocean. Most people would probably disapprove of these practices, though in times past, men have dressed in clothes far more ornate than ballgowns, castor oil was once a fashionable disciplinary tool, and dropping bodies from airplanes is really not so different from dropping them overboard from ships. Custom restricts all of these things, but such restriction is not justified by our basic belief in individual liberty.

If we agree that some restriction on freedom is necessary, where do we draw the line? We obviously approve of controlling people *beyond* just preventing them from doing harm, especially if the restriction is for the good of the person being restricted. This is why we hire traffic cops, dental hygienists, and gym teachers. Each tries to control the behavior of others for their own well-being. In deciding what controls should be allowed and in improving methods of such control, we need a clear understanding of individual differences. To reach this kind of understanding requires a more formal and technical approach than untutored reason and goodwill alone can bring to the task.

The scope of individual differences

Almost no one realizes the extent to which people differ biologically from each other. But just as there is enormous *variety* of kinds of plants and animals on this planet, there is also enormous variation *within* almost every individual species. The more complicated a species is, in fact, the greater the variations among its members. And people are by far the most complex biological organism on earth. So it is no wonder that the variation among them is great.

Human variability starts before conception, before sperm meets egg, in the process of germ cell division, called **meiosis;** this process makes it impossible for any offspring to receive more than half of the genetic material of either parent. But the arrangements even of that half are so varied within each germ cell, and so different from one sperm or egg to another, and there are so many of them, that the variety of human beings which result, viewed only in terms of genetic endowments, is for all practical purposes, *infinite.* This is the reason that fingerprints, like most of the rest of you, are never repeated identically. The chances of any two separate matings of human beings producing identical offspring are about one in several trillion, which is considerably smaller than the total number of people that have ever lived or that could be born on this planet in the next several million years.

With those kinds of odds, you can understand why our physical features differ so much from one person to another. Even identical twins can usually be told apart rather easily by

Figure 12.1 Human beings, like their fingerprints, are each different, and never repeated identically.

people who know them well. Our internal physical features differ just as much as our external ones. The sizes, shapes, colors, textures, and positions of heart, lungs, stomach, kidneys, intestines, and so forth are just as varied among us as the sizes, shapes, colors, textures and positions of noses, kneecaps, eyes, hair, lips, skin, fingers, ears, and all the rest (Williams 1956).

Most physical features are mostly genetically determined. Most of our behavior is not, though some of our abilities are dictated as much by our genes as is the shape of our noses. The almost infinite physical variety among us is small compared to the variety of human *behavior* because the genetic determinants of behavior are compounded many times by the variability which *learning* makes possible. Do you remember learning in mathematics or logic about the manipulation of infinite numbers—is the square

of an infinite number bigger than the infinite number or not? That is the kind of problem you face trying to identify the variety of human behavior traits.

The technology of individual differences

In psychology, the concept of individual differences is used in a specialized sense to mean, not just the differences between people in general, but especially the **differences in people's responses to the SAME STIMULI.** As a practical matter, this usually reduces to the study of their more or less consistent responses to a particular kind of situation. Trying to study these responses systematically gets psychologists involved in averages, frequencies and distributions, plotting curves, drawing graphs, and generally getting preoccupied with statistics. Ironically, it turns out, therefore, that the study of individual differences is often really the study of group trends, that is, of statistical comparisons of individuals to averages.

The approaches to individual differences: Cross sectional, longitudinal, normative, and ipsative There are basically two ways of studying individual differences in behavior. You can look at many people to see how much they differ from each other or you can look at just one person over and over again and see how much variation they show on different occasions. In the first instance, where you study *cross section* of people, you gain the advantage of studying the behavior comparatively so you can say that some people act more one way and some people the other. But you cannot say, from such a one-shot approach, how characteristic the behavior is of any single person at different times. So you gain knowledge of individual differences *between* people, but you lose information about what goes on *within* them. In the second case, the advantages and disadvantages are just the opposite. Approaching a person *longitudinally* (over a period of time), you get perspective on the range of their behavior. But if you study *only* that person, there is no way you can make comparative statements about how the behavior characterizes people in general. Each approach is more useful in some situations than others, and their combination is most valuable in still others.

The cross-sectional method is sometimes called the *normative* approach because it tries to discover standards of measuring and understanding behavior among different people. The longitudinal method is called the *ipsative* approach, from the Latin word for "same," because it tries to understand the behavior of the same person in many situations (Allport 1937). The first method is also called *nomothetic,* from the Greek word for "law," because it tries to discover laws of behavior, and the second *"ideographic"* because it tries to understand a single event or individual (an *ideogram* is a written symbol that represents a specific thing, like a hieroglyphic) (English and English 1958).

Nomothetic methods are commonly used for studying characteristics which can be more or less clearly identified in people and, therefore, can be compared from one person to another. Things like height, weight, color of eyes, hair, or skin can be satisfactorily studied this way. Even though things like height and weight change, they are still easily compared from one person to another because, at any one time, they are quite stable in each individual. This stability permits the use of the nomothetic approach, for unless there is some point of departure applicable to

Figure 12.2 The average of weight for different height and build is a cross sectional or normative method of comparing people.

Men:	Low	Average	High
5 feet 3 inches.............118		129	141
5 feet 4 inches.............122		133	145
5 feet 5 inches.............126		137	149
5 feet 6 inches.............130		142	155
5 feet 7 inches.............134		147	161
5 feet 8 inches.............139		151	166
5 feet 9 inches.............143		155	170
5 feet 10 inches...........147		159	174
5 feet 11 inches...........150		163	178
6 feet.......................154		167	183
6 feet 1 inch...............158		171	188
6 feet 2 inches.............162		175	192
6 feet 3 inches.............165		178	195
Women:			
5 feet.......................100		109	118
5 feet 1 inch...............104		112	121
5 feet 2 inches.............107		115	125
5 feet 3 inches.............110		118	128
5 feet 4 inches.............113		122	132
5 feet 5 inches.............116		125	135
5 feet 6 inches.............120		129	139
5 feet 7 inches.............123		132	142
5 feet 8 inches.............126		136	146
5 feet 9 inches.............130		140	151
5 feet 10 inches...........133		144	156
5 feet 11 inches...........137		148	161
6 feet.......................141		152	166

Note: Height is without shoes, weight is without clothing.

everybody, it is hopeless to try to make comparisons.

Ideographic methods are useful for studying things which are slippery and unstable, either because they change rapidly or because they happen to people in such unique ways that there is no meaningful point of comparison between them in that respect.

Which method is best depends on the use to be made of the information. The ideographic method might be more useful to a doctor who is concerned about someone's blood pressure, but the nomothetic method is more valuable for predicting the course of an infection.

In general, the more complicated the thing being studied, the more you need *to start* with the ideographic approach. If you want to study creative artists, for instance, you will probably learn more at first by examining their individual lives than by comparing them with most other people. Most other people do not compose symphonies, paint pictures, or write novels, so there is not much basis of comparison in those respects. At some point, however, the nomothetic approach generally takes over from the ideographic one in scientific work because the characteristics of one person are almost always variants of characteristics which everyone has to some degree—and we would want to find out if there are general laws that apply to everyone and might explain why this person is different from others. Sometimes there is no other sensible way to go. If you want to understand musical genius, for instance,

Genius—more easily recognized than understood.

you cannot reasonably limit yourself to studying *only* Mozart's life, though that might be a good place to begin. You would want to study the lives of other musical geniuses also so that you could compare them—and in doing so, you would be moving from an ideographic to a nomothetic approach. What is more, at some point you would want to study the abilities that underlie musical composition, like the ability to repeat tones, to remember tunes, and the like. These exist to some degree in everyone and can be examined *only* by nomothetic methods. If you wanted to select children for training as musical composers, in fact, you almost *have* to use this approach because a child probably could not learn to compose music if they could not recognize the harmonic differences between one sound and another.

One thing you ought to realize from the fact that the nomothetic approach can be applied to so many things is that there are some *limits* to individual differences. Every person's *total* experience is unique, but their individual traits and experiences may be quite predictable and quite comparable with anyone else's—that is why it is possible to make statistical plots and frequency distributions in the first place—to calculate what any given individual will probably be like *relative* to other people. Most people, in fact, deviate from each other in most respects only by relatively small amounts. Just as it is possible to evaluate people's *average* characteristics relative to each other, it is possible to evaluate standards of deviation from those averages, and to predict that most people who are not in the average range of anything will not deviate from it by more than a certain amount. (More of this in *More Statistics,* at the back of the book).

Even the ideographic method assumes that there is some lawfulness and limitation to individual activity—there is no point in comparing an individual to themselves over time unless you figure that there is some typical aspect to their behavior about which you can make some kind

of comparative statement when they act differently.

The point is that while we are different from each other, we are not entirely different in every way—or in any single way! The assessment of individual differences really begins with the analysis of the **central tendencies** of behavior, and with the calculation of the descriptive statistics that show how all of us are average in some respects and different from the herd in others. The uniqueness of every human being is a byproduct of the common condition of humanity.

ASSESSMENT

Both nomothetic and ideographic methods are approaches to **assessment**, which means **measurement** or **evaluation**. The problems of assessing individual differences are basically the same problems of scientific measurement we discussed in Chapter 1 and will, in more detail, in the Appendix on statistics). First, how do you know? How do you find out anything? How do you make and record observations? Second, how do you know whether to trust what you find out? This is the problem of finding dependable tests or measuring instruments or, as they are called in this business, **assessment devices,** and then finding some way to tell if the measurements made with them are accurate. Both for technical and social reasons, this is harder to do in studying individual differences in personality than it is in other areas of psychology, like psychophysics or perception, where it is, in turn, harder to measure anything than in the physical sciences.

Not that it is so easy there. The whole business of measuring differences in individual performance, in fact, began with a mistake in astronomy! In 1796, an assistant at the Greenwich Observatory in London was fired for constantly making mistakes in some routine timing of celestial observations. The times he recorded were always later than they should have been. Twenty years later, the German astronomer F. W. Bessel, hearing the story, got the idea that there might be *systematic differences* in people's speed of reacting to their observations. Tests on his colleagues showed that such differences did exist and, more important, were fairly consistent in each individual. He labeled this effect the "personal equation" (1830); we now call it *reaction time.*

Anyhow, the technical problems of measurement are bigger in personality because the things you are trying to study are usually intangibles like "personality," "intelligence," "aggressiveness," and so on. Such concepts are very hard to define for *operational* purposes, and if you cannot be sure what you mean by them in the first place, you cannot develop a test to measure them (Cronbach 1970). And since the concepts are intangible and abstract, even if you can come up with a useful practical definition, from which you can construct dependable measures, it is hard to be sure that what you are measuring is really what you are interested in.

Socially, personality measurement is touchier than other kinds because its consequences may be very serious for people's lives. If you want to admit students to college on the basis of their intelligence, for instance, and you are not really sure what intelligence is, you may do a lot of people a lot of damage by taking a very concrete action on the basis of a very vague criterion. Other kinds of measurement may have serious effects as well, but it is easier to justify the standards for their use. For example, you can make an awfully good case, and an awfully good measure, for giving driver's licenses on the basis of visual acuity, or for arresting someone for drunk driving on the basis of a breathometer test. But using IQ tests as a standard for admission to college may be unfair discrimination against Black students because IQ scores are questionable measures of intelligence in the first place.

Another social problem with personality measurement is that the intangibles being measured are often part of people's private lives. Emotionality, sexual inclinations, attitudes towards life, career, human relations, emotional stability are things which most of us regard as "no one else's business," at least no one who has to judge us in school, at work, or in our public roles. Some personality measures look into just these things and label people with respect to them in ways which can be embarrassing and harmful. On most jobs, it does you no harm if your personnel profile says you have slow reaction times or are colorblind—but if it says you are "emotionally unstable" (which may simply mean you are enthusiastic and excitable, as you see yourself) or "tend to be aloof and withdrawn" (which to you may simply mean that you are quiet and respectful of others' privacy), then your career may be jeopardized in many ways. Personality measurement is a problematic business.

Reliability and validity

The biggest technical difficulties of measuring individual differences are summed up by two important concepts—*reliability* and *validity.*

Reliability means the *consistency* or *repeatability* or *dependability* of the assessment you are making, that is, of the information you are collecting. In Chapter 1, where we discussed *significance* and *significance testing,* we were talking about the reliability, that is, the dependability, with which a statistical inference could be made. In evaluating the tests and measurements that are used to assess individual differences, we mean the same thing. There are several different ways of asking whether a measure can be depended on, however, and some different perspectives from which you can make the judgment. All of them reduce to two basic questions:

1. If you ask someone the same questions at different times, will you get the same answers?
2. If you put the same question different ways, will you get answers that are consistent with each other?

The first question is called technically, **test-retest reliability;** the second is generally called, **split-half reliability,** or **alternate-form reliability,** or **inter-item reliability.** All of them refer to the **dependability** of the measuring instrument, and *only* to its dependability—not to its **truth,** or **accuracy,** or **meaningfulness.** Remember, all sane observers, using the naked eye alone, can agree that the earth is flat and the sun goes around it; the observation is perfectly **reliable,** and perfectly **untrue.** In the same way, if someone lies consistently on a test, the test is reliable, but inaccurate.

The technical term for truth, accuracy, or meaningfulness is **validity.** In any kind of fact-finding endeavor, from personality testing to murder trials, the reliability of any information is more important, at first, than its validity because **validity depends on reliability,** while reliability has nothing to do with validity. Everyone's reliable observation that the sun goes around the earth, from Joshua's making it stand still through the bookmakers' permanent farewell to Columbus, was invalid. But Galileo's **valid** observation that the earth goes around the sun would have continued to be merely an invitation to a weenie roast (with him as the weenie) if it had not been proved absolutely reliable by everyone else who got their hands on a telescope. Referring back to Chapter 1 again, reliability means **degree of consensual validation. Validity** means **meaningfulness or accuracy of the consensus.**

The relationship between reliability and validity is dramatically evident in criminal law in the principle of **corpus delicti,** Latin for "the body of the crime." It means that you cannot arrest somebody and accuse them of a crime unless you can show that a crime has been committed in the first place. Suppose, to use a common whodunit theme, Mr. Jones is missing and the police think Mrs. Jones has done him in. Now, Mrs. Jones cannot be guilty of having murdered Mr. Jones (a question of validity) unless he is dead to begin with (a question of reliability). The best evidence, of course, would be his body or substantial fraction thereof full of bullet holes or knife wounds or poison. Next best, a note in Mr. Jones' handwriting that said "My wife is going to murder me," found a week after he disappears without having taken any luggage, while another man is living with his wife in his apartment and wearing his clothes, would be *less* reliable evidence of such a crime. And finally, his mere disappearance, with no note, no new occupant, and none of his personal things or suitcases remaining, would leave us with no reliable evidence at all that he had been done in.

The problems of reliability and validity in the measurement of individual differences are less dramatic, less interesting, and more technical. But they are of substantially the same quality, and you need to be familiar with them.

Test-retest reliability: Play it again, Sam
For most of the practical situations where psychological tests are used, **retest reliability,** or **temporal stability,** that is, the ability of the test to elicit the same answers from the same person at different times, is the most important kind. If you were testing someone's intelligence, for instance, in order to decide whether to give a scholarship, and they scored among the top 1 percent of applicants at one testing and among the bottom 1 percent at another testing, what decision could you make? Throw out the test or throw out the applicant? Or if someone decided that Uncle Louis were crazy and should be locked up, and the court ordered a diagnostic examination of his[2] emotional stability, including psychological testing. Suppose you gave him a

---

[2] Uncle Louis', not the person who thinks he is crazy.

test on which his first performance looked wildly insane and his second performance, a day, a week, or a month later, looked very sane and reasonable. What would you report? That he had changed or that the test could not be trusted?

Because of such problems, good testmakers try to determine *in advance* that the questions on their tests are of a kind that people will answer the same way on different occasions. This is not an easy goal to achieve, however, and irresponsible testmakers and testgivers sometimes publish and use tests which do not meet reasonable standards of retest reliability.

Internal consistency: Testing the test In addition to retest reliability, it is important to know whether a test is reliable in another sense. *Is it really asking the questions it meant to ask?* In almost any good personality measure, the testmaker tries to ask the same question in several different ways, hoping by this means to get a broader and more meaningful view of people's responses than they would otherwise. Suppose, for instance, that you wanted a "grump index" on someone, that is, you wanted to measure the extent to which they tended to be grumpy, moody, irritable, and a general pain to have around. If you were to get this information by having the person report on themselves, you would probably get a more reliable answer by asking the question in several ways than by asking once, plain and simple. "Are you a grump?" You might use a combination of questions, such as: "Do things put you in a bad mood very often?" "Do you think you are more sensitive to irritating situations than most people?" "Do other people mistakenly consider you a kvetch?" "Do others recognize what a wonderful person you really are?" "Do you hide your real personality under an irritable exterior?" And so forth.

If you are studying something like intelligence, it is even more necessary to ask many questions, and to ask questions of different types because, since it is hard to define intelligence very precisely in the first place, it is important to try getting at it from different angles. A good vocabulary may be part of high intelligence, a good memory might be, ability with numbers might be, and a good sense of humor might be. So many different things are potentially important that a good test might try to sample all of them and sample each one in several ways.

When good testmakers have collected a lot of questions that they believe get at the thing they want to study, they not only examine their retest reliability by giving them to the same people twice. They may also then divide the test questions up, making two **alternate forms** of the same test, and give both forms to the same people to be sure the tests are both reliable. This is called alternate-form reliability. They may also just give all the items to one group of people, then divide the items in two, score each half as if it were a separate test, and correlate the two scores each person would now have. If the different items get at the same things dependably, then there should be a high positive correlation between the two sets. This is called inter-item or split-half reliability." Like alternate-form reliability," it is a measure of the **internal consistency** of the test, the second main kind of reliability.

As you may have realized by now, reliability is expressed numerically by a reliability coefficient, which is just an ordinary correlation coefficient. Validity can also be expressed this way, to some extent. But remember the principle from Chapter 1: the actual degree of correspondence between two variables, from which we would judge **validity** here, cannot be greater than the square of the reliability coefficient. **Reliability sets the limit on validity.**

Constructs and criteria: The meanings of validity We said before that validity means the truth, accuracy, or meaningfulness of something. When we look at these terms precisely, as we must here, those words do not all mean the same thing. **Truth** and **accuracy** *can* mean the same thing. As we shall use them here, something is *accurate* if it corresponds precisely to some quantifiable standard of consensual validation, and something is *meaningful* if it fits a definition that has been assigned to it. In technical language, which may be easier to understand here, there are two kinds of validity: *accuracy,* called *criterion validity,* or *predictive validity,* which means that a test is valid for some practical purpose, by some useful standard; and *construct validity,* which means that a test makes sense in terms of some abstract idea, even if there is no practical standard with which to judge it.

Criterion validity is easy to understand, but it is not always easy to tell whether a test has it. A test's criterion validity is the extent to which it predicts something accurately. So, if you design a test of artistic ability, and everyone who gets a high score on it becomes a famous artist, while everyone who scores low becomes a professional "bad taste" or "color clash" demonstrator, then the test has high criterion validity. It predicts what it is supposed to predict.

Constructing a test with high validity gets harder when the criterion gets complicated, or abstract. If your standard of artistic ability, for instance, is the ability to *sell* the pictures people paint, then the test could be designed to see how close art students come to the work of commercially successful painters. But if you are trying to assess artistic ability in terms of a more permanent value than today's art market, a merely practical standard like commercial potential will not be good enough. You must find a way to *define* artistic ability *meaningfully.* To do so, you must have an *idea* of what artistic ability is, and the idea must go beyond the simple matter of market value. The measure you design for this purpose need not predict how well someone will do practically, but tests the meaningfulness of the idea itself. How well it does so defines its *construct validity* (Meehl 1973).

In the case of artistic ability, some of the components will probably be things like a good sense of color and color combinations, a good sense of form and of spatial relations, and so forth. But a lot of the things that go into artistic ability may not be easy to define or to measure—such as a good imagination, a keen choice of what subjects to paint, or of what situations, or countless other important but hard-to-specify things that make the difference between a great artist and a hack. *Construct validation* is the effort to figure out the possible components, the possible relationships between them, and the extent to which they are really present in good artists, absent in poor artists, and more relevant in combination than they are separately to the work of good artists. The test which results may not be a good predictor of success in the artistic marketplace, but it may be a very good means of assessing whether people have the kind of talents, training, and inclination which has led great artists of the past to create the kinds of products we have inherited from them.

The trouble is that a construct is an idea, not a concrete thing. It is an *abstraction* that tries to capture the essence of many related concrete things that express themselves in different ways from one person to another and one situation to another. "Anxiety," "intelligence," "aggressiveness"—all the key concepts of personality—are intangibles, abstractions, constructs. A test with high construct validity approaches the concept from many different angles which should be logically related to each other, if the construct is meaningful, and tries to see empirically if the logical relations are supported by the facts of behavior.

If you were assessing peoples' tendency to become anxious, for instance, you would define anxiety in different people and different situations and then try to study the relationships of those feelings and acts and people to each other to see if your definition was sound and if the component parts were related in the way you expected. Starting with the notion that anxiety means "fear," you might go out and find a group of people who had recently been exposed to frightening situations, and others who had not, and give the questions to both — predicting that people who had been frightened more would answer more questions in the fearful direction. If they do, then the construct of anxiety, as you have defined it, has some validity — it is meaningful.

The only difference between construct and criterion validity in this test so far, is that the anxiety criterion used here has no practical application. Good construct validation goes further, however. In this case, the next step might be to argue that anxiety should be reflected in people's galvanic skin responses (GSR), a measure of how easily their skin conducts electric current (see Chapter 8). The electrical resistance of the skin drops dramatically when people are emotionally aroused or frightened. So if the anxiety test is any good, then you might expect that people who are easily aroused according to the GSR, would have high scores on the anxiety test, while more phlegmatic performers on the GSR would have low scores. If this proved true, you would have a second demonstration of the meaningfulness of the measure.

Then you might simply ask people whether they consider themselves prone to anxiety or not, predicting that those who say "yes" will score higher on the test than those who say "no" — and that GSR scores, and statements about disposition to anxiety, and anxiety test scores, will all be positively correlated with each other.

And on and on. The only limit on the number of steps one may take in construct validation is the number of different things you can think of that should be related to the construct you are studying. The process of testing the relationships among different aspects of a construct is called casting a "nomological net," that is, establishing a network of lawful relationships which validate the meaning of a construct (Meehl and Cronbach 1955).

Faults and pitfalls Well constructed personality tests generally give better information than newspaper horoscopes, but they are far from perfect. Even the most carefully validated test will show up with some *false positives* — people who the test wrongly says are anxious, smart, aggressive, artistic, or whatever, when they are not; and some *false negatives* — people whom the test wrongly says are not anxious, smart, or whatever, when they really are. The variability of human beings is so much greater than the sensitivity of tests that even the best validation will not prevent a lot of errors in evaluating subtle or complex behavior.

Anyhow, many of the tests which are published and widely used in education, industry, and government, are not well constructed or carefully validated and their use falsely reassures some people that they are getting objective information. The American Psychological Association has published standards of test construction which specify the minimum requirements of reliability and validity which honest test makers should strive for (APA 1956), and there are some critical evaluations of tests published in works like *The Mental Measurements Yearbook* (Buros 1972). But the APA standards are voluntary; so some test makers do not observe them, critical evaluations are not always read by test users, and some people make a lot of money hustling tests, so they may promote bad ones without caring about the damage they can do.

THE MEASURES

There are only a few ways to gather information about someone; all the thousands and thousands of psychological tests, measures, and assessment devices use only three classes of inquiry.

The first has to do with *who* is asked — you can ask a person about themselves or you can ask *someone else* to tell you about them.

The second has to do with *how* you ask—you can ask questions *directly,* making clear exactly what it is you want to know, or *obliquely,* either by making unobtrusive observations, where the subject does not know you are studying them, or by using tests where you infer the answer to the questions without ever asking them explicitly (Webb et al. 1966).

The third has to do with the *kind* of question you are asking—you can press someone to give a *maximum performance* or inquire into their *typical performance.* Which kind of test you use on whom, and when, depends on what you want to find out, how precise the information needs to be, and whether you think you can get it better from one form of inquiry than from another. There are some good general rules for deciding what form a test should take.

In general, it is preferable to ask someone about themselves rather than to ask others about them, and better to ask directly than obliquely. But it isn't always possible. Sometimes people can't or won't tell you about themselves as well as other people can tell about them. For example, other people are better judges than you of how much *they* like *you* (your popularity), whether *they* consider *you* trustworthy, loyal, and honest (your integrity or responsibility), or whether *they* would vote for *you* in an election or choose you for their supervisor or team captain (your leadership value or charisma). These are known as *sociometric ratings.* So are *letters of recommendation.* When someone wants to know your own view of things, or people, or of yourself, however, it makes most sense to ask you directly—by interviews, questionnaires, self-ratings, and the like. In most cases, you do not need very precise information and cannot get it anyway; so you want a general impression—or a consensus of people's impressions.

Whether you want to observe maximum per-

Figure 12.3 A sociogram.

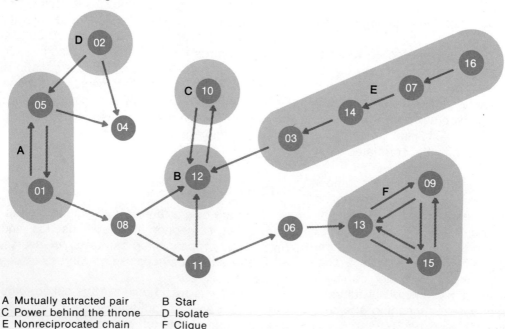

A Mutually attracted pair   B Star
C Power behind the throne   D Isolate
E Nonreciprocated chain   F Clique

formance or typical performance depends on the kind of information you seek. Most measures of personality try to see what a person is typically like, while most measures of ability are efforts to see what they are like at their very best. Of all maximum performance tests, the kind that requires the most precise information, and in which it is most difficult and complicated to get it, is measures of *intelligence.* For these, the most controversial of all measures of personality or of individual differences, every test in use is important and none is foolproof.

ASSESSMENT OF INTELLIGENCE

Of all assessment problems in psychology, intelligence has received the most systematic treatment for the longest time and been the most debated. There is practically no type of assessment device that is *not* used to estimate intelligence and none that has satisfied everyone that is fair, accurate, or even reasonable. Every kind of test method has been tried with intelligence, every plausible form of question has been used. Even so, it has not been possible, in almost a century of work, to devise a test which is entirely suitable to any good definition of intelligence, and therefore has high construct validity, or that entirely meets any practical standard for predicting whatever an intelli-

gence test ought to predict, and therefore has high criterion validity. Intelligence tests are *culture bound* (as opposed to *culture free,* or *culture fair*), meaning that people's performance on them depends largely on whether they have had good educational opportunities. And they are sensitive to the conditions under which they are administered, so people will not always show their true intellectual ability at a single testing. There are plenty of other things wrong with them too. With all of this, they are still among the best psychological tests around, and they have proved very valuable for some purposes.

Intelligence testing began in 1895 with the work of Alfred Binet, who was asked by school authorities in Paris to find a means of separating children who needed special help in school from those who would do well without it (See Chapter 1). The test which he published with Theophile Simon eight years later worked well enough to become a model for psychologists throughout the Western countries. In 1916, Lewis Terman, a psychology professor at Stanford University, created an American revision of Binet's test, from then on called the Stanford-Binet. This test, revised in 1937 and 1960, has been in continuous use ever since.

The Stanford-Binet is designed primarily for evaluating the intellectual ability of children. It is the prototype of *individually ad-*

Figure 12.4 The normal curve of intelligence distribution.

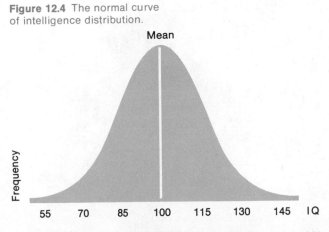

ministered psychological tests, which have the virtue of permitting the examiner to establish a personal relationship which may encourage the subject to do their best. In a *power test* (another term for maximum performance test), this should provide a more valid result than a group test could get.

The test itself consists of a bunch of questions and problems for which there are objective right and wrong answers; finding them requires such intellectual skills as comprehension of stories and pictures, vocabulary, and mathematical ability. The scoring system of the Stanford-Binet establishes a "mental age," a score comparing this child's performance to that of most children at a certain age. To make this comparison possible, the test is composed of a series of suitable questions for each age-level, such that most children of that age or above can pass them and most younger children cannot. If a child passes every item on one level, the examiner goes to a higher one, and keeps on going to higher levels until one is reached where the child fails all of the questions.

Wilhelm Stern invented the concept of IQ to express the meaning of such test performance (Stern 1911). Summing all the right answers gives the child a score equivalent to a certain intellectual level. That is the mental age. The mental age is then compared with the child's true chronological age to see how bright, dull, or average their abilities are. The ratio between the chronological and mental ages is called the *intelligence quotient* or *IQ* because it is obtained by dividing the mental age by the chronological age and multiplying the result by 100 (to get rid of the decimals). Thus the child with a mental age of five and a chronological age of five has an IQ of 100. The Binet is the only important intelligence test scored this way, but the term IQ has become so popular that now people use it in a general way to mean the *level of intelligence* rather than the score on the Binet.

For adults, the *Wechsler Adult Intelligence Scale* (WAIS) is the most widely used individual test. This test was developed in 1939 by Dr. David Wechsler at Bellevue Hospital in New York and revised in 1953. It is like the

IQ testing: Bead stringing from Stanford-Binet and block design from WISC.

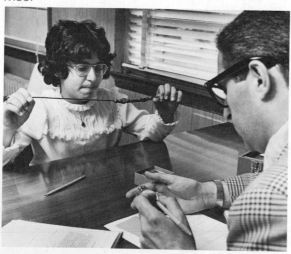

Stanford-Binet in that it is individually administered and contains a great variety of different kinds of problems. Rather than being arranged according to levels of difficulty, however, the items are grouped into *verbal* and *performance* subtests, with all the items of one kind given together. Each individual is scored separately on each kind of ability tested and the IQ is computed from the results. In fact, separate IQs are provided for *verbal* and for *performance* tests. There is also a *Wechsler Intelligence Scale for Children* (*WISC*), which uses the same format as the adult scale.

In World War I, the need to screen mental abilities among several million men drafted into the United States Army gave rise to the creation of *group* intelligence tests. They were pretty useful for screening low levels of intelligence, and since then, most psychological tests have been designed for group administration because it is so economical. Where greater precision is considered important, group tests are sometimes used for preliminary screening and individual ones for pinpointing whatever is being studied. You probably took one such group test, the SAT, (Scholastic Aptitude Test) or "college boards," as a credential for college admission. Similar tests are used to screen applicants to graduate school, law school, and medical school. Group tests often have low predictive validity, however, and intelligent university admissions policies do not rely too much on these test scores in selecting applicants.

SAT scores have been falling steadily since 1964 throughout the U.S., and some people interpret this fact to mean that students are getting poorer educations than they did in the "good old days." It may or may not mean that. There is some evidence that scores on such tests are negatively correlated with family size, for uncertain reasons, and families were getting bigger from the end of World War II until 1963. This could mean that SATs will start rising again around 1980 (Tavris 1976).

The measurement of general intelligence has generated a lot of controversy because intelligence is so elusive a quality and such an important one. Tests like the Stanford-Binet try to measure a wide range of qualities and to predict performance in terms of *general ability.* A great number of other tests have been designed to measure single aptitudes, such as mathematical, artistic, or clerical ability. Tests which predict the potential for developing specific skills are called *aptitude* tests. Like intelligence tests, aptitude tests are maximum performance measures, but their aims are specific, not general.

Maximum performance tests include tests for *speed* and tests for *power.* Speed tests have time limits and the person who can work the fastest without sacrificing accuracy gets the best score. Power tests measure ability to solve problems without regard for speed. In practice, time limits are placed even on power tests.

Achievement tests, measuring what you have done, differ from *aptitude* tests, which measure what you might be able to do. Intelligence tests are tests of general aptitudes. As anyone who has ever taken college boards knows, however, aptitude tests are largely measures of achievement. Scores on them do not really show a person's *ability* because they are always loaded with material which depends on particular kinds of *training.*

Projective tests are used more for measuring personality than for intelligence and will be covered a bit more thoroughly in Chapter 14. Such tests of *typical* performance as the Rorschach "inkblot" test, however, have been shown to provide good estimates of intelligence, which is to say they compare nicely with scores made on conventional intelligence tests. Administering and scoring these tests is complicated, and they are not used widely to measure intelligence because they are not really designed for that. Also, projective tests are oblique measures, in which subjects are unaware of the kinds of inference to be made

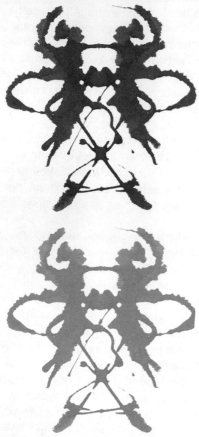

Figure 12.5 The Rorschach inkblot test is the most popular projective test. Rorschach made his blots the same way this one was made. He folded paper down the center of a blob of ink. What does this one look like?

from their responses—and there is rarely any need to use oblique measures for studying intelligence.

What do IQ tests test?

The biggest problem in the measurement of intelligence is defining what we are talking about in the first place. We commonly speak of intelligence as if its meaning were obvious,

but it is not. IQ tests are really tests of problem solving, or of knowledge or comprehension— they may predict grades in school or some other *function*—but what do they say about an underlying *ability,* which is what we want to mean when we talk about intelligence? Some scholars speak of intelligence in terms of "g," a *general ability* that supposedly pervades everything we do in life; others speak of it as logically unrelated sets of "s" factors reflecting *specific abilities;* and one of the outstanding students of measurement, L. L. Thurstone, declared: "intelligence is what intelligence tests measure." He was not being arrogant or silly, but simply saying that intelligence had to be defined by the construct validity of intelligence tests.

The idea of intelligence as a *general ability* was introduced by an influential British psychologist, Charles Spearman (1927). Spearman and his followers tried to isolate purely intellectual components of mental endeavor. This pure intellectual capacity turned out to be more elusive than its supporters were willing to admit, but psychologists have not broken away from this kind of thinking. Most of them do tend to view intelligence as a general ability, and IQ tests as efforts to tap it.

Another widely accepted definition of intelligence was developed by L. L. and Thelma Thurstone. In 1941 they published an analysis of test results which broke intelligence down into seven "primary" mental abilities: (1) verbal comprehension (V) based on vocabulary tests, (2) word fluency (W) based upon facility in verbal thinking, (3) number (N) based on arithmetic tests, (4) space (S) based on seeing relationships and drawing from memory, (5) memory (M) based on recall, (6) perceptual (P) based on tests of visual details, and (7) reasoning (R) for finding general rules, principles, or concepts. The Thurstones examined the relationship between the seven primary mental abilities and came up with a single intelligence measure. But no real agreement has been reached as to whether intelligence *is* a single ability or a combination of abilities.

The notion that intelligence can be *defined* by the tests that are currently used to *measure* it is intolerable today because it is inescapably clear that WASPs (White Anglo-Saxon Protestants) and their socio-economic equals of upper middle-class education and income, do considerably better on IQ tests than other folks do. This means either that tests are discriminatory against such groups as blacks, chicanos, and Indians—or that they are intellectually inferior to the rest of us!

This issue is not new, but it is more popular now than it used to be because concern over equal opportunities for minority groups has made some people think that they can justify discrimination if they can prove the inherent inferiority of blacks or other minorities. The topic first became a subject of scientific inquiry in 1860, when Sir Francis Galton (1822–1911), something of a genius himself, began a study of genius in an attempt to identify its hereditary components. His results were published partly in 1869 as *Hereditary Genius* and in 1883 as *Inquiries into Human Faculty*. His investigations traced the family relationships and pedigrees of eminent men and showed that intellectual superiority tended to run in families. Of course, this classic study suffers from the same shortcoming that still besets genetic studies—the inability to separate the influences of common heredity from those of a common environment—but its conclusions nevertheless have some merit. Extreme "smarts" does run in families. Somewhat. So does wealth.

Galton was criticized because he could not rule out the possibility that men were eminent because they came from superior social and cultural environments rather than because they were the heirs of a favorable biology. He had several answers to this criticism. (1) In America, where education was available to all (he thought), there was not a large number of superior people, as one would expect to find if favorable environmental conditions alone could produce superior intelligence. (2) Some of the eminent men he studied came from poor homes, but their abilities allowed them to rise above environment. (3) The relatives of the pope, who were accorded all the social advantages, were not all superior individuals.

At the opposite end of the scale from the abilities Galton had studied, the beginning of this century saw some influential studies on the hereditary nature of **feeble-mindedness** by H. H. Goddard and A. H. Estabrook. These were the case histories of the Jukes and the Kallikak families. The Jukes family was traceable back to five sisters, whose descendants after 130 years numbered 1,258 living people, all of whom Estabrook (1916) reported to be social misfits of one kind or another. He did not assign primary causation to either heredity or environment but, quite modern in viewpoint, indicated that both had some part in determining those personality types.

Goddard (1912) made a case for hereditary determination of social undesirability in his report on the two Kallikak families. He traced both back to one man, whom he called Martin Kallikak (Greek for good-bad). As an Army officer during the Revolutionary War, Kallikak had an affair with a feeble-minded barmaid who consequently gave birth to a son, after whom came a family of social misfits which included 480 descendants very much like the Jukes family. When Kallikak returned home from the war, he married a "normal," upper-class girl and sired a family of average and superior individuals. Both families were begun by the same wealthy man, and the social misfits occurred only among the descendants of the impoverished feeble-minded girl, but Goddard concluded that inheritance of feeble-mindedness, not of social deprivation, was responsible for the degenerate family.

These studies of families suffer from the handicap common to all work in human genetics. The effects of heredity and environment cannot be completely separated. Members of the same family share not only a common ancestry but also a common environment. In trying to overcome this difficulty, investigators long ago began to use twins as their subjects (see Chapter 2). Here it seemed was a clear-cut way to separate heredity from environment. It is not, of course, because there is no way to be brought up without an environment any more than it is possible to grow up without any heredity. Even so, twin studies have been useful in showing that there is a hereditary component as well as an environmental one in intelligence.

They are not all equally useful, however; in some of the most famous ones, Sir Cyril Burt claimed to have shown that identical twins raised apart have IQs corresponding more closely to their biological parents than to their foster parents, and closer to each other than to either parents or other siblings. Fraternal twins have IQs corresponding to each other about as much as to other siblings; ditto parents and their offspring. On the other hand, children raised in homes where the IQ level of their foster parents was higher than their real parents, showed higher IQs than would have been predicted from information about their real parents; so environment is also a

Efforts have been made to devise a culture-free test of intelligence, which does not penalize those whose background is different from that of the testmaker.

The Migration of the Negro, Jacob Lawrence

factor. Burt's results may have been flawed, but many other studies have substantiated similar claims (see Chapter 2).

The most conspicuous influence of environment on intelligence is seen in the difference between cultures. Anthropologists long ago became aware of how hard it is to meaningfully define intelligence when they realized that it was impossible to assess the relative abilities of people in different tribal cultures around the world by means of any of the measures available at home (Boas 1940). Asking someone what they would do if they "found a stamped, addressed envelope on the street" (Wechsler 1955) might be an index of social intelligence in New Jersey, but it would tell you nothing about turtle-snaring ability in the Guachapeepee Islands. If the natives of foreign cultures are approached with problems meaningful to their own lives, they handle them with the same variations of ability that are found anywhere. Early in the development of intelligence test-

ing, this knowledge gave rise to efforts at the construction of *culture-free* tests. These were essentially *nonverbal* IQ tests, and they were not successful. They could not be, of course, for everyone grows up in a culture. There is no IQ test that examines the quality of the brain tissue that has to do with intelligence—and that is what a truly culture-free test would have to evaluate. Today, test developers try to design instruments which are culture-*fair,* that is, which do not handicap a test subject for aspects of their upbringing which might make it hard to solve some of the problems of conventional IQ tests, even though they are plenty smart enough to do so (Metfessel and Sax 1969).

Systematic efforts to relate intelligence to race and culture became possible, of course, only with modern intelligence testing. The idea that black people might not be as intelligent as whites got a big impetus from the work of H. E. Garrett, a distinguished professor of psychology at Columbia University and later,

Figure 12.6 Culture-fair tests are generally nonverbal. They try to avoid handicapping people for lack of schooling.

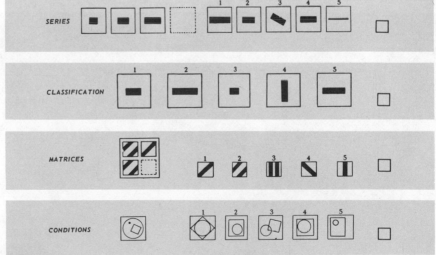

Source: From the IPAT Culture Fair Intelligence Test. Copyrighted by The Institute for Personality and Ability Testing. Used by permission.

at the University of Virginia. Garrett believed that Jews were smarter than other people and blacks dumber, and he then went about trying to prove it with IQ tests. This controversial position did not get very much public attention until it was seconded in 1969 by Arthur Jensen, an educational psychologist at the University of California at Berkeley. In a very scholarly article in the *Harvard Educational Review,* Jensen reviewed the literature on intelligence test differences between blacks and whites and reported that, though the range of intelligence is precisely the same between racial groups —so that there are geniuses and idiots alike among both blacks and whites—the average IQ test score of blacks is lower. Everyone already knew this. More important, Jensen said that the consistent difference between the groups on a great variety of IQ tests suggests that the lower average of blacks may reflect a genetic intellectual inferiority rather than being entirely due to cultural disadvantages. This possibility, he said, should be studied scientifically.

The storm that broke around this article included outraged intellectual reactions from the scientific and scholarly world and threats on Jensen's life from the outside world (Horn 1976). The chances are that Jensen is wrong for three reasons. First, IQ tests really are "loaded" against deprived people such as most blacks are. Second, to whatever extent intelligence is genetic, it is almost certainly **polygenic.** This means that there are many different genetic characteristics that combine to express intelligent behavior, and the chances are very small that the complicated combinations involved are related to the traits that define race. Third, and most important, the concept of race itself is pretty ridiculous in connection with problems like intelligence. If it is to be thoroughly examined, then we will have to see if IQ scores are lower among blacks who are very dark than among those who are very light, if flatter noses and thicker lips correlate with lower vocabulary ability and numerical reasoning power, if kinkier hair or wavier hair is significant, and a whole bunch of other such prob-

A storm of controversy followed Jensen's claim that there were genetic differences in intelligence between races.

Four Studies of a Negro's Head, Peter Paul Rubens

lems. At some point, if all this works out, we will have to turn it around also, and see what racial features of whites go with their keen mentalities. Blue-eyed, blond-haired Slavs are a lot whiter than swarthy Arabs or the almost pure Aryans of Iran and India. Are they smarter too? Does this mean the end of Polack jokes? Only research can tell. Meanwhile, from the storm, you wonder if the threats of violence may be coming from people who are afraid that Jensen is right and should therefore be shut up before he spills any more!

The issue is clouded, unhappily, by the fact that many distinguished students of intelligence, including such "biggies" as Terman and Goddard, were quite convinced themselves, early in this century, that all kinds of socially inferior groups were also intellectually inferior. Terman believed that Indians, Mexicans, and Negroes were all genetically inferior. Goddard thought it was obvious that laborers, Jews, Italians, and most other new immigrants from Eastern Europe were feebleminded. And one such work in the United States, paralleling research in England which proved the intellectual inferiority of immigrant Jewish children (Pearson and Moul 1925), became the basis for a quota system of immigration laws designed to restrict the influx of people from countries which produced "biologically inferior" people (Bingham 1923). What all those "inferior" groups had in common, of course, is that they were *poor.* This raises the suspicion that what all the intelligence scholars were doing, in their nasty pontifications, was justifying the social system from which those people came, thereby denying them access to its upper strata. Combined with the fact that some research results may have been "fudged,"[3] one must take very seriously the argument by Leon J. Kamin, in *The Science and Politics*

of IQ, that these tests have been used ". . . more or less consciously as an instrument of oppression against the underprivileged—the poor, the foreign-born, and racial minorities (1974)."

Pygmalion in the classroom Whether or not colored genes are important in IQ, colored expectations certainly are! There has been considerable research (also accompanied by storm, but no threats of violence this time) on the effects of teacher expectancy on IQ scores. A study by Robert Rosenthal and Lenore Jacobson (1968) of Harvard University showed that teachers who have been led to expect a certain performance from their students help make it come true. When they were told that a test showed that they should expect great improvement during the year from certain "late blooming" students, they apparently encouraged those students to do well and thereby made the prediction come true. Some scholars question the conclusions of Rosenthal's original study, but some of his subsequent studies, at least, have supported his original claims.

This suggests that expectation as well as discrimination may account for differences in performance by different ethnic groups. Considerable effort has been made to erase the test difference between people from different cultures and subcultures by "culture-fair" tests. Such tests would show the same average intelligence distribution no matter where they are given or to whom.

There is a small proportion of children who, by IQ test standards, are intellectually gifted. They tend to be healthy and emotionally adjusted as well, to do well in school and college, and to enter the professions and upper echelons of business, where they continue to do well. They also tend to come from upper middle-class families, which shows the environmental side of giftedness.

The most comprehensive study of gifted children was begun by Lewis Terman in California soon after World War I. He began studying over 1,500 high-IQ children from pub-

---

[3] Arthur Jensen, by the way, was directly responsible for opening the investigation which led to the exposure of Sir Cyril Burt's twin studies as being "not kosher." He noticed some oddities in Burt's statistics which seemed very unlikely.

lic schools, and the study has continued, with regular follow-ups, to this day, though Terman died in 1956. In 1972, the average age of these gifted "children" had risen to 62. On the whole, they were still doing well (Sears 1977).

Vive les differences: Sex and age and IQ
Cross-racial comparisons are not the only IQ studies that are done; they are just the most controversial. Of greater interest, I think, and likely to show greater and more meaningful differences in the long run, are comparisons of males and females on ability tests. A number of these have been done. On the Thurstone primary mental abilities tests, for instance, women tend to do better than men on verbal comprehension, word fluency, and perceptual skills, while men do better on spatial relations and number tests. Overall IQ results average out about the same for both sexes.

Any number of other studies have found similar results, and at different ages among people of different backgrounds. In general, it seems that females are slightly but significantly better at verbal skills of all kinds and that men are slightly but significantly better at numerical skills of all kinds (Maccoby and Jacklin 1974). Since *sex* is a far more real biological entity than *race* is, it makes sense to think that there may be biologically based differences in intellectual skills between the sexes. If there are, however, they are of historical, not practical interest; they may reflect on the differences in evolutionary functions which may have created a selective pressure on women to be able to communicate, perhaps with their children and with other women, and on men to understand spatial relations, a skill that would be valuable in hunting and foraging. They may even help to explain why there have not yet been great women mathematicians or musical composers, though women have been denied opportunity for so long in so many things that suppression alone may be plenty of explanation. But in any case, they do not allow any reasonable person to think that either sex should be encouraged or discouraged in one or another type of skill. The tests are not that good, the differences are not that big, and the overlap between males and females on test scores is complete, even when the average scores differ.

Finally, to shift briefly to oppressed majorities, today's youthful population tends to score higher on IQ tests than its parents did, again varying from one test to another. Better schooling, cultural advantages, "the tube," decent nutrition, and other factors probably account for this trend.

The picture is not so favorable with old age, however. Intellectual abilities do not continue to increase throughout life, though ***wisdom*** might and, with it, maybe the ability to live intelligently. Anyhow, the kinds of skills and abilities which tests measure reach a peak of development in early adulthood, remain stable for some years, and then some of them decline—at different rates for different abilities in different people. Some scholars argue that certain aspects of intelligence actually increase with age (Baltes and Schale 1974), but these things may reflect education more than skill (Horn and Donaldson 1977). Most old people agree with the scholars who feel they are less "quick-witted" than they used to be.

Whatever their shortcomings, intelligence tests are useful instruments for some purposes—where they get information more quickly and efficiently and with less bias than would be available otherwise. All tests are limited either by the difficulty of defining the thing to be measured or the difficulty of measuring it once it is defined. People are infinitely more variable than even the most ingeniously varied set of test items can possibly hope to measure. Before using any test, the first consideration must be the ethical issue of whether or not such a test may potentially infringe on the rights to individual differences each of us is entitled to possess, and most of the time, to guard in privacy.

SUMMARY

1 Individual differences has two meanings: First, a political meaning, that people are obligated to honor the rights of others to differ from them. The second, or technical meaning of individual differences is that people differ in their abilities and needs. The second meaning is important politically because people justify giving or denying others their rights on the basis of the technical differences. The denial of rights to blacks and women, for instance, is often justified by arguments that genetically they cannot manage equality happily. Blacks would rather eat watermelon than vote, and women would rather have babies than careers.

2 On a technical level the human being is the most complex and varied biological organism in the world. Most physical features are genetically determined while most behavior is not. Behavior is influenced by the infinite number of stimulating possibilities in the environment. For this reason, *individual differences* has the specialized meaning in psychology of differences in people's responses to the same stimuli.

3 Individual differences are studied in two main ways. The *normative* or *nomothetic* approach compares the same behavior among different people; the *ipsative* or *ideographic* approach studies the same person in different situations. Both approaches are usually necessary to understand behavior comprehensively.

4 All measurements are judged by their *reliability* and *validity*. Reliability means dependability; it can be assessed by comparing results of the same test given at different times (test-retest reliability); asking the same question in different ways (inter-item reliability); giving the same test in two different forms to the same people (alternate form reliability); or correlating two halves of the same test among many people (split-half reliability). Reliability sets the limit on validity. A test can be reliable and not valid, but it cannot be valid if it is unreliable. Validity means accuracy or meaningfulness; its accuracy can be assessed in its predictive value (criterion validity) and its meaningfulness in terms of some abstract idea (construct validity).

5 Since tests are used for important practical purposes, both their reliability and validity need to be established carefully before they are published. Even well constructed tests will produce some *false positives*, people whom the test says have qualities which they really lack, and some *false negatives*, people who the test says lack qualities which they actually have. Poorly constructed tests are doubly dangerous to society.

6 There are three dimensions of inquiry in psychological tests. The first concerns who is asked for information. Some tests ask a person to tell about themselves and others ask for information about them. The second concerns how information is requested. Some tests ask questions directly, making clear what information is sought, and others ask oblique questions and draw inferences from them. The third concerns the kind of information being sought. Some tests assess a person's maximum performance and others inquire about their typical performance. Most tests ask people to tell about themselves, but sociometric ratings and recommendations are third person assessment devices. Most tests also ask questions directly, but projective tests and other unobtrusive measures ask them obliquely. Tests of intelligence, achievement, and aptitude are maximum performance measures; tests of personality are measures of typical performance.

7 Intelligence has been studied more systematically than any other individual difference problem. Intelligence cannot be measured definitively, because it is an abstract concept and because ability to do well on IQ tests depends on educational opportunities and social backgrounds. All intelligence tests are culture-bound, and efforts to develop culture-fair tests have not been completely successful. The Binet Scale of Intelligence was the first individually administered intelligence test. Originally developed in France by Alfred Binet in 1903, it was revised several times in the U.S., and the *Stanford-Binet* has since become the most popular individual IQ test for children. The *Wechsler Adult Intelligence Scale* (*WAIS*) is the most widely used individual test for adults, and the *Wechsler Intelligence Scale for Children* (*WISC*) is also very popular.

8　Scholars disagree about whether intelligence involves a *general ability factor* which gives a person competence in many areas or whether it involves many unrelated specific abilities. Spearman argued that intelligence was a general ability and most intelligence testmakers agree with that position. Thurstone, however, proposed that there are seven separate primary mental abilities: verbal comprehension, word fluency, number, space, memory, perception, and reasoning.

9　The dispute about the hereditary versus environmental nature of intelligence goes back a century to the studies of genius done by Sir Francis Galton. The same argument today is whether race and intelligence may be linked. The polygenic nature of intelligence plus the polygenic nature of race makes this unlikely.

10　Teachers' expectations may have an important influence on the IQ test scores as well as on the classroom performance of many children. This finding may be particularly important in the education of children from deprived backgrounds, indicating that encouragement and the expectation of good performance could substantially influence their aspirations and achievement in school.

11　There are sex and age differences in IQ scores. In general, females do better than males on verbal tests, and males do better than females on spatial relations and numbers tests. In general, also, young people today do better on most IQ tests than their parents did a generation ago, probably because of better educational opportunities. The sex differences may have a biological basis. Neither difference has any practical implication. Intellectual abilities reach a peak of development in early adulthood, it seems, and some of them decline in old age, at different rates for different people.

Human development

13

13

Human development

Human *beings* have interested scientific psychologists for quite a while, but human *development* did not develop fully as a scientific discipline until recently. "Child psychology" had long existed by 1950 and was, in fact, then the only division of the American Psychological Association in which women outnumbered men. But it was not a very popular subject among professional psychologists. There really was no such thing as a psychology of adulthood or aging until then, probably because there were not enough old people organized to be politically important or to draw the attention of many scholars to them. All this has changed dramatically since 1950, and developmental processes, from the cradle to the grave, are now among the most intensely studied research topics in all of psychology. They should be. You cannot fully understand such basic processes as perception or motivation or emotion without knowing something about their development, *because they are always developing,* never static events which get to be a certain way and stay there. And you cannot have much perspective on human beings as a whole unless you get some perspective on the sequential course of their lives. This chapter tries to scan that sequence.

Development refers to change over time. It is the whole sequence of life, from conception to death. And it is not merely *what* happens, but how it happens—the order of its unfolding, the rules which govern it, and the variations and irregularities that separate individuals and cultures and whole species from one another.

All living creatures develop. The more complex the creature, the more development it has to go through to achieve much of its evolutionary potential. Single-celled creatures go through less then multi-celled ones. And among multi-celled ones, development is largely cumulative (each part gets added to previous ones), increasingly complex (you started as a single cell, and look at you now), and differentiated (you have separate parts for breathing, digesting, locomoting), and integrated (they all work in harmony, sort of) in a succession of syntheses (growth processes) which are not reducible to the parts from which they emerged.

Mammals, as you would therefore expect, develop more slowly than other animals; humans, as you would further expect, more slowly than others mammals. Along the same lines, human infants, among all animals, have the longest period of development before they are capable of adult behavior. (Humans live longer than other animals too, by and large, so the length of their immaturity, relative to that of their lives, is not so very great.)

The pattern of human development is also more variable than that of other species, and sometimes harder to measure, because human behavior is not all cumulative and because human perceptual faculties are so plastic and learning abilities so great that diversity is enormous within individuals and across the species. Some elementary skills, for instance, like eye-hand coordination (which makes it possible to grasp what you see) and sensory-motor coordination (which makes walking possible) and imitation (which makes most social behavior possible) all appear early in infancy, then disappear a few weeks afterwards, and do not surface again for months (Bower 1977). Culture has even more diverse effects. Within a culture, events that are normal at one age are bizarre at another. In America, when a baby burps after eating, the guests are amused; when you do, they are appalled. Across cultures, it may be different. When you belch after eating in a Bedouin home, you have honored the host; when you fail to, you may have spurned his hospitality.

Development always involves both change and continuity, sameness and variety. But the emphasis which is necessary to survey the sequence and span of development is not so much on **individual differences,** as in the last chapter, as on the **commonalities** of changing behavior over time (Wohlwill 1973). We will focus on those commonalities.

THEORIES OF DEVELOPMENT

Ages and stages

No one had to wait for a science of psychology to realize that development occurs in some kind of progression. There is a long literary tradition, not even counting common sense, which says so. The most famous expression of it, no doubt, is Shakespeare's:[1]

> All the world's a stage,
> And all the men and women merely players;
> They have their exits and their entrances;
> And one man in his time plays many parts,
> His acts being seven ages . . .

The questions that are not so easily answered are: "What governs the unfolding of the seven or three or however many ages there are? What makes them happen? What marks the end of one and the beginning of another? How can you tell them apart?" The answers are not self-evident.

Everyone agrees that behavior develops in some orderly way. A baby must babble before it can talk, must speak a little before it can think a lot, and must think a lot before it can write a poem. You must crawl before you can walk, and walk before you can dance. Scholars agree that *the order* of developmental events is much more uniform than *the age* at which they occur. There is less agreement about whether this order unfolds in a relatively smooth and continuous way, or whether it goes through more or less clearly marked levels. It is the difference between a ramp and a

---

[1] From *As You Like It,* Act II, Scene 6. The speech is recited by a character named Jaques, pronounced "Jack-iss." How do you like it?

staircase. The steps, in the staircase arrangement, are called stages.

In part, the continuities and discontinuities of development are simply unknown so that dividing them into phases of any kind is a convenient fiction. And where they are known, it is often impossible to be sure what their determinants are. This makes the facts of development a rich breeding ground for arguing the nature-nurture controversy, especially when they are conceived in stages. Some scholars see development chiefly as the unfolding of the built-in genetic codes which evolution has created—this is a *maturational* view, focusing on acquisitions that occur during sensitive periods. An alternative view focuses on the situations which occur at different points in the life cycle, from which one learns this or that habit, expectation, or feeling. This is an *environmental* view, focusing on learning and socialization processes.

A third position, sometimes called the *epigenetic,* or *interaction,* point of view, emphasizes the interaction between heredity and environment which leads to development, a point of view that does not commit itself to the notion that a meaningful argument can be made about which contributes most of what to it. This position is typical of the Swiss psychologist, Jean Piaget, whose work is the most prominent focus of contemporary research in developmental psychology (Ginsburg and Koslowski 1976). Most scientific students of development, whether or not they subscribe to the theories of Piaget, and whether or not they are convinced that there are clearcut stages, subscribe to this position.

The idea of a stage says more than simply that development is orderly. It implies that, at different ages, large segments of behavior are organized around a major theme, which differs from the theme or activities of other stages. It also suggests that there are spurts of development from one stage to the next, rather than a smooth transition.

Stages are not as firmly fixed as sensitive periods, that is, their effects are generally considered more reversible. Still, the notion of relative fixity is central to the stage concept. In theory, at least, if you are *fixated* at an early stage, that is, if you have not completed the growth process for that stage, you will be disabled, more or less, from mastering the developments waiting at the next. When you do advance to a new stage, moreover, you do not abandon the patterns learned in the previous one, but build on them.

Even among stage theorists, there is no clear agreement as to what all the stages of development are or what happens during them. Every stage theory, in fact, deals with special aspects of development, such as personality or cognition or moral development, and most of them only deal with what happens during infancy and childhood, because those periods do so much to shape adult behavior.

The first, and perhaps still the best known stage theory is Sigmund Freud's *psychosexual* stages of personality development, which says that children focus their interest on different pleasurable parts of their bodies as they mature. Freud's stages begin with an *oral* period in infancy, when feeding and sucking are main events, and proceed through *anal, phallic,* and *latency* periods. The *genital,* or adult stage, is reached after puberty as the child's attention begins to focus on adult interests. The best known variant of Freud's theory is Erik Erikson's theory of *psychosocial* stages, which cover the entire life span and which revolve around socially generated feelings rather than around sex (see Chapter 14).

The stage theory which commands most scientific attention today is that of the *mental growth periods* during which, according to Jean Piaget, cognitive development occurs. One offshoot of it has been the *moral development* theory of Lawrence Kohlberg, which says that children develop morally in six stages, from the time they can first make moral judgments until about the age of sixteen, when they can respond morally to their own consciences rather than merely to social convention.

Personality stages and cognitive periods: Freud and Piaget

Piaget's periods cover the same time span as Freud's, infancy to adolescence, but the theories do not touch each other very often in emphasis or interest. Freud's stages describe *personality* (emotional) development; Piaget's periods address the growth of *intellect.* Also, Freud's stages were far more culturally determined than he realized, while Piaget's periods do seem to occur in the same sequence across different cultures, regardless of education (Goodnow and Bethon 1966). The age at which children reach each intellectual period, however, may differ greatly from one culture to another (Piaget 1970).

Infancy Freud calls infancy the *oral stage* because the infant's basic source of pleasure, at this time, is its mouth. In Freud's view, thinking at this stage is a *primary process,* that is, a cluster of *autistic* (unrealistic, self-centered) mental images which express the infant's wishes for comfort and pleasure. Piaget calls this the *sensorimotor period,* lasting from birth until about 18 months. In it, he believes, the infant acts on the environment, and does not build mental images symbolizing reality

The oral stage.

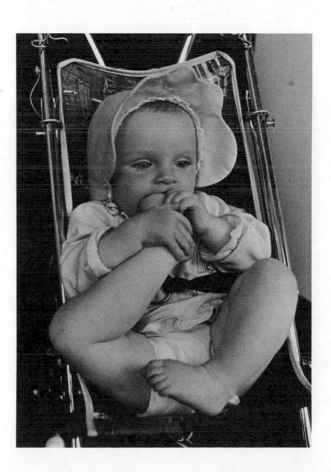

until the latter part. At first, these images, called *schemes,* are mere representations of the infant's own motor behavior; gradually, they give way to realistic thinking. In this stage, Freud's focus is on the emotional aspect of thinking, that is, its aim at wish-fulfillment, while Piaget's is on how the infant perceives events rather than how it feels about them.

Early childhood After infancy, the theories diverge more and more. Piaget goes on to what we might call human computer functions, that is, reasoning and logical thinking, while Freud goes on to the refinement of emotion and impulse into personality traits and character structure.

For Freud, toilet training is the key to the second, or *anal* stage, in which the child makes its first steps towards autonomy and runs into its first serious conflict with parents. For Piaget, language learning, which blossoms at the same time, is the key to the *preoperational* stage of his second period, called *concrete operations,* which includes all of Freud's *anal, phallic,* and *latency* stages. The preoperational part goes from about age two to seven. At this time, Piaget notes, all of the child's symbolic abilities grow. Dreams and night terrors and symbolic play, which Freud relates to anal and phallic conflicts and ego development, and Piaget to symbolic growth, all start occurring now. Representational drawing starts now, and two sticks at right angles become an airplane (Elkind 1974).

Later childhood The second half of Piaget's concrete operations period, from about seven to eleven, is Freud's latency stage, a relatively conflict-free time. In this period, the child grows capable of figuring out things in its head that previously required overt actions. Counting mentally instead of on your fingers is the simplest case. Later, this ability extends to understanding the relations among classes of things, so that doing thought problems becomes possible.

Pubescence: Formal operations The last stage of intellectual development occurs from age 12 to 15, when Freud's *genital* stage begins. Piaget calls it the period of *formal operations* because adult thinking now becomes manifest—the capacity to think about your thoughts, to formulate ideals, to reason about the future, to reason logically and hypothetically about such things as contrary-to-fact propositions. At this time, metaphors become meaningful—satire makes no sense before adolescence, which is why books such as *Alice in Wonderland* ". . . are enjoyed at different levels during childhood than in adolescence and adulthood, when their social significance can be understood (Elkind 1974, p. 25)."

By this time, the child is thinking systematically, and both personality and cognitive stages are complete, as these theorists see it, and so no radically new patterns will occur.

Freud's and Piaget's stage theories are quite compatible with each other. They cover the same time periods with quite different objectives, more often than not making unrelated observations of parallel aspects of children's behavior. Freud originally saw his stages as maturationally determined, but they are plainly products of the interaction of maturation and environmental events. Piaget denies that his periods are maturationally determined, but he also speaks of acquisitions to behavior occurring without learning, which sounds like maturation to me. Between them, in any case, the macro-theorizing of developmental psychology is about complete. No one else has advanced bold schemes to yield a single picture of the course of development. This is an area rich in empirical findings, but poor in theories for putting them together (Hetherington and McIntyre 1975).

Regardless of how many different stages there are, or precisely which aspects of development occur in stages and which do not, the whole business of living always goes in one direction—from start to finish. The start comes when sperm and egg unite; the finish, if all has gone well, when the ripened years have piled up, and the aged welcome the quiet of eternal rest. In between go infancy, childhood, and youth, and adulthood, always in that order. And that is how we shall look at them. It may seem like too obvious a classification scheme to bother stating, but it is not. People did not always see things this way.

The history of life phases

Shakespeare may have recognized human life as a sequence of "acts" divided into

"seven ages," but most people, until quite recently, did not. Childhood was clearly separate from adulthood, but in most places, throughout the recorded history of Western Civilization, the separation was to the great disadvantage of children (deMause 1974). By and large, they were the property of their parents (or of priests or government), nothing more, and could be left to die, in infancy or later, brutalized, sexually abused, or mistreated in any other way their elders wished. And so they were. In England, at the end of the 17th Century, John Locke recommended that they should go to work no

The world of adults has never been shaped to the needs of children.

later than age three (Laslett 1971). He was not unusual and not cruel for his time—or for the next 200 years. Children had no rights and no defenders. Infanticide was so common in every European country that foundling homes, in one case opened by a man who could not stand the sight of dying babies in the gutters of London, ran out of space soon after they opened. In 1890, the sight of dead babies in London streets was still common.

Youth was not childhood and was recognized everywhere as adulthood. Many cultures had special rites of passage into adult life, early versions of the communions and bar mitzvahs and graduations we still celebrate. But adolescence had no special status of its own either, separating it from adulthood legally or socially. Until well into this century, when social security laws and retirement pensions started to make it practical, neither did old age. Child-labor laws and mandatory school attendance everywhere did the same good turn for adolescence.

Professional interest in life phases followed social changes which made them more apparent. Freud's stage theory of development, the first of its kind, Binet's intelligence test, and the increasing interest in children which they represented, were social byproducts of trends towards universal free education, limiting child labor, and recognizing children more as people than as economic property. Until about 1950, however, scholars and the public alike tended to assume that, once you got to be an adult, you stayed whatever way you had become, and that was that. Since then, the elderly have become an important social and political force, and scholars accordingly have realized that there are adult developmental stages, just as there are childhood ones, and begun studying them (Erikson 1963; Peck 1955). This was "news" to the public as late as 1975, when *Time* magazine reported the fact, and in 1976, when the first popular book on it became a best seller (Sheehy, 1976).

FROM ZERO UP: PRENATAL AND NEONATAL GROWTH

Development in the womb

From conception to delivery, the period called *gestation,* takes about nine months, and with the astonishing number of things that have to happen and dangers to be averted in that time, it is a wonder we get born at all. Most of the fetus' metabolism and sensory system is functioning within four months, but important processes like respiration and digestion are not ready to go until the eighth month or so (Meredith 1975). If you were born before the end of the sixth month of pregnancy, your chances of survival would be almost nil; at seven months, they would be about 50–50.

The womb is a protected environment, but not a perfectly protected one. The only connection between fetus and mother is through the placenta, and its pores are so fine that they form a "placental barrier" by means of which most of mother's metabolic dangers are kept out while nutrients are passed in. Even so, there is some chemical communication between mother and fetus and even some behavioral communication which can affect the fetus' life and well-being, sometimes badly.

Drugs, viruses, X-rays, vitamin excesses or deficiencies, and many other chemical or physical agents in the mother can harm the growing fetus in different ways. If the mother gets German measles in the first three months of pregnancy, the baby could suffer blindness, deafness, or brain damage. Some sleeping pills or anti-nausea drugs in the fourth to sixth months have caused deformities (that is what Thalidomide, a tranquilizer, was famous for in the 1950's). Poor nutrition in the last three months can be damaging. If the mother is addicted to heroin, the baby will be born "hooked" and has to be withdrawn gradually. And alcohol, smoking, coffee, and possibly LSD, taken by the mother, all have some effects, of unknown duration or extent, but probably not wonderful, on the unborn child. The kind of damage a given substance will do varies largely with the stage of development at the time, a good example of the effects of sensitive periods on development (Gottlieb 1976).

Mother's body makes chemicals as well as takes them, and the behavioral events which reflect this process also may indicate that the growing creature within her is affected. Chronic strong emotions felt by the mother, for instance, eventually send adrenalin and other hormones into the fetus' blood. In the embryonic stage of development (the first three months), when most organs are formed, the results of severe maternal stress may be a harelip and cleft palate in the baby. Later on, the fetus responds to maternal stress with increased movement, and such infants tend to be overactive. No one knows why.

What *is* clear is that there is some kind of *chemical* communication from mother, reflected in her feelings and transmitted into the fetus' arousal patterns; maternal anxiety has an arousing affect, maternal serenity a soothing one. The fetus starts moving naturally, turning and kicking, from the fourth month; even earlier, however, it will produce a reflex movement of trunk and head when touched. And there is some evidence that avoidance learning can occur in the last two months before birth (Spelt 1948). The claim has been questioned, however, because of poor methodology, and because its results do not seem to have been replicated (Stone, Smith, and Murphy 1973). Premature infants, in any case, *can* be conditioned, though more slowly than full-term babies, and many of the actions which a baby is born ready to do are first practiced in the womb (Stevenson 1970; Meredith 1975).

The newborn

Newborn babies in America average around 7 pounds in weight and are around 20 inches long, about a quarter of which is head and a third, legs. By adulthood, the legs have become half a person's full height and the head about a tenth of it. Soft cartilage, which lets baby bounce instead of breaking on long falls, turns to hard bone; muscle grows about 40 times heavier; nerves grow larger, more interconnected, and more sheathed in protective myelin coatings. The brain grows fastest for about two years, then more slowly. At birth, it is about 25 percent of its adult weight; by six months, 50 percent; and by 30 months, 75 percent (Tanner 1970). Its biggest workload is organized in those couple of years.

When you realize what baby is capable of doing at birth, or just after, it is obvious that development has been going on for quite a while, and that maturation has been the main factor so far. The *neonate* (newborn) has several reflexes ready to work, beyond breathing, digesting, and eliminating (Wolff 1959). Some of them will disappear forever in a few weeks or months, such as the Babinski reflex—in which the foot withdraws and toes fan out when the sole is touched with a pin; the *Grasping,* or "Darwinian" reflex—in which the newborn will tightly grasp a rod put in its hand, like its primate ancestors maybe had to do to not fall out of trees; and the *Moro* reflex, in which the baby will go into a tense hugging movement, like its ancestors may have done to stay in mamma's lap.

More practical responses are also ready at birth, however; the *Rooting* reflex—you touch the side of its mouth, and baby's head turns towards you, and sucking starts, which allows the mouth quickly to substitute for the placenta as a feeding tube. Baby's eyelids will shut reflexively to a bright light from birth on; and within two hours, its eyes will follow a moving light.

Visual acuity isn't much at birth, around 20/200; the baby has poor depth perception; and baby's eyes tend to operate independently for some weeks. Still, the newborn sees, can

Infants can attend and recognize
some forms soon after birth.

focus on things about ten inches off, shows
some preference for visual contours or patterns
(see Figure 13.1) over blank space from the very
first (Bronson 1974; Fanz 1961), and can imitate facial gestures 12 to 21 days after birth
(Meltzoff and Moore 1977).

Some other senses are in good shape at
birth. Baby can hear 40 to 60 decibels, the
normal speaking range of sound, and can discriminate some tones (Bridger 1961). It also
withdraws reflexively from strong bad smells
and strong bad tastes, such as saline solution,
important capabilities, in evolutionary terms,
because they reduce the likelihood of poisoning.

Individual differences Newborns are not
all the same in any of these respects, of course.
They have different sensory thresholds and
different levels of responding. Some need firm
stroking, others respond to gentle. Some are
startled by softer sounds, others only by louder
ones. Some are placid, some active and restless (Korner 1969).

No one knows how much differences at
birth account for differences in infant behavior,
let alone through later life. But some *congenital*
(seen at birth) individual differences in activity level and the like may reflect differences
in temperament which start becoming measurable after two months or so, and which do seem
to last at least through much of childhood. By
that time, some babies seem to be dependably

easy to handle and responsive, others slow to warm up, and still others difficult (Thomas, Chess, and Birch 1970).

It is a mistake to place too much faith in temperament differences, though. The variability of infant behavior, in many respects, is enormous, both with respect to the age at which it first appears, the regularity of its occurrence, and the ease with which it can be measured. This is partly true of physical growth, more true of neuromuscular development, and most true of behavior. Infant intelligence tests, for instance, even at their best, are still very poorly correlated with later measures of intelligence in children and adults. Temperamental or personality measures are likely to be equally undependable.

Figure 13.1 Importance of pattern rather than color or brightness was illustrated by the response of infants to a face, a piece of printed matter, a bull's-eye and plain red, white and yellow disks. Even the youngest infants preferred patterns. Dark bars show the results for infants from two to three months old; light bars, for infants more than three months old.

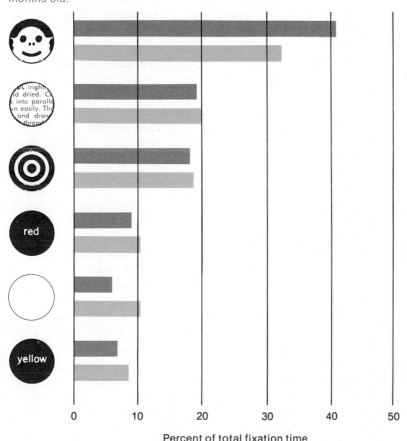

Percent of total fixation time

INFANCY AND CHILDHOOD

One textbook defines human *infancy* as the period during which a baby cannot survive without its mother, and *childhood* as the period when language development and socialization occur. (*Developmental Psychology Today* 1971). No clear boundaries exist between them.

The Latin word from which "infant" comes means "one unable to speak." It is the groundwork time for everything else, the setting in which all the stages to come are prepared. Here, the effects of maturation are most influential, and those of the environment are chiefly remarkable as they facilitate or interfere with early growth.

The normal course of infancy produces rapid, giant steps towards all the functions baby will need to become an independent animal and, hopefully, a human being. Learning ability increases drastically from two or three months on, as baby becomes capable of more attention. It facilitates everything else. Speech sounds such as "pa" and "ba" are already discriminable at two months (Eimas, Siqueland, Jusczyk, and Vigorito 1971). Social smiling (i.e. at faces) becomes notable by the age of four months, though it may be seen earlier (Kagan 1971). Baby will smile more and more at human features, even portrayed on cardboard, and even with the parts scrambled, for another couple of months (Gewirtz 1965). By seven months, it will smile more readily to real faces than fake ones, and still more readily to familiar than to strange ones. Now, it is ready to become emotionally attached to familiars—and sometimes fearful of strangers.

By seven or eight months, it has made a lot of progress towards locomotion; has attachments to particular people; and babbles in language sounds by about nine months. It sits, creeps, stands, and walks between 7–15 months, signifying nothing about later competence at anything, but a joy and a hope to doting parents.

So much for the ordinary course of infant development. The question which puzzles, and interests, scholars is: What happens when extraordinary situations occur, when the baby is deprived of normal stimulation? Will that hurt development? Or, conversely, will it speed up development if you can give the baby more than ordinary stimulation? What effect, after all, does early environment have?

Early environment

Deprivation, restitution, and enrichment There is some danger that, if a baby's early environment does not provide enough sensory, motor, and social stimulation, it may be impossible later on to compensate for these deficiences and for the baby to learn the skills needed for effective functioning. The evidence is mixed. A number of animal and human studies alike suggest that sensory and perceptual abilities, including pain perception, social and sexual competence, and language and intellectual functions may all be permanently damaged by prolonged lack of stimulation or an excess of stress early in life (Stone, Smith and Murphy 1973). There is also good evidence, on the other hand, that monkeys and people, anyway, have great elasticity early on which does not lock them into the mishaps of sensitive periods as much as other animals, but keeps their developmental potential plastic enough so that they can compensate for many privations and catch up with infants who had normal environments to begin with. Russian babies kept swaddled up to the neck, for instance, Indian babies strapped to a board, and Guatemalan children kept indoors and relatively immobile for the first year of life (Kagan and Klein 1973), all catch up with American babies who have had freedom of movement all along, and the nonAmerican babies seem none the worse for it thereafter.

Evaluating such studies, however, is not a simple matter. On the face of it, they make it

Cultural difference in handling infants makes no difference in the success of development.

seem like the maturation of nerve and muscle is more important than the restrictions of the environment. But that is not clear at all. The babies in swaddling cultures do get stimulation when they are not swaddled; and the swaddling itself provides a certain amount of stimulation. So it is not certain that these babies are really deprived of motor stimulation significantly. And they certainly are not lacking in the sensory and social stimulation of maternal care. If the environment is restricted severely enough for long enough, however, as happens in some orphanages and similar institutions, the damage may not be made up for so easily. And even fairly mild deprivations in these settings can retard development somewhat, while even

mild efforts at restitution can enhance it. Oddly, the same thing is true of premature infants; the incubator simulates the womb but, in doing so, it deprives babies of stimulation on which they clearly thrive as soon as they are airborne.

There is also some evidence, both among humans and other animals, that enriching the infant's environment by increasing sensory stimulation and opportunities for exploration and play may have an accelerating effect on the development of infants who have not been deprived in the first place (see Chapter 4) (White 1971). This too, is a mixed bag, because some studies, both of humans and other animals, suggest that exposure at least to mild stress in infancy may speed up some kinds of physical growth (Levine and Mullins 1966). Among humans, in fact, such stresses during infancy may cause an increase in adult height (Landauer and Whiting, 1964)—or, in rare cases, death from a condition called Sudden Infant Death Syndrome (Haith and Campos, 1977). It is not always obvious how much of any stimulation enriches the infant's environment and how much assaults it.

Were there a rule for the optimum amount of stimulation needed in early infancy, it might be: "not too little and not too much." A mildly deficient environment may not interfere permanently with most maturational effects, and a mildly enriched one may enhance their occurring without delay. Too much deprivation may do permanent damage; too much "enrichment" may do no real good.

It is useful to remember, in this connection, that when we talk about deprivation and enrichment of the *infant's* environment, we are asking, largely, whether any **neurological** damage is done by mild isolation and deprivation and whether there is some permanent booster given the maturational process by enriching the infant's surroundings. The answer to both those questions is a very qualified "no." When we ask about enriching the environment of *children,* however, we are really asking about influencing their interests, attitudes, and inclinations towards one or another kind of *learning* or *performance.* There, the answer is a much less qualified "yes." The kind of stimulation involved here is educational, broadly speaking, not only neurological. The most important stimulators, or educators, or manipulators of the environment, in this connection, are parents. Their function too begins in infancy, but grows apace as the baby does.

Parenting

The main manipulation of the environment, from nutrition and temperature control, through the opportunities for sensory experience, motor development, and language and social learning, comes from the action of parents. Parenting is the most significant environmental event of infancy and early childhood.

Caregiving Notice that "parenting" is a verb, not a noun; it describes an activity, a function, not a person. Ever since the need for stimulation and the dangers of stimulus-deprivation became known, scholars have debated whether the caregiving acts that define parenting in early infancy actually require a mothering *person* in attendance or whether the need for stimulation is independent of who delivers it. In the latter case, mother would be "a vehicle of sheer stimulation," and the contact comfort of terry-cloth mothers with their feeding nipples might satisfy some elementary needs of human infants, as of monkeys (Stone, Smith, and Murphy 1973). It does not. Nonsocial stimulation is important for some aspects of development, as we have seen, but the main things that mothering *people* do for infants cannot be done by impersonal means. It takes people to set the stage for the social interactions which are later associated with love, security, and competence in personal relationships. Children who spend their infancy in orphanages, by and large, become less sociable, more poorly adjusted, and colder emotionally than children raised in more homey atmospheres, including foster homes (Tizard and Rees 1974).

Attachment There seems to be a reciprocal tendency in infants and mothers which works to maximize chances of the infant's getting as much caregiving as mother has in her. Called **attachment,** it is the tendency to stick close to familiar figures, seeking attention and soothing from them. It is evident in the monkey babies who scamper into the bosom of the terry-cloth mother when they are frightened, and who keep hugging her with one arm as they reach out fearfully with the other to explore new things in the world around her. It is equally apparent in human infants, though more complicated and variable, like everything human. And you have met with it among lower species, where it is clearly inherited, as *imprinting* (see Chapter 2). In mothers, attachment is the disposition to be sensitive and accessible to the infant, to respond promptly to its crying, which reduces its frequency, and so forth (Bell and Ainsworth 1972).

Infant attachment to mothers is generally noticeable by seven months of age, and to fathers a month or so later (Lamb 1975), but the ability to detect and discriminate the emotional signals from adults which would indicate whether the infant could safely cling to them develops some months earlier. Maternal attachment has been studied less. Separation of mothers and infants among some mammals causes the mother to lose interest in the infant and stop caring for it when they are reunited. This may not be true of humans, but there is some evidence that mothers who have had very extended contact with their babies during the first three days after bearing them report more attachment to them (soothing them when they cry, missing them when separated) than do mothers who had more limited contact (Kennell, Trause, and Klaus 1975).

Attachment probably has an evolutionary function of maintaining closeness between infant and mother against dangerous separations (Bowlby 1969, 1973). The helpless young of the herd who get separated and fall behind either starve or get eaten. The comfort of attachment, on the other hand, makes it possible for babies to start exploring frightening new situations as they get used to them. Fearful monkey and human babies will go out on little expeditions to look over new toys and places, keeping a close eye on mother, ready to dash back any time. Gradually, they become bolder and more independent. Mother too becomes less anxious about baby's moving away from her. Thus *detachment* is born of secure attachment.

Attachment is not sustained only by its fear-reducing properties, of course, but by the positive feelings that are connected with it as well. This makes it reasonable to believe that even after independence is achieved, feelings of attachment endure, now experienced perhaps as affection, longing, and interest. Maybe that is why you write letters, as an adult, to people you were once attached to, even if you do not expect to see them again or need to. And maybe too that is why, if you do see them, you suddenly feel stronger bonds with them than you have felt for quite a while.

Stranger distress and separation Sometimes in the second half of the first year, usually after attachment is seen, many babies become fearful of strangers, and within another few months, they may become fearful of separation from mother. No one knows exactly why either of these things occur. Explanations vary from the ethological, which says that stranger fear represents the end of a sensitive period of attachment (Hess 1970), to the methodological, which says that it may not really exist (Rheingold and Eckerman 1973). Most studies do conclude that stranger fear exists, but it is not entirely predictable and consistent when it does occur, and it certainly is not universal, occurring in perhaps 50 percent of infants (Haith and Campos 1977). Infants can discriminate mother's face from that of strangers somewhere between two or three weeks and four months; so it is not mere strangeness that does it. (Mills and Melhuish 1974). Fear of strangers disappears, in any case, within a few months.

Separation-anxiety reaches its peak at around 18 months. It is, of course, a corollary of attachment, and its course often depends on what the quality of the mother-child attachment is to begin with. Secure babies are upset when mother disappears and happy when she returns; insecure babies are frightened when she leaves, but may show no pleasure when she comes back (Ainsworth 1973). Brief separations are not terribly hard on most children. Toddlers in day-care centers show some separation-anxiety, at first, but in the hands of competent and loving mother-substitutes, it dissipates in two or three days. Long separations can have longer lasting effects, especially if they occur at younger ages, again depending on the quality of substitute-care the infant gets.

Abused and neglected children are often victims of the worst effects of separation-anxiety. Because threat is a natural stimulus for attachment, mother's abusiveness or neglect may make them more clinging and attached to her by its very frightening quality. At the same time it wrecks their ability to trust her (Sameroff and Chandler 1974). The sense of trust that most babies develop from secure relationships with mother is, in Erikson's view, the cornerstone needed for building satisfying relationships and the ability to handle frustrations throughout life. Lasting bonds with other people are necessary for its development (Bowlby 1969, 1973). If they are seriously disrupted or fail to develop, the results may be painful and lasting (Rutter 1972).

Infancy sets the stage for the molding of a person. The greatest physical changes of the whole life-span come then. Nothing so con-spicuous happens again to the body with such dramatic speed until adolescence. Much of what happens in infancy is evidently a maturation process, as nerves and muscles begin to coordinate and mind and emotion to form (Kagan 1971). Maturation once again comes center stage a few years later, as puberty alters the child's appearance, its actions, and its experiences of self, while the once little boy or girl stands by, watching in the mirror for each new sign, a self-conscious onlooker at the mystery of its own growth. The time between is childhood, when most of what occurs goes slowly, and most depends on learning.

CHILDHOOD

It is a busy time. In a dozen or so years, language and thinking develop from the near babbling of late infancy to the sophisticated speech and abstract logic and moral capacities of adolescence, and social behavior grows from the primitive attachments and anxieties of babies to the complex skills of family member-

Childhood is a busy time. During this period children develop complex language and socialization skills.

ship and peer group negotiations. We shall look briefly at the processes of socialization and moral development.

The socialization process

Development unfolds as hereditary and environmental influences interact. In infancy, the maturational part of the interaction is most evident; as growth continues, environmental pressures become more obvious and learning a more and more obvious determinant of developmental patterns. Infancy "works," so to speak, without anyone trying to make it work except, perhaps, by providing the comforts of mothering. Certainly, its normal development does not depend on people putting systematic pressure on the infant. Childhood, on the other hand, "works" by the active pressure of family on the developing baby to learn the rules which govern life with other people and to develop the skills which allow those rules to be observed. Mothering *protects;* family *prescribes.* Protecting the infant permits maturation to take its course; prescribing to the child forces learning to occur.

From an evolutionary point of view, it is sometimes argued, the very purpose of the individual's existence is merely for passing on the genetic code from one generation to the next by mating and bearing offspring (Wilson 1975). The family, from that perspective, is the evolutionary medium for insuring that our young survive long enough and well enough to mate and generate. Humans, like many other species, are familial creatures. We have always been. The difference between us and other animals in this connection is that learning is so paramount in the organization of human behavior that we alone among the social animals have no firm and final intraspecies pattern of relationships which defines the human *nuclear family.*

Nuclear family means what you would call "the immediate family," and *extended family* means the rest of your relatives. Different cultures define membership in the nuclear and extended family differently. In Western cultures, the typical nuclear family, until well into this century, consisted primarily of biological mother and father, the children they bore, and maybe some of the children's grandparents and some of mother's or father's unmarried sisters (or, more rarely, brothers). Now, grandparents and maiden aunts are not very common residents in the American nuclear family home, and even the presence of both biological parents is less frequent than it was. As the divorce rate continues to climb, more children are being reared primarily by one biological parent, usually the mother, with stepfathers and assorted full-, half-, and step-siblings playing more prominent roles than they used to, but not roles which are well defined by any social norms. These changed family-patterns could make a difference in child-rearing patterns in our society, but no one yet knows just how or how much.

Discipline, reinforcement, and self-control Before most children reach age two, their parents have shifted from being "primarily caretakers to disciplinarians who put considerable pressure on the child to change his behavior (Hoffman 1977)." Discipline means training that aims to produce a specific behavior pattern. In a stable family, working to promote the child's optimum development, discipline consists of rewards and punishments which are administered dependably enough so that the child learns a *pattern of expectations* in relation to its own behavior. *Social reinforcements,* that is, rewards and punishments administered by people, especially ones that affect the child's relationships with those people, are more useful means of discipline than any others. Praise, encouragement, hugs and kisses, scoldings, and spankings are primary means by which parents (and older siblings) control small children. As the child learns to correlate its own activity with these things, and becomes aware of what actions produce what consequences, it develops self-control. This mastery, or competence, combines with the values which it learns from watching other people and from internalizing the emotional states that get connected with them, to make it a socialized person.

The self-control part of that combination is largely a matter of reinforcement. Learning to walk is a good illustration. The child experiments with standing movements, holding on and letting go, take a tentative step, or a couple of running steps, wobbling, falling, and trying again. Each success provides positive reinforcement and each failure a punishment; this part of the process proceeds by shaping, that is, by successive approximation, (see Chapter 6). Correct movements tend to be repeated because their success is reinforcing; inept movements tend to be eliminated because the falls and bumps they produce are punishing.

Now, there are some social incentives and reinforcements connected with learning to walk — one reason children attempt walking is because they see others walk; and parents and siblings praise their awkward first steps, soothe their wounds, and so forth. The social rewards and incentives for some aspects of language usage, such as "please," "thank you," and "shut up"[2] — if not of language learning itself — are even greater. They can be practiced with more people, the social reinforcement is more immediate, and the enormous variety of possible situations for using them makes them ultimately more interesting as devices for producing social interaction. In the long run, you can get more response out of people by talking to them than by walking for (or on) them.

A more complex kind of self-control, marking the shift from infancy to childhood, is toilet training, for here the incentive for new behavior is entirely social. There is no reason to withhold eliminations in diapers or on carpets or to dispense them into potties or toilets except that

parents don't like it done on the carpet and do want it done in the bathroom. What is more, they punish children for doing it in the one place and praise them for doing the very same thing in the other. The problem requires that the child develop an ability to *discriminate* the places, *inhibit* the behavior in one, and *exhibit* it in the other. This is a tall order. Achieving it is a master stroke in the development of self-control because the different parts of the total response which is necessary are not maturationally possible at the same time. A baby can be taught to release its excretory sphincters on the toilet as early as six-months old, but it likely cannot learn to inhibit those muscles until six to twelve months later. Mothers who push too hard for toilet-training at too early an age are teaching their babies things they probably don't want them to learn, such as that they cannot control their own bodies — but they may not be teaching them toilet-control.

Toilet-training, speech-habits, the rules of conduct, manners for using utensils when eating, for conveying food from plate or hand to mouth, and for washing and dressing, are all instances of the *explicit* learning demands which all families place on all children. One of the chief tasks of early childhood is learning to conform to such demands. The family continues to provide a broad protective atmosphere in childhood, of course, as the mothering agent provided a narrow one in infancy. Even so, its chief developmental value increasingly comes from its instructive function, and this is fulfilled as much by placing demands on the child for conformity as by nurturing it while it explores.

Some of the demands which the family places on the child are *implicit,* that is, built into the life situation of the family. The socioeconomic status of the family, for instance, dictates in part what kinds of manners the child will have to learn and at what age in order to get along with parents and siblings. Poor families run larger than middle-class families, which means that

---

[2] As in, "'Shut up,' my father explained." (Ring Lardner)

Toilet training.

housing conditions are likely to be more crowded, and so the child is likely to have to make concessions to the demands of many siblings and get less personal attention from parents than would be true in a wealthier household. The "emotional ambience" of a household, that is, whether its atmosphere is warm or cold, whether parents are stern and forbidding, are punitive, or permissive, or indifferent, are all factors which place implicit demands on the developing child for responsiveness or restraint, for docility or spontaneity, and so forth.

Another such implicit demand factor is *birth order.* No one instructs the oldest child in a large family to be the most conscientious or the youngest child to be the most pampered, but it often works out that they are that way. One reason is simply that the oldest child typically has to help mother in caring for the household

and for the younger children. The child learns this role as a result of mother's demands, the praise she gives No. 1 child for meeting them, and the disapproval she shows for failure to shoulder responsibilities. The youngest may get "spoiled" by the same process—by not having to take on burdens which it sees are expected of the older children, by getting attended to on demand, and therefore by coming to expect whatever it wants whenever it wants it. Learning such roles in early childhood helps create personality patterns which affect many aspects of behavior throughout life. There is conflicting evidence about the contribution of birth order to these roles, but it does seem that young children, at least, show sex-role preferences corresponding to the sex of their older siblings. And there is evidence from some studies, completely contradicted by equally good evidence

Older children may learn more responsibility than their younger siblings.

from others, that later born children have lower IQ test scores than first born children (see SAT stuff in Chapter 12) (Hetherington and McIntyre 1975).

The socialization process includes all the means by which infants change into socialized instead of merely social creatures. The most conspicuous of those means is through the process of learning. At first, classical conditioning may be the most important kind of learning, for emotions are formed by that means, and therefore basic attitudes towards other people in the infant's life evolve. Instrumental conditioning becomes more important as the infant begins to develop skills. And imitation and observational learning become increasingly important as it becomes aware of the other people in its life and begins to use them as models for its own action. Reinforcement is important in all these kinds of learning because it strengthens the new behavior, sealing it more firmly in the child's memory by directing its attention to the things to be learned and motivating the acquisition and maintenance of them. As the child grows older, the role of cognition becomes increasingly important in ascribing values to the things it does and the things it wishes or fears to do. It is not clear just how cognitive processes interact with the reinforcement aspects of social learning and social development. The field of cognitive development, as two scholars put it, "has much more to say about **cognition** than **development** (Ginsburg and Koslowski 1976)." But however they do interact, it is clear that one of the areas in which they do so most interestingly is that of the development of moral sensibility.

Moral development

Both Freud's and Piaget's stage theories have been the basis for speculation about the origins of moral sensibility in childhood. Freud saw it as a product of personality development, the **superego,** from which both conscience and ideals of personal accomplishment arise during the preschool years. (see Chapter 15). Piaget sees it as a function of the child's cognitive development in which the ability to assess moral situations depends on the child's ability to see things from the perspective of other people, something which does not happen until the period of concrete operations (age 7). Piaget's empirical studies led to more elaborate research by Lawrence Kohlberg, who theorizes that moral reasoning develops in six stages from about age seven to sixteen (Kohlberg

1963). The first two stages are called **Preconventional** morality; they are characteristic of children under seven. They obey rules, not as a matter of right and wrong, but first, to avoid punishment, and next, to gain rewards. By age ten, most children have largely replaced their earlier crude pragmatism with a more **conventional** sense of morality. At the beginning of this level (Stage 3), they want to "be good" in order to gain the approval of others; at the upper end of it (Stage 4), their morality has a more general quality of "doing one's duty" by respecting authority and maintaining the social order. Conventional morality dominates most children's attitude by age 13, and by then, the **Postconventional** level starts to become important. This is the level of respecting moral principles. In its beginnings (Stage 5), the basis for moral action is recognition of the rights of others, concern for the welfare of the community, and acting in ways that an impartial observer would respect. In the upper part of this level (Stage 6), the child's morality is based on its personal conscience, its own standard of justice. By age 16, *Postconventional* morality is far more prominent than Premoral thinking, but it never achieves the popularity of Stages 3 and 4, Conventional morality. Most of us stay bound to our moral conventions.

Kohlberg's theory, though intriguing, is not well supported by the evidence. Longitudinal study results do not support the stage sequence he describes; Stage 4 is, in fact, predominant at all ages above about seventh grade, and that inconsistently. There is backsliding from higher to lower stages among many subjects, which the theory says there should not be. And, anyway, the theory says nothing about what motivates the moral judgments of the different stages in the first place.

Social learning theory does. A very large body of studies indicates that moral **behavior** is learned largely by imitating models and being reinforced for it, and that moral **judgments,** contrary to the belief of the Piaget/Kohlberg cogni-

The inner character of children, like their outward appearance, is closely modeled after their parents.

Helene Fourment and Two of Her Children, Peter Paul Rubens

tive position, are effectively altered by imitation as well (Hetherington and McIntyre 1975). A number of studies, in fact, indicate that children's understanding of the moral principles involved in their judgment is increased in the imitation situation, and that the effects may last up to a year (Hoffman 1977). Like so many things in this crass world, the development of moral sensibility seems to depend more on children's observations of payoffs than of statements of principle.

ADOLESCENCE

There is no universal definition of adolescence. The term comes from a Latin word meaning "youth," as opposed to child or adult. It is a period of youth, all right, but the precise points at which it begins and ends depends on who is making the definition, what place they are talking about, and even the period of history involved.

In the United States, the phase of life we generally call adolescence, begins with *puberty.* Puberty is the time when boys and girls develop the physical characteristics of adulthood. These include some changes in the sex organs: boys and girls both grow pubic hair and hair on the genitals. Girls' breasts develop, menstruation starts, and their ovaries begin to release mature eggs. Boys' genitals grow larger and they begin to produce sperm. There are other changes in sexual physiology also, called *secondary sex characteristics* because they are not directly related to sexual behavior or childbearing capacities. In girls, for instance, as the mammary glands develop, there is an increase in fat deposits in breasts, hips, and other areas, giving them the rounded appearance typical of women. In boys, there is a rapid increase in skeletal musculature, the voice tends to deepen, and they begin to grow facial hair, a distinctive feature of adult males. In both sexes, there is a very rapid spurt in growth, visible to everyone, and all kinds of internal metabolic changes corresponding to it, visible to no one but affecting the behavior and feelings of the growing youth.

The physical growth of adolescence is a maturational matter, of course, but even here, the influence of environment is remarkable. Nutrition, for instance, is an important determinant of growth rate. So is the weather. In the frigid Northern regions of Scandinavia, children tend to come into their pubescent growth a good deal later than in the warm countries of the Mediterranean basin. In large parts of the Western world, moreover, there has been a continuing trend for almost two centuries for both boys and girls to mature earlier than they once did. The average age of menstruation, for instance, has dropped from 17 in 1830 to less than 13 now (Tanner 1970). It seems to be levelling off about here.

Adolescence is governed by cultural characteristics as well. Some scholars, indeed, consider its status as a distinct era of life to be a product of affluence, one which does not exist in societies that cannot afford it. It is true that poor societies generally lack any distinct adolescent period. You start working in childhood, you get married at puberty, and you continue the pattern of your life without any interim phase of "not-childhood" and "not-yet-adulthood."

Whether adolescence is a stormy or calm period also depends on the particular culture. In the South Pacific, it is generally a happy, easy time. In our society, perhaps because sexual awareness generally involves sexual conflict, and because the teen years are the time when children test the authority of parents and their own ability to be independent, it is often stormy. The storm, in any case, is built into the circumstances of the adolescent's life, not into the maturational events of adolescent growth.

Some important conflicts are connected with adolescent growth, however, because of the common preoccupation in our society with physical attractiveness, popularity, and dating, which becomes paramount in these years. Some children mature later than others and become embarrassed by developing secondary sex characteristics much earlier or much later than their peers. Girls who start menstruating in the fourth grade, for instance, or have not started by the tenth, are embarrassed and shy with other girls about it. Boys who mature sexually and begin masturbating at age ten or eleven, are often fearful that they are abnormally different from their fellows; and boys who are not yet shaving by their college years may be likewise embarrassed. Both sexes, moreover, have a hard time coping with the fact that maximum growth for girls occurs around age 12, and for boys around 14, so that in the seventh and eighth grade, the girls tend to be taller than the boys, with some mutual embarrassment resulting. Finally, while it is not true that adolescents are awkward and clumsy, it sometimes is true that they look less evenly proportioned than they did in childhood or than they will again in later adolescence and adulthood. The reason is that the growth rate of different parts of the body differs so that arms and legs may grow faster than trunk and head for a while and have to wait to get caught up with. Acne is another symptom of the metabolic disruptions of adolescence.

Sex and self-awareness: The motifs of adolescence From an evolutionary perspective, adolescence is the peak period of human life, the time that bursts with maximum energy and strength. It is the time when sexual capacities and urges not only mature, but are also capable of the most enduring and repeated expression. From the cold vantage of evolution, we were meant to grow into adolescence, bear children at its end, and then decline and die. Nowadays (the past million years or so, that is), these "declining" years are half or more of our lives. But adolescence is still the springtime of it.

The two major psychological themes of adolescence are sexual awareness and the conflicts resulting from it, and the need for independence and the conflicts that result from it. We shall deal at length with several aspects of them in Chapters 16 and 17 (personal psychology), but a word must go here about independence, which is probably the overriding theme of one's concerns as adulthood approaches.

The adolescent struggle for independence leads in many directions at once. For one thing, it often puts adolescents in direct conflict with parents in a way more serious, perhaps, than any they have encountered since the long forgotten conflicts of toilet training. One consequence is a shift in their perception of parents from all-powerful and ideal models to wrong-thinking, somewhat backward, and inept persons who interfere with the adolescents' striving for freedom and an identity of their own. The process of *de*identification with parents is accompanied by the substitution, often, of other adult hero figures, such as teachers, coaches, or more far removed figures, like movie stars or political leaders, who seem to be free of the human frailties of parents. Even more commonly, parental models are replaced by the cultivation of a **peer culture,** that is, by an increased sharing of experiences with friends who are going through the same kind of conflicts and crises that they are. Oddly, the intense energy of adolescence can combine with the intense need for identity that occurs then to make adolescence a very **dependent** state, emotionally and intellectually. In many adolescents, this intensity and dependency is seen only as extreme reliance on their peer group. In others, it may take the form of extreme religious devotion or committment to some other form of idealism. Priests, prophets, and revolutionaries often find their inspired callings in their adolescent years. True believers and fanatics, for better and for worse, are commonly adolescents. The Red Guard of China, which caused enormous violent destruction in the 1960's, consisted of hundreds of thousands of fanatical adolescents who, upon instruction of their political leaders, turned violently upon "old" reactionaries. The Freedom Riders of the American South, who were instrumental in the early 1960's in bringing about equal opportunities for black people in this country, were also largely adolescents. So were the Jewish pioneers at the turn of the century who gave up urban intellectual lives in the oppressive tyrannies of Eastern Europe to become farmers and clear the malaria infested swamps of Israel to build a Utopian democracy which they had envisioned (Elan 1970). When Romeo and Juliet turn from sex and romance to politics and religion, they remain as passionate as ever. Without this passion, however, they would be poorly equipped to endure the trials of adulthood and would be forced into lives of quiet desperation. With it, adolescents develop aspirations which sometimes lead them to great personal achievements.

ADULTHOOD AND OLD AGE

The universal concern among scholars with the different stages of child development has not extended until very recently into the observation that there are also adult stages of development. As Roger L. Gould, a leading scholar in this area, puts it: "Adulthood is still seen as a period of marking time and is not seen as a progression of stages much like the phases of rapid and slow growth of childhood and adolescence" (1972, p. 33).

As soon as you reflect on it, however, common sense indicates plainly that adulthood also has its developmental stages. Young adulthood, for instance, is the time when people commonly marry and begin families and is also the time when they generally become established in what may be their life work. Middle age is a period when the professional careers of men reach their peak, when the financial burdens of family also peak (as children go through adolescence), when parents become grandparents, and increasingly in our society, when

families are broken up by divorce and widowhood. Old age, as everyone also knows, is the period of retirement, decline, and death.

In all these periods, physical changes occur as well as personality changes. The physical changes have, if anything, been more carefully observed than the psychological ones. Eyesight changes with middle age, as does hearing, physical strength begins to decline, blood pressure begins to rise, and the individual to become more and more susceptible to a variety of ailments which presage gradual decline towards death. Likewise, there is a gradual decrease in sexual interests and activities, as in other more purely physical functions. All of these have been charted and mapped with endless precision and rigour.

Psychological changes have not fared so well. Erik Erikson was the first personality theorist to address the fact that there are adult stages of personality development. The last three of his "seven stages of man" are adult ones. The first adult stage is that in which a person finally experiences success or failure in their ability to have trusting, intimate relationships with others. The second phase of adulthood, according to Erikson, going from the mid-20s on, is that in which an individual elects to participate in the world as a caretaker, rather than to stagnate or merely remain a consumer. Erikson's final stage, which goes from later adulthood to death, is called the stage of integrity. Then, the individual is concerned primarily with evaluating the course of their own life and its uniqueness.

These are not very precise stages, as you notice, and most other attempts at describing adult stages have been equally loose and imprecise. Recently, however, a number of scholars have done careful empirical studies on adult phases of development and a number of rather clearcut stages have emerged from their researches (Neugarten 1968; Gould 1972; Sears and Feldman 1973). All of these schemes more or less approximate the time spans of Sears and

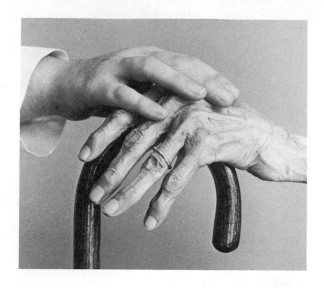

Life stages.

Feldman, which put the **young adult** period from 18 to 30 years, the **prime of life** from 30 to 42 years, **middle age** from 42 to 60 years, and **old age** beyond 60 years (1973).

Roger Gould did several studies of development from age 16 through 60. He found, as others have, that 16-to-18-year-olds are concerned with getting away from their parents, but have not actually done so. Eighteen-to-22-years-olds have largely done so, but are still afraid of being pulled back into the family and have not yet outgrown their adolescent concern with autonomy. In his studies, the first true adult phase goes from age 22 to about 28. People in this group feel established and autonomous, separate from their families and directed on the true course of their lives. They feel themselves as well defined, even if they are not fully satisfied with themselves.

The group aged 29 to 34 is in a later phase of development. These people are already established in marriage, family, and career lines but are now wondering whether these are the only options available to them. At this age, also, people start to become aware that they are the victims of forces within themselves other than their own volition. They want to be accepted "for

what they are," and try to accept their children in the same way.

In the 35 to 43 group, there is a more painful tendency to look within oneself and what Gould calls "a change of tone toward quiet desperation and increasing awareness of a time squeeze," that is, an awareness that life is finite and no longer full of unlimited possibilities.

The 43 to 50-year-old group has shifted again in its feelings. Now people feel that the patterns of their lives have been set beyond much changing. And though this is hard to accept in some ways, it is also "seen as a relief from the internal tearing apart of the immediately previous years." In some respects, this period is the opposite of adolescence, for now "there is an increase of interiority," that is, of preoccupation with one's own inner feelings as opposed to the wishes of one's peer group, and "there is a decrease in personality complexity (Neugarten 1968)."

Marriages that have not broken up by this time tend to improve, and this goes on into the 50's. Gould sees the 50's as a period of "mellowing and warming up" in which people are more aware of the time limits on their lives but feel less pressure with respect to them. The meaningfulness of life is again questioned seriously in this period, and people now start to become preoccupied with problems of health.

Old age "may be called the age of uncertainty (Sears and Feldman 1973)," because it is now uncertain both how long life will last and what the rest of it will be like. Physical deterioration starts to become perceptible during this period and may continue to the point where invalidism and general incompetence sets in. People age at remarkably different rates, however, and there is no telling how fast or slow the decline of aging may be. The rate is clearly affected by life circumstances, though. Men and women who are optimistic and enthusiastic

about life in the first place tend to remain active and involved in things long after they formally retire. This activity probably keeps them functioning well until very late in life, maybe until they die. The number of old people in the United States has increased enormously in this century, and more and more resources are now being devoted to studying the aging process. It is possible for people to grow old gracefully. Whether or not they do so depends partly on the attitudes they bring with them into old age, but it also depends on the conditions which society establishes for their declining years. If old people are esteemed and valued for what they

In Roger Gould's first true adult phase from age 22 to about 28, people become established and autonomous.

Baron Schwiter, Eugéne Delacroix.

Rembrandt's Mother, Rembrandt

Old age is "the age of uncertainty";
no one knows how long life will last
or what the rest of it will be like.

can still do well rather than dismissed for the things they cannot, then they may decline gracefully and with dignity. Our youth-centered culture has not yet paid very much attention either to aging or to the meaning of dignity in connection with it. So the problem of what to do with the aged is a major one in our society.

SUMMARY

1 Development refers to change over time. It covers the whole sequence of life from conception until death. Among more complex animal species, the period of development is slower than among simpler ones, with human development the slowest of all. The pattern of human development is also more variable than that of other species, both because of biological differences and cultural differences in rates and contents of development.

2 Development occurs in an orderly sequence, but it is not clear whether the progression involved is relatively smooth and continuous or whether it goes through distinctly marked levels. The view that there are levels is sometimes viewed as a "stage theory," which says that specific types of behavior develop at certain stages and are characteristic of the growing individual from that time on. Two of the most famous theories of this kind were formulated by Sigmund Freud, in the study of personality development, and by Jean Piaget, in the study of cognitive development.

3   Throughout most of the history of Western Civilization, children were the victims of whatever kind of treatment adults wished to inflict on them. They were brutalized, set to work barely past infancy, sexually abused, and often murdered in infancy when they were an embarrassment to parents by being illegitimate or when their parents were too poor to feed them. Since the late 19th century, widespread public education and child-labor laws have caused society to be more attentive to children's need for special treatment and care.

4   Development in the womb is not complete enough for premature infants to survive until about seven months after conception. The womb is a fairly protected environment; so most of mother's metabolic dangers are kept away from the fetus, but there is some chemical (and possibly behavioral) communication between them which can potentially endanger the baby. Some drugs, viruses, X-rays, and illnesses in the mother can be passed to the fetus directly (such as heroin addiction) or can cause indirect damage, depending on the fetus's stage of development at the time the chemicals are ingested. Very severe stress in the mother may also produce excesses of hormones in the fetus's blood, which could be damaging, especially in the first three months of development.

5   Newborn babies are well equipped for many perceptual and motor functions. Several reflexes, such as those involved in sucking, grasping, and hugging, are ready to work at birth. Some perceptual skills, such as the ability to perceive patterns or visual contours, are available at birth or very soon after, and so is the reflexive ability to hear as well as see and to withdraw from some bad smells and strong bad tastes. Within a few months, the newborn can make some speech sounds, smiles socially, and can distinguish human features. If it is deprived of normal stimulation during these first months of life, or subjected to excessive stress, development of language, motor, and social skills may all be retarded, sometimes seriously.

6   Some of the *caregiving* which infants require can be done impersonally, but most of the interactions which are later associated with love, security, and competence in personal relationships requires the personal attention of a parenting figure. Typically, around seven months or so, infants develop very strong *attachment* to their mothers, and within a month or so later, often to their fathers as well. This behavior is commonly reciprocated by the parent and may remain intact, in altered form, into later life. After attachment is formed, some babies will also become fearful of strangers and sometimes also of separation from mother. When those do occur, they generally disappear within a few months. Abused and neglected children sometimes suffer more from separation anxiety than do those who have had sufficient parenting.

7   Socialization in childhood is largely a matter of learning to deal with the *prescriptions* and requirements for living laid down by the child's *nuclear* family, that is, "immediate family." Before age two, most parents have shifted roles from being primarily caretakers to being primarily the child's disciplinarians. Social reinforcements and punishments are the primary disciplinary means by which children learn mastery and self-control over such important activities as toilet functions, some speech habits, and many of the rules of conduct for eating, dressing, and interacting with others. Some of the disciplinary demands placed on the child are taught explicitly, but others are implicit in the family situation, determined by things like *socioeconomic status* or *birth order*.

8 The development of moral sensibility has been viewed differently by different theorists. Freud saw it as a product of personality development, called *superego*, from which both conscience and the ideals of personal accomplishment arise during the preschool years. Piaget argues that moral development is an outgrowth of cognitive development, depending on the child's ability to see things from the perspective of other people, beginning around age seven. Kohlberg has developed a stage theory of moral development based on Piaget's ideas, but it is not entirely supported by the evidence. Social learning theory has produced extensive research which indicates that moral *behavior* is learned by imitating models and being reinforced for it, and moral *judgment* may be a byproduct of such observations and imitations.

9 There is no universal definition of adolescence, and it is not a separate developmental period in some cultures. In the United States, it is generally regarded as the period from the beginning of puberty until young adulthood, that is, the "teens." Both boys and girls reach their full adult physical development during this period. There are enormous variations in the ages of sexual and general physical maturing in both sexes, though girls generally go through a maximum growth spurt around age 12 and boys around age 14. Also, growth rates of different parts of the body differ, giving people the mistaken impression of adolescent awkwardness.

10 The main psychological themes of adolescence are sexual awareness and self-awareness, which are sources of conflict and confusion and of aspirations and ideals alike. The struggle for independence from parents and adult authority and the struggle for personal identity are two of the most evident problems of the adolescent years. The process of deidentification from parents tends to make adolescents into hero-worshippers of teachers, coaches, or political or religious figures and to make them very dependent on their peer culture as well.

11 Scholars now recognize that the adult years are also characterized by developmental phases, just as childhood and adolescence are. Young adulthood is distinctly the time when people marry, begin families, and launch their careers. Middle age is a time when professional careers peak, when the burdens of rearing young children are lifted, and when the personal crises of confronting old age begin. This is also the period when divorce and widowhood become common sources of crisis. Old age presents the crises of retirement, physical decline, and impending death. Research into the adult life phases is still a relatively new area of developmental psychology.

Personality

14

14

Personality

Have you looked at your baby pictures lately? Or even at a group photograph of your first or second grade class? It would be interesting to do. You have changed a lot since then, mentally and physically.[1] Your tastes have changed, your opinions are different, your body cells have mostly been turned in and replaced several times over, and your physical appearance has changed most of all. But you can still recognize yourself in those old photos, and so probably could everyone who knows you well, even if they just met you in college. They might recognize a facial expression, or a kind of look about you, which stayed the same from when you posed bare-bottomed on a rug until today—and that may make you just as recognizable 40 years from now, with your top bare and your bottom covered and the features in between all changed again. The things that stay the same compose your personality.

All the synonyms for personality convey this same idea; something is **characteristic** of a person, or **typical** of them, they have such-and-such **traits,** or **temperament,** or this-or-that kind of **nature**—these are all different ways of saying that someone is dependably the same person over time. Gordon Allport once collected dozens of different common English words for personality. You use many of them in everyday speech. Basically, they all mean about the same thing—**the stable aspects of your behavior.** Personality is the **continuity of the individual,** the things about them that make them recognizably the same creature to themselves and to other people. We will explore that definition and how the difficulties inherent in it give rise to different theories of personality, to different tactical methods of measuring it, and to different puzzlements and controversies surrounding its description. The upshot of all this will be that our definition will get sort of tattered by the time we finish the chapter, but it will remain too meaningful to abandon completely.

---

[1] I hope.

Van Gogh painted these self-portraits over a period of several years. The things about you that stay the same compose your personality.

The prehistory of personality

Personality is the oldest subject of psychological interest because it is concerned with understanding people comprehensively, not just in bits and pieces. For thousands of years, people have been looking for a royal road to such understanding, for "the key" to personality. Partly they hoped to use it as a basis for *controlling* others, partly as a means for *understanding* and *predicting* their behavior. No one has had awfully good luck finding one because there is no single key, but no one has given up trying, usually by inventing a theory of personality. There have always been plenty of salesmen and plenty of customers for such theories.

From ancient times, there have been two general kinds of theorizing about personality. One was to think of it as the product of people's *physical structure.* This is represented in the theory of *temperaments* of Hippocrates, the Greek father of medicine. The other was to think of personality as the result of events in the *environment* that determined what a person would be like. This is represented in the attempts of Babylonian astrologers, long before the Greeks, to understand behavior from the positions of the constellations at a person's birth.

Both points of view remained popular throughout history as, indeed, they do today in fancier forms. All kinds of new theories about personality have developed since those days, but few of the old ones have gone out of business. Modern scientific studies of the relationships between physiology and behavior are logical extensions of Hippocrates' thinking. And while astrology does not have the kind of support from today's scientific establishment that it enjoyed in Babylonia 4,000 years ago, it certainly has the methodology! In New York's Grand Central Station, a very sophisticated computer will give you a detailed analysis of your personality in 20 minutes, on IBM printout paper, if you can supply it with your exact time and place of birth, and two dollars and fifty cents. The system is called Astro-Flash.[2]

In the 19th century, *phrenology* was looked on as the scientific key to personality. It was not, but it was a forerunner of physical anthropology. *Graphology,* the analysis of personality from handwriting, is still used in some circles (it is much more popular in Europe than in the United States) as a tool for personality analysis. As a practical matter, fortune tellers, spiritualists, stage hypnotists, confidence men, and everybody whose business depends on gaining other people's trust, all use some

---

[2] For another couple of dollars, it will also tell your fortune.

implicit theory of personality from which to launch their ventures. All practical students of personality have recognized that human beings have some basic consistencies about them and have staked their careers, and sometimes their hides, on their own ability to divine those consistencies and take advantage of them.

One reason business is so good in the confidence game, in fact, is because people are so willing to believe authoritative sounding things about their personality and their prospects. In experiments where college students took personality tests and then, unbeknownst to them, were all given the same interpretation, most of them rated the interpretations as accurate evaluations of their own personalities, especially if the interpretation had ostensibly been made by a psychologist (Ulrich, Stachnik, and Stainton 1963).

In modern psychology, personality underlies some kinds of applied psychology—such as clinical psychology and psychological testing—in much the same way that physiology and anatomy underlie medicine and physical therapy. It has three main topics: first, the meaning of "personality," which turns out to be more complicated than it sounded a couple pages back; second, the theories that try to explain what human nature is and how personality develops and operates in our lives; and third, how personality is studied and measured.

Defining personality and pinning down the definition

The *general* definition of personality as "the consistencies of a person's behavior" is OK as far as it goes. But when we get down to specifics, it is not so easy to say exactly which consistencies, or changes, are important, and which ones are not, in anyone's personality. When we look for specific continuities in a person over time, in fact, they are sometimes hard to find. Even physically, people change a lot with growth—in height, weight, skin texture, hair color, . primary and secondary sexual characteristics. So are persons physically continuous with themselves or not? Yes and no.

Figure 14.1 Handwriting is as individual (and hard to forge) as fingerprints. Graphologists try to analyze personality traits from it.

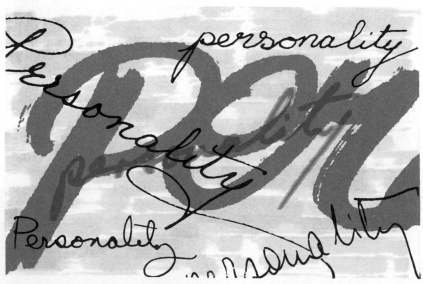

Some physical characteristics change more than others—eye color changes very little, hair color a little more, height and weight a whole lot, body build not a whole lot. As we shall see, one of the earliest kinds of personality theories, still very popular, treats body-build as the basis of the most important consistencies in behavior. But the theory has not held up well against the evidence.

The most definitive things about personality are not physical, anyhow, but are the consistencies of attitudes, mannerisms, and behavior that people show over long periods of time, and in many situations. When we think about personality, or gossip about it, in everyday life, we usually think of it in terms of people's **traits,** that is, their characteristic **styles** of behavior. For most people, these vary from time to time and place to place, but they are consistent enough so that we identify them with that person in general. For example, some people always seem to get angry when they are frustrated, whether in small matters like having to wait in line at the movies or in big things like being rejected in love. There may be plenty of situations where they are frustrated and do not get angry, of course, but the ones in which they do are so common that we come to expect it of them—or in other words, we associate anger-in-response-to-frustration with that person so consistently, that we come to see it as a trait of their personality.

The term **trait** means about the same thing in technical psychology and in everyday usage—it means **characteristic.** But there are two things about it which you must be aware of when using the term, or you will misunderstand it. First, a personality trait represents a person's **average** or typical behavior; it is not an absolute and unchanging quality they have. When we say that someone is an "angry" person, for instance, we are not saying that they are always angry or even that they are angry every time they get frustrated. We say that anger is one of their personality traits because, **on the average,** we expect them to get angry more often than not when frustrated and to get frustrated more often than we expect most people to—so they are angry a lot.

Second, the events which make up personality traits are not really *things* at all—anger is not an entity that a person carries around with them all the time and lets out on special occasions. It is an *act,* a *behavior* that comes into existence only when the person is stimulated in certain ways. Eye-color is a thing, height is a thing, the shape of your skull is a thing; but personality traits are not things; they are *labels,* names that you give to the actions a person takes, or the behavior they show, or feel, pretty consistently in many situations. Intelligence is a personality trait, aggressiveness is, hypnotic susceptibility is, ambitiousness is. None of them are things. They are names we give to people's characteristic reactions to certain kinds of situations.

Virtually all the questions we ask about people's characteristics, other than their physical attributes, vital statistics, or appearance, are questions about personality. "What is this person *like?*" "Nice? Smart? Mean? Interesting? Sexy? A nerd?" All of these are requests for personality descriptions. If you ask for information about more than one, in psychologese, it is called a **personality profile.**

If we were to describe the personality of most people, we would classify them on each of several *traits;* we would say they have this much intelligence, that much aggressiveness, so much ambition, such and such sex needs, and so forth. In most people, none of these traits would stand out enough by itself to give much impression of what the total person is like. In some people, however, one or another characteristic is so glaring and so dominant in shaping other aspects of their behavior and of the impression they make on people, that we ordinarily do not speak of *it* as a trait, but of *them* as a certain **type** of person. When we say that someone is "a lethargic type" or "a

Anger.

cheerful type" or "an aggressive type," we mean that lethargy, or cheerfulness, or aggressiveness is such a dominant factor in their behavior that it influences the expression of all their other traits. The term "type," in other words, is a much broader, more comprehensive notion than "trait." People *have* traits; they *are* types.

THEORIES OF PERSONALITY

Personality, like everything else, does not spring full blown from some chemical or neural reservoir in the brain or body. It develops, in some respects in fits and starts, in others, quite smoothly, from the interaction between the maturing physical apparatus of a child and the experiences by which its environment teaches it, shaping and molding its thoughts, feelings, and expectations. Personality development occurs in much the same way that body chemistry interacts with the nutritional and hygienic conditions of a child's environment, shaping and molding their physical development. There are several questions. What part of your personality is built in to your physical constitution? What contribution does the genetic or constitutional attributes of a child make to its adult personality? What part of later personality can be attributed primarily to the events of one's upbringing? If a boy grows up to be a viciously aggressive, hostile, destructive adult, for instance, shall we blame his parents for the *fact* that they bore him or the *way* that they raised him?[3] Is his nature or their nurturing responsible?

The question might seem academic here, but it is not. In several criminal cases in the 1960s, for instance, defense lawyers pleaded that their clients could not be held responsible for violent crimes they had committed because of their genetic structure; they had an extra male chromosome. It was argued that the XYY chromosome in their bodies disposed these people genetically to become violent—so they could not help it. While it turns out that the argument is not supported by the evidence in this case (Sarbin and Miller 1971), the problem is important enough so that some modern theories of personality are still based on the "structuralist" or "organic" position and a great deal of applied research has attempted to make some practical predictions about people's abilities and skills on this basis. Even environmental theories of personality, however, which argue that adult personality depends more on learning experiences than on biological dispositions, recognize that people are not infinitely plastic. In other words, there are limits to personality development that are set by our biological nature and that no amount of teaching will overcome. You can shape a person's experience, for instance, so that they will become very industrious, but there is no way you can teach them to totally do without sleep, no matter how hard they want to work. We have made this point repeatedly; it is still correct.

Few genetic factors in personality have ever

been proved, but pedigree studies and twin studies suggest that at least two aspects of personality have some hereditary basis: ***intelligence*** and ***temperament.*** As we have seen (Chapter 12), some kinds of mental retardation result from genetic problems, and intellectual genius, which tends to run in families, may also have some genetic basis. The genetics of temperament have not been demonstrated in human beings (it is not true that Scotsmen are naturally dour, Blacks full of joy and rhythm, or Orientals inscrutable), but they certainly have been in animals. Breeders raise some dogs for gentleness, others for viciousness, others for alertness, and so forth. Robert Tryon (1940) bred rats for maze running ability; and horses have long been selectively mated and bred for courage, high spirits, or docility, and still other species for social dominance and sexual vigor.

In humans too, the disposition to be alert, or calm, or sluggish, sometimes quite apparent

Figure 14.2 It has been thought that XYY chromosomes made some males violent; apparently, it just makes them tall.

---

[3] We had better blame them for something!

in newborn babies, may color many aspects of their developing personalities. Some infants, you recall, are more easily startled than others, some cry more readily and for longer, some get colic (gas pains, or indigestion) more than others. All these things may be determinants of later adult personality traits. The evidence is unsure, but many scholars, and all mothers, think so anyhow.

There is one aspect of constitutional traits which almost everyone admits has a marked effect on personality development. It is the normal part of our physical selves which is critically important to our lives, like being male or female, growing tall or short, maturing very early or very late, being endowed with good looks, or talent, or handicapped by lameness, blindness, pimples, or whatever else matters to us personally in our physical selves. Some theories of personality make a great to-do about constitution—and all growing people do.

The *organic* or structural factors in personality, such as genetics and constitution, have been much less studied than the *dynamic* or environmental and social factors that contribute to personality development. There are two general orientations towards the dynamics of personality development. The first, and best known, describes the dynamics of development in a biological framework which is sometimes called *sensitive periods* or a variant of it called *psychosexual stages.* The second describes personality development almost entirely as a matter of *social learning* or *reinforcement history.* These positions are expressed in different *theories of personality,* which is any theory that tries to explain what adult personality is and how it comes to be that way. There are many theories of personality, but you can usefully order them in your mind according to the emphasis they put on child development or on adult personality. In general, *organic* theories do not have much to say about growth and development. They concentrate on the biological determinants of adult personal-

ity. *Dynamic* theories, on the other hand, focus heavily on the processes by which personality is shaped in childhood. Organic theories emphasize what adult personality is like; dynamic theories focus on how it got there.

Organic personality theory

When Hippocrates invented the first theory of temperament, some 2500 years ago, scientific ideas of body chemistry and metabolism were not what they are today. Temperament means a person's "susceptibility to emotive situations; the tendency to experience changes in mood," especially as they are related to chemical changes in glands and other body tissues (English and English 1958). The ancient Greeks believed that the body was a compound of the four elements—earth, air, fire, and water—which took the forms of yellow bile, black bile, blood, and phlegm. The proportions of each of these *humoral* fluids in your body determined your temperament. If you had a lot of blood (Latin for which is *sanguis*), then you would have a *sanguine* disposition, that is, be cheerful and *good humored* (get it?). Yellow bile produced a *choleric,* or irritable temperament; black bile causes a *melancholic,* depressed personality. And an excess of phlegm makes you *phlegmatic,* that is, calm, imperturbable, and maybe sluggish. No one believes today that Hippocrates had the right bodily fluids in mind, but the temperaments they named are still commonly accepted descriptions of people, as you can see from the way the terms have become part of everyday language.

Plenty of constitutional theories of personality have been put forth since then (London and Rosenhan 1968), but the most famous was published in 1925 by a German psychiatrist named Ernst Kretschmer, in *Physique and Character.* It claimed that temperament was linked to physique or body type in such a way that you could tell a person's disposition, and even the kind of emotional disorders they

Ectomorph.

The Old Guitarist, Pablo Picasso

were prone to, by observing whether they were short and fat, tall and thin, or average in body build. This theory is a refined version of the popular belief that fat people are jolly and good-natured, and thin ones nervous and high-strung. The theory was further refined in 1942 by an American psychiatrist, William H. Sheldon. Sheldon's main work, with S. S. Stevens, is *The varieties of temperament*. It gives a refined and scientifically testable version of Kretsch-mer's theory. Sheldon names the three body types (he calls them "somatotypes"; *soma* is Greek for "body"): *endomorphic, meso-morphic,* and *ectomorphic,* according to what part of the embryonic endoderm, meso-

derm, or ectoderm dominates the adult physique (i.e., whether you have a big gut, or big muscles, or a lot of skin).[4] Depending on how much you are one body type or the other, or what kind of mixture you represent (since short, fat types sometimes marry tall, thin types, and mediums will marry most anyone) your temperament will be *viscerotonic* (*viscus* is Latin for innards), *somatotonic,* or *cerebrotonic* (*cerebrum* is Latin for brain). Viscerotonics take pleasure in eating, joking, and relaxing; somatotonics in athletics, competition, and energetic move-

---

[4] It still comes out short and fat; medium; and tall and thin, no matter how fancy the names get.

ment; and cerebrotonics in restraint, caution, and sensitiveness. In short, the theory says that fat people are jolly and good-natured and thin people nervous and high strung; muscular people are athletic; and most people are assorted mixtures of the pure physical and temperamental types (Scheinfeld 1965).

There is something appealing to most of us about constitutional type theories. Maybe it is that they make it seem so simple to understand personality. Maybe they simply fit our familiar stereotypes of behavior; so we like them because they confirm what we think we already know. In any case, Sheldon's typology has the rare merit of being highly measurable. He

developed a seven-point scale to rate how much of each type a person has, since most people fall somewhere in between the basic types. Thus a rating of 3–5–3 would indicate middling amounts of endomorphy and ectomorphy but strong mesomorphy—predicting temperamental characteristics in the same proportions.

The theory seemed so plausible, and the rating system so sensible, that the United States War Department spent a lot of money supporting Sheldon's research during World War II, hoping that somatotyping thousands of young men and correlating physique with temperament would make it possible to select them wisely for assorted military training and mis-

Endomorph.

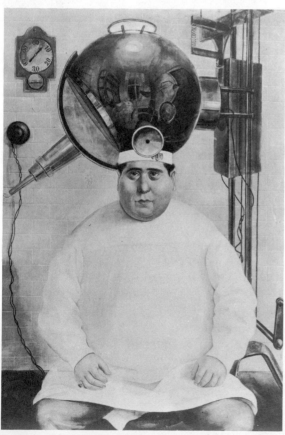

Dr. Mayer-Hermann, Otto Dix

sions. It did not (Stagner 1953). Not only are the relations of body-type and personality elusive, but the ratings of personality type are themselves unreliable, unless they are done by *untrained* people! Untrained raters are more influenced by the "fat-and-jolly" sterotypes they keep in their heads than by the actual behavior they observe in the subjects. Studies which make raters avoid such stereotypes do not produce reliable somatotypes (Tyler 1956). The correlation of body-type and personality has not proved useful for predicting anything else either, even in those cases where reliable ratings are obtained (Humphreys 1957). Like many other theories in psychology, this one is better to discuss than to examine.

A second kind of *type* theory does not depend on any connection between physique and temperament, but classifies people directly into psychological categories. The best known is the type theory of Carl Jung, a Swiss psychiatrist who was one of Sigmund Freud's earliest followers and later one of his severest critics. Jung believed that people could be classified as *introverts* or *extroverts* and subclassified as *thinking* or *feeling* types, *intuitive* or *sensation* oriented, and *perceptive* or *judgmental* in their ways of evaluating the world. An introvert, or "introversive type," tends to be into their own head, that is, to look within themselves for stimulation, interest, and values. Socially, they might be aloof and withdrawn. Extroverts, on the other hand, would be aroused by external stimulation and interests, and would evaluate things, including themselves, in terms of their interactions with the external environment. Socially, they would be quite outgoing. Some introverts would rely primarily on thinking, that is, on intellectual processes, for evaluating their inner experience; others would rely more on their feelings. The same holds for extroverts in evaluating their relations with the outside world. Introverts and extroverts alike might depend more on

Carl Gustav Jung.

intuition or on sensations for verifying their thoughtful or emotional conclusions; and finally, they might be more inclined to view the world either perceptively, that is, with impartial curiosity and interest, or judgmentally, that is, with the need to reach conclusions from which to act.

Each of the *polar attributes* (i.e., extremes) mentioned here is a kind of pure type which is not common in real people, just as the extremes of Sheldon's body and temperament types are relatively rare in real life. Most people are not pure introverts or pure extroverts, pure thinkers or pure feelers, and so forth. But whereas Sheldon thought that people were mixtures of body types, Jung did not believe that the personality types he described really existed in mixtures. Instead, he thought some characteristics were weaker or stronger than others in different people without being mixed together at all. As he saw it, you might be a slight introvert, or an extreme introvert, but you could not be part introvert and part extrovert at the same time.

Some people are natural extroverts — the outgoing, easygoing kind who make friends easily wherever they go.

Young Men by the Sea, Max Beckman

Jung's theory is even more widely known than Sheldon's, but less research has been done to test it, largely because his descriptions of the types were too abstract to pinpoint how they could be told apart and exactly how they differ in behavior. Even so, some important studies were done by Hans J. Eysenck, a British psychologist. He tried to identify the introversion-extroversion dimension of personality scientifically, and to prove that it was related to different kinds of neurotic behavior disorders. He claims to have succeeded in this task, but most behavior scientists who evaluate the results of his study feel that the case is not proven (1960).

An interesting practical application of Jung's type theory was made by Elizabeth Briggs and Joseph Myers. They created a personality test called the Myers-Briggs Type Indicator Test (Myers 1962). A self-administered, self-scored paper and pencil test, it was designed largely to aid in counseling high school and college students. Different personality types, the authors argue, tend to be happier in different kinds of occupations, and the test makes it possible for students to identify their type dispositions and to evaluate how their career interests seem to fit their personality profiles. There is no way to tell, from the published research, how well these comparisons predict job success. But the test is interesting to take and gives you a fresh perspective on things you should already know about yourself but may not have thought about systematically.

Jung does not call his theory an organic or biological personality theory, but *all type theories* are, and his is no exception. He discusses introversion-extroversion and the other dimensions of personality as if they are *natural* dispositions of different people, not *learned* behavior patterns. They have been shaped and molded, to some extent, by experience, especially by social relationships and the exigencies of living; but they are created in the womb, or in the germ cells, he believed, along with many other characteristics of personality and mental life which he called "the collective unconscious," and lie dormant until the individual's own maturation (Jung called it "individuation") permits them to blossom.

Dynamic personality theories

Most students of personality believe that people's make-up is so flexible that almost any kind of behavior pattern could become characteristic if the right experiences occur to produce it and maintain it. *Dynamic* personality theories are based on this idea, that personality changes, shifts, and grows with experience. The most popular dynamic theories are *psychoanalytic* theory, which has grown out of the work of Sigmund Freud and his students, and *social learning* theory, derived chiefly from experimental studies of learning, growth, and development. A third kind of dynamic theory is called *organismic, humanistic,* or *existential* theory of personality. All dynamic theories are based on the idea that personality is shaped by the interaction between the growing child's efforts to fulfill its basic biological needs and the life experiences which channel it along different routes for fulfilling them (Murphy 1947). Psychoanalytic theory pays particular attention to the process of biological maturation in which different kinds of experience have different meanings. Social learning theory attends more exclusively to social experiences, interpreting the rewards and punishments they provide as the basis for the personality patterns children develop. Other dynamic theories, including the organismic, deal mostly with adult personality, not with the developmental process.

Psychoanalytic stage theory Psychoanalytic theory is the oldest dynamic theory, and sometimes is called "psychodynamic theory," as if it were the only one. The theory starts from the idea that the most basic biological drive is the drive towards **tension reduction,** that is, the need to remove irritating and painful stimulation. The most elementary stimulations threaten life itself; they are painful irritants like hunger, thirst, and cold. But the same need to be "at peace," free of tension, occurs in situations where life is not at stake, but comfort and satisfaction are—when one is sexually aroused, or needs affection or attention, or tries to learn something. Whenever we experience tension, we want to be rid of it. Reducing that tension gives a feeling of relief or gratification, which Freud named the "pleasure principle." It is the dominant motive of all behavior, he argues, in man as in all other animals.

Human infants, far more than infants of other species, must learn to fulfill their needs in the channels prescribed by society. They must learn not to reduce the tension of a full bowel on the living room carpet and to reduce the tension of hunger using utensils, dishes, and napkins in America, chopsticks and rice bowl in most of Asia, and two fingers only of the right hand in Beduin tents, wherever they may be. The chief agents of this "socialization process" are the child's parents. This makes them the child's best friends and worst enemies—parents help children to reduce their tensions and gratify their needs, but they restrict the ways in which they can do it. So they are the chief objects of childhood conflict just as they are the chief sources of childhood happiness.

In addition to having parents to contend with, says psychoanalytic theory, infants develop different outlets for their attention and interest as they mature neurologically. The main source of pleasurable feeling is sexual, and at different stages of maturation children's sexual feelings and desires interact and sometimes conflict with the requirements of social living their parents have instilled. This makes for different behavior patterns at different stages of growth, as we saw in the last chapter, which Freud called the **psychosexual stages of development.**

Freud described four main psychosexual stages, the **oral** stage, the **anal** stage, the **phallic** stage, and the **genital** stage, according to the zone of the body on which pleasurable feeling gets concentrated at different times. The oral stage occurs in the first year or so of life when children are dependent on others for everything and take greatest pleasures and interest from the activities of their mouths. Children who do not outgrow this stage by having their oral needs properly met become, to use Freud's term, **fixated** on oral concerns and tend to develop very dependent personalities.

At around one and a half or two years old, the anal stage begins, and with it comes the child's first experience with independence and with parental restriction. They learn to walk and get around efficiently, making trouble as they go. But now, parents start to make trouble for them in return by demanding that they learn bladder and bowel control. This is the time when children become fascinated with excretory functions, taking pleasure in their ability to "make" or withhold and in the feelings that go with the acts—and this is the time when they learn to feel frustrated and resentful at their parents' intrusions on their pleasures. The foundations of adult attitudes towards independence, miserliness or generosity, and orderliness are all laid down during the anal stage.

The phallic stage, around the age of four or five, is the next launching platform for adult personality, according to psychoanalysis. At this time, children start to notice strong feelings of pleasure from their genital area, and it becomes the pleasure center of attention. If their parents are very repressive about sexual matters, they may arouse sexual anxiety in kids which will later interfere with their ability to form mature love relationships. In any case, this is the stage in which young children start to see the opposite sex as potential sexual objects—with the most likely candidate for their affections being their own opposite sex parent. For little boys, mother becomes the prototype of the desirable female partner,[5] and for little girls, father, so that the sexual love relationships they form in later life may be efforts to find partners who can emulate the wonderful qualities they fancied in their parents.

The delights of phallic living diminish around age six or seven and the child then enters a *latency* phase, according to Freud, which is a period when nothing much happens on the psychosexual scene. Plenty of other things happen in these primary-grade years, of course, but psychoanalysts do not believe it is as critical for adult personality as were the events of the earlier stages.

With puberty, sexuality is rearoused, now in adult form, with the capacity for sexual intercourse, orgasm, pregnancy, and childbearing. This period begins the *genital* stage, in which adolescents develop the capacity for deep love relationships and the career ambitions from which their life work will come. This stage, hopefully, lasts a lifetime.

Neopsychoanalytic stage theory Some psychoanalytic personality theorists have proposed variations on Freud's developmental stages. Erik Erikson, perhaps the most important psychoanalytic student of personality development, does not believe that it revolves around *sexual* stages at all (Erikson 1952). Like Freud, Erikson believes that personality develops from infancy onward in several stages. But he argues, first of all, that these stages are a result of conflicts between the developing person and the social environment, rather than the outcome of sexual conflicts. Second, he believes that there are distinct stages throughout the whole course of life, not just up until

adolescence. Personality develops as the individual resolves the conflicts arising in each of these *psychosocial* stages.

Erikson believes that there are eight stages, each characterized by a central social conflict. The issue of the first year of life, is *trust versus mistrust.* As a result of its experiences with nurturant, warm, mothering figures who meet its basic needs or with indifferent parenting agents who do not, the infant develops attitudes of basic trust or distrust towards others which will remain with it throughout life. In the second and third years, as it learns to walk and talk and gets toilet-trained, the young child passes through the second stage, the central theme of which is *autonomy versus doubt.* The third stage, in the fourth and fifth years, is that of *initiative versus guilt.* Stage four, from age six until puberty, when schooling and skill learning are central, deals with conflicts between *industry* and a sense of *inferiority.* Puberty and adolescence, when heterosexual relations and career choice and religious and other values become issues, is the stage of *identity versus role confusion.* Young adulthood, when marriage and family emerge, brings conflicts of *intimacy versus isolation.* Middle adulthood is the stage revolving around *generativity versus self-absorption.* And *integrity versus despair* is the main problem of old age.

Each conflict, as you can see from the names of the stages, is typical of people as they pass through the corresponding stage of life. Erikson's concept of *identity crisis* as the main conflict of adolescence, for instance, has become very popular in describing the problems of teenagers and college students.

What actually happens to a Western child, in Erikson's view, does not differ very much from Freud's ideas of what happens during those same years. What they have in common, with each other and with all *stage* theories, is probably more important than the differences between them. It is the idea that personality is

---

[5] Freud named this phenomenon the oedipal situation after Sophocles' tragic King Oedipus, who slew his father and married his mother, both by accident.

shaped by the interaction of *social experience* and *biological maturation.* The actual stages are created by the *interaction* because the effects of experience are pretty much the same at any period of maturation—pleasurable and rewarding experiences are learned and remembered and sought again; punishing and painful experiences are suppressed and avoided as much as possible. That simple rule is the basis of the social learning theory of personality development.

Social learning of personality Social learning theory emphasizes learning as the basis for personality development rather than the interaction between learning and biological development (Bandura 1977). It does not contradict stage theories, but rather argues that the specific *reinforcement history* of a child, that is, the history of rewards and punishments they have had, explains how they learn the patterns of emotions, attitudes, defenses, and skills which make up their personality. Since the most important determinants of personality are the things we learn in relations with other people, *social learning* is the main interest of this theory, not learning in general. So classical conditioning is of interest here only for its role in teaching emotions, and instrumental and operant conditioning for their roles in teaching social skills. We have discussed these at length in Chapters 6 and 13, and there is nothing new to say about them here except that social learning theory puts them into the specific context of personality development. It addresses the single question, *how do you learn your personality?*

The main emphasis of social learning theory is on how the socialization process is shaped (Chapter 13). As children strive towards maturity, they get approval and rewards directly from people, first from their parents, then from society. These *direct positive social reinforcements* make them feel secure and confident, and they learn to act in ways that will bring more social rewards. When children disobey grown-

ups, or displease peers, they disapprove or punish them. These direct *negative social reinforcements* make them feel insecure and anxious; so they learn behavior patterns to avoid such pains in the future.

Vicarious social learning also plays a great role in personality development. Vicarious learning, you recall, means learning by *observation* and *imitation*—by watching others do something you have not yet tried, and seeing what happens to them. If they get positively reinforced, you are more likely to try it yourself; if they get punished, you are more likely to avoid doing it. Many personality traits are learned this way—we learn the attitudes and dispositions of our parents by watching them and what happens to them as a result of their outbursts of emotion, their expressions of disdain, of affection, or of trust, their openness or secretiveness with others, and so forth. Children tend to be like their parents *are* rather than like parents *tell them to be* because they are so good at learning by observation and imitation. Parents may tell them that one kind of behavior is good for them, but children *see* what kind of behavior is good for the parents. Few children are so stupid that they *listen* to their parents without *watching* them. When parental words and actions contradict each other, most children imitate the actions.

Character All dynamic theories of personality development agree that personality is continuously being formed, from infancy throughout life. This is the main thing that makes them *dynamic.* Even so, they all place great emphasis on *childhood,* both as the arena for the creation of personality and as its proving ground. The most stable aspects of personality which give an individual the distinctive attributes that make them recognizable throughout life are called "character" (London and Rosenhan 1968, p. 252). Psychoanalysts argue that character is more or less completely formed by about age six, when the oedipal conflicts of the phallic stage are alleviated. Other dynamic theories make no specific claims, but it is clear that they agree on early childhood as the period of greatest importance. Neither the organic theories we have already looked at nor the organismic and trait theories we shall now study make any such claims. The dynamic theories alone, believing that "the child is father of the man," have tried to uncover the roots of personality in the formative period of life.

Organismic theories of personality

In some ways, *organismic* or *holistic* or *humanistic* theories of personality are not dynamic theories any more than Sheldon's constitutional theory or Jung's typology are. They do not deal with personality *development* at all, and they do stress our *inherent biological needs* for growth and for seeking meaningful goals in life. The best statement of this position is found in the work of Abraham Maslow (1954), which was introduced in Chapter 7. But the basic theme, that humans strive to fulfill themselves through meaningful relationships and aspirations, is emphatically stated in the writings of Kurt Goldstein (1947), Carl Rogers (1961), Erich Fromm (1947), and many later writers on psychotherapy, personality, and social philosophy.

Organismic personality theory grew out of the work of the early Gestalt psychologists, which showed that perception tends to be highly organized, and that some aspects of perceptual organization seem to be inborn (see Chapter 5). The *genetic* basis of perceptual organization is the basis for the *biological* orientation of organismic theory. Surprisingly little research has been done, however, to show that people do strive to fulfill themselves in the ways that organismic theorists claim, though most of us feel that the claim is true of our own lives.

Maslow himself did a very interesting study on this subject, in collaboration with Evelyn Raskin and Dan Freedman (1954, pp. 199–260).

They studied 43 apparently self-actualized, or potentially self-actualized cases. The technical report Maslow gives is very careless; so it is difficult to tell who was interviewed, or how, or over what period. Thirteen of the cases were such historical figures as Abraham Lincoln, Thomas Jefferson, Baruch Spinoza, and Walt Whitman, all studied through various writings. Twenty were young people, apparently college students who seemed to have a high potential for self-actualization. The other 13 were living adults, apparently well known personally to the authors. The subjects were selected partly on the basis of negative criteria —the *absence* of neurosis or other serious behavior disorders—and partly on the basis of positive evidence of self-actualization, which Maslow says:

> may be loosely described as the full use and exploitation of talents, capacities, potentialities, etc. Such people seem to be fulfilling themselves and to be doing the best that they are capable of doing, reminding us of Nietzche's exhortation, "Become what thou art!" (Pp. 200–201.)

They also studied some less fulfilled college students, but it is not clear who they were. Both groups were studied impressionistically, through "fortuitous contacts of the ordinary social sort. Friends and relatives were questioned where this was possible."

Because of the loose way in which data were gathered, the authors present their conclusions as "composite impressions . . . offered for whatever they may be worth." They may be worth plenty; so here are some of the important ones.

Self-actualized people have a greater tendency than others to perceive reality efficiently and have comfortable relations with it. They could judge other people accurately and efficiently.

Self-actualizers are more accepting of themselves, with all their faults and quirks, and have a sense of gusto and vitality in living their lives. They lack defensiveness, and they dislike such "artificialities" in others.

Self-actualizers are relatively spontaneous in behavior and even more so in their thoughts and impulses. They are not especially unconventional in action, but "conventionality is a cloak that rests very lightly upon his shoulders and is easily cast aside" when it might "inhibit him from doing anything that he considers very important or basic."

Self-actualizers are "in general strongly focused on problems outside themselves . . . they are problem centered rather than ego centered . . . customarily have some mission in life, some task to fulfill . . . which enlists much of their energies."

Self-actualizers can handle solitude without discomfort, and even like solitude and privacy more than most people do.

They tend to be independent souls, who remain stable in the face of drastic changes in the external environment and in social situations.

They maintain "the wonderful capacity to appreciate again and again, freshly and naively, the basic goods of life, with awe, pleasure, wonder, and even ecstasy, however stale these experiences may have become to others."

Self-actualizers tend to have a good deal of **mystic experience,** as described by William

Carl Rogers.

James in *The Varieties of Religious Experience.* Some of them describe the sensations of sexual orgasm in particular as expressing these feelings most deeply, ". . . the feeling of great ecstasy and wonder and awe . . . so that the subject is to some extent transformed and strengthened even in his daily life by such experiences."

Self-actualizers have a deep feeling of identification, sympathy, and affection for human beings in general. They have deeper and more profound interpersonal relationships than other adults. They are "democratic people in the deepest possible sense." "They are strongly ethical, they have definite moral standards, they do right and do not do wrong. They have a philosophical, unhostile sense of humor. And they are, without exception, creative."

There are many more goodies that go with self-actualization in Maslow's description, but you should get the picture already. Self-actualization is the collection of ideal personality traits towards which people strive, or towards which they would strive if they were not hampered by pathology or inhibition as they grew up. Maslow, and all other organismic theorists, are finally dynamic theorists because they do believe that the **developmental process,** which they never describe, *is* critical in the shaping of adult self-actualization — but it is critical **only in a negative way** by interfering with the natural process of growth which would lead to fulfillment if left to itself — or perhaps watered just a little. Freudians and social learning theorists believe that you are born an animal and shaped into a human by the combination of love and fear, of reward and punishment, which parents and society administer, sometimes cunningly, sometimes blindly and stupidly. If it is not shaped, the little animal becomes a big savage. Organismic theorists are both more optimistic and more vague about how one gets from animal infancy to human civilization; they believe that the best of personality will blossom from within us all if we are left alone to become ourselves.

Dynamic theories tell us more about development than they do about the adult personality that is created by it. Organismic (and type) theories describe adult personality traits without saying much about what produced them; both kinds are based on theories about human nature. Many behavior scientists reject both positions and try to explore personality by direct observation, unburdened with theories of humanity's nature or development. They have created what are called *trait-factor* theories of personality.

Trait-factor personality theories

If personality refers, as we have said, to the consistencies of behavior that make a person recognizable throughout life, there should be some coherent scheme for describing those consistencies in detail. But it is not an easy task to find one, and no theory has been terribly successful at it. So some scholars have given up the idea of *first* constructing fancy theories and then making detailed observations, and have gone the opposite route. They make detailed observations and see if, by putting them together systematically to identify personality traits, they can then gain a comprehensive understanding or theory. Such methods do not worry much about either the developmental or the biological determinants of personality; they concentrate on the individual *facts* and the general *factors* in behavior from which we infer the existence of personality *traits.*

These *empirical* approaches work by gathering hundreds of individual items of behavior, most often through personality tests. These items are then *correlated* with each other to see the consistencies among them. Then, the clusters of items which are most highly correlated with each other (and unrelated to items outside their cluster) are further examined, in a complex mathematical process called *factor analysis,* to see how much whole clusters are related to each other. The mathematical "factors" that result are then examined to see what their contents are about, and the factor is *named* accordingly.

Trait-factor scholars try to be purely empirical, but they end up with theories which are just as theoretical as psychoanalysis or social learning theory or type theory. What betrays the effort at pure empiricism is that you have to *name* the factors in order to interpret them. Then, inevitably, you start taking the name seriously and, before you know it, you are *theorizing* about what one factor-idea has to do with another. Humans are theorizing animals, especially when they try to understand themselves.

The father of trait theory was Gordon Allport (1897–1968), a Harvard psychologist who believed that traits had a neurological basis, different for every individual, that biologically disposed them to respond to several stimuli in the same way. Allport proposed that different kinds of traits operate at different levels of personality organization; some traits, in other words, affect more of your life than others. The broadest ones, called *cardinal traits,* are so important that they influence everything a person does. Such "superordinate common traits," in Allport's view, are the same thing that Jung means by personality *types.* Introversive and extroversive *types* of people, in other words, would be people in whom introversion or extroversion are *cardinal traits.* Actually, Allport felt that not everybody has a cardinal trait. Instead, he thought, most people's personality is actually organized by 5 or 10 *central traits,* broad characteristics which influence many of the things we do, but without any single one being more powerful than any other. Introversion, would be such a central trait, in Allport's view; so would such things as dependency, authoritarianism, and masculinity. The next lower level he called *secondary traits,* which still organize people's responses into consistent patterns, but less conspicuously and dependably than the more general traits do.

More important than the hierarchy of traits is Allport's distinction between *common* and *personal* traits. *Personal* traits, he says, are the *real* characteristics of an individual, and they are *uniquely different* from one person to another. *Common* traits, on the other hand, are the similarities between people that we observe and measure, the things which give us a basis for making comparisons between them. Personality assessment is the measurement of common traits. It is useful to measure them, Allport believes, because they tell us something about the gross similarities and differences in people's personalities. But they are very gross. If we look at the specific behavior underlying any common trait, we will find that people really are uniquely different from each other. *Personality measurement is always a rude approximation of a person.*

Although Allport founded trait *theory* and made many distinctions between one kind of trait and another, he was not really interested in *measurement,* especially in comparing common traits (Baughman 1972). He thought it much more useful to study individuals over long periods to find their unique attributes than to study large groups of people on a small number of traits. He felt that this individual, or *ipsative* approach, was more valuable in understanding personality than *normative,* or cross group comparison, ever could be (see Chapter 12).

Trait measurement has had many distinguished representatives, of which the University of Illinois' Raymond B. Cattell is among the best known. Like Allport, Cattell also believes

Abraham H. Maslow.

St. Augustine Reading Rhetoric and Philosophy, B. Gozzoli
St. Augustine had himself been a big sinner before his conversion;
afterward he condemned others for the same sins.

that traits are the underlying factors in personality and that there are both common and unique traits. He also believes that traits operate at different levels, and some have more general influence on behavior than others. He gives the name *surface traits* to the less important ones. The underlying forces at work in personality he calls *source* traits (Cattell 1965).

Unlike Allport, Cattell has made exhaustive efforts *to measure* a wide variety of people and, principally by means of mathematical factor analysis, to identify source traits in particular. He claims to have found some important ones. Cattell's best known personality test, is

called the 16PF (personality factors), referring to the main source traits he claims to have identified. He believes he has discovered that *intelligence* and *susceptibility to threat,* are primarily determined by heredity, while *ego strength* depends more on environmental factors. Most other scholars, even if they agree with these conclusions, would say that they cannot be proved by Cattell's methods.

So it goes with personality measurement in general, and with trait-factor theories in particular. The statistical methods of trait assessment are among the most sophisticated in the behavioral sciences, but the best methods of

Gordon Allport.

analysis will not yield better information than the instruments and observations permit. We have met this problem in Chapter 1; we will not be rid of it anywhere, nor plagued worse by it anywhere than in the assessment of personality. The most refined trait measurements have yielded very little useful information about what people are like or useful predictions about how they will behave in practically any situation (Mischel 1968). All the elegant empirical studies of personality traits have not told us much more than Gordon Allport theorized about them in the first place. Nor have they given us a better total understanding of personality than type theories, or psychoanalysis, or social learning theory.

This is not to say that the other theories have done so well by the field, especially in recent years. "Personality theory," to quote Lee Sechrest's review of the topic, "is, in my estimation, in sad shape. . . . In no other field purporting to be scientific are the current heroes of theory nearly all dead. And in every other field of science the current basic research is directed toward the testing of the theories being taught to students (1976, p. 3)." In personality, the research payoffs lie elsewhere.

BASIC PROCESSES IN PERSONALITY

Most of what we actually know about personality comes from studying single aspects of it rather than from building big theories or doing grand empirical studies on everything at once. Some of the most interesting topics are the process of **identification,** the study of **sex role** and **sex typing,** and the **sense of control.**

Identification: Growing up like Papa

There are several technical uses of the term "identification," but they all refer to the same thing—trying to be like another person, in speech, manner, attitude, action, or appearance. Students of all theoretical leanings agree that identification is one of the most important processes in the formation of adult personality. Largely by means of it, the growing child learns to be masculine or feminine in interests and outlook, learns to be aggressive or dependent in relations with others, and learns many of the preferences and attitudes which will later dominate their choices of things like a spouse, a political party, a religious creed, and a taste for beer.

Freud and his followers were the first to recognize that identification is a form of **learning by observation and imitation** in which children learn many of the attributes of their parents without being specifically taught them. Parents serve as unintentional **models** for such learning. Children also learn to imitate other important figures, like older siblings, teachers, and playmates. But parents are generally the most important identification models because, in children's experience, they come first, last longest, and have more power over them (and the world) than anyone else. By the time they discover (if they do) that parents are not the potent figures they thought, it is too late to shake the impressions they already have—or to throw off most of the habits and attitudes they learned in imitation of parents. Parents are not always good models for children to imitate, but they are generally the most impressive ones.

The psychoanalytic view of identification emphasized its function as a means by which

In some societies, children were encouraged to be little-sized copies of the adults around them.

Las Meninas, Diego Velásquez

children defended themselves against anxiety. Fearful of the hostile power his father has over him, for example, a little boy would make himself be like daddy, both to placate the father by imitation, "the sincerest form of flattery," and to get some of that power for himself. In ancient primitive tribes, Freud thought, sons ate their fathers in order to absorb some of their strength (1913). Modern cannibals do the same things sometimes with their enemies, evidently for the same reason. Psychoanalytic theory sees identification as a defense mechanism of the phallic stage, when little boys start becoming fearful of father's jealousy because of their own sexual attraction to their mothers (Freud called this the "oedipal conflict"). After a while, the child internalizes the behavior he has copied and makes it a part of him. Freud was somewhat less clear, and a lot less correct, about how identification by defense takes place in little girls.

Social learning theorists have observed, in any case, that imitative learning begins long before kindergarten and is not usually a defensive maneuver, though it may sometimes be. Children learn to imitate because their attention is focused on their parents, in the first place, and because they are vicariously reinforced for doing so in the second. One motive for imitation is that they love their parents; they see parents as loving, nurturant, rewarding figures that make them feel good. So being like them makes the children feel good too, reminding them of the good feelings that parents arouse. A second motive for imitation is that the child realizes that the parent is *powerful,* not only in a threatening sense, but in the control and dispensation of rewards as well as punishments (Bandura and Walters 1963). This is similar to the psychoanalytic notion of defensive identification, but it begins much earlier than the phallic stage, it has no sexual implication, and it applies to either parent. Finally, children imitate the *same sex parent* most because they see themselves as most similar to that parent. Early in childhood we learn to like the people whom we think are most like ourselves, and then to make ourselves be like the people we like most. This tendency bursts into bloom again in early adolescence, when children develop crushes and "hero-worship" teachers or other adults, usually of the same sex, and try to model their lives after these adored figures.

Sex typing: The child is father of the man

One of the main effects of imitative learning is that little boys and girls begin to play the roles that are stereotyped for them by the culture; girls start learning to do the things which are popularly regarded as *feminine* and boys the things considered *masculine.* Learning to prefer one or the other kind of activity is called *sex typing;* performing sex-typed activity is called *sex role* taking.

Some sex-typed behavior is learned by direct instruction and reinforcement; parents may punish little boys for playing with dolls and doilies and praise them for playing with tractors and hand grenades, while they will reverse the process with little girls. The patterns of reward and punishment get fouled up sometimes—you may have heard of families, for instance, where the mother wanted a daughter, bore a son, and then dressed him up in little girl clothes and

taught him to develop the mannerisms and interests of girls.

The unhappy results of intensive sex-role training are that it tends to stick too much, that is, to be internalized by children and to dominate their interests throughout life, sometimes putting them in terrible conflict. Adult homosexuality or transvestitism (the desire to dress and appear like a member of the opposite sex) may be one outcome of this process. The intensity of sex-role training may be more important than its direction, by the way. Parents who are over-anxious about their little boys' masculinity may cause just as much trouble for their super-masculine sons as parents who teach the reverse of conventional sex roles may cause their confused children.

Most sex-typed behavior is learned by observation and imitation rather than by direct instruction. Boys learn to imitate their fathers and other men; girls do the same thing with their mothers.

Sex-typing occurs in the first five years or so. Preschool children label "boys" and "girls" easily enough, but their concept of gender is superficial, addressing such physical features as dress and hair. By the time they start school, they have some idea of more basic differences and know that, among adults, men are bigger and stronger than women (Tavris and Offir 1977). There are some behavioral differences between the sexes from infancy: Girls vocalize more, smile more, and show more different reactions to facial stimuli than boys soon after birth. In the early school years, moreover, girls are generally somewhat better at verbal and language skills, while boys tend to surpass them in quantitative skills and spatial relations. It is not known to what extent the sex differences are genetic, though there is some evidence of a sex-linked chromosome for spatial ability. But nongenetic factors, such as parental "shaping" and imitation of other people's sex-typed behavior, probably contribute as much or more to

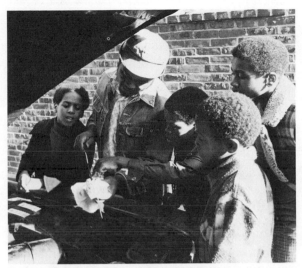

Modeling and imitation are the basis of sex typing.

most sex differences (Maccoby and Jacklin 1974). Some evidence to that effect comes from the fact that hermaphroditic children, having both male and female genitalia, turn out to be male or female in orientation depending entirely on how they are raised, regardless of which sex their chromosomes belong to (XY is male, XX female). And children who have been accidentally raised as the opposite of their biological sex also turn out to behave like the sex they were raised to be, and think of themselves as such (Money and Tucker 1975). The biological elements in sex-role behavior are far less important than the child-training practices. Boys and girls *learn* to be masculine or feminine in outlook and action regardless of whether they start off as biologically male or female.

The one area of personality development in which sex typing is probably the most important is *aggression.* As early as age three, boys show more physically aggressive behavior than girls, are more negativistic and more quarrelsome, get into more fights, and fight back more. This tends to be true across many different cultures, and to remain true from early childhood throughout life (Maccoby and Jacklin 1974). Although there is a widespread stereotype of girls as more dependent than boys, the data does not strongly support this belief.

With both aggression and dependency, as with any learned behavior, sex roles differ according to situations and cultural backgrounds. Aggression is probably the area in which boys and girls are most consistently raised differently in most cultures, but sex-role expectations within a single culture vary greatly in different settings and at different stages of development. Parents and teachers may permit little boys to be more physically aggressive than little girls in kindergarten, for example, but the courtesy does not extend to fistfighting in college classes a dozen years later. And while dependency may be a feminine attribute in love relationships, young men do not lose their "masculinity" by feeling deep needs for the company and comfort of their loved ones. Sex typing provides behavioral guidelines for conventional social roles. Learning them is important to wholesome personality development, but being locked into them is not.

Androgyny We commonly think of masculinity and femininity as if they were opposite ends of the same sex-role scale; so if you scored high on one, you would necessarily score low on the other. More and more evidence is coming forth nowadays which says that is not true, and that they are independent qualities so that you could have a lot or a little of either or both of them. The ability to respond in both masculine and feminine ways is called androgyny, from the Greek words for "man-woman". Sandra Bem has developed a Sex-Role Inventory for measuring androgyny (1974). It shows that people who are rigidly masculine or feminine are very distressed at the idea of doing things which they think belong to the other role, and that they may be deficient in some important social skills (Bem 1975; Bem and Lenney 1976). People who score high on **both** qualities, moreover, have higher self-esteem than low scorers on both and may be generally more responsive and open to others (Bem 1977). This seems to imply that "the androgynous person is better adjusted than the nonandrogynous person. While the androgynous reader may agree, the nonandrogynous reader may not (Phares and Lamiell 1977)."

The sense of control

Personality research has become increasingly attentive in recent years to the importance of the sense of control in people's lives. In order to function well, for most purposes, and to function at all, for some, people must feel that they have some control over their lives, that they can affect what happens, that they can influence events. The significance of this need has been widely recognized in personality theory, taking different labels from different authors. Alfred Adler referred to it as "the striving for superiority," Robert White as "competence" or "effectance" motives, Ives Hendrick as the "instinct to master," and Richard de Charms as the "striving for personal causation" (Langer 1975). This need prevails both in the short and the long views that people take of their lives. In the short view, they describe it to themselves as "volition" or "choice," and, in the long view, as "purpose" or "plan." No matter to what degree people feel enslaved or beholden to others, they always feel, on reflection, that they have some choice over what movement to make, what object to seize, what answer to give — the immediate consequences of their choices are under their control, as they see it, even if the more distant ones are not. By the same token, the more people see themselves as capable of favorably influencing the distant events of their lives, the less they feel constrained, enslaved and beholden by the events of the moment, and the more in control of things. The subjective measure of their confidence in these outcomes is the feeling of "hope."

The illusion of control The sense of control is so strong in most of us that we sometimes confuse luck and skill. "While they may pay lip service to the concept of chance," says Ellen Langer, "they behave as though chance events are subject to control (Langer 1975, p. 311)." Langer summarizes a considerable literature demonstrating the existence of a common "illusion of control," that is, a disposition of people to expect a probability of success in their endeavors which is "inappropriately higher than the objective probability would warrant (p. 313)." She cites several studies of chance situations, such as gambling, in which crapshooters are noted to typically roll soft when trying "to make" low numbers, and hard for high numbers, bettors place higher bets before the dice are tossed than after, and so forth. In an effort to account for this phenomenon, she hypothesized that one source of the illusion of control is a misplaced generalization which people commonly make from skill situations to chance situations. Some aspects of skill situations, in other words, also appear in chance situations (though they are, in fact, irrelevant there), and these apparent similarities mislead people into thinking that the chance events also can be influenced by skillful performance. In a series of six brilliant experiments, Langer confirms the notion that elements of *competition, choice, stimulus familiarity, response familiarity, active involvement,* and *passive involvement* in chance situations all tend to mislead people into the illusion that they can exercise some control over those events, as they might indeed over skill problems with those same characteristics.

The origins of control sense No one knows just how the sense of control originates in childhood. Presumably, however, it is an outgrowth of discrimination learning. Elementary acts of discrimination are the most primitive kind of choices. And all choices, if you think about it, are acts of control. The broad sense of control develops from success at making them.

The sense of control develops from childhood on, as discriminatory acts become more and

Although the artist calls this "Genuflexion of the Bishop," you could ask several hundred people what they see in it, add up the answers, and *voilà,* a new standardized projective test.

Genuflexion of the Bishop, Jean Dubuffet

1. I like mechanics magazines.

2. I have a good appetite.

3. I wake up fresh and rested most mornings.

4. I think I would like the work of a librarian.

5. I am easily awakened by noise.

6. I like to read newspaper articles on crime.

7. My hands and feet are usually warm enough.

8. My daily life is full of things that keep me interested.

9. I am about as able to work as I ever was.

10. There seems to be a lump in my throat much of the time.

11. A per___ ___'d try to understand his dreams ___ ___ take ___ from them.

Figure 14.3 Samples of the 566 true-false questions in the Minnesota Multiphasic Personality Inventory.

more deliberate, reflecting a person's experience of making choices and getting rewarding feedback for them. Each time a discriminatory choice is followed by a positive outcome, or reinforcement, the child's expectancy grows that such discriminations or choices will be successful in the future. The generalization of this expectation becomes the individual's sense of control. Control sense is thus one measure of people's positive reinforcement history rather than of the degree of control which they realistically can exercise over the environment. The broad sense of control is an *attitude* toward one's self and one's relation with the world, not an *assessment* of it. It is a disposition to see the world as a relatively manageable thing and one's own life as a relatively manipulable part of it.

Sense of control and locus of control The notion that the sense of control is a generalized expectancy that events will have a favorable outcome because of one's influence on them is part of a theory formulated by Julian Rotter. Another part of his theory says that whether people see the control of events as resting within themselves or in forces outside themselves is an important determinant of their personality. The *locus* of control, as it is called, has been the subject of about a thousand research papers between around 1965 and 1975, mostly using a scale which Rotter constructed for distinguishing whether people's sense of control was *internal* or *external* (called the I-E Scale). These studies continue to flourish, but the significance of locus of control in personality is not yet clear (Phares 1973; Phares and Lamiell 1977; Rotter 1975).

The most vital thing about the sense of control, in any case, is probably *having* it, not *locating* it. Some people will have the favorable expectancies involved in the sense of control because they think they are themselves powerful, and these people will manifest an internal locus of control. Others will have favorable expectancies because they see outside forces working in their favor, such as the will of God, the movements of the planets, or the turn of the weather, and theirs will be an external locus of control. Locus of control, as such, does not necessarily determine one's confidence of winning. The Arab conquerors of the Middle Ages saw themselves as instruments of Allah's will, not as actors in their own dramas; but they were as fierce in combat and as confident of victory as they could be, without looking backward, or inward, to any other source of inspiration.

Losing self control The sense of control is maintained, for the most part, quietly and unreflectively. Its loss is noisy and anguished. When a person's sense of control is threatened, anxiety results. When the threat deepens into the feeling that control is lost, demoralization and despair follow. Even in lower animals, Richter has shown that the loss of "hope," that is, of being able to effect a change in a situation from which no escape route is evident, causes rats to stop struggling and die; Mowrer and Vieck have shown that rats who cannot control electric shock differ subsequently from rats who can control shock, the latter developing a long-standing apprehension, which they label "fear from a sense of helplessness"; and Seligman, Maier, and Geer have shown the same experimental phenomenon in dogs, carried over, in

Seligman's speculation, to account for reactive depression in human beings (for an excellent summary of most of this work, see Lefcourt 1973).

In the extreme, the feeling of lost control may lead people to suicide, wanton destructiveness, or other impulsive and meaningless acts, as well as to clinical depression. At best, it produces the symptoms of misery that are expressed in variety ranging from simple discomfort to neurosis, to psychosomatic, and to psychogenic illnesses.

PERSONALITY MEASUREMENT

You have probably heard a lot about "personality tests," perhaps even taken some; so we should not close the chapter without a word about them. There are two kinds of instruments used to evaluate personality ("evaluate," "assess," and "measure" all mean the same thing): *objective* tests and *projective* tests.

Objective tests have specific questions and answers, much like the objective examinations you get in school, but the questions are more personal: "How do you usually feel in the morning?" for instance. Check one: "good, bad, awful, worse." Or they may be statements: "Most mornings, I wake up eager to study psychology." "true, false, ridiculous." And so forth.

Projective tests do not ask specific questions and do not have definite answers to choose from. The *Rorschach,* or ink-blot test, for instance, consists of ten cards with symmetrical ink blots. They are shown to you with the instruction: "What do these remind you of? What might they look like?" (Rorschach 1919; Klopfer 1954). The *Thematic Apperception Test,* a collection of 30 pictures, mostly of people in different situations, is given with the instruction: "Make up the most dramatic story you can about each of these pictures. Tell what led up to the scene in the picture, what the characters are thinking and feeling, and how the story will come out." Still other projective tests, such as *word-association* or *sentence-completion* tests, respectively, require the subject to say whatever word comes to mind when the examiner says a "stimulus" word, or to fill in the blank in such sentences as "I sometimes wish I could ——————."

All personality tests are really a kind of *interview,* standardized so that different people can be compared on the same questions and answers.

Objective personality tests use several different formats, such as *questionnaires, rating schedules,* and *inventories.* They are constructed in either of two ways, and both look alike to the person taking them. One kind is constructed by finding clusters of items that are similar to each other—this is the trait-measurement kind of test we discussed earlier.

In the second kind of objective personality test, the content of the question is not important, but only the way it is typically answered by people who are known to have the trait you are looking for. For example, take the true-false statement, "The color yellow always reminds me of despair." If this item was given to a great number of artists, say, who consistently answered "true," it could be used as an indicator of artistic temperament even though the ques-

tion has nothing to do with art. This kind of test is used most for practical situations where you are less interested in learning anything about the trait than you are in predicting something about the people to whom you give the test. The *Minnesota Multiphasic Personality Inventory* (MMPI) is the best known test of this kind. It was constructed by collecting patterns of answers to personal questions which more or less uniquely characterized normal, or neurotic, or other emotionally troubled people. When you take this test, your answers are not examined for their *meaning,* but only for how the pattern of your answers *corresponds statistically* to the pattern of the different standardization groups.

Most personality tests, whether objective or projective, are less reliable than they ought to be and *some of them are of doubtful validity.* Some businesses and some branches of government have used personality tests in the past to *screen* employees, letting them in, keeping them out, promoting them, or making other decisions about them through the use of these tests. There has sometimes been little justification for doing that. If that seems to be true in a situation where you are required to take them, do so with caution. They may be hazardous to your health.

SUMMARY

1 Personality means the stable aspects of behavior, the continuity of the individual over time. There are dozens of synonyms for personality, such as "character," "temperament," "nature," and "type."

2 Since ancient times, there have been two general trends in personality theory. One was to think of personality as the product of physical structure and the other was to think of it as the product of the environment. These trends are represented in modern personality theory by organic or constitutional theories of personality on the one hand, and dynamic theories on the other.

3 Most personality characteristics are considered *traits,* that is, styles of behavior. Traits are abstract terms which connote the statistical averages of people's behavior. If someone is an "angry person," for instance, the trait of anger refers to a typical behavior pattern, rather than to a physical property the person carries around within them. A personality description in terms of many traits is called a "personality profile."

4   The most popular modern organic theory is the Sheldon-Kretschmer theory. It claims that temperament and personality are linked to three basic body types: the endomorphic, or short, fat, type, goes with viscerotonic personalities, who take pleasure in eating and relaxing; the mesomorphic, or middle type, goes with somatotonic personality, which takes pleasure in athletic competition and energetic movement; and the ectomorphic, or tall, thin type, goes with cerebrotonic personality, which is restrained, cautious, sensitive and intellectual. The evidence supporting this theory is weak.

5   Carl Jung's personality-type theory is also an organic theory. Jung believed that people were born introversive or extroversive. Introverts tend to look within themselves for stimulation and interest while extroverts are more oriented to the external environment. Within these basic types, people tend to lean more in the direction of thinking versus feeling, of intuition versus sensation, and of perception versus judgment in their ways of viewing the world. Jung did not believe that the personality types existed in mixtures. You might be a slight introvert or an extreme introvert, but you could not be part introvert and part extrovert at the same time.

6   Dynamic personality theories are all based on the idea that personality changes and grows with experience. The three main ones are psychoanalytic theory, social learning theory, and organismic theory. Psychoanalytic theory emphasizes the interactions of biological maturation and social experience. Social learning theory emphasizes reinforcement histories, the pattern of rewards and punishments that determine personality. Organismic theory is not concerned with child development, but with adult goals.

7   Psychoanalytic theory proposes that personality develops in four psychosexual stages. The oral stage occurs in the first year of life, when children are dependent on others for everything and get greatest pleasure from the activities of their mouth. The anal stage begins around one and one half to two years; it is the child's first experience with independence (they learn to walk and get around), and with parental restriction, primarily in the form of toilet-training. The phallic stage begins around four or five, when the child's feelings of pleasure center around the genital area. At age six or seven the child enters a latency phase of relative psychosexual calm. The genital stage begins with puberty. It is the period of adult maturity in which the capacity for love relationships and career aspirations is fulfilled.

8   Erik Erikson proposed an important variation on Freud's developmental personality theory. Erikson argues that personality develops as a result of conflicts between the individual and the social environment rather than as a result of sexual conflicts, and that it continues developing throughout the life span. His eight *psychosocial* stages are (1) trust versus mistrust (the first year of life), (2) autonomy versus doubt (second and third years), (3) initiative versus guilt (fourth and fifth years), (4) industry versus inferiority (from age 6 until puberty), (5) identity versus role confusion (puberty and adolescence), (6) intimacy versus isolation (young adulthood), (7) generativity versus self-absorption (middle adulthood), and (8) integrity versus despair (old age).

9   Social-learning theory emphasizes reinforcement history as the basis of personality development. It is primarily concerned with how classical conditioning, operant conditioning, and learning by imitation, all contribute to the formation of personality.

10 Organismic personality theories propose that our entire development is aimed at the fulfillment of an inherent need for growth. Abraham Maslow, Kurt Goldstein, and Carl Rogers are major figures in organismic theory. Organismic theorists agree that our best capacities develop spontaneously if growth is not inhibited by bad child-rearing practices.

11 Trait factor theories are empirical approaches to personality which identify traits by questionnaires and behavioral observations, which are then subjected to a complex mathematical process called "factor analysis." Gordon Allport was the father of trait theory. He believed that people have cardinal traits, which influence everything they do, and that there are subordinate classes of traits, which are less conspicuous in determining behavior patterns. Ultimately, Allport believed all traits are individual, but that some common traits are grossly similar from one person to another. Raymond Cattell and Hans Eysenck have developed empirical trait-factor approaches to personality.

12 Identification is a basic process in personality development. It is learning by imitation, in which the parents serve as the model for children's development. Psychoanalytic theory argues that children learn to identify with their same sex parent, largely as a defensive measure, but social-learning theorists observe that identification also has many positive motivations.

13 Sex typing is the learning of stereotyped masculine and feminine roles within a culture. It occurs in the first five years of life. Confusion over sex roles or too intensive a training in one sex role may cause great difficulty in the emotional development of children. Aggression and dependency are strongly sex-typed behavior in almost every culture.

14 Masculinity and femininity may not be opposite ends of the same sex-role scale, but independent qualities, so that you could have a lot or a little of either or both. The ability to respond in both masculine and feminine ways is called *androgyny*.

15 In order to function effectively, people need to have a sense of control over their lives, that is, a feeling that they can influence the outcome of events which affect them. This need is so powerful that they will often attribute control to situations which really depend on luck; this "illusion of control" results from apparent similarities between chance and skill situations. In our society, the sense of control is commonly associated with the idea that the control of events is *within* oneself, called an *internal locus of control*. But in societies where control is felt to be outside oneself, such as in the will of God, or in other forces, the need for control sense is just as strong. Its loss produces anxiety, depression, and despair.

16 The two main kinds of tests used to evaluate personality are objective and projective tests. Objective tests, such as questionnaires, rating schedules, and inventories, have specific questions and answers. Projective tests, such as ink-blot tests, thematic tests, and word-association tests, ask general questions and do not have definite answers. Most personality tests are fairly unreliable, and all of them are of doubtful validity. They are often used by business and government to spy on people's private lives, and you should refuse to take them or cheat on them if they are used on you in this way.

Adjustment

15

15 Adjustment

"You've got to live. You've got to get along as best you can," says one of the characters in Lillian Hellman and Leonard Berstein's musical version of *Candide*. In the technical language of psychology, getting along as best you can is called "adjustment"; it is the name of the game of life. The general ways in which it operates throughout the animal kingdom, and the special ways in which it is played among human beings, especially in Western society, are the subjects of this chapter. All the basic processes of behavior we have studied up till now—sensation, perception, learning, motivation, emotion, and the rest—are significant in our lives for the ways they contribute to the processes of adjustment. ***Adjustive behavior is all behavior which tries to solve the problems of living.***

At the most elementary levels, all living creatures are faced with the same problems of adjustment, as we shall see. These problems become more complicated and the ability to solve them becomes more elegant as we move from plant to animal kingdoms and as we rise in the animal kingdom from the simplest phyla up to the mammals and, finally, to human beings. In humans, a new dimension of adjustment problem is added to all the old ones we already share with lower animals by the fact that language gives us the capacity to remember a lot, to worry a lot, to have opinions about ourselves, which shake our confidence something awful, and to lie a lot, both to ourselves and others. It gives us the corresponding ability to reason things out, however, and to plan our affairs; so it does not turn out to be a dead loss.

In this chapter, we shall take up the processes of adjustment in their evolutionary order, starting with the basic stresses of life and how they are met and proceeding upwards through human anxieties, self-doubts, and the psychological defenses we construct for dealing with them. The next two chapters will deal with some adjustment problems which especially preoccupy young Americans. And Chapters 18 and

19 will discuss the extreme adjustment difficulties called behavior disorders and the special techniques for treating them called psychotherapy, behavior modification, and behavior control.

STRESS AND ADAPTATION: THE BASIC FACTS OF LIFE

No living thing has it too easy. Life is a struggle, always, and for everything that lives, and the price of failure is death. All that lives pays that price eventually and dies. The effort to live and be satisfied is called *adaptation.* Everything in the environment which makes it hard to live is called *stress.* The basic adaptive needs of plants are for water, minerals, light, and warmth. The basic stresses on them come from too little or too much of these, and from constant threat of change in the environment. Too much rain one year, and the plants drown; too much sun, and they wither; too much of good conditions, and they grow so wildly that they choke each other or lure swarms of animals who eat them, multiply too much, and kill all the plants or the earth's capacity for growing them.

The same principles of stress and adaptation apply to animals as plants. The difference is that locomotion gives animals a greater chance to adapt than most plants get, while their more complex needs for food and appetites for each other put more stresses on them, too.

Ecology studies the **contemporary** balance of stress and adaptation among plant and animal life. *Evolution* studies the **historical** successes and failures of different species in adapting to changing stresses in the environment. A species becomes extinct when it cannot adapt successfully to the stress of new conditions, as the mastodons and saber-toothed tigers could not to the ice ages, or the dinosaurs and great ferns to the swamplands draining or climates changing. "Survival of the fittest" means that organisms survive which are best able to "fit" their patterns of living to the requirements of their surroundings, that is, to adapt themselves to the stress of their environment.

It is easy to understand the importance of stress and adaptation in extreme conditions and to overlook their significance in the routine course of living. Many common illnesses, including some serious ones, like ulcers, and

Stress.

Stress.

some deadly ones, like heart disease, are often connected with common life stresses (McQuade and Aikman 1974). And there is some reason to think that even aging and natural death are results of the body's failure to adapt to stress rather than an inevitable process. Maybe we get worn out and exhausted by lifelong efforts to cope with stress, in other words, and then collapse like any other machine. If so, then it may some day be possible to retard aging and lengthen the natural life-span of humans by discovering the chemical basis of stress resistance in the body's tissues.

The general adaptation syndrome

At the most elementary level of life, stress is experienced as *irritation* or *discomfort.* The "tissue irritability" of living matter is what makes plants turn towards light and even the simplest animals move away from noxious stimuli in their environment (London 1977). At a slightly more advanced level, stress is experienced as the *anticipation of harm,* called *threat* or

alarm or, in animals with well developed nervous systems like us, as *fear.* This emotional response to stress is the first part of a pattern which goes from alarm to *resistance,* and finally, if the stress is not overcome, to *exhaustion.* The alarm-resistance-exhaustion sequence is called the *general adaptation syndrome* (Selye 1953).

Alarm The feeling of threat has to be interpreted before any response to stress is possible. One's *appraisal* of the stressful situation is the first thing that determines what reaction we will make to it. Fear and anger are two of the most common emotional responses to stress. Fear mobilizes defense or escape responses, and anger arouses aggression or attack.

Resistance Either defense or attack will be more effective in resisting stress if they are *task-oriented,* that is, concentrated on the problem itself and not on how the individual feels about it. In fact, very strong emotional responses to stress tend to disorganize a person and make them react blindly instead of thoughtfully. If the disorganizing emotional responses are very prolonged, moreover, or repeated very often, they can cause psychosomatic disorders such as peptic ulcers or high blood pressure.

Exhaustion Stress can "get" you in the long run if it is severe enough, or if it lasts long enough to grind you down. The process of collapse which then takes place is called **decompensation.** It starts with disorganized responses and continues until exhaustion or death results. Even with good stress resistance, coping responses are costly. Under stress, our general functioning tends to become less efficient, we become more vulnerable to new forms of stress, and the continued mobilization of energy needed to combat prolonged stress eventually produces physical damage. In the long run, stress "gets" us all (Levi 1967).

In human beings, certain kinds of stress produce **ego anxiety,** a special form of fear connected with our capacity for language and self-consciousness. Ego anxiety sometimes produces ego-defensive responses, which are mental efforts to reduce this kind of stress. Ego defenses are generally poor methods of adjustment because they do not actually change the stressful conditions, but everyone uses them to some extent anyhow. We shall discuss them at length in this and the next two chapters.

FRUSTRATION AND CONFLICT

We have been describing stress as if it were always imposed on the organism by the external environment. When that is so, the only way to cope with it is either to *avoid* it or *adapt* to it, that is to get out of the stressful situation or get used to it.[1] But there are two important kinds of stress which animals help to create, largely because they can move about, and therefore

---

[1] Notice that adaptation has two meanings. As a technical term, it means *all* methods of adjustment to stress, including both avoidance and "getting used to." Adjustment has the same double meaning, that is, technically meaning *all* methods of coping and generally meaning "getting used to."

have *goals* which they try actively to fulfill. These are **frustration** and **conflict.** Frustration means that some *block* stands between you and your goal, preventing you from reaching it. Conflict means that you cannot choose among different goals. Both states arouse tension. The hallmark of frustration is the feeling of *anger;* in conflict, it is the feeling of *indecision.* From an evolutionary point of view, frustration is a more primitive problem than conflict. Even amobae experience it. Conflict is a more sophisticated experience because you cannot be conflicted until you have a sufficiently advanced nervous system to be able to pay attention to more than one goal at a time.

Frustration

Frustration can be dealt with in three different ways: (1) you can **circumvent** the block, that is, go around it to reach the goal; (2) you can **attack** the block, that is, remove it or go through it to the goal; or (3) you can **withdraw** from it, that is, give up the goal and turn to something else.

How you typically cope with frustration depends on what kind of animal you are and what kind of frustration you are facing. If reaching your goal is a life-or-death matter for instance, then almost no creature selects option number (3), withdrawal, no matter how dangerous it may be to pursue the goal. If the animal has been schooled in timidity, it will probably try circumvention rather than attack. If it has been trained to be aggressive, it will probably attack the block rather than go around it. When a lion wants to drink from the local water hole and other animals are there, it roars them away. When the gentle gazelle wants to drink, it waits for night to fall and the fiercer beasts to leave.

Predatory, carnivorous animals tend to respond to frustration with aggression since they learn to eat by ferocity to begin with; vegetarians and scavengers go in more for circumvention. But size, strength and temperament are more important determinants than feeding habits.

Elephants and buffalo, both vegetarians, tend to get their way in a hurry, and meat-eating jackals and hyenas, among others, tend to give it to them. Hitler was a vegetarian.

People cope with frustration in about the same ways animals do, with the vital difference that people are much smarter than animals and, therefore, are capable of much more discriminating responses to frustration. People from different families and cultural backgrounds may have learned to be aggressive or timid in general, but they also learn to handle one kind of frustration with circumvention, a second with aggression, and a third by withdrawal, depending on how important the goal is and what they think their chances are of reaching it by one means or the other. People also can deal with frustration symbolically, instead of directly, by talking and thinking over responses to frustration rather than by having to take direct action against it.

In some situations, there is no way at all to get relief from frustration. As we said in Chapter 6, animals who are subjected to painful shocks in a situation where there is no way to escape — that is, no way to resolve their frustration —

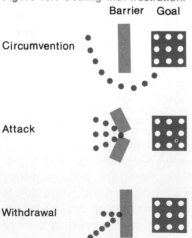

Figure 15.1 Dealing with frustration.

become passive and helpless and stay that way even when barriers to escape are removed. The same thing happens in experimental situations to college students. So it is reasonable to generalize that when most people are confronted with large scale unresolvable frustrations, they learn to respond in similar ways — by becoming passive, helpless, and depressed (Seligman 1975).

Conflict

Conflict exists whenever two goals are incompatible, so that choosing one causes stress from the failure to deal with the other. There are only three kinds of conflict situations: (1) approach-approach; (2) avoidance-avoidance; and (3) approach-avoidance (Lewin 1935).

Approach-approach conflict: Eat your cake and have it, too The easiest kind of conflict to handle is called the *approach-approach* conflict, because it involves two goals which are both desirable, but where you cannot get one without losing the other. This is the eat-your-cake-and-have-it-too situation. Lower animals do not face it very much, or at least they resolve it fairly fast, because one goal tends to outweigh the other pretty quickly. There is a classic story by the French philosopher Jean Buridan, that a dog supposedly starved to death because he could not choose between two equal-sized piles of food. But no four-legged animal would be caught on the horns of such a dilemma for long. Hunger would conquer indecision quickly in one direction or the other.

Human beings, on the other hand, can get stuck more seriously with double-approach conflicts because their ability to discriminate between goals lets them weigh the advantages and disadvantages of each at great length. Choosing between two boy or girl friends when both are appealing, or between which of two movies to attend, or which of two cars to buy, or whether to go away on vacation or to spend the same money on some other long sought

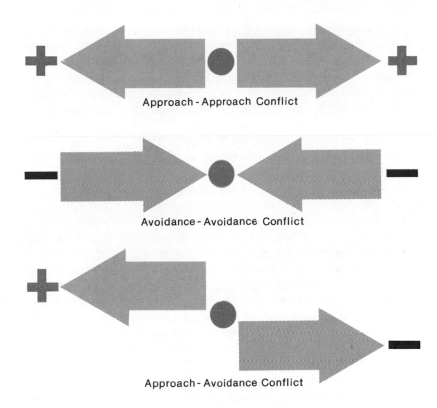

Approach - Approach Conflict

Avoidance - Avoidance Conflict

Approach - Avoidance Conflict

Figure 15.2 Dealing with conflict.

goodie—all these are double-approach conflicts. The resolution is usually fairly easy, because either goal is satisfying, but it is distressing to be caught in the process of decision for very long.

The actual decision that is made in a conflict depends on the *valence,* that is, the strength of either goal. In a double-approach conflict, we say that both goals have *positive valence,* meaning they are both desirable. The inability to decide, both in English and in psychology, is called *ambivalence,* meaning "both strong" or equally strong.

Avoidance-avoidance conflict: Between the devil and the deep blue sea Ambivalence is a more serious problem in the second kind of conflict. It is called *avoidance-avoidance* conflict because both goals have a negative valence, meaning both are undesir-

able or frightening and it seems impossible to avoid one without getting trapped by the other. This is the "out-of-the-frying-pan-into-the-fire" kind of conflict, also known as getting caught "between the devil and the deep blue sea." If you don't want to study this chapter, for instance, and you also don't want to fail the test your teacher might give on it, you have a double-avoidance conflict. It is more difficult to handle usually than a double-approach conflict because as you come close to one of the unwanted goals, the desire to avoid it grows stronger, pushing you back to an undecided state of mind. In a double-approach conflict, on the other hand, getting closer to one of the goals helps to resolve your indecision in its favor; since it is something you wanted in the first place, getting near it helps you forget how much you wanted the other goal.

The only happy resolution of double-avoidance conflicts is to *leave the field* and escape from both horns of the dilemma which creates the conflict. In everyday language, we try to find "a way out" of the conflict. If you don't want to study for the courses you enrolled in and don't want to fail the tests given in them, a "way out" may be to withdraw from the course. Another way may be to cheat on the tests. If you don't want to starve and don't want to work, a way out may be to find a rich (and maybe stupid) marriage partner—or a way of staying on welfare.

Unhappily, there are many real-life situations where it is impossible to leave the field, or where doing so may turn out even more miserably than staying in conflict. If you don't want to be fat, for instance, and you don't want to diet or to exercise a lot, you are just out of luck. There is no way you can leave the field; circumstances will force you to one alternative or the other, and you will end up either fat, hungry, or tired. Worse still, if you *remain* ambivalent about the alternatives, as often happens in such dilemmas, and waver back and forth between them, you may end up fat, hungry, *and* tired!

Approach-avoidance conflict: To eat but not work Stated differently, the diet-problem represents the third and most difficult of all conflicts, *approach-avoidance* conflict. In this situation, the same goal has both a positive and negative valence, that is, it is appealing in some respects and repulsive in others. If you want to eat a lot, but don't want to get fat, you have an approach-avoidance conflict. If you want to become a surgeon because of the money and prestige involved, but you can't stand the sight of blood, you have an approach-avoidance conflict. So too if you want to marry the boss's daughter to gain advancement in the company but you can't stand the sight of her. Or want to pursue the campus queen but fear being rejected by her. Or want to be a lawyer but not to spend years studying law. And on and on. Any choice situation in which there are positive and negative sides to the same goal in balance is an approach-avoidance conflict.

What makes it so hard to resolve approach-avoidance conflicts is that they promote endless ambivalence. Since both the appeal and the revulsion revolve around the same object, there is no way to satisfy one side of the conflict without intensifying the other. As you come close to the goal, both sentiments increase at the same time. Even worse, as you get very close to it, the revulsion generally increases faster than the appeal, which tends to make you retreat from it again. Ambivalence is stronger and more enduring in approach-avoidance conflicts than in any others. And unlike the others, there is no way to resolve it neatly.

In practice, it turns out that the only way approach-avoidance conflicts really get resolved is by *acting* on one or the other side of the ambivalence and paying the price of anxiety or unhappiness that is caused by doing so. If the course you choose has some rewards, eventually the bad feelings tend to dissipate. Once you become a lawyer, the travail, or boredom, of studying law tends to be forgotten, especially if you enjoy the work. Anxiety over the sight of blood eventually diminishes if you force yourself to study surgery (that happens, incidentally, whether or not you like the work). It is not always so simple, however. If you pursue the campus queen and are successful, you may feel twice repaid for the anxiety you suffered. But if you fail, the conflict will probably be even worse the next time you face a similar situation. And in some situations, the conflict gets sustained by short-term rewards and punishments that drive you back into the ambivalent position. Sticking to a reducing diet is not so easy, for instance, because the appeal of fattening foods and the pangs of hunger may overwhelm you periodically, restoring the conflict in full force.

The main virtue of trying *to act* in approach-avoidance conflicts is not so much that the conflict is likely to be resolved favorably as that the ambivalence of the conflict itself is likely to be as distressing as the results of most action—and it is almost sure to last longer.

HUMAN ADJUSTMENT: SOCIAL LEARNING AND SELF-DISCOVERY

If adjustment is defined as all efforts to cope with the stresses of living, all the stresses of living, in turn, could be defined as irritations, or stimulations, or tensions. You need to adjust yourself to something only if it has gotten you riled up in the first place. In that sense, adjustment means the reduction of tension. But most *motivation,* as we saw in Chapter 7, is the effort to reduce tensions. That's right. So we can define adjustment as the satisfaction of motives and motivation (for the most part) as the effort to adjust. It comes out to mean the same thing. When needs arouse tensions, adjustive demands are placed on you. The success of your efforts to meet those needs and reduce those tensions is the measure of how well you have adjusted.

Threat, frustration, and conflict are all basic adjustment problems. When you feel the stress of your needs not being met, you feel threatened. When your efforts to meet your needs are blocked, you are frustrated. And you are in conflict when, *no matter what you do,* one of your needs will go unsatisfied. Each kind of problem occurs to animals as well as people. In fact, the different types of conflict have all been demonstrated in lower animals, such as rats (Miller 1948).

Even so, the adaptation problems of lower organisms are far simpler than the adjustment problems of human beings. We have more conflicts than other animals because being human gives us a huge variety of response capacities which lower animals do not have. We can *choose* between more different alternatives.

Even at very primitive levels of functioning, our adaptive capacity is bigger than that of other animals. We have a broader range of sensory abilities, we have more diffuse and time-less sex drives, we have more complex perceptual systems, and so on. These abilities vastly increase the number of adjustments we can make and the number we must make. A rule governs the evolution of adjustive abilities: *the more you can choose, the more choices you must make.*

Since we have thought and language, moreover, our choices become infinitely great and endless trouble—because we can *invent* choices as well as *select* among alternatives in the outside world. We can fantasize possibilities, make fictional choices, and imagine contradictions. Language and thought also create culture, which is an entire new environment, and personality, a whole new set of adjustment patterns for dealing with it.

In fact, humans have changed the whole evolutionary adaptation game by fighting the stress of changing environments in a previously unknown way—we create *counter*environments to serve our special needs! The prehistoric invention of clothing and agriculture and the discovery of the practical uses of fire were all means of bringing warmth and food *to* us instead of having to move us to them. Now, air-conditioning and rapid travel and a huge technology reshapes the external environment, adjusting *it* to *us,* instead of vice versa. The next step, already started in genetic engineering experiments, may be the restructuring of our bodies by design instead of by evolutionary accident. The ability to adjust the environment to human needs makes it reasonable to judge the quality of a whole civilization, or the state of adjustment of a whole society, in terms of how much it is devoted to improving the lives of its citizens. Modern societies are capable of doing that, which has led some scholars to speak of them as more or less "sane" according to how much they strive towards that goal (Fromm 1956).

In any case, problems of human adjustment do not stop with basic biological needs—for which we will use the term *adaptation* exclusively from now on—but go on into the special needs entailed in being human. Needs for food, water, air, and so forth, are about the same for people and animals, and the frustrations and conflicts surrounding these "primary drives" are about the same as well. It is the threat to the satisfaction of our "secondary drives," that is, to our social and interpersonal needs, that creates the special adjustment difficulties of human beings. These too have their hierarchies of importance, you recall (see Chapters 7 and 14), starting with the need for love and nurturance and advancing to higher order needs to find meaning in life and to fulfill one's potential for valuable experience. At all levels, the values attached to these needs are learned from other people and **internalized** by the child, becoming part of the **sense of self.** It is the key to most of the satisfactions, and most of the adjustment problems, of the rest of life.

The growth of adjustive patterns

The first few years of life are the most important in the growth of adjustive patterns, and the interactions of children with parents are the most critical ones that take place in those years. We tend to rely our whole lives on the adjustive patterns we acquire in early childhood.

Culture and adjustment patterns Many of the adjustment patterns which children learn, both by explicit instruction and by imitation of their elders, reflect the attributes of the culture in which they are reared rather than just the personal traits of parents or teachers. This is why we develop *cultural stereotypes* about people and talk about *national character*— because different cultures and even different subcultures within a larger society foster some different behavior patterns in their children. Italians tend to be openly emotional, for instance, while the English are more reserved in their public behavior. In both cultures, children get reinforced and rewarded for adopting the

behavior of adults and get punished or ignored for failing to. So little Italian children are emotional and outgoing and rowdy, while little British children are publicly well-mannered and sort of shy. Not all of either group acts just that way, but enough do for the cultural tendency to be widely noticed.

Psychoanalysis and social learning Culture works through individuals, of course, and the values of a culture are transmitted to children primarily by their parents, along with the special features of personality which differ from one family to another. Parent-child interactions are the main area from which *individual* adjustment patterns develop. This is why psychoanalytic and social learning theories of personality both focus on the study of child development. They share a common perspective on motivation and on individual adjustment. They are in basic agreement about (1) the nature of motivation, (2) the importance of social learning in the development of adjustive patterns, (3) the role of threat and anxiety in placing adjustive demands on the individual, and (4) the importance of a person's self-concept, self-esteem, conscience, and image of their ideal self in developing satisfying adjustments. The theories differ in some important ways too. Psychoanalytic theory stresses childhood experience and psychosexual development in the origins of adjustive patterns and emphasizes symbolic adjustments, especially the **ego-defense mechanisms.** Learning theory tends to emphasize more the recent past in the perpetuation of adjustment patterns, and also tends to see adjustive patterns in terms of habits more than of symbolically meaningful events.

Social learning theory has contributed most to understanding adjustment by analyses of the role which learning plays in its development. In general, conditioning and imitation play the same roles in learning adjustment as they do in developing the rest of your personality. Classical conditioning is the basis for learning emotional adjustments; instrumental conditioning is the

British pre-adult persons practicing national character.

basis for learning most other adjustive behavior, especially skills and habits. Observation-imitation is a short-cutting process for instrumental learning. All learning largely depends on reinforcement; so it is correct to say that all our patterns of adjustment are largely a result of our *reinforcement history.*

Psychoanalytic theory offers a much more global and colorful description of personality development, part of which is already familiar to you in the psychosexual stages of personality development (see Chapter 14). Another part, more important to the growth of self-consciousness and the adjustment mechanisms connected with it, is the psychoanalytic theory of *id, ego,* and *superego.*

The psychoanalytic theory of self: War inside your head

At birth, says Freud, an infant has no awareness of itself as a creature distinct and separate from the rest of the world. All it "knows" is the feeling of comfort and discomfort. When it feels discomfort, it gets aroused and irritated until it is gone. This primitive capacity for arousal Freud named the *id.* He meant by it the repository of instinctive urges, such as hunger, thirst, warmth, and later on, sex and aggression, which demand immediate gratification in all animals. In humans, he believed, this "energy pool" provides the basis for infantile dreams and fantasies from which logical and realistic thought eventually grows.

As language and thought develop, Freud argued, the infant gradually becomes capable of distinguishing between itself and the world around it. It begins to recognize its separateness from other objects, and to discover that its needs can be met by negotiation with the world around it, which requires controlling its impulses. This all starts at the end of the oral stage. Hopefully, it never stops. Freud called the process of negotiation and control the development of *ego,* or *self.* The ego is the portion of personality that governs one's realistic, rational behavior, trying to get the most pleasure out of life at the least cost. The ego, in other words, controls adjustment, partly by curbing the id, partly by changing the outside world so its impulses can be gratified.

Ego is the sense of reality, including the awareness of self. As it grows, however, the child also develops a sense of morals and of ideals. The moral sense is **conscience.** The other sense, called **ego ideal,** is the feeling of wanting to be the kind of person who approves of themself. Together, conscience and ego ideal make up the **superego,** as Freud called it, which is part of the sense of self but has an evaluative, judgmental function over it.

To be happy with themselves, people have to strike some balance between the demands of their id, the demands of reality, and the demands of their superego. They have to have enough of their impulses gratified not to feel frustrated all the time, they have to do it without getting themselves killed or injured, and they

The Freudian theory of self or ego developing. The self or ego develops as the child becomes aware that its existence is separate from the rest of the world.

have to do it in a way that will allow them to feel, by and large, that they are nice persons. This is not easy. To the extent they can manage it, they develop a favorable **self-concept,** an image of themselves as lovable, worthwhile people. They then have high **self-esteem.**

There is a good-sized literature on "the self" and several different terms used for different aspects of it. The most popular ones, **self-concept** and **self-image,** both mean the way you see yourself; **self-esteem** means how much you like yourself or how highly you value yourself.

High self-esteem is just about the most valuable adjustment tool a person can have.[2] With it, you can enter new and tense situations without losing courage, you can face rejection in love and work without long depression or collapse, and you can sustain yourself in adversity by telling yourself that anyone so worthy cannot be meant to suffer long. People with low self-esteem tend to be defeated even before they start in new or difficult situations, because they are prone to feel hopeless in advance and defeated in restrospect.

Most of us have variable self-esteem in different things, just as our self-concepts vary in different situations. I may place high value on myself in interpersonal relations, think I am pretty inadequate intellectually, and feel that I am of middling worth as a worker. But in all situations, regardless of the initial value they assign themselves, people try to behave in ways which bolster their self-esteem. This is sometimes very hard to do, because our impulses, our moral sensibilities, and our opinions about what is realistic often conflict with each other. Such conflicts threaten self-esteem because it looks like there is no way out of them without either going unsatisfied (rejecting the id impulses), doing something wrong (rejecting the superego demands), or getting hurt (rejecting the ego). The result is **anxiety,** a feeling of fear-

---

[2] Good sense may be more valuable, but this is unproved.

fulness, even of dread. In psychoanalytic terms, we would say that the threat to self-esteem is a threat to the ego, which tries to balance the conflicting needs. There is no easy way to handle the conflict; so what the ego does (meaning what you do) is try to shield itself from the anxiety which the conflict causes. It does so by some remarkable methods by which we all lie to ourselves.

THE EGO DEFENSES: GAMES WE PLAY ON US

The ego combats anxiety through mechanisms of defense. There are many of them, but all share two important properties. First, they operate unconsciously; they are thrown into gear automatically by anxiety-provoking situations; so we become defensive without even knowing necessarily that we are feeling threatened. Second, these mechanisms neutralize the upsetting impact of threatening ideas by distorting reality. The defenses purchase comfort at the price of self-deception.

A defense is "effective" if it protects you from anxiety, but most of the time, most of us would be better off without them. For one thing, their distortion of reality makes it harder to combat stress than might be true if you could really tell what it was that was stressing you. For another, excessive reliance on them can result in the symptoms of neurosis, which are miserable in their own right.

But some capacity for defensiveness can be a good thing to have. When the stresses and strains of reality are so threatening to one's self-esteem that recognizing them would make life unbearable, you may need some ego defenses to shore up your morale. The use of defense mechanisms is universal, in any case, and whether a particular defense is helpful or harmful really depends on the circumstances in which you use it and the purpose it serves in your life.

It was through the psychoanalysis of various neuroses that the ego defense mechanisms were first conceived and described. Anna Freud, Sigmund's daughter, spelled out many of them in *The Ego and the Mechanisms of Defense* (1937), and many students of psychoanalysis, psychiatry, and the psychology of adjustment have identified others since. As a result, the number and definition of defenses varies among different authors. Here are some representative ones and some idea of how they work.

How defenses work: Making it go away

All the defenses are efforts to do away with things that threaten self-esteem. Some such threats occur in early childhood, when the child has barely learned to walk, or talk, or control bowel movements. Others happen later, when verbal taunts or personal rejections are more meaningful and the child's relationships more complicated than in the toddler years. Different kinds of defenses are learned at different stages of development. A child much threatened at an early age will master the defenses appropriate to that age and keep relying on them as it grows. If it was not threatened much in early life, it will rely more on defenses that it learns later. Either way, as it gets older and smarter, it pools the different mechanisms and, in most adult encounters, combines and uses several at once.

All ego defenses are designed to protect against, or ward off, some threat to our mental well-being, whether real or imagined.

The Night, Max Beckmann

434

The main difference between the earlier level and the later level defenses is that the former are more primitive. They are more **action-oriented** and less **verbal,** more massive and less subtle. The more primitive defenses, in other words, tend to be **regressive,** and the more mature ones **repressive.**

Regressive defenses

When a baby is frightened, it yells or cries or crawls away. When it expects to be frightened, it does about the same. The most primitive ego defenses are **withdrawal,** physically or in fantasy, or some other action intended to relieve the fear. Acting out childlish impulses, reverting to infantile modes of "harmlessness" or to endearing acts, such as baby talking (called **regression**), or getting sick (called **somatization**), are all efforts to **do something** that will prevent anxiety from bursting into consciousness. They are all things learned very early but which, in slightly altered form, can be kept up for a lifetime.

Withdrawal is sometimes a sensible course of action, but it is damaging when a challenging situation threatens your self-esteem so much that you withdraw into fantasy and solitude without even a modest risk of failure. In small children, it often takes a **negativistic** form in which they sharply refuse to try things and get mean and sassy if urged to do so. In adults, it is often accompanied by some kind of **rationalization** to the effect that the activity is not really interesting or engaging enough to be worth trying. Sometimes, indeed, the rationalization will be **overcompensatory,** such as: "It looks too easy to bother with," or "It's no challenge."

Fantasy, like **withdrawal,** is only a defense when used defensively, to obscure the anxiety that the person cannot afford to recognize over unfulfilled goals. Most fantasies, even when defensive, are pretty harmless; fantasies of fame, riches, sex, and what have you are all common and normal experiences. And fantasy is used creatively by some people to turn dreams into concrete achievement. But it can blend into the pathological process of **delusion** and **withdrawal** if a person comes to believe their fantasies on insufficient evidence or substitutes them for actual accomplishment.

Acting out refers to any aggressive, sexual, or self-damaging behavior performed as a means of reducing anxiety. "Acting out" is a defense mechanism, as opposed to simply "taking action," when it expresses an unconscious conflict rather than merely representing something a person wants to do—like the adolescent with hostility toward authority, who defaces the statue of a general. Or the guilt-ridden thief who bungles a crime in order to get caught. More commonly, acting out reduces tension by enabling a person to "blow off steam." It is in just that form that it is usually seen in small children, who sometimes block anxiety out through temper tantrums.

Compensation can be constructive when it propels a person to master skills or accomplish things that they might not otherwise do. It is defensive, however, because it is motivated by the need to "make up" for deficiencies which, unconsciously, make a person fear they are inferior. In small children, compensatory defenses often have a fantastic character, rather than a constructive one. In adults, the popular stereotype of compensation is the "97-pound weakling" on the beach who, after taking the Charles Atlas body-building course, becomes a "he-man," able to kick sand in other people's faces. Alfred Adler (1870–1930), a student of Freud's, built his whole theory of neurosis around the idea that most human striving is an effort to compensate for the terrible inferiority of infancy. He later held that the best expression of compensation was interest in the common social good (Adler 1929).

One of the most common compensatory acts among children is **regression** itself, that is, a returning to early, immature kinds of gratifying behavior. One familiar place to see it is in a family where a second child is born. The first child, suddenly dethroned as the sole object of parental attention and affection, may revert to baby talk and action long since outgrown. The throwback is motivated by anxiety over the apparent loss of parental love. Returning to babyhood is a defensive effort to restore No. 1 child's position in the family and with it, its confidence.

Regression is not used much by adults because it is so gross that it would not reduce your anxiety in the first place and would not be reinforced by other people in the second. Often, however, when you are depressed or disappointed, you may find yourself sleeping excessively, craving sweets more than usual, or doing other things that are regressive efforts to make yourself feel better in ways that may have worked very well in your childhood.

There is a nondefensive kind of regression also, called "regression in the service of the ego." It refers to the kind of situation in which artists fall back on childhood fantasies to find inspiration for their creative efforts, or scientists go to bed with their problems unsolved and find that somehow, in the course of their dreams, the answers turn up (Hartmann 1950).

Perhaps the most popular regressive defense is simply getting sick, feeling bad physically to ward off anxiety. Technically, this is called *somatization.* In more or less persistent form, somatization neuroses are called **neurasthenia** (thinking you are sick all the time when you are not). A very extreme tendency to somatization can give rise to **conversion hysteria,** in which a person may actually be paralyzed, or blind, or whatever, without any organic damage (see

Hypochondriacs enjoy the care and attention from others brought on by their complaints of illness.

The Sick Lady, Jan Steen

436

Chapter 18). Conversion hysteria is rare in the United States, but somatization is not. The small child who has a stomach-ache on the day of a school test it is not ready for, or you with the same symptom under the same circumstances, are somatizing.

Repressive defenses

Repression is the general term for keeping things out of consciousness, and is also the specific term for one kind of defense, namely "forgetting" unpleasant thoughts, feelings, and experiences. In its more general sense, repression is the master defense mechanism. It is the first one Freud proposed, and it gave him the key to psychoanalytic theory. In fact, he argued that all the defense mechanisms are outgrowths of repression in that their aim is to prevent the eruption of repressed material into consciousness.

In its narrower sense, *repression* refers to the inhibition of memory, that is, to an active process in which people selectively forget things which would be anxiety-provoking to recall (see Chapter 10). They push them "into unconsciousness," so to speak, and are unaware of them, even though the memory is perfectly clear to other people. Everyone represses some things; you may have noticed how, for instance, long-time friends could not recall some old incident in which they had once been very embarrassed, try as you might to remind them. Traumatic experiences of childhood are often repressed, and so are many of the most painful experiences of adulthood, physical and mental. People don't remember the physical pain of accidents, or of giving birth, and if, in childhood, you were frightened badly in an accident, or by an embarrassing public spanking which your family recounts forever after, you may not even remember that the episode occurred.

Some of the most interesting events of psychotherapy occur in uncovering repressed material, as Freud first found out. It can come up in an emotional explosion, called "abreaction" or "catharsis," which may itself be frightening and is always surprising when it happens to you.

Repression is a more mature defense than the earlier ones because it arises after verbal and memory skills are already well developed. There is a primitive kind of repression, however, in which the mechanism is not selective forgetting but blanket *denial* of any negative feelings at all. It differs from repression mainly by being more massive and more naive. If you question the feelings of someone about to take their first parachute jump and they deny being frightened, or someone screaming at his wife, who denies being angry, you will probably conclude either that they are big liars or very defensive. The only difference is that in the first case, they are lying to you, and in the second, to themselves. Lying to oneself is the essence of defensiveness.

Talking it away: Verbal defenses Repression and denial mechanisms both work by "not noticing" things which would arouse anxiety. Some of their offshoots are more sophisticated in that they make use of verbal and intellectual skills to aid the defensive maneuvers. They aid repression by "talking away" the anxiety stimuli as well as by other means of obscuring and retreating from reality. *Insulation, isolation, rationalization,* and *intellectualization,* are among the many variants of these defensive manipulations.

Emotional insulation is perhaps closer to repression and denial than the others in this group. It is the process by which a person reduces emotional involvement in painful situations; in other words, they cut off their feelings, and keep a "cool" pose all the time. Professional diplomats have to do that as a matter of course in order to conduct their negotiations effectively. When you do it while a boy or girl friend is explaining that they are not going to date you any more, it defends you against the anxiety that feeling rejected would create. Some people stay

Verbal defenses.

insulated all the time, stuck in their cool pose, even in an emotional block of ice. They avoid the anxiety of rejection that way, but it also closes them off to affection and intimacy.

Isolation is a variant of insulation, in which a person separates their contradictory feelings and ideals to avoid the anxiety that would come from exposing their hypocrisy. The churchgoing storeowner who gouges his ghetto customers with inflated prices and interest payments, or the lascivious judge who passes harshest sentence on sex offenders, both maintain their equilibrium by compartmentalizing these contradictory aspects of their lives, isolating them from each other and the contradiction from consciousness.

Rationalization and *intellectualization* are more explicit means of "talking away" anxiety. *Intellectualization* is simply an intellectual form of insulation, in which you cool off an anxious situation by "talking it up" in abstract generalities which make it distant and impersonal. Intellectualizers tend to talk in very complicated sentences. Putting things plainly and directly frightens them; so they control anxiety by dressing up their thoughts and speech in complicated, circuitous ways.

Rationalization is the invention of fictitious but acceptable reasons for your irrational, immoral, or inept behavior and attitudes. It means, in short, making excuses for yourself. One common way people do this is by making a virtue of necessity—"I'm so lucky not to have a big thriving business; this way I avoid all the ulcers and headaches and heart attacks big executives get." Another common form of rationalization is the "sour grapes" phenomenon from Aesop's fable about a fox who could not reach the ripe grapes nailed to a trellis above it and finally decided they were green and sour and not worth having. Rationalization is probably the easiest to recognize of all the verbal defenses. It is a special case of *dissonance reduction* (Brehm and Cohen 1962; Festinger 1957), a process whereby a person reconciles conflicting attitudes and actions by forcing them to be consistent with each other (see Chapter 21).

Exorcism and expiation: Ritual defenses There are many defenses which combine the action of regressive mechanisms with the mental gymnastics of repression. *Obsessive-compulsive rituals, undoing,* and *reaction formation* are the main ones.

Obsessive-compulsive rituals often have an important verbal component, but they are really much more primitive defenses than rationalization or isolation. *Obsessions* are urgently repeated thoughts, and *compulsions* are urgent impulses to action. Obsessive-compulsive defenses are meaningless rituals that have to be repeated many times to keep the sufferer from being overwhelmed by anxiety. A person may have to repeat a jingle over and over in their head, straighten their tie whenever they enter a room, or wash their hands 63 times a day. Failure to perform the prescribed ritual makes them anxious, and doing it brings relief. These rituals are almost universal among children at some time—you may remember having to skip the cracks in the sidewalk or count telephone poles on the bus, and they are normally found in the "good luck" gestures of gamblers who blow on their dice. Only their anxiety-reducing function makes them defenses, and that is only a serious matter when it becomes extreme, giving rise to obsessional neuroses (see Chapter 18). Freudians usually interpret obsessive-compulsive behavior as symbolic of underlying conflict or guilt; a symptom such as repetitive hand-washing is seen as a symbolic effort to "undo" the guilt-arousing thought of doing some "filthy" thing. Obsessive-compulsive traits are useful in many occupations when they take the benign form of attention to detail, punctuality, and orderliness.

Ritual acts are not the only form that *undoing* defenses take. *Undoing* refers to any unconscious guilt-inspired attempt to atone for the damage done by one's misdeeds. For instance, if a child felt that its "bad" thoughts or behavior were to blame for the death of a parent, it might strive singlemindedly to become a doctor. On a more common level, we strive to be especially nice to someone we have inadvertently slighted. Religious rites for the expiation of sins are examples of undoing. Compensation may also be a form of undoing; so may reaction formation.

Reaction formation is exaggerated action or concern in the opposite direction from one's underlying motives. Small children who are murderously jealous at the birth of younger siblings sometimes show an exaggerated preoccupation with protecting them. Alcoholics "on the wagon" may go out of their way to denounce drink. People who get rejected in love may decide they really hated their paramours all along. St. Augustine, once he gave up sex and sin, spoke violently against them. Mothers who covertly reject their children may become smotheringly controlling and overprotective of them. Reaction formation differs from isolation because here the person is not being hypocritical, but really has abandoned the behavior they are reacting against. In isolation, the unacceptable impulse is momentarily laid aside; in reaction-formation, it is abandoned. The isolator is a hypocrite; the reaction former is a fanatic.

They are not necessarily self-righteous, however. They may compensate or undo their sins by another defense, *turning against the self,* that is, accepting guilt and blaming themselves for everything bad. In extreme form, this defense

Clara Barton gave up a comfortable life to devote herself to a life of service.

Clara Barton Raising the Flag, August 17, 1865 Sketched by I. C. Schotel

may lead to depression, self-punishing acts, or even suicide.

Reaction-formation and undoing can work in a constructive direction too, propelling people into great busyness at work or play; the frantic activity blocks out feelings of anxiety. This defense is sometimes called "flight into reality" or "flight into health." In mild form, it may be constructive. In extreme form, it becomes a *manic* disorder, which can be quite destructive (see Chapter 18).

Substitutive defenses: Displacement and sublimation Reaction-formation has an element of compensation or substitution in it; an anxiety-provoking attitude or act is buried and its opposite carried out instead. Two of the most important defenses, sublimation and displacement, function entirely by substitution, reducing anxiety by substituting new goals for those originally sought.

Sublimation is a special case of substitution in which the substitute goals are more socially useful than the original goals. For instance, a nun may sublimate her unfulfilled maternal drives by becoming a teacher or nurse. Sublimation is a relatively desirable defense, but some forms of it may still cause trouble. A person who sublimates hostile impulses by becoming a soldier or a surgeon may abuse the role under the influence of this unconscious motivation. For Freud, sublimation was the basis for all altruistic motivation, and most civilized behavior. He held that all such "exalted" motives are derivatives of sexual or aggressive drives.

Displacement is the transfer of feelings or actions from their original object to a less frightening one. The objects may be animal, vegetable, body part, or relative. If someone is very concerned about their mouth, for instance, they may be displacing worries about their genital organs (Menninger 1947). "Scapegoating" is a kind of displacement in which you blame helpless people for failings that you are afraid to blame powerful villains for. The most

Three Witches Hanging

Witch hunting, another word for scapegoating, was especially popular after crop failures and other natural disasters.

common displacement occurs where anger is aroused by a parent or authority figure and "taken out" on a weaker person, an animal, or helpless object. Bosses yelling at their secretaries when they are angry at their wives is that kind of thing. Displacement of aggression occurs among animals as well as people. Miller (1948) trained two rats to attack each other in order to turn off an electric shock in their cage. When one of the rats was taken out, the other one attacked the rubber doll that was put in the cage.

Identity and defense: The growth defenses
Several defenses differ from the rest by being vital processes in personality growth; their defensive aspect, though sometimes quite damaging, is less important than the service they provide in socialization. The main process here is *Identification,* and its corollaries, *introjection* and *projection.*

Identification, you recall, is a process in which one person believes themselves to be like another, experiences the other's successes and defeats as their own, and models their own behavior after the others. Freud held that the child normally resolves oedipal conflicts by repressing desire for the parent of the opposite sex and identifying with the same-sex parent. From then on, he thought, the child emulates the same-sex parent and adopts his or her sex roles, ambitions, and ideals. We have discussed this process in some detail in Chapter 14 as an important form of learning by observation and imitation. What is interesting about Freud's theory is that he believed that normal identification *originates* as a defensive process. The little boy hopes to reduce papa's anger at him for lusting after mamma, and simultaneously to curry papa's favor, by being like papa. What starts as mere defense thus becomes a key to personality formation.

Identification gives rise to two mechanisms,

introjection and *projection.* In introjection, you adopt and internalize the beliefs, attitudes, and behavior patterns of others. In projection, you attribute your own beliefs, attitudes, and characteristics to them. The small boy, for instance, identifying with papa, introjects papa's mannerisms, walks like him, talks like him, plays at smoking his pipe, and tells himself that he is strong and wise, like papa. At the same time, he projects his own fantasies and feelings, good and bad, onto papa, and onto other people—figuring that they too know about the bogeyman, that they may really die if he gets uncontrollably angry at them, and that they sometimes feel the soft tender lovingness for him that he does for them. From these alternations and interactions of introjections and projections, he learns a style of facing the world and whatever capacity for empathy and reciprocity with other people that he is going to have.

As defenses, however, both in childhood and adult life, introjection and projection can be devastating. Introjection generally means adopting the beliefs or attitudes of powerful figures after an initial period of resistance to them. It works by helping you to avoid anxiety over how much they can hurt you. Prisoners in Nazi concentration camps sometimes displayed the same brutality, and even the same mannerisms, as their guards toward other prisoners. And survivors sometimes reported that they dreaded those turncoat comrades even more than the Nazis themselves. This kind of introjection is called "identification with the aggressor."

Projection as a defense means the attribution of one's own unacceptable traits to other people. A person with unconscious homosexual impulses, for instance, might think others are making subtle homosexual advances towards them. Sometimes the term *projection* is used to describe scapegoating. By projecting one's own hostility onto others and accusing them of being hostile, a person may "justify"

aggressive impulses against them; this occurs often in racial or religious prejudice and in some international tensions that lead to wars. Projection is one of the most destructive defenses, but one form of it, *idealization,* is an important basis of romantic love. *Idealization* is the attribution of *desirable* traits to another person. It is a defense because you use it to hide from yourself those faults in others which might make you anxious. The person who is idealized often cooperates in maintaining their admirer's impression; sometimes they exploit it.

Paranoid defenses are commonly based on projection. They involve unwarranted feelings of personal importance or the false belief that others are hostile. Paranoid symptoms severe enough to produce gross distortions of reality are called *delusions.* Delusions are false beliefs which resist all argument or evidence. A *delusional system* is a set of interlocking false beliefs. "Delusions of grandeur" and "delusions of persecution," tend to make the believer feel more important or to rationalize their failures. Persecutory ideas may result from *projecting* one's own hostility onto others; the idea that one is important then helps to rationalize why others may be "out to get" them. Freud thought that paranoid thinking was a defense against latent (unconscious) homosexuality. To control repressed homosexual impulses, a person may come to believe that they are hated by others of the same sex, thus building a self-protective wall of hostility.

Self-protection: The function of defense

In most situations, people would be better off without ego-defenses, because their function, no matter how politely stated, is really to distort reality so that we do not have to face unpleasant truths about our own feelings and motives or those of other people towards us. But most of us do not always have sufficiently high regard for our own value as human beings to accept the fact that we are imperfect creatures and to face ourselves humbly and honestly. If we could do so, then we would have an easier time improving ourselves so that we would then have more choice about how to carry on relationships with other people. If we were more complete in self-understanding, we would feel more able to confront other people honestly — or to lie to them more effectively if we felt that were necessary. As it is, we are what we are, usually by a pretty early age, and most of us spend more energy cushioning our imperfections than we do facing them and changing them. By the time you are old enough to read a book like this, you are probably deeply entrenched in whatever ego defenses you have learned throughout childhood and early adolescence. They make up a large, and unfortunate, part of your "personality style."

The ego-defenses help make it possible for you to muddle your way through your own anxieties only by lying to yourself or hiding from yourself. They never make you happy, in a positive sense, but they can prevent you from feeling as miserably frightened as you otherwise might. For some people, that must be considered a relatively satisfactory life arrangement because their underlying perception of the world is so terrifying that it would be too hard for them to get along without these unconscious props. For them, self-deception is the price they must pay for a tolerable adjustment to life. For others, even that price is not enough, and they must suffer from continuing maladjustments. When those become serious enough, they are given the formal label of "behavior-disorders," "psychopathology," or "mental illness." We shall spend Chapter 18 discussing them.

The basic problems of adjustment, in any case, arise from the stresses to which we are subjected by both the external environment and the conflicts we experience over our motives and desires. The way we respond to them depends largely on the skills we have developed at problem-solving and on our good opinions of ourselves, which depend in turn on our reinforcement histories. When the problems that face us threaten our self-esteem, we may respond to them with the self-deceptive mental tricks which Freud called "ego-defense mechanisms."

This chapter discussed the general framework of the adjustment process, and some of the mechanisms commonly used to help it run smoothly. Now we turn to survey some of the areas where people face their most serious adjustment crises and must resolve them as best they can. These are the areas of *love* and *work,* which consume most of the energies of adult life and which start to preoccupy most people for the first time in adolescence.

SUMMARY

1 *Adjustive* processes include all behavior which tries to solve the problems of living. The successful effort to live and obtain satisfaction is called *adaptation.* Everything which makes adaptation difficult is called *stress. Ecology* studies the contemporary balances of stress and adaptation among living things; *evolution* studies their historical successes and failures at adapting to changing stresses.

2 The most primitive forms of life experience stress as irritation; creatures with more advanced nervous systems experience it as *alarm.* Alarm is followed by efforts at *stress-resistance.* If these fail, then *exhaustion* follows and eventually, death. The sequence of alarm-resistance-exhaustion is called the *general-adaptation syndrome.*

3 Two important kinds of stress result from the fact that animals move about and have goals—*frustration* and *conflict.* Frustration exists when some *block* stands between you and your goal. Conflict exists when you cannot choose among different goals. Both states arouse tension. Frustration is felt largely as anger; conflict is felt more as indecision. Frustration is a more elementary evolutionary problem; conflict is more complicated because it requires the ability to attend to two goals at once.

4 Frustration can be dealt with in three ways: (1) *circumventing* the block, i.e., going around it to reach the goal; (2) *attacking* the block, i.e., removing it or going through it to the goal; and (3) *withdrawing,* i.e., giving up the goal and seeking a new one.

5 There are three kinds of conflict: (1) *approach-approach* conflict, where both goals are desirable, but you cannot get one without losing the other; (2) *avoidance-avoidance* conflict, where both goals are unwanted, but it seems impossible to escape one without getting trapped by the other; and (3) *approach-avoidance* conflict, where the same goal attracts you in some ways and repulses you in others. Approach-approach conflicts are the easiest to resolve, because moving towards one of the goals tends to make it more attractive, which helps you forget the attractions of the other one. Avoidance-avoidance conflicts can only be resolved by leaving the field, that is, by escaping from the situation altogether. Approach-avoidance conflicts are the hardest of all to handle because they arouse the most *ambivalence,* i.e., vacillation between moving towards and away from the goal.

6 Humans have greater problems of adaptation and adjustment than other creatures because our enormous response-capacities give us so many alternatives to choose from. But they make us capable of better adjustments as well. In fact, we have reversed the evolutionary pattern of stress and adaptation by creating environments to suit our needs instead of adapting to the environments which nature puts us in. The chief instrument of this invention is culture, and the chief training agent for individual adjustment within it is the family.

7 The psychoanalytic theory of *id, ego,* and *superego* gives a better picture of the development of adjustment patterns than other theories do. The id is the newborn infant's capacity for arousal by such basic urges as hunger, thirst, and discomfort. It demands immediate satisfaction, and stirs up infantile dreams and fantasies when not gratified instantly. Those reactions are the basis from which the *ego,* or self, develops. Ego includes all the processes of realistic thinking, in which the child recognizes its separateness from the rest of the world and develops language and logical thought. From the ego, conscience and a sense of ideals develop; their content depends on the reinforcements and models his parents provide. Together, conscience and ideals make the *superego,* so called because it evaluates and judges the self.

8 To be happy with one-self, a person must have a favorable *self-concept,* also called *self-esteem,* which means one must see one's-self as a worthwhile person. In psychoanalytic terms, this means you must balance the demands of your id impulses against the restrictions of your conscience without damaging your ability to function in the world. The threat to this balance is called *ego-anxiety.*

9 The ego has a number of ways to protect itself against threats to self-esteem, called *ego-defenses.* They are mechanisms for distorting a person's perception of reality so that they will not feel threatened. Anna Freud, who developed the theory of ego-defenses, accepted her father's idea that *repression* is the basic defense, and that all the others are variations of it. Repression means forcing anxiety-provoking thoughts out of consciousness. The uncovering of repression is the basic activity of psychoanalytic treatment of emotional disorders.

10 Some ego defenses manifest themselves mainly in distorting people's *thinking;* others are manifested chiefly in disruptions of their *overt behavior.* Some of the most common thought defenses are *rationalization,* the invention of fictitious reasons for your irrational, immoral or inept behavior; *displacement,* the transfer of feelings or actions from their original anxiety-provoking object to a less frightening one; *projection,* attributing your own unacceptable impulses to other people; and *denial,* refusing to recognize negative feelings about yourself or something you value. Some of the most common action defenses are *regression,* returning to early, immature modes of behavior; *acting out,* doing aggressive, sexual, or self-destructive acts in the effort to reduce anxiety; and *reaction-formation,* exaggerated action or attitudes in just the opposite direction from one's genuine feelings.

Personal psychology: One-sex and popularity

16

16

Personal psychology: One-sex and popularity

Have you ever thought of committing suicide? Have you ever tried it, planned to try it, thought of planning to try it? Or have you not been that explicit with yourself in moments of despair and loneliness, but simply thought: "Life is a painful, sad, and bitter burden—better not to have to bear it." If so, you are not alone in those thoughts. Suicide is the second biggest cause of death today among American college students (Cantor 1976). And that is only *known* suicide. The first cause of death is auto accidents, and who knows how many of them may come from suicidal carelessness or indifference (National Safety Council 1972)? The same is true of death from overdose of drugs, and perhaps from other causes that look accidental, or heroic, like death in combat.

Late adolescence and young adulthood are, in many ways, the most exciting times in people's lives—when their minds and bodies become adult, and they are not yet saddled with adult responsibility or locked into adult life-styles. It is the time when growth and groping of every kind, about the world, about one's self, and about the relations between them can be pursued most sensitively and energetically. This is the period when psychology and its meaning for one's own life becomes a matter of greatest personal interest. This chapter examines some of the technical topics of that interest and their personal implications for people's lives.

SELF-AWARENESS AND EXISTENTIAL CRISIS: WHO SHALL I BE WHEN I GROW UP?

Babies do not have self-consciousnes—looking at its fingers, the infant does not associate them with itself; they are just another interesting object, like its rattle. Self-consciousness comes with body consciousness, and that develops in childhood. In experiments where they ask kids, "Where is Johnny?" the child

Self-consciousness comes with body
consciousness.

points to different places at different ages—
finally, to its head, or to the center line of its
body (Murphy 1947).

Gradually, the child begins to think of its
body as something it *has* instead of simply
taking it, and its own existence, for granted.
At around that time, children start using personal
pronouns, referring to the self as "I" where they
previously called themself only by name. They
are starting to perceive themself as an entity, a
thing which is separate and distinct from the rest
of the world, even somewhat distinct from their
own physical parts. The thing is their self,
their I, their ego.

Ego is the Latin word for "self." Self really
means self-consciousness, that is, our own

awareness of what we are really like, how we
really feel, who we really are. This awareness
grows slowly from childhood on. It develops
with language, and with increasing skill and
control in the use of our mental and physical
abilities. In a well-developed, well-adjusted
person, the sense of self probably continues
to grow throughout life because experience
and memory enrich the knowledge of who one
is long after skills have passed their peak of
development. Old people have history. In most
animals, a sense of self may not develop
because, lacking the capacity for language,
they probably cannot use their imaginations
and physical skills to understand themselves
in a way that can be remembered or communi-

cated. Some primates, especially chimpanzees, are a notable exception. Alone among all other animal species except our own, they can recognize themselves in a mirror and use it for grooming and for self-inspection. Other animals react to mirrors as if they were seeing someone else, and then engage in the social behavior typical in their species for such interpersonal situations (Gallup 1977).

In adolescence (roughly from puberty until around 20), the sense of self is at its most painful, and it is in that period of life that the term "self-consciousness" has the unhappy connotations of awkward, ill at ease, embarrassed, and pretentious. It is not certain why adolescence is such an era of self-consciousness in Western society. In some cultures, adolescence is a relatively painless and happy period (Mead 1935). The pangs of adolescence are probably becoming milder in our society, too, but at the present time, it is still an awkward age.

The ordinary self-consciousnes of adolescence probably results from the fact that rapid life changes are taking place, mentally and physically, and new social situations, opportunities, and risks are opened up by the development of sexuality and of career interests.

With adolescence comes a growing self-consciousness. How do I look? How do I smell? Hours are spent at the mirror.

Girl before a Mirror, Pablo Picasso

Adolescence is the era of self-consciousness.

The business of children is play, but the business of adults, in our society, has traditionally been love and work. Adolescence is an introduction to them, and the awakening is often painful.

Above and beyond the normal stresses and strains of this growth period, however, there is an internal force at work in everyone that tends to keep them from experiencing themself fully — it is the tendency we discussed in the last chapter to defend oneself against anxiety, especially the anxiety connected with our self-esteem. The more one is defended against the recognition of their fears, their weaknesses, and their faults, the less capable they are of recognizing where their true strengths lie and of correcting their failings or compensating for them. Most important, the more defended a per-

son is, the less capable they are of realistically appreciating and liking themself because the less capable they are of knowing themself.

If a person is extremely defended, the bad results for their life can become like a row of dominoes. If I do not know who I am, or what I am like, it is hard for me to know what I want, or why, or who I want to be with, or what I want to do with my life. People who do not know how they feel in emotional situations or relationships — people who are vaguely restless or very unhappy with their jobs or careers, but do not know why they are dissatisfied or what they would prefer doing — people who are unhappy with their lovers or wives or roommates but cannot specify the source of the unhappiness, or cannot get relief from it by taking up with other people — all these suffer in large measure, probably, from not knowing their own selves. And their ignorance usually comes from years of indulging themselves in defending against anxiety and closing themselves up instead of experiencing reality inside and outside their heads.

There is no sure-fire formula for being open and undefended, but it is usually a pretty simple matter to see what arouses anxiety in yourself and to observe how you go about defending against it. Then it is a matter of finding the courage to let down the defenses, always a frightening experience because letting down defenses means letting in anxiety. In the long run, however, doing so opens up the doors of self perception in a way that can make your life richer and more fulfilling than it could otherwise be.

Being fully self-conscious is not an abstract goal. Nor does it mean being aware of yourself only in a special setting, like an encounter group, or a church service, or when viewing a glorious sunset and being glad you are alive — though all those may be grand experiences that are enriched by self-awareness while you are having them. To be most valuable, self-awareness is something that must be *a routine part of everyday living,* in work, in love, and at play. There is no real understanding of it except in those contexts; so discussing it in depth means discussing it in connection with those categories of experience. It is in them that you live your life.

Existential crisis

In most crises, a person is threatened by *circumstances,* such as illness, accident, or other acts of God. An *existential crisis* is one where the *meaning* of their existence is threatened rather than their *physical state* of existence (May 1961). Existential crises are always connected with choices that one must make. Deciding whether to marry a certain person, or follow a certain career, or have children, are

all existential problems because our solutions to them express the meaning we think these problems have in our total lives. Existential problems become existential crises most often when there are painful decisions to be made, especially decisions to *change* the pattern of our lives. Whether to divorce one's spouse and abandon an apparently happy family, to break up with a lover who would be hurt by the separation, to leave a successful career because it no longer seems meaningful to pursue it, to end one's own life because it does not feel worthwhile anymore — these are all existential crises.

The existential crises of adolescence and early adulthood are not always taken very seriously because the tremendous energy and resilience of young people often lets them muddle through crises unscathed by their sometimes idiotic choices and misjudgments. Even so, the existential crises of youth are very real and very many — revolving around the meanings of sex, love, marriage, and family, of work, success, achievement, and accomplishment, and of citizenship, the meaning of membership in society, and the obligations of people to each other. Resisting war, or joining the army, refraining from sex, or indulging freely, and with the opposite sex only, or with one's own as well, dropping out of the larger society to experiment with Utopia, or religion, taking drugs or not, are all existential problems common among young people.

The big existential question, "what does it all mean?" almost never turns into an existential crisis, if it gets asked at all, unless a person is having big troubles. Happiness and contentment do not turn most of us into philosophers. The stress of having to make important and difficult decisions or the distress of having things go badly in one's life is most likely to set them thinking about whether the struggle is worth the effort. There is no single answer equally acceptable to everyone.

The great risk of self-consciousness is that,

Whence Come We? What Are We? Whither Go We? (details), Paul Gauguin
Adolescence is traditionally a painless and happy period in the South Seas.

when you become more aware, you get more inclined to raise existential questions, especially as you face painful decisions, but you are not necessarily going to find more satisfying answers or become happier as a result. Quite the contrary, you may find yourself more naked emotionally in the face of the pain and tragedy that is built into human existence by death, illness, poverty, and endless ways of suffering. If the journey into self "pays off," it will do so by helping you deal with the exigencies of life more bravely so that you can take joy more deeply from its blessings even as you suffer deeply from its pain.

In either case, the problems of existence, like the problems of awareness, must be faced in the context of love, work, and play if they are to be taken seriously. So we must explore the psychological mechanics and meanings of these things, which are the main contents of our waking lives.

FRIENDSHIP, LOVE, AND SEX

When people find themselves happy in interpersonal relations, especially when they are in love, they tend to be happy with everything else too. There are at least two reasons. First, so much of our egos depend on our feeling lovable and loved, that when we do feel that way, it reinforces our image of ourselves as worthwhile, valuable people. That reinforcement in turn makes it easier for us to face the world with strength and good cheer.

The second reason that feelings of being loved have such a "spread of effect" onto other things[1] is that sexual and affectional drives are so powerful in most of us that their satisfaction produces tremendous feelings of relief, relaxation, and well being—with the rest of the world around us the beneficiary of our glow.

Very short phylogeny of love and sex

Love, you recall, starts getting learned in infancy by classical conditioning through the "contact comfort" of a warm, cuddly figure who also relieves hunger, removes the discomfort of wet and soiled diapers, and provides a variety of creature comforts. Once the infant recognizes this mother figure as a separate thing ("person" would be too strong a word at this stage of development), it feels pleasure in her presence and need for her when she is absent. Later, these feelings get labeled "love," "affection," and, in psychologese, "adience" (i.e., attraction, the desire to move towards). They generalize to other people, whom the child also sees as helpful, protective, and loving, and they form the basis of the attractions it will feel towards others in adolescence and adulthood and the maneuvers it will make to become attractive to them.

What starts as a very simple process of emotional conditioning becomes increasingly complicated, if not an absolute mess, when the child starts exploring friendships in depth, usually before puberty and junior high school. The complexities get worse when these explorations get colored by concerns with sex, beauty, and popularity, which generally start around the eighth grade and last forever, though less intensely as youth passes, ambitions settle, and energy flags. For many young adults, the period of marriage and childbearing and rear-

ing is a relatively quiet one in these respects, but the troubles of adolescence crop up again at the threshold of middle age, as doubts about one's attractiveness arise again, with wrinkles instead of pimples the symptom of concern.

The morals and mores of friendship, courtship, love, and marriage are changing so rapidly nowadays, that there is probably no period from puberty on when anyone is entirely free of concern with their sexual conduct and their love life. Our awareness of ourselves as creatures who need love and the pleasures and securities connected with it, is probably greater now than at any previous time in history. Fulfillment of that need is a basic aspiration of almost everyone.

The mechanics of attraction

Most people have a fantasy about themselves in which they are irresistibly charming, beautiful, and popular, never embarrassed, never frightened at a party, or with a new date, never fearful of making a rotten impression, and never needing to find a hole to hide in after making some incredibly stupid remark or other social blunder. It is a fantasy almost no one fulfills in real life. Short of achieving such perfection, most of us would settle for finding some reasonably certain route to *popularity,* because that is the reason we want to be beautiful and irresistible in the first place—so we will be popular.

Popularity is a quality that, colloquially speaking, "turns people on" and keeps them turned on. It is the ability to attract favorable attention and hold it. Popularity takes many forms and has many motives. Some people are popular because of their personal attributes, such as wit, beauty, intelligence, or the ability to listen sympathetically. Others are popular because of the resources they command, such as money, power, or influence over important people who are hard to reach.

Among college students, popularity revolves

---

[1] Remember the principle of *generalization* in Chapter 6? This is what it's about.

primarily around social and sexual attractiveness; beauty, "personality," and publicity from accomplishments in athletics, academic work, or campus politics are therefore primary criteria for it. Of these, physical beauty is the most obvious, the most inaccessible, and the most deceptive.

Beauty: The physics of attraction There is a good deal of agreement, in Western society, about *who* is very beautiful or ugly, but few people can define exactly *what* the attributes of beauty are. Even if they were defined, it would turn out that almost no one is either so beautiful or so malformed physically that all or none of the characteristics would apply to them. Most of what we call beauty is indeed "in the eye of the beholder." To some extent, in fact, it is a reflection of the beholder's eye turned inward — because if you see yourself as attractive, you tend to see people of the opposite sex as generally more beautiful than

you otherwise would (Morse, Gruzen, and Reis 1976).

If you examine carefully the things that go into most conventional descriptions of physical beauty and ask yourself what it is about them that makes them attractive, you will find that it is not artistically or esthetically obvious. What makes most aspects of one's physique attractive is the implications they have, in our minds, for attractive behavior (Berscheid and Walster 1972; Miller 1970). We associate sexual pleasure, for example, with youth, energy, and health. A trim figure and glowing skin and hair are largely attractive because they reflect these qualities. We associate friendliness, acceptance of others, responsiveness, harmlessness, and easy affection with childlike innocence. Big eyes, open facial features, and apparent symmetry of limbs and lines of body and face are appealing by representing these things. So adolescents and adults who combine such

Everyone wants to be beautiful.
Some work at it more than others.

Woman at her Toilette, Edgar Degas

traits are often seen as more "beautiful," i.e., attractive, than others.

There are other aspects of physical beauty that replace some of the above catalogue as adolescents grow into adulthood and middle age; they too are appealing largely because of what they seem to imply about the person's *behavior,* not because of any esthetic quality. Mature women, for example, are more likely than young girls to think beards and hairy chests are attractive in men because these things are associated with a common stereotype of sexual potency or masculine strength, which tends to replace youthful prettiness in women's evaluation of male beauty as they grow older.

The function that beauty fills is that it invites favorable attention from strangers (Sigall and Landy 1973). But in the long run, what makes beauty beautiful is the attractive behavior it implies. By itself, beauty cannot sustain popularity. And even without much beauty, certainly with no more than most people have, it is possible to gain and hold as much popularity as anyone can handle, and to develop casual encounters into profound experiences of friendship, intimacy, and love. It just takes a little more work to arouse interest and start things moving.

Mood: The chemistry of attraction Sullen beauties and taciturn heroes may look great in some movies, but they are hell to consort with. They have little to offer in social situations, so they cannot help to start or keep the action going. Worse than that, they are easy to annoy and hard to please, and their reactions are hard to predict; so one must tiptoe around them.

Almost everyone tremendously values cheerfulness, enthusiasm, intelligent attitudes, and kindly good humor. We like and admire it in others and like ourselves better for seeing it in our own conduct. Similarly, people are easily "turned off" by other people's depression, hostility, and anger if such bad feelings are aroused very quickly or last very long. Even the most sympathetic friends get tired out eventually and find themselves resenting the suffering mood, no matter how understandable or legitimate it was to begin with.

Mood is contagious, transmitted by voice, gesture, facial expression, or other action. The mechanisms are not entirely clear, but the fact could not be clearer. "Upbeat" spirits in one person arouse up-beat feelings in another and make them feel strong attraction to the source of these good feelings. "Downbeat" feelings cast a pall on others, which they experience as gloom or anxiety in the presence of people they like, and discomfort, or resentment, or revulsion in people they don't know or dislike. We all want to feel good, and we do not take kindly to people who undermine that need instead of supporting it.

This is not to say that everyone loves a Pollyanna. Unrealistic optimism is stupid or insincere, and therefore leaves a bad taste in the mouth. It also does not imply that a person should hide bad feelings as if they are unsightly, because doing so may reflect foolish distrust of other people's caring for you and wanting to communicate their sympathy. The point is simply that, once contact is made with potentially interesting people, the most important step one can take towards creating a relationship is to communicate the attitudes and enthusiasms that make people feel good about themselves and about others. Interest, anticipation, eagerness, and joie de vivre are radiant qualities. Other people feel their vibrations and resonate to them. That is what *popular* (from "people") means.

Role: The psychology of attraction A nice appearance attracts by implying pleasant behavior. A good mood attracts by creating a pleasant atmosphere for the behavior. But the behavior itself proves the pudding. To do so attractively, it must conform to certain social *roles* or *role-expectancies,* as they are called. A role is a behavior pattern that fits other people's stereotype or expectation.

Traditional female roles are learned—tending baby and home.

La Marquise de Pastoret, Jacques Louis David

Some roles are *sex typed,* that is, more characteristic of males than of females, and vice-versa; others are *age-graded,* that is, more characteristic of children than adults; and still others are general, and considered equally appealing or repulsive at any age and from either sex.

Feminine roles, which generally attract men to women, are fulfilled by behavior which implies sweetness, receptiveness, softness, docility, and perhaps passiveness, but certainly nonaggressive, nonhostile attitudes. *Masculine* roles, which make men most attractive to women, involve behavior which shows strength of character, courage, toughness, decisiveness, gentleness, generosity, and perhaps aggressive, but certainly assertive, active attitudes.

Sex roles evolved slowly in history, largely by making virtues of necessity. Until recently, women were a subjugated minority almost everywhere; so the behavior traits that came to be seen as desirable for them were ones which implied that a woman would be happy in her obedient role, as housekeeper, sex object, mother, or servant. She could compensate for her economic and legal helplessness by becoming all the things that would secure male protection for her—an inviting, accommodating, helpmate, sweetly desiring her own submission in return for her lord and master's protection. It still works. Men give seats to women on the bus, adore their incompetence at changing tires, feel tenderness and lust at their easy tears, and underpay them at work.

Pre-Columbian Golden Age, José Clemente Orozco

Traditional male roles are learned — the worker, the builder.

Male social roles evolved in similar ways. The desirable traits that came to be considered masculine were those which implied that the man was capable of functioning as protector, lord, and master all at once. He needed to be gentle towards his helpless helpmate, decisive and assertive in managing the affairs of the household, and courageous and tough in defending her and it against the ravages of a cold and cruel world.

Notice that some important personality characteristics, such as intelligence, humor, and cheerfulness, *never* were sex typed and *always* were critical in attracting the attention of other people, regardless of sex. They were never sex-typed because they had nothing to do with the social or economic functions which sex roles served in the first place. In modern times, the same thing is becoming true of formerly sex-typed roles. Women are no longer dependent economically on men; so docility is no longer an important aspect of femininity. Men no longer have to be able to defend their castles, wives, and other property, by force of arms; so aggressiveness is no longer a part of masculinity.

Traditional sex roles die hard and slowly, however; at present, sweetness and softness is still commonly regarded as a more desirable trait in women than in men, and strength and courage are still considered more masculine than feminine. Girls who "come on" tough and aggressive and boys who appear passive and docile generally make bad first impressions on people. But the lines that demarcate sex-roles are becoming more and more wholesomely blurred so that the behavior traits which make for popularity are increasingly **androgynous** (the same for both sexes); openness, gentleness, generosity, sincerity, strength of purpose (not rigidity), enthusiasm, sympathy, tolerance (not indifference), and many others (see Chapter 14).

The roles which promote popularity, when all is said and done, follow very simple rules. Other people tend to like in you the same traits that you tend to like in them and in yourself. Boys and girls tend to like the same traits in each other. Physical attraction is important in arousing interest, but mostly because of its behavioral implications. Most people become quite attractive enough by good grooming, good bearing, and a receptive, interested, and sympathetic manner. The rest is a matter of trying to be your best self and present it most effectively. That is sometimes difficult because what seems best about ourselves is not always the same as that which seems most real. When the reality we see in ourselves is anxious and unsure instead of gay and confident, it is hard to know what to present. Some people present a lie.

Putting on, showing off, faking out: The social defenses We all want to be loved and we all fear being rejected. How we approach most interpersonal situations depends on which we emphasize more. If we are lucky enough to be very self-confident (without merely being too stupid to feel anxious), we may present our best and most genuine selves as one and the same. Most of us have felt somewhat shy, at one time or another, and have tried to deal with our shyness in different ways. If we are frightened but honest, we may express our anxiety openly but gently enough so that we come across as tentative rather than impossibly fearful or obnoxiously anxious. If, however, we are ***afraid to seem afraid,*** a common sickness in our society, then we are likely to present neither our interest nor our anxiety, but a cloaked image, which is not fish, not fowl, and not real.

There are many ways to disguise anxiety in interpersonal encounters, some more tolerable than others. Perhaps the most common way is to show exaggerated self-confidence in the form of aggressiveness, boasting, sarcasm, or loud "enjoyment." Many shy celebrities use this method to hide their anxiety at having to perform before large crowds. Carol Burnett, Nancy Walker, Barbara Walters, and Johnny Mathis all say they have spent most of their careers trying to overcome their shyness in front of audiences (Zimbardo 1977). Less conspicuous methods include being very quiet, impassive, expressionless, and inscrutable, or else constantly smiling, laughing, or otherwise adjusting one's appearance and expression to what is apparently expected by whoever is dominating the company. While the loud methods are pretty obnoxious and the others pretty innocuous, they all have one main feature in common. They are false images designed to serve as armour against discovery of the person's anxiety.

The armored or defended self is endless trouble. People sometimes use it consciously, thinking to hide their fears just long enough to make a good first impression. Then they find themselves stuck in the roles they have taken and, fearful of being considered phony, try to play them further, at the cost of great energy and great discomfort—and generally little gain. People do not really like you for your pretensions, and the ones who like you best are the ones most likely to see through them anyway.

Most people use their social armor in a semiconscious or unconscious way, that is, they automatically go into a defensive "act" in an anxious social encounter without even trying to figure out whether or not it is needed (or will work). Longstanding habits of instant self-defense have conditioned them so thoroughly to some standard pose that they no longer quite realize it is phony. Sadly for them, other people often do, and as a result either shy away or approach them with needless caution. Even when the protection "works," it is sad—because just as it protects against anxiety, it insulates against communication.

There is nothing very mysterious about the social defenses. They aim to protect a person from anxiety about possible rejection by making them seem invulnerable to it. When they work well, they may even make them feel invulnerable. In some situations, where "cool" is everything, these defenses may be useful. But in relationships directed at love and friendship, they can only be damaging in the long run. You cannot be open without being vulnerable, and you cannot feel much depth of love without being open to all your sentiments — including anxiety. The deepest experience of love in adult life comes from immersing one's own consciousness in the life of another person. But to achieve immersive love, the people must be open to each other's deepest feelings.

It is understandable that people approach new relationships with caution, ready to defend themselves, fearful of rejection, aware of their faults and defects. No human being of any sensibility is free of such fears. No human being alive is free of faults. And there *is* some danger of being rejected for them. But the risk must be taken, sooner or later, if love is to be won. For people who have won it, the risk has always seemed worthwhile.

SEX: TO DO OR NOT TO DO — AND WITH WHOM, WHEN, AND HOW

Of all our many drives and needs, none makes more trouble or gives more pleasure than sex. It is the most primitive expression of the impulse to live, the chief motive underlying love, tenderness, and compassion, and the most intense experience of fulfillment in those things. Sex is the drive which sponsors much of the human need to play and explore, discover, and create. At the same time, it is the source of much of our worst anxiety, the cause of some of our profoundest guilt, the reason for many of our deepest pains. In most of us, the sex impulse will not be denied, try as we might to suppress it — but it may not be expressed in straightforward ways. For sex is tied to love, to pleasure, and to physical dangers and moral prohibitions all at once. How to treat one's sexual impulses, oneself, and other people in this supercharged area of emotion and action is a problem that grows in importance each year from puberty on and which offers greater challenges to the development of adult self-consciousness than perhaps any other experience of college years.

Sex and the social order: Birth and death of the double standard

Attitudes towards sex and standards of sexual conduct in Western society have been changing steadily since the beginning of this century. From about the end of World War II until now, the rate of change has increased so fast that there are few clearcut standards any more (London 1978). Young people becoming aware of their own sexuality are finding, therefore, that with the exhilaration of having sexual freedom goes the anxiety of having to decide what to do with it.

This situation differs enormously from that of a generation ago, and almost incredibly from a generation before that. Having a very strong sex drive and being preoccupied with sexual thoughts and fantasies was then considered "abnormal" (it is not). Masturbating was considered dangerous to physical health (it is not) and a doubtful reflection on one's mental health (it is not that either). Homosexuality was considered a serious disorder, and such sexual problems as male impotence, sexual dysfunction in women, and the like, were not considered fit topics for discussion among even the most intimate friends. There is more, but it is better dismissed as an unhappy chapter in the misguided efforts of civilized people to improve themselves. Of all the peculiarities of sexual practices in the recent past, the most important to be aware of are those which restricted and penalized sexuality in women. Most of these are contained under the label of "double standard."

The double standard said, in essence, that men could enjoy sexual activity that women could not. Premarital sex relations were considered somewhat improper for well-bred boys, but scandalously immoral for girls. The same was true of extramarital relations. It was quite common for husbands to visit prostitutes or, if they could afford it, to keep mistresses, but it was unthinkable for wives to have serious lovers—and casual ones, or male prostitutes, were virtually unknown. The so-called "unwritten law" said that a man could kill another man for consorting with his wife, and maybe kill his wife in the bargain; but no redress existed for the wounded vanity of a wife whose husband ran around with other women, except perhaps divorce. And she could not begin divorce proceedings usually without risking scandalous publicity, which was enough to deter most women.

What she could do, if she had the nerve, was keep her husband out of her bed. Here too the double standard operated. A wife's refusing to have sex with her husband was considering punishing to *him*—not to her—because it was taken for granted that she did not find sex pleasurable in the first place! Women were supposed to *endure* sex in order to please their husbands and to become pregnant, not to *enjoy* it. The sex urge was normal in men, and its absence was equally normal in women. Most people did not know that nice women could have orgasms, and most nice women, accordingly, did not have them.

The breakdown of the double standard occurred gradually over the past couple of generations, partly as a result of the increasing emancipation of women in politics and economics, partly as a result of technological changes. Modern contraceptive methods enabled women to have sex without great risk of pregnancy and with control of contraception entirely in their own hands. Affluence and automobiles further liberalized sexual conduct by enabling people to find privacy for lovemaking. Advances in contraception now enable women to prevent conception even *after intercourse,* and easing of abortion laws now makes it possible to avoid childbirth even if pregnancy occurs. The technical conditions of sexual conduct are becoming virtually identical for men and women, and the technical, emotional, and moral problems connected with it are largely the same ones for boys and girls.

The sex acts: Stimulation to consummation

Awakening and exploration Nobody knows when the first tingle of sexual awakening occurs. Some scholars, like Freud, argue that it begins in infancy and simply concentrates in the genitals at puberty (Freud 1905). Others believe that true sexuality begins as adolescence approaches and the primary sexual characteristics develop their mature form.

Regardless of when it begins, adult, genital sexual feelings and abilities—the capacity for arousal and for orgasm—are present in almost everyone before the end of high school. The desire for sexual activity generally increases for several years, evidently reaching a peak in boys during their late teens and in girls in the late thirties. The sex drive remains active throughout adult life, however, in both sexes, and may continue very late into old age (Katchadoürian and Lunde, 1975).

All the statistics on rates of sexual activity at different ages and in males versus females must be taken lightly. Sexual behavior depends so much on attitudes which were conditioned in childhood and upon the sexual norms of different societies, that there are not really any pure *biological* statistics of sex, only psychological and sociological and biological ones all mixed together (Ford and Beach 1951). In general, the more people like sex and their sex partners, the more often they do it and the longer they continue doing it through life. The better their health, the more this is true, and the happier their feelings about living and loving, still more is it true. The main determinant of sexual activity is the way you feel about it—not age, menopause, vitamin intake, or the positions of the planets.

A Bridal Pair, Anonymous

Shakespeare's Juliet was 14 years
old when she and Romeo
consummated their passionate and
tragic union.

Sexual activity tends to stimulate more of
itself and abstinence, at least total abstinence,
probably reduces sex drive. It is also true that
sexual fantasy, including pornographic books
and dirty movies, stimulate sexual appetites
in males and females alike. This was not known
about women until recently because girls have
been conditioned in our society to a kind of
"modesty" which made it improper for them to
respond positively to sexy talk, books, and the
like. For boys, that kind of stuff has long been
acceptable. It is now becoming so for girls
as well.

When young people first become aware of
genital sex urges, they may go through some
turmoil trying to figure out how to handle them.
They may find sex constantly on the mind, their
attention easily distracted by uncontrolled
lustful thoughts. Boys find themselves having
wet dreams at night and embarrassing erections
at awkward times and places by day. Girls go
around mooning romantically, with or without
overt sexual content to their fantasies, depending usually on attitudes they have absorbed at
home. Both sexes find themselves drawn
cautiously to discussions with close friends to
see if the same things are happening to them
and, if they can approach them, to then worry
or experiment together about what to do with
these urges. Masturbation, the most ready to
hand behavioral outlet for these urges, may
become a joint activity at this time, along with
some experiments in homosexual and heterosexual play.

Autosexuality: Masturbation Masturbation
is reportedly far more common among boys
than among girls (Kinsey et al. 1948 and 1953).
This is probably true in Western society, partly
because the cultural hangover that denied female sexuality made masturbation a more awful
"perversion" of little girls than little boys. It may
be true for a biological reason as well. From
infancy on, the little boy can hardly fail to be
tantalized by the sight of his penis flopping
around in front of him and, having handled it
thousands of times to pee, there is nothing
unique about fondling it to play. Current evidence, on the other hand, indicates that masturbation is probably increasing among women,
though it is still surrounded with guilt for many
(Barbach 1976). Some of them, moreover, are
reporting that they find it more satisfying than
sexual intercourse (Hite 1976).

Masturbation is harmless, physically and
psychologically, for boys and girls, to orgasm
or not, and by any variety of ways and means.
Some people feel anxious and guilty about it,
often for reasons they cannot state. Anxiety
and guilt are painful experiences, and if you
cannot masturbate without feeling bad about
it, maybe you should stop. Not masturbating is

462

also harmless. But if your concern over masturbating involves fears for your health, for your ability to bear children, for your later sexual potency, for your obsessional preoccupation with sex, or for any other of the known ills that flesh is heir to, then set your mind at ease and enjoy yourself. It will not hurt you in this world. There is a Biblical passage about a man named Onan (onanism is a polite Victorian word for masturbation) whom God killed for "spilling his seed on the earth," and many religious people have used this passage as a basis for condemning masturbation ever since. Strictly speaking, God was angry, in the Biblical story, because Onan refused to impregnate his sister-in-law, not because he played with himself (Genesis 38:8–11). But if you wish to avoid masturbation for religious reasons, that is your business. This is a psychology, not a theology book.

Heterosexuality, Phase 1: Necking and light petting Most youngsters are introduced to heterosexual behavior gradually, sometime between puberty and the end of high school, through parties and dates. There is no connection at all between heterosexuality and masturbation. Either may start before the other and progress nicely despite it. There is tremendous variation in the age of onset and the kinds of heterosexual behavior engaged in by normal children. A very small proportion, largely of children from poverty-stricken backgrounds, will be experienced at intercourse before they reach puberty. And a very small proportion will not have kissed anyone by the time they reach college. The vast majority, however, will begin their heterosexual encounters in junior high school and have done some necking and light petting before they finish 12th grade.

Necking is often considered an acceptable means of expressing affection by boys and girls who have doubts about whether they should pet. Many allow themselves to engage in "light petting," usually defined as petting above the waist. Traditionally, the problem of whether to permit petting has been considered the girl's responsibility because it is assumed that the boy would naturally do it if she let him. This is untrue, of course. Boys and girls have the same moral dilemmas about "how far to go."

The decision is not an easy one to make because the physical contact of necking stimulates desire for more intense physical relations. Physically, the lips and mouth are among the body's more sensitive "erogenous zones," and psychologically, the act of kissing, especially repeatedly and prolongedly, expresses the partner's desire, if not willingness, to go ahead. The nipples of the breast, moreover, consist of the same erectile tissue as the penis; they are very excitable in response to stimulation, and the fingertips are among the most exquisitely sensitive organs of touch in the body. The whole system is designed "to go" physiologically. The gentle beginnings of sexual activity, in other words, invite its passionate intensification.

Heterosexuality, Phase II: Heavy petting In heavy petting, the "action" shifts from kissing and fondling of face and breasts to fondling each other's genitals. When this is done in deliberate preparation for intercourse, it is called "foreplay." Fondling the girl's clitoris and vagina and the boy's penis causes both of them to become lubricated and makes them increasingly sensitive to further touch. Sensations of great pleasure accompany these physiological events and grow more and more intense, finally culminating in orgasm, also called "climax" (colloquially: "coming"). Orgasm in the mature male involves ejaculation of semen and is generally felt as an explosive peak of sexual feeling. In the female, little additional fluid is produced by the orgasm; it is felt also as somewhat explosive, but apparently more in wavelike rhythms than the male orgasm. It also generally lasts longer and recovery (being able to get aroused to orgasm again) occurs faster.

The physical events of orgasm are the same in masturbation, heavy petting (which is, technically, being masturbated by another person), and sexual intercourse, but the psychological differences may be so great that they mislead people into some false interpretations. Some people believe, for instance, that if a boy is aroused for a long time during petting and does not have a climax, the result will be harmful to him. It is true that he may feel uncomfortable and even have some slight pains in his groin (called in slang **blue balls**), and perhaps he can use this to persuade his sympathetic and affectionate girl friend to bring him to climax—but no harm will come from stopping short except, perhaps, to his vanity. Similarly, some people think it is unhealthy to have orgasm in one situation, such as masturbation, but healthful in another, such as intercourse—or that one kind of orgasm during petting is better or worse than another. None of this is true. Physiologically, orgasm is orgasm, no matter how you get to it. Whether it is good or bad for you psychologically depends on how you feel about the situation that leads you there.

The problem created by heavy petting is the same as that of light petting, only more so. "The more you eat," to borrow from the Cracker Jack ad, "the more you want." Just as light petting attracts you to heavy petting, heavy petting may make you want sexual intercourse. The issue now, across virtually all religions, cultures, and moral codes, is no more child's play.

Heterosexuality, Phase III: Copulation The majority of American youth, at this writing, apparently have not had sexual intercourse by age 20, but it is a dwindling majority. In 1953, according to the Kinsey report, something like 23 percent of women reported they had had intercourse before age 21. By 1973, a comparable study found the figure had risen to 45 percent by age 19. Kinsey reported, moreover, that in 1953, only 3 percent of girls reported had had intercourse by age 15; in the later study, over 25 percent had done so by age 17 (Sorenson 1973). A small proportion of the difference can be accounted for by the fact that youngsters talk about sex more freely than they used to—but not *that* much more freely. Any fool adult who looks around can see that there has been a sexual revolution in our society; any intelligent youngster has either participated in it, is about to, or is worrying about it.

The myths surrounding sexual intercourse are too voluminous to deal with here, and the basic facts which high school and college students need, and pathetically often do not have, are simple and clear.

Dangerous facts: Venereal disease You really can get venereal disease from having intercourse, and you are more likely to get it from another teenager than from anyone else. Despite the existence of very effective antibiotics for controlling syphilis and curing gonorrhea (there are other forms of VD, but these are the most common), there has been a steady rise in the incidence of these diseases over the past generation—and the chief carriers are teenagers (Gordon 1973). Gonorrhea is a very, very painful condition which usually becomes evident a few days after intercourse and usually is quickly cured by antibiotics. Not always—more and more cases of gonorrhea, especially in women, are not showing symptoms until the disease is quite advanced, and some strains of the disease are showing up which are resistant to penicillin (Culliton 1976), making gonorrhea a more dangerous condition than it used to be. Syphilis is even more dangerous because it is more likely to go undiagnosed until it reaches a fairly advanced stage, when it can produce severe brain damage and death. Its only symptoms, also occurring generally within a few days of intercourse, are very small sores in the infected area, usually in the genitals or mouth, and in fairly inaccessible, hard to notice places—syphilis is an anaerobic bacillus; it can only grow where there is no air.

If you have had sex relations, including heavy petting where there has been genital contact (you can get it through the mouth or off a toilet seat, too, but not easily), and especially with strangers, wash yourself thoroughly with soap and water; also urinate—both kill VD germs (Brecher 1973). Then inspect yourself closely for several days; and if you see sores or retain doubts, go to your doctor, health clinic, or one of the VD clinics maintained by virtually every big city as well as by church groups and youth organizations. If you are scared about being identified, telephone first to find out the doctor's or clinic's policy. If you are still scared, talk to a counselor—or at least a friend with a cool head. Most treatment agencies have respect for your privacy, and your embarrassment; but in any case, it is worse to be ill with these conditions than to be embarrassed.

Dangerous facts: Pregnancy A girl really can get pregnant from intercourse. If she does, it will be from one sex act, and only one. The chances of getting pregnant are statistically greatest if she has relations around the middle of her menstrual cycle (when ovulation is most likely to occur) and if no contraception is used; but she *can* get pregnant right in the middle of her period, even if both partners are using contraceptives, and even if the boy practices "coitus interruptus" (that is, takes his penis out before coming). The chances of impregnation under those circumstances are not great, but it is important to understand that they are real (Cohn 1974). Most girls do not ovulate around menstruation time, but some do. It takes one sperm and one fertile egg to do the job, no more. Most sperm is released only during the ejaculations of orgasm, but some can seep out earlier or later—most will not make it up the vaginal passage into the womb, but only one has to. There are documented cases of girls being impregnated from a semen-soaked finger of boys who came completely outside the girl's body. If a boy has intercourse very often, the chances of his sperm being very active and plentiful are greater the first time he ejaculates than the second or third time in the same day;

but the rate of sperm production in healthy males is quite rapid, and a few days abstinence will replace the sperm-supply fully. Also, sperm will be more active if the boy's testicles are cold than if they are warm. I do not know if this means the chances of getting pregnant are greater from sex in the woods than in the bedroom.

Playing it safe: Contraception The safest way to avoid pregnancy is to avoid intercourse; but if you choose not to go that route, then contraception is the next surest means. Male prophylactics, usually made of rubber or lambskin (called "rubbers" or "condoms"), are among the safest and are purchased cheaply and easily in any drugstore. The lambskin kind are best because they are virtually unbreakable and are very thin so they do not reduce sensation much for the male; but they are more expensive than the rubber kind, which are also generally quite strong, especially the lubricated ones (Hatcher et al. 1976.) The virtue of condoms is that they are cheap, easy to get, and can be used safely with no experience. They sometimes break, however, and sometimes slip off during intercourse (more often, after it, so there is rarely cause for alarm). Also, many boys feel that they reduce the pleasurable sensations in the penis by preventing direct contact with the walls of the vagina.

All the other effective common contraceptives have to be used by the girl. The only easily available one (in any drugstore), is contraceptive jelly or foam—the foam works somewhat better, but is squishy, and some couples find it unpleasant.

A diaphragm is generally even safer than rubbers when used correctly. It needs to be fitted by a doctor and has the disadvantage of requiring correct placement before each use and having to remain in the vagina for several hours after intercourse. It does not interfere with normal toilet functions—but you have to carry it around with you unless you know for sure that you will or won't have sex relations that day.

The Orgy (Scene III) from Rake's Progress, William Hogarth

A young man should know how to protect himself against trouble in sexual encounters—and so should a young woman.

The IUD (Intra-Uterine-Device) requires no such planning and is perhaps even safer than a diaphragm, but its insertion can cause extreme pain and discomfort for days (it only needs to be checked about once a year) and some women get pains and infections from it. (*Population Report* 1975).

The *almost* perfect contraceptive is "the pill," but in most places it is available only by prescription (generally easy to get), it must be taken with great regularity and adjusted to the menstrual cycle, it may have unpleasant side effects, and it may, in the long run, be dangerous to health. Some women get nausea from the pill, some store excessive water in the body cells and get bloated (called edema); and research now in progress is exploring whether its prolonged use may cause some kinds of

cancer or vascular problems. Most women can take it without side effects, but most doctors recommend that they go off the pill every two or three years for at least a year.

A more nearly perfect pill would be one that either sex could take immediately before intercourse. The perfect one would be a pill that the girl could take safely for hours or days after intercourse.[2] That would eliminate pregnancy as a deterrent to sex and permit people to make love or not on personal instead of technical grounds. Research is being done on such pills, and they may be available soon.

Dangerous facts: Abortion Some couples are casual about contraceptive precautions because they figure that if the girl does get

---

[2] Such pills exist now, but are not perfected (*Population Reports* 1976).

pregnant, she can always get an abortion. This is increasingly true, and increasingly safe, as abortions become legal in more and more states and are therefore under responsible medical control. But abortions are not always safe or always easy, and even if you have no moral or religious qualms about them, it is still far better to avoid pregnancy than to court abortion.

For one thing, abortions can only be performed safely in the first several weeks of pregnancy. For young women, in fact, the risk of death from abortion in the first 12 weeks is actually lower than the risk from childbirth (Tietze and Lewit 1977). After about the third or fourth month, however, abortion increasingly carries the danger of causing placental hemorrhaging, which could be fatal. Second, however simple it may seem, abortion is surgery, and all surgery has some risk. Finally, having to spend several weeks anxious about being pregnant, then anxious about having an abortion, and anxious throughout about possibly becoming a parent, perhaps getting married, and maybe having to confront parents, friends, and others with the situation, must put an awful strain on the relationship between boy and girl. Such stress is more likely to make them draw apart than grow together, especially if either one has lingering resentments about the other's failure to take precautions. That often happens because most unwanted pregnancies are products of such irresponsibility.

Dangers or no, most people who want to have sex relations manage to do so without getting veneral disease, pregnant, or psychologically undone in the process. For them, sex is a continuation of their childhood experiments in friendship, intimacy, and love. Eventually, for them, it may become a new form of play, as traditional sexual morality gives way in our society to a growing view of sex as the expression both of love and recreation. For others, however, the awakening of sexual awareness is the beginning of trouble with family, society, and most of all, with their perceptions of themselves as worthwhile people capable of fulfillment and happiness. For them, sexual awakening may be a painful arousal to the knowledge that they are different from other people.

Sex and deviance: Homosexuality

Our whole culture takes so much for granted that courtship, romance, and marriage are heterosexual activities (whereas biologically, only reproduction is) that we often have trouble understanding that some people are physically attracted to members of their own sex and some are repulsed by the opposite sex. When we do observe this deviant (i.e., uncommon) behavior, we sometimes view it as perverse or pathological and figure that it shows a bizarre indifference to good norms of social conduct or is a sign of mental illness. The casual observer's surprise may be nothing compared to the frightened shock of the individuals themselves on discovering that they have homosexual impulses. Chances are that they, like most other people, grew up thinking that such things were signs of depravity (whatever that means) and, seeing them in themselves, that there must be something very wrong with them. Worse, whatever it is that's wrong is shameful as well; so there is no way to seek counsel without exposure to contempt. For many people, the discovery of their homosexual impulses is the beginning of a long sentence to loneliness.

There are many theories about the origins of homosexuality. Some of them make a case for or against it as "natural," "normal," "neurotic," and what have you. The facts are interesting, but the theories are all inconclusive. Homosexuality has been observed in sophisticated cultures, such as ancient Greece, and in some relatively primitive ones, such as the Berber tribes of North Africa. It has been prominent among warrior castes, such as the Japanese Samurai or the Prussian Junkers, who associated it with masculinity; it has also been

Homosexuality is becoming widely recognized and accepted in American
society.

found in other warlike societies where it is associated with femininity, as among the American Plains Indians. It occurs in some societies where sex is repressed and in others where it is free. And it is very common in some cultures and very rare in others. And so forth. It has also been observed a lot among some primates. Sometimes monkeys do it for fun, and sometimes to show submission to bigger monkeys who threaten them.

Most human and animal studies of homosexuality have concerned relations between males more than females. Male homosexuality has been considered more important because males have been considered more important in most human societies until just lately. It is possible that there actually is less homosexuality among females than among males, as some studies claim, but it is more likely that they simply "get away with it" more easily since what girls did mattered little anyhow, and since feminine roles in Western society have always allowed women to express affection to each other more than has been permitted men. The problems of homosexuality in our society, in any case, are the same for males and females.

Some theories propose that the basis of homosexuality is in genetic traits which dispose the individual towards masculine or feminine preferences. Others claim that it is a matter of simple conditioning in childhood and youth—if you are positively conditioned toward your own sex and aversively conditioned towards the opposite sex, you will be inclined towards homosexuality. Still others argue that it is a matter of the individual dynamics of childhood relations with one's parents—a boy whose mother is overbearing and whose father is passive, for instance, may identify with passive feminine sex roles which permit him to emulate mother in some ways and protect himself against assault from her in others (Fenichel 1945). Each of these theories has different implications for how to "cure" homosexuality,

but none of them says anything about whether there is anything wrong with the homosexual in the first place that needs curing.

For some people, it is clearly an undesirable condition because it violates their religious beliefs or because it interferes with their aspirations for marriage and children or because it prevents them from developing the kinds of feelings and relationships they would like with the opposite sex, and because it represents an uncontrollable compulsion for them. Such people properly view homosexuality as an emotional disorder, or at least see themselves as troubled and disordered because of their homosexuality, and they are wise to seek professional counseling for it. For others, however, the problem is not that they are unhappy with themselves for being homosexual but that other people are unhappy with them on that account. For them, the problem is learning how to manage their lives as "gay" (homosexual) citizens of a "straight" (heterosexual) society. It is the secretiveness required by their jobs, families, and social situations which places the burden of guilt and anxiety on them, not their sexual tendencies. Counselling may be useful for these people as well, but it would more likely help them learn to handle their homosexuality rather than to get rid of it.

Adjusting to homosexuality is probably easier now than it has ever been in American society because the liberal attitudes Americans are adopting towards sex in general extend to their feelings about homosexuality as well. More and more states are passing laws which permit free sexual contact of any kind between "consenting adults," that is, adults who find it mutually agreeable. In 1973, the American Psychiatric Association officially decided that homosexuality is no longer considered an illness or emotional disorder. Most people in this country still see it as a sickness, however, despite the increasing acceptance of "gay liberation," as it is called (Weinberg and Williams 1974). Homosexual organizations, both of men and of women, are active in educating the public to the idea that homosexuals are not mentally ill and not socially irresponsible, but ordinary citizens who are entitled to all the rights and privileges of other citizens, including the right to conduct their private sexual lives any way they please and their public social lives with whatever partners they please. Efforts at establishing the equal rights of homosexuals have received the endorsement of responsible politicians of all parties.

In the past, homosexuals have tended to cluster in metropolitan areas where they can find large numbers of companions and live with some integrity by having a social life within the "gay" subculture. As homosexuality becomes more accepted, it is less necessary to live a "shadow" existence, and homosexuals increasingly live openly in society, even operating some homosexual community centers, churches, and health clinics and, in some cases, formally marrying their sexual partners.

There is no way of knowing whether homosexuality is more common today than it was a generation ago, or whether the liberal sexual trends which exist now have merely made homosexuals talk more openly about themselves (Hunt 1974). Homosexuality has long been much more common in American society than people realized. The original Kinsey study indicated that about one third of American males had had at least one homosexual experience since puberty (with the experience defined as having orgasm through contact with a male partner) (1948). The figures for females are much lower. Most such experiences do not stimulate long-term interest in one's own sex, but individuals strongly disposed towards homosexuality who have been previously unaware of it sometimes find themselves overwhelmingly interested after only one encounter.

Homosexual inclination may become apparent to someone at any time of life, but most homosexuals discover it in their early teens, though they may not act on it for years, some-

times never. The awareness may come gradually, by realizing, for instance, that one does not share the common enthusiasms of other kids for the opposite sex, or that one is actually afraid of physical contact with them, or repulsed by it. Some youngsters are led to the discovery by their great fondness for the clothing, cosmetics, or behavior patterns of the opposite sex. Still others see it by feeling sexually aroused at the sight of another person of the same sex, or by chance physical contact, or by their unexpected responsiveness to sexual seduction.

One thing that frightens people about homosexuality is the possibility that the seduction of young children may lead them permanently into homosexual behavior-patterns. No one knows how likely this is, but it is probably true that a pleasurable introduction to any sexual pattern in childhood will dispose the child to look favorably on it in later life. Most homosexuals do not report that seduction was critical in their initial attraction to their own sex, though it may have helped the discovery or reinforced the desire to act on it.

Homosexuals have a reputation for being more promiscuous than heterosexuals and for being less constant in their living arrangements. If this was ever true (there is no direct evidence for it), it would probably have resulted from the same factors which make extramarital heterosexual affairs unstable and which are now unstabilizing marriages throughout Western society and causing great increases in divorce —secrecy, which strains any social relationship, and the absence of contractual bonds and of children, that is, of responsibilities which give people a sense of commitment and permanence in their mating relationships.

In fact, the differences between "gay" and "straight" subcultures seem to grow more narrow all the time. We live in an era of increasingly permissive sex, where experiments are becoming more popular—and mating arrangements less permanent. The differences between homosexual and heterosexual people seem to lie increasingly in the choice of partner, not of life-style.

It is possible also that differences in sexual behavior may be diminishing as sex roles become less rigidly stereotyped in our culture. Shifting standards for sex-role conduct are probably an important factor in making homosexuality more acceptable than it once was, and they may also contribute to an increase in the incidence of "bisexuality," that is, attraction to both sexes. But no one knows for sure whether either kind of *activity* has actually increased or not in recent years, or only publicity about it. Heterosexual conduct surely has increased, however, according to virtually all surveys, and the more permissive attitudes towards sex in general which exist now make it reasonable to think that there have been increases in other kinds of sexual conduct as well.

Sexual deviance and you If you are aware of having homosexual inclinations, or wanting to dress in the clothing of the opposite sex (transvestism), or are sexually stimulated by the idea of feeling pain (masochism), or of inflicting it (sadism), or find yourself aroused by any other sexual impulses which frighten and shame some people, you have probably had some pleasant or stimulating experience in the past which turned your attention accidentally in that direction. It does not mean that you are emotionally disturbed or unbalanced or that you are condemned to a deviant or unhappy future, sexually or otherwise. It may mean only that you are more conscious than other people of the wide variety of impulses that people have—and that they often fear to recognize in themselves or admit to others. In any case, impulses are not acts and not aberrations; they are only feelings. It is up to you what you do with them.

If you dislike the feelings, or are afraid of being overwhelmed by them, you certainly should not experiment with them, but instead should seek the wise counsel of someone who has probably had experience with similar feel-

ings in other young people—a doctor, minister, teacher, or counselor—tell about them and see if clarifying your feelings doesn't help you figure out how to cope with them. For most people, it does. It may *not* be useful to talk it over with your friends at first, because they may have the same problems you do without any more wisdom than you about what to do. Peers lack knowledge [3] It also may not be useful to discuss them with your parents at first, even if you are close to them, because they may be too frightened by your fears to be very helpful. Parents care too much. Once you have clarified your feelings, however, there is probably nothing as helpful to your handling them as discussing them with intelligent, sympathetic people.

If you are strongly inclined in unconventional directions, such as homosexuality, it may be even more important to talk out your feelings than if you are merely afraid of them, because there is more at stake. You are more likely to act out homosexual impulses if they intrigue you than if they frighten you. Doing so, you risk unhappy encounters with the law (homosexuality is still illegal in many places), embarrassing dealings with doctors (homosexuality is the most prominent source of venereal disease), and the contemptuous rejection of "straight" society, let alone the pain you may give some people you love. Times have changed a lot, and homosexuality is less condemned than it used to be —but things have not changed that much, and the risks are real.

The most unhealthy thing about deviant sexuality psychologically, however, is not the sex act but the secrecy that accompanies it, which causes endless anxiety about being discovered and resentment against society for making it necessary to hide. The cost to a person's dignity and integrity may be far

---

[3] I worried terribly about whether masturbation was harming me (I couldn't seem to stop) from age 11 until 14, when I found the nerve to talk to one of my best friends about it. Then I really worried! He said it weakened your body.

greater, in the long run, by hiding their difference, than the cost to their public position of revealing it, especially to people they love, value, and want to trust. Communicating your feelings to those people, without flaunting them, may prove that they are worthy of your trust and that your private sexual behavior need not cripple your personal relationships.

SUMMARY

1 Mental and physical development are greatly accelerated in adolescence, stimulating great personal crises. The main activity of childhood has been play; but the meaning of adult love and work now assume primary importance. The crises of adolescence create an exaggerated sense of self-consciousness, a tendency to build up defenses and a preoccupation with existential crises.

2 The importance of love in people's lives is probably more widely recognized today than in any previous period in history. There is no time from adolescence through middle age when people are not concerned about love and sex, and their capacity to attract other people and fulfill their needs in these regards.

3 Everyone wants to be attractive to other people, chiefly so they can be popular. Popularity can come either from a person's personal attributes or from the resources they command, which make other people seek them out. Among college students, social and sexual attractiveness is the main source of popularity. This kind of attraction revolves primarily around beauty, mood, and role. Beauty is largely attractive because of its implications for attractive behavior. Mood or attitude is even more important because everyone puts high positive value on cheerful, enthusiastic, and kindly behavior, and because both positive and negative moods are contagious. Meeting role expectancies is the most critical factor in attractiveness; in general, people tend to like others for traits they like in themselves.

4 Social defenses develop in an attempt to prevent rejection in new relationships. They take different forms, all of which are efforts to appear emotionally invulnerable. Even when effective, these social defenses cause problems for the people using them by creating a role expectation in other people that they will continue acting this way.

5 Sex is an elaborate expression of the impulse to live, but is also the source of much anxiety, guilt, and pain. Attitudes towards sex have been changing more and more rapidly in this century, especially towards the "double standard" which said that sexual freedom was permissible to men, but not to women. Sexual development, drive, and activity differ greatly among individuals. In general, it reaches a peak in boys during the late teens and in girls in the late 30s, but remains active in both sexes throughout life.

6 Heterosexual activities begin gradually around puberty, usually with kissing and light petting. The next step in sexual exploration is generally heavy petting, i.e., the fondling of each other's genitals. Stimulation of the genitals in both sexes causes them to become lubricated, and makes them more sensitive to further touch. Continued stimulation eventually culminates in orgasm or climax. In the male this involves ejaculation of semen and is felt as an explosive peak of sexual arousal; in the female, it is felt more in wave-like rhythms, which last longer and recur more rapidly than male orgasm.

7 The age of first sexual intercourse is becoming younger in the United States; about 45 percent of girls have had intercourse by age 19, and an even larger percentage of boys. Many myths surrounding copulation are passing, but two age old problems are not diminishing: venereal disease and unwanted pregnancy. Contraceptives can help prevent both conditions, and are easily available. Safe abortions are also easier to obtain today than ever before, but abortion has some element of risk.

8 Homosexual behavior presents complicated problems. Society has labelled it "deviant" in a bad sense, but it is known to be deviant only in being uncommon, not mentally unbalanced. It has been found in many cultures, among all age groups, and in males more than females. Some theories argue that the basis of homosexuality is physiological, others claim it develops like any other learned behavior, as a result of childhood experience. It may become apparent at any stage of life. Homosexuality is physically harmless, but creates serious psychological problems for many people, because it puts them in conflict with social or religious standards which condemn it.

Personal psychology: Two-love and work

17

17

Personal psychology: Two—love and work

The last chapter discussed the *mechanics* of popularity and of sexual relations; this one will concentrate on their meaning.

WARM ENCOUNTER: FRIENDSHIP, LOVE, AND FAMILY

The basic function of popularity is *social;* in childhood, it gets the other kids to come out and play with you; in adolescence and adulthood, it gives an index of your status and prestige. With sex, the basic function it serves is *biological;* relieving the intense drive of sexual arousal makes you feel good and also propagates the species. Neither of these functions is very personal; by mastering the right mechanics, almost anyone can get popular and have sex safely—without intimacy. Some people can "enjoy" popularity without friendship, and making love without feeling love. Most of us find, however, that unless we have some very intimate love relationships, we suffer from harrowing loneliness or from the listless feeling that life has little meaning and little value. For most people, the form in which their deepest and longest lasting intimacies evolve is romantic courtship, marriage, and raising children. The "nuclear" family, as sociologists call it, has been the focus of love-relationships in our society for many centuries, but since the family served other purposes as well, its role as the harbor of affection was often obscured. Rapid changes in American society may change the function of the family drastically again in this century. But at present it remains the culmination of the striving for interpersonal intimacy in most of our lives (Blankenship 1976).

Friendship: The sharing of interests

From an evolutionary point of view, the need for intimate personal friendship is a highly advanced one. It does not aid biological sur-

The love of friends for each other is one of the most cherished themes of literature since ancient times.

Hamlet and Horatio, Eugène Delacroix

vival of the species — sexual reproduction works just as well with strangers as with friends; and it does not aid economic survival of the individual — being socially acceptable enough to get a job or live in a community does not require intimacy with anyone. Intimacy serves the need for "fulfillment," not for survival. It is what Maslow calls a higher-order need, one which characterizes people more than animals and adults more than children (Maslow 1954). It is the basis for adult love.

"Friend" comes from an Anglo-Saxon word which means "lover," appropriately enough, implying that friendly relationships are the basis for love. Friendship begins to develop in childhood, but for a long time does not have the quality of later friendships, which are predominantly the sharing of experiences. Tod-

dlers first engage each other in *parallel play,* that is, they play separately in the same sandbox, hardly aware of each other's presence. Months later, they notice what each other is doing and start interacting, but not deliberately cooperating or caring about the other child, rather just "nosing in" to its activity. A lot of tugging, hitting and crying occurs at this stage. By pre-school age, they engage in cooperative play, doing vaguely structured things together by a kind of primitive agreement ("Let's play doctor. I'll be the nurse, and Janie can be the patient.") Finally, by the primary grades, they are able to play highly structured games with complicated rules, requiring teamwork, such as relay racing, and soon, baseball (Hartup 1970).

Children start off as *playmates;* they only

become friends as they mature enough to feel a sustained emotional response to the other person, such as missing them when they are away (as opposed to merely feeling there is no one around to play with) or feeling pleasant anticipation about being with them (with no idea about what they will actually do together). Friendship is quite a different experience from the love children feel for their parents, which is largely feeling securely dependent on them. It is more the feeling they have for siblings; but friendship with siblings gets complicated, and often goes unrecognized, by competition for parental attention, by age differences, by the trouble siblings make for each other in sharing resources, and by the fact that your brothers and sisters are always around, so you never know you would miss them if they weren't.

Emotionally secure children make better friends than insecure ones because feeling safe in the love of parents makes them secure about their own value. This in turn gives them confidence that other people will respond favorably to them and will want to befriend them. They are right. Insecure children approach potential friendships with fear of rejection as a powerful motive; this makes them too cautious and prone to defensiveness and withdrawal at the slightest threat. It might seem that very dependent children (and adults) make the best friends because they feel such great need for the other person. But theirs is a *fearful* need, for avoiding abandonment rather than securing pleasure, and it makes its victim ultimately undependable. The best friendships are with people who *want* your company, not with those who fear losing it.

Friendship consists of the **sharing of interests** between people who **feel positive emotions** towards each other independently of their specific interests. The sharing of interests may include doing things together, sharing material goods, and sharing thoughts, especially anxieties, confidences, and fantasies. The more sharing there is of all three things, the

Friendship. The sharing of interests which marks friendship in childhood . . .

stronger or deeper the friendship (Derlega and Chaikin 1975). The role that positive emotions plays is that it motivates the person to want to be with this particular friend and it sustains that *adient* (approach) tendency through times when there is little of mutual interest to share (Byrne 1971).

People deceive themselves easily about the permanence and depth of their friendships because they typically underestimate the changeability of their circumstances and overestimate the reliability of their feelings and memory. Children leave summer camp bathed in tears and sworn to oaths of eternal devotion and weekly letters to bunkmates whose names, let alone addresses, may be fuzzy two months later. High school graduation parties are steambaths of life-long friendship pledges between people, a few of whom really *will* come to the reunion 25 years later and will leave it musing

over whether they really did feel so close to old Charley back then in the first place. The continued sharing of interests is critical, with the positive emotions sustaining it—when the sharing stops, the emotions weaken because memory by itself is almost always too fragile to sustain them without more tangible reinforcement.

Some people fool themselves into thinking they have deep friendships merely because they share important interests, even though they really do not like their partners much. This happens, evidently, because we are trained so much "to be friendly" that we feel it is somehow treacherous *not* to be friends with people we cooperate with. People also lie to themselves about friendship with people to whom they are powerfully drawn without really having much interest in common. Here, too, we feel we have to claim "friendship" because we feel it is im-

. . . leads to the sharing of self in adolescent intimacy.

proper to admit that desires for sex, status, or reward are all that motivate us. Friendship is probably the most socially acceptable of all motives for anyone having anything to do with anyone else; so we cover a lot of other motives with that name.

The capacity for deep and permanent friendships increases from the elementary years through early adulthood because the number of sharable interests in anyone's life increases steadily during those years. By middle age, however, it becomes difficult for some people to make new friends because they are so entrenched in their habitual lifestyles and routines that they cannot open themselves up to the new interests needed for forming new friendships. This problem becomes even more severe in old age, when new friendships must be constructed on the overlay of a lifetime of memories which cannot be shared. Old people are often lonely because as children grow and old friends leave or die, there are no replacements. And memory is no substitute for company.

Children are rarely burdened with such problems. Their friendships grow more robust as they approach puberty and adolescence. There is more and more to talk about as their intellectual horizons expand; there is more and more to do as their skills develop; there is more and more to wonder at as their bodies change, their minds improve, their feelings grow more subtle and varied. There is more to share all the time, and their ability to understand and appreciate the people with whom they share grows too as emotion and memory expand and enrich each other.

As the capacity for friendship reaches its peak, sexual awakening occurs too. And the sharing of interests and of positive feelings which nurtured friendship are now transmuted by sex into the capacity for adult love.

Love: The sharing of self

People who have never been in love sometimes have trouble understanding just how powerful a feeling it is. The 15th-century political philosopher Niccolo Machiavelli felt that love is ultimately responsible for much of the evil done in the world. For lovers, it seems responsible for most of the good.

Adolescence is when romantic love commonly first blooms, though it may happen at any time in later life and it may recur over and over again regardless of when it starts. The word "romantic" has different connotations in different places, but I am using it here to speak of relationships in which "falling in love" leads to greater and greater intimacies, ordinarily reaching their peak in sex, love affairs, and sometimes marriage.

Falling in love is a somewhat painful experience and a somewhat deceptive one as well. It is painful because you feel a terrible longing for the loved person, a passionate desire to be with them all the time, to share everything with them, to immerse your whole existence with theirs. It is deceptive because people who fall in love think that if their love is requited, the relationship will be an enduring one; while the truth is that for endurance one must *grow* in love, which is harder to do than young people may think. Love affairs that are fallen into often get fallen out of. The growth of love, like any growth, requires roots in experience and careful tending over time in order to blossom and bear fruit.

People fall in love with remarkable speed. First, they find themselves interested or amused by someone or struck by the person's appearance (more often because it is interesting than because it is "pretty"). Then, they find themselves thinking a lot about the person, wondering what it would be like to be with them more, and starting to spin a web of fantasy about the pleasure of their company. The fantasy may or may not have a sexual content (it likely does not at this point); what makes it romantic, and what makes the person aware that they are in *love*, is generally a suffusion of tender, often longing, feelings towards the other person, coupled with a great desire to express the feelings to them. The tenderness and the longing may take many forms—a feeling of protectiveness, a desire to be responsible for the loved one, to help them in work, to nurse them in illness, console them in sorrow. The fantasies of romantic love frequently take the form of heroic encounters, such as saving the "damsel in distress," or "Florence Nightingale" situations, where "an angel of mercy" nurses the fallen warrior back to health and thereby wins his undying love. The classic themes of romantic chivalry did not get to be classics by accident, but because they recounted so well the classic fantasies people have had about winning the love of some adored person. They were the same as yours.

There are several features of romantic love that differ from the prior experiences of simple friendship which you may have had. First, the fantasies themselves are different. Children have plenty of fantasies about their friends, but they are generally about doing things together and they generally lack the painful urgency of romantic fantasies. Second, the feeling of love makes the beloved person an object of supreme importance, around whom one's entire life seems destined, hopefully, to revolve; so the fantasies are almost constant rather than occasional, and awareness of the other person is always near the forefront of consciousness. Third, the desire to share is more extreme and more complete than one feels towards friends because it is a desire to blend oneself completely in the experience of the loved one. Precisely that need makes sexual relations in love far richer and more rewarding than sex can be under more im

Romantic love—a classic, timeless ideal—or fantasy?

The Lovers, Pablo Picasso

personal circumstances; for the urge of lovers to immerse themselves completely in each other comes nearest fulfillment when they blend their bodies, thoughts, and feelings in the act of love. A scale which measures the components of romantic love finds three main factors in it: Intimacy (the ability to confide), attachment, and caring (Rubin 1975).

Clearly, the difference between friendship and love is the intensity of the feelings in the first place and the commitment one feels towards the other person because of them in the second. The more passionate the feelings, the more timeless the need for the other person becomes, and the more involved one feels in the other person's life and sensitive to their concerns. This sensitiveness accounts for the constant delighted discovery of lovers that they seem to think and feel alike about so many things with so little discussion or communication about them. The truth is that they are so finely tuned to each other's thoughts and feelings, and so eager to respond positively to them, that they pick up small nuances of meaning without noticing how carefully they are looking for them— and are then wondrously pleased to "discover" the sympathetic communication they have so carefully constructed.

The sympathetic mutual responsiveness of lovers is not a trivial byproduct of early romance which dies with familiarity. In a love relationship where the partners grow together over time, the sympathy between them may increase and spread to other areas of experience—so old married couples who have lived through a lot together and are still in love may communicate great reams of meaning with a nod, a glance, or a smile, and sometimes are observed to gradually look more and more alike over the years, and even to have more and more similar handwritings. Personality is largely shaped by circumstances, as we have seen (Chapter 14), and the chief circumstance in the life of loving partners is each other—so they really do become more alike.

People differ a lot in how easily they fall in love; how deeply, that is, how all-encompassing it is when it happens to them; and how realistically, that is, how much their attraction towards the other person correctly predicts their ability to get along together in different situations and over a long time. Some people are afraid of the intensity of feelings involved, either because they fear that the feelings will get "out of control" and they will be overwhelmed with anxiety, or because they fear that exposing themselves very deeply to another person will expose such faults and weaknesses that the other person will no longer love them. Such people are likely to say that they don't know if they can ever love anybody or that they don't know for sure what love is. They are right, but it is fear, not ignorance, that makes it so.

Some people go to the opposite extreme and are constantly falling in love with one person and out of it with another. Their friends may think that they are hypocritical, but if they have been lying, it is more likely to themselves than to anyone else. What generally happens is that they fall in love with very little knowledge of the other person or of their own deeper needs; a pretty face, a charming manner, a glib front is all they actually see of the other person and, with nothing more to go on, they project a huge fantasy that the person has other wonderful qualities which really are not there. When it turns out that the fancied qualities are missing, or worse, that the loved one has a lot of repugnant traits that they never noticed in the first place, they quickly fall out of love with that person and start looking elsewhere. Such people learn little from experience, it seems, and tend to get in the same mess over and over again. Sometimes they are so blind that they attribute their falling out of love to the fact that the other person misled them, or perhaps really was at first the romantic idol they fantasized, but then came to take their love for granted and changed into a schnook.

Still a third group of people tends to fall in

love repeatedly with new people, but without abandoning their love for previously established partners. In some cases, this behavior is self-deceptive; they really do not retain their love for the first partner, but they are too guilty about abandoning them to admit it, or else too fearful that the new relationship will not work out to give up the old one. In other cases, however, this capacity may represent a kind of maturity in love, wherein the experience of deep satisfaction in one love relationship makes the individual more open to love with others as well. Whatever motivates it in each case, this phenomenon is becoming more and more common in American society, creating problems of jealousy and insecurity when both partners to a relationship don't feel the same about extra relationships, and promoting the breakdown of the exclusive monogamous relationships which have dominated law and custom in sex and marriage for many centuries in Western society.

Long before they have established strong patterns of belonging to either of the above groups, however, most young people who fall in love find that their feelings are reciprocated by someone they love long enough for both parties to want a permanent commitment to each other. In the ardor of romantic love, they may not inspect too carefully what they mean by "permanent" or by "commitment" and they may not worry much about whether either of them will change. Convinced enough of their present feelings, they launch themselves together on the road to marriage and family.

Marriage and family: The sharing of responsibility

Since the end of World War II, the divorce rate of Americans has risen higher and higher, and more and more people who live together are unmarried (U.S. Bureau of Census 1977). Some people see this as a bad omen for the future of society. It is clear, in any case, that the meaning of marriage has been changing dramatically.

Few people realize today how much marriage has traditionally represented an **economic,** rather than an **emotional relationship;** but the reason that the legal and religious ceremonies of marriage use the language they do is just that. Marriage is a **contract,** that is, a binding agreement between two parties based on an "exchange of value." The value which the wife received, historically, was economic security, protection, and, in male-dominated societies (i.e., everywhere), a legitimate source of sexual activity. The man, who did not need to get married for any of those purposes, received exclusive possession of the woman's body, her services, and her children—in short, he secured property rights. While this may sound like a cold and heartless arrangement to you, it was actually a pretty good deal for both sides. Women really did gain something by shifting owners (they were their father's property before becoming their husband's), because they could have sex, children, and a chance to become partners to the arrangement if their husband was a kindly person. Men gained too because if they had only ordinary financial means (that is, next to nothing), it was their big chance economically—children could work, and marriage gave the man regular housekeeping care, let alone a dependable sex partner. For both parties, of course, marriage meant having company, and in the world of alternating overwork and boredom in which most people spent their entire lives (Russell 1930), the value of a companion was inestimable. This fact, more than any other, led to the emotional closeness which still characterizes good marriages and which generally made it possible for "arranged" marriages, in which the betrothed couple never met until the wedding day, to work out reasonably well.

The institution of marriage itself, like the incest taboo which is virtually universal in human society, probably developed for psychological as well as economic reasons. It reduced jealousy and conflict among male competitors

The Golden Wedding, Adriaen van Ostade

The celebration of marriage as a happy institution was prominent even when most marriages were arranged.

for the possession of women and children. Monogamy (having only one wife) probably developed for sheer economic reasons (most men could not afford more); but over time people made a virtue of necessity, increasingly recognized the wife's right to exist as an individual rather than as the mere property of her husband, and thus made monogamy into a mutual agreement between *partners:* the wife and husband would each be available sexually to their marriage partner *and to no one else.* At this point, wives could divorce their husbands for "sexual infidelity." The double standard was dealt another blow.

The meaning of marriage today among edu-

cated middle-class people (*you*) has become more and more questionable as traditional motives for it have become less and less important. The *economics* of marriage have changed drastically. Women no longer need male support in order to survive, and men no longer need the labor of their wives or of a lot of children in order to tend their farms or run their mills. The *sexual* benefits of marriage have diminished for many people and the sexual restrictions have become more uncomfortable for them. More women and men both feel, nowadays, that they are entitled to have sex relations outside of marriage, just as they feel increasingly that it is all right to have sex-relations before marriage, even with people you do not expect to marry (Hunt 1974). While religious prohibitions on premarital and extramarital sex are about the same now as always, many laymen take them less seriously than they used to, and so do many clergymen. The morality of premarital and extramarital sex has shifted as the practical problem has declined; with little danger of pregnancy, and relative ease of abortion, women need not fear coming home with children who have been sired by other men.

The domain of *mutual responsibility* which the marriage contract can meaningfully cover, therefore, may be shrinking. Marriage can still provide economic comfort, social status, and a dependable sexual liaison, but the value of a binding **contract** between the parties to see that those things get done is less than it has ever been. For this reason, laws have been passed in many of the United States, over the past few years, making it easier than it has ever been to dissolve marriages legally. One of the primary remaining motives for marriage—the desire for affectionate companionship—is not really subject to contract. The other—the joint rearing of children—is still very much so, so much in fact, that if parents separate legally or divorce, the possession of their children and the financial arrangements for supporting them are primary issues in the courts.

Childrearing may be the last area of mutual concern that clearly requires people's binding themselves together contractually and remaining together through the strains of conflict and disagreement which arise in any partnership. Undoubtedly, many marriages are kept intact by the mutual feelings of parents that the positive value of the complete family for the welfare of the children outweighs the unhappiness caused by remaining with an unsatisfactory spouse. It is hard to know; in fact, unbroken but unhappy families may produce more delinquency than happy broken homes (Nye et al. 1958). Among intact families, some children suffer a lot from the strain between their parents, no matter how sincere the efforts are to protect them from it. Others are not affected much by the ongoing conflicts but are later shocked and torn to discover that the parents whom they love are going to separate. There is no way for marital unhappiness to be good for children.

People are more sensitive today than they once were to the fact that they do not need to get married in the first place to have most of the benefits of companionship, sex, and so forth. Since it is possible to get divorced more easily, moreover, and with little social stigma, it is also possible to enter marriage more casually than in the past and, until children get into the act, to leave it more casually too. For thoughtful people, the *voluntary* quality of contemporary marriage has created an ongoing problem for maintaining it: how to make of marriage an experience of mutual growth rather than one of mutual restriction.

The problem arises because the responsibilities of husbands and wives shift over the years, their expectations of themselves and each other change, and the romantic passions that led them to marriage in the first place get strained by familiarity, which leads them to take each other for granted, and by outside stresses, which makes the other person's needs and weaknesses into a burden. Either partner may find that the other is no longer very interested in their problems so that their burdens of responsibility are felt as unshared, their needs as unspoken, their partner as uncaring, and themselves as unappreciated. What has happened, in that event, is that the *sharing* which led them from friendship to love to marriage in the first place has become weak or lost in the routines of married life. The enterprise has then defeated its own purpose. It is possible that there are gross inequities to begin with in who gets what from marriage; the evidence suggests that men profit more from it than women. Married women, even those reporting themselves happy with marriage, have more physical illness and

The Wedding Dance, Pieter Bruegel the Elder
Traditional marriage—the whole community acknowledges and celebrates the transfer of ownership. The bride, formerly her father's, is now her husband's.

emotional disorders than unmarried women, whereas just the opposite is true with married and unmarried men (Bernard 1971). If the values of marriage are in such imbalance when the partners are happy, the potential for disaster must be even greater when one of them is not.

The situation is worse if conflict is precipitated by money problems, by a loss of sexual interest on either part, or by terrible difficulties in either partner's job or social life. Perhaps the most common source of dissolution is when the wife's interests are turned more and more towards housekeeping, childrearing, and the routines of neighborhood social life, while the husband's are increasingly engaged by business or professional activity which draws him into new social circles and new roles. He then starts to find her boring, and she finds him strange and distant.

Some people try to solve these problems of marital "ennui" by deliberately finding new things to share and by encouraging each other to grow in ways which will make them more interesting partners to have around. A common means of encouraging growth is by each partner pursuing separate professional or recreational interests, taking vacations independently, having separate as well as common social activities and, more rarely, even encouraging each other to have extramarital sexual relationships. Sharing experiences also takes a variety of forms, including, sometimes, joint sexual activity, called "swinging," in which couples exchange partners to have sex relations or participate together in group sexual activity. This is not very common; it is reported by less than 4 percent of the married women of the United States (London 1978), but it is more widely acknowledged, at least, than it used to be, to judge from the literature on the subject. Its advocates claim that it improves relations in marriage by reducing jealousy, depersonalizing extramarital sex, and making marital partners more sensitive to each other's sexual needs and desires. In a small number of cases, people also attempt group marriage, that is, sharing the responsibilities for housekeeping, childrearing, and sexual relationships among several people living under one roof.

All these experimental variations on traditional marriage go under the common name of "open" marriage, implying that the act of getting married is not intended to restrict each other's life, but to open up the possibilities for common growth and enrichment (O'Neill and O'Neill 1972). Open marriages may be good for some relationships, especially where one or both partners would otherwise feel that they had foolishly imprisoned themselves by getting married. For others, however, marriage serves primarily as a means of satisfying their dependency needs, especially their needs for security in a single love relationship where they are the stable target of loving attention — and for them, open marriage arrangements are a source of constant threat, fear, and jealousy.

One of the biggest questions concerning experimentation with marriage is the effect it will have on family life, that is on patterns of child rearing (obviously, it is already having an effect on patterns of sexual relations). It is too early to say how children are affected by communal child rearing of the kind that goes on in group marriages[1] because there are still very few such marriages and few progeny from them. The high divorce rate among American families causes a lot of children to be raised by one parent only,

---

[1] People sometimes mistakenly compare child-rearing in communal marriages to child-rearing in the Israeli kibbutz, or commune movement. They have nothing in common but the word "communal," so forget it. There are no group marriages in the kibbutz, and children maintain very close primary relationships with their parents, not their "metaplot" (caretakers).

which is often hard on the parent but not necessarily harmful to the child. Experimentation in family life may move increasingly in the direction of more women deliberately bearing and rearing children alone, without getting married in the first place. This probably would have happened more in the past if women had a choice in the matter, but their general subjugation to men made it unthinkable that they could be permitted to produce and control such valuable property as children by themselves, even if they could have found the economic wherewithal to do it. Nowadays it *is* thinkable, some women are thinking of it, and a few, especially those with independent careers, are doing it.

It would have been relatively easy to write about the meaning of marriage a generation or two ago when it was plainly the "normal" ob-

Social acceptance of the single — unmarried — mother (by choice), is increasing.

Gypsy Woman with Baby,
Amedeo Modigliani

jective of the growth of love for almost everyone. It may become easy again a generation from now if patterns of marriage and family life in America again start to stabilize. At present, however, we have not abandoned traditional monogamous marriage, on the one hand, while changes in sexual conduct and morals, the liberation of women, and the existence of many alternative lifestyles have all challenged the meaningfulness of the tradition, on the other. The possibilities for continued personal development through marriage have never been greater. Neither have the risks of disillusion, disappointment, and divorce.

WORK, VOCATION, CAREER

Until you look closely at it, work seems like a less complicated and mysterious topic than love; people are not afraid of the subject, it is not shrouded in mystery, and everybody ends up, at some time or other, working. But a lot of them end up hating their jobs, feeling like work is drudgery or torment, bored silly, not knowing how they fell into what they are doing, and un-

able to escape from it because they need the money and don't know what else they could do that would be less wretched anyway.

Work is not a simple subject; it has a developmental sequence for everyone, much like the sequence in which love and friendship develop, and with the same variable results. Some people find themselves with a "life work," a "calling," that gives them endless satisfaction. They may discover it in childhood or fall into it in school — or in adulthood, in the course of working. Others never even understand the term, and spend their lives detached from their work or miserable in it. A third group, apparently growing in our society, masters some kind of work, thrives on it, succeeds at it, tires of it, and switches in middle age to something new. Whatever the outcome, the sequence of thinking about work, preparing for it, and finding it is a common one.

Imitation, aspiration, and achievement-need: The sources of vocation

Very small children do not want to be doctors, lawyers, and merchant chiefs. They want to be

As women become more liberated, sex role stereotypes apply less and less to their vocational choices.

Children, in their play, try out many vocational roles. Doctor, lawyer . . . Indian chief.

Big Elk, George Catlin

garbagemen, firemen, and mailmen, people they can see and with whom they can identify (nowadays, add astronauts, cowboys, and other "tube" heroes of your choice). If the heroes have uniforms, so much the better—their role is clear. Ditto if they are very active and big and powerful —activity is easy to understand, and children are small and powerless.

The first basis of vocational choice, and perhaps the one that remains strongest at all times, is the imitation of adult roles. We see what adults do, we want to be like adults we admire or love, so we think about playing the same roles they do. "Playing" the roles, in fact, is exactly the way that children think about them, fantasizing the action that goes with the role and, wherever possible, acting it out, alone and with other children. Play is the medium in which careers are conceived. Play and fantasy remain the media through which they are rehearsed. And for some very fortunate children, the conduct of their adult work, if not its preparation, always retains the character of play.

While the idea for being one *specific* thing or another seems to come from adult models, the *general* motivation for achieving success seems to originate elsewhere. Studies of the achievement motive suggest that it comes from early childhood training towards independence administered by positively reinforcing figures (McClelland 1955; Winterbottom 1953; Rosen and D'Andrade 1959; Heckhausen 1967). Wherever it comes from, some children are motivated to do well only in very specific areas which capture their fancy, while others seem generally inclined to strive hard—or not to.

Girl in Front of Mirror, Norman Rockwell

"Someday I will be a big lady, like Mommy."

Preparation

Serious ideas about career start to occur in most children around the end of the primary grades and the approach of puberty. Then they begin to forecast themselves in adult roles. This is still fantasy, of course, but now the fantasy is connected not only with a person to be emulated but with an interesting subject that can be explored directly. This is the age of chemistry sets, science kits, and stamp collections—in short, of **hobbies.** Hobbies are still forms of play; the child's object in pursuing them is entertainment, not instruction, but they are instructional too because they require you to pay disciplined attention to what you are doing. A lot of hobbies go by the board this way because children discover that they get bored by having to do it right. But if interest remains high as discipline develops, skill is created and the basis for a vocation has been laid.

Hobbies do exactly the kind of thing that school should be doing for discovering one's vocation, that is, providing a ground for exploring interests, developing skills, and measuring one's own strengths and aspirations. Hobbies often succeed in doing it because the experience of **input, feedback,** and **reinforcement** from them is very straightforward and meaningful— you try to build a wobblestoppit (input), discover by doing so how difficult it is, and how well it

Imitation of adult roles is a step in growing up. Affectation of seemingly "adult" habits—like smoking a pipe—is one way.

Man Lighting a Pipe, David Teniers the Younger

works (feedback), and finally you see how rewarding the experience can be by using it or selling it or getting praise from other people for its excellence (reinforcement).

No such luck obtains in most school situations. Even the important things that you learn in elementary school, such as reading and arithmetic, are usually only indirectly related to your specific interests; so the incentive to learn them may not be great. And most of the requirements of high school, with the exception of trade school curricula, are fairly useless for any skillful work anyhow. College should be an exception, but often it is not. Liberal arts programs, like college-preparatory high schools, prepare you for nothing specific, though they have many course requirements. Preprofessional programs, as in medicine and law, provide background which is interesting to scholarly students of these disciplines but not of much use to practitioners of them. More important, you cannot tell from the background studies whether you have any aptitude for the real thing. Chemistry courses, for instance, are not good predictors of medical aptitudes.

The truth is that no one really knows very much about how to prepare anybody academically for anything except by teaching them the thing itself. A century ago, defenders of the liberal arts curriculum insisted that everyone should study Latin because it sharpened their general intellectual skills. (Actually, it sharpened their Latin.) Today, for equally doubtful reasons, some PhD programs in universities still require that students have a reading knowledge of one or two foreign languages.

Nor is much known about what makes for high or low aptitude in most professions. Psychologists once did an elaborate study trying to predict who would be good clinical psychologists, with the view of establishing good standards for admission to graduate school. They found out that the only really good predictor of performance in graduate school was performance in undergraduate school. They could tell next to nothing from studying the personalities of the psychology trainees or their knowledge of the field (Kelly and Fiske 1951; Kelly and Goldberg 1959).

If there is a single moral to this story, it is this. If you know what you want to be when you grow up, go for it! Don't give up because aptitude tests tell you that you are unfit for it, or because you do poorly in the prerequisite courses, or because learned and established authorities in the field say you have no talent. They may be wrong, and you cannot find out without trying. The purpose of formal education in preparation for most trades, including medicine, law, business, and wobblestoppitry, is to teach the rudiments of the trade and provide "union cards" for admission to it. If you have a "calling," you must not permit yourself to be deterred in pursuit of it by the hardships of securing your union card.

On the other hand, there are limits to individual aptitudes, and they do not always correspond perfectly to individual desires. That may be true of you. You may want to be a doctor worse than anything in the world and really not be able to do the things that are necessary to get into medical school or through it. And then, you should consider whether there might not be other things in this world that you could do and be happy at without breaking your head or your heart in a fruitless struggle.

Profession

The work people do helps to shape their adult personalities, in part because they play the professional roles that are common to their business and partly because the kind of work makes them look at people in certain ways. Policemen can hardly help becoming cynical about human kindness after seeing all the horrible ways that people assault, violate, and torment each other. Accountants and lawyers watch greed and selfishness constantly at work on their clients. Social workers and psychotherapists confront ignorance, weakness, frailty, and irrationality all the time. People in the service and helping professions (as opposed to manufacturing and selling) are more affected by human frailties than other workers because, since their job is to help, they think-that-other-people-think that they are supposed to know what they are doing. The less they do know and the more insecure they feel about it, the more likely they are to "play roles," that is, to put on airs of authority, wisdom, and self-confidence. Lots of people are fooled by the pose, and where it works well, it often becomes a standard mannerism of the whole industry, which calls it "professionalism." Some aspects of professionalism reflect skill at the craft, but role-playing does not. It is merely a means of getting prestige, often at the expense of the customer's dignity. The most offensive professions in this connection are probably medicine and academia. Professors often play the role of "great intellectual" and doctors of "all-knowing counselor." In doing so, they may fool themselves as well, mistaking the role for the skill.

In general, you only become skillful at any craft by practicing it—a lot and self-critically. The preparation you get in school for your work does not make you good at it. Only doing it will.

A famous failure, as predicted from his undistinguished childhood.

One great danger in getting good, oddly, is that success itself makes some people *lose* their self-critical faculty, and their skill may then deteriorate. Experience is the best teacher, all right, but only if you are willing to learn from it. Many fine artists, craftsmen, and professionals have fallen into the trap of permitting the praise of their admirers to replace their own tough judgments of their work. Really skilled professionals are most skilled at evaluating their own products.

In the past, being successful at your work almost always guaranteed that you would continue doing it the rest of your active life. If you tended to give up one kind of work to try another, it usually meant that you were failing at the first. This is changing today, and many people who are successful in their careers abandon them to face the challenge of new work. This seems to happen most to people in their early 40s, who are old enough to have fully established themselves in one kind of work but still young enough to have a long work life in another. Chances are that the trend will grow in the future. It is probably a good thing because it suggests that people are still seeking personal growth long after they are able to settle into comfortable routines of activity.

The need to continue productive work of some kind, once its value is established in a person's life, seems never to end. When work is satisfying, it may take up so much of a person's "life space" that interrupting it for long becomes unsettling. That is why some people get fidgety on a vacation; they would be more rested back on their jobs. The permanent termination of work, moreover, as in retirement, can be devastating. If retired people do not find some really valuable activity to replace the satisfactions they formerly obtained from work, they may start getting all kinds of ailments, some of them very serious—and probably die earlier than they otherwise would have.

For such people, work is the most fulfilling routine of life, the highest form of *play,* or of *vocation* (the Latin word for "calling" or inspiration). Few people are so lucky. Some are lucky if they find their work is anything more than a "stale, flat, and unprofitable" drudgery, needed for survival. For them, it is something to be escaped from, and the time they can spend away from it is, indeed, *re*creation—it permits them to come alive again. Their lives are split in time, and, while work has priority for survival, their fulfillment can only come through leisure.

LEISURE, PLAY, RECREATION

Since the end of World War II, American society has become increasingly a culture of leisure. Most societies throughout the world remain cultures of poverty, in which people "have nothing to do." In ours, people increasingly do not "have to do anything." The results are not entirely happy. As the work week gets shorter (it averages close to 35 hours now, half of what

it was a century ago), leisure time becomes a burden to millions of people who find that they have nothing to fill it with. They may not much like to work, but they have forgotten how to play—and they grow fearful of boredom. The problem may grow much worse in the near future. It is serious because the need to rigidly split work and play time, the inability to fill leisure time happily, and the fear of boredom all signify a lack of integrity in a person's life.[2]

Curiosity and exploration: The origins of play

Curiosity is a basic drive, common to animals as well as human beings. The need to snoop around, to explore, and to do new things, is less dramatic than the need to eat, drink, or sleep, but it is just as real. Our common language recognizes the fact. We speak of "satisfying curiosity" in the same way we say "satisfying hunger." Needs arouse tension; meeting the needs satisfies or resolves it. In the course of doing so, the basis of everything novel, inventive, and creative in human activity is established.

In children, the curiosity drive is expressed early in the form of play—it is sometimes even called the "ludic drive" (Berlyne 1960), from a Latin word meaning "play." Children's play has two important characteristics. First, it involves a fairly frequent shift from one activity to another. Their attention span is short and they need a good deal of stimulus variation to remain interested in something. Secondly, their play is largely a matter of *doing* things, not merely watching or listening for very long. Children get fidgety when they have to sit still for long in play, just as in other things.

Before school age, children start to form *habits* of play, most of which are not well understood. Some favor imaginative and fantasy activity, for instance, perhaps including imagi-

_____
[2] See what *dis*integrate means?

Leisure.

nary playmates with whom they do things together. Others are more inclined to action
games and large-muscle activities. Still others
favor sensory and fine-muscle activities, drawing, molding clay, building things, manipulating
objects. There is a large age factor determining choice of play activity, and almost all
children like to do all kinds of different things;
but preferred habits of play are probably important determinants of the kinds of work and
leisure that the child will favor later on. In general, the more different kinds of play they are
exposed to, the more aroused and curious they
will be, and the more exploration they will do.
Their preferences will combine the different
kinds of stimulation, and the interests they end
up with will be broader and richer as a result. If
they are lucky, then they may become in adulthood what they first learned to be at child's

play—a **dilettante,** one who takes delight in
many different things. It depends largely on
how much they are encouraged to see education
as the means to play.

Education: The channeling of play

To learn almost anything very well, you have
to get interested in it, engrossed in it, motivated
by it. The thing that separates work from play
for many people is that play means something
they want to do whether they have to or not; work
is something they have to do whether they want
to or not. What education should do is help you
develop skills for doing things that are useful
as well as interesting. There may be some difficulty or drudgery involved in that, but the interest of the goal makes it worthwhile. Kids
learning to ride a bicycle will tolerate enormous

amounts of failure, bruises, and falls because they want the skill badly enough to make them worthwhile. If they are absorbed enough in what they are doing, in fact, they may not even notice that the bruises hurt.

When the drudgery part of education is done, and the skills are learned, people should be able to take pleasure in using them. To the extent they do so in their careers, their work is their play and doing it is a rich source of fulfillment. This is important in choosing a career because you need to separate what you want to *do* from what you want to *be*. A career can only be fulfilling if the activity you perform is fulfilling. If your aspirations to become one thing or another revolve around the role rather than the function, chances are you will not be very happy with it. If you want *to be* a doctor, but not to *practice medicine,* you may be bored and miserable.

You may have noticed that highly successful people in business, the professions, and the creative arts tend to be preoccupied with their work. Their spouses complain that they are never home, their friends that they "don't know how to relax." Sometimes this is so, but often the simple truth is that they are vitally and delightedly preoccupied with their work, and would simply rather be doing it than most other things.

People for whom vacations, coffeebreaks, and sick leave are important may be people for whom the job is effort rather than diversion. There are many such jobs, of course, and almost no one can be fulfilled by them. Leisure periods are really necessary for them to get recreation. For the lucky ones whose work is their play, leisure may serve well enough merely by giving rest and relaxation.

The uses of leisure

The two main uses of leisure are **rest** and **play.** Rest is recreating even if your work is fulfilling because all work tends to develop its own routines and you eventually feel stale doing it if you don't get enough stimulus-variation. In this case, stimulus-variation just means getting away from the familiar situation before it becomes fatiguing, or boring, to the point where you don't do it as well as you can and don't like it as much as you should. If your work is drudgery or difficult to begin with, then you get bored and fatigued quickly anyhow, and you probably need more frequent rest periods, though perhaps no more total rest than the person with interesting work. The "coffeebreak" of American business and industry has been recognized by the U.S. Supreme Court as a rest period to which workers are entitled in addition to the lunchtime break. In fact, the pause from routine probably makes them more efficient at their desks and assembly lines.

The function of rest is not so much to change stimulation as to *reduce* it so the person's level of arousal will drop. Obviously it is more wearing to be excited than relaxed. Since sleep is the lowest state of arousal healthy people experience, it is therefore the most complete and refreshing way of resting for most people. Many people who have the habit of taking short naps report that they can awaken from them after only 10 to 30 minutes feeling refreshed. Such naps can help people work more efficiently and improve their mood. (Taub, Tanguay, and Clarkson 1976). Since you also probably work best at logic-related tasks (such as math problems) earlier in the day (Folkard 1975), a short afternoon nap may be particularly valuable for college students.

Lots of people who would like to take naps don't because they cannot fall asleep easily or cannot wake up shortly without feeling more tired. There are physiological differences in sleep and waking patterns, of course, but most people can teach themselves to nap without much trouble, just by practicing doing it at about the same time every day.

Some useful substitutes for short sleep periods are meditation, relaxation exercises, and yoga. They all work fine, though they will not provide as much rest as a nap unless you are quite adept at them. Like napping, they can all be learned pretty well with a little practice, and most of the paperback books on these subjects give reasonably good instructions on how to practice. You may skip the parts of the books that claim these disciplines will change your whole outlook on life, teach you the secrets of the universe, make people stop laughing when you sit down at the piano, or clear up pimples. But the books are restful—and may even help you learn how to nap.

Rest has to be passive in order to be refreshing. Mind and muscles both need time in which to do nothing but recuperate from alert and active states. Listening to soft music, light conversation, or watching television, while less restful than sleep, are more so than going shopping, playing tennis, or watching a football game, even if those things are very enjoyable. It is the quiet that restores here, not the joy. Doing nothing can be good for you.

Play recreates you by changing the familiar stimulus pattern of work in pleasurable ways. They may be more exciting and more active than work, and in that sense, more fatiguing; but they are refreshing anyway because they are enjoyable, even if they are not restful.

The kinds of play available to adults are broader than those of children because adults have more skills, capacities, and interests than

Games were part of the religious life of classical civilization, and play was an important institution of human behavior long before recorded history began.

Croquet Scene, Winslow Homer

children and because they don't have adults hanging over them telling them not to do things (well, some things). Some adults have a problem in this connection; they have become so immersed in their habitual social roles that they are embarrassed to abandon them, even for short periods. They are self-conscious in the protection of a phony self. Such people may take advantage of new situations to drop their customary roles. If they have been constricted enough at home, they may even act completely abandoned. Sober businessmen may become obnoxious infantile drunks at conventions, the delightful people you met on vacation in the mountains may be boring creeps when you go to dinner at their house back in town, and the nice boy you dated in high school may be a loudmouthed boor when he takes you to his fraternity house. It is also why away-from-home **vacations** may be good experiences for adults and pretty pointless for children. Vacations offer the chance to play without the role-restrictions of home base.

Adults can enrich the play things of childhood in all categories of activity. In **large-muscle play,** they have the whole gamut of sports. In **mind-play,** they can add a deeper appreciation of *drama* and *reading* to the fantasy and gameplaying of childhood without giving up any of it. In *sense* (and **fine muscle**) **play,** they can make far richer use, both actively and as spectators, of music and art. [Sometimes too, of perception-altering chemicals such as alcohol and marijuana.]

Most important, adults can engage in **people play** in greater depth than children because they can make more use of *interpersonal encounter,* of *sex,* and of *conversation.*

Many of these activities, moreover, combine many play functions and therefore exercise many faculties at once. Participation (as opposed to watching) in sports, drama, music, art, and sex, variously combines muscle, mind, sense, and people games. In so doing, they may fill many needs at once, and thus be richer, more rewarding, and more recreating than other kinds of play.

This is not to say that it is good for everybody to play at everything. It often is not, for varied reasons. Alcohol is damaging to health, for instance; some other drugs, though perhaps harmless, are illegal; encounter groups are emotionally risky for many people. Sex play has the moral and religious disapproval of many people, and they should not pretend to treat it casually just because some other people do.

In general, the more open you are to yourself, the better you can prejudge what kinds of play to try and the better you can evaluate what kinds of experience are most fulfilling for you. For some people, a wide range of play is necessary, but for others, a few choice things are quite enough. It usually takes some experimenting to find out—but the object is to find out, not to experiment. When you know, quit.

LIFESTYLE AND PERSONAL VALUE

There is a story, apparently undocumented, that when Sigmund Freud was once asked what the proper goals in life were for normal people, he said simply: "Love and work."

In the past, love, work, and play have been very separate events in people's lives. But nowadays the parts of work that are necessary drudgery take less and less time from most people's lives, and may take still less if technology and the distribution of wealth both improve. And the parts of work that are fun can be major preoccupations; so work and play can merge in people's lives. And perhaps both of them, with effort and with luck, can be shared with people whose interests are similar to yours and with people you want to share your self with—friends and lovers. Then the meaning of life, to restate Freud's dictum, becomes: "the things you do and the people you do them with." And then the answer to most existential questions about how to find personal fulfillment becomes: "Find things you want to do and people you want to do them with. Then do them."

As you should realize by now, that simple formula is not so easy to apply. It is frightening in many ways, and arduous in many others, to find the things and engage the people, and the hardest and most honest efforts sometimes fail. And the lies in your own head sometimes prevent you even from acknowledging the fears.

There is no painless way to force honesty (integrity) upon yourself, no way to abandon defenses without feeling anxiety, and no way to be self conscious (aware) if you are very defended. But without integrity and awareness you are crippled to seek fulfillment in love or work. You may find it by dumb luck. Some people do. But most, it seems, are not that lucky, and go through life wandering unsteadily between being almost happy and almost miserable and generally puzzled about why. The reason they are puzzled is probably because they are not facing their feelings that:

They do not want to do what they are doing, or
They do not know what they want to do, or
They fear they cannot do it;
They do not want to be with the people they are with, or
They do not know with whom they would like to be, or
They fear they cannot be with them as they would like.

There are endless sources of unhappiness outside people's heads but only a few sources of puzzlement inside them. The puzzlement which comes from not facing these feelings creates its own special brand of unhappiness because it leaves you feeling that you are not in firm control of your self. You are not, of course, because you are keeping an important part of your self, that is, your anxieties, out of consciousness. In doing so, you are not **whole;** you lose your **integrity.**

The more self-confident you are, of course,

the easier it is to face your anxieties and lower your defenses because the fewer the things are that scare you in the first place.[3] But the more you can force yourself to lower your defenses and face your fears, the more self-confident you may become, because you will find that most anxieties are magnified by hiding them and diminish with exposure. Also, you may gain confidence because your functional intelligence increases, that is, your ability to figure out what is going on in your life and to plan rationally for what you want. Finally, you may gain confidence because when you face your anxieties, you are more likely to borrow the further courage to test them—and you will sometimes come out ahead for doing so. Success increases your estimation of your own value; that gives you confidence; that makes it easier to face yourself. It is a benign circle.

Everyone lies to themselves sometimes. If you can pursue an integral life-style, in which you are always trying to be in honest touch with your head, then you will only be a victim of circumstances, like everything else in the universe. But if you make a life-style of defense, your inner life becomes the victim of your own folly and your total life is twice victimized— by outside circumstances you cannot control and by inner ones you do not know. In the long run, you gain nothing by defense except a brief relief from pain; it will not help you love or work happily, it will not make you live longer, and it will not help you die! To give up the defensive life-style means to take big risks, but the big gains go with the big risks in living. The point of trying to win, of aiming for success, not merely avoiding failure, is that luck, age, infirmity, and death make us all lose anyway in the end. Integrity, awareness, and openness are the instruments of meanwhile.

---

[3] Some apparently self-confident people are really quite anxious, and self-confidence is merely their social defense; they generally act like toads and are recognizable. Some other people are truly self-confident because they are unusually stupid; they generally are recognizable as fools. I am not talking about either of those types.

SUMMARY

1 The role of the *nuclear family* in society is changing rapidly, though it is still the main object of love relationships for most people. The sequence of romantic courtship, marriage, and childrearing has its basis in the development of friendship in childhood. Friendship emerges from the parallel play of toddlers, which gives way to the cooperative play of young children, and in turn, to the general *adient* tendency friends maintain towards each other. Friendships are not constant throughout life, but people often find it hard to recognize this fact because our society places such a high value on friendliness.

2 Friendship develops into romantic love with puberty and the awakening of sexual interests. Falling in love is a painful experience because of its urgency, characterized by the passionate desire to immerse one's whole existence in the loved one's self. All romantic love is marked by sympathetic mutual responsiveness, but the depths and permanence of love relationships varies enormously.

3 The meaning of marriage is changing dramatically in the United States, as the average age at which Americans marry drops and the divorce rate rises. The liberation of women is an important factor in the weakening of marriage, since the economic, sexual, and social needs of both partners can increasingly be fulfilled through other means than marriage. The rearing of children may be the last area of mutual responsibility that can be meaningfully covered by contractual marriage. The long-range effect on family life of the changing patterns is not foreseeable.

4 Choosing a vocation, training for it, and becoming competent in it is a major life activity, not always satisfying. The motivation to succeed comes from early childhood training, but serious career thoughts often do not begin until puberty. Hobbies play an important role in molding vocational interest and skills, but academic training is often unrelated to the needs of many jobs or to people's ability to succeed at them. Efficiency at most work comes more through practice and self-criticism, probably, than through innate talent.

5 Since World War II, American society has become increasingly a culture of leisure, in which the boundaries between play and work have shifted and weakened. This is one reason that an increasing number of adults is changing professions in the middle of their careers. Play is an outgrowth of the curiosity drive, which gets channeled into systematic skills in childhood. The only difference between play and work comes in the definition of one as desirable and the other as necessary. Either recreates the individual by changing their environment-stimuli. Rest recreates for the same reason.

Behavior disorders

18

18

Behavior disorders

A wide variety of disturbances in people's lives collectively make up the field of **abnormal psychology,** also called **psychopathology, mental illness,** and **behavior disorders.** None of these names, strictly speaking, are correct for all of this field, except perhaps "behavior disorders." Abnormal psychology technically means the study of any behavior that deviates from the average, that is, the study of extreme individual differences (see Chapter 12). While that covers behavior disorders all right, it should also include the study of genius, creativity, and all kinds of good things like that. But those are never discussed in psychiatry[1] textbooks and hardly ever in abnormal psychology books (London and Rosenhan 1968). Psychopathology (from the Greek words for mental illness) refers precisely to behavior disorders connected with disease or damage to the brain or nervous system, but a lot of behavior disorders are not illnesses at all, and it is misleading to use the term for them.

What all the behavior disorders have in common, whether they involve trouble in the nervous system or not, is the fact that something is wrong with people's thoughts, feelings, or actions. Usually, they know about it and are made miserable by it; sometimes, they think they are all right, but others are made miserable by their unusual conduct. It makes no difference, in any case, whether the basis of the disturbance is physical or not, whether it comes from a misplaced gene, a toxin (poison) floating around in one's brain (like alcohol), or a brick falling on their head—nor whether the trouble originates in one's experience, and is attributable to their reinforcement history or to the wrongheaded attitudes they may have learned by imitating, or defying, the norms of parents, playmates, or teachers. Behavior disorders go together, more or less, because they all involve

---

[1] Psych = mind; iatry = treatment. Psychiatry is the branch of medicine that treats behavior disorders. A psychiatrist is a *medical* doctor; a psychologist, ordinarily, is not an M.D. but a Ph.D.

malfunctions or *maladjustments* that prevent people from getting along in life as well as they ought to. They are the subject of this chapter.

EVOLUTION AND BEHAVIOR DISORDER

Animal trainers, zoo keepers, and veterinarians generally know a whole lot about *learning,* and special kinds of animal trainers, like the ones who train seeing eye dogs and teach blind people to live with them, know a whole lot of practical things about animal personality development, especially about the process of identification. But there are no animal psychiatrists to speak of because there are no behavior disorders worth mentioning below the level of mammals. You can frustrate anachnids, but you can't make them nervous about it, evidently, whether they circumvent, attack, or withdraw in response. Among mammals, and perhaps some lower vertebrates, you can produce conflict situations which require a certain amount of complex response capacity to get into. And among all kinds of lower animals, genetic troubles and toxins or traumas (poisons and accidents) will produce neurological and perceptual troubles. But to have complex behavior disorders, one needs a sufficiently complex nervous system to get screwed up when it is tampered with. This means a central nervous system, called an "adjuster" system because it integrates the nervous activity in the receptor and effector systems (Gerking 1969). Among lower organisms, the worms are the lowest phyla to qualify. The *phylum chordata,* of which we are members, is defined by having a spinal chord, the beginning of the complex central nervous system from which the brain developed. All vertebrates qualify.

Fish, amphibians, reptiles, and birds get frightened, angry, and frustrated, but they do not get conflicted much, and they do not get neurotic at all. Rats, as we saw in Chapter 15, can be taught to experience conflict in experi-mental situations. Pavlov was able to produce the equivalent of a "nervous breakdown" in dogs and also what psychiatrists would have to call a masochistic perversion. Gant, an American student of his, enticed dogs into what he called "experimental neuroses," and Liddell did the same with sheep. They were "experimental" only in the scientist's view; the animals were miserable. These effects were all produced by putting animals in stress situations where they had to make very subtle perceptual discriminations, or try to avoid painful shocks, or otherwise to solve insoluble problems. When they could not do so, and could not escape, previously lively, friendly animals would go

The words *insanity, madness,* or *mental aberration* used to—and maybe still do—conjure up an image of maniacal violence to some people.

Guardian Figure, Japanese Kamakura Period

into the sheep or dog equivalent of collapse. They would stop trying to cope with the problem, become irritable and morose, go off their feed, mope and sulk, and grow listless (Gantt 1944; Liddell 1956). Basically, the same thing happens to people. But since people are more complicated creatures than other animals, the form of their behavior disorders may also be.

The extent to which you can develop complex behavior disorders depends on the extent to which you are capable of complex behavior, which in turn depends on how complicated an "adjuster" system you have. As you climb the phylogenetic ladder, and the adjuster system grows more and more complex, so does the potential for varied behavior—and varied trouble connected with it. In mammals, even more in primates, and most of all, in human beings, that capacity has become so elaborate that many of the disorders connected with it have no *functional* (meaning "practical") connection with any known disorders of the brain or nervous system at all. This was not widely understood before Freud's writings, starting at the end of the 19th century, and it was not widely accepted for many years thereafter. The discovery of functional disorders was the most important turning point in the study of psychiatry, and perhaps Freud's greatest contribution to human knowledge. But before discussing it, we should look briefly at the historic events that led to it.

The prehistory of psychiatry

Until fairly modern times, almost nothing was known about behavior disorders. "Madness" was generally considered either a divine inspiration or a supernatural affliction, depending on who was considering it and when. In the Golden Age of Greece, Hippocrates wrote that such disorders resulted from natural rather than supernatural causes, and that these natural causes were to be found in the brain, but he knew nothing about the brain. Five hundred years later, Galen said much the same thing, knowing as much as Hippocrates did about the brain. Both of them gathered case material, however, and wrote descriptions of different mental ailments. The only other important classical student of behavior disorders was Soranus, a century before Galen, who said the first sensible things ever about *treating* mental illness—provide some comfort for the sufferers and keep their interests alive.

The Middle Ages In the Dark Ages, when Christianity became the dominant religion of Europe, classical ideas were discredited in favor of the belief that mental illness was caused by evil spirits, possession by demons, and so forth. Monks became the psychiatrists and monasteries the mental hospitals of the day, and prayer and incantation became the main treatment. Torture and burning at the stake later replaced them as better means of chasing out demons and combating witchcraft. A lot of harmlessly insane people were legally murdered as witches and warlocks.

The Age of Reason By the beginning of the 18th century, these brutal practices had diminished, but they were not replaced with good care for the mentally ill. Often their families just threw them out to wander around and manage as best they could. In fact, they were probably a lot better off that way than they were going to one of the few hospitals that were around to give them "asylum." The Hospital of St. Mary of Bethlehem in London (founded as a hospital for the insane in 1547) for instance, has given us the word *bedlam* (the way Bethlehem was popularly pronounced), meaning "a situation of noisy uproar or confusion; a madhouse" (American Heritage Dictionary 1970). It accurately describes what went on there. The patients were treated like animals, running around wildly or chained in their own filth, brutalized by the keepers hired to control them, and targets of great mirth and entertainment from the heartless public that paid a fee to go watch them cavort. The purpose of such in-

Until fairly recent times, little was known about behavior disorders. Patients with mental illness who were institutionalized were often chained and treated like animals.

stitutions was to remove the mentally ill from society, not to help them.

The ugly institutions began to become mental hospitals through the work of Philippe Pinel (1745–1826), the chief physician of La Bicêtre, France's equivalent of Bedlam. He struck the chains from the patients in 1792 and began a regimen called *moral treatment,* which meant being kind to patients, talking with them, and setting a model for sane and reasonable conduct. It was a great success. A lot of patients got well and went home. When the same treatment program was applied in other places, it worked equally well. Worcester State Mental Hospital,

in Massachusetts, for instance, began to record a discharge rate of mental patients that it did not again equal until a few years ago (Bockoven 1963). Benjamin Rush (he was Benjamin Franklin's father-in-law), and after him Dorothea Dix (1802–1887) also improved conditions greatly in mental hospital care in the United States, and William Tuke (1832–1922) did so in England.

Modern psychiatry Ironically, the quality of treatment got worse in mental hospitals when scientific psychiatry came into existence, more or less officially, with the publication of Griesinger's textbook in 1845 (see Chapter 1). The main belief of scientific psychiatry was that

Philippe Pinel. His "moral treatment" was the humane handling of mental hospital patients.

the cause of mental disorders was physical. If someone became mentally ill, they must have had some hereditary or constitutional defect or have suffered some kind of damage to brain or nervous system through disease, poisoning, or accident. Psychiatry, in that perspective, was simply part of neurology, itself a branch of physiology and anatomy. So psychiatric research would be physiological and anatomical.

With this approach as a guide, the physical basis of paresis, a disabling psychosis, was discovered to be syphilis, by Gournier (1857–1914) and Krafft-Ebing; Korsakov (1845–1900) discovered that another psychosis, named for him, resulted from chronic alcoholism; and several other physical bases of behavior disorders were discovered and speculated on. Today, this orientation is called *organic* or biological *psychiatry* because it seeks the roots of the behavior disorders in physical causes.

It was assumed that heredity and brain pathology were the main causes of most disorders, but evidence was lacking in almost all instances —and it was abundantly clear that there were a lot of different disorders. Classifying them therefore became an important task of psychiatry. The most important figure in this work was Emil Kraepelin (1856–1926), who developed the scheme of psychiatric classification used, in revised form, to this day. Like almost everyone else at the time, Kraepelin believed that the root of everything was organic, but he had sense enough to recognize that the best way to classify the disorders was in terms of *observable*

Benjamin Rush. Benjamin Franklin's father-in-law, and a signer of the Declaration of Independence, he was the American equivalent of Pinel.

Emil Kraepelin originated the classification system of behavior disorders still in use today.

symptoms, since the supposed physical causes could only be inferred. He made two major groupings of psychoses: (1) *dementia precox,* which includes several conditions which today we call **schizophrenia;** and (2) *manic-depressive* psychoses, today called *affective* disorders.

The third important phase of modern psychiatry (the first two are the organic approach and Kraepelin's classification scheme) was the discovery that *dynamic* or psychological factors could be so powerful that they could create behavior disorders even in people who did not have any evident brain disease or hereditary defects. The basis for this idea lay in the work of a French psychiatrist, Charcot (1825–1893), whose studies of hysteria (see below) showed that its symptoms could be induced or removed by hypnosis. But he himself believed that hysteria had some organic basis, and it remained for two of his students, Pierre Janet (1859–1947) and Sigmund Freud (1856–1939), to develop the idea that hysteria results from mental processes which somehow produce the symptoms of physical illness. Freud's work became far more popular than Janet's, partly because its implications extended to many conditions other than hysteria, including some of the everyday peculiarities of speech and action which he named the *Psychopathology of Everyday Life*—and partly because of the psychoanalytic treatment method he developed for these conditions. But both Freud and Janet may be regarded as the fathers of what is now called *dynamic psychiatry.* The experimental work of Ivan Pavlov and Edward Thorndike was being published at the same time that Freud and Janet were writing, but the implications of *learning* for dynamic psychiatry did not become apparent until 20 or 30 years later, and the importance of so-called behavioral or learning principles in the dynamics of behavior-disorders has only become widely recognized since 1950. In any case, both the psychoanalytic and behavioral approaches to disorder are parts of the functional or *dynamic* approach, as opposed to the *organic.*

CLASSIFYING THE DISORDERS

The foundations of modern psychiatry were laid by the beginning of this century, and the structure built on them since has not changed too much. The classification scheme which Kraepelin laid down has been expanded and broadened, both by the recognition of *functional* disorders (i.e., those which do not involve physical defects) and by the expansion of the number of different human problems that are today regarded as psychiatric in nature. In 1952, the American Psychiatric Association published an official classification scheme, called the *Diagnostic and Statistical Manual of Mental Disorders* (DSM-I for short), which was almost universally accepted as the best system around, despite its many shortcomings. It was revised and improved in 1968. DSM-II has received even more general acceptance than the first edition did. DSM-III is now in the making (1977).

According to DSM-II, there are seven major categories of behavior disorders: (1) *neurosis,* (2) *psychosomatic disorders,* (3) *personality disorders,* (4) *special symptom disorders,* (5) *Psychoses,* (6) *brain damage,* and (7) *mental retardation.* For the most part, conditions are grouped together according to how severe they are and to what their common symptoms are, not according to whether their origins are functional or organic or how they can best be treated. Even so, there are some common biases about many of them among mental health experts. *Neuroses,* for instance, are put in one group largely because of the common belief that they have no physical basis, that anxiety is their main symptom, and that they are among the most treatable of behavior disorders. *Psychosomatic disorders* are grouped together on the basis of the physical symptoms

Behavior disorders as depicted in a scene from *The Persecution and Assassination of Marat as performed by the Inmates of the Asylum of Charenton under the direction of the Marquis de Sade* by Peter Weiss.

involved, that is, because they are medical conditions—but they are called *psycho*somatic only because of the common belief that they result from psychological stresses. *Psychoses,* on the other hand, are grouped together only because of their common symptoms, and there is a vigorous debate about whether they originate in the dynamics of early parent-child relationships or in some genetic or constitutional predisposition, or both.

There is much uncertainty about the meaningfulness of many psychiatric classifications and much evidence that diagnoses are often unreliable (Zigler and Phillips 1961). In some places, for instance, people tend to get classi-fied as neurotic if they are white middle-class types and psychotic if they are black or immigrant lower-class types (Redlich and Hollingshead 1958). In others, psychiatrists tend to rely on one kind of diagnosis for almost everyone. In still others, there is a tendency never to change a diagnosis, once it is made, regardless of how the patient changes. If you are diagnosed as having a schizophrenic psychosis when you enter the hospital, in such places, and then you get well, they don't change your record to say that you are well, but now merely call you a schizophrenic "in remission," meaning "not crazy for the time being" (Rosenhan 1973). And in still other places, they go back and "correct" the original diagnosis to fit your present condition. It is well known, for instance, that everyone recovers from severe depressions in a pretty short time, but it is widely believed that schizophrenics stay psychotic indefinitely. So in some hospitals, if you are diagnosed schizophrenic on admission, and then you feel well and act normally a week later, the original diagnosis may change to "depression."

Perhaps the most troublesome thing of all about the diagnoses of behavior disorders is that, even when they are made reliably and accurately, they do not always contribute much to planning treatment. The first impressions that patients make on the hospital staff are even more important than their diagnoses. Patients who make likable first impressions get more personal attention from the staff and fewer tranquilizers than patients with the same problems but less appealing ways (Katz and Zimbardo 1977).

For all these reasons, some scholars feel that it is practically useless, if not harmful, to make diagnostic evaluations at all. Maybe so. But other scholars argue, equally strongly, that the diagnostic categories *are* useful descriptively and that, on some occasions, they are vital indicators of the severity, and possible danger involved in some disorders (Meehl 1973). And most mental-health experts continue to use them. We shall discuss enough major ones to give you some familiarity with them.

THE NEUROTIC REACTIONS

Neuroses are conditions in which people go to extreme efforts to escape anxiety, fail to pull it off, and feel anxious or damage their functioning because of it. Neurotic reactions are important only when they cause serious problems in your life. Anxiety about grades is not a neurosis, having headaches doesn't make you hysterical, and counting cracks on the sidewalk does not make you a compulsive neurotic. Neuroses can often be helped quickly by psychotherapy or medical treatment.

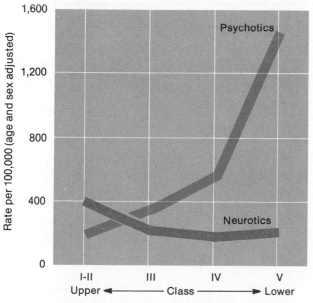

Figure 18.1 Your official mental health status may depend as much on your color, income, and education as on your symptoms.

Source: Hollingshead and Redlich, Social Class and Mental Illness: A Community Study, New York: John Wiley & Sons, 1958.

The three main kinds of neuroses are (1) *conversion* and *dissociative reactions,* called *hysterical neuroses;* (2) *obsessions* and *compulsive reactions,* called *obsessive-compulsive neuroses;* and (3) *phobic* or *fearful reactions,* which make up the *anxiety neuroses.*

Hysterical neuroses

Hysterical neurotics use repression and denial defenses to the extreme. The two main hysterical neuroses are *conversion reactions* and *dissociative reactions.*

In conversion hysteria, a person suddenly *loses sensation,* such as pain sense or sight, hearing, or touch; or they lose *motor abilities,* becoming paralyzed or unable to talk; or they undergo *internal changes,* such as headaches, lumps in the throat, choking sensations, or having trouble breathing. Whichever the particular symptoms, the general effect is that the person becomes physically disabled with no apparent physiological basis for it.

Conversion hysterics are not *malingering,* that is, not pretending to be ill. But there are some things about their symptoms that usually make it clear that the illness is *functional,* not *organic.*

First, hysterics often seem untroubled by their ailment, while most people would be terrified to suddenly find themselves blind or paralyzed.

The Absinthe Drinker, Pablo Picasso

In conversion hysteria, patients find themselves suddenly blind or paralyzed. This is becoming less common as people become more knowledgable.

Second, conversion symptoms often differ from the usual medical patterns. Hysterically paralyzed limbs don't waste away like organically paralyzed ones, and the areas affected in hysteria don't match the nerve pathways in the limb.

Third, conversion symptoms are inconsistent. Hysterical paralyses may disappear during sleep, unlike organic ones, and hysterically blind people don't bump into things, while physically blind people do.

Fourth, conversion symptoms often can be manipulated by hypnotic suggestions or drugs, while most organic symptoms cannot.

Conversion hysterics are highly suggestible, dramatic people, emotionally very dependent on others, and manipulative and seductive in relations with them. The conversion reaction helps them repress anxiety by getting sick, and the sympathy they then get gives them a new motive to stay sick. The symptoms are often those of organic ailments which the patient has actually had or has seen.

Freud's notion that repression was the underlying cause of conversion hysteria was the basis for psychoanalytic theory, which says that the unsuccessful repression of unacceptable *sexual impulses* is responsible for conversion hysteria. The failure of the repression efforts starts to produce anxiety and, in a process which Freud did not claim to understand, the energy of these impulses is *converted* into the symptoms of physical illness, with the result that the repression is maintained, the anxiety staved off, and the person disabled.

Dissociative reactions are the second main hysterical neurosis. Dissociation means separating yourself from threatening thoughts. Instead of becoming physically ill, the victim gets one of four symptoms: *amnesia, fugue state, multiple personality,* or *somnabulism.*

In *amnesia,* you forget your past, maybe even your name and home. Amnesia is sometimes faked by people trying consciously to escape from unpleasant situations, and it sometimes results from brain damage. But in hysterical amnesia, most of a person's behavior patterns remain the same as always, and the amnesia may be lifted by drugs, hypnosis, or psychotherapy.

Some amnesia victims escape even further from their problems by going into a *fugue state,* which means that you combine amnesia with actually running away. When people find you in this state, you don't know who or where you are. People sometimes recover spontaneously from this condition, and they may then have amnesia for what happened during the fugue. It is as if they wake up from a dream, knowing *who* they are, but unsure of *where,* or how they got there.

Multiple personality is a very rare, dramatic dissociative reaction in which the person develops two or more distinct personalities. The new personality is commonly socially extroverted, outgoing, or wild, and the original one shy and inhibited. What's more, while the person is in one condition, they may not know the other personality exists. Multiple personality is thought by some workers to be a way of handling conflicting impulses without feeling guilty or responsible for our behavior. The inhibited personality is dissociated from the wild action of the other one.

There are only a few well documented cases of multiple personality, and among them are some accounts of three or more personalities developing in the same individual. The most famous of these are *The Three Faces of Eve* and *Sybil.* Eve was discovered, treated and reported by Corbett Thigpen and Hervey Cleckley and portrayed in a very successful Hollywood movie by Joanne Woodward (1957). Sybil was a young woman with three main personalities and thirteen auxiliary ones. She was successfully treated over a period of many years by a combination of psychoanalysis and hypnosis (Schreiber 1973). In the splendid 1976 television-movie version of Sybil, Joanne Woodward played the psychiatrist. Multiple personalities were first described in the literature at the turn of the century by the American psychiatrist, Morton Prince (1901). The prototype of all multiple personalities is, of course, *Dr. Jekyll and Mr. Hyde* (Stevenson 1886).

Somnambulism, or sleep walking, is a dissociative state in which a person acts when their conscious controls are relaxed in sleep. Young people are more prone to sleepwalk than adults. Most sleepwalking episodes last less than a half hour. It is not dangerous to awaken sleepwalkers, but they rarely know where they are or what has been happening. Unlike the hysterically blind, sleepwalkers *are* in danger of being hurt; they often have accidents.

Obsessive-compulsive reactions

Obsessions are persistent thoughts that interfere with a person's normal activity. In obsessive neuroses, they may be fears of being overwhelmed by uncontrollable impulses of sex or hostility, or by fears of sickness, or death overtaking you or those you love. Even though you know they are nonsense, you cannot get rid of the thoughts, and they make you guilty and anxious.

Compulsions are *rituals* a person feels they must do even though they seem senseless (see Chapter 15). The ritual may be a trivial thing, such as humming a tune over and over, or it may be a complex pattern, such as getting out of bed only on the left side, brushing your

A compulsion to wash the hands constantly and endlessly may mask an underlying fear of being so hopelessly dirty—perhaps from sexual thoughts or acts—that they will never wash clean.

Woman Washing Her Hands, Gerard ter Borch

teeth a certain way, always putting on the left shoe before putting on the right sock, counting every fourth telephone pole you walk past, starting over each time a girl passes you in the opposite direction wearing sandals, and on and on. The troublesome thing about compulsions is that the person feels anxious, guilty, and uncomfortable until they have done the ritual act. Then they feel relieved and satisfied — for a while.

Obsessions and compulsions are ritualistic attempts to defend against anxiety, perhaps aroused by sexual, aggressive, or other impulses a person cannot accept in themselves. By inventing "busywork" behavior-patterns, they try to make their inner world secure, preventing the impulses from bursting forth by the compulsive barriers they erect against them. The obsessions and compulsions may be substitutes for the dangerous thoughts and acts one fears they would do if they were to "let themselves go."

Obsessive-compulsives have rigid consciences, tend to be very guilty, and generally try to cope with their unacceptable impulses by *reaction-formations* of seeming very kind, considerate, and scrupulous, or by *insulation* defenses like *intellectualization* and *rationalization,* which make them emotionally insensitive and therefore less prone to guilt.

The seeds of obsessional neuroses are innocently sown in childhood in the harmless rituals that you probably remember doing yourself — such as not stepping on a crack in the widewalk; instantly reciting such incantations as "needles, pins, triplets, twins. . . ." If you and a friend said the same thing at the same time; holding a button and lifting your feet when you cross a railroad track;[2] and many others. The function of obsessive and compulsive acts in childhood is the same as in adulthood: to prevent harm from having done something wrong. It makes no difference whether the harm

comes from God, parents, or random demons, nor whether the wrong is mild or serious or the guilt you felt over it small or great. In all events, the magic ritual of thought or action has the same defensive function, undoing the danger involved and thus relieving your anxiety. The roots of such feelings are buried in the dark past of human history, and have been institutionalized since time out of mind, in religious rituals for propitiating the gods.

Psychoanalytic theorists feel that obsessional neurosis is a more infantile problem than the hysterical neuroses are. They believe it results from an emotional *fixation* at the anal stage of development, meaning that the child simply never outgrew the preoccupations of that stage. Hysteria, on the other hand, is thought to come from fixation at the phallic stage, when sexual impulses start to concern the growing child. Some thinkers believe that the sudden development of obsessive-compulsive neurosis in adulthood represents a *decompensation* of personality, a mental "falling apart" which if unchecked can eventually degenerate into psychosis (Fenichel 1945).

Of all the neuroses, these are the most difficult to treat by psychotherapy. One reason is that obsessive-compulsives tend to be very smart and very intellectual; so they tend to fence intellectually with their psychotherapists and not to let themselves get opened up emotionally to the anxiety which their symptoms are defending against in the first place. Another reason is that they tend to be passive in a subtle way and unwilling to confront themselves emotionally, which is the "hard work" of psychotherapy. They want the therapist to do the work of treatment, so to speak, while they sit back and watch it. As you might expect, success rates in treating these problems are low.

Anxiety neuroses

All neurotic symptoms are abortive attempts to avoid anxiety. There are three kinds of

---

[2] Failing to do this, you will lose a friend.

neuroses, however, in which the primary symptom actually *is* anxiety. These **anxiety neuroses** are named **acute traumatic neuroses, anxiety states,** and **phobias.**

In **acute traumatic neuroses** a person is suddenly overwhelmed with anxiety and remains disturbed for some time. This can happen in combat, where it is sometimes called "shell-shock"; or it can happen to people who are assulted, raped, or in a violent accident. It is called **traumatic neurosis** because violence is involved, and it is called acute because its onset is sudden and intense. Its victims feel fearful, dejected, hypersensitive, and irritable; their sleep may be disturbed for some time and they may suffer tremors while awake. Fortunately, they soon recover even with little or no treatment.

Anxiety states are more **chronic** conditions, meaning they last a long time. People with chronic anxiety are nervous, depressed, unable to concentrate, have trouble sleeping, and generally cannot enjoy life. They may suffer sexual malfunctions and may have a lot of aches and pains, such as headache or dizziness or upset stomach or even the panicky feeling that they're having a heart attack. About a third of all neurotic complaints are anxiety states. Most people probably suffer from them in mild form at one time or another. These are the conditions for which mild tranquilizers are commonly prescribed; anxiety states have made these pills the most widely sold drugs in the world. Anxiety states are vaguely fearful conditions in which the victims cannot specify exactly what they are afraid of. Phobias and traumatic anxiety, in which there is a feared object, are also forms of anxiety state.

People with long-standing anxiety states are called **anxiety neurotics.** In addition to all the symptoms indicated above, they also tend to feel apprehensive about the future. They lack self-confidence, can't make decisions easily, and are easily discouraged. This makes them feel guilty and increases their anxiety and pessimism about themselves.

Sexual impotence has become a widely acknowledged problem among American males in the past decade or so, partly perhaps in reaction to the "sexual revolution" which has made women the sexual equals of men and therefore made it legitimate for them to initiate sexual activity. This has been anxiety-provoking to some men. They feel called upon to prove themselves in sexual performance, fearful that they will not be able to do so, and therefore that they are not "masculine" enough to be admired and respected by their lover. Then, as if in proof that their fears are justified, they find themselves sexually impotent, and are embarrassed and humiliated by it.

The reason for "psychic impotence" is that sexual arousal in males comes from the action of the parasympathetic nervous system (see Chapter 3), which dominates relaxed states. Arousal is inhibited by the sympathetic nervous system, which dominates the body in alert, tense states. A male become impotent **when he is tense** either from anxiety, anger, or revulsion.[3] If he is genuinely attracted to a female and simply lets himself relax in a sexually exciting situation, he will get aroused. If he is too busy with fantasies of his own inadequacy to relax, he can usually be helped a lot by psychotherapy (Kaplan 1974). Almost all cases of impotence are treatable (Masters and Johnson 1970). One of the things that may be most valuable for him to learn, in this connection, is that to most women, "masculinity" does not mean sexual athletics but the ability of a man to be tender, gentle, and loving towards her. Developing these feelings in oneself is a powerful antidote for impotence.

Phobias are extreme fears, usually of relatively harmless things. There are dozens

---

[3] Impotence can sometimes have a physical basis, but it is relatively rare.

of useless Greek and Latin names for phobias, like **claustrophobia** fear of closed places; or **acrophobia,** fear of high places. Most of them are not worth remembering.

Phobias are very common disorders. They happen more to young than to old people, and more to women than to men. People with severe phobias go to great lengths to avoid situations that arouse their fears. This can make life very difficult. In a big city, people with phobias for elevators or for driving on freeways are limited in where they can go, and fear of airplanes interferes with the business and pleasure of many people.

Some phobias involve displacement mechanisms in which the feared object is a substitute for a different source of anxiety, too frightening to recognize. Such phobias may develop like an obsession, as a defense against some unacceptable impulse. A person may become phobic for high places to defend against recognizing the impulse to throw their professor off a cliff. But some phobic reactions are probably a result of simple conditioning (Davison and Neale 1978). If a child is attacked by a dog, it learns to fear dogs, even friendly ones, maybe even stuffed toy dogs, or furry toys in general, though it knows they are harmless.

Most phobics know their fears are irrational, but the knowledge doesn't relieve them. Phobias are best treated by behavior therapies, which we shall discuss in the next chapter.

Psychosomatic disorders

As we have seen, physical illnesses sometimes result from emotional stresses a person cannot cope with. Some of these conditions are major health problems, affecting millions of people. They are called **psychosomatic** or **psychophysiological** ailments because both mental and physical processes are involved. No age or sex group is immune to these reactions. Some of the most common psycho-

somatic disorders are asthma, ulcers, migraine headaches, hypertension, colitis, and obesity

Asthma is a form of allergy in which breathing is very difficult (Purcell and Weiss 1970). It occurs most among children and among males. As in other allergies, a constitutional predisposition may be an important factor in getting asthma. The psychological factor is thought to be connected with unsatisfied feelings of dependency (Rees 1964). The child's asthmatic attack, for instance, is sometimes considered an unconscious appeal to mother for help. But these and other possibilities are still only hypotheses (Davison and Neale 1978).

Millions of Americans have stomach or intestinal **ulcers,** which are painful sores in the lining of the stomach or intestine. Four times as many men as women get ulcers. There is clear evidence that ulcers develop in connection with feelings of dependency, insecurity, and anxiety in people (and monkeys) who feel heavy responsibility and some helplessness about their ability to fulfill it (Seligman 1975). Ambitious, driving career men and women are more prone to them than other people, but some data point to a constitutional disposition as well (Davison and Neale 1978).

Migraine headaches are mostly a female disorder. More than 10 million people in the United States have chronic migraines, mainly produced, it seems, by tension and frustration over interpersonal relationships and social roles. Perfectionistic, intelligent, rigid, conscientious people seem most prone to migraine. There is so much of it around that a society of migraine sufferers has created a foundation to support research on the care of this devastatingly painful condition.

Hypertension means high blood pressure. It appears most in ambitious, striving, alert people who are always on guard. It is most

---

[4] In fact, DSM-III has dropped this category altogether, in the belief that *all* medical illnesses can have psychological components.

likely to develop in middle age, and it may come about as a purely physical condition as well as a psychosomatic one.

Colitis, also called "nervous stomach," happens more to women, especially to tense people with depressive personality traits. It seems connected with anxiety and hostility towards maternal figures.

Many other illnesses and disorders may have psychosomatic components. There is even some evidence that such diseases as tuberculosis and cancer might be influenced by stress and personality factors, though this is not accepted by most medical experts. But there is no doubt that allergies, backaches, respiratory ailments, and some skin disorders and heart conditions may be aggravated, if not induced, by psychological stresses. And some general practitioners of medicine have told me that they estimate as much as 85 percent of the complaints that people bring to their family physicians are for things that must be considered psychosomatic, if not purely psychological.

Many of the problems that involve the interactions of behavior and body processes cannot exactly be called psychosomatic, on the one hand, and cannot be treated by psychotherapy any more readily than by medical attention, on the other—but still may be **behavior disorders** in the truest sense of both words. The *DSM-II* does not even try to find labels for all these conditions. Alcoholism, drug addiction, and some sex preferences[5] are considered fairly serious and classed together as "Personality Disorders and Certain Other Nonpsychotic Mental Conditions." Bedwetting, speech problems, overeating, undereating, smoking, nailbiting, and what have you, all considered less serious, are lumped together as "Special Symptoms." What they all have in common is that they are not neuroses, not psychoses, and not psychophysiological re-

actions, but are all functional behavior problems, which do not come from any known bodily defect or disease.

Special symptoms

The special symptom reactions have sometimes been called **habit disorders** when they involve what your grandma might dismiss as mere "bad habits." Most of them are not very serious in comparison with the other kinds of functional disorders. But all of them are serious enough to make their victims miserable and often need professional help. Here are some of the most common ones.

Stuttering—About 1 percent of people stutter; most are males. Stuttering usually begins at preschool ages. If not treated, it can last a lifetime. Some people believe there is a hereditary or neurological factor in stuttering, but the evidence for this is weak. *All* stutterers have an important *psychological* problem; their fear of stuttering makes them tense before speaking; this may actually cause the stuttering or make it worse when it starts. Most stutterers speak clearly when they are alone or with people who are not threatening to them, and when singing.

Enuresis (bedwetting) is a more common problem for boys than for girls; it is not rare among young adults, but is among people over 30. Sometimes enuresis results from organic conditions, but most bedwetting has a psychological cause. In children, it may be a sign of general anxiety. In adults, it creates anxiety because it is so embarrassing.

Tics are habitual small muscle twitches or movements, like blinking hard, licking your lips, and clearing your throat. They are most common in grade school children but are widespread among adults as well. These nervous mannerisms occur most in uncomfortable social situations. People are often unaware of their tics until it is brought to their attention, and then may be embarrassed and self-conscious about them. **Nailbiting, finger**

---

[5] Fewer and fewer.

drumming, and **knuckle cracking** are also nervous mannerisms, but they are more conscious and voluntary than tics. All such movements seem to originate as anxiety-reducing responses to mild stress. Once they become habits, they are maintained for the same reason.

There is no special classification for garden variety **overeating** or for compulsive **smoking.** There is a "special symptom" grouping called "feeding disturbance," but it refers to things like **anorexia nervosa,** which is pathologically starving yourself, or **bulemia,** compulsively stuffing yourself, both fairly rare conditions.

Ordinary overeating and smoking are not included because their ill effects are not primarily *behavioral.* Even so, the effects are so serious in both cases and result so directly from eating and smoking *habits,* that they certainly are habit disorders, or special symptoms.

Smoking a lot may produce addiction, but there is no proof it does. Without a doubt, though, it develops into a habit rather quickly, and seems to serve the same anxiety-reducing functions as tics and nailbiting. Unlike them, however, smoking is socially acceptable and

Smoking.

Obesity.

often socially reinforced. "Have a cigarette" is considered a friendly, not a hostile gesture. Many treatment methods have been developed for smoking, but none has lasting success with most people. This does not mean it is impossible to quit smoking, by any means. Millions of people have stopped permanently—it simply means that there is no special treatment method more likely to work than any other. If you try one, and it fails, try another.

Overeating is a more complicated problem because it is more difficult to treat. *All* smoking is bad for you, and treatment succeeds when you stop completely and stay stopped. But some eating *is* good for you, and successful treatment means learning to control eating, not to give it up. Obesity has become one of the biggest public health problems in America in recent years, with an estimated 90 million Americans suffering from overweight. Present knowledge indicates that most overeating is a simple habit disorder, like smoking, with no profound psychodynamic implications (Stuart and Davis 1972). As with smoking, how-

ever, this means that there is no single treatment method clearly able to work. Successful control of one's weight can be managed best by some combination of calorie-restricting diet and exercise; a balanced diet of fats, proteins, and carbohydrates is probably best for most people and is the kind most available; but whatever works for each individual is good enough, and no one knows what works best for whom.

Personality disorders (and other big troubles)

If you are not psychotic, not neurotic, not brain-damaged, but still suffering from very big behavioral trouble, the psychiatric manual will probably have you classified under "Personality disorders and certain other nonpsychotic mental disorders." The "certain other" disorders are **sex, alcohol,** and **drugs.**

"Personality disorders" used to be called "character disorders," or "personality pattern disturbances," or "personality trait disturbances" because, in all of them, the person's general character and lifelong behavior patterns, not any specific symptoms, are the cause of serious trouble in their lives. The different types are[6] *inadequate* personality, *schizoid* personality, *cyclothymic* personality, *emotionally unstable* (hysterical) personality, *passive-aggressive* or *passive-dependent* personality, *compulsive* personality, *paranoid* personality, *explosive* personality, *asthenic* personality, and *antisocial* personality.

Inadequate personality means a "sad-sack" character who is inept intellectually, socially, and emotionally.

Schizoid personality means someone who is emotionally aloof, shallow, and perhaps eccentric also, but without the disordered thinking or other symptoms of schizophrenia.

Cyclothymic (also called "affective") personality means manic or depressive tendencies in someone who is not psychotic.

Emotionally unstable (or *hysterical* or *histrionic*) personalities are people with poor control over their excited emotions; they are vain and self-dramatizing, and they switch from feeling hostile to guilty to anxious with excessive ease.

Compulsive personalities are tense, rigid, super-conscientious, and obsessed with trivial details.

Passive dependency is also a sad-sack character trait of people who behave helplessly in most life situations. They rely on others to take care of them and do nothing to manage their own lives. *Passive-aggressive* people, on the other hand, combine dependency with hostility towards the people they depend on. They get on people's nerves because, instead of expressing their hostility openly, they do it passively, procrastinating, obstructing, and not lifting a finger to help themselves, while com-

plaining that other people are indifferent or unfair to them.

Paranoid personality is the name given people who are rigid and hypersensitive about themselves, suspicious of other people's motives, jealous, self-inflated, and tending to blame others for things.

Explosive personality (also called "epileptoid") refers to someone who has uncontrollable outbursts of rage strikingly different from their usual behavior. In rare cases, such people have actually been found to have epilepsy (Mark and Ervin 1971); the term "epileptoid" means that this condition looks like epilepsy.

Asthenic personality is easily fatigued, low in energy, and unenthusiastic—the way you must feel by the time you get through this list.

Note so far that most of the conditions called personality disorders are variations of neurotic or psychotic conditions in which the person simply does not have the neurotic symptoms of anxiety-run-wild or the loss of reality which is supposed to define psychosis. Supposedly these are less serious problems, but that is not always true. They can ruin people's lives or jobs or relationships. This is obvious when you look at the personality disorders which are not connected to the conventional neuroses and psychoses: *antisocial personality, sex deviation,* and *addictions.* All three conditions were once subtopics of *sociopathic personality disorder,* meaning "socially ill" people, like "criminals, gamblers, prostitutes, dope peddlers," and everyone else who would be considered unsavory by polite society. *DSM-II* recognizes that being socially unacceptable does not mean you have a behavior disorder; some people commit crimes for profit, not because they are disturbed. So this manual drops the term "sociopathic personality" and calls some of these things "conditions without manifest psychiatric disorder."

Antisocial personality, once called "psychopathic personality," is another story. These are emotionally immature people motivated by

---

[6] The conditions actually named in *DSM-I* and *DSM-II* differ somewhat; so I have taken interesting ones from both.

momentary impulses. Impulsive and irresponsible, they have little feeling for other people. Many psychopaths have great personal charm and use it to become professional "con" men. They have little love or loyalty for others and little guilt or anxiety about it. Most psychopaths are failures, even at confidence games, because their impulsiveness leads them into frequent error and prevents them from learning anything from it.

Addictions *Alcohol* and *drug* use were both discussed at some length in Chapter 11. They are considered personality disorders only when their prolonged use causes trouble, not because of their effects on consciousness.

The psychiatric manual, like many other writings, avoids the term *addiction,* and prefers to use the term *dependence,* especially when discussing drugs. The distinctions between them are not always clear, even in the technical literature. As far as you are concerned, in any case, they both mean "getting hooked."

Alcoholism is the most serious mental health problem in the United States, statistically speaking, and the fourth most widespread disease, affecting over 10 million people. About five times as many men are alcoholic as women, though a large number of women alcoholics

The asthenic personality tends to take to its bed, languish, and not to get very much done.

Resting, Antonio Mancini

are able to hide the fact. The average age of alcoholics is in the 40s, but it occurs in all age groups, and shortens the average life span by almost a dozen years (see Chapter 11).

Alcohol inhibits the functions of higher brain centers when used even in small amounts. But acute psychotic reactions, like delirium tremens or DTs, may result from prolonged heavy drinking. It usually happens to chronic alcoholics on a long drunk. They develop uncontrollable tremors, become terrified, hallucinate, and lose their orientation to time, place, and people. The DTs last a few days and are followed by a deep sleep, after which the patient is all right if the other effects of being so "pickled," such as malnutrition, have not yet taken a permanent toll.

Addiction to alcohol usually occurs gradually. It may begin by a person accidentally finding that social drinking relieves tensions. Over many months they gradually get to drinking more and more, start drinking alone, think more and more about getting liquor, feel guilty about it, but keep on drinking. Slowly they lose control over drinking, and their physical tolerance for it drops greatly. By then, they are fully addicted and will suffer physical **withdrawal** symptoms if they try to stop drinking.

Drug treatment sometimes works with acute alcoholism, as does psychotherapy, but neither works very well. **Alcoholics Anonymous** has offered the most successful treatment so far.

Drug addiction is less common than alcoholism and has been declining (see Chapter 11). Drugs derived from opium, such as heroin and morphine, and barbiturates, such as phenobarbital or seconal, are physically addicting, you recall. But such drugs as LSD, marijuana, hashish, and cocaine, the *amphetamines,* and the *tranquilizers,* are not addicting. Users may become psychologically dependent on them in the sense that they crave them or feel uncomfortable about not having them available, but they do not suffer physical danger when they are withdrawn.[7] It isn't hard for most people to stop using the habituating drugs, with or without treatment, but treatment for the addicting drugs is very difficult.

In small doses, heroin and morphine do not seem to be physically harmful, but the barbiturates are. Most psychedelic drugs seem to be harmless in small doses. With many drugs, overdose is a more serious danger, perhaps, than addiction itself. Most addicts buy heroin from street peddlers, for instance, in highly adulterated lots. They develop a tolerance for the drug in those amounts. If they then, accidentally, are sold a batch of pure heroin and take what they think is the usual dose, they may kill themselves from the overdose. Since they cannot analyze each batch chemically, there is no way to be sure what they are getting. Ditto with LSD and cocaine.

Sexual deviations are listed as a class of personality disorder, but many of them are not. A sexual deviation, technically, is any kind of sex activity which is commonly disapproved; so the only thing wrong with some sexual deviants may be that they are unconventional. Some sexual patterns do involve emotional disturbances. Others are called personality disorders only because they are not socially accepted; from their own point of view, their perpetrator may simply be having fun. More likely, however, they find themselves drawn to the activity even if it is distasteful to them. If they feel guilty and anxious about it, the sex acts in question are more symptoms of neurosis than of personality disorder, but since sex has such a history of taboo in our society, sex acts have been set apart as objects of special significance. Some such deviant acts are **exhibitionism,** the desire to show off one's genitals; **sadism,** getting sexual pleasure from hurting someone; **masochism,** getting sexual

---

[7] At least one common tranquilizer, *meprobamate,* is an exception. It produces withdrawal symptoms like those of barbiturates (Huff 1977).

pleasure from being hurt; and *fetishism,* concentration of sexual attraction on things like hands or feet or inanimate objects, like clothing.

PSYCHOSIS

Psychosis is the modern term for insanity.[8] The psychoses are considered the most serious of the behavior disorders. They often require long hospitalization, and sometimes are never cured. Psychotic people have lost contact with reality so that their perceptions and thoughts are disordered and inaccurate. Some psychoses result from neurological damage or disease, but some of them cannot be connected with definite organic or hereditary factors, though continuous research goes into that subject.

Some common symptoms of all psychoses are *delusions,* false beliefs which the person adopts and sticks to despite evidence that they are wrong; and *hallucinations,* strange perceptions and sensations, like hearing voices when no one is around, or seeing things that, to other people, aren't there.

The two main kinds of psychoses are the *schizophrenias* and the *affective* or *manic-depressive* psychoses. Schizophrenia is considered a *thought* disorder; affective psychosis a *mood* disorder. In schizophrenia, the main symptoms are *disordered thinking* and *perception* combined with an apparent lack of feeling, called *emotional withdrawal* or *flattened affect.* In affective psychoses, the main symptoms are *disordered feelings* and *emotions. Depressed* people are given to despair, hopelessness, and lethargy, while the much rarer *manic* psychotic is overactive, excited, and elated, and has grandiose feelings of power, invincibility, and supreme self-confidence. Occasionally, these symptoms alternate

in the same person, and the disorder is then called *circular* or *manic-depressive* psychosis.

Affective psychoses: Depression and mania

Everyone has felt depression sometimes and is familiar with some of its symptoms. Depressed people feel dejected and "down," guilty, inadequate and worthless, unloved and unlovable, and often full of vague aches and pains. Frequent experience of this kind is called *neurotic* depression. *Psychotic* depression occurs when this mood is so deep that guilty feelings turn into agitated delusions or when slowed down motor activity, called *psychomotor retardation,* becomes so lethargic that the person seems stuporous. The stuporous condition is called *retarded depression,* and the anguished condition is called *agitated depression.*

Manic psychosis is sometimes called *acute mania* or *hypomania.* It is an excited emotional state in which people appear superficially happy and in good spirits, but are really just wildly excited rather than happy. Manics tend to be grandiose and self-confident, self-assertive in irritating ways, and indifferent to ordinary rules of social interaction. They tend to sleep very little, have *flights of ideas* from one subject to another too rapidly to follow them, and get involved in hare-brained adventures and business schemes before anybody can stop them. Acute mania sometimes turns into *delirious mania,* in which activity gets so frenzied that the victim loses all self-control, becomes incoherent, and starts tearing things to pieces. People wear themselves out quickly from manic episodes, but until they do, delirious manics are terrifying to watch, and may be quite dangerous. The expression "raving maniac" comes from this condition.

Most affective psychoses occur in middle age or later. Depressions are much more common than mania, and women get them somewhat more than men. People generally recover

---

[8] Nowadays, "insanity" is a legal, not a medical term. It doesn't mean just psychosis, however, but something more like "legally not responsible because of craziness." That concept sometimes includes things which you and I might think quite sane.

Portrait of the Artist's Mother, James A. Whistler
A common time for women to experience depression is when all the children have left home to live their own lives—the "empty nest" syndrome.

spontaneously from affective psychoses in weeks or months, but there is danger of suicide among depressives. ***Electro-convulsive therapy,*** or ECT, which consists of tiny electric shocks into the brain, is effective in treating depressions, but no one knows why. It is quite unpleasant.

Schizophrenia

The schizophrenias are the most common functional psychoses; more than half the beds in American mental hospitals are occupied by schizophrenics. Schizophrenia is called a *thought* disorder because its primary symptoms are distortions in thinking and perception. These take three major forms: ***withdrawal*** of interest from the outside world; ***autistic thinking,*** or concern with inner fantasies and ideas which make no sense to other people; and ***flattened affect,*** which means a loss of emotional responsiveness.

The ***secondary symptoms*** of schizophrenia, such as delusions and hallucinations, are more dramatic than the main symptoms but are not always seen. Some extreme schizophrenics may show completely regressive behavior and be unable to take care of the simplest functions, such as dressing, feeding themselves, and using the toilet.

There are four main types of schizophrenia: *simple, catatonic, hebephrenic,* and *para-noid.* There are several more subtypes, including childhood schizophrenia, but most cases are accounted for by these four types.

Simple schizophrenia is easily confused with mental deficiency because its victims act indifferent, irresponsible, and apparently stupid, with none of the dramatic secondary signs of schizophrenia and often without apparent suffering. They do not talk much, or about anything important, take poor care of their grooming and hygiene, don't get interested in anything, and can manage only simple work, if that. Since they are not very active or troublesome, simple schizophrenics are often cared for at home instead of being hospitalized. This condition occurs mostly in late adolescence and early adulthood. Many hobos, prostitutes, and petty criminals are simple schizophrenics.

Catatonic schizophrenia is less common than simple schizophrenia. It may develop quickly and if treated early shows a higher rate of recovery than the other schizophrenias. There are two subtypes of catatonia, *withdrawn* and *excited.* The former is more common. Its main symptom is *catatonic stupor,* in which the patient is mute and motionless. In this state, they often show *waxy flexibility,* meaning that they remain in whatever position they are put for long periods of time, even if their arms and legs are positioned in unusual and tiring ways. The stuporous condition may alter with periods of *catatonic excitement,* a frenzied state in which the patient is quite dangerous. It is the second rarest form of schizophrenia.

Hebephrenia is the rarest schizophrenic psychosis. It develops early, like a catatonic condition, but comes on more slowly, with more personality deterioration and less chance for recovery. The main sign of hebephrenia is very regressive behavior together with a constant silly grin. Hebephrenics look idiotically happy, giggle or babble at times, and have bizarre delusions, often that their sex is changing. They are active, but not manic, and their regression is so extreme that they may be found in the back wards of hospitals playing with their feces, masturbating openly, and so forth.

Paranoid schizophrenia is the most common schizophrenic psychosis. More than half of all schizophrenics are paranoid. (There is another functional psychosis called *paranoia,* but it is very rare.) It tends to start between ages 25 and 40, and the main symptom is delusions of persecution. The patient feels spied on or endangered, often by friends or relatives, who are "out to get them," either naturally or by magic, because they are jealous of their wonderful qualities. People who think they are Caesar, Napoleon, or Christ are paranoid schizophrenics. Paranoids may also have hallucinations and do strange or destructive things to obey hidden voices commanding them. Most paranoid schizophrenic episodes are acute, requiring relatively short hospitalization.

The origins and dynamics of schizophrenia are not well understood. The dispute about its possible organic versus functional origins is a lively one. There is some evidence of genetic and metabolic differences between schizophrenics and others, and there may be an inherited disposition towards both schizophrenia and manic-depressive illnesses (Davison and Neale 1978).

BRAIN DAMAGE

Organic behavior disorders involve damage to the brain and central nervous system. This may come from natural events like aging, or from infections, brain tumors, head injuries, or toxic processes.

Three infectious diseases cause serious brain disorders: *syphilis, encephalitis,* and *meningitis.* Syphilis causes *paresis,* a condition which destroys brain tissue and leads through several stages of bizarre behavior to deterioration and, finally, death. *Encephalitis,* or sleeping sickness, is a virus infection which destroys brain tissue. *Meningitis* is a bacterial infection. Most of its aftereffects are physical, but it may harm the development of intelligence in children.

All brain tumors are destructive because they put pressure on the skull bones. Since bone can't give way, brain tissue gets destroyed. Many behavior changes may result, none of them good. Surgery is generally the only treatment.

Head injuries and *toxic psychoses* from drugs and poisons cause mostly acute reactions and only minor brain damage, but they are increasingly common in modern society and sometimes permanently damaging. *Nutritional deficiencies* and disturbances of the *endocrine glands* can also cause brain damage.

Epilepsy is one of the oldest illnesses known. It results from disturbances in the electrical activity of the brain. Its main symptoms are *convulsions* or *seizures,* which are uncontrollable motor spasms, with some loss of consciousness. Some epileptics get a warning signal before the seizure, called an *aura;* it may be a visual or auditory signal, or mild nausea, dizziness, or anxiety.

There are four main types of epilepsy. *Grand mal,* or "great illness," is the commonest kind; its seizures are severe, with complete loss of consciousness, intense convulsions, and some danger of injury. *Petit mal,* or "little illness," involves milder seizures, with partial loss of consciousness and small convulsions so that the person may not even know they had a seizure. Petit mal occurs most in children and adolescents; it is rare in adults. *Jacksonian epilepsy* is like grand mal, but the seizure starts in one part of the body and spreads as it gets more intense. *Psychomotor epilepsy* involves small lapses of consciousness, usually for just a few seconds, while the person continues activity. Some people become violent during these attacks, but this is not common.

Epilepsy occurs in about 1 percent of the population, equally often in all sexes, races, and nationalities, but more in children than adults. It can be controlled more than half the time by drugs and surgery.

MENTAL RETARDATION

About 3 percent of the population are considered mentally retarded, meaning that they are not intelligent enough to get along without special training or institutional care. The different degrees of mental retardation, mild, moderate and severe, are defined by IQ tests, but IQ is not a very good measure of a person's potential ability.

Most mental retardates fall in the *mild* category, with IQs from 50 to 70. With special training, they may become self-sufficient members of society.

Moderate retardates have IQs from about 30 to 50. Their adult performance is about that of a seven-year-old child, and they often have physical abnormalities as well as behavior deficits. They can learn simple work, but they learn slowly. Moderate retardation usually requires a lifelong sheltered environment.

Severe and *profound* retardations involve IQs below 35. Children in these groups develop intellectually to about the three-year level, do not learn fluent speech, and can master only simple tasks.

Moderate and severe mental retardations result from biological disorders; mild ones are generally thought to result from social conditions which keep children from having good learning opportunities.

Primary or *endogenous* mental retardation is biological. It includes: (1) *mongolism,* (2) *cretinism,* (3) *microcephaly,* and (4) *phenylketonuria. Mongolism* is the most common kind of moderate and severe retardation. The condition comes from a chromosome deficiency, and the name comes from the fact that mon-

Dutch Joe, Robert Henri

Many mental retardates are in the mild-to-moderate range and can learn to fend for themselves. Retarded children may be very affectionate and return many measures of love for the effort spent on their care.

goloid babies are born with almond-shaped slanting eyes. *Cretinism* results from a thyroid gland deficiency. It can be corrected with early treatment. In *microcephaly,* brain development is impaired, and the child's head and brain are abnormally small. The resulting mental retardation is severe, but the condition is fairly rare. *Phenylketonuria,* or PKU, results from the lack of a vital enzyme. Detected early, it can be prevented or controlled by special diet.

A lot of mental retardation comes from environmental conditions, not from genetics or brain damage. Called *cultural-familial* retardation, it includes: (1) social deprivation, in which opportunities and incentives to learn are missing, and (2) poor nutrition or poor care which interferes with neurological development.

There is also an unknown amount of so-called "normal" retardation, where the genes for intelligence may just be of low quality and not damaged or diseased.

A lot of research is aimed at improving teaching methods for mental retardates, developing drugs and medical techniques for raising intelligence, and improving social conditions for deprived children so they can make better use of educational opportunities.

SUMMARY

1 Different technical terms are used for the behavior disorders, including *abnormal psychology,* and *psychopathology,* or *mental illness.* Strictly speaking, *behavior disorders* is the most correct usage because it includes both disorders of the brain and central nervous system and behavior problems without known organic components.

2 There are no behavior disorders to speak of in phyla lower than the vertebrates because a complex central nervous system (called an "adjustor system" because it integrates sensory and motor functions) is prerequisite to complex behavior problems. Only among mammals does conflict become sufficiently complex for neurosis to occur. In dogs and sheep, it takes the relatively simple form of disorganized activity and feeling miserable; in primates, psychosomatic disorders such as ulcers occur; and in humans, behavior disorders may be so complicated that the physical conditions underlying them are completely unknown.

3 Hippocrates, Soranus, and Galen, classical fathers of medicine, said that the behavior-disorders had nautral causes, but nobody listened. In the Middle Ages, they were considered forms of demon-possession and were generally treated by prayer and torture. These did not help. In the 18th century, the mentally ill were thrown into asyiums where they were treated like wild animals. This did not help either. Humane treatment began in France with the work of Philippe Pinel, whose *moral treatment* emphasized being kind and reasonable with patients, and setting a model for sane conduct. This helped a lot. It was dropped in the middle of the 19th century, however, because contemporary psychiatrists then believed that all behavior disorders had an organic basis and required organic treatment.

4 Emil Kraepelin began modern psychiatric classification by grouping psychoses according to their symptoms. He identified the two major groupings today called the *schizophrenic psychoses* and the *affective disorders*. Subsequent classifications included the *functional disorders*, discovered by Freud and Janet. Today, the American Psychiatric Association's *Diagnostic and Statistical Manual of Behavior Disorders* (DSM-II) is generally accepted as the best system of classification around.

5 The seven major categories of behavior disorders are (1) *neuroses*, (2) *psychosomatic disorders*, (3) *personality disorders*, (4) *special symptom disorders*, (5) *psychoses*, (6) *brain disorders*, and (7) *mental retardation*.

Conditions are grouped together primarily because they have common symptoms. The reliability of psychiatric diagnoses is often poor and so, accordingly, is the validity of diagnosis. There is evidence that patients are sometimes given diagnoses according to their socio-economic status, that some psychiatrists tend to diagnose almost everyone alike, and that some diagnoses, once given, are never changed, regardless of how the patient's behavior changes.

6 The three main kinds of neuroses are (A) *conversions* and *dissociative reactions*, called *hysterical neuroses;* (B) *obsessive* and *compulsive reactions*, which are the *obsessive-compulsive neuroses*, and (C) *phobic* or *fearful reactions*, which make up the *anxiety neuroses*.

A. In *Conversion hysteria*, a person suddenly loses physical function or develops physical symptoms without organic basis. In *dissociative reactions*, the victim gets one of four symptoms: (1) *amnesia*, forgetting one's own past; (2) *fugue state*, running away without knowing it; (3) *multiple personality*, developing a new personality which operates without the customary personality being aware of it; or (4) *somnambulism*, sleepwalking.

B. In *obsessional* and *compulsive neuroses*, persistent thoughts or compulsive urges interfere with normal activity; these are sometimes fears of being overwhelmed by one's own evil impulses, or urgent rituals one feels they must perform, suffering guilt and anxiety until they are completed. Obsessive-compulsive neurotics tend to be very intelligent and very intellectual; treatment of this condition often fails.

C. In *anxiety-neuroses,* fear itself is the primary symptom. The anxiety-neuroses are named *acute traumatic neuroses, anxiety states,* and *phobias.* In acute traumatic neuroses, a person is suddenly overwhelmed with anxiety and remains anxious for some time. People recover from this condition with little or no treatment. Anxiety states are more chronic conditions whose victims are nervous, depressed, and generally cannot enjoy life. Most people suffer from mild anxiety states at some time in life.

Phobias are extreme fears, usually of relatively harmless things. Some phobias involve displacement mechanisms in which the feared object is a substitute for an even more frightening source of anxiety, but other phobias develop by simple conditioning, and are effectively treated by behavior therapy.

7 Some of the most common *psychosomatic disorders* are asthma, ulcer, migraine headaches, hypertension, and colitis. These are all physical ailments which may have psychological components as well. Asthma, for instance, is an allergy whose arousal may be related to unsatisfied dependency needs. Ulcers may be caused in part by anxiety in people who feel burdened by excessive responsibility. Migraine headaches and colitis seem to be connected with tension over interpersonal relations. There are many other psychosomatic conditions, all of which reflect the effects of mental stress on body processes.

8 *Special symptom reactions* were formerly called *habit disorders.* They are generally less disabling than other functional disorders. Stuttering, enuresis, and tics are typical of problems in this category. Excessive smoking and compulsive eating may also be considered habit disorders.

9 *Personality disorders* are serious functional conditions such as personality pattern disturbances; sexual deviation; alcoholism; and drug addiction. In *personality pattern disorders,* a person's life-long behavior pattern is the cause of the trouble rather than any specific symptoms. Excessive dependency, chronic aggressiveness, or general emotional instability are typical of this group. Antisocial or psychopathic personality is among the most serious of the personality pattern disturbances.

10 Some *sexual deviations* are considered personality disorders only because they are not socially acceptable. In others, the deviant feels compulsively drawn to the activity but is anxious or guilty about it. *Exhibitionism,* the desire to show off one's genitals; *sadism,* getting sexual pleasure from hurting someone; *masochism,* getting sexual pleasure from being hurt; and *fetishism,* sexual attraction to objects rather than to people, are all grouped in this class.

11 *Psychosis* is the modern term for insanity. It is considered the most serious of the behavior disorders because it often requires hospitalization, and is sometimes not cured. Some psychoses result from neurological damage or disease; others are functional. Delusions and hallucinations are common symptoms of all psychoses.

12 The two main functional psychoses are *schizophrenias* and the *affective psychoses.* Schizophrenia is considered a thought disorder: affective psychosis, a mood disorder. The main symptoms of schizophrenia are bizarre thinking and perception combined with emotional withdrawal, called *flattened affect.* In affective psychoses the main symptoms are extreme moods and disordered emotions, either of *depression* or of *manic* excitement.

There are four main types of schizophrenia: *simple, catatonic, hebephrenic* and *paranoid. Simple schizophrenics* are often confused with mental defectives because they may act indifferent, irresponsible, and apparently stupid. The main symptom of *catatonic schizophrenia* is a stupor in which the patient is mute and motionless. This condition may alternate with periods of frenzied excitement. It has a high rate of recovery. *Hebephrenic psychosis* is the rarest kind, and has the least chance for recovery. Its main symptom is extreme regressive behavior, together with a constant silly grin. *Paranoid schizophrenia* is the most common schizophrenic psychosis. Its main symptom is delusions of persecution, combined with bizarre thinking.

13 *Organic behavior disorders* involve damage to the brain and central nervous system. This may come from aging, infections, brain tumors, head injuries, or poisoning. Three infectious diseases cause serious brain disorders: *syphilis, encephalitis,* and *meningitis.* Brain tumors are destructive because they put pressure on the skull bones and destroy brain tissue. Head injuries and poisoning tend to cause acute reactions and do only minor brain damage, but they are sometimes permanently damaging. *Epilepsy* is a disturbance in the electrical activity of the brain that produces convulsions and seizures. The commonest kind of epilepsy is *grand mal;* its seizures are severe and cause unconsciousness. *Petit mal* involves milder seizures with partial loss of consciousness. It occurs most in children and adolescents. *Jacksonian epilepsy* is a variation of grand mal. *Psychomotor epilepsy* involves seizures of only a few seconds, usually while the person continues activity.

14 About 3 percent of the population are mentally retarded, usually only to a *mild* degree; with training, they can become self-sufficient. *Moderate* retardates can learn simple work but slowly; they usually require a life-long sheltered environment. *Severe* retardates develop intellectually only to about the three-year-old level. Some mental retardation results from biological disorders, called *primary* or *endogenous* retardation. Much mental retardation comes from environmental conditions, called *secondary* or *cultural-familial retardation;* it results from social deprivation or poor nutrition or poor care which interferes with neurological development. There is also an unknown amount of "normal" retardation where the genes for intelligence may simply be of low quality and not damaged or diseased.

PERSONAL ADVICE 4¢

4¢

THE "DOCTOR" IS IN

Treatment and control

19

19

Treatment and control

There are so many different kinds of treatment for people's psychological problems that it would take about a chapter just to name them, let alone discuss them. So this chapter will concentrate only on the main kinds of treatment and how they work rather than trying to cover them all. The most interesting treatments are psychological ones, chiefly *psychotherapy,* so most of the chapter will be about it. But something will also be said about *medical* and *educational* treatments because they are important, too.

THE NATURE OF MENTAL TREATMENT

As you have seen from the last four chapters, there is a great variety of psychological troubles in the world. Some of them can be considered pure **behavior disorders,** such as the neuroses and most psychoses, and some can be considered **medical** problems, such as brain damage, paresis, and so forth. But most human conflicts and frustrations are not really behavior disorders at all, as you could see from Chapter 15, and most of the existential conflicts and questions discussed in Chapter 16 and 17 are not either. A large part of the psychological treatment professions is dedicated to helping people solve such personal problems. The treatment of true **mental illness,** and of non-medical **behavior disorders,** takes up a large part of the treatment industry, but not all of it by a long shot.

Each of the many different treatments in use is commonly applied to many different problems, often regardless of what their causes are. **Medical** treatments such as drugs may help relieve anxiety in someone who has an anxiety neurosis or a frightening job interview or a conflict about whom to marry. **Psychoanalysis** may do the same; so might **behavior therapy.** Each of the treatments may work on a different aspect of the problem—the drugs on the chemistry of anxiety, psychoanalysis on the motivational causes of it, behavior therapy on the habits or reaction patterns which sustain it. In practice, just about every kind of treatment is used by one practitioner or another for just about every kind of disorder. You cannot tell from the type of disorder how best to cure it. Psychosomatic symptoms, such as asthma or hypertension may be, sometimes respond very well to psychotherapy and not as well to medicines—or vice versa. Mental retardation is most often approached by educational techniques; yet medicines can be as much help. Psychosis,

neurosis, and character disorders are commonly treated by all three means.

Categories of treatment

Classifying the treatments as (1) medical, (2) educational, and (3) psychotherapy, is actually a lot less exact than it sounds. We will use *medical* treatments to mean only *chemical* and *physical* manipulations of the body. By *educational* treatments, we mean *instructions* or *demonstrations,* but some kinds of educational treatment, like "guidance" and "counseling," can be considered forms of psychotherapy.

Psychotherapy and counseling— the helping professions.

The Good Samaritan, Heinrich Nauen

Psychotherapy is a hard-to-describe collection of methods, not exactly like the practice of medicine, not the same as most teaching, more than giving advice, and less than religious revivalism—but still a means of changing people's lives. It will take a lot of describing.

Assessing treatment effects

The main problem of all the treatment methods is not classifying them but finding out if they work. This is not simple, for several reasons. First, the best treatment for a disorder must not just work but must work better than any alternative. It must especially work better than no treatment at all, called the **spontaneous recovery rate.** And it must also work better than a **placebo,** that is, a phony technique which looks like a real treatment but is not intended to be. Lots of people recover spontaneously from what ails them, and lots recover with placebo treatments. A valid treatment must do better than either.

When the effects of treatment are understood, however, you cannot always tell whether they have been beneficial or harmful. This is often a moral question to which scientific answers are irrelevant (London 1964). If an alcoholic who is treated with antabuse (a drug that causes vomiting if alcohol is taken while it is in the body) gives up drinking but takes up heroin instead, how do you evaluate the treatment? Good, bad, or nil? If a sexually dysfunctioning woman undergoes psychotherapy and, freed of her fears of sex, becomes promiscuous, should we count her improved or impaired? The answer depends on the moral perspective of the patient, the therapist, and society. And since these may all conflict, it is often an ambiguous answer.

MEDICAL TREATMENTS

There are two kinds of medical treatment: (1) **assault** treatments, mostly shock-therapies and surgery; and (2) **drug** treatments, which nowadays are mostly "weak" tranquilizers, antipsychotics, and mood elevators.

Assault treatments

Shock treatments, as they are popularly called, have been used mainly with hospital patients, although electric-shock treatment (electroconvulsive therapy or ECT), the most widely used assault method, is occasionally used in office practice. Chemical shocking agents were in use long before electrical ones—perhaps as early as the 18th century. The first modern treatment by this means was by L. J. Meduna in 1935. He induced convulsions by injections of camphor in oil and later of metrazol, a synthetic camphor. Both were terrifying to patients; they would get feelings, when they were injected, of impending death and sudden annihilation, even before the convulsions started. Even if no convulsions occurred at all, in fact, they still felt anxiety, restlessness, nausea, and general discomfort for hours. Insulin-coma therapy was another popular chemical shock treatment of the same kind. Neither is used much anymore (Goldenberg 1977).

Electricity has been used for treatment almost from the time it was discovered. It has been used to treat almost everything, usually without success. In 1938, Cerletti and Bini found that the brain tissue of dogs was not damaged by electrically produced convulsions, and shortly thereafter, the same thing was observed in people. Next came the observation that some people's psychiatric symptoms diminished after the experience, and ECT was in business. As currently practiced, it consists of sending a small electrical current through the front part of the patient's head, producing unconsciousness, convulsion, and on rare occasions, wrenched muscles or broken bones. Most patients hate the treatment or find it terrifying, though it seems to be painless, because they awaken with temporary loss of memory and feeling disoriented.

Until 1950, ECT was the most common treatment for schizophrenia, but most schizophrenics are not helped by it. It is sometimes effective for treating depression, particularly severe or agitated depression, but nobody knows why.

Since the 1950s, most assault treatments have been abandoned. ECT, insulin, and metrazol have all pretty much given way to antidepressant drugs and antipsychotics.

Psychosurgery

Most people do not think of **surgery** as a method of psychiatric treatment, but prefrontal lobotomy, in which the patient's frontal brain lobes are partially separated from the thalamus, was fairly widely done during the late 1930's and 1940's, chiefly to calm down unmanageable patients. It sometimes had the opposite effect, arousing calm ones. Other dramatic side effects were that from 1 to 4 percent of the patients died. Variations of the prefrontal lobotomy have been introduced since (Freeman and Watts 1942; Freeman, 1949), but most psychiatrists feel that the risks far outweigh the potential benefits, particularly since damage from brain surgery is not reversible.

Most brain surgery is done to treat medical problems, such as tumors or head injuries, and the term **psychosurgery** has come to mean brain surgery **done for the purpose of changing behavior.** It is not used much yet, but it may come to be done more as techniques develop for finding the exact centers in the brain that control different aspects of behavior (see Chapter 3). Experimental work on animals has shown that many aspects of mood, emotion, sex, and social behavior can be controlled in this way. A number of operations have been done on human beings as well, mostly to control helpless outbursts of rage in people who do not respond to any other treatment. It has also been used to improve speech, manipulate sexual interest, and some other things. This work is quite controversial, you recall, because the techniques are not perfected and because there are moral and legal problems in its use (Gaylin et al. 1975).

Although it is not widely discussed as such, **plastic surgery** is sometimes a treatment for psychological conditions. Often, people will request cosmetic surgery to alleviate anxieties over a marred appearance. The usefulness of this treatment is another story. In some cases, it is of immense value. In others, where the person's desire for surgery reflects an unrealistic fantasy that changing their appearance will somehow give them a new and happier personality, the results are nil, or worse. Sometimes, the fact that the person's difficulties are not relieved may disturb them even more than they were to begin with because the fantasy no longer shields them from their underlying fears.

Mood-control drugs

In 1955, chlorpromazine, the first modern tranquilizing drug, entered the American market, producing an explosive change in psychiatry, reducing the use of physical restraints in mental hospitals, and eliminating most psychiatric surgery, with its permanent damage, and most shock therapies, with their terror.

By now, drugs are the most common medical treatment for all psychological disabilities, in or out of mental hospitals. By themselves, they generally do not cure anything; but they do relieve many symptoms and make patients accessible to other kinds of treatment.

The main psychiatric drugs are antipsychotics, or "strong" tranquilizers, such as chlorpromazine (commercially called Thorazine); "minor" tranquilizers, such as diazepam (Valium is its commercial name); antidepressants, such as Elavil, which tend to induce euphoria; and sedatives such as phenobarbital, which have been in use since before World War I. All of them work on the central nervous system in the way each type-name suggests. Energizers and tranquilizers are valuable for people who are lethargic or agitated; they help to alleviate feelings of depression and often of anxiety. Unlike such old-fashioned sedatives as the barbiturates, they tend to change mood without disturbing other aspects of consciousness, such as intellectual functions, and without any permanent effects.

Most prescriptions for *psychotropic* (mood changing) drugs are for the minor tranquilizers, or antianxiety drugs, such as Valium and Librium, but their effectiveness is very limited. They do not influence psychoses or most neurotic conditions. They do help to relieve short-lived tension and anxiety induced by stress, as aspirin and placebos may also do (Klerman 1974). They are pharmacologically similar to barbiturates, but a little more effective and a lot less dangerous (Julien 1975). Also, adaptation to their effects occurs rather quickly; so even their benefits, such as they are, may not last long. Their widespread and growing use, therefore, is highly questionable.

The strong tranquilizers, or antipsychotic drugs, present another, and more optimistic picture. Since they have been widely used, discharge rates from psychiatric hospitals have risen, and the net inpatient population has declined. In the hospital, moreover, patients are more manageable, show fewer bizarre symptoms, and hassle the staff less than they used to. Schizophrenics at least, have been relieved of many symptoms by the use of tranquilizers in hospital treatment. Informed opinion also seems to conclude that tranquilizers delay rehospitalization, allowing patients to stay outside the hospital longer than they could otherwise.

Less is known about both tranquilizers and energizers than one might guess from the number of them prescribed. In some cases they seem to have no demonstrable effects at all; in others, the effects are just the opposite of those usually expected. A hyperactive child, for example, who is absolutely uncontrollable by means of tranquilizers or sedatives may be calmed by ritalin or benzedrine—or by coffee—all stimulants! The reason is not known, and the selection of particular drugs for particular conditions is often done on a trial-and-error basis.

Effective energizers and tranquilizers are described all too precisely by the slang terms "uppers" and "downers" because they affect only the *direction* of your mood, not the thoughts or acts that accompany it. An "upper" may support aggression, lust, giggling, or tearful weltschmerz, and there is no telling from the drug alone which is most likely to result. Even so, the drugs are potentially important treatment and behavior-control devices. As doctors use them more, the public wants them more and, wanting them, expects to get them. Their proliferation is assured by a growing technical ability to produce them synthetically.

EDUCATIONAL TREATMENTS

You can tell educational treatments apart from medical ones by the fact that they do not involve medicine or surgery. But you cannot easily distinguish them from psychotherapy at all. It is only a convention of naming them differently that separates them. The main treatments labeled educational are (1) remedial teaching of skills, especially reading; and, (2) speech therapy.

Remedial reading

Any kind of remedial teaching can be considered an educational treatment, but remedial reading is the best known and the most practiced. There are four main kinds of reading problems: (1) word recognition, (2) vocabulary, (3) reading comprehension, and (4) reading speed. Special techniques exist for treating each kind.

Most reading deficiencies probably result

from bad training, but some may be symptoms of children's anxieties, of perceptual problems, or of minimal brain damage. What is more, reading handicaps in children often *create* emotional problems. Retarded readers get a lot of negative reinforcement in school, for instance, and may have a strong sense of failure and incompetence by the time they come for treatment. For this reason, most reading clinics use a method aimed to reduce readers' anxieties by using materials of gradually increasing difficulty and giving a lot of sympathetic encouragement.

Speech therapies

So much of our interpersonal competence depends on our ability to speak that we take our complex speaking abilities for granted. People suffering speech impediments do not. They are so painfully aware of their stuttering or stammering that they often avoid talking rather than risk the embarrassment of exposing their problem.

The dynamics of stuttering are unknown. The most popular view is that it reflects an emotional conflict. Psychoanalysts see it as psychological immaturity involving oral needs; others describe it as an approach-avoidance conflict, in which the fear of speaking competes with the desire to do so. With the two tendencies equally strong, the speech comes out with hesitancy—and stuttering.

Until recently the main treatment for stuttering was interview psychotherapy. Now several psychologists are applying principles of learning to the problem. One experiment (Flanagan et al. 1958) tried to control stuttering by changing the reinforcements related to it. Sometimes a loud noise was sounded each time the subject stuttered; at others, the noise played continuously *except* when the subject stuttered. In the first case stuttering decreased; in the latter, it increased.

In later research, Goldiamond substituted delayed auditory feedback for the noise. Delayed auditory feedback means you record someone's voice as they speak and you play it back to them through earphones a fraction of a second later than they would normally hear themselves—very annoying! This procedure forces stutterers to use slow, prolonged speech, which prevents stuttering; when encouraged to speed up this new speech pattern, the stutterer can speak more normally (teaching people to pace their speech to a metronome or produce a smooth flow of air while speaking has similar effects).

Auxiliary treatments

Some educational treatments are designed to interest patients in things other than their problems. In a hospital, this may take the form of teaching them useful skills, such as clerical work, gardening, housekeeping, and carpentry. This stuff was once thought of as "busywork," but now it is considered a valuable part of treatment. Nowadays, it often includes training patients for outside jobs and establishing relationships with local businessmen to allow patients to work outside while they still live in hospitals. Some vocational rehabilitation programs try to help patients find permanent employment outside when they are ready to be discharged.

Other auxiliary therapies, such as group psychotherapy, try to teach patients better social interaction, especially the norms of socially accepted behavior they need to get along independently. Still others, like dance therapy, art therapy, and music therapy aim to teach them satisfying ways of self-expression.

PSYCHOTHERAPY

Psychotherapy consists of different ways to help people solve personal problems primarily by talking.

There are millions of people getting psycho-

These people are not dead—they are in sensitivity training. Can't you tell?

therapy all the time in the United States. There are several dozen psychotherapeutic systems or schools of thought on how it can best be done. Most psychotherapy is done by psychiatrists, psychologists, and social workers, but a lot of it is also done by clergymen; marital counselors; guidance counselors in schools and businesses; family doctors; nurses; and laymen whose work or life experience have qualified them for doing it, often working in organizations such as Alcoholics Anonymous or Synanon. A lot of psychotherapy is done also in situations which are not supposed to be treatment, such as sensitivity training or personal encounter groups.

Regardless of who conducts it, or in what setting, psychotherapy is still a systematic means of *persuasion;* in some respects, it is salesmanship elevated into a technology. It is also a way of educating people about themselves. Some physicians do not accept that idea because they would like to view psychotherapy as a branch of medicine, and some psychologists do not because they would like to consider it a unique discipline. They are both wrong.

People seek psychotherapeutic help for a huge variety of troubles. These include problems in relation to society, other people, one's own inner life, mood, feelings, aspirations, ideals, or even physical ailments. They range over every possible subject and every degree of severity and urgency.

What all psychotherapeutic problems share is that they are all *behavior* problems in the broadest sense — that is, they are all problems of action, emotion, and attitude (though they may also involve problems of body functioning). The most common psychotherapeutic problems involve behavior which is *out of control* from someone's point of view, such as drinking too much or drug addiction; trying to restrain sexual impulses or express them; to concentrate on schoolwork; to stop obsessing over trivia; not to wet the bed at night; to free one's self from over-

Somebody to talk to: that is what a great part of psychotherapy is all about. Paraprofessionals are being used increasingly in this capacity, after some training.

Tahitian Women, Paul Gauguin

dependency; to assert one's rights; to quell irrational fears; to be able to feel good; to restore physical health in the face of stresses which cause fits of asthma or scale one's skin or cover it with hives or knot one's stomach into ulcerous aches; to shake the delusion that one is being watched or persecuted or chosen, or the strange sensation that one's sex is changing magically —all these and many others are the common province of the psychotherapeutic arts. And the goal of therapy in every case is to restore control of the disordered behavior to the patient or to eliminate it so that they will not be troubled by it any more.

These goals are not always met, by a long shot. And this fact creates a constant need to find and test new kinds of treatment and to constantly evaluate how well the old ones are working.

The origins of psychotherapy

Psychotherapy began with gadgetry and gimmicks in the wealthy salons and courts of Europe. The treatments were not much like the kinds used today, but the problems they addressed were similar. Not counting the frankly occult arts such as witchcraft and black magic,

Reunion of the Soul and the Body.
From Blair's Engraving by Schiavonetti.

The aim of much psychological treatment is the restoration of harmonious functioning in life, work, love, and play—the reunion of body and soul, as it were.

there were still many treatments which would today seem more like frauds, or what we would now call "placebo treatment," than like psychotherapy. The most glamorous of these was the 17th century "celestial magneticoelectro bed" of John Graham, O.W.L. (Oh Wonderful Love). The purpose of Graham's bed was to restore sexual potency to the flagging roués of Restoration England. You just lay down on it, surrounded by contraptions, and rose up to find your own contraption fixed.

A more important forerunner of psychotherapy was the "animal magnetic" treatment of Friedrich Anton Mesmer, a Viennese doctor. His treatment was to make various hand movements in the air around the afflicted body parts of his patients, who suffered from all kinds of aches, pains, and paralyses. Mesmer's movements would induce a trance-like condition in the patient, after which many ailments would disappear. He called the curative force animal magnetism. Mesmer became famous in the court of Louis XVI of France for his enormous successes in the wealthy salons of Paris and in the free clinic which he operated, where he would treat whole crowds of people at once. He became so famous, in fact, that a royal commission was appointed to investigate animal

Friedrich Anton Mesmer.

magnetism. Benjamin Franklin, then in France for the Continental Congress to get support for the American Revolution, was a member. The commission discredited Mesmer because there was no such thing as animal magnetism and his cures were achieved "merely by suggestion." This put him out of business, even though his cures worked. Mesmer was the father of modern hypnotism, which for some time was called mesmerism, after him.

Modern psychotherapy grew chiefly from psychoanalysis and from the psychoeducational clinic, both introduced at the very end of the 19th century. The psychoeducational clinic was the forerunner of school psychology and of guidance and counseling. Today almost every big university in the United States has a counseling center to help students with personal and educational problems. Supporters of psychoanalysis, on the other hand, fought a largely uphill battle from the beginning of the century until World War II to get it accepted in psychiatry. They were eventually so successful that psychoanalysis became the most popular kind of psychotherapy, and most new treatments were compared with it as a measure of their value.

Originally psychoanalysis meant only the treatment developed by Sigmund Freud and his students. But a few years after psychoanalysis got started, a number of heresies occurred, and some important offshoots developed as therapeutic techniques between about 1910 and World War II, such as the individual psychology of Alfred Adler, the analytical psychology of C. G. Jung, the will therapy of Otto Rank, and indirectly, the client-centered therapy of Carl Rogers. All of these, plus still others, are commonly called "insight therapy."

Psychoanalysis has been so influential in America that many people still do not realize that the therapy systems that have arisen from research on learning are mostly derivatives of Ivan Pavlov and E. L. Thorndike, both contemporaries of Freud. Pavlov and Thorndike were laboratory scientists rather than clinical practitioners, which is one reason that their work was not translated into clinical situations for some years. By now, however, the "behavior therapy" methods derived from them are widely studied in universities, clinics, schools, and hospitals everywhere. They are called behavior therapy after the behaviorism of John B. Watson.

Insight and behavior therapies overlap a lot in how they are done. In both, people may be seen one at a time or in small groups. Similarly, both systems may use auxiliary methods such as dramatic acting (called "psychodrama"), hypnosis, or drugs. And in both, talking is the main activity. Most of the time, a psychoanalytic therapy session (insight) might look about the same as a desensitization session (behavior).

There are differences between insight and behavior therapies, however, in their activities and in their objectives and effects. One system aims to foster insight or understanding into the problem-relevant aspects of people's lives, the other tries to produce some change in their actions. Insight therapy addresses people's "internal behavior systems" (motives, feelings, attitudes), using techniques for expanding consciousness; behavior therapy works on "symptom clusters" or "external behavior syndromes" (the overt problems presented for treatment) by methods designed to affect them directly. Behavior therapists talk about stimulation, response, and reinforcement. Insight therapists are more concerned with the inner lives of their patients. Neither method is certain

Group therapy.

to heal anybody, but each has developed a useful "first stage" of therapeutic technology.

Insight therapy

The basic idea behind all insight therapy is that **motives dictate behavior;** this means that disordered behavior comes from peculiarities **inside** the individual. To treat it successfully, it is argued, the therapist must find the inner states beneath the surface difficulties and, by bringing them to light, loosen the bond between them and the disordered behavior they produce. The therapist does this by helping patients gain insight into their motivations and their behavior with the idea that this insight will give them greater control over themselves.

Insight means understanding. All the techniques of insight therapy try to lead the patient to greater self-understanding, especially of things about themselves which have not been conscious or which they have been unable to face directly. As patients see it, they are trying to find out why they act and feel the way they do, expecting that the discovery will free them of the troubles that brought them to therapy.

In the course of the inquiry, which can take hundreds of hours over several years, they will probably explore not only the reasons for the original problem, but all their feelings and experiences in all their important relationships and in many less important ones; and they may experience these same feelings over again in the therapy session itself and in relation to the psychotherapist. With luck, patience, and effort, they may get rid of the symptoms, too, but they will gain self-understanding in any case.

Understanding the basis of one's own behavior, of course, makes that behavior more meaningful; for this reason, most advocates of insight therapy see it as a technique which not only frees patients of disabling symptoms but also helps to make their whole life more meaningful by seeking the meaning of those symptoms. This characteristic of insight therapy is very appealing, but the method's actual potency for reducing troubling symptoms has been often challenged, doubted, and denied.

Techniques of insight therapy

Insight therapy works essentially by a variation of the **socratic** teaching method, in which a person's ideas, attitudes, and feelings are questioned and challenged until they are confirmed, reformulated, or rejected. Called "maieutics" by philosophers, the method is supposed to draw out of a person thoughts and ideas that are already within them; this would mean that any conclusions they come to are ultimately under their own control and, therefore, are their own responsibility.

This reasoning pervades all insight therapies; details of techniques vary among different brands, but they all share a primary rule. The patient alone is responsible for the subject matter of the therapy sessions. In general, it is *the patient's* job to initiate discourse and to conduct it, with the therapist there to guide the stream of the patient's consciousness, not to interfere with it. Everything the therapist does is supposed to promote the patient's self-exploration, not to put new contents in their life. So insight therapists not only avoid pressing their own opinions on the patient, but in general also avoid telling much about themselves. This anonymity further forces patients to be responsible for themselves; otherwise, by knowing too much about the therapist's personal life, patients might pattern their own behavior after this model. In its purest form, insight therapy is a guided dialogue between the patient's outer and inner self. Its Platonic ideal is to **Know Thyself,** and its belief is that, in the process of doing so, the truths you learn will make you free of the troubles you brought with you into treatment.

It may sound as if the "compleat insight therapist" does nothing but sit passively while patients get well by talking to themselves, or to a sympathetic-looking lump. This is not true. But Carl Rogers, in his major work, *Client-Centered Therapy,* does cite one case in which a girl came to therapy a few times and said very little to a therapist, who, in turn, said little back; eventually she declared that her problems were worked out so that she no longer needed to see him. Reports from others indicated that she was right. Similar stories have come from a counseling program which the Western Electric Company conducted for its employees; several people said they felt better after talking to a counselor who did little but grunt sympathetically. And the abundance of jokes (and complaints) about therapists who fall asleep during sessions (along with some serious papers which should be jokes) also illustrates the relatively passive, tentative, or restrained behavior of insight therapists. The drama of insight therapy is not seen in any animated dialogue; at its best, it may be visible only to the mind's eye of the patient who goes through it.

The influence of insight therapy comes from the subtle methods it uses. Subtlety is at once the greatest asset and liability of insight treatment. When it works, it may produce profound and lasting changes in the patient—of feelings, attitudes, values, and activity. When it fails, patients may have wasted their time, energy, and money—and it sometimes fails because its very gentleness makes no impression or because, by giving patients their own reins, it makes bad impressions on their life. At all events, three specific techniques are used most in insight therapy; we may call them **association, interpretation,** and **relationship.** Their respective purposes are to help reveal the problem areas, to promote understanding, and to redirect behavior.

Association In most psychoanalytic therapies, an association technique is commonly used to get people to disclose themselves.

Sometimes the therapist asks questions about whatever seems important or, when the patient has said something of interest, asks, "What does that bring to mind?" In some therapies, such as Jungian analysis, the therapist has the patient write down dreams or compose fantasies or fairy tales as gateways to their inner self; Freud called dreams the "royal road to the unconscious." All these procedures serve much the same purpose, but none of them is quite so formal as free association.

Free association is the main psychoanalytic method for exposing unconscious thoughts. The analyst tells the patient to say *everything* that comes to mind; then sits back, usually out of sight, and waits. It is hard to free-associate. Merely keeping track of all one's thoughts is hard; telling them to someone is even harder. One purpose of the analytic couch is to relax patients so they can free-associate more easily. The analyst may occasionally prod the patient's association, but the responsibility for doing it rests with the patient. The same thing that makes it hard to free-associate makes it valuable for discovering hidden thoughts. Unlike ordinary discourse, in which the speaker tries to keep to a train of thought and move logically from item to item, in psychoanalysis the very thoughts that would usually be suppressed as irrelevant or embarrassing are the most useful. The reason is because thoughts occur in associative chains, the more conscious ones coming first and more repressed ones coming later. Free association permits your consciousness to move gradually from more open to more hidden thoughts, uncovering anxiety-laden ideas and feelings unavailable to consciousness.

But free association is also useful because it violates ordinary conversation manners. By encouraging what Donald Ford and Hugh Urban call the "urge to utter," patients are led to value their ideas and feelings.

Interpretation As patients develop skill at associating and as their problems become clear, the therapist increasingly *interprets* what is happening. Sometimes these are interpretations of what the patient has said, sometimes of feelings they have exposed but not stated, sometimes of things they have not revealed which the therapist infers. One kind of interpretive remark, called "reflection," is the main tool of client-centered therapy. In reflection, the therapist *restates what the patient has said* in a way that exposes their feelings and also communicates understanding and acceptance of them. This reinforces the patient's own pursuit of ideas and associations and of responsibility for the therapeutic discourse. Interpretations which are not reflective may also have the same effect. By gauging interpretations to what the patient is prepared to understand and accept, the therapist encourages patients to continue their self-initiated exploration.

Interpretations give insight therapists great opportunity to affect the patient's behavior by giving them latitude to direct the patient's thinking. Patients choose their own problems, so to speak, and most of their own associative material, but the therapist chooses the interpretations to make of them. The patient's acceptance of them shows acquiescence to the therapist's influence.

Relationship How much the patient buys of the therapist's interpretations probably depends more on their relationship than on the wisdom or accuracy of the interpretation. The importance of the therapeutic relationship is widely recognized by insight therapists. The main tool for producing a warm, friendly atmosphere is simply listening sympathetically to what the patient says. It makes people want to reveal themselves to therapists and to change because of them. If someone expects to be criticized for exposing thoughts or feelings, they become anxious and clam up. If they do reveal themselves, however, and nothing unpleasant results, the anxiety diminishes (is extinguished) and they feel more free to open up (Dollard and Miller 1950). By listening to patients without reacting negatively to what they say, the therapist reduces their anxieties about self-revelation and makes it easier for them to talk.

Sympathetic listening has a strong seductive effect on people in ordinary life, too. If it is hard for someone to talk to others, then the more need persons feel to do so and the more they expect an unsympathetic response from them, the more likely it is that unloading to a sympathetic listener will make them feel grateful or affectionate towards that person. The shrewd listener who so chooses can exploit those feelings to get money, sex, or other bounty from a grateful "client"—and may claim, in so doing, not to have actually "done anything" to the other person. Professional confidence men intuitively recognize this principle, which is one of the main things that send them after *lonely* victims who have nobody to talk to. In a similar vein, James H. Bryan, of Northwestern University, and I found, in an interview study of American call girls, that an important reason that some girls stay attached to pimps, give them all the money they earn, and stay hopelessly and futilely in love with them despite generally shabby treatment at their hands is that they provide a sympathetic ear. A pimp is "somebody to talk to," especially for a girl who fears to discuss her work publicly, and especially in the cold and lonely hours before dawn. For many people, loneliness mostly means "not having somebody to talk to."

Transference Most psychotherapists use sympathetic listening to promote a good relationship with patients, but psychoanalysts make more precise use of it, together with their deliberate anonymity, to produce *transference* reactions. "Transference" means projecting onto the analyst the attributes of other people who are important in one's life and then feeling the same emotions toward them which those people arouse. A man may feel that the analyst is just like his cruel father, and then feel furious and fearful toward him just as he feels toward his father. Transference occurs in any intimate relationship to some extent, but psychoanalysis makes ingenious use of it to help patients expose feelings that have been impairing their relationships. Once exposed, they can be analyzed and the transference resolved.

The therapist's personal anonymity helps foster the transference by withholding information which would give the patient a realistic basis for responding. Since the patient knows little about the analyst's life or what the analyst is really like, the things they attribute to the analyst and the emotions they have toward them must come from experiences with other people. One reason Freud began sitting out of sight of his patients was to minimize the influence of his own gestures and appearance (he also found it wearing to have to look at and be looked at for many hours every day).

Critique of insight therapy

Insight therapy has been criticized a lot on both technical and moral grounds. The technical critics say that it is an ineffective means of controlling behavior; the moral critics say that, where it does work, the effects are obtained immorally by seducing patients away from their original purposes. Both arguments have some merit.

Insight therapy is sometimes a poor means of symptom control; uncovering motives and expanding self-understanding by themselves apparently do not have much power to cure most symptoms. Most of the studies of insight therapy's effectiveness have proved equivocal. A few report fair results; others do not. The fact that intelligent, educated people tend to stay in it for a long time anyway suggests that therapy works in some other sense than curing symptoms, which is not measured by most research. It is here that the morality of insight therapy is challenged.

Because they assume that problems of moti-

vation underlie the symptoms that bring people to them, insight therapists try to get patients concerned with their motivations. But it was concern with symptoms, more than with motives, that brought them to treatment in the first place. So, if it turns out that treating motivation fails to cure the symptom, then the therapist ends up selling a different product than the patient intended to buy—understanding instead of relief!

The product may still be worthwhile, of course, because insight therapy helps to solve people's existential problems even when it fails to cure their symptoms. Many patients who enter therapy wishing at first only to be free of symptoms later discover that "the quest for meaning" or what James Bugental calls the "search for authenticity," is really more important in their lives. When that happens, the patient may now be in the position of saying that though the symptom is still there, it no longer bothers them. Therapy has then changed the patient's needs to suit the symptom instead of curing the symptom to suit their needs.

The nature of insight therapy makes it function this way; it tends either to radically change people's lifestyles or to leave them unaffected. A person is more likely to switch careers as a result of insight therapy than to lose a nervous tic, more likely to leave home, change their politics, or alter their religious convictions from being psychoanalyzed than to give up phobias, smoking, homosexuality, or compulsive hand washing.

One man, who entered therapy because he was afraid to drive on Los Angeles freeways, changed his wife, his job, and his friends after a year of treatment, but he still could not drive on the freeways. He considered his therapy successful, even though it never met his initial purpose.

Both the assumptions and methods of insight therapy make it work best only on broad targets. Its first assumption is that only the patient can really decide what is good for them and only they can achieve it—the only proper behavior control is self-control. Second, it assumes that self-control results from expanding consciousness; and third, that consciousness can be expanded by verbal means. All the techniques of insight therapies serve these ends, promoting patients' search of self, with the therapist not sharing much responsibility for what they find. Free association and reflection both leave patients in control of their own activity; the therapist, by maintaining anonymity and interpreting the transference, avoids influencing them too much. "Too much" means anything the therapist does that dictates what patients should do, even if doing it might help cure their symptoms. The *source* of control is more important than the *act* of control; it must remain in the patient's hands to be legitimate. The aim is not simply to treat people, but to do so without *manipulating* them.

Insight therapists regard manipulation as immoral, and this gives them a good defense against some critics. They may be selling something the patient did not originally intend to buy —self-understanding instead of symptom relief —but they are still selling something of value in itself; and the patients alone are responsible for whether or not they want to take it. Uncovering motives may not always relieve symptoms, but it is still wrong to remove symptoms by indecent means, even if they work. Finally, the quest for meaning is more important than the need for relief, and if patients meaningfully change themselves and now can live with their symptoms, the therapy *has* been of value. If someone loses their ability to make money, talks to a therapist because of it, and discovers that their life is improved by a new career that can never make them rich, it is stupid to say the treatment failed.

Most observers of insight therapy, on the other hand, would say that it is not quite so pure as it claims and that insight therapists use far more influence on their patients than they realize. There is some evidence to that effect in research reports that patients tend to develop personal values like those of their therapists.

It is no wonder that they should. For no matter how tentatively they approach the patient, nor how pure their motives *not* to control or dominate, insight therapists still have to work on what they consider the most important material presented to them. If patients' ideas of what is important don't correspond with their own, sooner or later, then the treatment has to stop. Also, the natural imbalance in the relationship, where the therapist is always giving help and the patient is always receiving it, makes patients look up to the therapist as authority, model, or inspiration, no matter how little they know of the therapist's outside life. After all, they know plenty about the therapist's attitudes toward the important things in *their* life, and it makes sense that they should absorb those attitudes.

In short, insight therapy works by a combination of subtle persuasion and benign neutrality; the one turns patients' attention to what the therapist thinks is important; the other encourages them to adopt the attitudes they think the therapist has. All this happens without therapists *trying* to exert control; were they to try, they might have more powerful effects than they usually do.

Even if they do not wish to control their patients, however, insight therapists do have some responsibility for relieving symptoms as long as they hang out shingles telling symptom-ridden people to come to them for help. And it is over symptom relief that behavior therapists have registered a legitimate complaint against insight methods. Making this their sole standard of therapeutic success, they have invented some valuable treatment methods for problems where insight therapy often works poorly.

Behavior therapy

The procedures of behavior therapy sound like the opposite of insight therapy. Instead of concentrating on the motives that produce a person's symptoms, they focus directly on the symptoms. Instead of placing responsibility for treatment on the patient, they place it on the therapist. Instead of focusing on patients' personal relationships or existential concerns, they attend only to their functioning and the way their symptoms interfere with it. Instead of viewing therapy as a tool of self-understanding, they see it as a *planned* attack on disorder in which it hardly matters whether any insight comes about. Most symptoms, they believe, are really habit patterns which are learned, according to Hans Eysenck, the British psychologist who coined the term "behavior therapy," "through a process of conditioning. . . . Treatment is directed primarily to the symptoms, as distinguished from psychotherapy with its stress on hypothetical underlying complexes and disease processes."

Two of the pioneering leaders in behavior therapy, Joseph Wolpe of Temple University and Arnold Lazarus of Rutgers, once defined it as the use of "experimentally established principles of learning" for overcoming "persistent maladaptive habits" (O'Leary and Wilson 1975). Most advocates of these methods would apply them to many things they would not call bad habit patterns, but all of them would agree that the language of learning theory is common to all behavior therapists. The principles of learning *are* guidelines for planning their work moreover, even if the work itself is not always as scientific as they claim (London 1972).

A wide number of programs using these principles are now in use in prisons and schools, among other institutions, which aim at the *modification* of behavior, generally in socially desirable directions, and the terms *behavior therapy* and *behavior modification* are therefore sometimes used interchangeably. A lot of ethical concern over behavior modification has revolved chiefly around its coercive use, infringing on people's rights (Goldfried and Davison 1976). For our purposes in this chapter,

we are discussing only *behavior therapy,* meaning the treatment system which is used essentially for the same problems and on the same people as insight therapy, differing only in how it works, not in what it tries, or on whom.

Techniques of behavior therapy

The main rule of all behavior therapy technique is *be specific!* First, define the problem precisely; next, calculate a specific way to attack it; then, do what you planned; finally, see how it worked. The problems to be defined and the ins and outs of evaluating how the treatment worked are the same for all kinds of therapy; the behavior therapist's specific ways of attacking them are less familiar to many people. Two of the main ones, "counterconditioning" and "extinction," are used chiefly on phobias, anxiety, and sexual problems. The third is "behavior shaping" or *operant* methods," used mostly for training habit patterns or skills (see Chapter 6).

Counterconditioning Counterconditioning means replacing one feeling or behavior with another that is opposite to it. In treatment, this means replacing a useless or bad feeling with a constructive or pleasant one. The anxiety of a Milquetoastish employee is replaced with justified, constructive anger at an unreasonable boss. The helpless need to guzzle whiskey is converted to nausea at the sight of it. A college girl's obsession over what people think of her is exchanged for a realistic recognition of what difference it makes in different situations.

There are several ways to do counterconditioning; most of them are associated with the work of Joseph Wolpe, but they originate, as he points out, in treatments reported as early as 1924.

Sexual impotence, for instance, can be helped by *discriminative training.* It consists of teaching a man to recognize sexual encounters which are likely to be frightening, to tell them apart from those likely to be gratifying, and to adapt his behavior to his understanding. As Wolpe describes it, the patient is taught to attempt sexual relations *only* when "he has an unmistakable, positive desire to do so, for otherwise he may very well consolidate, or even extend, his sexual inhibition." He is taught to seek out people with whom he can be aroused

> . . . and when in the company of one of them, to "let himself go" as freely as the circumstances allow. . . . If he is able to act according to plan, he experiences a gradual increase in sexual responsiveness to the kind of situation

of which he has made use . . . (and) the range of situations in which lovemaking may occur is thus progressively extended as the anxiety potentials of stimuli diminish.

Sexual therapy has become very popular since Wolpe described it in 1958. Most current sex therapy methods such as those of Masters and Johnson (1970), involve special applications of counterconditioning, but some of it combines insight and behavior therapy methods (Kaplan 1974).

Assertive training is a behavioral method

Figure 19.1 One of the distinguishing features of behavior therapies is that its results can sometimes be quantitatively scheduled. Here is a case of the successful application of behavior therapy to a common clinical problem. Public-speaking phobia was treated by counterconditioning, by an "insight" method and by a placebo treatment. There was also an untreated control group. The chart gives the percent of subjects who showed decreased anxiety (according to three different criteria).

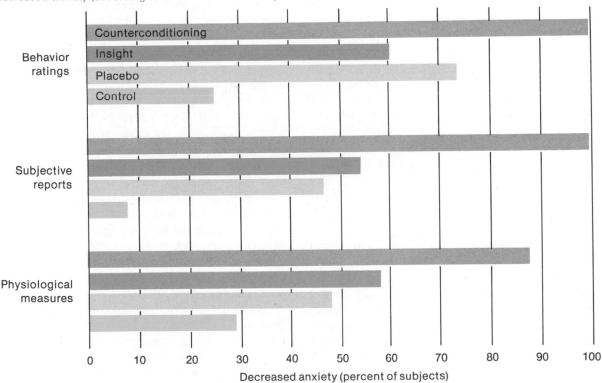

used for people who are easily intimidated and exploited by others, a common complaint of psychotherapy patients. Here, people are taught when and how to respond to others with (verbal) aggression. They practice it in the therapy sessions and apply the training to real life, reviewing and rehearsing it with the therapist's coaching. Assertion is not only used to teach aggression; Wolpe also used it to teach "the outward expression of friendly, affectionate, and other nonanxious feelings" and for "gaining control of an interpersonal relationship by means subtler than overt assertiveness." He takes Stephen Potter's *Gamesmanship* as a text and recommends Potter's works "to patients who seem likely to profit from reading them."[1] Like all counterconditioning methods, assertive training works on the assumption that anxiety inhibits self-expression. Practicing assertion inhibits anxiety, which gives people greater freedom to express themselves in dealings with others.

Assertiveness training, like sex therapy, has also become very popular since 1970, both in the form of classes and popular books, many of them excellent, for learning how to do it. Some of the best are written specifically for women, who may need assertiveness training more than men because the sex roles traditionally assigned to them in society are submissive ones, and the requirements of contemporary social behavior are for women to be more independent (Bloom, Coburn, and Pearlman 1975).

Aversion therapy   Conditioned avoidance methods, now called "aversive therapy," were originally used to reduce "free-floating anxiety." Wolpe describes one which works by giving patients repeatedly a harmless but painful shock. Before shocking them, the therapist tells them that if the shock is too strong, they can end it by saying "calm." Over many trials, the word

"calm" becomes associated with (conditioned to) pain reduction so that merely thinking or saying it has a soothing effect. Presumably, this conditioning generalizes beyond the consulting room so that whenever people start getting anxious, they can feel better by saying "calm."

Conditioned avoidance can also be used to get rid of undesirable behavior patterns. To free a man of homosexual desires, for example, the electric shock is connected with pictures of nude males. Each time the patient is aroused by a picture, he is shocked, till eventually the pleasure of the picture is destroyed by its connection with pain. The resulting "unlust" generalizes to real-life situations where he faces homosexual stimulation.

Aversion therapy, you recall, is a form of classical conditioning (see Chapter 6). It has been used increasingly over the past several years to treat such things as alcoholism, smoking, and overeating, and has been the main method in a number of commercially successful clinics. Ethical criticisms of behavior therapy have often been aimed at aversive treatment because its punishing aspects are so repulsive to most of us. But the truth is that it generally has been used only for voluntary treatment; so such ethical criticisms may not all be justified. A more important criticism is technical — it often does not work, or its effects do not last very long (Sansweet 1975).

Extinction Extinction methods work by making head-on attacks on problems rather than by replacing old feelings with new ones. Three main techniques are used. Where the symptom is pleasant or gratifying, as is common in children's behavior problems, remove the reward; this is called "reinforcement withdrawal." Where the problem is anxiety, as in phobias, eliminate the fear, either by gently manipulating the patient's imagination with "systematic desensitization," or by "burning out" their capacity for neurotic anxiety with "implosive therapy."

Reinforcement withdrawal The treatment

---

[1] They wouldn't hurt you either; see *Gamesmanship* and References: Potter, S. *Lifemanship* and *One-upmanship*.

Assertiveness training teaches people to overcome shyness.

of bedtime temper tantrums uses this method. When children have such tantrums, typically, they scream and rage after their parents have left the room; this brings the parents back and permits the children to stay up longer, which reinforces (rewards) their having yelled in the first place. But if the parents calmly put the child to bed, leave the room, and do not respond to rages, the child will gradually give up the tantrum. C. D. Williams (1959) charted such changes in one case. On the first night of this "cold turkey" treatment, the little boy in the case screamed for 45 minutes before falling asleep. On the second, he went to sleep immediately; on the third, he only cried for 10 minutes. By the tenth night, he smiled when his parents said good night and left his room, and he went quietly to sleep.

Systematic desensitization The most successful technique of behavior therapy is systematic desensitization. It is a method of using imagination particularly to reduce anxiety, such as in phobias. It works as follows: The patient and therapist jointly compose a list of things that arouse anxiety, ranking them from least to most frightening. The patient is trained, sometimes with hypnosis, to relax deeply; then, the therapist describes the lowest ranking item on the list and asks them to imagine it vividly. If they can do so without getting upset, the therapist goes on to describe the next item. And so forth. If an image starts to arouse tension, the patient signals the therapist, who then backs up to an earlier one. This goes on from session to session until the most frightening item finally fails to disturb the patient's relaxed state. This calm state then generalizes to the real-life fears outside the session.

The range of problems to which desensitization has been applied is simply enormous: nightmares, compulsive hand washing, auditory hallucinations, chronic diarrhea, kleptomania, excessive urination, and every conceivable kind of clearcut fear do not exhaust the list by far. Well over 250 studies of this treatment method have been published by now. Most of them show that systematic desensitization is a good treatment method, but it is not always better than other treatments. The oddest thing about this method, however, is that the reason it works cannot be stated with certainty! A number of studies, for instance, have found that it may work very well without either relaxation or the rank-ordered presentation of the list of frightening items (Kazdin and Wilcoxon 1976).

Implosive therapy This treatment, devised by Thomas Stampfl, serves the same purpose as densensitization but by an opposite means. Instead of letting the phobia wear itself out, this method tries to create an internal explosion (implosion) of anxiety, frightening patients without actually hurting them. As in desensitization, the therapist and patient decide what things are anxiety-arousing, and the therapist then gets the patient to imagine them. Unlike desensitization, however, implosive therapists start at the top of the list, with the *most* frightening items; they describe them as fearsomely as they can, trying to terrify rather than soothe the patient. The principle involved is an elegant variation on the saying: "Sticks and stones may break my bones, but words will never hurt me." Since phobic anxiety is "neurotic"—that is, unrealistic—getting frightened repeatedly from mere words, where nothing ever comes of the fear, causes its extinction. Treatment is completed when the therapist can no longer

frighten the patient with scary images (Stampfl and Levis 1967). Implosion is also called **flooding,** that is, overwhelming the patient with anxiety.

The fact that desensitization and implosion both seem to work on the same types of problems is hard to explain since they appear to be opposites, the one soothing, the other terrifying. One possible explanation is that both methods provide a **cognitive** basis for reducing fears by allowing people to discriminate mentally between real and fancied dangers (London 1964). Physiologically, implosion is a means of classically conditioning extinction by stimulating fear without reinforcing it, so that habituation takes place (McCutcheon and Adams 1975).

Critics of implosive therapy sometimes fear that a dramatic practitioner may frighten some patient into a heart attack or "overwhelm them with anxiety"—that is, scare them "out of their wits." No such event has yet been reported. Perhaps frightening words don't really hurt as much as people fear they will.

An interesting practice with extinction methods is for therapists to assign homework to patients or go with them to face the things that frighten them, riding together in elevators, airplanes, or subways, or giving them other live practice with experiences that help overcome their fears. The University of Southern California's Dr. Ronald McDevitt, cured a case of extreme claustrophobia by having the patient practice staying alone in a tiny room, locked from the outside, while bound hand and foot in a zippered sleeping bag. As everyone knows who has learned any dangerous skills, people adapt to frightening situations if they are exposed enough to them without being hurt.

Behavior shaping B. F. Skinner is not a psychotherapist, but behavior shaping still has many promising applications to psychotherapy. It is used not only for many symptoms of neuroses and psychoses, but for a variety of behavior problems ranging from stuttering to juvenile delinquency, school failure, and general social adjustment (see Chapter 6).

All behavior-shaping operations, you recall, are based on two learning principles: *reinforcement,* which says that an organism will learn to repeat an act for which it is rewarded and to avoid one for which it is ignored or punished; and learning by *successive approximation,* which says that complicated habits or skills are learned gradually in small steps that come closer and closer to an optimal level of performance.

To make practical use of these principles, therapists must know what patients find rewarding or unpleasant. They must have enough control over the environment so that they can provide or withhold these rewards at will, increasing them when the desired behavior increases and withholding them when undesirable behavior appears. They might also, of course, use punishment to control undesirable behavior. But punishment, unless applied with great skill, often has unexpected effects. The Skinnerian therapist, therefore, commonly avoids using punishment in most situations.

The technique requires more ingenuity and inventiveness than any other behavior therapy and may take longer to work. Some impressive results have nevertheless been achieved by behavior shaping. At the University of Virginia, for instance, Bachrach, Erwin, and Mohr were able to induce a lady with anorexia nervosa (a form of neurotic self starvation) to eat and gain weight by controlling the availability of things she enjoyed, such as listening to music and chitchatting with people (1968). Willard Mainord, at the University of Louisville, and others, have used behavior-shaping methods for therapeutic groups and therapeutic hospital wards. People have used them to teach parents and teachers how to manage behavior problems in children. Since each unit of behavior that can be taught by behavior shaping tends to be very small, however, the method has not yet proved as effective with chronic psychotics

as was orginally hoped. Still, Ivar Lovaas and his collaborators at the University of California at Los Angeles have had more success in teaching schizophrenic children different intellectual and social skills than have most other workers; they have succeeded in teaching nonprofessionals to perform the same therapeutic functions that Lovaas's senior team members can do—which gives behavior-shaping methods tremendous economic promise.

Token economies are, of course, the most widespread methods by which behavior-shaping principles are applied, mostly in mental hospitals and institutions for the intellectually retarded. These programs have had varying success, and have been criticized on ethical, practical, and historical grounds (Gagnon and Davison 1976; Kazdin 1973).

Critique of behavior therapy

The techniques of behavior therapy take for granted that the responsibility for treatment rests with the therapists. They must decide what needs to be done to help (change) people, and they are obliged to direct the doing. Their job is to give patients symptom relief, not self-control, and they can do it by many different means; whatever works without damaging the patient is acceptable. The expansion of consciousness, they sometimes say, is usually irrelevant, and occasionally harmful, and rarely valuable for this purpose. The emphasis of behavior therapy is on finding practical applications, planning therapeutic work precisely, and judging it by standards that everyone can understand. In doing so, behavior therapists sometimes overlook or oversimplify complexities of human nature and experience. Even so, they have been more successful with many problems than insight treatments have been. One technique is best for sex, they say, another for tantrums; this for timidity and that for terror; and a third for aggression or stuttering or delinquency. Both good sense and evidence suggest that they are right. But the extent to which they are right in saying that different treatments should be used for different problems goes beyond the expectations of some behavior therapists because some of the problems which are most responsive to psychotherapy yield to insight treatments and to hypnosis more than to counterconditioning or desensitization. This means that the evaluation of psychotherapies should compare them method by method, rather than grouping them under *insight* and *behavior* therapies and trying to evaluate them as realistically opposing positions (London 1972).

Evaluating psychotherapy

The differences between the systems are far less important to the patients than to the doctors. Therapy patients do not usually care whether they are suffering from motivational problems or habit disorders so long as their anxieties get eased and their capabilities, desires, and functions are all right. Any treatment method that satisfies those needs is sure to have their wholehearted approval, regardless of how the doctors bicker among themselves.

There is a growing body of evidence that the bickering among insight and behavior therapists about which is the better treatment does not have much basis. One well controlled study of behavior therapy and psychoanalytic therapy, for instance, showed that, over a two-year follow-up period, both kinds of treatment were more effective than no treatment at all, but that they did not excel over each other. There are some data to indicate, however, that one treatment method might be more suitable for some kinds of patients, and the other for other kinds (Sloane, Staples, Cristol, Yorkston, and Whipple 1975, 1976).

A review of a large number of studies of psychotherapy in the treatment of psychosomatic disorders confirms this notion. It shows that such conditions as peptic ulcers might respond best to insight therapy, warts and some cases of asthma might be treated best by hypnosis, most asthma by a combination of desensitization and relaxation training, and migraine headaches by a combination of desensitization and assertiveness training (Kellner 1975)! Still another review of the many studies comparing therapies to each other finds that most patients do benefit from psychotherapy, that the difference in numbers of people who benefit more from one kind than from another is insignificant, and that the combination of any kind of psychotherapy with drugs often is more worthwhile than either therapy or drugs by itself (Luborsky, Singer, and Luborsky 1975).

It seems clear, from many sources, that psychotherapy "works," which has been a longstanding concern among professional people and is a growing one to the public (Strupp and Hadley 1977). But it is also clear that there is no clearcut explanation of when it works on whom or why to be found in the conventional theories either of insight or behavior therapists. Some behavior therapists have responded to this situation by trying to expand their theoretical ways of talking to include cognitive processes, calling the whole business "cognitive behavior therapy" (Mahoney 1977). In reality, they are simply moving in a direction which early behavior therapists paid too little attention to and which psychoanalysts paid too much attention to—namely, noticing that people's thoughts and fantasies are powerful determinants of their behavior.

Other psychotherapy students, however, are trying to find some general rule which accounts for why all kinds of people with all kinds of problems get better through all kinds of treatment. An interesting idea, in this connection, is the "demoralization" hypothesis of Jerome Frank (1974). It says that the main thing that brings everyone into psychotherapy is a sense of demoralization, and that the main thing that psychotherapy does is to restore morale by restoring people's *sense of mastery,* that is, the sense of control we discussed in Chapter 14. There is some evidence supporting this idea in the fact that a common component which explains the success of treatments as diverse as desensitization and meditation is the expectation people have that the treatment will help them (Kazdin and Wilcoxon, 1976; Smith 1975). The expectation that help is coming goes a long way toward restoring morale.

SUMMARY

1 There are three main kinds of treatment for behavior disorders: (1) medical treatment; (2) educational treatment, and (3) psychotherapy. Medical treatment means chemical and physical manipulations of the body. Educational treatment means instructions or demonstrations used to treat disorders. Psychotherapy refers to a variety of treatment methods which rely primarily on talking to produce their effects. All three kinds of treatments are used for all kinds of behavior disorders.

2 Treatments must be evaluated in effectiveness against the *spontaneous recovery rate,* that is, the rate at which people get better without receiving treatment, and against the effects of *placebos,* that is, phony techniques which look like real treatments but are not intended to be. A satisfactory treatment must produce higher recovery rates than either of them. Also, whether a successful treatment is beneficial or harmful often depends on the moral position of the observer. If you cure alcoholism by "turning on to pot" for instance, many observers would regard the treatment as harmful.

3 There are two kinds of medical treatment: (1) assault treatment, mostly shock therapy and surgery, and (2) drug treatment. Several different chemical assault treatments, especially injections of insulin and metrazol, were once thought to be helpful in treating schizophrenias. They were replaced by ECT (electro-convulsive therapy), which consists of sending a tiny electrical current through the brain. ECT does not help schizophrenics much but it is effective for treating depression. No one knows why. Psychosurgery was once limited to prefrontal lobotomy, done chiefly to quiet unmanageable patients. It is not done much today. Modern psychosurgery consists largely of ESB (electrical stimulation of the brain) by means of radio and chemical transmitter and receiving devices, which activate or inhibit different brain centers.

4 Drug treatments have become the main medical tools since 1952. The major psychiatric drugs are (1) *antipsychotics* or strong tranquilizers, (2) weak tranquilizers, (3) antidepressants, and (4) sedatives. The tranquilizers tend to change mood without interfering with intellectual functioning or motor coordination. The most commonly prescribed weak tranquilizers, however, have not proved to be very effective. Some antidepressant drugs such as energizers, are also of questionable value.

5 The main educational treatments are (1) remedial teaching, especially of reading, and (2) speech therapy. Most reading deficiencies are probably the result of bad training, but some may be symptoms of children's anxieties and other problems. Also, reading handicaps may create emotional problems because they induce a sense of failure. The dynamics of many speech problems are unclear, and different treatments have been used for them accordingly. Verbal psychotherapy has generally proved inadequate for stuttering, the most common speech problem, and current workers use behavioral treatments more. Occupational therapy, dance therapy, and art therapy, are auxiliary educational treatments used largely in mental hospitals.

6 Psychotherapy consists of many methods for helping people solve personal problems, mostly by talking. There are millions of people getting psychotherapy in the United States, several dozen systems for doing it, and many different professions conducting it, primarily psychiatry, psychology, and social work. All psychotherapy may be regarded as forms of persuasion or education to help people with behavior which is out of control.

7 Psychotherapy originated with gadgetry and quackery in the wealthy salons of Europe. Today we would call the methods of the 17th century *placebo* treatment. The forerunner of psychotherapy was the *animal magnetism* of Anton Mesmer, a Viennese doctor who practiced in Paris. The modern name for his methods is *hypnosis*.

8 Modern psychotherapy grew chiefly from psychoanalysis in Europe and from psychoeducational clinics in the United States, both at the end of the 19th century. A number of offshoots of psychoanalysis have subsequently become important kinds of psychotherapy and the psychoeducational clinic has given rise to guidance and counseling systems. Behavior modification methods also originated at the turn of the century, but did not become very popular until after World War II. Therapies deriving from psychoanalysis are called *insight therapies;* those deriving from learning studies are called *behavior therapies*.

9 The basic idea behind all insight therapy is that motives dictate behavior. The treatment of disordered behavior therefore requires helping clients to understand their hidden motives so that they can free themselves of their effects. The most popular insight therapies are psychoanalysis and client-centered therapy. The latter, also called non-directive therapy, originated in the work of Carl Rogers. In insight therapy, the client is primarily responsible for the content of the therapy session. The therapist's job is to guide the person in searching themselves.

10 The three main techniques of insight therapy are (1) association, (2) interpretation, and (3) relationship. Free association is the main psychoanalytic method for exposing unconscious motives by getting the patient to say everything that comes to mind. Repressed thoughts gradually come out as the process goes on. Interpretation is done in two ways. In one, the therapist works out with the patient what the meaning of different thoughts, feelings, or dreams is. In the other method, called *reflection,* the therapist exposes the patient's feelings and communicates the therapist's acceptance of them. The establishment of a sympathetic, understanding and open relationship is the most important tool of all insight therapy. In psychoanalysis, it leads into a *transference* relationship, in which patients feel the same emotions towards the analyst as toward other people who are important in their life.

11 Behavior therapy concentrates on the treatment of symptoms rather than motives. It also places the main responsibility for treatment on the therapist, not the patient. Among the many different techniques of behavior therapy, some of the main ones are (1) counterconditioning, (2) extinction, and (3) behavior shaping. Counterconditioning means replacing one feeling or behavior with another that is opposite to it. Usually this means replacing anxiety with a constructive or pleasant feeling. *Extinction* methods work by head-on attacks on problems rather than by replacing old feelings with new ones.

Systematic desensitization is the most popular extinction method. It works by exposing patients to increasingly anxiety-provoking images under circumstances where they are not frightened. This gradually accustoms them to feeling relaxed in face of those situations. *Behavior shaping* is operant conditioning. It is used for a variety of behavior problems, including stuttering, juvenile delinquency, and school failure.

Groups, crowds, and cultures

20

20

Groups, crowds, and cultures

The next two chapters are about social psychology. It is not an easy subject to define because almost anything about people's behavior in relation to each other can legitimately be considered social psychology. In general, however, there are two things of main concern to most social psychologists. First, people's behavior in relation to groups—how they form them, act within them, and change them. And second, the effect of groups on people's individual behavior—how we become social creatures, experience most of our needs and satisfactions as parts of our social life, and even do most of our private thinking much more socially than we usually realize. How we become social animals has occupied much of the earlier chapters in this book on learning, language, and personality. This chapter will discuss how groups evolve, how they are structured, and how small groups operate. The next chapter will discuss attitudes, beliefs, and opinions, and how they come and go.

THE EVOLUTION OF SOCIAL BEHAVIOR

Social life begins with sex—not for you personally, but for the evolution of most organisms, which requires mating for reproduction. Even some plants and flowers reproduce sexually, but since they are rooted down and wind and bees do the mating, their social life never gets far. Locomotion increases the possibilities for sociality, and social organization increases the chances for survival. So it is an *animal* function, in evolutionary terms, and the more complex the animal, the more important its social functions are to its survival, individually and as a species.

Social life among the beasts

Almost all species have some social life, and the interactions involved are generally more than merely mating. Some insects, such as ants and honey bees, have complex colonial organizations with extensive divisions of labor and of communication. Some birds roost in colonies, and even more migrate as groups. Wolves hunt in packs, seals gather in great tribal consortiums, some whales travel in schools, and some primate species live in social aggregations similar to those of human beings.

All social life evolved to promote the survival of species, but the way it works towards that end differs greatly among them. V. C. Wynne-Edwards (1962) proposes that social organizations all serve their evolutionary purposes by creating mechanisms for controlling the population of a species in relation to such things as its food supply. Migration, casting out older members, cannibalizing babies, territoriality, social dominance, and still other aspects of social life practiced among different animal species, all seem to serve this end.

Every species has developed some means, for instance, of **testing population density,** which means being able to recognize its own members. Certain kinds of movements are recognition signals in some species; brightly colored species tend to have color vision; songs, shrills, and howls provide auditory recognition signals for others; odors for still others. And some have signal methods undetectable by human senses.

Territoriality functions largely as a means of controlling dispersion within a species. It exists among many species. Among anthropoid apes, which are nomadic, territory is a group rather than individual matter. Within a fixed domain, baboons, as a group, will resist invasion by other bands of baboons.

Social dominance is more important. It exists in all classes of vertebrates. In any group, dominance gives precedence in *feeding* and *mating* (also in territory, which is itself license to feed and mate). Contests for dominance among other species than our own, incidentally, are rarely settled by actual combat —usually by preening and threatening. Where there is actual fighting, it is usually harmless. Wynne-Edwards believes it is a mechanism of group survival, a "social guillotine" for cutting off the lower ends of society when food gets short. Brown calls it a *"peaceful convention* guaranteeing that *some* members of the group will endure" (1965). Whoever dominates, eats, propagates, and thereby endures.

Human beings have done about the same things as other animals to control populations—and we still do. Remember, for instance, the classical tradition of leaving deformed babies to perish on the hillside? Even today, laws and customs are made and changed deliberately to affect the populations of different societies. Egypt and Japan, for example, have long had legalized abortion—both are heavily overpopulated countries. Australia, Israel, and Brazil, on the other hand, all underpopulated, give great financial advantages to potential immigrants in hopes of getting them to settle—and some countries even pay special subsidies to citizens for having large families. The bitter reality of how warfare and starvation have systematically prevented humanity from overcrowding the planet (until recently) was turned into economic doctrine almost two centuries ago by Thomas Malthus.

The evolution of human groups

Human groupings undoubtedly began the same way animal groups did, and for most of human prehistory, their organization was probably much the same as it is today among the anthropoid apes.

That changed dramatically with the development of language because language made **culture** possible. Culture means all the conventions of a group that get transmitted from one generation to the next. It includes common language, manners, dress, religion, and manner of working, fighting, playing, lovemaking, and child rearing. Broadly speaking, every human society can be considered a culture, that is,

American Gothic, Grant Wood

Traditionally the starting point for the social development of human beings, the nuclear family, is based on the economic unit of father, mother, home, and livelihood.

every human group which recognizes itself as a common group—primarily by sharing a language, a living space, and a commonly agreed upon set of relatives.

Language is the most important aspect of culture because it extends memory beyond the lifetime of individuals so that a large part of everyone's experience can be transmitted from one generation to another. This possibility creates enormous complexities in the *structure* of human groups. It made possible the extension of *functional groups* to a very large size by extending the boundaries of communication beyond the immediate limits of familiar faces. A functional group is a bunch of people mutually involved in achieving some common goal. The earliest groups of humans, like contemporary groups of apes, were essentially families that roamed a small territory and kept together for gathering food, for mating, and for mutual protection. This tiny grouping, the family, is still the basis of most human society, and is called the *primary group,* or *primary kinship group.* Originally, it needed only simple methods of communication and mutual recognition. You were a member if the other members considered you one; otherwise, not.

Language removed the need for face-to-face familiarity as the basis for membership. It extended kinship bonds by extending memory, and this was done by *naming* people and relationships. You did not have to know a man personally to believe he was a member of your family if you were told that he was the son of your mother's brother's son—because you knew your mother, and probably knew her brother, so you could accept that her brother's son was connected to you, and therefore not an enemy. In preliterate societies, to this day, kinship names and relationships are still the main basis of determining mutual social obligations. It is common for little children to be able to reel off the names of their ancestors for 30 or 40 generations and of several dozen contemporary uncles, aunts, and cousins of different degrees. Nor is the significance of kinship so far removed from our own practices. Only late in the Middle Ages, did people take on *last names.* Until then, a person was usually identified as so-and-so, son-or-daughter-of-so-and-so. Even when last names became common, they were most often the names of important progenitors (e.g., John*son*, Davido*vitch*, Maimon*ides*, all mean "son of"), and they are still called *family names.*

Language extended the primary kinship group so much that **secondary groups** gradually developed, that is, groups in which membership was based on some common interest or purpose you shared with other people. In primary groups, membership is an end in itself. There is no *purpose* in your be-

Informal secondary groups may form when people gather at a place of recreation repeatedly. Their mutual interest in entertainment and companionship, which brought them there, is what they have in common — along with their styles of dress, coiffure, and favorite drinks.

At the Moulin-Rouge, Henri de Toulouse-Lautrec

longing to your family; you just *do*. But you don't just *happen* to join a club; you join it because you want something from it.

In the evolution of human societies, it was a long distance from primary kinship groups to secondary social clubs. In between came the evolution of tribes, kingdoms, nations, empires, and the whole complex of social structures which humans have invented everywhere.

Tribes grew out of families, usually united by a patriarchal relative. They expanded by marriage across families, and eventually gave rise to kingdoms. Kingdoms are extensions of tribes in which the kinship bonds are weak, and other cultural bonds, like language and religion, are strong, and the geographic limits of the group are pretty definite. The king is a tribal patriarch whose family relationships to most of his subjects is unknown.

Nations and empires are less continuous with families; most nations are not tied together by any traceable kinship bond, and empires not even by a bond of common language.

Racial and ethnic groups The great limiting factor in the early history of human social organizations was geography. With us, as with lower animals, there is only so much food to go around in so much space, and therefore only so many people can survive there. What we call racial groups today are the offspring of kinship groups that clustered together for a long time in relatively remote areas, were

A common interest, or shared loneliness, can forge people into a long lasting, stable "secondary" group.

The Card Players, Paul Cézanne

As ethnic groups assimilate into American society, they are able to assert their differences more proudly.

seldom invaded by other groups, and did not have to move much in order to survive. In such situations, people intermarried relatively close to their own kinship groups, and the resulting cultural groups shared many physical features as well as common languages and customs. Throughout human history, however, language and custom were always more important considerations in the intermarriage of different groups than were physical similarities or differences. *Custom* determined the relative positions of dominance and familiarity within each group and from one social group to another. All human societies, in other words, have always shared some common characteristics of social structure; the universals of social structure are the heart of mankind's universal tendency to band together.

UNIVERSALS OF SOCIAL STRUCTURE

It is almost impossible to put two human beings together for long without a group developing. A *group* differs from a loose aggregate like a *crowd* or a *mob* by being *organized.* Every group has some leaders and some followers, some roles that people have to play to get status with the other people in the group, and some rules for who can play what roles under what conditions. Whether the group you are studying is one that has been created for some special purpose, such as an army or a college faculty or a social club, or whether it just came together naturally, as people happened to gather at one place, as many towns do, it still will have a *hierarchy* of roles and status positions and rules. What is more, these hierarchies have remarkably similar structures across

The Village of the Mermaids, Paul Delvaux

Strangers who find themselves together are not necessarily a group. Each
individual may be wrapped up in private thoughts, needs, or problems
and have no relationship at all with others in the same room.

all kinds of groups. We shall look at some of
them here.

There are two kinds of group membership—
ascribed or **attributed,** and **acquired** or
achieved. An ascribed group member is someone who has no choice about belonging.
You are a member of your class at school, for
instance, because you are a certain age and
live in a certain neighborhood. An acquired
group member, on the other hand, chooses to
join a group and gets membership by some
voluntary means.

Roles and role differentiation   A role is a
function of society, that is, a behavior pattern
expected of a person according to their social
position. Roles depend on the values a society

attaches to age, sex, kinship, or occupation as
leader, follower, teacher, student, or whatever.

Most people play many roles, switching from
one to another in different social situations.
This sometimes causes role conflict, but
usually does not.

Status: Caste, class, and situation   Status
means the "standing" of an individual in a
group. It refers to a person's value, that is, to the
relative worth of a group member.

Every social group has a **status hierarchy,**
that is, a distribution of status positions. In the
most rigid social structure, a **caste** system,
status is always **attributed**— you are born with
as much or as little of it, ordinarily, as you are

Georgia Jungle, Alexander Brook

Ascribed group membership is what we are born into—family, racial group, nationality. We have no choice about it.

going to get. In an ***open class*** structure, which most Western societies are, it is often attributed, but can sometimes be achieved. There is more mobility in social class systems, which may allow you to move from a position of low status to one of high status—or vice versa.

In a completely functional group, that is, a group which exists to do a job, ***status*** depends on a member's contribution—the more one contributes, the higher it is. Few such groups exist. In an open society, however, most people belong to several kinds of groups at once, which gives the individual more than one chance for high status. If you can't get it in one group, you still might in another.

Caste has been officially abolished in India, but for all practical purposes it still exists. In Western society, ancient civilizations were organized along caste lines wherever there was a hereditary priesthood, nobility, or slave system—in short, almost everywhere. The fact that slaves could become free helped move society somewhat towards an open class system, but did not help much. The position of a freeman (called "yeoman" in England of the Middle Ages) in society was not a great deal better than that of a serf or slave, and the status of freeman was usually hereditary. The main purpose of a caste system is to keep people "down," which largely means keeping them *physically* as well as *socially immobile*. The medieval serf, for instance, had no right to leave his lord's lands. The rise of ambitious kings and the creation of a merchant or middle class began to weaken the caste system of medieval Europe, and it broke down even more when the opening of the New World after Columbus gave people the opportunity to *emigrate*. America developed as a relatively classless society largely because its open frontier permitted people who were dissatisfied in one place to leave it for another.

At any time, in any society, wealth is an important factor in determining social class, but other forms of prestige are important too, such as power and achievement. There tends to be pretty general agreement in any given society about who belongs in which class, especially when people are ranked by occupation (Cattell 1942). Source of income is more important than amount of it, for instance; upper-class people are more likely to live on inherited wealth than middle-class people, even if it totals to less money (Warner et al. 1949).

Child rearing practices differ somewhat from one class to another, so people in any one class tend to share some personality traits which distinguish them from members of other classes (Bronfenbrenner 1958). One of Kinsey's most curious findings had to do with sexual behavior

In every society wealth confers high status.

differences in individuals from different classes (Kinsey et al. 1948, 1953). People tend to exhibit sexual behavior typical of the class to which they belong!

Social mobility is the ability to shift from one class to another or from one role to another. It is the key to shifting social status, on the one hand, and to a society of maximum opportunity, on the other. The fewer restraints a society has to prevent people from changing home, occupation, social circle, manners, or morals, the more opportunities they have to find what they want in life and to be the kind of social creature they like best. Social mobility promotes high achievement, which is the best route to higher status in an open society because it gives access to the main source of status in any society—the acquisition of *power.*

Children adopt their social roles by imitating their parents, as they learn to be members of a group—the family—from birth.

The Family, Adriaen van Ostade

Third Class Carriage, Honoré Daumier

In a nonmobile society, being born into a poor or working class virtually dooms people to living out their life in that class. Their opportunities, the places they can go, and the people they can associate with will always be bound by their class position.

POWER, LEADERSHIP, AND POLITICS

Any group, regardless of size, has a *power structure;* some people in it are more powerful and influential than others. The main determinants of a person's power are their *resources* in relation to the other people's *dependencies* and *alternatives* (Raven 1965; Collins 1970). Your *resources* are anything you have that is of value to other people—money, property, weapons, or personal qualities of intelligence, education, or leadership ability—in short, any-

thing that puts you in a position to *reward* people by sharing your bounty with them or to *punish* or *coerce* them, either by withholding whatever it is that you have and they need or by forcing them to submit to your will. A resource is a means of getting power only to the extent that other people *depend* on it in the first place and have no *alternative* means of getting it other than by yielding to your demands. If they have other ways of satisfying their needs, and can get along without your resources, then you gain no power by having them. A dressmaker in a nudist colony gains no power from such skills. If you are dissatisfied with your local telephone company's service, on the other hand, there is not much you can do about it—it controls all the resources for instant communication.

Control of resources can be a great source of conflict. The water and grazing rights disputes of Biblical times and the range wars on the American frontier were problems in the control of resources. So were the Trojan Wars and the Punic Wars (between Carthage and Rome) and many other of history's greatest conflicts. Most struggles for **power** are struggles to control the resources which permit one to dispense rewards and punishments.

Having control of resources, however, does not guarantee that you can make wise or effective use of them, just as it does not imply that you have any skills at getting them in the first place. Until very recently in the history of civilization, most wealth and most power was inherited. (Wealth still is.) The rare individuals who succeeded in *gaining* power and in *maintaining* it in the face of conflict have had to demonstrate the special skills of persuasion and coercion which constitute **leadership.**

Leadership

The progress of human society has not come from the herd characteristics of our species but from the superior **organization** that human intelligence has enabled us to impose on ourselves in groups. The creation of that organization and its maintenance has always depended more on the quality of **leadership** than on any other single event. It still does today, and perhaps it always will.

The birth and growth of leadership The great question about leadership is how it arises and how it is maintained. This has been debated by scholars and biographers for at least a couple thousand years; there are two opposing views predominant. The first is a **historical view;** it says that leaders arise in response to historical necessity, i.e., they grow out of social situations which demand leadership. The second, or **psychological view,** says that leaders grow out of the personal experiences of individuals that dispose them throughout life to seek opportunities for power or to make the most of them when they occur. The historical view suggests that the great events of history make great leaders of ordinary people who merely rise to the occasions they seem to command. In the psychological view, history is made by great people whose strokes of genius or great blunders move the rest of our lives in directions they otherwise never would go. Both positions are overstated in their extreme form; obviously, the drama of history and the personalities of its main characters interact—the Napoleonic Wars could not have happened had Napoleon not wanted an empire. But Napoleon might not have risen to power if the events of the French Revolution had not made it possible —and he had nothing to do with starting that. History and personality must converge at just the right points for great people to express their leadership potential.

Very little, in fact, is known about when and how someone becomes a potential leader. When you observe the behavior of adults in small groups, it seems clear that some people have a more "natural" disposition towards leadership than others, meaning that they tend to talk more, to assert themselves more, and to be more willing, sometimes eager, to tell everyone else what to do. In disasters, such as floods or bombings or shipwrecks, the tendency of some people to assume leadership roles and of others to follow is even more dramatic. The personal qualities that dispose some people towards leadership are probably some combination of self-assertiveness, or aggressiveness, on the one hand, and of charisma, on the other, that propel them into leadership situations. Intelligence, initiative, and a couple of other things were identified as general leadership traits in a 1940 review of some 20 studies, but except for intelligence, none of those traits were highly correlated with leadership (Bird 1940). Studies since then have reached the same conclusion—that with the possible exception of intelligence, there is no consistent pattern of personality traits that predict leadership (Davis 1969; Gibb 1969; Mann 1959; Stogdill 1948). Whatever elusive qualities of personality may be involved, they probably are developed in childhood, in the course of the role-typing activities that establish sexual and occupational preferences (see Chapters 14 and 17); the reinforcements children get in those activities must establish their interpersonal styles of conduct as well. But little is known about them. Leaders are probably made, not born, but it not clear how.

Varieties of leadership Different personal qualities make for good leadership in different

This task-oriented group also shares an informal relationship. The pleasure of sharing a meal after working hard together is also ensured by cooperation—one man is cutting bread, another brings a jug of water, all relax and chat or rest—the task too will be pleasurable.

The Harvesters, Pieter Bruegel the Elder

kinds of situations. Modern research focuses on the kinds of leadership important for particular goals (Jenkins 1947). This is usually studied in small group situations, both in laboratories and real life. One of the first major laboratories for studying the dynamics of small groups was that of Harvard's Robert F. Bales (1950). By a method called "interaction process analysis," he came to the conclusion that there are two main kinds of leader. One is a "task specialist," whose leadership comes by virtue of being active in the group and effective in performing whatever job the group has to do. The second kind of leader is a "socioemotional specialist," who may be less *competent* and active than the task specialist but becomes a leader anyway by being more likable (Bales 1958). There also is a third kind of leader who combines activity, ability, and likability. Borgatta, Couch, and Bales call him the "great man" type of leader (1954). In leadership, as in all other things, greatness is rare.

The most sophisticated and subtle studies of leadership in small groups have been conducted by Fred E. Fiedler and his associates at the University of Illinois and University of Washington. Fiedler's group has examined almost every kind of small group imaginable, from collections of college students who get wheedled into experiments to the real life activities of basketball teams and tank crews. From almost two decades of research, he developed a theory of leadership effectiveness (Fiedler 1967). It says that there is no such thing as an *absolute* quality of leadership. The most effective leadership depends on the kind of problems a group faces and the circumstances under which it has to solve them (Graen, Alvares, Oriis, and Martella 1970). In relaxed conditions, or in a group which does not have a special task to perform, the best leader is someone who is sensitive to the personal feelings and relationships of group members. Under stress or, in groups which have a common problem to solve, a task-oriented

leader, perhaps somewhat insensitive to the personal relations among group members, is most effective (Yukly 1971).

Whether personal style of leadership is task-oriented or social-emotional, a leader may direct a group in either a **democratic** or **authoritarian** manner. Here too, the value of either kind of leadership depends on how you look at it. Authoritarian groups tend to operate slightly more efficiently for some work purposes, but democratic groups tend to inspire more good feeling among the membership with little loss of productivity. **Laissez-faire** groups, in which no leadership is exercised, tend to be most dissatisfying, both in the feelings of group members and in what the group accomplishes with tasks set for it (Lewin et al. 1939).

Politics is the exercise of leadership over a group. Some political leaders maneuver their way into power by being task-oriented and organizing a political machine that can influence, persuade, or coerce people's support. Other leaders are effective mostly because their personal qualities are emotionally appealing to people, so that their **charisma** (Greek for "grace" or "favor"; in English, "charm") makes people want to follow them or fear opposing them. In American history, George Washington and Woodrow Wilson are good examples of task-oriented political leaders; people followed their political leadership because they seemed to be so **capable,** not because they seemed **lovable.**[1] Washington demonstrated his great military abilities in the French and Indian Wars, 20 years before the American Revolution, so the Continental Congress had some confidence that he could pursue the war against the British. What's more, he was the richest man in the Colonies; so they figured he could help pay for the troops and arms to fight (he did). Franklin

---

[1] It is easy to get confused here because lots of people love a winner and adore the most scurvy characters once they gain power or get close to it. I am talking about the personal qualities of potential leaders that make people support them *in search* of power.

Oarsmen on the Schuylkill, Thomas Eakins

A task-oriented group. The speed and smoothness of the vessel depend
entirely on the cooperative work of the four men.

Delano Roosevelt and Dwight D. Eisenhower, on
the other hand, were **charismatic** leaders.
People followed them because they loved them,
not because they were especially good civil or
military administrators. In fact, they were not
very distinguished in those capacities, though
they had both held important jobs.

Whether a political leader's personality is
task-oriented or charismatic has nothing to do
with whether they exercise democratic or authoritarian leadership, no more than it does
among small group leaders. Political institutions
are not like laboratory groups or social groups,
however, because there is a lot of power at
stake and because they tend to be self-perpet-
uating. So one important problem of political
leaders is that of leadership **continuity,** that is,

preparing new leadership for the groups they
now govern.

This may be easiest to do in a democratic
society because it probably will have a richer
supply of potential leaders than an authoritarian
one—democratic societies tend to have greater
social mobility and to offer more people more
experience at leadership. The key to leadership
continuity in any society is probably not political
democracy, however, but the training of a
capable civil service which can continue working through a wide range of shifting governments. The Roman Empire, the dynasties of
Imperial China, and the British Empire, all had
long histories of successful government because they all had a sophisticated and well
educated corps of bureaucrats, or mandarins,

or civil servants, who could keep the wheels of society in motion through many changes of political leadership. Of the three, only the British government was democratic, and only within the British Isles. Empires which depended on the skills and charisma of a single great leader generally collapsed immediately after his death—so it went with King Solomon, and Alexander the Great, and Charlemagne. The same thing happens today among the developing nations of the "third world," whose often inspired political leaders cannot govern effectively because they lack the administrative apparatus of educated and dedicated officials necessary to keep the wheels of government turning. Some people think that these governments are unstable because their leaders are too revolutionary. The real reason is sometimes that their followers are too inept.

Group communication

The roles people play in social situations, the status they obtain, and the leadership or power they exercise, all depend, in the long run, on their ability to communicate effectively with their peers, henchmen, and **constituents** (an elegant term for subjects, citizens, voters, or members). Patterns of communication (also called communication structure) give a good index of the way status and power are distributed in a group. In almost any social system, high-status members initiate and receive more communications than low-status members. They talk to each other more than to those beneath them, and when there is communication with people lower than themselves in the status-power hierarchy, it is generally from the top down, not from the bottom up. This tends to be just as true in a democratic political system as in a totalitarian one. The difference is that, in a democracy, elections give the citizens a periodic chance to communicate forcibly with the people they have set above them to govern.

There are four basic communication structures common to all social systems, whether they are small and informal, as in a social group, or large and structured, as in the government of a city or country. They are (1) the **circle,** (2) the **wheel,** (3) the **Y,** and (4) the **chain.** Each has different uses and value in one or another circumstance.

In the **circle** pattern, the flow of communication moves from one group member to another and circulates throughout the system. This is the kind of social system where everyone knows everything and where all the members of the group tend to be equal. This kind of arrangement is ideal for small groups which have no special problem to solve, such as a discussion group, or where the common problem is one in which the discussants all need to feel that they are in equally good positions to bargain. When the contending parties in the Vietnam War began to negotiate peace terms with each other in Paris in 1968, they spent months arguing about the proper shape of the tables they would sit at. To the public, it seemed like a stupid argument; to the negotiators themselves, however, it was important to the flow of communications from them to their antagonists and to their own assistants—and they were not willing to sit at tables in which a bad seating arrangement might lead them into making a bad deal.

In the **wheel** pattern, communication flows from one central member, at the wheel's hub, down the spokes to each individual group member. The wheel is generally considered the most efficient communication pattern (and the circle the least efficient one) for "problem-solving" or "task-oriented" groups (Shaw 1955; Trow 1957). It is the basic communication system for small organizations with highly centralized leadership, such as a tank crew or a football team. The reason it "works" so well for problem solving is that there is little confusion in communication from the leadership down. Since only a single message gets sent, and there is only one stage of transmission, it is more likely to travel accurately than it would in another

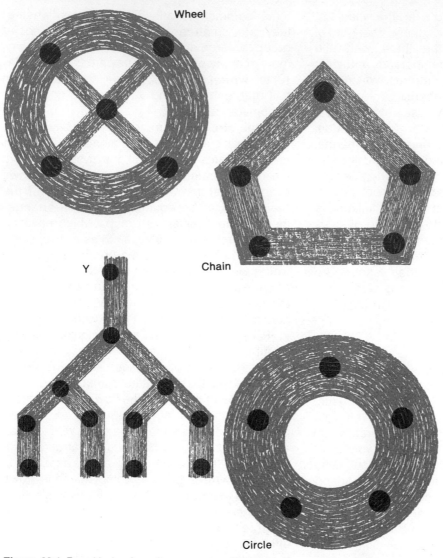

Figure 20.1 Four kinds of small group organization.

communication structure. And when there are errors in communication, it is easier to find them than it would be in a system where the messages have to go through many people. In small groups, with authoritarian leadership, it is the communication pattern of choice.[2]

The **Y** pattern is typical of most large-scale communication structures; it is the system by which most organizations are administered and, most societies governed. It starts from one person and then branches out to others, in an

<hr>

[2] "Authoritarian" is not used here as a dirty word, but simply as a descriptive term for any situation in which the

leader, or boss, has the right to decide how employees, subordinates, or colleagues should work without necessarily having to consult them in advance for each decision.

upside-down Y, with the branches forming branches beneath them. Communication starts from one person, in other words, goes simultaneously to one or two or three people beneath them, as in the wheel, but then goes from each of them to the people beneath them in the communication structure. This is a *hierarchical* system, meaning that it passes through different levels of responsibility, authority, and status. The whole structure, in pure form, takes the shape of a pyramid, as communication branches outward from the original source through more and more levels of transmission. At any point, of course, a branch may operate in a circular, wheeled, or *chain* fashion, rather than continuing directly to branch out in more Ys. It depends on the kind of power or administrative structure that operates at that level.

The wheel pattern, on a small scale, and the Y pattern, on a large one, are the communication structures used most in *centralized* administrative or communication network. A centralized system is one in which responsibility and power may be traced back to a single source rather than being diffused among many people.

In general, groups in which individuals have maximum communication with each other are the most satisfying to most members. For group productiveness in solving simple group problems, the most effective structure is a "differentiated" or hierarchical one, i.e., one where some members are more central than others and where communication takes place through a chain of group members. For more complex problems, on the other hand, a relatively undifferentiated informal structure is more effective (Trow 1957).

SOCIAL NORMS: HOLDING "OUR CROWD" TOGETHER

The main reason for studying group behavior is that people do not act just the same way in group situations as they do individually. Put a person together with other people, either in an organized group or an unorganized crowd, and you do something to their thoughts and feelings which moves them towards a different kind of action, and gives them a different perspective on it, than the same person will have when you view them alone.

As people form groups, and the groups develop structure, pressures grow on the individual members to maintain that structure. People get used to definite patterns of social interaction, and once they do, it bothers them if those patterns are not kept to by everyone else. We are all creatures of habit, in large part, and many of the *habits of social interaction* we develop with each other or learn in growing up become such a deep part of our expectations and perceptions that we are shaken to see them disregarded. *Social perception* is as much part of a person's private definition of reality as visual or auditory perception is.

The mutual social expectations people have of each other give rise to *social norms,* that is, standards of conduct implicitly agreed upon by the group and expected of all its members. When a group becomes so large and well organized, over a long time, that it gets impractical for each member to remember *all* the standards that apply to everyone, then some of the norms are made *explicit* and become *rules* or *laws.* This happens most when there is uncertainty or conflict between people about how they are supposed to behave. Between roommates, or in a family, for instance, most routine interactions are routinely learned and governed by expectations that have not been talked over much. But when there is confusion or disagreement occurs, the discussion which settles it makes those norms into explicit rules by which to act—who can use the car when, what the priorities in the bathroom are, or with the television set, and so forth. When the *reference group* (the group you are interested in, i.e., *refer to* in your thoughts, feelings, or discussion) is too large, or spread out, or diffuse in its interests and activities for such simple management, as in a *society,* then laws tend more and more to replace norms.

A law is usually *explicit,* so that everyone can understand what it demands, and *general,* so that it can be applied to anyone at any time. Like a law, a social norm is an instruction to conform, but it is commonly *implicit,* understood rather than stated. As a society becomes more complicated and sophisticated, it develops more and more laws but it does not *stop* having norms. There are no laws in our society, for instance, that say you must cut a steak with knife and fork instead of eating it with your fingers, or that you may not pick your nose in public; most social conduct everywhere is determined by norms, not by laws. In a very civilized society, violating norms may get you socially ostracized, but it will not get you jailed or killed — there are laws for the things that will. In a more primitive society, some norms may have the force of laws, so that their infraction may subject you to harsh penalties by common consent. This is most true, of course, in preliterate societies, where the absence of writing blurs the distinction between norms and laws.

Common law Even where writing exists, and laws are written, some norms are considered so important and so universal that the action you take on them is considered a matter of law, which everyone is expected to under-

Crowd.

stand and abide by, no matter what kind of formal education or explicit warning they have had about it. Such norms make up what might be called *common law,* because it is assumed that they are known to everyone (as in the expression, "it is common knowledge that . . .") and understood by everyone (as in "a matter of common sense"). It is for such matters that we say, "Ignorance of the law is no excuse." Killing someone without provocation, or taking someone's property without their permission, are forbidden almost everywhere by common laws. In many places, if a man and woman live together for a long time, especially if they have children, they are considered married by common law, even if they have not obeyed the explicit laws requiring them to get a license and go through a ceremony. The common law, it is thought, has a universal quality.

In fact, there is nothing universal about common law at all, only about the egotism of human beings. In every society, people tend to regard

The symbolism in clothing and ornaments can communicate the wearer's group affiliation, status in that group, and many other aspects of personal identity.

Portrait of a German Officer, Marsden Hartley

their own common practices as the "right and proper" way for everyone to behave everywhere. The common law is a society's formal stamp of approval on its own normative customs.

In every society, the *bandwidth* of norms varies a great deal. That means that standards of conformity vary; some of them are rigid and narrow and must be adhered to very carefully. In modern America, for instance, the restrictions on violence are rigid and narrow. Not only may you not kill someone you dislike, but you also may not knock their teeth out, slap their face, spit at them, or even threaten them with violence. The only people who are permitted to be physically violent are people with licenses and generally uniforms showing that they have such rights, and even then, they can only express it is certain situations that have been defined as part of their "duty."

Other norms have a relatively broad bandwidth, meaning that there is a lot of leeway in what a person must do to conform to them. American norms in clothing, for example, are pretty liberal now and getting more so all the time. Everyone is expected to appear in public with their genitals covered, but almost everything else is permissible by way of color, material, and style. Interestingly, clothing trends have moved in the direction of permitting women to wear the same kinds of clothes that men do more than vice versa. So slacks are now worn by both sexes, and so are shirts and ties — but skirts, dresses, and head scarves are still pretty much restricted to women. The reason may be that since women have always had lower status than men, their moving towards slacks is upgrading, while men's wearing skirts would be stepping down.

Conformity

Norms develop in a social group because people seem to have a strong need to be like each other, to feel that they are in agreement with one another and with the group they belong to. People vary individually in the extent of their need to conform, as they vary in everything else; those with strong feelings of inadequacy, for instance, are more inclined than others to be conforming in a lot of situations, probably because being like everyone else helps reduce their feelings of not amounting to much by themselves. People who feel more self-confident are likely to be more individualistic in their own behavior and more tolerant of deviant behavior in others.

Even so, the pressure to conform is so strong, both in the individual who thinks of deviating and in other members of the group, that deviating seems to throw it off balance. When this happens in a small group, there is more communication among the members, especially in the direction of the deviants, and generally aimed at restoring them to the common practice or opinion. The function of conformity seems to be to hold groups in balance (Brown 1965). Thus, *conformity is the individual need from which social norms are born.*

A lot of experiments have been done to see how group decisions are reached and social norms created. They make it clear that the tendency for group members to conform to each other's judgment is not a matter of outside pressure but of personal need. A classic experiment by Muzafer Sherif demonstrated this fact (1935). He brought people into a dark room, first individually, then in groups of two or three, to observe the *autokinetic effect* (see Chapter 5), that is, the apparent movement of a pinpoint of light which is actually stationary against a dark background. The people did not know about the effect; they were told that a point of light would appear, move a short distance, and then go out. They were to estimate how far it moved. In individual trials, they developed very different but self-consistent opinions. But then, when they were put in groups, hearing each other's guesses, over the course of many trials, their estimates gradually would

Conformity.

narrow down to within an inch or two of one another. People reach some consensus of judgments, evidently, because they turn to each other for guidance. In doing so, they establish a group norm which then serves as a reference point for each individual's behavior. As we would expect also, people's sense of social status, power, identification, and self-confidence influence the developing norm as much here as they do anywhere else. So everyone's final judgments tend to conform more to people high in those attributes than they do to the judgments of "sad sacks" or "oddballs" or shy, retiring subjects. People

get their confidence bolstered, and their opinions validated, by being like each other.

The confidence that comes from being like the other members of your group has some practical effects beyond making you feel good. It also may have a *disinhibiting* effect on people's sense of responsibility, so they will make decisions and take actions in a group which are far more extreme than those they would do individually. We meet this phenomenon in its most active form in the behavior of crowds and mobs, but it occurs even in well-organized, purposeful groups whose members are generally responsible as individuals. When the group extreme favors action, it is called the "risky-shift phenomenon" (Stoner 1961; Marquis 1962; Wallach et al. 1962). But whether the movement is towards risk-taking or is a shift towards caution, which also sometimes happens, the group decision will be more extreme than the individual decision (Brown 1965). No one has a single explanation for the whole business.

So far, we have been talking about people's tendency to conform to the group when there is no special pressure to do so outside the individual's own head. In such situations, the extent of conformity depends on things like how much the individual needs the group and wants to live up to its expectations. That in turn may depend not only on such personality factors as self-esteem and self-confidence, but on the attractiveness of the group itself. Some groups are more attractive than others because they are more **cohesive,** that is, there are more things about them that make their members want to stick together and be part of a single unit. They may see the group as important, or the people in it as congenial, so they get a lot of satisfaction from interacting with one another and feel rewarded by participating. The more cohesive a group is, the more pressure a person will feel to conform to it. The point is that the human disposition to huddle together in groups is so strong that the formation of norms to keep it in operation in every group is virtually inevitable. Roger Brown sums it up neatly:

> There seems to be an almost ineradicable tendency for members of a group to move toward agreement. It occurs when there is no instruction to reach a consensus. It occurs when there is no opportunity to argue. It even occurs, incipiently, when the members do not know one another's opinions but can only guess at them. It occurs when the positive relations among the members are weak (1965, p. 669).

On the other hand, you may say, the conformity situations described above are ones where there is no **objective truth** to make judgments of. Of course we tend to agree with each other in social situations where there is no obvious standard for decision or for disagreement—because we are all reared to be **sociable.** But we are also reared to be truthful, honest, and accurate in our judgments where there *is* some objective basis for decision; so we can expect a lot of disagreement within a group in those circumstances. That argument makes sense, but it is often sadly wrong.

Group pressure to conform: The Asch studies The most important findings about people's public judgments in situations where there is an objective right and wrong answer were conducted by Solomon Asch. His results teach us a lot about people's response to pressures from a group to conform.

Asch did several experiments with the same general design (1956). People were recruited to participate in what they thought was a visual perception study. They went into a room where several other subjects (actually stooges of the experimenter) were already seated and sat down with them. Everybody looked at a line in the front of the room and at three cards next to it, each containing a line of different length. One of the lines was the same length as the standard one in the front, and subjects were to guess which, starting from the right, and stating their judgments aloud. The real subject was always next to last in this arrangement.

Now the comparison was not really difficult; the standard line was distinctly more like one of the three cards than like either of the others. But the phony subjects, starting their guesses, would always name the same wrong line as being identical with the standard—and over a third of the real subjects denied the plain evidence of their senses and gave the same response as the unanimous majority!

There was little possibility of real error in this situation; when control studies were done to see if people made such mistakes in comparing lines when there was no group around to refer to, nobody did. The experimental result occurred because the individual felt pressured to conform to the opinions of the majority, and for no other reason. And in doing so, people were not deliberately lying, but actually adjusted their perceptions, it seems, to be agreeable.

The Asch experiment has been repeated with many variations, and on hundreds of subjects, and with many different experimental tasks ranging from solving logical syllogisms to counting the beats of a metronome (Blake et al. 1956). Rosenhan, DeWilde, and McDougal (1963) did the same basic study Asch did, and on virtually the same population of students. They used logical syllogisms instead of lines as the judgment problem, on the logical grounds that people could honestly disagree on the length of lines, so that the real subjects could easily doubt their own judgment. But logical problems have a mathematical character— everyone knows that two plus two is four, no matter what other people say about it. Well, everyone doesn't know. Subjects in this study yielded to majority errors in logic as readily as their predecessors had done to misjudging lines. Howard Lim and I repeated the syllogism experiment, varying the difficulty of the problems (London and Lim 1964). But doing so did not change the quality of the answers much; as expected, people acquiesced more to the majority when the problems were hard because they were less certain of the answers—but they acquiesced plenty when the problems were easy as well.

The conforming responses observed in these experiments were clearly responses to **social pressure,** not to the subjects' simple misjudgment, because the more consistent the majority was, the more subjects would acquiesce; if there was a break in the majority, and two or three stooges disagreed with it, more real subjects would disagree also. What is more, if the pressuring majority consisted of fewer people, then the real subject would find

it easier to be independent—although the presence of even one person making phony judgments would elicit a higher rate of error than if the subject was alone.

Not everyone acquiesced, of course, and gave the wrong answers—but everyone paid an emotional price for the stress of resisting, and both in Asch's original study and in that of Rosenhan, DeWilde, and McDougal, some bright subjects who *had* yielded to the majority seemed terribly distressed over the entire situation, apparently because they were unconsciously sensitive to what had gone on.

The difference between the Asch-type experiments and the Sherif-type, as far as norms are concerned, is that in the Sherif studies, the group is asked to **construct** a norm; in the Asch studies, it already has one, and the question is whether the individual will abide by it or deviate from it. The pressure to abide, to be agreeable, to acquiesce, and to "fit in," is enormous. Everybody, it seems, has the deep need to "be good," however mother or father or God or society or whoever-is-one-up on us has defined it. Just how deep this need goes, and what it can do to our behavior, is more dramatic, and more frightening than you would ever guess from experiments on lines and syllogisms.

Just following orders: The Milgram studies
The readiness with which people obey authorities is astonishing; they often do so without examining how legitimate the authority is or how meaningful the commands are that it sets down. Stanley Milgram demonstrated this effect, both of individual authorities and of group pressures, in a shocking series of experiments. The basic pattern of these studies was that a man was told he was going to participate in some experiments studying the effects of punishment on learning. A phony "subject" was brought in; he drew straws with the real subject to see who would be the "teacher" and who would be the "learner." The drawing was actually rigged so that the

real subject always became the "teacher." The "learner" was then taken into an adjoining room and, in the presence of the subject, was strapped into an "electric chair" with electrodes attached to his wrists. The "teacher" (subject) was then taken back outside and seated before a control panel with a series of phony switches indicating increasingly higher voltages. He was given a real sample of a moderate shock so that he would have an idea of what the "learner" supposedly would have to endure. When the experiment began, he was told it was his job to give a shock for each wrong answer to some simple tests and to increase the shock to the next higher voltage with each mistake. The experiment proceeded with the "learner" making occasional mistakes until the shocks reached 300 volts. At this point, the "learner," who had previously complained of a heart condition, began to scream and pound on the wall, begging for the experiment to stop. The "teacher" was instructed to continue administering the shocks, and in 65 percent of the cases he did—even when the screams ceased and nothing more was heard from the other room! This is not to say that the "teacher" did so gleefully. The conflict between their consciences and their orders was obvious in the subjects' trembling, stuttering, groaning, and nervous laughter—but most did continue obediently to shock the "learner." The implications of such discoveries have been applied to the understanding of such things as the mass murder of Jews in World War II. But this was not Germany in the 1930s; it was America in the 1960s. The effect was greatest, moreover, when the naive subject was teamed with two other "teachers," who could suggest different shock levels to use for each mistake. The subject always had the option to use a lower level than they suggested, but with few exceptions, he did not. Only when the subject had no companions, and no instructions to increase the shock, did 38 of 40 people stop the shock at the point where the victim's complaints became serious (Milgram 1963 and 1964).

The effect of the confederate (i.e., the experimenter's stooge) works in the opposite direction as well, of course. In an experiment where the stooges refused to go along with the punishment when it became severe, 36 of 40 subjects joined them and quit "shocking" the victim. The point is that the group is a strong influence in *either* direction. It is not that the individual is willing to be punitive or that he wants to be helpful—but that he needs, more than anything, to *belong,* and at almost any price. Deviance is the role that most people feel they cannot afford to play, for better or for worse. This is probably why, in experimental situations where an unknown person is screaming for *help,* people sitting in a nearby room are less likely to give it if there are other people in the room than if they are alone (Latane and Darley 1970)! The net effect of the group is that *it inhibits individual action.* When all is said and done, the only thing more important than belonging, maybe, is not doing anything that shows that we do not belong!

The upshot of the previous section ought to be pretty depressing if you place much value, as most of us think we do, on individual initiative, independence of thought and action, and personal integrity. From the impressive body of evidence social psychologists have collected, it looks as if we are largely victims of our own need to be members of the "in-group," regardless of how we are trained, who we are, or how vile the in-group is. When you consider that it is only in recent history that one of the most educated and civilized peoples in the history of the world, the Germans, committed the most massive and horrible massacre of innocent victims in the history of the world—and that the most popular defense of Nazis brought to trial after the War was that they were doing nothing worse than "following orders" in carrying out these atrocities, the most pessimistic conclusions about human nature seem to be in order. Our **herd** instincts seem more significant than our **human** ones. Maybe they are, indeed, but you cannot reach this conclusion with too much certainty from the evidence at hand.

There is some reason to think that the experimental results obtained in the Milgram study, for instance, do not represent sheepish obedience on the part of amoral subjects, but rather illustrates their blind confidence in the benevolence of experimenters. In a series of ingenious experiments, Martin Orne has shown repeatedly that experimental subjects will do a great variety of meaningless, idiotic, and vicious things in response to instructions, not because they are dolts or villains, but because they think that experimenters are neither of those things. They must have some decent and sensible purpose in mind, subjects figure, when they ask them to do apparently indecent and senseless things, or they would not be asking them. The naive faith that scientists have people's welfare at heart, and that they will protect the experimental subject from doing anything excessively dangerous or harmful, permits otherwise sensitive, conscientious and responsible people to do these things, which Orne titles the "demand characteristics" of the experimental situation (1959 and 1962). Were the same people to be asked the same thing in real-life situations, says Orne, they would probably not comply with unreasonable or improper requests (Orne and Holland 1968). There is no final way to test this hypothesis, of course, even in experiments which use the kinds of "deception design" described in the studies above, because subjects take for granted, once they enter an experiment, that they should stick to their instructions regardless of what unexpected events occur. If Orne is correct, then the unhappy results reported here are really a testimonial to our belief in the goodness of scientists. Let us hope so, since it seems we cannot find out for sure.

But do not assume so just because you hope so. One of the demand characteristics of the Milgram studies, according to Orne's argument, might be the fact that the study was being done at a classy institution like Yale University, making subjects therefore feel more secure in the experimenter's benign intentions. To test this possibility, Milgram repeated the experiment in a sleazy office building in a run-down area of Bridgeport, Connecticutt. Fifty per cent of the men still went all the way in shocking the "learner." So the prestige of Yale had some effect, but not enough to explain away the general results (Milgram 1974). So far, nobody has done so. Just as nobody has yet explained away the Nazis or any other mass murderers in history.

As you can imagine, Milgram's experiment raised a storm of ethical as well as technical controversy. Part of the criticism involved the ethics of subjecting human subjects to traumatic experimental situations, as a result of which the awful self-perceptions and social perceptions they had acquired during the experiment might stick (Baumrind 1964). Were subjects in these studies to have gotten the notion that they were brutal and sadistic people, the subsequent "debriefing"[3] in which they learned what had really been going on might not be enough to return their self-images to normal (Bem 1970). Such debriefings do, in fact, tend to be ineffective (Ross, Lepper, and Hubbard 1975). Another criticism is that deception studies are not justified altogether, even if subjects are not subjected to traumatic experiences. Partly as a result of such controversies as this, psychologists are rightly much more wary about doing deception studies than they used to be, universities and government agencies are rightly much more concerned about protecting human subjects than they used to be, and traumatic deceptions of the kind used in Milgram's studies are generally forbidden.

---

[3] A term derived from law via bureaucratese. "To brief" means to inform succinctly; to "debrief" originally meant to get back information from the person who had been briefed. Here it means "to dismisinform."

It is hard to tell if the last is such a good thing. Maybe something worse happened than that the subjects were traumatized—maybe they weren't! Maybe they were just upset for a few minutes, or a couple of hours, or a few days. Maybe the social life of human beings is really like that for many of us, where we will do whatever we are told by an apparently wise authority, even if it seems awful and repugnant. And afterwards, living a normal life again in the company of normal people and situations, we recover entirely from our traumas so, if the need arose, we could do it all over again. The Milgram studies have done a great unhappy service to social psychology by suggesting that this is so.

Social psychology as history A more optimistic possibility is presented by Kenneth Gergen who, fittingly enough, teaches at Swarthmore College, where Solomon Asch earlier taught and did his line-judgment studies. Gergen suggests that the dissemination of social psychological knowledge has a self-correcting influence on the things it theorizes about (1973). In other words, as people get to know about the general tendency to conform to social norms, to acquiesce too readily to the demands of the majority, and so forth, the knowledge makes them guard against these tendencies in themselves. As he puts it:

> sophistication as to psychological principles liberates one from their behavioral implications . . . knowing that persons in trouble are less likely to be helped when there are large numbers of by-standers may increase one's desire to offer his services under such conditions; knowing that motivational arousal can influence one's interpretation of events may engender caution when arousal is high. In each instance, knowledge increases alternatives to action, and previous patterns of behavior are modified or dissolved (p. 313).

In effect, he says, "social psychology alters the behavior it seeks to study" in the long run, by informing people about it. So the very process of discovering such phenomena as the Asch effect, or the Milgram effect, helps to correct them in real life, even if they are more ominous then mere "demand characteristics" of psychological experiments.

If educating people about their own social dispositions tends to free them from conforming to senseless majority standards, then perhaps the general effect of education and sophistication in our technological civilization will be to reduce the number of social norms to which people feel bound. There is no way to know that, and you can make interesting arguments both ways. On the one hand, instant mass communications and automated production of goods makes our society more homogeneous so that we become more alike everywhere in much of our dress, manners, and customs. The "local color" of new places disappears when you find the same McDonald's and Colonel Sanders restaurants and Sears stores and Shell gas stations in all of them. At the same time, there is more variation everywhere—in our dress, our occupations, and our interests. It seems a toss-up.

The results of such a loosening of norms, if it does occur, would be a mixed bag. We have spoken of conformity, and the research on it, as if it were an unqualified evil, but that is not so. Social norms tie people together in more positive ways than negative ones; they are responsible for group loyalties that go beyond the immediate ties we have to family and close friends; they give us a sense of belonging to social institutions of value; they provide a sense of personal identity and self-esteem that allows people to know "who they are." The price of living with social norms, as we have seen, is that they are restrictive in some ways—but most people do not experience their social identity as being costly, and most people who are aware of the price are probably willing to pay it in order to belong.

SUMMARY

1 *Social psychology* primarily concerns people's behavior in relation to groups. This includes the ways in which they form groups, and act within them, and more importantly, the effect of groups on people's individual behavior.

2 Social behavior begins with sexual union, but the social life of most species is more complicated than merely mating. All social life evolved as a means of aiding the survival of species; it serves this function in different ways among different animal groups. Migration, territoriality, and social dominance are common aspects of social life in different species, including human beings. Social behavior serves primarily to guarantee that some members of the group will endure a variety of difficult circumstances.

3 Human groups undoubtedly began the same way that animal groups did, and were probably organized much the way anthropoid apes are today. Human social life changed dramatically when *language* developed because language made *culture* possible. Culture means all the conventions of a group that get transmitted from one generation to the next.

4 Functional human groups were able to become very large, because people could identify each other in terms of *kinship*. The *nuclear family* (two parents and their children) is the smallest *primary kinship group*. Language made possible the extension of primary kinship groups to include many other degrees of relationship. Ultimately, secondary groups also developed, in which membership was based on common interests rather than on blood or marriage. Tribes, kingdoms, nations, and empires are more complex social structures which evolved from family groupings. Racial and ethnic groups developed from kinship groups which were geographically isolated and therefore intermarried to the point where their members shared some common physical features more or less distinguishable from people in other groups.

5 A *group* differs from a *crowd* or a *mob* by being *organized*, that is, by having a distinct structure of rules and customs. *Membership* is the most basic aspect of structure. The two kinds of group membership are *ascribed* or *attributed* membership, in which you have no choice about belonging to the group; and *acquired* or *achieved* membership, in which you join a group voluntarily. National, religious, and cultural group membership is mostly ascribed, while belonging to the Democratic or Republican Party reflects acquired membership. Every kind of group membership implies some kind of social role, and everyone plays several roles in every society.

6 *Status* means the standing of an individual in a group. It refers to a person's value, that is, to their relative worth as a group member. Every social group has a *status hierarchy,* that is, a distribution of status positions. In a caste system, status is always attributed. In an open class system, however, it is often possible to move from a position of low status to one of high status. In most societies, wealth is a vital factor in determining social class, but other forms of prestige are important, too, including birth, power, and achievement. Increasing social mobility generally promotes achievement in every society, ultimately enriching both the individual and the group as a whole.

7 Every group has a power structure in which some people are more powerful and influential than others. A person's power depends mostly on their *resources* in relation to other people's needs, that is, the things they have of value to others, that they can bestow or withhold as they choose. If other people have alternatives for satisfying their needs without depending on your resources, then the resources are not sources of power.

8 The achievements of human social organization have depended largely on the *leaders* which arise to direct groups. Different qualities make for good leadership in different situations. In groups which do not have special tasks to perform, the best leader is a person who is sensitive to the feelings and relationships among group members. In groups which have a common problem to solve, however, especially under stress, a task-oriented leader is most effective. Either kind of leader may administer their group in a democratic or authoritarian or laissez-faire (letting everyone do what they want) manner. Authoritarian groups are sometimes a little more efficient than democratic groups, but generally not enough to make up for the bad feelings they create among group members. Laissez-faire groups are the most dissatisfying in all respects.

9 *Politics* is the exercise of leadership in securing power over a group. Some political leaders are more task-oriented, others more personally oriented, but all political leaders must command enough personal loyalty from others to remain in power. Leadership continuity is especially important in political groups. In complex societies, continuity of a political system is guaranteed by the existence of an efficient civil service or bureaucracy rather than by the appearance of new leaders.

10 Four basic communication structures common to all social systems are (1) the *circle,* (2) the *wheel,* (3) the *Y,* and (4) the *chain.* In circle patterns, communication moves from one group member to another and circulates throughout all the members of the group. Circle arrangements are best for small, person-oriented groups. The wheel pattern flows from a central member at the wheel's hub down the spokes to each individual member. This pattern is most efficient for problem-solving groups with highly centralized leadership. In the Y pattern, communication starts from one person and then branches out to others in an upside-down Y. It is a hierarchical system, with different levels of responsibility, authority, and status. Most organizations and societies are administered by this pattern. The chain pattern is a simple one-way transmission from one individual to the next to the next.

11 Social *norms* are standards of conduct implicitly agreed upon by the group and expected of all its members. *Laws* are social norms which have been made explicit in a society. Most social conduct is determined by norms, not by laws. The *common law* is a group of social norms which have the status of law but which have not been made into explicit rules because it is assumed that they are known to everyone.

12 Social norms are the product of people's need to conform to each others' behavior. Although there is some pressure to conform in any social group, many experiments have demonstrated clearly that the need to conform exists in us even when there is no outside pressure from others. This tends to make people feel less responsible in groups than they do as individuals for their actions. As a result, the decisions made by groups are often more extreme than those which the individual members would make on their own. This is called the *risky-shift phenomenon.*

13 Solomon Asch began a series of experiments which demonstrate the effect of pressure from a majority on the conformity of individual group members. He found that individuals tended to give the same response as the majority of people in their experimental group, even when the majority response was clearly wrong. The extent of conformity needs was shockingly demonstrated in experiments by Stanley Milgram, where subjects administered supposedly dangerous shocks to other people merely on his instructions. These compliance responses have been compared to the behavior of Germans in carrying out the Nazi mass murders of World War II. The point is that people seem to be motivated more than anything else by the need to *belong*.

14 There is some reason to doubt the validity of these conclusions about conformity. Martin Orne has conducted numerous experiments which show that people respond to the *demand characteristics* of the experimental situation, meaning that they perform apparently senseless, irresponsible, or dangerous acts because they think the experimenter has some benevolent purpose in mind, and that experimenters will protect them from harm or from doing any damage. This may have been the case with the Milgram studies, but it has not been proved.

WOMEN STRIKE • aug. 26
WOMEN ♀

Opinions, beliefs, and attitudes

21

21

Opinions, beliefs, and attitudes

At first glance, a person's attitudes may seem like the most individual, private part of their experience, not part of *social* psychology at all. But the study of attitudes, beliefs, and opinions has long been a major area of social psychology, and for good reason. They are derived almost entirely from our social experiences, they are maintained or changed by the social support or criticism we get for them, and they are the target of inquiry and manipulation all our lives by advertisers, opinion pollsters, politicians, and sales personnel. These people know perfectly well, without having read this book, just how much these things *do* belong to social psychology. The whole marketing and advertising and public relations and propaganda industry is devoted to manipulating people's *attitudes* so that you will buy what they want, vote for whom they want, and like or dislike the people they say you should. Much of the education industry does the same thing, often in a subtler way. Attitude change is one of the main industries of the modern world. This is most true in a democratic society because in a democracy, where you cannot force people to do what you want, you can only try to persuade them. So the attitude changing business is the chief instrument of behavior control in democratic society.

An attitude is a person's disposition to feel, think, and act in a certain way. The word means "leaning" or "inclination"; it describes how you lean towards something—what your inclination towards it is. **Beliefs, opinions, values,** and **prejudices** are terms for special aspects of attitudes. You **believe** something when you are inclined to accept it as true. When you say that you have an **opinion** about something, you mean that you know your own attitude towards it. The same is true of **prejudice,** but used precisely, it means opinions for which evidence is lacking; it means "prejudging." You **value** something by thinking well or ill of it, and you value it a lot or a little depending on how strong your positive or negative feeling is.

The main word in the whole bunch is *attitude*. It contains all of the others within it. When we study attitudes, we are also looking at beliefs, opinions, values, and prejudices. Understanding them gives us better means of preserving the ones that are useful, dumping the ones that are not, and distinguishing between them.

ATTITUDE FORMATION

Attitudes are more than beliefs and opinions. They are mostly learned, not inherited, but they start to get absorbed in your system with your mother's milk, and they are such a pervasive part of your personality from infancy on that you cannot really separate their *emotional, intellectual,* and *behavioral* components. There are temperamental aspects of attitude underlying much of their emotional character; these are largely constitutional rather than learned. The general disposition to be cheerful or glum, to be energetic or lethargic, to be active or passive are all attitudes in the most profound sense. We shall confine our discussion, however, to the development of *social* attitudes, that is, of those attitudes which specifically affect our interactions with other people.

Social attitudes start to get learned in infancy, but their intellectual component doesn't become apparent until later, when intellect does. They start getting learned by classical conditioning which, you recall, is the basic process for the learning of emotion. This is why all attitudes have an emotional component—they start off as emotional responses in the first place.

Children learn their earliest social attitudes from their parents and usually adopt the same attitudes through love or fear (see Chapter 6). The child associates the expressions, gestures, and words the parents use about other people with the emotions it feels about them, and generally comes out in early life with the same attitudes. If the child senses hostility, contempt, or disparagement in the parents' description of others, then it may mimic those attitudes. If the relationship to the parents is loving, the child mimics them because it thinks their opinions are all-wise; if the relationship with them is fearful, it is afraid to differ with them very much. The earlier an attitude is observed in parents, the more likely it will ape them. Children sometimes rebel against parental attitudes in adolescence, and a few kids make their lifework revolve around the need to "get back" at their parents for teaching them wrongheaded attitudes—but this is more the exception than the rule. Most of us tend to become remarkably like our parents were. Political attitudes, as reflected in voting patterns, are also very consistent from one generation to the next. Most attitudes are *instilled* a lot more easily than they are *changed.*

While most basic social attitudes come from relations with parents, plenty come also from peers, teachers, and other admired figures in the child's world. A few come from books, movies, and television heroes too. Notice that attitudes do not come much from *ideas,* but from *people.* Also, they come less from what people *say* than from what they *do,* as in all learning through identification (see Chapter 14). The learning process involved is a much more fundamental one than "book learning." Attitudes are not very easily learned, it seems, beyond the age when it is easy to make new identifications. That may be why they are not easily changed either, except by very powerful influences exerted over a long time.

The uses of attitudes

We maintain attitudes which serve some useful function in our lives by directing our attention towards objects that fill our needs. In so doing, the attitudes themselves are reinforced. Daniel Katz and Ezra Stotland propose that there are four motivational functions for any attitude (1959). They have labeled these the *adjustive function,* the *ego-defensive function,* the *value-expressive function,* and the *knowledge function.*

The *adjustive* function is the tendency everyone has to develop *favorable* attitudes toward things which reward them and *unfavorable* attitudes toward things which lead to punishment. Everyone always seeks to maximize their positive experiences and minimize the negative ones anyway, and attitudes are used adjustively to support their perceptions accordingly. Attitudes are especially useful tools for social adjustment. By means of their attitudes, people cultivate the variety of roles that make them socially acceptable in circles where they want to to go. If someone wishes to be admitted to the "country-club set," for instance, they will develop attitudes of preference for champagne over beer, skinny girls over plump ones, and elegant grammar over plain talk. They may also cultivate contemptuous attitudes towards things they associate with "lower-class" values.

The *ego-defensive* function of an attitude helps protect one's self-concept from threat. A person who doubts their own intelligence may adopt a negative attitude about the value of IQ tests, without even knowing how well they score on one. More broadly speaking, all the ego defense mechanisms we discussed in Chapter 15 are *attitudes* by which a person defends themself against a negative self-image.

Attitudes are not always defensive, of course. One of their main functions is to **express** people's **values**, especially values that are most relevant to their self-concepts. People develop a network of related values for this purpose. If someone thinks they are politically liberal minded, for instance, their attitudes will favor liberal or left-of-center political parties, they will read books and newspapers identified with those causes, will cherish friends who share their politics, and they may, if a very appealing political hero arises, develop personal habits and attitudes like those of their idol (note again how the personal quality sneaks in).

Finally, the **knowledge** function of an attitude motivates a person's attempts to understand their experience. They tend to develop attitudes that make sense of their experience. Someone who has been the victim of job discrimination by a large corporation may develop negative attitudes toward the firm, the people who work there, and large corporations in general.

Because they work so pervasively in our lives, our general inclination is to maintain our attitudes unchanged in the face of changing circumstance. Most of us, in fact, go to remarkable lengths to preserve our attitudes—we will, for instance, learn and remember arguments that support our own positions much more readily than we will arguments that contradict them. And we will learn readily arguments that make opposing attitudes look stupid, but not arguments that make them look good (Jones and Kohler 1958). We need to see ourselves as consistent, and attitudes are a critical testing ground for self-consistency because they are so pervasive. Since *every* attitude involves feelings, beliefs, and a tendency towards action, in other words, we anchor the happy image of our self-consistency to the integration of the attitude components in our lives. We like to feel that it reflects the integrity of our characters.

Even so, situations often arise in everyone's life which challenge their ability to maintain long-standing attitudes. Understanding how this happens, and trying to find lawful formulas for predicting when people will change their attitudes and in what direction, has been a major preoccupation of social psychologists for many years. They have advanced some ingenious theories and done countless experiments to this end. Their findings are often inconclusive because it is so hard to measure attitudes in the first place.

Measuring attitudes

The main instruments for measuring attitudes are called **attitude scales.** They typically consist of a number of opinion statements with which you may agree or disagree in varying degrees. The responses are added together, and the resulting score reflects your over-all attitude on that subject. All the different questionnaires and inventories you have taken where you must state your opinion, such as "all wobble-stoppers should be cadgiformed—strongly agree, mildly agree, neither agree nor disagree, mildly disagree, strongly disagree" are attitude scales.

Two of the best known kinds of attitude scales are the Thurstone (1929) and the Likert (1932) scales, named after their inventors. The Thurstone-type scale consists of a large number of statements which judges have already rated as representing positive or negative attitudes toward something. To take the scale, you merely check off whether or not you agree with each statement. The measure of your attitude is how your responses add up to what the judges have rated as favorable or unfavorable.

The Likert-type scale is more commonly used. It measures *your own degree* of positive or negative attitude towards something, rather than assuming that your simple agree-disagree statements mean the same things that judges think they mean. You respond to the items by indicating *how much* you agree or disagree with the statements.

Two more recent measurement approaches are now widely used. The first, called the **Guttman Scale** (Guttman 1947), uses a **hierarchical order** of questions in which the answers at any point on the scale imply the answers to all the points beneath it. The questions, in other words, are arranged in increasing order of difficulty, or agreeableness, or whatever. If you agree with the fifth question, then most likely you agree with all those beneath it—if you disagree with it, then you probably disagree with all those above it. Most of our attitudes involve a hierarchy of preferences; so Guttman scaling seeks a more sensitive index of attitudes than the earlier types.

One thing wrong with attitude scales is that they are largely restricted to measuring the *intellectual* aspect of attitudes and cannot very well get at the *affective* side of them. The *semantic differential* tries to overcome this problem (Osgood et al. 1957) by rating each thing on many feeling qualities, such as **good** or **bad, strong** or **weak,** and **warm** or **cold,** not merely as **favorable** or **unfavorable.** The resulting scores hopefully give a more precise evaluation of a person's attitudes than a simple statement of whether they are positive or negative; they may be "good" on the one hand, but at the same time "cold" and "weak," or any other combinations of the different dimensions.

These four approaches to the measurement of attitudes are the most widely used for research exploring attitude change. Most of the studies you will read about shifting attitudes *congruently* (in the same direction they already were, i.e., making them stronger) or *incongruently* (in the opposite direction, i.e., making an attitude weaker or getting someone to change their mind) have used one or another of them to measure the attitudes in question.

CAUGHT OFF BALANCE: THEORIES OF ATTITUDE CHANGE

Several theories try to explain when and why people change their attitudes—and all of them agree that they do not change very readily. People tend to change their attitudes only when they feel *forced* to reexamine them. This happens only when there is some *inconsistency* or *disharmony* between the person's attitude and their perception of what is going on in the world —and only when the inconsistency is such that the person's world is so shaken, or thrown off balance, that the attitude does not serve their needs any more. Attitude change is an attempt to restore the person's psychological equilibrium, to put them back in balance. You can use a "balance principle" to describe the relationships among different attitude components. A balanced state means that all things about a person's attitudes are in harmony. If you like someone, for instance, you expect that person also to like the other people you like, and that all these folks will like each other. In real life, it doesn't quite happen that way. Often your attitudes are threatened by pieces of information that upset the balance. One of your friends may not like another friend of yours. When that happens, your attitude toward each must change in some way to adjust to this new knowledge.

You have come upon this notion before, first in *homeostatic theory* (see Chapter 7), and again in the theory of adjustment (see Chapter 15). It says that organisms tend to maintain a state of internal equilibrium. Now the same principle is extended to the domain of attitudes. It says: your attitudes are challenged when you feel a disequilibrium, or imbalance, or conflict resulting from the *incongruity* or *inconsistency* or *dissonance* between your attitudes and your perceptions. You can correct this situation by changing your perceptions or changing your attitudes. There are no other ways. So theory of attitude change is essentially adjustment theory, applied to the special province of social psychology.

The basis of attitude problems is, as social psychologist Roger Brown puts it that:

> human nature abhors inconsistency. A situation of inconsistency is one that calls for mutually incompatible actions . . . inconsistency in the mind threatens to paralyze action (1965, p. 606).

The most prominent theories of attitude change are based on the *balance theory* of Fritz Heider (1958). It says that balance exists in a person's mind when the elements they deal with are in harmony with each other; when they are not, the mind tries to shift towards a balanced state. Heider used the theory to explain how people make their positive and negative thoughts and feelings about the same object

work in harmony. Suppose, for instance, that I like my Uncle Louis (+), but detest my cousin Fensterwald (−), his son — if Uncle Louis also detests Fensterwald (−), then the system is in balance, that is, his negative opinion is congruent with my own; so I feel more justified in my positive opinion of him. If I like my Uncle Louis (+), and love my cousin Fensterwald (+), and Uncle Louis also loves Fensterwald (+), the system is again in balance — everyone's opinions are positive and therefore mutually compatible. Finally, if I dislike Uncle Louis (−), and I also detest cousin Fensterwald (−), and Uncle Louis likes Fensterwald (+), the system is even yet in balance — the positive regard of these two creeps for each other justifies my negative view of both.

The system gets unbalanced only when there is an *odd number* of negative impressions. If I like Uncle Louis (+) and dislike Fensterwald (−), but Uncle Louis likes him (+), then my

Figure 21.1 Balance theory says that attitudes are harmonious when the number of negative opinions involved is even; they are unbalanced when there is an odd number of negative opinions.

	Balanced	
A.	+	I like Uncle Louis.
	+	I like his son Fensterwald.
	+	He likes Fensterwald.
B.	−	I hate Uncle Louis.
	−	I hate Fensterwald.
	+	He likes Fensterwald.
C.	+	I like Uncle Louis.
	−	I hate Fensterwald.
	−	He hates Fensterwald.
	Unbalanced	
A.	+	I like Uncle Louis.
	−	I hate Fensterwald.
	+	Uncle Louis likes Fensterwald.
B.	−	I hate Uncle Louis.
	−	I hate Fensterwald.
	−	Uncle Louis hates Fensterwald.
C.	+	I like Uncle Louis.
	+	I like Fensterwald.
	−	Uncle Louis hates Fensterwald.

opinions of him and of Fensterwald become incongruent—neither one is supported by the other. The same thing is true, though maybe to a smaller degree, if I dislike both of them (−) (−) and they dislike each other (−)—their mutual antagonism gives no support to my opinion. Or if I like both of them (+) (+) and they dislike each other (−)—their antagonism makes me uncomfortable.

Balance theory has been expanded and refined in some very useful ways, all of which retain the same basic premise. The best known of such theories is probably Leon Festinger's theory of *cognitive dissonance*. According to Festinger (1957), any two thoughts (cognitions) are dissonant if, to use the technical phrase, "the obverse of one follows from the other." For example, the thought "I want a cigarette" is dissonant with the thought "smoking is bad for me." The feeling of dissonance is uncomfortable; it creates conflict, which causes pressure to reduce it. Dissonance can be reduced either by changing your behavior or by changing your thinking. Thus, the person who experiences dissonance because they smoke, despite their belief that smoking is bad for their health, may reduce the conflict either by giving up smoking or by changing their belief about its ill effects. The smoker may find reasons to discredit the arguments that smoking is bad for them; they may focus attention on the pleasures of smoking; or may actively avoid situations that highlight the negative aspects of smoking. The pressure to reduce cognitive dissonance depends on how much dissonance you feel.

Another well known balance theory is the *theory of congruity*, proposed by Osgood, Suci, and Tannenbaum (1957). It states that ideas have different intensities of positive or negative value to an individual. *Congruity* exists when the relationships among these ideas are balanced. If a person has a positive attitude towards the president, for instance, and finds that the president has a negative attitude toward wobblestoppers, congruity theory would predict that this person too will develop a negative attitude toward wobblestoppers. The intensity of their negative attitude would depend on the intensity of their attitude toward the president and on their perception of how strong the president's attitude was toward wobblestoppers. The congruity model is more precisely stated than the dissonance model, and it tries to provide quantified statements about attitude change. It is not very successful in this respect. It does propose correctly, on the other hand, that extreme attitudes are harder to change than moderate ones, which balance theory and dissonance theory do not offer.

Another important theory of attitude change is Rosenberg's theory of *affective-cognitive consistency,* which says that the *feelings* we have toward an attitude object are closely related to the *thoughts* we associate with it. Rosenberg (1956) has developed what he calls a "cognitive index" of a person's beliefs about an attitude object. He finds that the cognitive and emotional components of attitudes correspond most for a person's most important values. If you feel satisfied with your particular mode of verbal expression, for instance, such as constantly chattering, you will probably have a strongly favorable attitude towards it even if others do not.

THE FACTS OF ATTITUDE CHANGE

The major theories of attitude change try to explain what happens when people face attitudinal conflict. Whether or not these general accounts are valid, there are a number of specific principles that have been pretty well established about changing attitudes. Some of these concern characteristics of the attitudes themselves and of the situations in which change is attempted; others concern the personalities of the people who are trying to induce the changes and the people they are trying to influence.

Seven factors seem to be most important in determining how changeable an attitude is. They are (1) extremeness, (2) multiplexity, (3) consistency, (4) interconnectedness, (5) consonance, (6) strength and number of wants served by the attitude, and (7) centrality of the value to which the attitude is related (Krech et al. 1962).

Extremeness Political extremists are always complaining about "wishy-washy liberals," meaning that their liberal attitudes are not very fixed and firm and are therefore very changeable. They are often right—because extreme attitudes are more resistant to change than moderate ones, whether they are extreme in the sense of being intensely held, or in the sense of being extreme in contents or both. It is easier "to change the mind" of someone who does not have it much "made up" in the first place than it is to influence the attitudes of someone committed to a position.

Fanatics and "true believers" of all kinds have the advantage over other people, in conducting their lives, of being deeply committed to extreme attitudes which help them to endure enormous stresses and pressures of change. Probably one reason nobody likes a fanatic is because we are jealous of the security they get from being so absolutely certain about how to live; another reason, more relevant here, is that we all know there is no arguing with a fanatic, that is, little possibility of influencing their attitudes. Some people believe that the tendency towards fanaticism is a personality trait that underlies all of a person's attitudes rather than just their attitudes on certain subjects. If that is true, it would explain, perhaps, why people who abandon one extremist cause often get involved in another—such as devout Catholics who become militantly antireligious Communists and vice versa (Hoffer 1946). There was a vast research inquiry in this direction soon after World War II, trying to establish whether there was such a thing as an authoritarian personality type (Adorno et al. 1950).

It turns out that some people are more *rigid* than others in their attitudes, that is, less flexible in their opinions and, in some respects, even in their perceptions. The latter trait is called "intolerance of ambiguity"; in perception, it refers to a person's inability to see both versions of an ambiguous figure (see Chapter 5). In personality, it refers to peoples' need to take decisive positions on things because suspending judgment or otherwise "hanging loose" intellectually makes them anxious. The idea is plausible, but no one has proved that there is such a thing as an authoritarian personality or that extremism in one set of attitudes is highly related to extremism in other, unrelated ones.

At the other extreme of attitudes towards attitudes is the **Charlie Brown syndrome,** that is, the person who is easily influenced or persuaded, who gets hustled by used-car dealers and insurance salesmen, and who is generally "socially suggestible," or, more plainly, gullible and wishy-washy. A good deal of research has also tried to find out whether there is such a general "persuasibility" trait, but it has not been studied as much as authoritarianism, probably because it is considered a more harmless trait. As with authoritarianism, there is some weak evidence that some people tend to be more persuasible than others, especially if they have little self confidence and strong needs for social approval from others (Cox and Bauer 1964; Janis and Field 1959; Rozelle, Evans, Lasater, Dembroski, and Allen 1973).

There probably are some personality traits that are related to changeability of attitudes, but they are not so easy to identify or measure. It is likely that people who are generally insecure about themselves and doubtful of the value of their ideas, or feelings, or existence go to one or another extreme attitude positions. If they handle their insecurity by defensiveness, then they probably appear very decisive, or extreme, in their attitudes. If their insecurity is expressed by their being anxiously agreeable, then they probably seem easily influenced to change attitudes. But don't let this hypothesis run away with you—some people are quite decisive, if not extreme, in their attitudes because they are secure and self-confident. Being rich and powerful will do this just as well for you as being reared to fanaticism. And some people appear easily influenced because they are thoughtful and considerate of other people's opinions and at the same time so confident of their own that they can afford to shift back and forth with never a qualm for their self-esteem. You cannot account for anyone's inner dynamics simply by knowing the changeability of their attitudes.

Multiplexity This is a sort of psychological jargon term which refers to the number of component ideas an attitude has. A *simplex* attitude is one which involves a single idea. Multiplex attitudes have a *horizontal structure,* meaning that the different ideas involved bolster each other, making the overall attitude harder to change than it would be otherwise. (Bem 1970). If one argument gets discredited, there are others left to take its place. So multiplex attitudes are harder to change than simplex attitudes, but they are easier to strengthen. If someone opposes legalizing marijuana only because it is damaging to health, they might change their attitude in the face of evidence that it is harmless. But if their negative attitude involves other objections as well, such as the idea that it is immoral to induce changed states of consciousness by drugs, that people are more prone to driving accidents under "pot's" influence, and that "getting stoned" dampens people's interests in important life goals, then accepting the idea that the drug is medically harmless would not, by itself, change their overall attitude towards it. With the multiplex of negative ideas already operating, however, adding another one would serve to strengthen the total negative attitude. You can almost always strengthen attitudes in whatever direction they are already pointed by adding information which is *congruent* with the beliefs the person already holds.

Producing *incongruent* attitude change, that is, change in the opposite direction, is the big problem.

Consistency When the different aspects of a person's attitude are consistent with each other, their total attitude tends to be stable and therefore to resist change. If they have some inconsistent thoughts and feelings about it, then their ambivalence is good breeding ground for changing their attitude by strengthening one or another side of their doubts.

Interconnectedness The more an attitude is tied in to other attitudes, the harder it will be to change, even with powerful contrary pressures —the impetus of the other attitudes will "rescue" this one. A lot of unhappy marriages are preserved this way; when a spouse starts to develop negative attitudes towards the marriage partner, for instance, they get tempered by positive attitudes towards children, family life, and the social status that married life may bring.

Consonance This is the extent to which one attitude is similar to the others with which it is connected. The more an attitude is consonant with the other attitudes in its group, the harder it is to change it in an opposite direction. The more *dissonant* an attitude is with the others in its group, the easier it is to change it in the same direction as them. It is easy to convince us, for instance, that someone we already like has done a good thing, and hard for us to accept the notion that they have done something awful.

Strength and number of wants served A person's attitudes may serve many purposes, including some that they are unaware of, and the ease with which such attitudes can be changed depends on how important and how conscious those purposes are. If a person's hostile attitudes towards black people, or towards women, for instance, is serving their need to believe in their own masculinity, or competence, or self-esteem, then they will not easily change that attitude in a friendly direction. On the contrary, they will probably use whatever meager information they can find to reinforce their negative attitude, hoping to feel more satisfied with themselves by doing so.

Centrality of related values   A final factor determining the ease of changing attitude is its role in the person's values. An attitude which supports their important values will resist most efforts to change it in the opposite direction, while attitudes which are not related to important values will shift more easily. This is the reason that advertising is more effective in selling you a different brand of shirt than a different kind of religion—you have no important values attached to Arrow or Hathaway,[1] but presumably it matters to you whether you believe in Christ or Krishna. I started to use the analogy of changing attitudes towards shirts versus *politicians,* but nowadays that would not make a good comparison. Modern political campaigns revolve more and more around the *personal image* rather than the *political ideas* of candidates because many political managers are convinced that the American people do not have strong political values at all! With that in mind, campaign appeals try to change attitudes to favor candidates on the basis of appealing personal qualities instead of valuable political doctrines and programs.

Summing up the different factors in attitude change should give you some insight into the role that attitudes play in our lives: the ease or difficulty you face in changing any attitude depends on *how tightly it is integrated into the fabric of people's lives*—the more an attitude is integral to their consciousness, the harder it is to change. What that in turn tells us about attitudes is that *they are the chief psychological devices by which we experience and express our integrity as human beings.* That is why the earlier an attitude gets ingrained in someone, the more deeply it is learned, and the more it is part of their total value system, the harder it is to change. In many respects, a person's personality *is* the sum of their attitudes; so one does not give them up easily any more than one rejects their own personality easily, or turns it in for a new one.

How to change attitudes

None of this is to say that attitudes cannot be changed, only that is not an easy job. The processes by which they are changed, both in arguments and in other situations, have been studied a lot, and something is known about them. They can be divided into three main areas, namely: characteristics of the *communicator,* who is trying to exert the influence; characteristics of the *communication,* the message or information used to do the swaying; and characteristics of the *audience,* the recipient of the communication who, it is hoped, will change some attitude (Greenwald et al. 1969; Kiesler et al. 1969; McGuire 1969).

By far the thing most studied about communicators is their *credibility.* If we have good reason to believe what the communicator says, we will more likely be influenced by them. Their prestige, expertise, trustworthiness, and their known values all contribute to their credibility. The more credible the communicator is, the more effective in temporarily changing the attitudes of the audience. Over a longer range, however, the audience tends not to retain such changes, and the credentials of the speaker tend to have no lasting effect (Newcomb 1963). You seem to forget the source after a while.

Just as qualities of the communicator are important in attitude change, so are several aspects of the *communication.* If you are interested in winning someone over to your point of view, there are several issues that you should consider. Should you give both sides of the argument? Try to frighten your audience into changing sides? Present your side of the story only but with great enthusiasm? There are probably times when each of these approaches would work, but if you carefully analyze the

---

[1] I hope.

The characteristics of the communicator—the charisma or strength of character of the persuader—go a long way in influencing others.

San Roman, Francisco de Zurbaran

specific situation, you can increase your chances considerably.

First of all, assess how much change you are trying to get. If the opposing opinion differs only slightly from the one you are trying to put over, your tactics will be different from a situation in which the audience considers your position extreme. The way a communication is organized and presented is very important (McGuire 1969). Communications consisting of **one-sided arguments,** for instance, work best on people who **already agree** with the communicator, not on people who disagree with them. When the audience **disagrees,** they will be more affected by **two-sided** presentations (Hovland et al.

1949). Moreover, two-sided arguments have a more lasting effect; attitude changes resulting from them are more resistant to counterpressure later. So even if you succeeded in winning your point by a one-sided argument, chances are that a few weeks later you would find your accomplishment undone.

Primacy and recency In situations where both sides of the argument get presented, such as in a debate, the question arises whether *primacy* or *recency* is more to the persuader's advantage. Primacy means speaking first, so people hear your position before it has been criticized by your opposition. Recency means going last, so the listener has heard you more

Politics in an Oyster House,
Richard Caton Woodville

In informal conversation, people
sometimes do succeed in
changing attitudes, such as
political leanings.

recently than the opposition and can therefore
have your arguments fresh in mind. In general,
primacy is more effective if an argument is
being used to reinforce an attitude someone
already has (Luchins 1957). If you think the
audience already pretty much agrees with you,
you would do well to hit them with the full
strength of your argument right off the bat.
In a debate, you should try to present your case
first. Also, there is a strong primacy effect when
an audience has to take a public stand after
hearing only one side of an issue before it hears
the other side. In other words, after hearing your
arguments, a person who initially disagreed with
you may support your position because they
haven't heard anything subsequently which
supports their original contention. If both sides
of an argument are to be presented to an impartial audience, however, recency generally has
the advantage. If the audience will take a public
stand or cast a vote immediately after hearing
both sides of an issue, you are better off presenting your side last (Zimbardo, Ebbesen, and
Maslach 1977).

Other studies of the audience find that people
evaluate a persuasive communication by comparison with their own attitude. They may
assimilate what the speaker says as tolerable,
or they may *contrast* it to their own precon-
ceived notion and reject it. Communications
which fall into a listener's **latitude of rejection,**
that is, those which differ greatly from their own
position, may actually produce a boomerang
effect—making their original attitude even

stronger and more resistant to change (Lusko et al. 1966; Sheriff and Hovland 1961). So if the attitude you are trying to change is very different from the position you want to change it to, you will be wise to present your views moderately, pointing out the *similarities* of your position and theirs, rather than hitting them with how great the differences are. It is also important to remember that the more *involved* a person is in an issue, the greater their latitude of rejection becomes—that is, the more they care about something, the harder it is to change their attitude toward it.

But it helps in getting others to accept your position if you can arrange for them to become positively involved even in a small way. Once they have agreed to comply with a small behavioral request, that is, have taken some action or repeated some statement in support of your position, they are more likely to go along with a bigger demand. This is known as the "foot-in-the-door technique" (Freedman and Fraser 1966).

Strong appeals to fear generally do not work in producing attitude change. They apparently make people defensive and suspicious of the

Horse trading is a traditional euphemism for efforts at mutual persuasion.

Bargaining for a Horse, William S. Mount

communicator's motives. This is not always the case with mildly frightening arguments, however; a rational, objective communication which arouses just a little anxiety is sometimes effective (Janis and Feshbach 1953). Fear has been used effectively to promote the use of automobile seatbelts, disease prevention, and forest-fire prevention (Berkowitz and Cottingham 1960; McGuire 1969).

Emotion-charged words also have a positive effect on the persuasiveness of an argument. Calling someone a communist, or a troublemaker, or a saint disposes audiences to see them more in those ways than any amount of calmly accurate description may do. Carrying your argument to an *extreme* position can help produce some shift in attitude in your direction. If you can arrange to be *overheard* making your points instead of directly addressing your audience, you have a definite advantage. You should always state your position *clearly* before you end your communication, rather than leaving your audience to draw their own conclusions as to what you meant (Sargant 1939).

Some personality characteristics of the *audience* which influence attitude change have been suggested above, such as *influenceability*. But situational factors in audience reaction are also important, maybe more so. Whether an audience pays attention to what you are saying, for instance, is obviously an important factor in reaching them. If the audience is very prejudiced against what you have to say, they may tune out altogether by daydreaming or thinking about something else. Or they may choose to reinterpret what you say in line with their own viewpoint and thus accept only compatible parts of what you are saying.

Resistance to attitude change, like change itself, is generally a dynamic and gradual process, not a one-shot episode that happens suddenly. Some people become resistant to attitude change by a kind of *immunization* process—if they resist mild exposure to an opposing attitude, they tend to be even less

affected by further arguments for it than they had been previously (McGuire 1961).

PREJUDICE AND DISCRIMINATION: THE SOUR ATTITUDES

The most important area, probably, for which the study of attitudes should have important applications is **social prejudice** and **discrimination. Prejudice** means the attitudes that predispose a person unfavorably toward a whole group. **Discrimination** is the behavior which expresses prejudicial attitudes by treating members of certain groups badly.

In talking about prejudice and discrimination, it is important to recognize the role of the **ingroup** and the **outgroup.** Everyone has an ingroup or reference group with which they identify and to which they have a sense of belonging (see Chapter 9). The outgroup is any group which they consider not their own, generally a group that has some attributes which set it apart from their group. Because their own group is the source of their satisfactions and the repository of shared norms and pressures to conformity, the individual tries to view its members more favorably than those of the outgroup. They seem more like oneself and more like one another than do members of the outgroup. If the norms of the ingroup are prejudiced against outsiders, then its members are likely to discriminate against those outsiders without necessarily having strong personal motives for doing so (Allport 1954; Pettigrew 1961). So much are we all hungry to belong. If they *are* strongly prejudiced, moreover, then our anxious need for belongingness will make us more willing to put up with an unpopular consensus of the ingroup about us than to accept the support of an outgroup member (Boyanowsky and Allen 1973).

The impressions we tend to form of people in either group are generalizations usually formed from small segments of individual

Discrimination.

behavior and then applied across the board to everyone in the group. This tendency to cast people in a rigid mold is called a **stereotype**.[2] Everyone everywhere forms them, and they have some value. Stereotypes are convenient means of making generalizations about people without having to study them carefully. But they are often inaccurate. Because we share a common culture and live in a common society with others, we tend to agree on many stereotypes, especially about people of minority *national* and *ethnic* groups. Stereotyping people interferes with judging them on their individual merits.

This does not make a lot of trouble until situations arise where prejudice and discrimination are used against people, and negative stereotypes of them are invoked to justify their mistreatment. Whenever there is unequal status or power between groups within the larger society, such trouble is inevitable because the actions of the "down" group, which is the outgroup, to improve its status, threaten members of the "up" or ingroup, who then encourage prejudice and discrimination against the outgroup. The negative stereotypes that people

[2] Originally a printer's term for a mold-cast printing plate, it was introduced as a psychological term by a great political journalist, Walter Lippmann, in his book, *Public Opinion* (1922; reissued 1956; paperback ed., 1965).

bring into intergroup relations further cloud and confuse their dealing with each other.

The worst thing about such prejudices is not only that they are unfair and destructive, but that they are transmitted from generation to generation even when they no longer serve any function. The hostility that many white people feel towards blacks for wanting to move into white neighborhoods is rarely based on the economic motive that they use to rationalize it ("they run down real estate values"). Instead, it seems to result from an unreasoning fear and disdain unjustified by their personal experience with blacks, but comes from longstanding myths they have learned from other whites.

How are such prejudices learned in the first place? To some degree the different behavioral or physical characteristics of an outgroup is enough to start the process. Different clothing, language, food, religion, skin color—it hardly matters which. More important is the fact that parents tend to pass their prejudices on to their children (Allport 1954). Children also pick up these attitudes or get reinforced for them at school and through the mass media. While pressure from minority groups has helped to alleviate the problem in the media, stereotypes of lazy blacks, helpless women, mercenary Jews, and swishy homosexuals still prevail. Since much of the prejudiced stereotype is based on myth, exposure to the outgroup and its point of view often helps break down prejudice. Unfortunately, our distribution of housing and schools tends to cluster racial and ethnic groups together, which reduces such exposure. Interestingly, many studies show that *imposed* racial integration can help eliminate prejudice in some situations and circumstances (Rose 1946; Deutsch and Collins 1951). But not in all (Cook 1969).

Once attained, a prejudice is very hard to break down. It is bolstered by the need to feel superior. It seems to be a source of great comfort that an ingroup member of even the lowest status can feel superior to outgroup members.

One may be able to work out the frustrations and inferiority feelings of their own life by directing aggression against the outgroup. In racial conflict, such displaced aggression is known as *scapegoating.* A prejudiced person who suffers financial, social, or other frustrations may direct their aggressive wrath at a group toward whom they are already prejudiced. This is not the only form of scapegoating, but it is a widespread one.

Another evil of prejudice and discrimination is the tendency for the views the dominant ingroup has about the oppressed outgroup to become *self-fulfilling prophecies.* What happens is that the ingroup relies on its negative stereotyped notions when dealing with the outgroup, and this shapes the interaction in such a way that the outgroup really starts to act like the ingroup expected, thereby confirming the negative beliefs about it. If you treat children as immature, they behave immaturely. If you treat former mental patients as oddballs, you tend to convince them that they are (Farina et al. 1968, 1971). And on and on. In social prejudice, if it has the power to do so, the ingroup may well maintain social conditions to keep the outgroup on the low level of its prejudiced expectations, meaning "down." Over the course of American history, for instance, the white majority in this country has supported a social system providing poorer education, housing, and economic opportunity for the black minority than for whites. As a result, black people are less equipped to fill jobs requiring good education, and whites then accuse them of inferiority because of it. The solution is not easy to see because there is a vicious circle in the problem—to improve their lot, blacks must be given opportunity. To get opportunity, white discrimination must stop. To reduce discrimination, white attitudes must be changed. But white attitudes are reinforced by the "down" status of blacks, which reinforces the negative white stereotypes. Where might this ugly chain best be broken?

ATTITUDES AND ACTIONS: TENSION AND TUG-OF-WAR

Studies of how to change attitudes have used up an enormous amount of the time and energy of social psychologists, and they have not always paid off very well. It is hard to measure attitudes in the first place, even harder to formulate theories which will account for how they get shaped and what changes them, and hardest of all to tell whether or not the results of laboratory studies have any dependable application to real-life attitudes. So why have people broken their heads against this subject for so long? What makes it so important?

The reason is that psychologists, like every-one else, are convinced that people's attitudes determine their behavior—that is, that people's disposition to think, feel, and act in certain ways toward certain objects will determine the way they actually do act towards them. If that is true, then there can hardly be a more important and practical topic of study than attitudes and attitude change. If people discriminate against blacks, or women, or Jews because they have bad attitudes towards them, then we should try to change those attitudes in order to change their behavior. If people are kind and helpful to the aged and the lame and halt because they have compassionate attitudes towards them, then we should try to reinforce those attitudes in order to promote the behavior. If attitudes

It is hard to change political beliefs which protect our social status.

DAUGHTERS OF REVOLUTION

Daughters of Revolution, Grant Wood

are the dispositions which underly our acts, then there is no more reasonable way, it seems, to change or cement those acts than by manipulating attitude.

There is a long and honorable tradition, in the personal history of each of us and in the cultural history of humanity, supporting this idea. It is the notion that our beliefs, our opinions, and our thoughts determine the way we act, that *our ideas move our lives.* This truth seems so self-evident that it may hardly be worth stating. People go to war voluntarily and die for all kinds of causes; people plan their lives way in advance and suffer patiently for years in order to fulfill their dreams, ambitions, and goals. It is their attitudes, of course, which

Our common stereotype is that women are the best caretakers of young children, but this nursery school in California is run exclusively and successfully by men.

focus them on these goals and which make possible long years of self-sacrifice and suffering to reach them. So—can there be any doubt that manipulating attitudes is the key to controlling behavior?

Yes, there is plenty of doubt (Ajzen and Fishbein 1977)! A fair summary of all the research on attitude change would have to conclude that: (1) it is hard to change most attitudes towards most anything in most anyone, and (2) it is hard *to keep* attitudes changed even if you can get them changed in the first place. If you want to change the behavior that results from bad attitudes, the best way to do so is probably *to find some means of rewarding different behavior* and maybe not fool around with the cognitive part of the attitude at all! If you succeed in changing people's behavior so that it no longer fits their old attitudes, then you might *reinforce* the new behavior by propagandizing new attitudes. But it is very difficult, in most cases, to work the other way around, that is, to first change old attitudes and then reinforce the change by promoting new behavior (Festinger 1957). This makes sense if you think back about what an attitude is in the first place.

An attitude, remember, is an *inferred* disposition to behave in certain ways. It consists of an emotional or feeling component, an intellectual or cognitive component, and a behavioral or action component. Now, no one ever *sees* an attitude—all you can observe, in yourself or anyone else, is feelings, thoughts, and action tendencies. Usually, these are congruent with each other, and we have powerful mechanisms within ourselves to keep it that way, which is why we tend to stay so self-satisfied with our attitudes and why they are so hard to change. But when something happens to **unbalance** the feelings, thoughts, and actions that make up an attitude, the part we all view as most within our own control among the three, is *always* the action component. We all feel that we cannot help our thoughts and feelings, but that *we control* our actions! Because of that, we can use our actions as a kind of lever from which to shift our thoughts and feelings, *as long as we consider the action voluntary*. And we *always* consider our action voluntary if we are doing it for some reward! So it follows, if I want to change someone's attitude towards something, I can do so by first identifying the action component of their attitude, then rewarding a different action than the one they are used to. When they perform that different action for a while, they will start changing their thoughts and feelings to make them congruent with it.

Human beings are remarkably realistic that way; they adjust with comfort to all kinds of situations which they anticipate with dread. This is why arranged marriages used to work out pretty well—the choice having been made for the bride and groom by their parents, the couple themselves more often than not adjusted their attitudes accordingly to make the best of it. The same thing happened to most young men who were drafted into the army; given a choice, they would rather have stayed home, but since there was none, they learned to make the best of it.

Neither of these are the happiest of examples, but the practical problems of attitude change that society faces are not problems of happiness but of accommodation. In relations with minority groups, for instance, it is less important, to begin with, that prejudiced whites learn to like blacks than that they learn to treat them equally and decently. If the *behavior* required of them is undiscriminatory, then their attitudes are likely to shift in the direction of justifying what they find themselves doing already. This then makes it easier to develop positive attitudes from which relationships of genuine amity can grow.

SUMMARY

1 An *attitude* is a disposition to feel, think, and act in a certain way. Beliefs, opinions, values, and prejudices are all special kinds of attitudes. Every attitude has an emotional, an intellectual and a behavioral component; these are usually inseparable. Attitudes are learned, not inherited, and their learning begins in infancy.

2 Attitudes which effect our interactions with other people are called *social attitudes*. Children usually adopt the social attitudes of their parents, because they *identify* with parental attitudes and internalize them. Attitudes are generally more easily learned than they are changed.

3 Attitudes are maintained because they serve important functions in *adjustment, ego-defense, expressing values,* and *knowledge*. Attitudes help in social adjustment especially, by directing us towards playing the social roles which make us acceptable in circles we want to enter. The ego-defense mechanisms are attitudes by which people defend themselves against a negative self-image. The expressive function of attitudes helps us organize and integrate behavior consistent with our values, and their knowledge function motivates us to develop attitudes that make sense of our experience.

4 There are four kinds of attitude scales in common use: (1) The *Thurstone*-type scale measures the extent to which a person's attitude reflects the same degree of approval or disapproval as judges' ratings. (2) The *Likert*-type scale gives a person's own degrees of positive or negative attitudes towards something, rather than assuming that the statements mean the same thing that judges have thought they meant. (3) The *Guttman* technique uses a hierarchical order of questions, in which the answers at any given point on the scale imply the answers to all the points beneath it. (4) The *Semantic Differential* tries to study the affective side of attitudes, by rating things as good or bad, strong or weak, and warm or cold, rather than merely as favorable or unfavorable.

5 It is very hard to change attitudes once they are established, and there are several different theories of when and why attitudes ever change. In general, attitude change occurs only when people feel forced to reexamine their attitudes because their attitudes no longer serve their needs. Attitude change is an attempt to restore the person's psychological equilibrium, to put them back in balance. All the major theories of attitude change use such a *balance principle*.

6 The first major *balance theory* of attitude change is that of Fritz Heider. It explains how people make their positive and negative thoughts about the same object work in conjunction with each other. The best known balance theory is Leon Festinger's theory of *cognitive dissonance*. It says that the feeling of dissonance between two ideas creates discomfort and conflict, and the dissonance is reduced by the person changing their behavior or changing their thinking. The theory of *congruity* is by Osgood, Suci, and Tannenbaum. Congruity exists when the relationships among a person's thoughts are balanced, and incongruity occurs when they are not. Finally, Rosenberg's *affective cognitive consistency theory* describes the relationship between a person's thoughts and attitudes towards an object and how they fit their general beliefs and values.

7 Generally, extreme attitudes are more resistant to change than moderate ones. When people who are fanatically committed to an extreme attitude do change it, they often take extreme positions in the opposite direction. Some scholars believe that such extremeness reflects a personality trait, usually named *authoritarianism,* but the evidence is weak. Other research has explored an opposite personality trait, social suggestibility, or *persuasibility*. As with authoritarianism, the evidence for this trait is weak and inconclusive.

8 *Consistency, interconnectedness,* and the *consonance* of attitudes with each other are also important determinants of how easily an attitude can be changed. The more strongly attitudes are related and interconnected, the more resistant they will be to change of any kind, and the more easily they will be strengthened by new information. Also, the more an attitude serves a person's strong needs and central values, the more it helps to integrate their personality and consequently the harder it will be to change.

9 The credibility of the person trying to change one's attitude is a critical factor in short-term attitude change. Very credible speakers impress audiences favorably. In the long run, however, the audience tends to resume its original position.

10 Some aspects of the communication itself are also critical in producing attitude change. One-sided arguments work best on people who already agree with the communicator. When the audience disagrees, they will be more lastingly affected by two-sided presentations. *Primacy,* presenting your own argument first, is more effective than *recency,* presenting it last, under some circumstances. Otherwise, recency generally has an advantage. Also, people compare communications to their own attitudes. When their attitude is very different from the position you want to change it to, then your argument should be presented moderately.

11 Emotional involvement is another important factor in attitude change. If people become positively involved with your position, they are more likely to accept it. This is called the "foot-in-the-door" technique. Strong appeals to fear do not work to produce attitude change, but mildly frightening arguments may be effective. Also, emotion-charged words have a persuasive effect. Carrying your argument to an extreme can produce some attitude shift in your direction, by involving people emotionally. And, arranging to have your points overheard instead of addressing them directly to your audience, can also work this way. The process by which people develop resistance to attitude change is called *immunization*. This resistance tends to build up gradually, just as attitude change itself tends to occur gradually.

12 *Prejudices* are attitudes that dispose a person unfavorably towards a group; *discrimination* is the behavior which expresses prejudice by treating its members badly. *Prejudice develops from negative stereotypes* a person has about *outgroups*. A stereotype is a tendency to generalize about people's traits. Prejudicial stereotypes are used destructively, where the outgroup is inferior in status or power, to justify mistreating outgroup members.

13 Children generally absorb the prejudices their parents already have. Prejudice is very hard to break down, especially among low-status members of the ingroup, who gain some comfort in their inferior position by displacing aggression from socially superior ingroup members against the outgroup. This behavior is called *scapegoating*.

14 Attitude change is studied so much because attitude determines behavior, so changing attitudes seems like the key to changing behavior. Actually, the opposite is generally more true. It is easier to manipulate behavior patterns than to change attitudes, and the successful manipulation of behavior tends to produce attitude change.

The future of psychology

22

22

The future
of psychology

No one really knows what's going to happen to them tomorrow; so predictions about the future of anything are doubtful. Even so, it is important to try and make them. You don't *know* that the sun will rise tomorrow, but if it does, and you are caught with your pants down at high noon, you will get burned.

What happens to psychology depends, to begin with, on what happens to the world. If nations become so urgent in their hostility to one another that they blow us all up, there is no problem and nothing to predict. If a major war or other long-term catastrophe develops, short of total destruction, the results for psychology are also clear. Some of its technical branches, such as human engineering, will be diverted to the service of fighting the war or relieving the disaster. They will grow and develop tremendously as a result. Others, useful only in peaceful and prosperous times, may stagnate or wither. World Wars I and II each did more for the growth of professional psychology than all the educational needs of children or therapeutic needs of mental patients since the world began, because the tremendous emergencies of war mobilized everyone's energy and resources; every discipline that could potentially contribute to winning the wars was encouraged, and thrived accordingly. "War," as James Agee sadly said, "brings out the best in men."

For the most part, psychology is a luxury profession wherever the struggle for physical survival dominates people's lives. Neither the peasants of India nor the generals of the Pentagon are able to worry about their mental health or their personal fulfillment when they are struggling to feed their families or are fighting their wars. They may make some technical use of psychology to ease their misery — by Yoga, or meditation, or religous ritual — or to increase their fighting efficiency — by better tests for personnel selection and classification, or by improved training methods. But even these activities are luxuries for most peasants and for most generals when they are concerned with nitty-gritty matters of survival. Psychology becomes a necessity for people only when their physical existence is secure enough not to need all their attention and the conditions of life are leisurely enough to let them look into their heads and examine their lives. At the same time, they must be educated enough and sophisticated enough so that when questions occur about their goals in life, they are not easily satisfied with the answers that the local wise men or priests have always supplied. The well-fed, happy folk of the South Sea Islands, a century or so ago, were no more interested in psychology than the hungry cannibals of New Guinea were.

Psychology is the byproduct of economic success and technological advancement. This is probably the main reason Americans have become the most psychologically oriented people in the world. With all its inequities, the production of goods and the distribution of wealth in America has become so efficient that less work is required of people now than at any previous time in history. Americans have more education, more disposable income, more comfortable housing, better health, and a longer life span than ever before. And the manufacture and production of goods is so thoroughly automated that over two-thirds of working Americans are now in service occupations (Ginzberg 1976).

None of this means that survival needs are no longer important or that everyone is getting them met. Blacks, Indians, Appalachians, Chicanos, old people, and plenty of others (including some plain WASPS) still suffer from economic deprivation or the fear of it. But most of the population does not, or not very seriously —no worse, for instance, than most of you reading this book. The expectations of this well-fed

Survival needs come first. The members of this family may not mind missing their therapy session this week.

Tornado over Kansas, John S. Curry

majority determine the psychological orientation of our culture.

Enough people now take for granted that their survival needs will be met and exceeded, no matter what kinds of day-to-day troubles they have meeting them, so that they now think about the "quality of life" in different terms than their parents did and give the goal of "a better life" a somewhat different meaning. They worry more about population growth and pure air and energy shortages and less about buying a new car. The new car means less to them than it did to their parents (as does a college education) because they are more confident they can get it. They are not better people, or more nobly motivated, but their values have shifted. The promise of physical security makes people self-confident about it so that they put less value on it and become, in some degree, less *materialistic.*

THE AGE OF PSYCHOLOGICAL MAN

The transition we are going through from a production-occupied, work-oriented, industrial society to a service-occupied, leisure-oriented society is starting what sociologist Phillip Rieff calls "the age of psychological man" (1959). Other scholars, such as economist John Kenneth Galbraith (1960; 1967) and social philosopher Herbert Marcuse (1955; 1964), approaching the problems of social change from their own perspectives, reach much the same conclusions. Galbraith and Marcuse describe the "new industrial state" we are now capable of creating as a "nonrepressive" society where the meanings of love, work, and play, as we have traditionally known them, will change radically. Not all the changes will necessarily be happy ones, but they will be ones in which people's other needs will become more apparent and more important as their survival needs are more thoroughly met and taken for granted.

In such a society, psychology must become a paramount concern and an important occupation, as it becomes a more and more important preoccupation. So a good way to forecast what may happen to it is to explore what will happen to our society if it continues moving in that direction, and then to see how professional psychology may be called on to serve it.

America in your middle age

By the end of the 19th century, Americans were deeply imbued with the belief that technological progress would marvelously improve their lives. In terms of physical comforts, they were largely right. Rapid transportation, swift communication, and the endless convenience of electric lighting and indoor plumbing and water supplies (which most of the world still lacks), were just becoming commonplace then. Now, as the 20th century approaches retirement, Americans are so accustomed to technological novelty (did you know that most products you use were invented during your lifetime?) that they take it in stride. Most of them have lived most of their lives in relative comfort and convenience anyway so that they are not too impressed by the invention of new conveniences. There is a real threat to these conveniences from economic disasters and energy shortages, but its psychological impact is not yet predictable.

Three major events of American experience since mid-century, however, are already having great psychological impact on our society and will probably continue to do so through the next generation (yours): (1) career and family patterns are changing dramatically; (2) the lot of deprived minorities is getting sustained public attention; and (3) progress in medicine and the biological sciences goes faster and faster. Each of these will have a big impact on professional psychology.

Love and work in transition Our vocational patterns are moving in the direction of more leisure and fewer restrictions on what a person

Technology has been the prime influence on our lives in this century. Think of how much one invention—the telephone—has affected every aspect of our lives.

The Telephone, Morton Schamberg

can do for a living and how often one can change it. This sounds like a fine thing, but if you are the beneficiary of it, you may find yourself very easily irritated and frustrated with what you are doing, or bored by it, and all too able to get out of it and into something else— maybe even over and over again, until you are firmly established in nothing at all.

Work as a means of survival is becoming less important. As that happens, people will either have to find in work a means of personal fulfillment or else preoccupy themselves with leisure activities that they can find meaningful; they will have to find either work at which they can play or play at which they can work.

At the same time that leisure becomes a larger part of our lives, and partly because of it,

the patterns of sex, love, marriage, and family life are also shifting rapidly. For many Americans, sex today is primarily a means of getting pleasure and expressing love and only secondarily intended for reproduction, just the opposite of most people's feelings a couple of generations ago. Our tremendous mobility and the growing independence of women combine with our changing sexual mores and economic ease to make marriage less binding than ever. The near future may exaggerate the resulting trends—towards sexual experiments and open marriage. The number of young people who routinely live together without getting married, or expecting to, will probably increase—the ease of sexual relations without deep emotional involvement will probably grow—and the commitment to treat marriage as binding, a once-in-a-lifetime act, will probably diminish even more.

One kind of problem psychologists will have to help solve, as this trend grows, will be the problem of *transitional activity and changing values.* For many people, the work ethos will diminish without a meaningful replacement appearing, and the traditional goals of love relationships will disappear without new ones at hand. In some people, this transitional period will produce anxieties that take the form of more or less traditional neuroses. For others, it will produce feelings of depression, anomie, and existential crisis. A lot of the professional effort of psychologists, far more than at present, will therefore go into counseling and psychotherapeutic work. The problem, in any case, will be the redefinition of purpose in love and work.

The natives are restless tonight: Minorities in transition The possibilities for a better life have not gone unnoticed among our socially and economically deprived minorities—blacks, Chicanos, Indians, women, the elderly—and the rest of this century will see more and more attention directed towards giving them equal status with everyone else. For some such

Increasing leisure time will create deep changes in our life style in the decades to come.

Sunday Afternoon on the Island of La Grande Jatte, Georges Seurat

groups, equal status requires more than equal opportunities, just as their social deprivations, thus far, have been more than equal to the rest of ours. In the long run, of course, success in the social system is the best solution to feeling "put down" by it, but success can only come through a combination of education and political action—and minority members must use both means to assert themselves and demand what they require: help and support in their efforts at self-improvement and at securing their rights.

Psychology can play three roles in this effort. The first is to develop educational programs for training deprived people to function well in "establishment" society. The second is to develop methods of motivating them to use these programs. The third is political: counseling the agencies of government on the special needs of these groups and the dangers to their well-being, and to the entire society, that come from delays in securing their free and equal place in it.

Educational and developmental psychologists have been working for some years on special educational programs, but none of them, thus far, have been very successful, and the social progress of ethnic minorities has been inhibited terribly by the failure of their children to get a good educational start in the primary grades or to keep from dropping out before the end of high school.

Equal status for the elderly also requires

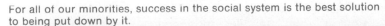

For all of our minorities, success in the social system is the best solution to being put down by it.

more than just equal opportunity; in this case, medical and psychological help rather than educational programs are needed. Psychological help would serve primarily to help older people adjust to retirement and develop new interests which could sustain them in old age—*emotionally,* not just economically. For many elderly people, the loss of their jobs means the loss of purpose in their lives, and they soon wither away, becoming ill, senile, and dying. Their problem in retirement is the same existential problem as in working—meaningful preoccupation. The difference is that old people have mostly been hard at work all their lives, and the shift to *retirement* can mean that *you* are useless now rather than that work is lacking.

The triumph of the biosciences When your mother was having children, one of the greatest tragedies imaginable to her was the thought that she might outlive them. To her grandmother, it was the thought that she might not. Throughout most of history, the chief cause of death among women was giving birth. That is probably why, in the course of evolution, females became physically so much stronger than males that today when they generally survive childbirth, they survive everything else better than men do too. The *chief* cause of death among everyone, historically, was not giving birth, however, but being born into infancy, which made your chances of dying before your first birthday about 180 per 1,000 births in 1900 in the United States; the rate has dropped rapidly to fewer than 21 deaths for every 1,000 births in 1972. Those sources of uncertainty in life are so long gone you may not even have known until now that they ever existed—or even, perhaps, that pneumonia, flu, scarlet fever, and polio, among others, were mortal illnesses that kept your grandparents alternately worried in winter and in summer for your parents' lives. Our expectations regarding life and health have been turned upside down in less than a century by the progress of medical science, and that progress is about to see the greatest spurt in its history in the next generation. Degenerative diseases and psychiatric disorders are two areas where its effects may be most dramatic.

The pattern of health expectations has changed so dramatically that it hardly occurs to couples planning families today that their children may not live and grow up in good health, no more than it occurs to you that your life may be cut short by unforeseen illness. The odds have indeed shifted heavily in favor of life and health. By the end of the century, they will have shifted even more, At the start of life, it will be possible to protect unborn fetuses better than now from the ailments transmitted during pregnancy. In infancy, childhood, and early adulthood, there will be much better control than now over infectious illnesses, ailments resulting from nutritional deficiencies, and disorders such as asthma and diabetes. In later life, degenerative conditions such as heart disease and cancer will pose less threat than they do now. Some of these improvements will come from discoveries in biochemistry, pharmacology, and nutrition, others from physics, engineering, and surgery—and the net effect will be better health and longer life for more people.

Psychiatric and psychological disorders also will benefit from these developments, especially of drugs and behavioral psychotherapy, both of which are becoming more efficient all the time. The drama of these new treatments for old problems will not always be obvious because the type of treatment is conventional. More effective pills for treating depression may soon be available, for instance, and some clinical depressions may then become run-of-the-mill conditions for which you can see your general practitioner rather than go to a mental hospital.

Psychosurgery and chemistry may offer dramatic new treatments for many conditions that cannot be handled well by current methods. Pills or brain implantation methods will exist by the end of the century for curbing many forms

622

of impulsive violence and other socially unacceptable outbursts. There may also be similar devices for improving memory and concentration; these would be used, to begin with, mainly for treating mental retardation, but they might also be useful for some of the problems of memory and concentration which normal people face in daily life. Such devices would, for all practical purposes, be viewed as "IQ Pills."

A lot of other aids for discomforts and disabilities, as well as instruments of pleasure, are sure to come out of biochemistry and medicine in the next decades. Aphrodisiac chemicals for reducing impotence or for prolonging the sensations of sexual arousal or climax are likely to be found. Chemical access may be gained to the pleasure center of the brain by oral means; it can already be reached surgically. Pills for controlling appetite, without producing disastrous side effects, may be found, making weight control an easier goal to reach. So too may harmless pills to help normal people control severe swings of mood.

Will all this make you a nicer person? Not by itself — but it certainly won't hurt!

Psychotechnology in a psychocivilization
You may have realized already that there is nothing in the description of likely events or probable contributions of psychology connected with them that is *unique* to professional psychologists, that is, nothing that requires the skills of a psychologist, as opposed to a social worker, or a physician, psychiatrist, or other person with training in the right service or technology. If you look back at Chapter 1, however, you will recall that this is true even now. It is

Will it happen in your lifetime — the dispensing of IQ pills in a public clinic, like vaccinations a generation ago?

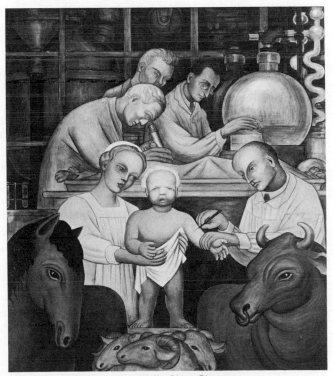

The Vaccination Panel (North Wall), Diego Rivera

going to be more and more true in the future.

The statement in Chapter 1 that all sciences work in essentially the same way, by systematically gathering and interpreting facts, was meant literally, not as a metaphor or simplification. The more knowledge grows within each branch of science, the less distinct that branch becomes from the one next to it. This is most obvious in the most advanced sciences. It would be foolish, for instance, to argue about whether a chemical physicist and a physical chemist were really students of different disciplines, or whether biochemistry is *more* about biology or about chemistry.

Science is interdisciplinary because knowledge is integral or unitary. In the long run, all subject matter flows from and into all other subject matter.

The behavior sciences, in the long run, are also integral, with each other and with the helping professions they serve. The more we know about every perspective on human behavior—social, economic, emotional, interpersonal, and physiological—the more interrelated this knowledge becomes, and the more integral the personal services we can design to serve personal needs.

It is useful to divide people and their problems into categories for purposes of study, and to divide services into professional groups with different expertise for dealing with different aspects of them, but the more society becomes concerned with the total experience of its members, the less rigid the categories are.

If you add up all the minorities in a benign society that need special attention, for instance, it turns out that they are a majority of the people in it—women, children, old people, racial and religious minorities, the poor—to name only the most conspicuous. It seems that the happy majority consists of four white Protestant middle-aged businessmen in Poughkeepsie—and of them, one smokes, one is overweight, one is sexually impotent, and one is actually Jewish (he changed his name).

Jokes aside, this is as it should be. A good society seeks the optimum development of all its members, not just the satisfaction of its dominant groups. Every individual is entitled, ideally, to the kinds of special attention that will help them develop themselves best. When we group people in terms of their common problems so that we can figure out the best means for helping to solve them, we should ultimately be including *everyone.*

The same thing happens when we try to classify problems according to type of disorder or classify services according to the type of profession needed to give them. Drug addiction and tuberculosis and alcoholism, for instance, can all be taken as medical problems, or as social problems, or as psychological problems—but calling it one or the other will make no difference to the human suffering involved or the need for service of perhaps many kinds to ease it. We could probably say much the same things of crime, or poverty, or poor schoolwork, if we knew enough about them to see the physiological basis of the vandal's aggression, or the derelict's despair, or the flunking student's apathy or restlessness. Or suppose, to make the point flamboyantly clear, that there were a pill that would turn black people's skin white, their hair blonde, and their accents upper-class New England—at the risk of occasional cancer, psychosis, mental retardation, and uncontrollable aggression. What kind of problem would we face then? A medical one? A social one? Or does the title matter? This may sound like science fiction, but the remainder of this century will see more and more problems of this kind develop as increased knowledge makes it possible to approach them from more and more different perspectives. Psychologists can probably contribute best to all of them by using their scientific skills, already highly sophisticated, in basic and applied research on these problems (Atkinson 1977).

Some people fear that the improvement of biomedical and behavioral technology will lead

The future?

to a more mechanized society in which people will be more indifferent to each other's human needs. If we do develop such a society, it will not happen because of advancing technology but because of lagging human concern. "Technical" does not mean mechanical, and "mechanical," in any case, does not mean either boring or cruel. The best *machinery* of medicine is used to save and enhance life, and the best machinery of psychology should serve the same purpose. Whether it does or not depends on the kindness and good sense of the people who use it, not on the machinery itself. If your personal interests combine service to people

with curiosity about electronics, engineering, computers and the "mechanics" of human behavior, then psychotechnology may be a good career for you.

The job of psychologists in the future will not be entirely technical, however, regardless of where their expertise lies. It will also be *political* in some important ways. As psychology helps develop tools for meeting people's needs in society, it also has to assume more responsibility for advising society on the uses of those tools. This is especially important in a free society, because the tools of psychology are instruments of behavior control.

FREEDOM AND BEHAVIOR CONTROL

The great social events like shifts in work patterns and the striving of minorities for equality are all expressions of a common goal. People want *freedom* and opportunity to live as they please and do what they want. They are willing to take some risks to get them too. That is why they seek more leisure, even without knowing how to fill it, engage in dangerous intimacies, without knowing where they will lead, and challenge the slowness of their progress on the gamble that they can gain more by impatient demands than by politely waiting for society to give them what they should have. The technology to which psychology belongs can help them gain that freedom. But it is also a technology of *behavior control.* While most of it is aimed at improving the human condition, some of the methods, such as drugs, brain surgery, and psychotherapy, can also be used to regiment, mislead, or abuse people. This problem will become greater as the means of controlling people become more efficient.

There are only two general ways to control someone. One is to supply them with *information* upon which to act. The other is to maneuver them physically, to *coerce* them. Some information is gentle and leaves them a choice of how to act, such as education, cajoling, persuasion, or even propaganda. Some is brutal and relentless, such as threats and hostile gestures. Some is in-between, like seduction. The same thing is true of coercion. Some coercion is horrible, such as torture or prison; some is soothing, like the act of making love or taking an alcoholic drink to relax.

Nobody objects to behavior control as such, of course, but only to brutality, to the denial of choice, and to the misdirection of one person's actions to serve another person's goals. This is the oldest problem in the social, political, and interpersonal history of humanity. Until recently, however, psychologists have not discussed it much nor been very alarmed by it because in the past, the means of control have always been crude and the effects of trying to control others have been uncertain. Today they are in a different ball game. There is increasing likelihood that we will be able, in the near future, to manipulate people's mood, emotion, desire, and need so precisely that large domains of behavior can be removed from their control and placed under the control of other people.

Most of them presumably will be doctors, teachers, psychologists, and others who work to serve people's expressed wishes. But some of the controllers will be legislators, police, and judges, who will have the same apparatus to use on behalf of society, whether or not the person it is used on likes it. The greatest danger of this technology, in fact, is that *one can be made to like it.*

Behavior-control technology increasingly makes possible a benevolent tyranny which can create a happy society, but at the possible cost of not having any deviation or dissent within it. In such a society, the problems of work, love, and equal rights would be solved by an elitist government deciding what is best for the good of society and the happiness of its citizens, and then using the technology of behavior control to implement it.

Psychology contributes to the problem by helping to develop behavioral technology. It can contribute to the solution by helping society to contain this technology, to prevent bad uses of behavior control, and to evaluate the need of a good society for any controls, technological or legal. To do this, psychology must broaden beyond its scientific and clinical role into social philosophy, social criticism, ethics, and law.

To handle behavior control intelligently, we must consider the future of its uses and misuses. Nobody is really willing to give up technological society, even though very many people are killed annually by automobiles, for instance, because it is too convenient to have cars and because the consequences in plague, illness, and economic disaster of living in a nontechnological society would be so fantastically worse that they beggar the imagination. And no one is really willing to give up behavior-control technology, because so much of it is plainly benevolent. One cannot oppose technology in general without condemning flush toilets, pasteurized milk, and penicillin. And one cannot condemn behavior control in particular without opposing education, traffic lights, and artificial lungs.

To confront the dangers of behavior control intelligently, we must distinguish between its **ethical** and its **technical** implications. Brain surgery that can remove hostile impulses, for example, may be a frightening thing—but for people who would otherwise go to jail because of their uncontrolled violence or who would be victims of epileptic seizures, it may be very beneficial. The ethical problem is not that the surgery exists, but that it can be used against people's will or for political purposes. In the same way, computer data banks that can store your secrets in a tiny space are the same kinds of facilities that can teach mentally retarded children to read or pay the social security checks of old people. The ethical issue is the invasion of privacy, not the capacity of the computer.

Science and technology are dumb things that will not control themselves or give answers to ethical problems. They can create new alternatives by their inventions, but they cannot select among them. Behavior control technology gives some people tremendous power over others, power that can be used to enslave, debase, and deny humanity the right to pursue its own destiny and development. The same instruments can be tools of dehumanization and debasement used one way, and facilitators of growth and fulfillment used another. It is the use, not the tool, which needs endless scrutiny.

The control of behavior is not *only* a technological problem; psychology can also contribute to the *policy* problem of what to control and what not to by helping to define the implications of different problems, the consequences of control, and the values inherent in the way legislative and law enforcement agencies want to handle them. As our approach to *crime* becomes less punitive, for instance, psychology can help find the causes of criminal behavior, the costs to individual and society of dealing with it in medieval ways, and new methods of prevention and rehabilitation which will serve both the individual and society best. As the pressure mounts for *drug* laws to change, and as *sexual* attitudes and practices do change, psychology can help guide the enactment of intelligent legislation to protect the innocent from dangerous exposure to these things, on the one hand, and free the adult population from needless restraints, on the other. As the trend towards divorce grows stronger and towards rearing children with only one parent, or with more than two, psychology can help define the proper role of social agencies in interfering with the private relations of parents to their children and the most beneficial limits of responsibility within families for the sake of their children. Some of this can be done best by psychologists in the role of researchers, others in the role of *lawyers* or other professional agents of social control. The assumption of direct social responsibility is relatively new for psychologists, but it is something they must do more of if they are to make their full contribution to the psychologically oriented society of the future.

THE LONG-RANGE FUTURE: DEEP IN THE CRYSTAL BALL

Once a civilization is as deeply immersed in technology as ours is, its future depends more all the time on the quality of its new technologies and the intelligence with which people put them to work. If we move intelligently in the most promising directions we are now headed, then the long-range future of our society will revolve around three main events:

The future of a culture may be shaped by the way its children are shaped.

1. The elimination of poverty.
2. Multiple socially acceptable patterns of family life and child rearing.
3. The improvement of health, increasing the life-span, and mastering the means of emotional self-control and of optimum intellectual functioning.

A century or two from now, drone work could be largely eliminated from our lives, and the Biblical curse of Adam—that he would have to toil in suffering (Genesis 3:15: "Cursed is the ground because of you; in pain shall you eat from it your entire life")—could be lifted. People would work because it was interesting to do so or because the work gave them pleasure. Garbage collection and government, drudgery and administration—the mindless tasks and great responsibilities that civilization needs to keep its wheels going, but that cannot be automated for one or another reason—could be done by people who are pleased to serve society in those capacities. And where no one wants to make a career of hauling trash or

wielding power, the work could be rotated among the citizenry, as military service and jury duty have long been done.

The curse of Eve could also be lifted (Genesis 3:17, "In pain shall you bring children forth"), not just in terms of safe and painless childbirth, already here, but of the whole pattern of marriage and child rearing. The nuclear family, as we have known it, might be only one of many acceptable family patterns. Much of family life has traditionally revolved around the helplessness of wives and children to survive without a husband and father, not around the idyll of happy families joined in a community of love. Where people are happy together, they would stay together—and where they were not, they would not be condemned to do so nor their children to suffer excessively by their separation.

Within that time, moreover, many of the personal ailments now tormenting people—such as most neuroses and anxieties and psychosomatic ailments, such as ulcers and asthma, and habit disorders, such as smoking or overeating—could become unknown (as hysterical neurosis already almost is in the United States) or could be controlled so easily that they would become trivial miseries.

Those things could so change the face of the world that many of our present concerns and preoccupations would be unrecognizable. In a rational, benign future, the confusion or anguish we go through today over racial integration, the equality of women, providing decent housing and education and job opportunities— and most of all, *war,* would be almost unintelligible reminders of a savage past.

With the economic resources already available to our society, and with the technology which now exists, or will before the century ends, we could be so far advanced towards meeting these utopian goals that it would seem conservative to speak of them as things a century or two away. With diligence, intelligence, and luck, *we* could be the prehistoric people of tomorrow's sane society.

If we were really to apply ourselves intelligently, in fact, then barring catastrophic acts of God, we could be a great deal more advanced even than the previous pages indicate. No one knows what the limits of individual development are for any human being, but it is very clear, whatever they are, that we have come nowhere near reaching them. As the nature of behavior is better understood, and the biochemistry underlying it becomes known, some marvellous possibilities for human growth appear. Learning could become a rapid process, and retention a more permanent one, as the keys to concentration and memory are found. People could develop more control over their untoward moods as the chemistry of emotion is uncovered and synthesized. Sleep could become an intensive, quick, and restful thing for everyone, and fatigue could be dissipated by a pill or its equivalent.

The individuals that would result from such knowledge would be, by today's standards, superb. Their functional intelligence would be great because it would combine quick learning and clear memory with the emotional control that would let them think imaginatively, without inhibition, and act rationally, without impulsiveness. Their capacity to pursue goals would be great because they would combine clear-

The curse of Adam and Eve may be lifted in our lifetimes.

Adam and Eve Driven out of Paradise,
Masaccio

headed purpose with great energy. Their ability to love would be large because their emotional life would not be dulled by neurotic anxiety or their perceptions of other people distorted by defenses. And their ability to cooperate with others would be great because they would not be doubtful of their own capacities and have to reassure themselves by seeking power over others. They would possess competencies and self-knowledge which would protect them against possession by the ghosts of ignorance, superstition, and fear which have plagued humanity since time began. They would be the masters of themselves and exercise their mastery on the environment around them, to the benefit and pleasure of themselves and others, and without designs for interfering with their goals. They would be the victims of circumstance alone, as everything in the universe must be, but not of the foolishness or avarice and despair that human beings dredge up inside themselves and smash their lives upon in senseless pain. They would spend their life fulfilling it.

This picture of society and of humanity is **utopian** (Greek for "nowhere") because it has not come to pass, but it is not fantastic in the sense that miracles would be required to make it happen. This vision of society is based on developments that are *now* occurring to make it possible, not on little green supernerds coming out of spaceships and making us all unite in amity. The vision of individual potential, likewise, is extrapolated from *current* events in the biological and behavioral sciences, not predicated on the notion that a lucky miracle for humankind will occur when Professor Klotz accidentally eats frammistan in his breakfast food and turns into Superblob! It says nothing, for instance, about the remarkable human being of the future having telepathic communication because today's behavior sciences have not been able to demonstrate clearly that telepathic ability exists, or that it can be learned if it does. It says nothing about future people living

forever or in perfect health because biological science today cannot forecast precisely how such things could happen, if they could. My image of human potential is not conservative, but it is not magical either. Our capacity for creating the "brave new world that has such creatures in it" is greater than it has ever been before. It does not require the magic of Heinlein's *Stranger in a Strange Land* and it need not be the meaningless pleasure cult of Huxley's *Brave New World*. It is a world we can reach for while we dream about it.

Meanwhile, the world we live in is in transition, and it is not too clear where it is going or whether the changes now occurring all represent progress. The potential for individuals to live a good life is probably greater in our present society than has ever been true before in human experience—but even so, most people who ever lived, live now, and most are abjectly miserable. Overcrowding, overpopulation, starvation, epidemic illness, and social deprivation are *pre*psychological problems, and most of the things that psychology can do most about become apparent only when the prospects for a decent life for everyone start looking up. This has happened in my generation—so psychology can come into its own in yours.

You will not have to anticipate the distant future of humanity, of course, to do your work; you will need only to understand the problems and people of your own time. In the perspective of history, whether already written or merely being forecast, they are problems of transition, of readjustment from one social norm to another, from one life-style to another, or from one phase of life to another. But from the perspective of the people you will confront, the problems you must deal with, as scientist, or teacher, or counselor, cannot be handled meaningfully in such a philosophical or academic way. Change is the law of life, and transition is a permanent condition for everyone. But like yourself, people experience their problems as immediate events requiring immediate concern, and to treat someone's live experience as an abstraction, is to dismiss it.

To deal with people from within their own perspective, however, or to get inside them enough to help them shift it usefully, requires a degree of self-consciousness and sympathy that cannot be learned easily from books, even psychology books, or from discussions of the future of psychology and the future of humanity. Still, it can be worth reading such books and thinking about such possibilities because, at our best and most self-conscious, we are constantly shaping our present-day lives to pursue future goals. The clearer the image of the future we would like to see, the clearer the prescription becomes for the action we can take today. This principle applies equally well to going on a diet, with a clear image in your head of your shapely figure in the future; to planning your college studies, with the image of what career you would like to pursue; and to planning the future of humanity, with the image of how you can contribute to it.

A great economist, John Maynard Keynes, once said, "Men are ruled by ideas and by little else." In terms of the way we experience ourselves, he was entirely correct—for all our needs and urges and impulses and longings, from receptors, or glands, or muscles, or brain, take shape within our minds, and are transmitted from them to the outside world, answering its stimulation and changing it to meet our vision of how it ought to be. In your own experience, you have probably not yet formulated any such vision for humanity, if indeed you have even settled clearly on the way you would like to shape your own future. But they go hand in hand, if you have a decent regard for the fact that "no man is an island" and that your time is now. So think about it. It is the first step in lending yourself to it and in fulfilling yourself by advancing the human enterprise.

SUMMARY

1 Psychology is a luxury enterprise for people who must struggle to survive. It becomes a necessity for people when their physical existence is secure and life is easy enough for them to start worrying about whether it is fulfilling. The economic success and technological advancement of American society may be moving us toward what John Kenneth Galbraith calls a "postindustrial state" which will be dominated by what Phillip Rieff calls "psychological man." In this society, psychology would be a paramount concern of almost everyone.

2 One of the main social developments likely to dominate society for the rest of this century will be dramatic changes in people's career and family goals. People will have more leisure and more mobility. They will become more preoccupied with making leisure activities into meaningful parts of their lives. Career switches in middle age and earlier will become more common and retirement a greater social problem. Patterns of sex, love, marriage, and family life will also continue to shift rapidly. Already, sex is primarily a means for getting pleasure and expressing love and only secondarily intended for reproduction among Americans. This, combined with the growing independence of women will make marriage less binding and the sanctity of traditional family life more questionable. A lot of psychological work will be counseling people who will need help to redefine their purposes in love and work.

3 The possibilities for a better life in this rapidly changing society will continue to arouse the demands of black people, Chicanos, Indians, women, old people, and other deprived groups to seek equal status. Psychology can play three roles in aiding these

efforts: (1) to help develop suitable educational programs for deprived people; (2) to develop methods of motivating them to use the new programs; (3) to counsel agencies of government on the special needs of these groups.

4 Dramatic changes will also come from discoveries in the biological sciences. Their net effect will be better health and a longer life span for many people. Some of these benefits will apply to psychological problems. Drugs and surgical techniques for relieving depression, curing uncontrollable aggression, improving memory, and improving sexual functioning may all exist before the year 2000. The contribution of psychology to society will be to help figure out the best uses for these developments rather than in inventing the things themselves.

5 The future work of psychology has some political aspects because the developing technology can be used to control human behavior in ways that violate people's freedom and dignity. Behavior-control technology helps make possible a benevolent tyranny in which people are happy but unable to dissent or deviate from social norms. The only way to prevent that from happening is to be constantly aware of the political and ethical problems which behavior technology creates.

6 The long-range future promises three main events if society moves intelligently in its most-promising directions. They include: (1) the elimination of poverty; (2) multiple, socially acceptable patterns of family life and child rearing, and (3) the improvement of health, increasing the life-span and mastering the means of mental adjustment. Drone work could largely be eliminated from people's lives. Marriage and child rearing could revolve around people living happily together rather than clustering together for protection. And most of the psychological ailments now afflicting people could be eliminated. The economic and political resources for such a utopian society already exist in contemporary American life. To marshal them, however, people must formulate a utopian vision for humankind. Psychology can play a major role in doing so.

Appendix:
More statistics

What follows in this section is more than you need to know for understanding the rest of this book. As a result, your instructors may not lecture on this appendix or may not insist that you read it. If they do, and you do, however, you may be better equipped to understand some important problems in the scientific evaluation of information, not only in psychology, but in business, politics, or anything else where the decisions people make depend on the quantitative reliability and validity of the information they get.

Some people are afraid that their ignorance of mathematics will make them helpless with statistics. But you will see, if you read this section, that understanding statistical descriptions and inferences requires only that you be thoughtful and logical, not mathematical. The section aims to make you a more intelligent consumer of statistics, not a computer of them.

Statistic comes from the Latin word *status,* which means the same thing as the English word *status*—position, standing, or state of things. Originally, in fact, it was a political term, which referred to "affairs of state"; now it is a scientific one referring to the "state of affairs" of scientific observations. Scientific method is the systematic observation, measurement, and recording of information; statistics is the variety of formal ways in which those measurements are made and recorded and summarized and evaluated.

Underline the word "formal" in the previous sentence, and you will begin to understand why statistics involves numbers and mathematics as much as it does. The big problem of scientific method is how to make *precise* observations, that is, observations which have a very dependable and accurate form. The common word for precise observation is *measurement.* The common language for recording measurement is numbers. Statistics is all the things that are done with those numbers; it is the mathematics of measurement.

Measurement scales: What the numbers mean

The physical world, you recall, is measured by scales, rulers, and clocks (see Chapter 1). They are the most precise kinds of measurements possible, and the numbers they use to record those measurements can consequently be compared in the most subtle and precise ways. If you are measuring distance, for instance, you can start counting from zero and can be sure that all the units of measurement are the same length. In the 100 metre race, the distance from metre 0 to metre 10 is exactly the same as the distance from metre 10 to metre 20, and metre 20 is exactly twice as far from the starting point as metre 10, metre 30 three times as far from it, and so forth. The same thing is true with scales and clocks—one ounce of prevention is worth exactly one pound of cure, and it weighs exactly one sixteenth as much; and three ounces is exactly triple the weight of one ounce. It is the same with time; all minutes are the same length, even though they seem longer when you are waiting for the dentist to finish drilling than when you are doing some happy task. Such precise kinds of measurements are called *ratio scales* because they start from some absolute zero point (such as zero height, weight, or time) and because the units of measurement from that point on are all identical with each other so that you can compute ratios from them (e.g., "A is twice as long as B," etc.). In psychology, they are used a lot for such things as psychophysics and physiology studies, but no one has been able to develop such precise scales as that for things like personality study.

If there is no absolute zero point to a measuring instrument, you can never talk about it in ratios—with temperature, for instance, you cannot say that if it is 80 degrees Fahrenheit outside, it is twice as hot as if it were 40 degrees because the zero point on your thermometer does not truly mean that there is no heat at all. Still, units of temperature all do mean the same thing; the *interval* from 40 to 50 degrees involves the same amount of heat units as does the *interval* from 50 to 60 degrees. Such *interval scales* do measure the amount of difference between the points on them, even though they do not start from any true zero point. In psychology, IQ tests and other ability tests are interval scale measurements.

Sometimes you cannot measure amounts of difference between things at all, but only the *order* of differences. If you measured popularity in a social group, for instance, you might find one person rated most popular, another next most popular, and so forth down the list. But there would be no way in that hierarchy to decide just *how much* more popular one person was than another. A measurement which put things in order from first to last but does not tell how much difference there is between them is called an *ordinal* scale (from the Latin word for "order"). It is perhaps the most common of psychological measurements.

Finally, there are situations where the only observations you can make are matters of simply classifying and counting things. Visitors from a foreign planet, for instance, studying the connection in human beings between wearing moustaches and bearing children would discover that all the people with moustaches and all the people giving birth to children fell into two separate groups, which they might label males and females. Membership in these groups, it turns out, is *mutually exclusive* — you cannot be both a male and female; also, the distinctions between them are *qualitative,* not *quantitative.* If you are a male, you are not less or more female than someone in the other group but, to mix a metaphor, are a horse of an entirely different color. Grouping things in this *qualitative* way, that is, by simply classifying them, is called *nominal* scaling (from the Latin word for "naming"). You could use numbers for it if you wanted, like calling males "1" and females "0," but the numbers here are just different *labels,* that is, *names* for maleness and femaleness. They represent *classes,* not *amounts.*

The different kinds of measurements give different amounts of information. A ratio scale will tell you everything that the other scales will, and more. A nominal scale will give you much less information than any other. The kinds of statistics that can be used to summarize and evaluate any observations depends on the kinds of measurement scales by which they were recorded in the first place.

Descriptive statistics

Measurement means a systematic way of making observations and recording them. Statistics begins where sheer measurement ends — at the point where observations are recorded and now have to be understood. The stuff that is acquired from the process of measuring and recording is called *raw data.* Statistics is the means by which it gets refined.

The basic process of refinement is that of organizing and arranging and portraying the data so that you can make some sense of it, that is, of summarizing it so you can *describe* it intelligently. The common ways of doing this are by pictures and by numbers. Numerical displays are generally called *tables;* pictorial ones are generally called *figures.* Each has its virtues and drawbacks.

Since measurements are made in numbers to begin with, you can summarize most raw data, after a fashion, by simply listing how many of each measurement occurred. Psychological measurements often involve tests of some kind; so we will use test scores as an example. Suppose there are 100 people in your psychology class and they all take a test on which they can score from zero to 20. Not everyone gets the same score, of course — they will be *distributed,* hopefully along the upper reaches of the test, with some scores being made more *frequently* than others. Ten people may get scores of 19, for instance; 15 people may have scored 18;

13 may have scored 17; and so on down, with a few poor stragglers way down below the rest. A **frequency distribution** table might display these scores in a list like Table A–1.

Table A–1 Frequency distribution

Score	Frequency
0	1
1	3
2	0
3	2
4	3
5	0
6	1
7	1
8	3
9	3
10	4
11	4
12	5
13	6
14	2
15	7
16	17
17	13
18	15
19	10
20	0
Total	100

Or, instead of showing exactly how many people scored at each single point, it might group the scores as well as the frequencies, like Table A–2.

Table A–2 Grouped frequency distribution

Score	Frequency
0–2	4
3–5	5
6–8	5
9–11	11
12–14	13
15–17	37
18–20	25
Total	100

Now, these lists summarize the raw data, all right, but not in a way that gives you an immediate and clear image of how the class as a whole did on the test. About all you can tell quickly from Table A–2 is that more people got high than got low scores, and you cannot even tell that much right away from Table A–1. You can provide a better and quicker image if you can literally picture the data summary. That is what *figures* (also called "graphs") do.

Graphic presentation: The shape of things
If you were to take Table A–2 and make a mark for each score at each frequency instead of summarizing them with numbers, the table would look like Table A–3. You could tell, at a glance,

Table A–3 Initial graph of Table 2

Score	Frequency
0–2	****
3–5	*****
6–8	*****
9–11	***********
12–14	*************
15–17	**************************************
18–20	*************************

how the scores tended to be distributed, even though you could not specify so quickly what the frequency was for each score interval. Now, turn Table A–3 on its left ear, put some calibration marks on the left side (called the **ordinate**) so you can tell what the exact frequency is for each score section, and you will have converted the table to a graph (see Figure A–1 on the opposite page). The ordinate is also called the vertical axis. The score intervals, which are now spread across the graph, are spread over what is called the **abscissa,** or horizontal axis.

Fundamentally, a graph is a precise pictorial display of a frequency distribution. The picture may be composed in different ways to emphasize different aspects of the data, just as a clock may have a round face which shows time by the position of the hands, or it may be digital, with no picture display at all, or it may be set up like an hourglass, to show time by the amount of sand in each part of the glass or the area of glass covered by sand (which means the same

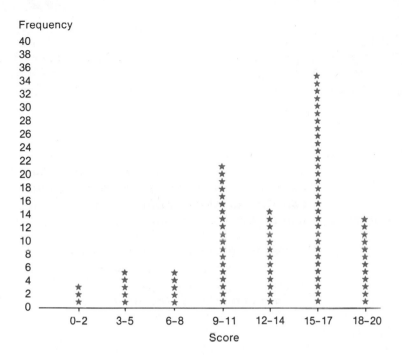

Figure A-1 Distribution of test scores

Time has many faces.

thing). The frequencies in Figure A–1 could be represented as **bars** rather than marks. This would be called a "bar graph" or "histogram" (see Figure A–2). Or they could be represented as connected high points, dropping the lines to the**abscissa** at each end of the distribution. The whole thing then looks like a polygon and, indeed, is called a "frequency polygon" (see Figure A–3). Exactly which portrayal would be best depends on your interpretation of the data. The frequency polygon is better for data which represent, in your opinion,**continuous** events; the histogram is better for emphasizing the**discrete** or discontinuous nature of the events represented by the data. Time, for instance, is a continuous event which we mark off in discrete segments as a convenience for measurement. Gender, on the other hand, is a more discrete event—people probably consider you either male or female, on the whole, rather than falling at some graded point between them. With much of the statistical data that psychology cares

about, however, it is unclear. Are masculinity and femininity discrete or continuous? Are scores obtained on IQ tests only reflections of discrete problem-solving activity, or do they represent some underlying abilities which are continuous in infinite degrees throughout the human species? The answers to such questions cannot be taken from the data but must be imposed on them in every effort one makes to understand the facts one has gathered.*There is no such thing as merely summarizing statistical information without also implying some interpretation of it.* To understand it best, you do best to examine it from many different angles, both numerical and graphic. Some of the most useful numerical descriptions are called "measures of central tendency."

Central tendency: The main point In some respects, graphs and frequency distributions tell you too much; they show patterns in the data, but they do not allow you to make summary statements about the individual scores which

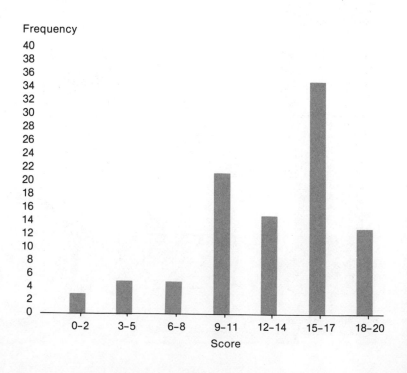

Figure A–2 Histogram

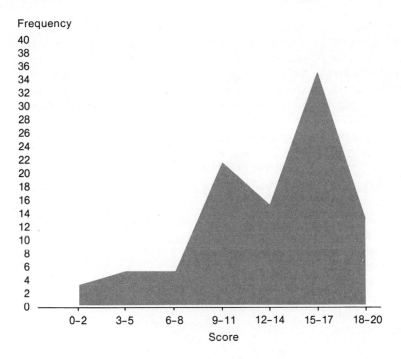

Frequency

40
38
36
34
32
30
28
26
24
22
20
18
16
14
12
10
8
6
4
2
0

0-2   3-5   6-8   9-11   12-14   15-17   18-20

Score

created the patterns. Knowing that the distribution of scores on your psychology test had more high scores than low ones tells you something, but it does not give you any specifics about the scores themselves, or about how well anyone did. Measures of central tendency are mathematical attempts to represent all the data in a single statement, a kind of "best guess" that you would make about any individual if you knew all the scores in the distribution but didn't know which person got which score. They are, in other words, statements about "the average individual," here meaning the typical individual.[1] The three most commonly used such measures are the *mode,* the *median,* and the *mean.*

The *mode* means about the same thing in statistics as it does in French—"fashion." In a

statistical distribution, the mode is the most fashionable score, that is, the single score obtained most often or, in a classification system (a nominal scale), it is the class with the most members in it. The mode can be a very deceptive figure, though. If you heard, for instance, that the modal income of Americans was $2,437.14 per year, it could mislead you into thinking that this country is much poorer than it really is. Most people earn more than $2,437.14 and that figure would simply represent the most common single income, with no hint of what most incomes were or of how many people made more money or less money than that. The most frequent score may not occur with great frequency and is not necessarily located near the middle of the distribution—so the mode is not a very useful measure of central tendency.

The *median* is generally more useful than the mode because it gives some information about how the cases are actually distributed. The statistical term "median" means the same thing as the "median line" painted down the

---

[1] "Average" has several dictionary meanings, one of which is "typical"—the way you typically use the term. "Arithmetic average," which you learned about in grade school, is typically called the "mean" or "arithmetic mean" in statistics, to avoid confusion.

center of many streets and highways, namely "located in the middle." And it has the same function, that is, it divides the distribution into two equal parts, such that half the individuals score above it and half below it. The median is the *middle score,* in other words, for that particular sample. In the test described in Table A–1, taken by 100 people, the median would be the score below which 50 people fell and above which 50 people fell — in this example, a score of 16 (see Table A–1). The median is among the most useful of all descriptive statistics because it gives you an instant way of comparing people to each other in percentages. The *percentile* scores with which you are probably familiar from scholastic aptitude and achievement tests have the same basic meaning as the median — they tell you what percentage of people taking the test got lower scores than that. The median is the 50th percentile point of any distribution.

Like all percentile scores, however, the median only gives ordinal scale information, which tells you nothing about how much difference there is between different points in it. If the median score on a psych test were 85, for instance, we would know that 50 percent of the class had done better than that and 50 percent worse, but nothing else. The half that scored below 85 could have scored anywhere below it — they could all have gotten scores of 12 or 23 or anything else below 85 without changing the median at all. In that instance, the median would mislead you badly about the shape of the distribution because it takes no account of the actual *scores* anyone gets, but only of the percentage of *cases* above and below a given point. The *mean,* or *arithmetic mean,* tries to do both.

The term "mean," like "median," also comes from a Latin word meaning middle, but it is a more ambitious kind of midpoint than the median. It takes account of the size of the scores as well as of the number of cases falling higher or lower in the distribution, and it is expressed as a combination of them. Instead of just counting up half the cases, from lowest score up, as you would to compute the median, you calculate the mean by adding up every single score and dividing the sum by the number of scores you have added together. In our example (Table A–1), the mean is 13.93 (see Figure A–4 for instructions on computing means).

Figure A–4 How to compute the Mean

To compute the mean, add up the scores, and divide the sum by the total number of scores.

$$\text{Mean } (\overline{X}) = \frac{\text{Sum of scores } (\Sigma x)}{\text{Total no. of scores } (N)}$$

Using the scores from Table A–1:

$$\overline{X} = \frac{1,393}{100} = 13.93$$

The Mean in this example is 13.93.

Like the median and mode, however, the mean too is an imperfect measure. For one thing, it becomes meaningless[2] if the scores are not obtained from an interval scale, that is, if the differences between score units are not exactly alike. Suppose you tried to calculate the average height of a piddle of puppies[3] using an elastic tape measure (Lipton 1968). Stretching the tape would have no effect on the *order* of the numbers (all you need to compute the median), but the distances between the numbers would be different at different points on the tape. One would still precede two and two come before three, for instance, but the numbers might be one inch apart one time and two or three inches next time, depending how hard you pulled on the tape.

Another drawback of the arithmetic mean is that it is sensitive to extreme scores, that is, it

---

[2] Ho, Ho, Ho!

[3] Or a slouch of models, a flush of plumbers, a wince of dentists, or most other things for which a tape measure would do.

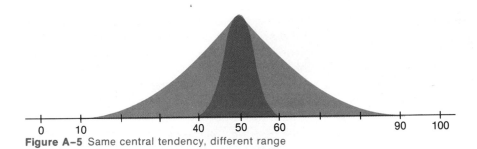

Figure A–5 Same central tendency, different range

is respectively increased or reduced more by very high or very low scores than by middle-range scores. Even so, the mean is the most favored of all central tendency measures in the social and behavioral sciences. Of the three, the mode, the median, and the mean, far more things can be done to the mean mathematically than to the others. The most important of such refinements involve measures of variability.

Variability Measures of central tendency tell us what is most typical about a frequency distribution, not what is unusual about it. But the atypical extremes may be just as important, even more so. If I am studying people's ability to learn some skill so that I can assign them to classes, I need to know something about who will be at the top and bottom of the class, not just what the average is. So most statistical descriptions of frequency distributions give some numerical information about variations within the sample as well as about its central tendencies.

The *range* is the simplest index of variability in a sample. It is the difference between the lowest and highest scores. Using it together with the measures of central tendency gives you a better idea of what a distribution is like than the latter would alone. If you can score anywhere from zero to 100 on a test, there is a big difference between a group whose scores range from 10 to 90 and one whose scores range from 40 to 60—though the central tendency measures of both groups may be 50 (Figure A–5).

You can only make use of the range, as of the mean, with scores obtained from an interval scale. Its great disadvantage, as with the mean, but more so, is that its size depends *only* on the extreme cases. On a test scorable from zero to 100, all but one student might score between 60 and 90, so the range would be 30—but that one person, scoring 30, let us say, would double the test's range, giving a false impression of how large the variations in people's scores really tended to be.

The best index of variability, as of central tendency, would be a number which took account of every individual score, not just of the extremes. The most commonly used measure for this purpose is called the *standard deviation from the mean* (also called *standard deviation,* also *s.d.*). It is a kind of average, but it does not tell the most typical scores; it tells something about the most typical departures from them. It is a "best guess" statement about variability rather than central tendency. If you did not know any individual score in a distribution, your best guess would be the mean; if you knew that someone had not scored at the mean, your best guess would then be that their score was within a standard deviation above or below it. The standard deviation, in other words, is an index of the typical deviation (that is, variation) of scores from the mean.[4]

---

[4] It is actually the average deviation, algebraically cleaned up. If you were literally to add up every deviation from the mean and divide by the number of scores (the way you compute the mean in the first place), the total would be zero. Look at Figure A–6 on computing the standard deviation and you will see why.

Figure A–6 Computing the standard deviation

The scores of 10 students on Test A are listed below. To find the standard deviation, s:

Find the mean of the scores, using the method described in Figure A–4.

$$\bar{x} = 89.6$$

Find the deviations of the scores from the mean by subtracting the mean from each score. The result is in Column 2 of the table.

Square each deviation in Column 2. The result is in Column 3.

Add up the squared deviations, and divide the sum by the total number of scores. This gives you the *variance*, s^2.

$$s^2 = \frac{\Sigma \text{ deviations}^2}{\text{Number of scores } (N)} = \frac{324.4}{10} = 32.4$$

The *Standard Deviation, s,* is the square root of the variance.

$$s = \sqrt{32.4} = 5.7$$

Column 1 Scores on Test A	Column 2 Deviation from the mean	Column 3 Deviation squared
98	8.4	70.56
93	3.4	11.56
90	0.4	0.16
87	−2.6	6.76
91	1.4	1.96
90	0.4	0.16
89	−0.6	0.36
75	−14.6	213.16
89	−0.6	0.36
94	4.4	19.36
		324.40

Comparison Scores Knowing in detail about the variability of a sample makes it possible to compare a single person's relative performance on two different measuring instruments, even if they use quite different scoring gauges or units. You would measure someone's long-jumping ability in feet or inches, for instance, and their ability to hold their breath in seconds, minutes, or hours.[5] If a person can

---
[5] Once people hold their breath for an hour, they continue doing so indefinitely.

hold their breath for five minutes and can broad jump six feet, there is no saying they are better at one than at the other. But if they have done these things along with many others whose ability has also been sampled in both areas, then their ability in each area *relative* to the other people can be assessed.

Percentile Scores One way of making this comparison is by ranking the scores on each measure from highest to lowest, counting the people at each score rank, and calculating what percentage they make up of the total. You may notice that, worded a little differently, here we are back at the median—or, to be exact, at **percentile scores.** It makes no difference that the measuring units are for breath-holding, long-jumping, or anything else; by converting each rank to a number which indicates the percent of people who scored below it on that test, we create a common means of comparing scores on all tests: "Jamie long-jumped farther than 73% of the kids and breath-held longer than 29%, and is thus a relatively better long-jumper than breath-holder."

Standard scores provide an even better means of converting people's **raw scores** on different tests into comparable units. Called z-scores, they are restatements of the original scores as standard deviation units. If you got a score of 80, for instance, on a test where the mean was 50 and the standard deviation was 20, your z-score would be 1.5, that is, one-and-a-half standard deviations above the mean. In practice, z-scores are often further transformed in a number of ways which enable them to be reported without decimal points or negative numbers (if you had scored 30 on that same test, for instance, your z-score would be −1.0, that is, one standard deviation below the mean). That is why such tests as the SAT and the Graduate Record Examination report your scores in hundreds and in per centiles. The hundreds number is actually a standard score, whose mean is fixed at 500 and standard deviation at 100. (See Figure A–7.)

Figure A–7 How to compute standard score

Find the mean, $\overline{X}$, and the standard deviation, s. In the case of Test A,

$$\overline{X} = 89.6$$
$$s = 5.7$$

The standard score is computed by subtracting the mean from each score, and dividing by the standard deviation.

$$z - \frac{x - \overline{x}}{s}$$

Standard scores for Test A:

Score (x)	Standard Score (z)
98	1.47
93	0.6
90	0.07
87	−0.46
91	0.25
90	0.07
89	−0.11
75	−2.56
89	−0.11
94	0.77

Just as standard scores permit comparisons of the relative position of a single person on two measures, they also make possible the comparison of everyone at once on those two measures, that is, *correlation,* which we began discussing in Chapter 1. A correlation scatter diagram is actually a *graph of two standard score distributions.* The dots are the scores each person got on *both* tests. A perfect positive correlation produces a diagonal slope upwards to the right, as you can see in Figure A–8, because every individual got the same z-score on both tests. A perfect negative correlation slopes downward from the left because each z-score on one test is matched by an inverse score on the other; if a person's score was one standard deviation above the mean on one test, it would have been one standard deviation below it on the other. In a moderate positive correlation, the scores scatter into an oval shape. And as a zero correlation is approached, the score pattern becomes a circle so that a line representing it on a graph would have a slope of zero—it would parallel the abscissa, because there is no correspondence at all between people's z-scores on the first and second tests. It is easy to compute the correlation (Figure A–9) between two tests once you know the standard scores. The correlation figure obtained from standard scores is called the *Pearson product-moment correlation coefficient,* also called *r.* Percentile and other ordinal scale scores can also be correlated by a method called *Spearman rank-order correlation.*

The normal distribution In all the biological and behavioral sciences, there is one kind of frequency distribution which occurs more than all the others; it is called the *normal curve* or *bell-shaped,* or *Gaussian curve.* Some of its properties make it very convenient for statistical descriptions; it also follows the empirical pattern of the way many biological and behavioral events occur in nature; and finally, it has mathematical properties which make it a model even for some events which are not normally distributed. For these reasons, it is an important tool of statistical inference as well as of description (see Figure A–10).

The descriptive properties of the curve are neat ones. Since it is perfectly symmetrical, the mean, median, and mode are all exactly the same. The mean, in short, is also the most frequently obtained score and the score which divides the cases in two—half of them scoring higher and half lower than it. As you go farther and farther from the mean, that is, as scores are higher and higher or lower and lower, there are fewer and fewer cases. Scores one standard deviation from the mean, above and below it, occur exactly at the *point of inflection* of the curve—the point where it switches from a concave to a convex shape. The curve has been divided in the diagram so you can see percentages of scores in each section. About two-thirds of all scores fall within one s.d. of the mean in a normal curve and more than 99

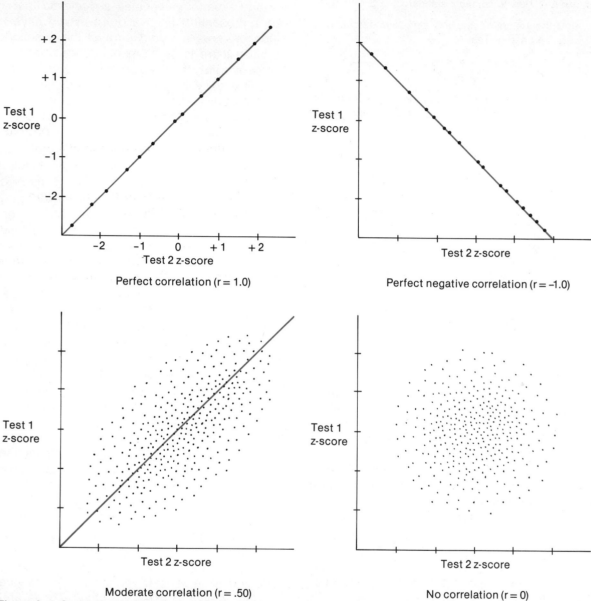

Figure A–8 Correlation scatter plots

Figure A-9 How to compute the correlation

In the table below are the scores of 10 students on Test A and Test B. To find the correlation between these two sets of scores:

Find the mean and Standard Deviation for each set of scores.

$$\overline{X}_A = 89.6 \qquad \overline{X}_B = 47$$
$$s_A = 5.7 \qquad s_B = 3.7$$

Convert the scores to standard scores. This is done in the table below.

Multiply the standard scores of each case. The results are in the table below.

Find the mean of the multiplied standard scores, $z_A \cdot z_B$. This gives you r, the correlation coefficient.

$$r = \frac{\Sigma z_A \cdot z_B}{N} \qquad r = \frac{9.08}{10} = .908$$

		Standard scores		
Test A	Test B	z_A	z_B	$z_A \cdot z_B$
98	53	1.47	1.62	2.38
93	49	0.6	0.54	0.32
90	48	0.07	0.27	0.02
87	45	−0.46	−0.54	0.25
91	48	0.25	0.27	0.07
90	47	0.07	0.0	0.0
89	46	−0.11	−0.27	0.03
75	39	−2.56	−2.16	5.33
89	45	−0.11	−0.54	0.06
94	50	0.77	0.81	0.62
				9.08

percent of all cases fall within three s.d.s on either side of the mean—so, for all practical purposes, a normal distribution contains six standard deviations.[6]

But the peculiar virtues of the normal curve do not lie so much in these descriptive properties as in the fact that there seem to be many events in nature which are actually distributed normally, as if the symmetry of the curve symbolized the symmetry of many biological structures. Take height and weight, for instance.

---

[6] Although it theoretically extends to infinity. This is called an asymptotic distribution.

There is an average height for males at given ages; more males probably are that height than any other single height; most of the rest are close to that height; and as you look for taller and taller and for shorter and shorter men, there are fewer and fewer at the extremes. So too for weight. This kind of fact permits the invention of industries for standardizing attention to people's needs, such as ready-made clothing, standard toothbrush sizes, and so forth. The amounts of clothing a manufacturer needs to produce items of each size can be figured out from knowing the averages in a population that is normally distributed. Psychological traits may be normally distributed also, such as intelligence, performance abilities, and personality traits. No one knows absolutely because there is no perfect way to measure everyone on anything. The best that one can do is collect samples and to infer the relationship between samples and the population from which they were drawn. The great value of the normal curve is the mathematical model it provides for inferring the relationship between samples and populations. Only part of its value, moreover, comes from the fact that nature imitates the normal curve; part also comes from the mathematical fact that, if you collect many, many samples from the same population, the distribution of the means of those samples will itself tend to be normal, regardless of the distributions of the samples themselves. The normal distribution is thus the most generally used tool of statistical inference.

Statistical inference

The problem which gives rise to statistical inference is the fact that scientific observations are always observations of **samples,** while the conclusions we want to draw from them are always generalizations about the populations from which those samples come. Technically, the measures derived from a sample are called **statistics** and the population characteristics

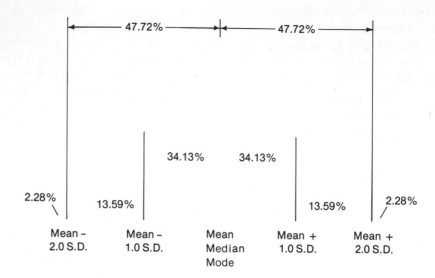

Figure A–10 The normal curve

| 2.28% | 13.59% | 34.13% | 34.13% | 13.59% | 2.28% |

Mean –
2.0 S.D.

Mean –
1.0 S.D.

Mean
Median
Mode

Mean +
1.0 S.D.

Mean +
2.0 S.D.

they are supposed to represent are called **parameters.** The problem is: with what degree of confidence can we generalize from sample statistics to population parameters?

The answer depends partly on how **representative** a given sample, or set of samples, really is of the population in question (see Chapter 1). There is no absolutely certain way to know this except by measuring the entire population. This is usually impossible, which is why samples are used in the first place. A very large sample is, accordingly, more likely to represent the population than a very small one, but as a practical matter, there are always limits on how large a sample one may take. The next best alternative to measuring the entire population is to sample as much *at random* as one can, which means to sample in a sufficiently unbiased way so that every possible source of error will have the same chance of getting into the sample. A variety of methods exist to insure that you are sampling at random. But just as you cannot be sure that a sample is representative merely because it is large, you also cannot be certain it is representative just because it is selected at random. Randomization will improve the chances that your efforts are not

biased, but you cannot *know* whether the sample has errors.

Statistically, the more samples you take, the better estimate of the population becomes possible. The mean of each sample is itself an estimate of the population mean, containing a certain amount of error. The distribution of all these means would tend to be a normal curve, as we have said, and the mean of the sample means would be the best possible estimate of the true population mean. Its standard deviation is called the standard **error** of the mean. It is used to calculate the **confidence limits** of the mean, that is, the range of scores within which we would expect most means to fall if they were drawn from further samples of the same population. The larger the sample we use, the smaller (that is, more precise) the range of values for a given level of confidence because increasing the size of the sample reduces the size of the standard error of the mean.

Statistical significance Estimating the probable attributes of a population parameter from a sample statistic by means of the normal curve is typical of the procedures of inferential statistics, all of which are designed to perform similar tasks by a variety of mathematical manipulations. For some purposes, especially for testing hypotheses by comparing groups in an experiment, we are really interested in seeing whether the overlap between the scores of the groups is so small and the distance between their means is so great that we *cannot* assert with much confidence that all the groups have come from the same population. When the mean of the experimental group falls outside the 95 percent confidence limits of the mean for the control group, for instance, meaning that it would be expected to occur in less than 95 out of 100 samples drawn in the same way if it were indeed from the same population, we say that its difference is *statistically significant.* The statistical assumption on which the comparison is based is called the *null hypothesis,* meaning that the observed difference between the groups is assumed to be a chance result of sampling error, that the two samples are really from the same population, and that the experimental group mean will therefore fall within the confidence limits of the control group mean. A significant result is one in which we *reject* the null hypothesis, that is, we accept the idea that the observed differences in means of the two groups reflect, not chance errors in sampling, but systematic consequences of their derivation from different populations.

Statistical significance, as indicated in Chapter 1, is a statement of probability, however, not of knowledge. It is a form of best-guess-under-the-circumstances, the circumstances being that there is no way to examine the entire population directly. It is conventional to reject the null hypothesis (that is, to assert that the differences between groups were lawful, not accidental) if the experimental mean falls outside the 95 percent or the 99 percent confidence limits of the control mean, which is stated as reaching "the 5 percent or 1 percent level of significance." But that rejection literally means that we have decided to reject the null hypothesis even though there is almost a 5 percent or a 1 percent chance that it is in-

deed true! This is called a *Type I error,* (also called alpha error) that is, believing that the statistical difference we have observed is meaningful when, indeed, it is simply the random fluctuation that occurred in this sample. The smaller the level of significance we require for rejecting the null hypothesis, the less risk there is of this kind of error.

But the less we risk the *Type I error* of believing the difference really means something, the more we risk the *Type II error* (also called beta error) of accepting the null hypothesis when it is false, that is, when the differences between the observed sample means really do reflect different population means. The errors are reciprocal. The common way this problem is dealt with is by setting the required significance level for avoiding Type I error quite small and making the sample size as large as practicable.

There are a large number of statistical techniques for testing the significance of differences between means; for testing whether correlation coefficients are significantly different from zero and for predicting one set of scores from knowing another; and for testing whether observed events differ from those which could be expected theoretically in situations where there is no model form of distribution such as the normal curve for comparison.

The most common method used for comparing two means is called the *t-test,* in which the model distribution is similar to the normal

Figure A–11 True state of the population

Decision based on confidence limits	Null hypothesis is true — results are due to random fluctuation	Null hypothesis is false — results not explained by random fluctuation
Do not reject null hypothesis	Correct	Type II error β
Reject null hypothesis	Type I error α	Correct

curve but not identical with it. The t-test gives a more accurate comparison of means for small samples and for samples taken from populations whose variance is not known. *Analysis of variance* is an extension of the t-test which is useful for comparing the means of more than two groups at once and for comparing several means within a single group.

The significance of a correlation coefficient can be tested both by the t-test and by other means. The value of one variable can be predicted from another by means of a *regression coefficient,* computed by a procedure similar to that for calculating correlation. Standard errors of the estimate of this prediction can also be computed and the confidence limits of the coefficient established, as with means.

A variety of *nonparametric* methods are used to test the significance of statistics for which there are no theoretical models like the normal curve. They are generally easy to use, especially with small samples, but are not as powerful as parametric methods and are considered less desirable when the latter can legitimately be used.

You do not need to know how to compute tests of significance at this point, only to understand what they are. They are the best methods around for conveniently determining whether to put any faith in the empirical observations one has made or not. "Putting faith" in them does not mean literally believing them—it would be silly to think that a complicated universe will give up its secrets so generously as to let statistical tests reveal reality with any ease. What it does mean is using the significant results of one experiment as a basis for deciding in what direction to turn one's attention for the next experiment—how to further explore the meaning of the results obtained so far, or whether to discard the line of inquiry which, until now, has not "paid off" in results which are statistically significant enough to make it promising. Inferential statistics are not judgments which verify results, but teasers, half-promises to promote further exploration, or gentle warnings against being overly impressed with the appearance of what one has found. They are minimal guides to scientific probing. Without statistically significant results, you must not accept that your findings are meaningful. With them, you need not dismiss your findings out of hand. Statistics are the most valuable tool available in the behavior sciences for guarding the practical belief by which science works—that reducing error, even more than increasing information, builds knowledge best.

Glossary

absolute threshold The weakest or lowest level of intensity of a stimulus in any sensory domain (e.g., sight, sound, etc.) that can be detected without any special aids.

abstraction An idea which has no corresponding concrete image.

achievement motive The social motive to accomplish objectives of value, or to compete against a standard of excellence.

acquired membership Group membership attained by some voluntary means. Also referred to as *achieved membership*.

acrostics A form of conceptual organization in which the first or last letters or lines of poetry (or prayer) are arranged so as to spell out some key word or alphabetical sequence.

acting out In psychoanalytic theory, the ego defense characterized by aggressive, sexual, or self-damaging behavior performed as a means of reducing anxiety.

acute traumatic neurosis State of a person suddenly overwhelmed with anxiety, such as may be induced by a violent accident, and remaining upset for some time.

adaptation The successful effort to survive and obtain satisfaction in life.

addiction An uncontrollable hunger—e.g., for food, alcohol, heroin, etc.

adient behavior Approach tendencies.

adjustment All of the processes directed toward the solution of problems of living.

affective cognitive consistency The theory of *attitude* change which postulates that feelings held toward an attitude object are closely related to the thoughts associated with it.

affective psychosis That form of *psychosis* involving extreme moods and disordered emotions.

affectothymia In Raymond Cattell's theory of personality, the most basic source trait. Refers to emotional expressiveness.

afferent (or sensory) neurons Those nerve cells which receive impulses from the sense organs and then transmit them to the central nervous system.

afterimage The visual experience that persists after the stimulus which produced it has been withdrawn.

all-or-none-principle Refers to the fact that a nerve cell always fires with the same intensity. Thus the neuron either fires at full intensity, or not at all.

alternate-form reliability Evaluation of the reliability of an assessment procedure by administering different forms of the same test to the same people.

altruism The social motive inferred from behavior apparently carried out to benefit another person, or people, without anticipation of rewards from external sources.

ambivalence Conflict expressed in vacillation between moving toward and away from a goal.

amnesia A dissociative reaction characterized by a forgetting of one's past.

anal stage In psychoanalytic theory, the second stage of psychosexual development, beginning at about the age of 18 months, during which the child's experiences with independence and parental restriction—particularly as concerns toilet training—are assumed to contribute heavily to the formation of personality.

analysis of variance A procedure for testing the statistical significance of the difference between means of more than two groups and for comparing several means within a single group.

androgyny The ability to respond in both masculine and feminine ways.

anger The emotion involving a temporary heightening of arousal accompanied by a tendency to attack.

anorexia nervosa Pathological self-starvation.

anthropomorphization The attribution of human characteristics to inanimate objects.

antisocial personality Personality pattern characterized by a tendency to be motivated by momentary impulses and indifferent to other people.

anxiety neurosis A long-standing anxiety state.

anxiety states Chronic conditions characterized by nervousness, depression, inability to concentrate, difficulty in sleeping, and general inability to enjoy life.

aphasia A language disorder involving inability to articulate or understand speech.

apparent movement Illusions of movement created by presentations of stationary visual stimuli in rapid succession.

approach-approach conflict Conflict between two desirable goals.

approach-avoidance conflict Conflict in which the same goal has both a positive and negative valence for the person, that is, is appealing in some respects and repulsive in others.

arithmetic mean The statistical measure of central tendency derived by adding up the scores in a distribution and dividing that sum by the total number of scores.

ascribed membership Group membership which is accorded automatically, that is, in which the person has no choice as to whether or not to "belong" to the group. Often referred to as *attributed membership.*

assault treatments The whole variety of "shock" procedures used in treatment of behavior disorders.

assertive training The *counterconditioning* method used in treatment of people who are easily intimidated by others.

assessment Measurement or evaluation.

associative (internuncial) neurons The "connecting wires" of the *central nervous system* which serve to connect neurons to one another.

association areas Those areas of the brain which integrate and interpret the information received from all the different senses.

asthenic personality The personality pattern characterized by a tendency to be fatigued easily, low in energy, and unenthusiastic.

attachment The tendency to stay close to and seek attention and soothing from a familiar person, such as occurs between an infant and its mother.

attention The mechanism by which *perception* is focused on certain features of a stimulus field, with the remaining signals being filtered out as background "noise."

attitude A person's disposition to feel, think, and act in a certain way.

attitude scales Instruments for measuring attitudes.

auditory area That area of the cortex of the brain located in the *temporal lobe*—which apparently plays an important role in the control of auditory processes. Stimulation of a part of this area known as the "interpretive cortex" results in the experience of auditory impressions from the individual's past.

autism A childhood disorder characterized by a severe inclination toward social withdrawal, absorption in fantasy, and profound disruption of language and thought.

autistic thinking A mode of thought reflecting wishes and desires of the thinker rather than realistic perceptions of the world.

autokinetic effect The apparent movement of a stationary point of light in a dark room.

autonomic nervous system A system of nerve fibers from the spinal cord, subordinate to the *central nervous system,* regulating glandular and smooth muscle (generally involuntary) activities.

aversive conditioning Conditioning procedures which involve the use of painful stimuli.

avoidance-avoidance conflict Conflict in which the individual is confronted with a choice between two unwanted goals with the seeming impossibility of escaping one without getting trapped in the undesirable consequences of the other.

axon The end of the nerve cell (*neuron*) from which electrical impulses are transmitted to other *neurons.*

balance theory The theory of *attitude* change designed to explain how people harmonize their positive and negative thoughts about related objects.

behavior genetics That area of psychology which focuses on the effects of biological heredity on behavior.

behavior therapy Psychotherapeutic methods concentrating on the treatment of symptoms rather than the understanding of motives, using the principles of learning as guidelines for planning therapeutic efforts.

being motives (B-motives) Motives toward psychological growth or self-actualization at the upper end of the hierarchy of human motives; they can be felt and acted on only after the deficiency motives (*D-motives*) are satisfied.

binocular parallax Aspect of vision in which the distance between the eyes gives the perceiver two somewhat different perspectives on the visual location of an object, thus providing a three-dimensional (stereoscopic) cue to depth or distance.

biofeedback The procedures in which individuals are trained to have voluntary control over internal physiological processes which are normally involuntary (e.g., their own brain-wave patterns). Involves the application of *instrumental conditioning* techniques providing the person with instantly monitored information about such physiological processes as they are occurring.

biological rhythms Patterns of physiological and

metabolic activity that follow various geophysical cycles.

brightness constancy The tendency for a familiar object to be perceived as unchanging in brightness in spite of changes in its illumination by surrounding light.

bulemia Compulsive overeating.

Cannon-Bard theory A theory of emotion named for the two scientists who developed it. Emphasizes the role of the *hypothalamus* in mediating emotional arousal.

cardinal traits In Allport's theory of personality, those traits of people so important that they influence everything they do.

caste system The most rigid form of social organization, in which *status* is always attributed.

catatonic schizophrenia A form of *schizophrenia* characterized by stupor, in which the person is mute and motionless.

central fissure A large crack on the top of each cerebral hemisphere of the brain separating the *frontal* and *parietal lobes*.

centrality The extent to which an *attitude* supports a person's important values.

centralized system A communication network or form of social organization in which responsibility and power may ultimately be traced back to a single source rather than being diffused among many people.

Central Nervous System (CNS) The brain and spinal cord in vertebrates.

central traits In Allport's theory of personality, those traits of individuals subordinate in importance to the cardinal ones, but still influencing much of their behavior.

cerebral cortex The convoluted (i.e., folded and wrinkled) outer surface of the cerebrum in the brain. This area, divided into two halves called *hemispheres*, apparently controls most of the higher functions.

cerebrotonic personality In the Sheldon-Kretschmer theory, the personality type characterized by a tendency to be restrained, cautious, sensitive, and intellectual.

cerebrum The "new brain," which is the center of all higher mental processes including perception, memory, reasoning, and volition (decision-making).

chain communication pattern A simple, one-way transmission from one individual to the next, and so forth.

chemical receptors The organs responsive to the sensations of taste and smell.

choleric The temperamental trait or type characterized by irritability.

chunking The basic coding process in *memory* in which percepts are organized into units or chunks.

circle communication pattern Path in which the flow of communication moves from one group member to another and circulates throughout the system.

classical conditioning A procedure for training or modifying involuntary processes. Results in the acquisition of a response to a neutral (or *conditional*) stimulus which was, before training, associated with another stimulus called the *unconditional stimulus*.

clinical psychology That branch of applied psychology specializing in the testing, diagnosis, and treatment of people with emotional problems and behavior disorders.

closure A perceptual grouping principle which refers to the tendency for the perceiver to somehow fill in the gaps between sensory events or group them together so that a closed, continuous unit is perceived.

cochlea A fluid-filled tube in the inner ear lined with tiny hairs from which auditory impulses are transmitted to the brain through the auditory nerve.

coding The mental process which facilitates *memory* through the generation and application of rules for defining and counting units of information.

cognate languages Language cousins based on the same historical mother tongue.

cognitive dissonance theory The variant of *balance theory* which postulates that an inconsistency between two ideas creates a feeling of discomfort and conflict referred to as "dissonance," which is reduced by the person changing their behavior or their thinking.

color constancy The tendency for a familiar object to be perceived as unchanging in its color in spite of changes in its illumination by surrounding light.

color spectrum The measured range of wavelengths of light.

common fate The Gestalt grouping principle which refers to the tendency for individual objects to be perceived as a single whole if they move together, whether or not they are connected.

common law A group of social norms which have the status of law but which have not been made into explicit rules because it is assumed that they are known to everyone.

community psychology That branch of applied psychology specializing in the human ecology of urban society. Objectives include research into community action strategies designed to facilitate adjustment of the individual to the social environment, and to create environments more optimally suited to the actualization of human potential.

comparative psychology That branch of *psychology* which compares the behavior of various species of animals to each other and to behavior of the human animal.

compensation In psychoanalytic theory, the ego defensive process whereby people somehow "makes up for" their deficiencies and inferiority feelings by striving for superiority along certain lines.

compulsions Ritualistic behavior which a person feels they must carry out, even though it may seem senseless.

compulsive personality That personality pattern characterized by tenseness, rigidity, superconscientiousness, and an obsession with trivial details.

concept A word representing several things having a single property or characteristic—i.e., a word which represents an idea.

condensation According to Freud, a form of concealment of *latent content* of dreams in *manifest content* in which several different themes are collapsed into a single word or image.

conditional (conditioned) response In *classical conditioning*, the acquired response to a *conditional stimulus* resulting from repeated pairing of that conditional stimulus with an *unconditional stimulus*.

conditional (conditioned) stimulus In *classical conditioning*, the stimulus which, through repeated pairing with another stimulus called the *unconditional stimulus*, comes to evoke a response similar to the one originally evoked by that unconditional stimulus.

conditioning An elementary form of learning, in which new connections are learned between stimuli and responses.

confidence limits The range of scores within which we would expect most sample means to fall if they were drawn from the same population.

cones Cells in the *retina* of the eye used for normal day vision, color vision, and sensitivity to fine detail.

conflict Difficulty in choosing among incompatible goals.

congenital Characteristics of a newborn infant that are present at birth.

congruity theory The variant of *balance theory* which postulates that a state referred to as "congruity" exists when the relationship among a person's thoughts are harmonious, and "incongruity" occurs when they are not.

consciousness The states of awareness, varying on a continuum of arousal from sleep at the low end to excitement at the high end.

consensual validation The tendency for people to try to determine the extent to which their own private perceptions of reality agree with the perceptions of others.

consonance In *cognitive dissonance theory*, the extent to which different *attitudes* are consistent with each other.

construct validity The meaningfulness of a test in terms of some abstract idea or principle, even if there is no practical standard by which to judge it.

continuity The perceptual grouping principle which refers to the tendency for the eye to follow continuous contours and to disregard abruptly changing ones.

control group That group in an experiment to which the experimental treatment is not applied.

conventional morality In Kohlberg's theory, the stage in moral development during which children want to "be good" at first in order to gain social approval, and later out of a sense of duty to maintain the social order.

conversion hysteria A disorder in which a person suddenly loses physical function or develops physical symptoms without organic basis.

cornea The tough, convex-shaped membrane which bends together light rays entering the eye.

correlation coefficient A numerical index of the strength of the relationship between two variables.

counseling psychology That branch of applied psychology specializing in information and guidance services in educational, occupational, vocational, and marital planning and adjustment.

counterconditioning The *behavior therapy* technique which aims to replace one feeling or behavior with another that is opposite to it.

covert rehearsal That form of practice in which verbal material is studied silently by the learner.

crackerjack effect "Tastes like more." The tendency for the taste of food to stimulate appetite; the operation of incentive motives.

creole language A hybrid language which becomes a mother tongue for later generations.

cretinism That form of *mental retardation* resulting from a thyroid gland deficiency.

criterion validity The accuracy of a test in making some practical predictions.

critical period A *sensitive period* of growth during which presumably irreversible behavior patterns are acquired.

cross-sectional method Where different strata of people are compared on a particular behavior. Identified with the *normative* or *nomothetic* approaches to the study of *individual differences.*

cultural-familial retardation Refers to those forms of *mental retardation* resulting from environmental conditions.

culture The body of common learning transmitted by a group from one generation to another. An integral component of man's evolutionary development.

culture-bound tests Tests on which performance depends on culturally determined learning experiences to which the person has been exposed.

culture-fair tests Intelligence tests which have been developed to minimize the extent to which performance depends on culturally determined learning experiences of the individual.

cutaneous receptors The skin senses of pressure, heat, cold, and pain.

cycles per second Units in terms of which the frequency of a wave is measured; abbreviated cps or Hz.

cyclothymic personality That personality pattern characterized by manic or depressive tendencies in a person who is not psychotic.

Darwinian Reflex The grasping reflex in a newborn infant.

data Information gathered in an empirical study.

decibels Units in terms of which the loudness of a sound is measured; abbreviated *db.*

decompensation The process of disorganization and deterioration which may result from exposure to severe or long-endured stress.

deficiency motives (*D-motives*) Those motives, such as the physiological needs for food, air, and water, which must be satisfied before higher human motives (*B-motives*) can be felt or acted on.

delusions False beliefs which resist all disconfirming argument or evidence.

demand characteristics The features of a situation which color people's expectations and lead them to act accordingly, especially in laboratory research in psychology.

dendrite That portion of the nerve cell (neuron) through which electrical impulses are received from other *neurons.*

denial In psychoanalytic theory, the ego defense mechanism involving a refusal to accept a negative evaluation of oneself, or of something one values.

dependent variable In an *experiment,* the thing that happens as a result of the experimental manipulation.

depression The psychological condition characterized by feelings of despair and guilt.

detection threshold A level of stimulus intensity detected by most people only 50 percent of the time under laboratory conditions.

development Refers to change over time throughout the whole sequence of life, from conception to death.

developmental psychology That branch of psychology dealing with psychological changes over the course of individual development. Traditionally, emphasis has been on the study of physical-maturational growth trends in children and corresponding changes in intelligence and personality.

dialect A recognizable variant of a language.

differential threshold The minimal degree of change or difference in stimulation necessary for a person to notice it. Referred to as the "just-noticeable-difference (j.n.d.)."

discrimination The behavior which expresses

prejudice by treating members of a given group badly.

displacement (1) According to Freud, a form of concealment of *latent content* of dreams in *manifest content* in which one object represents a related object. (2) The ego-defense mechanism involving the transfer of feelings or actions from their original, anxiety-provoking object to a less frightening one.

dissociative reaction A form of hysterical *neurosis* in which the person somehow separates themself from threatening thoughts.

dissonance reduction In *cognitive dissonance theory*, a process whereby a person reconciles their conflicting attitudes and actions by making them consistent with one another.

drive The tension experienced as the psychological counterpart of a tissue *need*.

dual coding hypothesis The hypothesis which assumes that both verbal and imagery coding are used to store some verbal information.

dynamic psychiatry The psychiatric orientation which emphasizes the search for psychological causes of behavior disorders.

dynamic theories Theories which emphasize the contributions of childhood social-environmental processes to the development of adult personality.

eardrum The taut membrane at the end of the ear canal which transmits vibrations from movements in the air to the middle ear.

ecological niche A "place" within the natural organism-environment scheme of things that can be defined in terms of characteristics required for the survival of any of its inhabitants.

ecology The contemporary balance of stress and adaptation among living things and their environment.

ectomorphic body type In the Sheldon-Kretschmer theory, the tall, thin body type associated with the *cerebrotonic personality*.

educational treatment Forms of treatment for psychological disorders involving instruction and/or demonstration. Mainly remedial training of skills such as reading and speech.

efferent (or motor) neurons Nerve cells which transmit impulses from the *central nervous system* toward the muscles and *glands*.

ego In psychoanalytic theory, the component of personality that governs one's realistic, rational behavior, trying to get the most pleasure out of life at the least cost.

ego anxiety In psychoanalytic theory, any threat to disrupt the balance between the demands of an individual's id impulses and the restrictions of their conscience (superego).

ego defenses In psychoanalytic theory, the personality mechanisms by which the individual's perception of reality is distorted in such a way as to reduce threats to their self-esteem.

eidetic imagery The sharpest form of *imagery*, in which the person imagines something more as if they were actually looking at it than as if they were merely remembering it. Not common in children and even rarer in adults.

electroconvulsive therapy (ECT) An *assault treatment* consisting of the delivery of tiny electric shocks into the brain.

electroencephalograph (EEG) A device for measuring electrical activity in the brain.

emotional instability The personality pattern characterized by poor control over excited emotions. Sometimes referred to as hysterical or histrionic personality.

emotional insulation In psychoanalytic theory, the process whereby a person reduces their emotional involvement in painful situations.

emotions States of physiological arousal accompanied by subjective feelings and attitudes—e.g., anger, fear, etc.

empiricist philosophy The view that perception is essentially learned.

endogenous retardation *Mental retardation* resulting from biological disorders. Also called *primary retardation*.

endorphins Opiate-like substances produced by the brain.

endomorphic body type In the Sheldon-Kretschmer theory, the short, fat body type associated with the *viscerotonic personality*.

energizing drugs Also referred to as "activators," "stimulants," "antidepressants," and "uppers"; produce alertness, euphoria, appetite-depression, and some ill effects. Include caffeine, nicotine, amphetamines such as dexadrine, benzadrine, methadrine, and others.

engineering psychology That branch of applied psychology specializing in improving the design of machinery, tools, and work environments so as to maximize safety and efficiency of human functioning in the work situation. Often called "human factors" psychology.

engrams *Memory* traces.

enuresis Bedwetting.

epigenetic view The developmental view which emphasizes the interaction between heredity and environment.

epilepsy A disturbance in the electrical activity of the brain that produces convulsions and seizures.

epistemology That branch of philosophy which deals with how knowledge is obtained.

error rejection The *memory* search-mechanism by which an incorrect response is dismissed or corrected by the person before receiving any external information showing it is incorrect.

ESB Techniques for controlling behavior through direct *Electrical Stimulation of the Brain* by means of surgically implanted electrodes.

Esperanto An artificial language, a combination of European languages, developed to facilitate international communication.

estrus Sexual "heat" or receptivity to sexual activity in female animals. Occurs only during ovulation in lower animals, but is virtually independent of the fertility cycle in humans.

ethological method The *field-study* method of naturalistic observation of animal behavior.

ethology The naturalistic study of whole patterns of animal behavior.

evolution (1) The genetic process by which species change and by which one species emerges from another. (2) The theory and documentation of the dynamics of this process as first outlined by Darwin, involving three main principles: (a) *heredity* — the tendency for like to beget like; (b) *random variation* — the tendency toward wide variation in characteristics of members of the same species; and (c) *natural selection* — the idea of "survival of the fittest."

exhibitionism The compulsive desire to show off one's genitals.

existential crisis A crisis in which the meaning rather than the physical state of one's existence is somehow threatened.

experiment A method of controlled observation of relationships between variables.

experimental group That group in an *experiment* to which the *independent variable* i.e., the experimental manipulation, is applied.

experimental psychology That branch of psychology concerned with the biological and psychological foundations of behavior.

explosive personality The personality pattern characterized by uncontrollable outbursts of rage. Also referred to as the "epileptoid" personality.

extinction The decrease in strength of an acquired response due to nonreinforcement.

extinction methods The *behavior therapy* techniques which make head-on attacks on symptoms rather than being directed toward the replacement of old feelings with new ones.

extrovert In Jung's theory of personality, the socially outgoing type of individual who tends to be aroused primarily by external stimulation and interests and to evaluate things, including themselves, in terms of their interactions with the external environment.

eye/head system The system which allows for the perception of movement when the eye is following a moving target.

false negatives Instances where a test shows that some individuals lack a quality which they actually have.

false positives Instances where a test shows that some individuals have a characteristic which they really lack.

fear That emotion involving a temporary heightening of arousal accompanied by a tendency to withdraw or flee.

feeling-of-knowing The tendency for feeling that one knows the correct response to be associated with truly correct recollections.

feral children Youngsters raised in the wilds by animals or isolated by cruel or insane parents from the normal socialization process that occurs through interaction with people.

fetishism The sexual deviation characterized by a tendency to concentrate sexual attention on inanimate objects, or on things like hands or feet, rather than on people.

field experimentation Experiments conducted in the natural environment.

field study Observation and measurement of behavior as it occurs in a natural setting without any intentional interference with that situation.

figure-ground Refers to the tendency for human perceptions to be organized in such a way that certain features stand out as figure against the general background in which they appear.

fixation Failure to have completed the growth process appropriate to a particular stage of development.

forgetting The process by which memories are lost.

formal operations In Piaget's theory, the last stage of intellectual development, during which adult modes of thinking are manifested.

fraternal twins Twins conceived at the same time but developed from two separate fertilized egg cells (zygotes). (*See* identical twins.)

free association The main psychoanalytic method for exposing unconscious motives by getting the patient to say everything that comes into their mind.

free nerve endings Cutaneous receptors capable of producing the whole range of skin sensations—warmth, cold, touch, itching, tickling, and pain.

frontal lobe The portion of each cerebral hemisphere of the brain located in front of the central fissure.

frustration Refers to the existence of some obstacle blocking goal attainment.

fugue state A dissociative reaction in which the person runs away without knowing it.

functional disorders Disorders of behavior which involve no apparent physical defects.

functional group People mutually involved in achieving some common goal.

galvanic skin response (GSR) An index of resistance of the skin to the conductivity of electrical current. Often used as an objective index of emotional arousal.

general adaptation syndrome The stress response pattern which follows the alarm-resistance-exhaustion sequence.

genital stage In psychoanalytic theory, that *psychosexual* period beginning with puberty, which spans the whole period of adult maturity, and during which the capacity for love relationships and career aspirations are assumed to develop.

Gestalt psychology The school of thought whose advocates emphasize the idea that we are all born with a natural tendency to organize our experience in meaningful ways, as illustrated in the operation of the so-called "grouping principles" in human perception.

gestation The period of prenatal development from conception to birth.

glands Small internal organs that secrete chemical fluids called hormones, which regulate activities such as sexual behavior, crying, and sweating.

grand mal epilepsy The most common form of *epilepsy*, characterized by severe seizures which often produce complete loss of consciousness, intense convulsions, and some danger of injury. (See petit mal.)

group An organization of individuals with rules and customs governing their activities.

Guttman technique An *attitude* scaling procedure which employs a hierarchical order of questions, in which the answers at any given point on the scale imply the answers to all the points beneath it.

habit disorders Special symptoms that may be regarded as "bad habits" which often make their victims miserable enough to need professional help.

hallucinations Unusual perceptions and sensations, such as hearing voices when no one is around or seeing things that, to other people, aren't there.

hebephrenia The rarest schizophrenic *psychosis*, involving extreme regressive behavior and a constant silly grin.

hierarchical system A communication network or form of social organization involving different levels of responsibility, authority, and status.

hierarchy of motives An ordering of motives in terms of their relative importance to the organism.

hippocampus That area of the old brain which seems to control the transfer of impressions from short- to long-term *memory*.

holography The neophotographic technique in which light from every point in a scene is distributed to every point on the film. Suggested by Pribram as a model for representing the neurological processes by which *memory* and *perception* occur in living organisms.

homeostasis Refers to the mechanisms by which internal metabolic and chemical processes are regulated automatically such that a relatively constant or balanced environment is maintained within the body.

horizontal structure Multiplex attitudes in which the component ideas support each other, thus making the overall attitude highly resistant to change.

human nature Innate, biologically-determined patterns of human behavior.

hypermnesia An induced (e.g., by *hypnosis*) increase in *memory*.

hypnosis A voluntary relinquishing of normal critical faculties under which extraordinary cognitive, emotional, and physiological feats are often performed.

hypnotic age regression The phenomenon in which under *hypnosis,* a person re-experiences some event of their earlier life.

hypochondriasis A form of *somatization* characterized by complaints about vague aches and pains, constant seeking of medical attention, and related behavior.

hypoglycemia A blood sugar deficiency producing feelings of weakness and/or fainting spells.

hypothalamus A structure in the upper region of the brain stem which apparently controls a variety of motivational and emotional activities such as hunger, thirst, fighting, and making love.

hypothesis A tentative statement or educated guess about the relationship between two or more variables.

id In psychoanalytic theory, the component of personality that is the repository of instinctive urges such as hunger, thirst, warmth, and later on, sex, aggression, etc., which demand immediate gratification.

idealism The philosophical view that there may be no reality beyond our individual subjective perceptions. Often contrasted with the view known as *realism.*

identical twins Twins developed from a single fertilized egg cell (zygote).

identification Process of learning by observation and imitation in which the parents serve as models.

ideographic method That approach to the study of *individual differences* oriented to understanding of the individual event or person. Sometimes called the *ipsative* approach. Identified with *longitudinal studies* of behavior.

idioms Peculiarities of expression and meaning in a language which lose their meaning when translated literally into other languages.

image/retina system The system which allows for the perception of movement when the eyes are stationary and a moving object crosses the field of vision.

imagery The process by which mental pictures are constructed.

imagery dominance Refers to the type of image, visual, auditory, etc., experienced most frequently by a person.

images Mental pictures generally created in the absence of an immediate external stimulus.

implosive therapy The *behavior therapy* extinction procedure in which a patient is frightened as much as possible, without being hurt, until anxiety disappears.

imprinting Species-specific types of behavior patterns acquired during *sensitive periods* early in development—e.g., the inclination for certain species of chicks to follow around after their mother soon after birth.

inadequate personality The "sad-sack" personality, characterized by intellectual, social, and/or emotional ineptitude.

incentive A potential reward, reinforcer, or need-reducer.

independent variable In an experiment, that variable (usually a set of stimulus conditions) controlled and manipulated so as to determine its effects upon some other variable(s).

individual differences Refers to both (a) the political idea that people are obligated to honor the rights of others to differ from them and to grant them liberty and equal opportunity despite their differences; and (b) the technical, psychological study of differences between people in their responses to the same stimuli.

induced movement The perception of apparent movement of a stationary object caused by movement of its surroundings.

industrial psychology That branch of psychology specializing in problems pertaining to work, such as job efficiency, worker morale and productivity, and interpersonal relations between people in work settings.

inferential statistics That branch of statistics concerned with the techniques by which direct observations of representative cases may be used as a basis for making predictions or drawing generalizations about things which have not been observed directly.

ingroup A *reference group* with which a person identifies, and to which this person has a sense of belonging.

inner ear That portion of the ear from which auditory impulses are transmitted from the membrane called the "oval window" to the cochlea and in turn to the organ of Corti from which the signal is then relayed to the brain.

insight A dramatic form of learning, occurring without any apparent rehearsal, in which the solution to a problem is suddenly understood in what is called an "aha! experience."

insight therapy Psychotherapeutic approaches which assume that effective treatment requires helping clients to understand the hidden motives underlying their disordered behavior.

insomnia A state of overarousal in which one is unable to fall asleep or stay asleep long enough to feel rested.

instinct A whole, often quite complex, pattern of unlearned behavior triggered by a single stimulus which continues until its function is completed—e.g., nest-building in birds.

instrumental conditioning The learning of new responses which solve problems or provide relief. Referred to as "trial-and-error" learning of voluntary behavior, in which successful responses are reinforced, and unsuccessful ones are eliminated by nonreinforcement.

intellectualization In psychoanalytic theory, a form of emotional insulation in which some sort of intellectual means is used as an ego defense against threatening feelings.

intelligence quotient (IQ) An index of intelligence test performance. Calculated by dividing an individual's "mental age" test score by their chronological age, then multiplying by 100.

interconnectedness The extent to which an *attitude* is related to other attitudes.

interference theory The theory of forgetting which assumes that some memories get blocked by events preventing their recall.

Interlingua An artificial, written language used for scientific communication.

interoceptive conditioning The conditioning of physiological processes such as stomach contractions.

interpretation The psychotherapeutic technique in which the therapist explains to the patient the meaning of their thoughts, feelings, etc., as these things relate to their problems.

interpretive cortex A term used by the neurosurgeon Wilder Penfield to refer to the *temporal lobes,* in view of the apparent function of this area of the brain in the integration of different impressions of the senses into meaningful experiences.

interval scale An instrument without an absolute zero in which differences between all points on the scale are equal.

introjection In psychoanalytic theory, adoption of the beliefs or attitudes of powerful figures after an initial period of resistance to them.

introvert In Jung's theory of personality, the socially withdrawn persons who tend to look within themself for their main source of stimulation.

ipsative method That approach to the study of *individual differences* which focuses on the behavior of the same person in different situations. Sometimes described as the *ideographic* approach. Identified with *longitudinal method* of studying behavior.

iris The two sets of muscles which regulate the amount of light entering the eye.

isolation In psychoanalytic theory, the ego defense process whereby incompatible beliefs or values are maintained without producing constant conflict by somehow keeping them separated within one's belief system.

item reliability Evaluation of the reliability of an assessment procedure by comparing the responses of people to the same questions asked in different ways.

Jacksonian epilepsy Like *grand mal epilepsy,* except that the seizures typically start in one part of the body and spread as they become more intense.

James-Lange theory A theory of emotion named for the two people who independently developed it. Proposes that the physiological changes or visceral events occurring in response to a given stimulus produces the experience of emotion.

kinesthetic receptors Nerve endings located in the body joints that are sensitive to movement of joints and muscles in the body. Such sensitivity (sometimes called "kinesthesia") is essential for maintaining balance and posture and the coordination of muscle activities.

lability Volatility or instability of moods or mental processes such as images which tend to come into and go out of consciousness with relative ease.

laboratory A specially designed environment in which conditions can be manipulated so as to achieve maximum control over selected variables in order to identify their relationships with other variables of interest.

latency In psychoanalytic theory, that period in development starting in the sixth or seventh year and lasting until puberty during which nothing much happens in terms of psychosexual development.

latent content According to Freud, the underlying content of a dream which is disguised or hidden in the *manifest* or *surface content* of the dream.

latent learning A type of learning which occurs in the absence of any apparent reinforcement.

lateral fissure A deep crack on the side of each cerebral hemisphere of the brain, below which is located the temporal lobe.

laws Social norms which have been made explicit in a society.

learning A more or less permanent change in behavior occurring as a result of experience rather than maturation.

lens The structure which adjusts so as to focus light precisely on the retina of the eye.

lexicon In a language, the words or sounds used to symbolize the various meanings.

Likert-type scale A type of *attitude scale* designed to measure a person's own degree of positive or negative attitude toward something rather than assuming that their statements mean the same thing that judges have thought they meant.

limbic system A set of structures in the upper region of the brain stem apparently involved in the control of a variety of motivational and emotional functions.

linear perspective The observations in horizontal distance that appear to make objects shrink and parallel lines converge.

lingua franca An international language, usually a trade or commerce language.

linguistics The study of language.

locus of control The extent to which a person sees the control of events in their own life as resting within theirself, or in forces outside of the self.

longitudinal method Where the behavior of the same person is measured at different periods in time to determine how much variation that individual shows from one occasion to the next. Identified with the *ipsative* or *ideographic* approaches to the study of *individual differences*.

LSD D-lysergic acid diethylamide, a powerful drug derived from a fungus which infects rye. Produces elation, pleasure, hallucinations or agitation, and an occasional psychotic reaction.

manic behavior An overdriven "busyness" in work or play which blocks out feelings of anxiety, depression, or hostility.

manic psychosis That form of *psychosis* in which the person is overactive, excited, and elated. Sometimes called "hypomania."

manifest content According to Freud, the content of a dream as it is recalled by the person, and from which the *latent content* can be inferred.

masochism Deriving sexual pleasure from being hurt.

maturational view The developmental perspective which sees development chiefly as the unfolding of the built-in genetic codes which evolution has created.

maturation The process of physical development of the organism, primarily a product of biological or hereditary factors.

median The statistical measure of central tendency which is the middle score in a distribution.

medical treatment Chemical and/or physical treatments for psychological disorders.

meditation The rituals of self-discipline in Zen Buddhism in which the person concentrates intensely on nothing, and the techniques aimed at complete control of body functions via controlled breathing in the Yoga system.

melancholic The temperamental trait or type characterized by depression.

memory The capacity for storage and retrieval of information.

memory span The absorption capacity of short-term memory.

mental growth periods Stages in Piaget's theory of cognitive development

mental retardation A condition involving insufficient intelligence to get along without special training or institutional care.

mescaline A natural hallucinogenic drug, derived from the flowering heads of the peyote cactus.

mesomorphic body type In the Sheldon-Kretschmer theory, the muscular body type associated with the *somatotonic personality*.

methadone A synthetic *opiate* used in the treatment of heroine addiction. It is addicting.

microcephaly A form of *mental retardation* characterized by impaired development of the brain and an abnormally small head.

middle ear That part of the ear containing the three tiny bones called the hammer, anvil, and stirrup, through which auditory impulses are amplified and transmitted to the oval window of the inner ear.

mnemonics The intentional use of mediating processes for enhancing memory.

mode The statistical measure of central tendency which indicates the most frequently occurring score in a distribution.

mongolism The most common kind of moderate and severe *mental retardation*.

motion parallax A perceptual distance cue produced by apparent differences in speed.

motivation Internal processes regulating the arousal, integration, and direction of purposeful behavior.

motor area That area of the *cerebral cortex* of the brain which apparently controls voluntary muscle activity. Located in the *frontal lobe,* just in front of the *central fissure.*

movement aftereffect Situation in which the sudden cessation of movement of an object in a given direction gives rise to the perception of movement in the opposite direction.

multiple personality A very rare, dramatic *dissociative reaction* in which the person develops two or more distinct personalities.

multiplexity Refers to the number of component parts of an attitude.

mutation A radical transformation of a gene resulting in the formation of a new characteristic, or even a new species.

myelin sheath The "insulating" layer of fatty tissue covering *neurons.*

naive realism The belief that our senses convey directly to us accurate impressions of reality.

name A word representing a single thing.

natural language A language which develops without any plan by being spoken rather than composed.

nature-nurture controversy The longstanding debate over the extent to which behavior traits (e.g., intelligence, temperament) are determined by characteristics which are inborn or innate to the biological nature of the organism, or learned as a result of the experiences to which that organism is exposed.

need A state of homeostatic disequilibrium due to physiological deficit in body tissues.

neonate a newborn infant.

neoteny The theory that, unlike other species, humans maintain an infantile capacity to learn throughout life, whereas this capacity diminishes rapidly in other animals as they mature.

nerves Bundles of *neurons.*

neurasthenia Constant feelings of weakness and fatigue without apparent organic basis.

neurologizing The analysis of all psychological processes through reference to brain physiology.

neuron The nerve cell, or basic element of the *central nervous system.* A highly specialized cell by means of which information is transmitted in the form of electrical impulses.

neuroses Functional behavior disorders with no medical component, and anxiety as the main symptom. Generally among the most treatable of behavior disorders.

nominal scaling Grouping things in some qualitative way.

nomothetic method That approach to the study of individual differences which seeks general laws of behavior. Applied to the design of individual difference measures which aim for high construct validity.

nonsense syllable A meaningless word-like letter sequence. Used in experimental studies of learning and memory.

normal distribution A symmetrical or bell-shaped distribution of scores.

normative method Method for the study of individual differences which focuses on comparisons of the same behavior among different people, called *cross-sectional* studies of behavior.

nuclear family The unit consisting of two parents and the children they bear. The smallest *primary group*, also called the "primary kinship group."

null hypothesis The statistical hypothesis that an observed difference is due to chance factors.

objective tests Those tests with specific questions having right and wrong answers.

obsessions Persistent thoughts that interfere with the person's normal activity.

obsessive-compulsive reactions Ego-defensive forms of thought or action repeated over and over again, to prevent the person from being overwhelmed by anxiety.

occipital lobe That portion of each cerebral hemisphere of the brain located behind the *parietal* and *temporal lobes*.

omission behavior The memory search mechanism in which a memory is not reported due to uncertainty about its correctness.

operant conditioning The best known form of instrumental conditioning, also referred to as "behavior shaping." Works by the principle of *successive approximation*.

operant technology The use of behavior shaping or *operant conditioning* to solve practical problems.

opiates Drugs such as opium, morphine, and heroin, derived from the common poppy, producing temporarily altered states of consciousness.

oral stage In psychoanalytic theory, the first of the *psychosexual stages* of development, occurring in the first year of life, during which the mouth is the body zone that serves as the center of pleasurable activity.

ordinal scale A measurement which puts things in order from first to last but does not tell how much difference there is between them.

organic behavior disorders Disorders involving damage to the *central nervous system*.

organic psychiatry The psychiatric orientation which emphasizes the search for physical causes of behavior disorders.

organic theories Theories which emphasize structural or biological determinants of adult personality.

organismic theories Personality theories which propose that human development is aimed at the fulfillment of an inherent need for seeking meaningful goals in life. Often referred to as the "holistic" or "humanistic" theories.

orienting response The alerting response to a stimulus above the absolute threshold.

outgroup Any group which a person considers not their own. Generally a group that has some attributes which set it apart from one's own group.

overlearning Practice of a task or skill beyond the point at which mastery has been achieved.

overt rehearsal Form of practice in which verbal material is repeated and reviewed aloud by the learner.

paradoxical thermal sensation The elicitation of a cold sensation produced by applying a warm stimulus to certain spots on the skin, or vice versa.

parameter A variable with a range of possible value that delimits a population of events.

paranoid personality The name given a person who is rigid and hypersensitive about themselves, suspicious of other peoples' motives, jealous, self-inflated, and tending to blame others for things.

paranoid schizophrenia The most common form of *schizophrenia;* primary symptoms include delusions of persecution and bizarre thinking.

parasympathetic division The part of the *autonomic nervous system* that controls relaxation or quiescent states of the organism. It complements the functions of the sympathetic division.

parietal lobe That portion of each cerebral hemisphere of the brain located behind the *central fissure* and between the *frontal* and *occipital lobes*.

passive-aggressive personality Personality pattern characterized by a combination of great dependency with great hostility toward the people depended upon.

passive dependency The tendency to behave helplessly in most life situations.

patterning processes Those perceptual processes which seem designed to permit rapid interpretations of sensory data.

perception The interpretive process by which sensory information is invested with meaning.

perceptual constancy Those perceptual mechanisms which produce the experience of continuity and stability of sense impressions — e.g., *brightness, color,* and *size constancy.*

perceptual grouping and patterning Organizing principles in human perception, such as *proximity, similarity,* and *closure.*

perceptual selectivity The reaction in which attention tends to be focused on some objects in a sensory field more than on others. The determinants include stimulus intensity, contrast, and change.

perceptual set A learned predisposition to perceive in a particular way.

perceptual style The constellation of personal characteristics, past experiences, and current motives of the individual which produces its own, unique mode of perceiving.

personality That area of psychology which deals with enduring behavior traits.

personnel psychology That area of applied psychology, specializing in problems such as vocational choice, aptitudes, interests, and the selection and training of employees.

petit mal epilepsy That form of *epilepsy* characterized by relatively mild seizures involving partial loss of consciousness and small convulsions.

phallic stage In psychoanalytic theory, the third stage in *psychosexual* development, beginning around age four or five, and during which period the child's feelings of pleasure start to center on the genital area.

phantom limb pain A feeling of sensation in a limb which has been amputated.

phenylketonuria (PKU) A form of *mental retardation* which results from the lack of a vital enzyme.

phi phenomenon The illusion of movement created (e.g., in "motion pictures") by the tendency of the visual movement detectors to fill in the blank spaces between lights flashed in rapid succession.

phlegmatic The temperamental trait or type characterized by calmness, imperturbability, and perhaps sluggishness.

phobia An intense fear, often of things considered harmless by most people.

phonology The intonation and pronunciation patterns of a language.

photographic memory *Eidetic imagery* in an adult.

photoreceptors Light-sensitive cells (the rods and cones) in the retina of the eye.

phrenology A 19th century theory of personality, now commonly regarded as pseudoscience, which said that individual differences in traits of character could be measured by studying the shape and contours of a person's head.

physiological psychology That branch of psychology which deals with the behavioral effects of physiological and anatomical processes and structures.

pidgin (patois) A trade language consisting of a blend of other languages.

placebos Phony techniques which appear to be real treatments but are not intended to be.

politics The exercise of leadership over a group.

postconventional morality In Kohlberg's theory, that stage in moral development during which a respect for moral principles emerges.

preconventional morality In Kohlberg's theory, the first two stages of moral development, during which rules are obeyed, first, to avoid punishment, and, next, to gain rewards.

prefrontal lobotomy Partial surgical separation of the frontal brain lobes from the thalamus. A procedure used quite frequently in the late 1930s and 1940s to calm down unmanageable patients, but now widely regarded as involving greater risk than potential benefit to the patient.

prejudice Attitudes that dispose a person unfavorably toward a group.

primacy In persuasion, refers to the first argument presented.

primary group The *nuclear family.* The basic unit of social organization in most human societies.

primary motives Physiological motives whose fulfillment is essential for survival, such as hunger and thirst.

primary odors The seven odors from which all other olfactory sensations have been found to derive: camphoraceous, musky, floral, pepperminty, ethereal, pungent, and putrid.

primary process Primitive imagery-dominated thinking reflecting the wishes and desires of the thinker rather than realistic perceptions of the world.

proactive inhibition The forgetting of things recently learned due to interference from prior learning.

probability theory The mathematical study of the likelihood of occurrences of events by chance alone. Provides the basis for tests of statistical significance, and thus for decisions and inferences about the dependability of research outcomes.

projection In psychoanalytic theory, the ego-defense mechanism which involves the attribution of one's own ideas, feelings, or attitudes to other people.

projective test A test in which the characteristics of interest are measured obliquely so that the individual is unaware of the kinds of inferences to be made from their responses.

prosocial behavior Behavior which serves the adaptational interests of the species—e.g., affection, altruism, cooperation, etc.

proximity A perceptual grouping principle; the tendency for sensory events which occur contiguously (close together) to be perceived as somehow belonging together.

psychedelic drugs The so-called "consciousness-expanding" drugs, such as marijuana, hashish and LSD.

psychology From the Greek words "psyche," meaning soul, mind, or spirit, and "logos," meaning study or discuss. Thus, literally, the "study of the mind." Most commonly defined now as "the science of behavior."

psychomotor epilepsy That form of *epilepsy* involving small lapses of consciousness, usually for just a few seconds, while the person continues activity.

psychophysics The study of relationships between physical characteristics of stimuli as they impinge on sense receptor organs and the psychological processes evoked by such sensory events—e.g., studies of relationships between physical intensity of a stimulus and evaluations of its intensity by the person to whom it is presented.

psychosexual stages In psychoanalytic theory, the stages of personality development, defined in terms of the body zone (oral, anal, genital) which functions as the main source of pleasurable feeling during that period.

psychosis The modern term for insanity. Considered the most serious of the behavior disorders in that it often requires hospitalization of the individual who has lost contact with reality.

psychosocial stages The stages of human development postulated in Erikson's theory; covers the entire life span.

psychosomatic disorders Physical ailments such as ulcers or migraine headaches which have a psychological basis.

psychosomatic pain The experience of pain in the absence of any identifiable physical basis for the painful sensation.

psychosurgery A term once used to refer only to prefrontal lobotomy, but which has come to mean brain surgery done for the purpose of changing behavior.

psychotherapy All treatments of psychological disorders which rely primarily on talking to produce their effects.

psychotropic drugs Drugs used to alter a patient's mood.

puberty The period in human development when boys and girls develop the physical characteristics of adulthood.

pupil The opening through which light enters the eye.

range The statistical measure of variability given by the difference between the lowest and highest scores in a distribution.

rationalization In psychoanalytic theory, the ego-defense mechanism involving the invention of fictitious reasons for one's own irrational, immoral, or inept behavior.

rationalist philosophy In the psychology of perception, the view that ideas (percepts) are inborn.

ratio scales Measuring instruments with an absolute zero point, with the units of measurement from that point being identical to each other.

reaction formation In psychoanalytic theory, the ego-defensive action process involving exaggerated action or attitudes in the opposite direction from one's genuine, underlying motives and feelings.

realism The philosophical view that human perceptions are interpretations of objective reality. Often contrasted with the view known as *idealism*.

recall The capability for repeating a response; one form of memory.

recency In persuasion, refers to the last argument presented.

recognition The capability for identifying the criterion events from among alternative events; a second form of memory.

redintegration A special kind of recall in which past events are reconstructed from single details.

reference group Any group to which one refers in one's thoughts, feelings, or discussion.

reflex An unlearned, fixed, specific, and automatic reaction of muscles or glands to the stimulation of a specific group of nerves. The most elementary form of organized behavior—e.g., the pupillary contraction response to a light stimulus, the knee-jerk response to a tap on the tendon just below the knee.

refractory period A period of temporary inactivity of a neuron following an excitation (firing) of that nerve cell.

regression In psychoanalytic theory, the ego-defensive process of action whereby a person returns to a developmentally earlier, immature mode of behavior.

reinforcement Stimulation following a response which strengthens or increases the probability of that response when the situation recurs.

relearning A recovery from long-term storage of memories which seem to have been forgotten altogether.

release mechanism The stimulus that triggers or sets off an instinctive pattern of behavior.

reliability The dependability or consistency of an assessment.

REM sleep That stage in sleep during which the eyeball twitches rapidly from side to side (rapid eye movement), and during which dreams apparently occur.

remembering The process by which memories are retrieved or recovered.

repression In psychoanalytic theory, the basic ego-defense mechanism out of which all of the others are developed; a forcing out of consciousness of anxiety-provoking thoughts.

response Reaction to a stimulus.

reticular formation (reticular activating system) An ill defined structure near the bottom of the brain stem which is apparently involved in the regulation of consciousness and attention.

retina The light sensitive surface of the eye at which light waves are converted into electro-chemical impulses that are carried to the brain by way of the optic nerve.

retroactive inhibition The forgetting of events learned earlier due to subsequent learning.

risky-shift phenomenon The tendency for decisions made by a group to be more extreme than those which the individual members would make on their own.

ritalin An energizing drug used extensively to calm down hyperactive children.

RNA Ribonucleic acid. A cellular nucleic acid which has been studied for its possible utility in facilitating memory.

rods Cells in the retina of the eye sensitive to achromatic light (i.e., only black, white, and shades of grey), particularly important in night and peripheral vision.

role A behavior pattern expected of people according to their social position.

rooting reflex The reflexive tendency of a newborn infant to turn its head and begin to suck as the side of its mouth is stimulated.

rote learning Memorization which is achieved by repetition alone without the support of associative or mediational processes.

sadism Deriving sexual pleasure from hurting someone.

sampling error Mistaken judgments due to observation not representative of the general class of events of interest.

sanguine The temperamental trait or type characterized by cheerfulness and good humoredness.

scapegoating A displacement of aggression, typically against innocent and helpless people who are blamed or made to suffer for frustrations of the scapegoater.

Schachter-Singer theory A theory of emotion named for the two scientists who jointly developed it. The theory emphasizes the importance of cognitive and social factors in determining emotional experience.

schemes In Piaget's theory of cognitive development, mental images symbolizing reality.

schizoid personality The personality pattern characterized by emotional aloofness, shallowness, and possibly eccentricity, but without the disordered thinking or other symptoms of schizophrenia.

schizophrenia A *psychosis* involving thought disorder reflected in distortions in thinking and perception, along with emotional withdrawal (flattened affect).

school psychology That branch of applied psychology specializing in problems of children in the school situation.

secondary group A group in which membership is based on some common interest or purpose.

secondary motives Motives not directly needed to sustain life or reproduce; mostly learned in a social context—e.g., the desire for wealth, prestige, or power.

secondary process An expression used by Freud to describe realistic, rational thinking aimed at problem solving rather than the creation of wish-fulfilling fantasies.

secondary sex characteristics Sexual physiological characteristics not directly related to sexual behavior or childbearing capacities—e.g., mammary glands in girls, and a deepening of the voice in boys.

self-actualization One of the higher order, learned motives in terms of which one's life goals are defined. Refers specifically to the tendency toward maximum fulfillment of one's potential.

self-concept The person's evaluation of themself. Also called "self-image."

self-esteem How highly an individual values themself.

semantic differential A technique for studying the affective as well as the intellectual side of attitudes by having the person rate things according to such qualities as good or bad, strong or weak, etc.

semantic generalization Conditioned responses to words of responses previously made only to objects or other words.

semantics The system of word meanings in a language.

sensation The mechanisms by which sense organs receive and process information about events occurring both within and outside of the body.

sense organs Receptors of the various forms of stimulus input which the organism is capable of sensing—e.g., the eyes, ears, etc.

sensitive periods Periods of time in the development of an organism which are optimal for the learning of particular response patterns. Prior to this period it may be too early and afterward it may be too late for adequate development of the relevant behavior.

sensorimotor period The period in human cognitive development which, in Piaget's theory, is assumed to extend from birth to about 18 months.

sensory adaptation The reduction in attention or sensitivity to an unchanging level of stimulation.

sensory deprivation Refers to experimental studies of adults under conditions of prolonged exposure to minimal sensory stimulation.

sex-role (or *sex typed*) behavior Behavior considered appropriate for individuals of each sex in any given cultural context—e.g., learned preferences for certain types of play or work.

sex-typing The learning of stereotyped masculine and feminine roles while growing up.

sexual deviations Any kind of sex activity which is socially-disapproved.

sexual impotence In males, inability to maintain erection in sex relations.

shape constancy The tendency for a familiar object to be perceived as unchanging in shape regardless of the visual angle from which it is viewed.

similarity A perceptual grouping principle which refers to the tendency for sensory events which are similar in some way to be perceived as belonging together.

simple schizophrenia That form of *schizophrenia* characterized by indifference, casual irresponsibility, and apparent stupidity.

size constancy The tendency for a familiar object to be perceived as its actual size, regardless of its distance from the viewer.

social attitudes Attitudes which affect our interactions with other people.

social class system The mode of social organization typical of most human societies in which status is often attributed, but can sometimes be achieved.

social learning theory The approach which emphasizes the importance of the individual's reinforcement history in the development of personality.

social mobility The extent to which people within a social system are free to move from one class or role to another.

social norms Standards of conduct implicitly

agreed upon by the group and expected of all of its members.

social psychology The branch of psychology which deals with the processes of interaction between people, especially the effects of groups and individuals on each other, and the ways in which attitudes are formed and changed.

social reinforcements Rewards and punishments administered by people.

somatization In psychoanalytic theory, all ego defenses which produce symptoms of physical illness — e.g., *conversion hysteria*.

somatotonic personality In the Sheldon-Kretschmer theory, the personality characterized by athletic tendencies and energetic movement. Associated with *mesomorphic body type*.

somnambulism Sleepwalking. Generally regarded as a dissociative state in which a person's repressed impulses induce them to act when their conscious controls are relaxed in sleep.

source traits Raymond Cattell's term for the underlying forces at work in personality.

spatial summation The firing of a neuron by the simultaneous action of a number of subthreshold stimuli, each of which individually is too weak to fire that neuron.

specific hungers Unlearned taste preferences which may reflect bodily needs.

speech area An area of the cortex which apparently plays an important role in the control of speech. Located in the frontal lobe, but in the left hemisphere of right-handed people and vice versa.

split-half reliability Evaluation of the reliability of an assessment procedure by correlating the scores on two halves of the same test taken by the same people.

spontaneous recovery The return in strength of an extinguished conditional response after the lapse of some time, without renewed reinforcement.

spontaneous recovery rate The rate at which people recover from any kind of behavior disorder without receiving any professional treatment at all.

stabilizing processes Those perceptual processes which seem designed to foster dependable interpretations of sense data under different environmental conditions so that irrelevant information can be disregarded.

standard deviation A statistical index of "typical" variability or deviation of scores within a distribution.

standard scores Restatements of original scores in standard deviation units.

statistic Quantitative measure derived from a sample.

statistical description A quantitative statement about any set of data — e.g., percentages, averages, etc.

statistical significance A probability estimate of the extent to which a given outcome is attributable to more than chance factors.

status The "standing" of an individual in a group.

status hierarchy The distribution of status positions in a group.

stereoscopic vision Three-dimensional vision.

stereotype A generalized statement about people's traits.

stimulus generalization The tendency for a conditional response associated with a particular conditional stimulus to be evoked by other stimuli similar to the original conditional stimulus.

stimuli (stimulus) Sensations or sensory data. Forms of energy which activate receptor organs sensitive to them.

stimulus contrast A difference in quality or intensity of stimulation.

stimulus intensity The strength of a *stimulus* — e.g., the brightness of a light, the loudness of a sound, etc.

stress Those events which interfere with the individual's *adaptation*.

stroboscopic motion Illusions of color and motion which can be produced by the sensation of flashing lights.

sublimation In psychoanalytic theory, a special case of substitution in which a substitute goal is more socially useful than the original goal.

substitution In psychoanalytic theory, the ego-defensive process involving the acceptance of substitute goals in place of those originally sought.

successive approximation The basic principle of *operant conditioning;* the reward of small steps in learning as they gradually come closer and closer to the desired performance.

superego In psychoanalytic theory, the component of personality which includes the individual's moral sense (or "conscience") and their sense of ideals.

surface traits Raymond Cattell's term for the less important traits of personality.

symbolization According to Freud, a form of concealment of *latent content* of dreams in which one object in *manifest content* represents a totally unrelated one.

sympathetic division That part of the *autonomic nervous system* that controls aroused or excited states of the organism. Regulates functions which complement those of the *parasympathetic division*.

Synanon Among the most successful of the self-help societies for the treatment of addiction.

synapse The tiny, fluid-filled space between adjacent *neurons* through which impulses must pass as they are conducted from *axon* to *dendrite*.

syntax In a language, the grammar or diction specifying the rules by which words are to be put together in meaningful ways for the purpose of communication.

systematic desensitization The *behavior therapy* extinction procedure which works by exposing patients to increasingly anxiety-provoking images under circumstances where they are not frightened.

temperament A person's innate susceptibility to emotive situations; the tendency to experience changes in mood.

template A hypothetical biological program or general behavioral disposition of thought or language which may be characteristic of human functioning in all cultures—e.g., thinking in pairs of opposites such as raw-cooked, strong-weak, etc.

temporal lobe That portion of each cerebral hemisphere located on the side below the *lateral fissure* and in front of the *occipital lobe*.

temporal summation The firing of a *neuron* by the repeated action of a single, weak stimulus.

testing population density A species' means of being able to recognize its own members.

test-retest reliability Evaluation of the *reliability* of an assessment procedure by comparing results of the same test given at different times to the same people.

tests of significance Statistical procedures designed to estimate the probability that a given empirical outcome would result again from a precise repetition of the conditions under which the results were originally obtained—e.g., the t-test, analysis of variance, chi-square, etc.

thalamus A structure at the top of the brain stem. Often referred to as "the great relay station of the brain" because it connects so many activities of the *cerebral cortex* and the brain stem.

thinking Internal, conscious representation processes including reasoning, wishing, talking, and imagining.

Thurstone-type scale A type of *attitude scale* consisting of a large number of statements about something which a number of judges have already rated as representing positive or negative attitudes toward it.

tics Habitual, small muscle twitches or movements such as blinking hard or clearing one's throat.

tip-of-the-tongue A memory search phenomenon, related to the "error of rejection" mechanism in which the person cannot recall the relevant information immediately, but has a clear feeling of knowing it and that it will soon come to mind.

token economies Environments designed according to *operant conditioning* principles in which tokens (e.g., poker chips), earned for performing particular acts, can be exchanged for different types of rewards.

trace-decay theory The theory of *forgetting* which assumes that some memories just fade away.

trait-factor theories Empirical approaches to *personality* which identify *traits* by a variety of questionnaire and behavioral observations which are then subjected to a complex mathematical process called factor analysis.

trait A characteristic style of behavior.

transcendental meditation Known as TM, a popular method of relaxation in which the person concentrates silently on a specially chosen word called a "mantra."

transference In psychoanalytic therapy, the tendency for the patient to project onto the analyst the attributes of other people who are important in their life and then feel toward the analyst the same emotions which those others arouse.

transsexual A person who is more comfortable in the role of people of the opposite sex, and who may choose to undergo surgery to change their own biological sex.

traumatic learning Where a frightening experience becomes associated with a neutral event such that, from that time on, the previously neutral event by itself evokes the fear.

t-test A procedure for testing the statistical significance of differences between pairs of means.

twin studies A research method used to provide empirical estimates of the relative contributions of hereditary and environmental factors to the development of various human *traits*.

tympanic membrane See *eardrum*.

type I error Inferring that an observed statistical difference is meaningful when it is actually due to random fluctuations.

type II error Acceptance of a statistical null hypothesis when that hypothesis is actually false.

unconditional (or unconditioned) response In *classical conditioning*, a response which is naturally evoked by a given stimulus (e.g., salivation produced by the presence of food in the mouth).

unconditional (or unconditioned) stimulus In *classical conditioning*, a stimulus that naturally evokes a given response (e.g., food in the mouth producing salivation).

undoing In psychoanalytic theory, the guilt-inspired attempt to atone for damage done by one's misdeeds or bad thoughts.

valence The strength and direction of a goal.

validity Accuracy or meaningfulness.

vegetative functions The basic, reflexive, life-sustaining functions such as respiration and digestion, under the control of the spinal cord, cerebellum, and brain stem.

vestibular sense The sense of balance or body position. Depends on structures located in the *inner ear*.

vicarious learning Learning that occurs, in the absence of any apparent reinforcement, through imitation of the behavior of others.

viscerotonic personality In the Sheldon-Kretschmer theory, the personality pattern characterized by pleasure in eating and relaxing. Associated with the *endomorphic body type*.

visible spectrum That portion of the color spectrum to which the eye is sensitive.

visual area That area of the cortex which controls visual processes. Located in the *occipital lobe*.

wave frequency Measured in cycles per second, the rate of vibration of a wave; dictates the tone or pitch of a sound.

wavelength The length of a light wave; dictates color or hue.

wheel communication pattern Where communication flows from one central member to each individual group member.

withdrawal Those response patterns typified by failure to accept challenge, narrowing of interests and activities, and retreat into fantasy and solitude.

Y-communication pattern A progression in which communication starts from one person and then goes, simultaneously, to one or two or three people beneath them, and then to people further down in the communication structure.

Zeigarnik effect The tensions or preoccupation associated with incompleted tasks which may dispose a person to remember such tasks better than completed ones.

References

Adams, J. A. *Human Memory.* New York: McGraw-Hill, 1967.

Adams, J. A. *Learning and Memory; An Introduction.* Homewood; Ill.: Dorsey Press, 1976.

Adams, J., and Dijkstra, S. Short-term memory for motor responses. *Journal of Experimental Psychology,* 1966, 71, 314–18.

Adler, A. *Problem of neurosis.* London: Routledge and Kegan Paul, 1929.

Adler, F. H. *Physiology of the eye.* St. Louis: Mosby, 1953.

Adorno, T. W.; Frenkel-Brunswick, E.; Levinson, D. J.; and Sanford, R. N. *The authoritarian personality,* New York: Harper & Row, 1950.

Aghajanian, G. K.; Haigler, H. J.; and Bennet, J. L. Amine receptors in CNS. III. 5 Hydroxytryptamine in brain. In L. L. Iverson, S. D. Iverson, and S. H. Snyder, (eds.), *Handbook of Psychopharmacology.* New York: Plenum, 1975. Pp. 63–96.

Ainsworth, M. D. S. Anxious attachment and defensive reactions in a strange situation and their relationship to behavior at home. Paper presented at meetings of the Society for Research in Child Development, Phil., Pa., 1973, as cited by M. M. Haith and J. J. Campos in *Annual review of psychology,* Vol. 28, 1977, pp. 277 ff.

Ajzen, I., and M. Fishbein. Attitude-behavior relations: A theoretical analysis and review of empirical research. *Psychological Bulletin,* 1977, *84,* #5, 888–918.

Alexander, A. B. Experimental test of assumptions relating to use of electromyographic biofeedback as a general relaxation training technique. *Psychophysiology,* 1975, 12, 656–662.

Allport, G. W. *The nature of prejudice.* Cambridge, Mass.: Addison-Wesley, 1954.

———. *Personality, a psychological interpretation.* New York: Holt, 1937.

———. As quoted in A. Richardson, *Mental imagery.* New York: Springer, 1969.

Allport, G. W., and Pettigrew, T. F. Cultural influence on the perception of movement: The trapezoidal illusion among Zulus. *Journal of Abnormal and Social Psychology,* 1957, 55, 104–13.

Altman, J., and Das, G. D. Autoradiographic and histological studies of postnatal neurogenesis. *Journal of Comparative Neurology,* 1966, 126, 337–89.

American Psychological Association. *Standards for educational and psychological tests and manuals.* Washington, D.C.: American Psychological Association, 1956.

———. *Psychology as a profession.* Washington, D.C.: American Psychological Association, 1968.

American Psychiatric Association. Committee on Nomenclature and Statistics (E. M. Gruenberg, Chairman). *DSM-II: Diagnostic and statistical manual of mental disorders.* (2d ed.) Washington, D.C.: American Psychiatric Association, 1968.

———, Committee on Training in Clinical Psychology. *Recommended graduate training program in clinical psychology.* Washington, D.C.: American Psychiatric Association, 1947.

Ammons, R. B. Effects of knowledge of performance: A survey of tentative theoretical formulation. *Journal of Genetic Psychology,* 1956, 54, 279–99.

Amoore, J. E.; Johnston, J. W. Jr.; and Rubin, M. The stereochemical theory of odor. *Scientific American,* 1964, *210,* No. 2, 42–49.

Anand, B. K.; China, G. S.; and Singh, B. Some aspects of electroencephalographic studies in Yogis. In Charles T. Tart (Ed.), *Altered states of consciousness.* New York: Wiley, 1969.

Ardrey, R. *Social contact.* New York: Atheneum, 1970.

———. *Territorial imperative.* New York: Dell, 1968.

Asch, S. E. Studies of independence and conformity: A minority of one against a unanimous majority. *Psychological Monographs,* 1956, 70, 9 (Whole no. 416).

Atkinson, R. C. Reflections on psychology's past and concerns about its future. *American Psychologist,* 1977 (March), 32, No. 3, 187–97.

Ax, A. F. The physiological differentiation between fear and anger in humans. *Psychosomatic Medicine,* 1953, 14, 433–42.

Ayllon, T., and Azrin, N. H. *The Token Economy: A Motivational System for Therapy and Rehabilitation.* New York: Appleton-Century-Crofts, 1968.

Babkin, B. P. *Pavlov; A Biography.* Chicago: University of Chicago Press, 1949.

Bachrach, A. J.; Erwin, W. J.; and Mohr, J. P. The control of eating behavior in an anorexic by operant conditioning techniques. In L. P. Ullman and L. Krasner (Eds.), *Case studies in behavior modification.* New York: Holt, 1968.

Bales, R. F. A set of categories for the analysis of small-group interaction. *American Sociological Review,* 1950, 15, 257–63.

———. *Interaction process analysis: A method of the study of small groups.* Cambridge, Mass.: Addison-Wesley, 1950.

———. Task roles and social roles in problem-solving groups. In Eleanor E. Maccoby, T. M. Newcomb, and E. L. Hartley (Eds.), *Readings in social psychology,* (3d ed.) New York: Holt, 1958.

Balter, M., and Levine, J., Character and extent of psychotherapeutic drug usage in the United States. In *Proceedings of V World Congress of Psychiatry.* Amsterdam: Excerpta Medica, 1971.

Baltes, Paul B., and Schaie, Warner, K. "The Myth of the Twilight Years" *Psychology Today,* 1974, (March) 35–40.

Bandura, A. *Aggression: A social learning analysis.* Englewood Cliffs, N.J.: Prentice-Hall, 1973.

————. Behavioral psychotherapy. *Scientific American*, 1967, 216, 78–89.

————. *Principles of behavior modification*. New York: Holt, 1969.

————. *Social Learning Theory*. Englewood Cliffs, N.J.: Prentice-Hall, 1977.

————. Social-learning theory of identificatory processes. In D. A. Goslin, ed., *Handbook of socialization theory and research*. Chicago: Rand McNally, 1969.

Bandura, A. and Walters, R. *Social Learning and Personality Development*. New York: Holt, 1963.

Barbach, Lonnie Garfield. *For Yourself; The Fulfillment of Human Sexuality*. Garden City, N.Y.: Doubleday, 1976.

Bard, P. A. A diencephalic mechanism for the expression of rage with special reference to the sympathetic nervous system. *American Journal of Physiology*, 1928, 84, 490–515.

Bash, K. W. Contribution to a theory of the hunger drive. *Journal of Comparative Psychology*, 1939, 28, 137–60.

Bateson, G. Redundancy and coding. In T. A. Sebeck (Ed.), *Animal communications*. Bloomington, Ind.: Indiana University, 1968.

Baughman, E. E. *Personality: The psychological study of the individual*. Englewood Cliffs, N.J.: Prentice-Hall, 1972.

Baumrind, D. Some thoughts on the ethics of research: After reading Milgram's "Behavioral study of obedience." *American Psychologist*, 1964, 19, 421–23.

Beach, F. A. The descent of instinct. *Psychological Review*, 1955, 62, 401–10.

Beary, J., and Benson, H. A simple psychophysiological technique which elicits the hypometabolic changes of the relaxation response. *Psychosomatic Medicine*, 1974, 36:115–20.

Beecher, H. Measurement of subjective responses. New York: Oxford University Press, 1959.

Bell, S., and Ainsworth, M. D. S. Infant crying and maternal responsiveness. *Child Development*, 1972, 43, 1171–90.

Bem, D. J. *Beliefs, attitudes and human affairs*. Monterey, Calif.: Brooks/Cole, 1970.

Bem, S. L. On the utility of alternative procedures for assessing psychological androgyny. *Journal of Consulting and Clinical Psychology*, 1977, 45, No. 2, 196–285.

————. Sex role adaptability: One consequence of psychological androgyny. *Journal of Personality & Social Psychology*, 1975, 31(4), 634–43.

————. The measurement of psychological androgyny. *Journal of Consulting and Clinical Psychology*, 1974, 42, No. 2, 155–62.

Bem, S. L., and Lenney, E. Sex typing and the avoidance of cross-sex behavior. *Journal of Personality and Social Psychology*, 1976, 33, No. 1, 48–54.

Benedict, R. *Patterns of culture*. Boston: Houghton Mifflin, 1934.

Benson, Herbert. *The Relaxation Response*. New York: William Morrow and Co., 1975.

Berkeley, G. *Works on vision*. Colin M. Turbayne (Ed.). Indianapolis, Ind.: Bobbs-Merrill, 1963.

Berko, J. The child's learning of English morphology. *Word*, 1958, 14, 150–77.

Berkowitz, L., and Cottingham, D. R. The interest value and relevance of fear arousing communications. *Journal of Abnormal and Social Psychology*, 1960, 60, 37–43.

Berlyne, D. *Conflict, arousal, and curiosity*. New York. McGraw-Hill, 1960.

Bernhard, C. G. (Ed.). The functional organization of the compound eye. London: Pergamon, 1966.

Bernard, J. The paradox of the happy marriage. In V. Gornick and B. Moran (Eds.), *Woman in Sexist Society*. New York: Basic Books, 1971.

Berscheid, E., and Walster, E. Beauty and the best. *Psychology Today*, 1972, 5, 42–46.

Best, J. B. The photosensitization of Paramecia Aurelia by temperature shock. *Journal of Experimental Zoology*, 1954, 126, 87–100.

Bettleheim, B. Feral children and autistic children. *American Journal of Sociology*, 1959, 64(5), 455–67.

————. *The informed heart: Autonomy in a mass age*. Glencoe, Ill.: Glencoe Free Press, 1960.

Bingham, C. C. *A study of american intelligence*. Princeton, N.J.: Princeton University Press, 1923.

Birch, H. G. The relation of previous experience to insightful problem-solving. *Journal of Comparative Psychology*, 1945, 38, 367–83.

Bird, C. *Social Psychology*, New York: Appleton-Century-Crofts, 1940.

Blake, B. G. A follow-up of alcoholics treated by behavior therapy. *Behavior Research and Therapy*, 1967, 5, 89–94.

Blake, R. R.; Helson, H.; and Mouton, J. S. The generality of conformity behavior as a function of factual anchorage, difficulty of task, and amount of social pressure. *Journal of Personality*, 1956, 25, 294–305.

Blankenship, J. *Scenes From Life*. Boston: Little, Brown & Co., 1976.

Bleuler, E. *Dementia praecox or the group of schizophrenias*. New York: International Universities, 1950.

Bloom, L. *Language development: Form and function in emerging grammars*. Cambridge, Mass.: MIT, 1970.

Bloom, L. Z.; Coburn, K.; and Pearlman, J. *The new assertive woman*. New York: Delacorte Press, 1975.

Bloomfield, H. H.; Cain, M. P.; and Jaffe, D. T. *TM: Discovering inner energy and overcoming stress*. New York: Delacorte Press, 1975.

Blumenthal, A. L. reappraisal of Wilhelm Wundt. *American Psychologist*, 1975, 30, 1081–88.

——. *Language and psychology: Historical aspects of psycholinguistics.* New York: Wiley, 1970.

Boas, F. *Race, language and culture.* New York: Macmillan, 1940.

Bockoven, J. S. *Moral treatment in American psychiatry.* New York: Springer, 1963.

Bodmer, Walter F., and Cavalli-Sforza, Luigi L. Intelligence and race. *Scientific American.* 1970, 223(4), 19–29.

Boneau, C. A. et al. *A career in psychology.* Washington, D.C.: American Psychological Association, 1970.

Borgatta, E. F.; Couch, A. S.; and Bales, R. F. Some findings relevant to the great man theory of leadership. *American Sociological Review,* 1954, 19, 755–59.

Boring, E. G. *A history of experimental psychology.* New York: Appleton-Century-Crofts, 1957.

Borkovek, T.; Steinmark, S.; and Nau, S. Relaxation training and single item desensitization in the group treatment of insomnia. *Journal of Behavior Therapy and Experimental Psychiatry,* 1973, 4, 401–403

Bower, Gordon H. Analysis of a mnemonic device. *American Scientist,* 1970, 58, 496–510.

——. Memory freaks I have known. *Psychology Today,* 1973, 7, 64–65.

Bower, G. H., and Winzenz, D. Comparison of associative learning strategies. *Psychonomic Science,* 1970, 20, 119–20.

Bower, T. G. R. Repetitive processes in child development. *Scientific American,* 1976, 235, 38–47.

——. The visual world of infants. *Scientific American,* 1966, 215, 85–92.

Bowers, K. S. *Hypnosis for the seriously curious.* Monterey, Ca.: Brooks/Cole, 1976.

Bowlby, J. *Attachment and loss.* Vol. 1. *Attachment.* New York: Basic Books, 1969. Vol. 2. *Separation.* New York: Basic Books, 1973.

Boyanowsky, E. O., and Allen, V. L. Ingroup norms and self-identity as determinants of discriminatory behavior. *Journal of Personality and Social Psychology,* 1973, 25, No. 3, 408–18.

Brady, J. V. Emotion and the sensitivity of psychoendocrine systems. In D. C. Glass (Ed.), *Neurophysiology and Emotion.* New York: Rockefeller University Press, 1967.

——. Ulcers in "executive" monkeys, *Scientific American,* 1958, 199(4), 95–100.

Brecher, E. M. Victims of the VD rip-off. *Viva,* 1973, 1, 42 ff.

Brecher, E. M., and the Editors of Consumer Reports. *Licit & Illicit Drugs.* Boston: Little, Brown, & Co. 1972.

Breger, L., and McGaugh, J. L. Learning theory and behavior therapy: A reply to Rachman and Eysenck. *Psychological Bulletin,* 1966, 170–73.

Brehm, J. W., and Cohen, A. R. *Explorations in cognitive dissonance.* New York: Wiley, 1962.

Bridger, W. H. Sensory habituation and discrimination in the human neonate. *American Journal of Psychiatry,* 1961, 117, 991–96.

Bridges, K. M. B. Emotional development in early infancy. *Child Development,* 1932, 3, 324–41.

Broadbent, D. E. The hidden preattentive process. *American Psychologist,* 1977, 32, No. 2, 109–118.

——. Perception and communication. London: Pergamon, 1958.

Bronfenbrenner, W. Socialization and social class through time and space. In E. E. Maccoby, T. M. Newcomb, and E. L. Hartley (Eds.), *Readings in social psychology.* (3d ed.) New York: Holt, 1958.

Bronson, G. Postnatal growth of visual capacity. *Child Development,* 1974, 45, 873–90.

Brown, B. New mind, new body. New York: Harper & Row, 1974.

Brown, Roger. A first language. Cambridge, Mass.: Harvard University Press, 1973.

——. *Psycholinguistics: Selected papers by Roger Brown.* Riverside, N.J.: Free Press, 1970.

——. *Social psychology.* New York: Macmillan and Free Press, 1965.

Brown, R.; Galanter, E.; Mandler, G.; and Hess, E. *New directions in psychology.* New York: Holt, 1962.

Brown, R., and McNeill, D. The 'tip of the tongue' phenomenon. *Journal of Verbal Learning and Verbal Behavior,* 1965, 4, 103–6.

Bruner, J. S.; Olver, R. R; and Greenfield, P. M. *Studies in cognitive growth.* New York: Wiley, 1966.

Bryan, J. Children's reactions to helpers: Their money isn't where their mouths are. In J. Macaulay and L. Berkowitz (Eds.), *Altruism and Helping Behavior.* New York: Academic Press, 1970, pp. 61–77.

Bryson, L. Graduate Lecture in Philosophical Foundations of Education, Teachers College, Columbia University. 1953.

Buckhout, R. Eyewitness testimony. *Scientific American,* 1974, 231, 23–31.

Budzynski, T. Biofeedback procedures in the clinic. *Seminars in Psychiatry,* 1973, 5, 537–48.

Bugental, J. *The quest for authenticity.* New York: Holt, 1964.

Buros, O. K. *The seventh mental measurements yearbook.* Highland Park, N.J.: Gryphon Press, 1972.

Burt, C. The evidence for the concept of intelligence. *British Journal of Educational Psychology,* 1955, 25, 158–77.

Burtt, H. E. An experimental study of childhood memory. *Journal of Genetic Psychology,* 1941, 58, 435–39.

Byrne, D. *The attraction paradigm.* New York: Academic Press, 1971.

Caggiula, A. Analysis of the copulation-reward properties of posterior hypothalamic stimulation in rats. *Journal of Comparative and Physiological Psychology,* 1970.

California State Ballot, Initiative Number 19, 1972.

Campbell, B. *Human evolution: An introduction to man's adaptation.* Chicago: Aldine, 1967.

Campbell, D. T. On the conflicts between biological and social evolution and between psychology and moral tradition. *American psychologist,* 1975, 30, 1103–26.

Cannon, W. B. *Bodily changes in pain, hunger, fear and rage.* (2d ed.) New York: Appleton-Century-Crofts, 1929.

————. Hunger and thirst. In C. Murchison (Ed.), *A handbook of general experimental psychology.* Worcester, Mass.: Clark University, 1934.

————. The James-Lange theory of emotions: A critical examination and an alternative theory. *American Journal of Psychology,* 1927, 39, 106–24.

————. *The wisdom of the body.* (Rev. ed.) New York: Norton. 1939.

Cantor, P. C. Personality characteristics found among youthful female suicide attempters. *Journal of Abnormal Psychology,* 1976, 85.

Cattell, R. B. The concept of social status. *Journal of Social Psychology, 1942, 15, 293–308.*

————. *The scientific analysis of personality.* Chicago: Aldine, 1965.

Cerletti, U., and Bini, L. Electric shock treatments. *Bulletin Academia Medica Roma,* 1938.

Chafetz, M. E., and Demone, J. W., Jr. Programs to control alcoholism. In S. Arieti (Ed.), *American Handbook of Psychiatry,* Vol. 3 (2d ed.). New York: Basic Books, 1974.

Chase, W. G., and Simon, H. A. Perception in chess. *Cognitive Psychology,* 1973, 4, 55–81.

Chomsky, N. *Language and mind.* New York: Harcourt, 1968.

————. Language and the mind. *Readings in Psychology Today.* Delmar, California: CRM Books, 1969.

————. *Syntactic structures.* S'Gravenhage, Netherlands: Mouton, 1957.

Chomsky, N., and Halle, M. *Sound patterns of English.* New York: Harper & Row, 1968.

Clark, H. H., and Clark, E. V. *Psychology and language: An introduction to psycholinguistics.* N.Y.: Harcourt, Brace, Jovanovich, 1977.

Clark, W. E. LeGros. *The antecedents of man: An introduction to the evolution of the primates.* New York: Harper Torchbook, 1959.

Cohn, F. *Understanding human sexuality.* Englewood Cliffs, N.J.: Prentice-Hall, 1974.

Coleman, J. C., and Broen, W. *Abnormal psychology and modern life.* (4th ed.) Glenview, Ill.: Scott, Foresman, 1972.

Collins, B. E. *Social psychology.* Reading, Mass.: Addison-Wesley, 1970.

Cook, S. W. Motives in a conceptual analysis of attitude-related behavior. *Nebraska Symposium on Motivation,* 1969, 17, 179–231.

Coons, E., Levak, M., and Miller, N. E. Lateral hypothalamus: Learning of food-seeking response motivated by electrical stimulation. *Science,* 1965, 150, 1320–21.

Cooper, L. M., and London, P. Sex and hypnotic susceptibility in children. *International Journal of Clinical and Experimental hypnosis,* 1966, 3, 13–19.

Corso, J. F. The experimental psychology of sensory behavior. New York: Holt, 1967.

Cox, D. F., and Bauer, R. A. Self-confidence and persuasibility in women. *Public Opinion Quarterly,* 1964, 28, 453–66.

Craighead, W. E.; Kazdin, A. E.; and Mahoney, M. J. Behavior modification: Principles, issues, and applications. Boston: Houghton Mifflin, 1976.

Cronbach, L. J. *Essentials of psychological testing.* (3d ed.) New York: Harper & Row, 1970.

Cronbach, L. J., and Meehl, P. E. Construct validity in psychological tests. *Psychological Bulletin,* 1955, 52, 281–302.

Culliton, B. J. Penicillin-resistant gonorrhea: New strain spreading world-wide. *Science,* 24, 1395–97.

Darwin, C. *The expression of the emotions in man and animals.* London: Murray, 1872.

————. *Origin of species.* J. W. Burrow. (Ed.). New York: Penguin, 1969. (Originally published 1859).

Davis, C. M. Self-selection of diet by newly weaned infants. *American Journal of Diseases of Children,* 1928, 651–79.

Davis, J. H. *Group Performance.* Reading, Mass.: Addison-Wesley, 1969.

Davis, W. S. *Life on a medieval barony.* New York: Harper Torchbook, 1928.

Davison, G. C., and Neale, J. M. *Abnormal psychology* (2d ed.) New York: Wiley, 1978.

Davson, H. *A textbook of general physiology.* (3d ed.) Boston: Little, Brown, 1966.

de Chauteaubriand, F. R. *Atala (1801) Rene.* Tr. by Irving Putter. Berkeley: University of California, 1952.

Delgado, J. M. R. *Evolution of physical control of the brain.* New York: American Museum of Natural History, 1965.

————. *Physical control of the mind: Toward a psycho-civilized society.* New York: Harper & Row, 1970.

Delgado, J. M. R., Roberts, W. W., and Miller, N. E. Learning motivated by electrical stimulation of the brain. *American Journal of Physiology,* 1954, 79, 587–93.

Dember, W. N. Perception, *Encyclopedia Britannica,* Vol. 14, 38–45. Chicago: Encyclopedia Britannica, Inc., 1975.

————. *The psychology of perception.* New York: Holt, 1960.

deMause, L. (ed.). Ch. 1, "The Evolution of Childhood" by Lloyd deMause *The history of childhood.* N.Y.: Harper & Row, 1974.

Dement, W. An essay on dreams: The role of physiology in understanding our nature. *New Directions in Psychology,* Vol. 2. New York: Holt, 1965.

de Moivre, A. *The doctrine of chances or a method of calculating the probability of events in play.* London: Woodfall, 1738.

Derloge, V. J., and Chaikin, A. L. *Sharing intimacy: What we reveal to others and why.* Englewood Cliffs, N.J.: Prentice-Hall, 1975.

Deutsch, M., and Collins, M. E. *Interracial housing: A psychological evaluation of a social experiment.* Minneapolis, Minn.: University of Minnesota Press, 1951.

DeVore, Irven (ed.). *Primate behavior; field studies of monkeys and apes.* New York: Holt, Rinehart, & Winston, 1965.

Dobzhansky, T. On methods of evolutionary biology and anthropology. Part 1. Biology. *American Scientist,* 1957, 45, 381–92.

Dollard, J., and Miller, N. E. *Personality and psychotherapy: An analysis in terms of learning, thinking, and culture.* New York: McGraw-Hill, 1950.

Ebbinghaus, H. *Uber Das Gedachtnis.* Leipzig: Duncker & Humblot, 1885.

Eibl-Eibesfeld, Iranaus. *Ethology, the Biology of Behavior.* Translated by Erich Klinghammer. New York: Holt, 1970.

Eimas, P. D.; Siqueland, E. R.; Jusczyk, P.; and Vigorito, J. Speech perception in infants. *Science,* 1971, 171, 303–6.

Ekman, P., Sorenson, E. R., and Friesen, W. V. Pan-cultural elements in facial displays of emotion. *Science,* 1969, 164, 86–88.

Elan, A. *The Israelis: Founders and sons.* London: Weidenfeld and Nicolson, 1971.

Elkind, D. *Children and adolescents: Interpretive essays on Jean Piaget* (2nd Ed.) New York: Oxford University Press, 1974.

English, H. B., and English, A. C. *A comprehensive dictionary of psychological and psychoanalytical terms.* New York: McKay, and London: Longmans, Green, 1958.

Engstrom, D. R.; London, P.; and Hart, J. EEG Alpha feedback training and hypnotic susceptibility. *Proceedings, 78th Annual Convention, American Psychological Association,* 1970, 837–38.

Epstein, S. Toward a unified theory of anxiety. *Progress in experimental personality research.* B. A. Maher. (Ed.). New York: Academic Press, 1967.

Erikson, E. H. *Childhood and society* (2nd Ed.; 1st Ed. published in 1950). New York: W. W. Norton, 1963.

Esdaille, J. *Hypnosis in medicine and surgery.* New York: Julian Press, 1957. (Originally titled: *Mesmerism in India,* and published in 1850.)

Estabrook, A. H. *The Jukes in 1915.* Washington, D.C.: Carnegie Institution, 1916.

Eysenck, H. J. *Dimensions of personality.* London: Kegan Paul, 1947.

———. (Ed.). *Behavior therapy and the neuroses.* New York: Pergamon, 1960.

Fanz, R. L. The origin of form perception. *Scientific American,* 1961 (May). Reprinted in R. Held and W. Richards (Eds.), Perception: Mechanisms and models. San Francisco: W. H. Freeman, 1972.

———. Form preferences in newly hatched chicks. *Journal of Comparative and Physiological Psychology,* 1957, 50, 422–30.

———. Pattern vision in newborn infants. *Science,* 1963, 140, 296–97.

Farina, A.; Allen, J. G.; and Saul, B. B. The role of the stigmatized in affecting social relationships. *Journal of Personality,* 1963, 36, 169–82.

Farina, A.; Gliha, D.; Boudreau, L. A.; Allen, J. G.; and Sherman, M. Mental illness and the impact of believing others know about it. *Journal of Abnormal and Social Psychology,* 1971, 77, 1–5.

Feldman, M. P. Aversion therapy for sexual deviations: A critical review. *Psychological Bulletin,* 1966, 65–79.

Fellner, C. H., and Marshall, J. R. Kidney donors. In J. Macaulay and L. Berkowitz (Eds.). *Altruism and helping behavior.* New York: Academic Press, 1970.

Fenichel, O. The psychoanalytic theory of neurosis. New York: Norton, 1945, and London: Routledge and Kegan, 1955.

Fenz, W. D. Conflict and stress as related to physiological activation and sensory, perceptual, and cognitive functioning. *Psychological Monographs,* 1964, 78.

Festinger, L. *A theory of cognitive dissonance.* Stanford, Calif.: Stanford University, 1957.

Fiedler, F. E. *A theory of leadership effectiveness.* New York: McGraw-Hill, 1967.

Field, M.; Magoun, W.; and Hall, E. *Handbook of physiology.* Washington, D.C.: American Physiological Society, 1959. 3 vols.

Finger, F. W., and Mook, D. G. Basic drives. *Annual Review of Psychology,* 1971, 22, 29.

Fischer, William F. *Theories of anxiety.* New York: Harper & Row, 1970, 167 pgs.

Flanagan, B.; Goldiamond, I.; and Azrin, N. Operant stuttering: The control of stuttering behavior through response contingent consequences. *Journal of Experimental Analysis of Behavior,* 1958, 73–77.

Flanders, R. E. *American century.* Cambridge, Mass.: Harvard University, 1950.

Flavell, J. H. *The developmental psychology of Jean Piaget.* Princeton: Van Nostrand, 1965.

Flavell, J. H., and Hill, J. P. Developmental psychology. *Annual Review of Psychology,* 1969, 20, 1–56.

Folkard, Simon. Diurnal variation in logical reasoning. *British Journal of Psychology,* 1975, 66, 1–8.

Ford, C. S., and Beach, F. A. *Patterns of sexual behavior.* New York: Harper & Row, 1951.

Ford, D. H. and Urban, H. B. *Systems of psychotherapy: A comparative study.* New York: Wiley, 1963.

Forer, L. *The birth order factor.* New York: McKay, 1976.

Fraenkel, G. S., and Gunn, D. L. *The orientation of animals.* Oxford: Clarendon, 1940.

Frank, J. D. Psychotherapy: The restoration of morale. *American Journal of Psychiatry,* 1974, 131, 271–74.

Franks, C. (ed.). *Behavior therapy.* New York: McGraw-Hill, 1969.

Freedman, D. G. Personality development in infancy: A biological approach. In S. L. Washburn and P. C. Jay (Eds.), *Perspectives on human evolution.* New York: Holt, 1968.

Freedman, J. L. Transgression, compliance, and guilt. In J. Macaulay and L. Berkowitz (Eds.), *Altruism and helping behavior.* New York: Academic Press, 1970.

Freedman, J. L., and Fraser, S. C. Compliance without pressure: The foot-in-the-door technique. *Journal of Personality and Social Psychology,* 1966, 4, 195–202.

Freeman, W. Psychosurgery: Retrospects and prospects based on twelve years' experience. *American Journal of Psychiatry,* 1949, 581–84.

Freeman, W., and Watts, J. W. Prefrontal lobotomy; the surgical relief of mental pain. *Bull. N.Y. Acad. Med.,* 1942, 18, 794–812.

Friedman, M., and Rosenman, R. F. Overt behavior pattern in coronary disease. *Journal of the American Medical Association,* 1960, 173, 1320–25.

Freud, A. *The ego and the mechanisms of defense.* London: Hogarth, 1937.

Freud, S. *The basic writings of Sigmund Freud.* New York: Modern Library, 1938.

———. *Die traumdeutung.* Leipzig: F. Deuticke, 1900. *The interpretation of dreams.* Tr. by A. A. Brill. London: C. Allen, 1913.

———. *The interpretation of dreams.* Tr. by James J. Strachey. New York: Basic Books, 1955.

———. *The psychopathology of everyday life.* New York: Macmillan, 1914.

———. *Three essays on the theory of sexuality.* In Strachey, J., *Standard edition of the complete psychological works of Sigmund Freud.* Vol. 7. London: Hogarth, 1953. (Orig. published 1905).

———. *Totem and taboo.* London: G. Routledge & Sons, 1919.

Fromm, E. *The forgotten language.* New York: Holt, 1951.

———. *Man for himself.* New York: Holt, 1947.

———. *The sane society.* New York: Holt, 1956.

Gagnon, J. H., and Davison, G. C. Asylums, the token economy, and the metrics of mental life. *Behavior Therapy,* 1976, 7, 528–34.

Galanter, E. Contemporary psychophysics. In *New directions in psychology,* Brown, R. E.; Galanter, E.; Mandler, G.; and Hess, E. New York: Holt, 1962, pp. 87–156.

Galbraith, G. C.; London, P.; Liebovitz, M. P.; Cooper, L. M.; and Hart, J. T. EEG and hypnotic susceptibility. *Journal of Comparative and Physiological Psychology,* 1970, 72 (1), 125–203.

Galbraith, J. K. *The affluent society.* Cambridge, Mass.: Riverside, 1960.

———. *The new industrial state.* Boston: Houghton Mifflin, 1967.

Gall, F. J. *Philosophisch medicinische untersuchungen uber natur und kunst im kranden und gesunden zustande des menschen.* Leipzig: Baumgartner, 1800.

Gallup, G. Gallup poll. Los Angeles, Calif.: *Los Angeles Times,* August 26, 1973.

Gallup, G. G. Self-recognition in primates: A comparative approach to the bidirectional properties of consciousness. *American Psychologist,* 1977, 32, 329–38.

Galton, F. *Hereditary genius.* London: Macmillan, 1869.

Gantt, W. H. *Experimental Basis for Neurotic Behavior.* New York: Hoeber, 1944. (Also published as *Psychosom. Med. Monogr.,* 1944, No. 7.)

Garcia, S. J. A. Black English in the schools: Controversy, confusion and conflict. Unpublished paper, 1973. Department of Psychology, University of South Florida, Tampa.

Gardner, R. A., and Gardner, B. T. Teaching sign language to a chimpanzee. *Science,* 1969, 165, 644–72.

Gaylin, Willard M.; Meister, Joel S.; and Neville, Robert C., eds. *Operating on the mind: The psycholsurgery conflict.* New York: Basic Books, Inc., 1975.

Genesis 38: 8–11.

Gergen, K. J. Social psychology as history. *Journal of Personality and Social Psychology,* 1973, 26, 309–20.

Gerking, S. D. *Biological systems.* Philadelphia: Saunders, 1969.

Gibb, C. A. Leadership. In G. Lindzey and E. Aronson (eds.). *Handbook of Social Psychology,* Vol. 4 (2d ed.). Reading, Mass.: Addison-Wesley, 1969. pp. 205–82.

Gibson, E. J., and Walk, R. D. The "visual cliff." *Scientific American,* 1960, 202, 64–71.

Gibson, J. J. *The perception of the visual world.* San Jose, Calif.: H. M. Gousha, 1950.

Gilgert, J. A., and Patrick, G. T. W. The effects of loss of sleep. *Psychological Review,* 1896, 3, 469–83.

Ginzberg, E. The pluralistic economy of the U.S. *Scientific American,* 1976, 235, 25–29.

Ginsburg, H., and Koslowski, B. Cognitive development. In M. R. Rosenzweig and L. W. Porter, Eds., *Annual review* of psychology. Palo Alto, Calif.: Annual Reviews, Inc., 1976.

Goddard, H. H. *The Kallikak family, a study in the heredity of feeblemindedness.* New York: Crowell-Collier and Macmillan, 1912.

Goldenberg, H. *Abnormal psychology: A social/community approach.* Monterey, Calif.: Brooks/Cole, 1977.

Goldenson, R. M. *The encyclopedia of human behavior: Psychology, psychiatry, and mental health,* Vol. 2. Garden City, N.Y.: Doubleday, 1970.

Goldfried, M. R.; and Davison, G. C. *Clinical behavior therapy.* New York: Holt, 1976.

Goldiamond, I. Fluent and non-fluent speech (stuttering): Analysis and operant techniques for control. In L. Krasner and L. P. Ullman (Eds.) *Research in Behavior Modification,* New York: Holt, 1965.

Goldiamond, I., and Hawkins, W. F. Vexierversuch: The log relationship between word-frequency and recognition obtained in the absence of stimulus words. *Journal of Experimental Psychology,* 1958, 56, 457–63.

Goldman, R.; Jaffe, M.; and Schachter, S. Yom Kippur, Air France, dormitory food, and the eating behavior of obese and normal persons. *Journal of Personality and Social Psychology,* 1968, 10, 117–23.

Goldsby, R. A. *Race and races,* New York: Macmillan, 1971.

Goldstein, K. *Human nature in the light of psychopathology.* Cambridge, Mass.: Harvard University, 1940.

Gomulicki, B. R. The development and present status of the trace theory of memory. *British Journal of Psychology Monograph Supplement,* 1953, No. 29.

Gordon, S. *Facts about VD for today's youth.* New York: John Day Co., 1973.

Gottlieb, G. Conceptions of prenatal development: Behavioral embryology. *Psychological Review,* 1976, 83, 215–34.

Gould, R. L. The phases of adult life: A study in developmental psychology. *American Journal of Psychiatry,* 1972, 129, 33ff.

Graen, G.; Alvares, K.; Ortis, J.B.; and Martella, J.A. Contingency model of leadership effectiveness: Antecedent and evidential results. *Psychological Bulletin,* 1970, 74, 284–96.

Green, D. M., and Swets, J. A. *Signal detection theory and psychophysics.* New York: Wiley, 1966.

Greenwald, A. G.; Brock, T. C.; and Ostrom, T. M. *Psychological foundations of attitude.* New York: Academic, 1968.

Gregory, R. L. *Eye and brain: The psychology of seeing* (2d ed.) New York: McGraw-Hill, 1973.

Gregory, R. L. *The intelligent eye.* London: Weidendfeld & Nicholson, 1970.

Griesinger, W. *Mental pathology and therapeutics.* (2d ed.) London: New Sydenham Society, 1845.

Griffin, S. B. Communist China's capacity to make war. *Foreign Affairs,* 1965, 43, 217–36.

Grissom, R. J.; Suedfeld, P.; and Vernon, J. Memory for verbal material: Effects of sensory deprivation. *Science,* 1962, 138, 429–30.

Grossberg, J. M. Behavior therapy: A review. *Psychological Bulletin,* 1964.

Grossman, S. P. Physiological basis of specific and non-specific motivational processes. In W. Arnold (Ed.), *Nebraska symposium on motivation.* Lincoln: University of Nebraska Press, 1968.

Guilford, J. P. *Psychometric methods.* (Rev. ed.) New York: McGraw-Hill, 1954.

Guttman, L. The Cornell technique for scale construction. *Educational and Psychological Measurement,* 1947, 7, 247–80.

Gwinnup, G. *Energetics.* New York: Bantam Books, 1970.

Haith, M. M., and Campos, J. J. Human infancy. In M. R. Rosenzweig and L. W. Porter, (Eds.), *Annual review of psychology, Vol. 28.* Palo Alto, Calif.: Annual Reviews, Inc., 1977.

Hall, C., and Van de Castle, R. *The content analysis of dreams.* New York: Appleton-Century-Crofts, 1966.

Hamburg, D. A. Emotions in the perspective of human evolution. In Peter Knapp (Ed.), *Expressions of emotions in man.* New York: International Universities, 1963, 300–17.

Harlow, H. F. The formation of learning sets. *Psychological Review,* 1949, 56, 51–65.

—————. Mice, monkeys, men and motives. *Psychological Review,* 1953, 60, 23–32.

Harlow, H. F., and Harlow, M. K. Social deprivation in monkeys. *Scientific American,* 1962, 207, 136–46.

Hart, J. T. Memory and the feeling-of-knowing experience. *Journal of Educational Psychology,* 1965, 56, 208–16.

Hartmann, H. Comments on the psychoanalytic theory of the ego. In Anna Freud et al. (Eds.). *The psychoanalytic study of the child.* Vol. 5. New York: International Universities, 1950.

Hartup, W. W. Peer interaction and social organization. In P. H. Mussen (Ed.), *Carmichael's manual of child psychology.* New York: Wiley, 1970.

Hasler, Arthur D., and Larsen, James A. The Homing Salmon. *Scientific American,* Aug. 1955, 193(2), 72–76.

Hatcher, R. A.; Steward, G. K.; Guest, F.; Finkelstein, R.; and Godwin, C. *Contraceptive technology, 1976–1977,* 8th Rev. Ed., N.Y.: Irvington Publishers, Inc., 1976.

Heath, Robert G. Electrical self-stimulation of the brain in man. In R. Ulrich, T. Stachnick, and J. Mabry (Eds.), *Control of human behavior.* Glenview, Ill.: Scott, Foresman, 1966.

Hebb, D. O. *The organization of behavior.* New York: Wiley, 1949.

———. *A textbook of psychology.* (2d ed.) Philadelphia: Saunders, 1968.

Heckhausen, H. *The anatomy of achievement motivation.* New York: Academic, 1967.

Heider, E. R., and Oliver, D. C. The structure of color space in name and memory for two languages. *Cognitive Psychology,* 1972, 3, 337–54.

Heider, F. *The psychology of interpersonal relations.* New York: Wiley, 1958.

Heimer, L. Pathways in the brain. *Scientific American,* 1971, 131, 48 ff.

Heinlein, R. *Stranger in a strange land.* Berkeley, Calif.: Berkeley, 1968.

———. I will fear no evil. Berkeley, Calif.: G. P. Putnam, 1970.

Held, Richard. Plasticity in sensory-motor systems. *Scientific American,* 1965, 213(5), 84–94.

Held, R., and Hein, A. Movement-produced stimulation in the development of visually guided behavior. *Journal of Comparative and Physiological Psychology,* 1963, 56, 872–76.

Henkin, R. I. The neuroendocrine control of perception. In *Perception and its disorders,* 1970, Res. Publ. A.R.N.M.D., 48. (The Association for Research in Nervous and Mental Diseases.)

Henkin, R. I.; Schechter, P. J.; Hoye, R.; and Mattern, C. F. T. Idiopathic hypoeusia with dysgeusia, hyposmia, and dysosmia: A new syndrome. *Journal of the American Medical Association,* 1971, 217, 434–40.

Hernandez-Peon, R.; Scherrer, H.; and Jouvet, M. Modification of electric activity in the cochlear nucleus during "attention" in unanesthetized cats. *Science,* 1956, 123, 331–32.

Heron, W. Cognitive and physiological effects of perceptual isolation. In P. Solomon et al. (Eds.). *Sensory deprivation.* Cambridge, Mass.: Harvard University, 1961.

Herriot, P. *An introduction to the psychology of language* London: Methuen, 1970.

Hess, E. H. Space perception in the chick. *Scientific American,* 1956, 195(1), 71–80.

Hess, E. Ethology and developmental psychology. In *Carmichael's manual of child psychology, 3rd Ed.* P. Mussen (Ed.). New York: Wiley, 1970.

Heston, Leonard L. The genetics of schizophrenia and schizoid disease. *Science,* 1970, 167, 249–56.

Hetherington, E. M., and McIntyre, C. W. Developmental psychology. In M. R. Rosenzweig and L. W. Porter (Eds.), *Annual review of psychology,* Vol. 26 Palo Alto, Calif.: Annual Reviews, Inc., 1975.

Hilgard, E. R. Hypnosis. In *Annual review of psychology, Vol. 26.* M. R. Rosenzweig, and L. W. Porter (Eds.). Palo Alto, Calif.: Annual Reviews, Inc., 1975.

Hilgard, E. R., and Hilgard, J. R. *Pain control through hypnosis and suggestion.* Los Altos, Calif.: Kauffmann, 1975.

Hilgard, E. R.; Kubie, L. S.; and Pumpian-Mindlin, E. *The scope of psychoanalysis: 1921–1961.* New York: Basic Books, Inc., 1962.

Hite, Shere. *The Hite Report.* New York: Dell Publishing Co., 1976.

Hoffer, E. *The true believer.* New York: Harper and Row, 1951.

Hoffman, M. L. Personality and social development. In M. R. Rosenzweig and L. W. Porter, (Eds.), *Annual review of psychology,* Vol. 28. Palo Alto, Calif.: Annual Reviews, Inc., 1977.

Hokanson, J. E., and Burgess, M. The effects of status type of frustration, and aggression on vascular processes. *Journal of Abnormal and Social Psychology,* 1962a, 65, 232–37.

———. The effects of three types of aggression on vascular processes. *Journal of Abnormal and Social Psychology,* 1962b, 64, 446–49.

Horn, John L. Human abilities: A review of research and theory in the early 1970's. *Annual Review of Psychology,* Vol. 27. Palo Alto, Calif.: Annual Reviews, Inc., 1976.

Horn, J. L., and Donaldson, G. Faith is not enough: A response to the Baltes-Schaie claim that intelligence does not wane. *American Psychologist,* 1977, 32, 369–73.

Horner, M. S. Fail: Bright women. *Psychology Today,* November, 1969, 3, 36–38.

Hovland, C. I. The generalization of conditioned responses. I. The sensory generalization of conditioned responses with varying frequencies of tone. *Journal of Genetic Psychology,* 1937, 17, 125–248.

Hovland, C. I.; Lumsdaine, A. A.; and Sheffield, F. C. *Experiments on Mass Communication.* Princeton, N.J.: Princeton University, 1949.

Howard, I. P. Perception of movement, *Encyclopedia Britannica,* Vol. 14, 45–46. Chicago, Encyclopedia Britannica, Inc., 1975.

Hubel, D. H., and Wiesel, T. N. Receptive fields, binocular interaction, and functional architecture in the cat's visual cortex. *Journal of Physiology,* 1962, 160, 106–00.

Hubel, D. H., and Wiesel, T. N. Receptive fields and functional architecture in two non-striate areas (18 and 19) of the cat. *Journal of Neurophysiology,* 1965, 28, 229–89.

Huff, B. B. (ed.). Physicians Desk Reference. Oradell, N.J.: Medical Economics Co., 1977.

Hulicka, I. M., and Grossman, J. L. Age-group comparisons for the use of mediators in paired-associate learning. *Journal of Gerontology,* 1967, 21, 46–51.

Hume, D. *Philosophical works.* T. Hill Green & T. Hodge Grose, (Eds.). New York: Adler, 1964.

———. *A treatise of human nature.* L. A. Selby-Bigge (Ed.)

Humphreys, L. G. Characteristics of type concepts with

special reference to Sheldon's typology. *Psychological Bulletin*, 1957, 54, 218–28.

Hunt, E., and Love, T. How good can memory be? In A. W. Melton and E. Martin (Eds), *Coding Processes in Human Memory*. Washington, D.C.: V. H. Winston and Sons, 1972.

Hunt, M. *Sexual behavior in the 70's*. Chicago, Ill.: Playboy Press, 1974.

Hurvich, L. M., and Jameson, D. An opponent-process theory of color vision. *Psychological Review*, 1957, 64, 384–404.

Huxley, A. *Brave new world*. New York: Harper and Row, 1932.

Huxley, T. H. *Collected essays*. Westport, Conn.: Greenwood, 1969.

Isaacs, W.; Thomas, J.; and Goldiamond, I. Application of operant conditioning to reinstate verbal behavior in psychotics. *Journal of Speech and Hearing Disorders*, 1960, 8–17.

Itard, J. M. G. *The wild boy of Aveyron*. Translated by George and Muriel (1797) Humphrey. New York: Appleton-Century-Crofts, 1962.

Jacobsen, A. L., and Kales, A. Sommambulism: All-night EEG and related studies. In S. S. Kety, E. V. Evarts, and H. L. Williams (Eds.), *Sleep and altered states of consciousness*, 1967.

James, W. The principles of psychology. New York: Holt, 1890.

———. *The varieties of religious experience*. London: Longmans, Green, 1902.

———. What is an emotion? *Mind*, 1884, 9, 188–205.

Janis, I. L., and Field, P. B. Sex differences and personality factors related to persuasibility. pp. 55–68. In I. L. Janis, C. I. Hovland, P. B. Field, H. Linton, E. Graham, A. R. Cohen, D. Rife, R. P. Abelson, G. S. Lesser, and B. T. King (Eds.), *Personality and persuasibility*. New Haven, Conn.: Yale University Press, 1959.

Janis, I., and Feshbach, S. Effects of fear arousing communications. *Journal of Abnormal and Social Psychology*, 1953, 48, 78–92.

Jenkins, J. G., and Dallenbach, K. M. Obliviscence during sleep and waking. *American Journal of Psychology*, 1924, 35, 605–12.

Jenkins, W. O. A review of leadership studies with particular reference to military problems. *Psychological Bulletin*, 1947, 44, 54–79.

Jensen, A. R. How much can we boost IQ and scholastic achievement? *Harvard Educational Review*, 1969, 39, 1–123 (Winter), and 273–356 (Spring).

Jones, E. E., and Kohler, R. The effects of plausibility on the learning of controversial statements. *Journal of Abnormal Psychology*, 1958, 57, 315–30.

Jones, M. C. Conditioning and reconditioning: An experimental study in child behavior. *Proceedings and addresses of the National Education Association*, 1924a, 62, 585–90.

———. The elimination of children's fears. *Journal of Experimental Psychology*, 1924b, 7, 382–90.

Juel, N. N. *Individual and environment*. Copenhagen: Munksgaard, 1965.

Julien, R. M. *A primer of drug action*. San Francisco: Freeman, 1975.

Jung, C. G. Archetypes and the collective unconscious. *Collected Works*. (2d ed.) Vol. 9, Part 1. (Bollingen Ser. Vol. 20). G. Adler. (Ed.) Princeton, N.J.: Princeton University, 1969a.

———. *Modern man in search of a soul*. New York: Harcourt, 1933.

———. *Psychological types*. London: Routledge & Kegan, 1923.

——— (Ed.). *Man and his symbols*. New York: Doubleday, 1969b.

Kagan, J. Do infants think? *Scientific American*, 1972, 226, 74–82.

———. *Change and continuity in infancy*. New York: Wiley, 1971.

———. Personality development. In P. London and D. Rosenhan (Eds.), *Foundations of Abnormal psychology*. New York: Holt, 1968.

Kagan, J. and Klein, R. E. Cross-cultural perspectives on early development. *American Psychologist*. 1973, 28, 947–61.

Kallmann, Franz J. *Heredity in health and mental disorder*. New York: W. W. Norton & Co. Inc., 1953.

Kamin, L. J. *The science and politics of IQ*. Potomac, Md.: Erlbaum Associates, 1974.

Kanellakos, D. P., and Ferguson, P. *The psychobiology of Transendental Meditation*. Los Angeles,: Maharishi International University, Spring 1973.

Kaplan, H. S. *The new sex therapy*. New York: Brunner-Mazel, 1974.

Karamyan, A. I. *Evolution of the function of the cerebellum and cerebral hemispheres*. Tr. from Russian by M. Roublev. Jerusalem: S. Monson, 1962.

Kasamatsu, A., and Hirai, T. An electroencephalographic study on the Zen meditation (Zazen). *Folio Psychiat. and Neurolog. Japonica*, 1966, 20, 315–36.

Katchadourian, H. A., and Lunde, D. T. *Fundamentals of human sexuality*, 2d ed. New York: Holt, 1975.

Katz, B. *Nerve, muscle and synapse*. New York: McGraw-Hill, 1966.

Katz, D., and Stotland, E. A preliminary statement to a theory of attitude structure and change. In S. Koch (Ed.), *Psychology: a study of a science*, 3, 423–75. New York: McGraw-Hill, 1959.

Katz, M., and Zimbardo, P. Making it as a mental patient. *Psychology Today*, 1977 (April) 10. 122–26.

Kazdin, A. E. The failure of some patients to respond to token economy programs. *Journal of Behavior Therapy and Experimental Psychiatry*, 1973, 4, 7–14.

———. Recent advances in token economy research. In *Progress in behavior modification*, vol. 1, M. Hersen, R. M. Eisler, and P. M. Miller (Eds.). N.Y.: Academic Press, 1975.

———. The token economy: An evaluative review. *Journal of Applied Behavior Analysis*, 1972, 5, 343–72.

Kazdin, A. E., and Wilcoxon, L. A. Systematic desensitization and nonspecific treatment effects: A methodological evaluation. *Psychological Bulletin*, 1976, 83, 729–58.

Keesing, R. M., and Keesing, F. M. *Perspectives in cultural anthropology*. New York: Holt, 1971.

Keller, M., and Rosenberg, S. S. (eds.). First Special Report to the U.S. Congress on Alcohol and Health from the Secretary of Health, Education, & Welfare. Washington, D.C.: US Government Printing Office, 1971.

Kellner, Robert. Psychotherapy in psychosomatic disorders. *Archives of General Psychiatry*, 1975, 32, 1021–28.

Kelly, E. L., and Fiske, D. W. *The prediction of performance in clinical psychology*. Ann Arbor: University of Michigan Press, 1951.

Kelly, E. L., and Goldberg, L. R. Correlates of later performance and specialization in psychology: A follow-up study of the trainees assessed in the VA Selection Research Project. *Psychological Monographs*, 1959, 73 (Whole No. 482).

Kennell, J.; Trause, M.; and Klaus, M. Evidence for a sensitive period in the human mother. In T. Brazelton, E. Tronick, L. Adamson, H. Als, and S. Wise (Eds), *Parent-infant interaction*. New York: Elsevier, 1975.

Kenshalo, D(an) R. (ed.). *The skin senses: Proceedings of the first international symposium on the skin senses*. Springfield, Ill.: Chas. Thomas, 1968.

Kenshalo, D. R.; J. W. Kling; and L. A. Riggs (eds.). The cutaneous senses. In *Woodworth and Schlosberg's experimental psychology*, (3d Ed.) New York: Holt, 1971.

Keppel, G., and Underwood, B. J. Proactive inhibition in short-term retention of single items. *Journal of Verbal Learning and Verbal Behavior*, 1962, 1, 153–61.

Kiesler, C. A.; Collins, R. E.; and Miller, N. E. *Attitude change: A critical analysis of theoretical approaches*. New York: Wiley Press, 1969.

Kimble, G. A. *Conditioning and learning*. New York: Appleton-Century-Crofts, 1961.

Kinsey, A. C.; Pomeroy, W. B.; Martin, C. E.; and Gebhard, P. H. *Sexual behavior in the human female*, Philadelphia: W. B. Saunders, 1953.

———. *Sexual behavior in the human male*. Philadelphia: W. B. Saunders, 1948.

Kissen, R. T.; Reifler, C. B.; and Thaler, V. H. Modification of thermoregulatory responses to cold by hypnosis. *Journal of Applied Physiology*, 1964, 19, 1043–60.

Klatsky, R. L. *Human memory: Structures and processes*. San Francisco: Freeman, 1975.

Klein, R. F.; Bogdonoff, M. D.; Estes, E. H., Jr.; and Shaw, D. M. Analysis of the factors affecting the resting FFA level in normal man. *Circulation*, 1960, 22, 772.

Kleitman, N. *Sleep and Wakefulness*. Chicago: University of Chicago Press, 1963.

Klerman, G. L. Are we an overmedicated society? Invited paper presented at Session on Ethical Aspects of Psychiatry, American Psychiatric Association, Detroit, Michigan, May, 1974.

———. Psychotropic drugs as therapeutic agents. In Controlling behavior through drugs. *Hastings Center Studies*, 1974, 2·1.

Klopfer, B. *Developments in the Rorschach technique*. Yonkers, New York on the Hudson: World Book Co., 1954.

Knight, R. P. Evaluation of the results of psychoanalytic therapy. *American Journal of Psychiatry*, 1941, 434–46.

Koestler, A. *Darkness at noon*. New York: Macmillan, 1941.

Kohlberg, L. The development of children's orientations toward a moral order. I. Sequence in the development of moral thought. *Vita Humana*, 1963, 6, 11–33.

Kohler, W. *The mentality of apes*. New York: Harcourt, 1925.

Korner, A. F. Neonatal startles, smiles, erections, and reflex sucks as related to state, sex, and individuality. *Child Development*, 1969, 40, 1039–53.

Kraepelin, E. Clinical psychiatry. Tr. by A. R. Diefendorf (Ed.). New York: Macmillan, 1907.

Krech, D., Crutchfield, R. S., and Ballachey, E. L. *Individual in society: A textbook of social psychology*. New York: McGraw-Hill, 1962.

Krech, D., and Rosenzweig, M. R. Environmental impoverishment, social isolation, and changes in brain chemistry and anatomy. *Physiology and Behavior*, 1966, 1, 99–104.

Kretschmer, E. *Physique and character*. New York: Harcourt, 1925.

Kuhn, T. S. *The structure of scientific revolutions*. Chicago: University of Chicago, 1962.

Lamb, M. Infant attachment to mothers and fathers. Paper presented at meetings of the Society for Research in Child Development, Denver, Col., 1975; as cited by M. M. Haith and J. J. Campos in *Annual review of psychology*. Vol. 28, p. 278. Palo Alto, Ca.: Annual Reviews, Inc., 1977.

Lamberg, Lynne. Help for those who have lost their senses. *Today's Health*, July–August, 1975.

Lambert, W. E.; Libman, E.; and Poser, E. G. The effect of increased salience of a membership group on pain tolerance. *Journal of Personality*, 1960, 28, 350.

Langer, E. J. The illusion of control. *Journal of Personality and Social Psychology*, 1975, 32, 311–28.

Lashley, K. S. Experimental analysis of instinctive behavior. *Psychological Review*, 1938, 45, 445–71.

Laslett, P. *The world we have lost. England before the industrial age* (2d Ed.). New York: Charles Scribner's Sons, 1971.

Latané, B., and Darley, J. Situational determinants of helping. In J. Macaulay and L. Berkowitz (Eds.), *Altruism and helping behavior.* New York: Academic Press, 1970.

———. *Unresponsive bystander: Why doesn't he help?* New York: Appleton-Century-Crofts, 1970.

Laub, D. R., and P. Gandy, (eds.). *Proceedings of the Second Interdisciplinary symposium on Gender Dysphoria Syndrome,* (Feb. 2–4, 1973).

Lazarus, A. A. *Behavior therapy and beyond.* New York: McGraw-Hill, 1971.

Leib, Warren. The ineffectiveness of alpha training in a psychiatric population. *Dissertation Abstracts International,* 1974 (Nov., 35, (5-B), 2438.

Leibovitz, M. P.; London, P.; Cooper, L.; and Hart, J. Dominance in mental imagery. *Educational and Psychological Measurement,* 1972, 32, 679–703.

Lefcourt, H. M. The function of the illusions of control and freedom. *American Psychologist,* 1973, 28, 417–25.

Lehrman, Daniel S. The reproductive behavior of ring doves. *Scientific American.* 1964.

Lenneberg, E. H. *The biological foundations of language.* New York: Wiley, 1967.

———. On explaining language. *Science,* 1969, 164, 635–43.

Lessac, M. The effects of early isolation and restriction on the later behavior of beagle puppies. Ph.D. thesis, Univ. of Pennsylvania, 1965, as cited in Melzack, R., *The puzzle of pain.* Middlesex, England: Penguin, 1973, p. 29.

Levi, L. *Stress.* New York: Liveright, 1967.

Levine, Seymour; Haltmeyer, Gary C.; Karas, George C.; and Denenberg, Victor H. Physiological and Behavioral Effects of infantile stimulation. *Physiology and Behavior,* 1967, 2, 55–59.

Levi-Strauss, C. *The raw and the cooked.* Tr. by John Weightman. New York: Harper Torchbook, 1969.

Lewin, K. *A dynamic theory of personality.* New York: McGraw-Hill, 1935.

Lewin, K.; Lippitt, R.; and White, R. K. Patterns of aggressive behavior in experimentally created social climates. *Journal of Social Psychology,* 1939, 10, 271–99.

Liddell, H. S. *Emotional hazards in animals and man.* Springfield, Ill.: Charles C. Thomas, 1956.

Liebeskind, J. C., and Paul, L. A. Psychological and physiological mechanisms of pain. In M. R. Rosenzweig and L. W. Porter (Eds.), *Annual review of Psychology.*

Palto Alto, Calif.: Annual Reviews Inc., 1977, pp. 41–60.

Likert, R. A technique for the measurement of attitudes. *Arch. Psychol.,* 1932, 140.

Lindzey, G., Lehlin. J., Manosevitz, M., and Thiessen, D. (eds.). Behavioral genetics. *Annual Review of Psychology.* Palo Alto, Calif.: Annual Reviews, 1971.

Livingston, A. *Newsweek,* 1971, 77(25), 65–67.

Lloyd, K. E. Retention of responses to stimulus classes and specific stimuli. *Journal of Experimental Psychology,* 1960, 59, 54–59.

Loftus, Elizabeth. Leading Questions and the Eyewitness Report, *Cognitive Psychology,* October 1975, pp. 560–72.

London, P. *Behavior control.* (2nd Ed.) New York: New American Library, 1977.

———. Developmental aspects of discrimination in relation to adjustment. *Genetic Psychology Monographs,* 1958, 57, 293–336.

———. Sexual behavior. *Encyclopedia of Bioethics.* 1978.

———. The end of ideology in behavior modification. *American Psychologist,* 1972, 27, 913–20.

———. Kidding around with hypnosis. *International Journal of Clinical and Experimental Hypnosis,* 1976, 24, 105–21.

———. *The modes and morals of psychotherapy.* New York: Holt, 1964.

———. Morals and mental health. In R. Plog, R. Edgerton, and R. Beckwith (Eds.), *Determinants of mental illness.* New York: Holt, 1969.

———. The rescuers: Motivational hypotheses about Christians who saved Jews from the Nazis. In J. Macaulay and L. Berkowitz (Eds), *Altruism and helping behavior.* New York: Academic Press, 1970.

London, P.; Hart, J. T.; and Liebovitz, M. EEG alpha rhythms and susceptibility to hypnosis. *Nature,* 1968, 219, 71–72.

London, P., and Lim, H. Yielding reason to social pressure: Task complexity and expectation in conformity. *Journal of Personality,* 1964, 32, 75–89.

London, P.; Ogle, M. E.; and Unikel, I. P. The effects of hypnosis and motivation on resistance to heat stress. *Journal of Abnormal Psychology,* 1968b, 6, 532–41.

London, P., and Rosenhan, D. *Foundations of abnormal psychology.* New York: Holt, 1968.

Long, R. A. From Africa to the new world: The linguistic continuum. *CAAS Papers in Linguistics,* No. 2. Atlanta: Atlanta University, 1971.

Lorenz, K. The evolution of behavior. *Scientific American,* 1958, 199(6) 67–78.

———. *King Solomon's Ring.* New York: Crowell, 1952.

———. *Studies in animal and human behavior.* Vol. 1. Cambridge, Mass.: Harvard University Press, 1970.

Lorge, I. Influence of regularly interpolated time intervals upon subsequent learning. *Teachers College Contributions to Education,* 1930, No. 438.

Lovaas, O. I. Behavior therapy approach to treating childhood schizophrenia. In J. Hill (Ed.), *Minnesota symposium on child development*. Minneapolis: University of Minnesota Press, 1967.

——. A program for the establishment of speech in psychotic children. In J. K. Wing (Ed.), *Early childhood autism*. New York: Pergamon, 1966.

Lowry, Richard. *The evolution of psychological theory.* Chicago: Aldine Publishing Co., 1971.

Luborsky, L.; Singer, B.; and Luborsky, L. Comparative studies of psychotherapies. *Archives of General Psychiatry*, 1975, 32, 995–1008.

Luce, G. G. *Body time.* New York: Bantam, 1973.

Luchins, A. S. Primacy-recency in impression formation. In C. I. Hovland et al., *The order of presentation in persuasion*. New Haven: Yale University Press, 1957.

Luria, A. R. The functional organization of the brain. *Scientific American*, 1970, 222, 66–78.

——. *The Mind of a mnemonist.* New York: Basic Books, 1968.

Macaulay, J., and Berkowitz, L. *Altruism and helping behavior*. New York: Academic, 1970.

Maccoby, E. E., and Jacklin, C. N. *The psychology of sex differences*. Stanford, Calif.: Stanford University Press, 1974.

Macfarlane, D. A. The role of kinesthesis in maze learning. *California University Publications in Psychology*, 1930, 4, 277–305.

Mahoney, Michael J. Reflections on the cognitive-learning trend in psychotherapy. *American Psychologist*, 1977, 32, 5–13.

Malinowski, Bronislaw. *The Sexual life of savages in north-western Melanesia*. New York: H. Liveright, 1929.

Mandler, G. Emotion. In R. Brown et al., *New directions in psychology*. New York: Holt, 1962.

Mann, R. D. A review of the relationship between personality and performance in small groups. *Psychological Bulletin*, 56, 241–70.

Mann, J.; Sidman, J.; and Starr, S. Effects of erotic films on sexual behavior of married couples. *Technical Report of the Commission on Obscenity and Pornography*, Vol. 8, Washington, D.C.: U.S. Government Printing Office, 1971.

——. *Motivation and personality.* New York: Harper & Row, 1954.

——. *Towards a psychology of being.* (2d ed.) New York: Van Nostrand Reinhold, 1968.

Marcuse, H. *Eros and civilization.* Boston: Beacon, 1955.

——. *One-dimensional man.* Boston: Beacon, 1964.

Marijuana (cannabis) fact sheet, 1967. The brain humanist forum. In C. T. Tart (Ed.), *Altered states of consciousness*. New York: Wiley, 1969.

Mark, V. H., and Ervin, F. R. *Violence and the brain.* New York: Harper & Row, 1971.

Marquis, D. G. Individual responsibility and group decisions involving risk. *Industrial Management Review*, 1962, 3, 8–22.

Maslow, A. H. Cognition of being in the peak experiences. *Journal of Genetic Psychology*, 1959, 94, 43–66.

——. *Motivation and personality.* New York: Harper & Row, 1954.

——. *Towards a psychology of being.* (2d ed.) New York: Van Nostrand Reinhold, 1968.

Mason, William A., and Lott, Dale F. Ethology and Comparative Psychology. *Annual Review of Psychology*. 1976, 27, 129–254.

Masters, W. H., and Johnson, V. E. *Human sexual response*. Boston: Little, Brown, 1966.

——. *Human sexual inadequacy.* Boston: Little, Brown & Co., 1970.

May, R. (ed.). *Existential psychology*. New York: Random House, 1961.

McCarthy, D. A. Language development in children. In L. Carmichael (Ed.), *Manual of child psychology*. New York: Wiley, 1946.

McClelland, D. C. (ed.). *Studies in motivation*. New York: Appleton-Century-Crofts, 1955.

McClelland, D. C.; Atkinson, J. W.; Clark, R. A.; and Lowell, E. L. *The achievement motive*. New York: Appleton-Century-Crofts, 1953.

McCutcheon, B. A., and Adams, H. E. The physiological basis of implosive therapy. *Behavior Research and Therapy*, 1975, 13, 93–100.

McGill, T. E. *Readings in animal behavior.* New York: Holt, 1965.

McGlothlin, W. H. Drug use and abuse. In M. R. Rosenzweig and L. W. Porter, Eds., *Annual review of psychology*, Vol. 26. Palo Alto, Calif.: Annual Reviews, Inc., 1975.

McGuire, W. J. The nature of attitudes and attitude change. In G. L. Lindsey and E. Aronson (Eds.), *The handbook of social psychology*. Vol. 3. (2d ed.) Reading, Mass.: Addison-Wesley, 1969.

——. Resistance to persuasion conferred by active and passive prior refutation of the same and alternative counterarguments. *Journal of Abnormal and Social Psychology*, 1961, 63, 325–32.

McKinney, F. Fifty years of psychology. *American Psychologist*, 1976, 31, 834–42.

McQuade, W., and Aikman, A. *Stress.* New York: Dutton & Co. 1974.

Mead, M. *Coming of age in Samoa.* New York: Mentor, 1949 (originally published 1928).

——. *Sex and temperament in three primitive societies.* New York: Morrow, 1935.

Meehl, Paul E. *Psychodiagnosis: Selected Papers.* Minneapolis: University of Minnesota Press, 1973.

Meehl, P., and Cronbach, L. J. Construct validity in

psychological tests. *Psychological Bulletin*, 1955, 52, 281–302.

Meglitsch, P. *Invertebrate zoology*. New York: Oxford University Press, 1967.

Meltzoff, A. N., and Moore, M. K. Imitation of facial and manual gestures by human neonates. *Science*, 1977, *198*, No. 4312, 75–78.

Melzack, R., and Wall, P. D. Pain mechanisms: A new theory. *Science*, 1965, 150, 971–79.

Melzack, R. *The puzzle of pain*. Middlesex, England: Penguin, 1973.

Melzack, R., and Scott, T. H. The effects of early experience on the response to pain. *Journal of Comparative and Physiological Psychology*, 1957, 50, 155.

Menninger, K. A. *The human mind*. 3d ed. New York: Knopf, 1947.

Meredith, H. Somatic changes during prenatal life. *Child Development*, 1976, 46, 603–10.

Metfessel, N., and Sax, G. Systematic biases in the keying of correct responses on certain standardized tests. In W. L. Barnehe Jr. (Ed.), *Readings in psychological tests and measurements*. New York: Holt, 1969.

Milgram, S. Behavioral study of obedience. *Journal of Abnormal and Social Psychology*, 1963, 67, 371–78.

———. Group pressure and action against a person. *Journal of Abnormal and Social Psychology*, 1964, 69, 137–43.

———. Liberating effects of group pressure. *Journal of Personality and Social Psychology*, 1965, 1, 127–34.

———. *Obedience to authority*. New York: Harper & Row, 1974.

Miller, David L. *George Herbert Mead: Self, language and the world*. Austin: University of Texas Press, 1973.

Miller, G. A. The magical number seven, plus or minus two; some limits on our capacity for processing information. *Psychological Review*, 1956, 63, 81–97.

———. *Psychology: The science of mental life*. New York: Harper & Row, 1962.

———. Role of physical attractiveness in impression formation. *Psychonomic Science*, 1970, 19, 241–43.

Miller, G. A., and Selfidge, J. A. Verbal context and the recall of meaningful material. *American Journal of Psychology*, 1950, 63, 176–85.

Miller, N. E. Learning of visceral and glandular responses. *Science*, 1969, 163, 434–45.

———. Physiological and cultural determinants of ·behavior. *The scientific endeavor*. New York: Rockefeller University, 1965.

———. Studies of fear as an acquirable drive. I: Fear as a motivation; fear reduction as reinforcement in the learning of new responses. *Journal of Experimental Psychology*, 1948, 38, 89–101.

Miller, N., and Zimbardo, P. G. Motives for fear induced

affiliation: Emotional comparison or interpersonal similarity. *Journal of Personality*, 1966, 34, 481–503.

Mills, M., and Melhuish, E. Recognition of mother's voice in early infancy. *Nature*, 1974, 252, 123–24.

Milne, L. J., and Milne, M. *The senses of animals and men* New York: Atheneum, 1962.

Milner, P. M. The memory defect in bilateral hippocampal lesions. *Psychiatric Research Report*, 1959, 11, 43–52.

Mischel, W. *Introduction to Personality*. New York: Holt, 1971.

———. *Personality assessment*. New York: Wiley, 1968.

Moffitt, A. R. Consonant cue perception by twenty- to twenty-four-week-old infants. *Child Development*, 1971, 42, 717–31.

Money, J. *Sex research: New developments*. New York: Holt, 1965.

Money, J., and Tucker, P. *Sexual signatures: On being a man or a woman*. Boston: Little, Brown, & Co., 1975.

Montagu, A. *Human relations*. Cleveland: World Press, 1959.

———. *The human revolution*. New York: Bantam, 1965.

———. *The natural superiority of women*. (Rev. ed.) New York: Macmillan, 1968.

Moray, Neville. *Attention: Selective processes in vision and hearing*. London: Hutchinson, 1969.

Morgan, E. *The descent of woman*. New York: Bantam, 1972.

Morison, S. E. *Admiral of the ocean sea*. New York: Atlantic Monthly Press, 1942.

Morris, D. *The naked ape*. New York: Dell, 1969a.

———. (Ed.). *Primate ethology: Essays on the socio-sexual behavior of apes and monkeys*. Garden City, N.Y.: Doubleday Anchor, 1969b.

Morse, S.; Gruzen, J.; and Reis, H. The "eye of the beholder": A neglected variable in the study of physical attractiveness. *Journal of Personality*. 1976, 44, 209–25.

Mountcastle, V. B. *Medical physiology*. (12th ed.) Vol. 2. St. Louis: Mosby & Co., 1968.

Mowrer, O. H. On the psychology of "talking birds": A contribution to language and personality theory. *Learning theory and personality dynamics*. New York: Ronald, 1950.

———. Hearing and speaking: an analysis of language learning. *Journal of Speech and Hearing Disorders*, 1958, 23, 143–51.

Moyer, K. E. *The psychobiology of aggression*. New York: Harper & Row, 1976.

Mueller, C. G., and Mueller, R. M. (eds.). *Light and vision*. New York: Time, 1966.

Munn, N. L. *Evolution and growth of human behavior*. (2d Ed.) Boston, Mass.: Houghton Mifflin, 1965.

Murphy, G. *Personality: A biosocial approach to origins and structure*. New York: Harper & Row, 1947.

Mussen, Paul H. (ed.). *Carmichael's manual of child psychology*. 3d ed. New York: Wiley, 1970.

Myers, J. B. *The Myers-Briggs type indicator.* Princeton, N.J.: Educational Testing Service, 1962.

Naruse, O. "Hypnosis as a state of meditative concentration and its relationship to the perceptual process." *The Nature of Hypnosis,* M. V. Kline (Ed.). New York: Institute for Research in Hypnosis, 1962.

National Safety Council *National center for health statistics,* Washington, D.C.: U.S. Bureau of Census, 1972.

Neugarten, B. L. *Middle age and aging.* Chicago: University of Chicago Press, 1968.

Newcomb, T. M. Persistence and regression of changed attitudes: Long range studies. *Journal of Social Issues,* 1963, 19, 3–14.

Nievergelt, J., and Farrar, J. C. What machines can and cannot do. *American Scientist,* 1973, 61, 309–15.

Norman, D. A. *Memory and attention: An introduction to human information processing.* New York: Wiley, 1969.

Nye, F. I.; Short, J. F.; and Olson, V. J. Socioeconomic status and delinquent behavior. *American Journal of Sociology,* 1958, 63, 381–89.

Olds, J., and Milner, P. M. Positive reinforcement produced by electrical stimulation of septal area and other regions of rat brain. *Journal of Comparative and Physiological Psychology,* 1954, 47, 419–27.

O'Leary, K. D., and Wilson, G. T. Behavior therapy: Application and outcome. Englewood Cliffs, N.J.: Prentice-Hall, Inc., 1975.

O'Neill, N., and O'Neill, G. *Open marriage: A new life style for couples.* New York: Avon, 1972.

Orne, M. T. The nature of hypnosis: Artifact and essence. *Journal of Abnormal and Social Psychology,* 1959, 58, 277–99.

———. The simulation of hypnosis: Why, how, and what it means. *International Journal of Clinical and Experimental Hypnosis,* 1971, 19 (4), 183–210.

———. As cited in G. H. Estabrooks (Ed.), *Hypnosis: Current problems.* New York: Harper & Row, 1962.

Orne, M. T., and Holland, C. C. On the ecological validity of laboratory deceptions. *International Journal of Psychiatry,* 1968, 6, 282–93.

Ornstein, Robert E. *The Psychology of Consciousness.* San Francisco: W. H. Freeman & Co., 1972.

Orwell, G. *1984.* New York: Harcourt, 1948.

Osgood, E. E.; Suci, G. J.; and Tannenbaum, P. H. *The measurement of meaning.* Urbana, Ill.: University of Illinois, 1957.

Paivio, A. *Imagery and verbal process.* New York: Holt, 1971.

Palvio, A.; Yuille, J. C.; and Madigan, S. A. Concreteness, imagery, and meaningfulness values for 925 nouns. *Journal of Experimental Psychology Monograph Supplement,* 1968, 76, no. 1, Pt. 2.

Palyak, S. *The vertebrate visual system.* Chicago: University of Chicago, 1957.

Parloff, M. B.; Iflund, B.; and Goldstein, N. Communication of "therapy values" between therapist and schizophrenic patients. *Journal of Nervous and Mental Diseases,* 1960, 193–99.

Paskewitz, David A. Biofeedback instrumentation: Soldering closed the loop. *American Psychologist,* 1975, 30(3), 371–78.

Paul, G. L. The production of blisters by hypnotic suggestion: Another look. *Psychosomatic medicine,* 1963, 25, 233–34.

Pavlov, I. P. *Animal intelligence.* New York: Macmillan, 1911.

———. *Experimental reflexes and psychiatry.* Tr. by W. H. Gantt. New York: International Publishers, 1928.

Pearson, K., and Moul, M. The problem of alien immigration into Great Britain, illustrated by an examination of Russian and Polish Jewish children. *Annals of Eugenics,* 1925, 1, 5–127.

Peck, R. C. Psychological developments in the second half of life. In J. E. Anderson (Ed.), *Psychological aspects of aging.* Washington, D.C.: American Psychological Association, 1956.

Peckstein, L. A. Whole vs. part methods in learning non-sensical syllables. *Journal of Educational Psychology,* 1918, 9, 379–87.

Pei, M. *World book encyclopedia.* Chicago: Field Enterprises, 1967.

Penfield, W. The permanent record of the stream of consciousness. *Proceedings and papers, 14th International Congress of Psychology,* June 1954, 47–69.

Perfield, W. *Speech and brain mechanisms.* Princton, N.J.: Princton University Press, 1959.

Perry, R. B. *The thought and character of William James: As revealed in unpublished correspondence and notes together with his published writings.* vol. 2. Philosophy and psychology. Boston: Little, Brown, 1935.

Pengelley, Eric T., and Asmundson, Sally J. Biological clocks. *Scientific American,* 1971, 224(4), 72–79.

Peterson, Donald R. Need for the doctor of psychology degree in professional psychology. *American Psychologist,* 1976, 31, No. 11, 792–98.

Pettigrew, T. S. Social psychology and desegregation research. *American Psychologist,* 1961, 16, 105–12.

Pfeiffer, J. E. *The emergence of man.* New York: Harper & Row, 1969 and 1972.

Phares, E. J. *Locus of control: A personality determinant of behavior.* Morristown, N.J.: General Learning Press, 1973.

———, and Lamiell, J. T. Personality, in M. R. Rosenzweig and L. W. Porter (Eds.), *Annual Review of Psychology* Vol. 28. Palo Alto, Calif.: Annual Reviews, Inc., 1977.

Piaget, J. *The child's conception of the world.* New York: Harcourt, 1929.

———. *The origins of intelligence in children.* New York: International Universities Press, 1952.

Population Reports a. IUDs Reassessed—A decade of experience. Intrauterine Devices, Series B, Number 2, Jan. 1975.

Population Reports b. Postcoital Contraception—An Appraisal. Series J, Number 9, Jan. 1976, Family Planning Programs.

Postman, L.; Bruner, J.; and McGinnies, E. Personal values as selective factors in perception. *Journal of Abnormal and Social Psychology,* 1948, 43, 142–54.

Postman, L., and Riley, D. A. Degree of learning and interserial interference in retention. *University of California Publications in Psychology,* 1959, 8, 271–396.

Potter, S. *Lifemanship, or the art of getting away with it without being an absolute plonk.* New York: Holt, 1951.

———. *One-upmanship, being some account of the activities and teaching of the lifemanship correspondence college of one-upness and gameslife-mastery.* New York: Holt, 1951.

———. *The theory and practice of gamesmanship or the art of winning games without actually cheating.* New York: Holt, 1948.

Premack, David. The education of Sarah. *Psychology Today,* 1970, 4(4), 54–58.

Pribram, Karl H. *Languages of the brain: Experimental paradoxes and principles in neuropsychology.* Englewood Cliffs, N.J.: Prentice-Hall, 1971.

Prince, M. *The dissociation of a personality.* London and New York: Longmans, Green, 1920.

Purcell, K., and Weiss, J. H. Asthma, C. G. Costello (Ed.), *Symptoms of Psychopathology: A Handbook.* New York: Wiley, 1970. p. 597.

Ramsay, A. O., and Hess, E. H. A laboratory approach to the study of imprinting. *Wilson Bulletin,* 1954, 66, 196–206.

Raven, B. H. Social influence and power. In I. D. Steiner and M. Fishbein (Eds), *Current Studies in Social Psychology.* New York: Holt, 1965.

Razran, G. H. S. Decremental and incremental effects of distracting stimuli upon the salivary CRs of 24 adult human subjects. *Journal of Experimental Psychology,* 1939, 24, 657–62.

———. The observable unconscious and the inferable conscious in current Soviet psychophysiology: Interoceptive conditioning, semantic conditioning, and the orienting reflex. *Psychological Review,* 1961, 68, 81–147.

Redlich, F., and Hollingshead, A. B. *Social Class and Mental Illness.* New York: Wiley, 1958.

Rees, L. The significance of parental attitudes in childhood asthma. *Journal of Psychosomatic Research,* 1964, 7, 253–62.

Reiff, R., and Scheerer, M. *Memory and hypnotic age regression.* International Universities Press, 1959.

Reik, T. *Listening with the third ear: The inner experience of a psychoanalyst.* New York: Grove, 1948.

Rheingold, H. L., and Eckerman, C. Fear of the stranger: A critical examination. In H. W. Reese (Ed.), *Advances in child development and behavior, Vol. 8,* New York: Academic Press, 1973.

Rheingold, H. L.; Gewirtz, J. J.; and Ross, H. W. Social conditioning of vocalization in the infant. *Journal of Comparative and Physiological Psychology,* 1959, 52, 68–73.

Richards, I. A. *World book encyclopedia.* Chicago: Field Enterprises, 1967.

Richardson, A *Mental imagery.* New York: Springer, 1969.

Rieff, P. *Freud: The mind of the moralist.* New York: Viking, 1959.

Riesen, A. H. Arrested vision. *Scientific American,* 1950, (July). Reprinted in R. Held and W. Richards (Eds.), *Perception: Mechanisms and models.* San Francisco: Freeman, 1972.

Riggs, Lorrin A. Human vision: Some objective explorations. *American Psychologist,* 1976, 31, No. 2, 125–34.

Riggs, L. A.; Ratcliff, F.; Cornsweet, J. C.; and Cornsweet, T. N. The disappearance of steadily fixated visual test objects. *Journal of the Optical Society of America,* 1953, 43, 495–501.

Riggs, L. A., and Schick, A. M. L. Accuracy of retinal image stabilization achieved with a plane mirror on a tightly fitting ·contact lens. *Vision Research,* 1968, 8, 159–69.

Rimland, B. *Infantile autism.* New York: Appleton-Century-Crofts, 1964.

Rogers, C. *Client-centered therapy: Its current practice, implications, and theory.* Boston: Houghton, 1951.

———. *On becoming a person.* Boston: Houghton, 1961.

Rogers, D. A. Factors underlying differences in alcohol preference among inbred strains of mice. *Psychosomatic Medicine,* 1966, 28, 498–513.

Romer, A. *Man and the vertebrates.* Baltimore, Md.: Penguin, 1962.

Rorschach, H. *Psychodiagnostics.* New York: Grune and Stratton, and Berne: Hans Huber, 1942.

Rosaldo, Michelle Z., and Lamphere, Louise (eds.). *Woman, culture, and society.* Stanford, Calif.: Stanford University Press. 1974.

Rose, A. M. Army policies toward Negro soldiers. *Ann. Amer. Acad. Pol. Soc. Sci.,* 1946, 244, 90–94.

Rosen, B. C., and D'Andrade, R. The psychosocial origins of achievement motivation. *Sociometry,* 1959, 22, 185–218.

Rosenberg, M. J. Cognitive structure and attitudinal effect. *Journal of Abnormal and Social Psychology,* 1956, 53, 367–72.

Rosenhan, D. On being sane in insane places. *Science,* 1973, 179, 250–58.

Rosenhan, D.; DeWilde, D.; and McDougal, S. Pressure to conform and logical problem solving. *Psychological Reports,* 1963, 13, 227–30.

Rosenthal, D. Changes in some moral values following psychotherapy. *Journal of Consulting Psychology,* 1955, 19, 431–36.

Rosenthal, R., and Jacobson, L. *Pygmalion in the classroom—Teacher expectation and pupils' intellectual development.* New York: Holt, 1968.

Rosenzweig, M. R. Auditory localization. *Scientific American,* 1961, (October). Reprinted in R. Held and W. Richards (Eds.), *Perception: Mechanisms and models.* San Francisco: Freeman, 1972.

Rozenzweig, M. R.; Bennett, E. L.; and Diamond, M. C. Brain changes in response to experience. *Scientific American,* 1972, 226, 22–29.

Rosenzweig, M. R. and Teiman, A. L. Brain functions. *Annual review of psychology,* Vol. 19. Palo Alto, Ca.: Annual Reviews, Inc., 1968.

Ross, L.; Lepper, M. R., and Hubbard, M. Perseverance in self-perception and social perception. Biased attributional processes in the debriefing paradigm. *Journal of Personality and Social Psychology,* 1975, 32, 880–92.

Rotter, J. *Social learning and clinical psychology.* Englewood Cliffs, N.J.: Prentice-Hall, 1954.

———. Some problems and misconceptions related to the construct of internal versus external control of reinforcement. *Journal of Consulting and Clinical Psychology,* 1975, 43 (1), 56–67.

Rousseau, J. J. *Emile* (1762), *Julie* (1761), *and other writings* S. E. Frost, Jr. (Ed.) Woodbury, New York: Barron, 1964.

Routtenberg, A. Current status of the two-arousal hypothesis. Paper presented at the International Congress of Psychology. London: July, 1969.

———. The two-arousal hypothesis: Reticular formation and the limbic system. *Psychological Review,* 1968, 75, 51–80.

Rozelle, R. M.; Evans, R. I; Lasiter, T. M.; Dembroski, T. M.; and Allen, B. P. Need for approval as related to the effects of persuasive communications in actual, reported, and intended behavior change—a viable predictor? *Psychological Reports,* 1973, 33, 719–25.

Rozin, P. Novel diet preferences in vitamin-deficient rats and rats recovered from vitamin deficiency. *Journal of Comparative Psychology,* 1967, 63, 421–28.

Rubin, Z. Liking and loving. In Z. Rubin (Ed.) *Doing unto others.* Englewood Cliffs, N.J.: Prentice-Hall, 1975.

Rugg, H. *Imagination.* New York: Harper & Row, 1963.

Rumbaugh, Duane M., and Gill, Timothy V. Reading and sentence completion by a chimpanzee. *Science,* 1973, 182, 731–33.

Russell, B. *The Conquest of Happiness.* New York: H. Liveright, 1930.

———. *Mysticism and logic and other essays.* London: Longmans, Green, 1921.

Rutter, M. *Maternal deprivation reassessed.* Harmondsworth, Middlesex, England: Penguin Books, 1972.

Sade, Donald Stone. The evolution of sociality. *Science,* 1975, 190, 261–63.

Safer, D., and Allen, R. *Hyperactive children: Diagnosis and management.* Baltimore, Md.: University Park Press, 1976.

Salapatek, P., and Kessen, W. Visual scannings of triangles by the human newborn. *Journal Experimental Child Psychology,* 1966, 3, 155–67.

Sameroff, A. J., and Chandler, M. J. Reproductive risk and the continuum of caretaking casualty. In F. D. Horowitz, E. M. Hetherington, S. Scarr-Salapatek, and J. Siegel (Eds), *Review of child development research,* Vol. 4. Chicago: University of Chicago Press, 1974.

Sanford, F. Across the secretary's desk: Statement on mental health legislation. *American Psychologist,* 1955, 10, 221–24.

Sansweet, S. J. *The punishment cure.* N.Y.: Mason/Charter Publishers, Inc., 1975.

Sarbin, T. R., and Coe, W. C. *Hypnosis: A social psychological analysis of influence communication.* New York: Holt, 1972.

Sarbin, T. R., and Miller, J. E. Demonism revisited: The XYY chromosomal anomaly. *Issues in Criminology,* 1970, 5 (2), 195–208.

Sargant, W. *Battle for the mind: The mechanics of indoctrination, brainwashing and thought control.* Baltimore, Md.: Penguin, 1961.

Schachter, S. *Psychology of affiliation.* Stanford: Stanford University Press, 1959.

Schachter, S., and Gross, L. P. Manipulated time and eating behavior. *Journal of Personality and Social Psychology,* 1968, 10, 98–106.

Schachter, S., and Singer, J. Cognitive, social and physiological determinants of emotional state. *Psychological Review,* 1962, 69, 379–99.

Schacter, S., and Wheeler, L. Epinephrine, chlorpromazine and amusement. *Journal of Abnormal and Social Psychology,* 1962, 65, 121–28.

Scheinfeld, A. *Your heredity and environment.* Philadelphia: Lippincott, 1965.

Scoville, W. B. Loss of recent memory after bilateral hippocampal lesions. *Journal of Neurology, Neurosurgery,* and *Psychiatry,* 1957, 20, 11–21.

Sears, Robert M. Sources of life satisfaction of the Terman gifted men. *American Psychologist,* 1977, 32, 119–28.

Sears, R. R., and Feldman, S. S. *The seven ages of man.* Palo Alto, Calif.: William Kaufman, Inc., 1973.

Sechrest, L. Personality. In M. R. Rosenzweig and L. W. Porter (eds), *Annual review of psychology,* Vol. 27. Palo Alto, Calif.: Annual Reviews, Inc., 1976. pp. 1–28.

Sebeak, T. (ed.). *Animal communication.* Bloomington, Ind.: University of Indiana Press, 1968.

Segal, M. H., et al. Cultural differences in perception of geometric illusions. *Science,* 1963, 139, 769–71.

Sekuler, R., and Levinson, E. The perception of moving targets. *Scientific American,* 1977, *236,* 60–73.

Seligman, Martin E. P. *Helplessness: On depression, development, and death.* San Francisco: W. H. Freeman & Co. 1975.

———. Chronic fear produced by unpredictable electric shock. *Journal of Comparative and Physiological Psychology,* 1968, 66, 402–11.

Selye, H. *The stress of life.* New York: Knopf, 1953.

Shaefler, K. and London, P. Differential effects of hypnotic susceptibility on cognitive and motor performance. *Proceedings, 77th Annual Convention of the American Psychological Association.* 1969, 4, 909–10.

Shaw, M. E. A comparison of two types of leadership in various communication nets. *Journal of Abnormal and Social Psychology.* 1955, 50, 127–34.

Sheinfeld, Amram. *Twins and supertwins.* Baltimore, Md: Penguin, 1967.

Sheldon, W. H., and Stevens, S. S. *The varieties of temperament.* New York: Harper & Row, 1942.

Shepard, R. N. Recognition memory for words, sentences, and pictures. *Journal of Verbal Learning and Behavior,* 1967, 6, 156–63.

Sheppard, J. R.; Albersheim, P.; and McClearn, G. E. Enzyme activities and ethanol preference in mice. *Biochem. Genet.,* 1968, 2, 205–12.

Sherif, M. A study of some social factors in perception. *Archives of Psychology,* 1935, 27 (187)

Sherif, M., and Hovland, C. I. *Social judgment.* New Haven: Yale University Press, 1961.

Siffre, Michel. Six months alone in a cave. *National Geographic.* March 1975, 426–35.

Sigall, H., and Landy, D. Radiating beauty: Effects of having a physically attractive partner on person perception. *Journal of personality and social psychology,* 1973, 28, 218–24.

Sills, D. (Ed.). *International encyclopedia of the social sciences.* Vol. 2. New York: Macmillan, 1968.

Simons, E. L. Ramapithecus. *Scientific American,* 1977, *236,* No. 5, 28–35.

Skinner, B. F. *Beyond freedom and dignity.* New York: Knopf, 1971.

———. *Contingencies of reinforcement: A theoretical analysis.* New York: Appleton-Century-Crofts, 1969.

———. *Science and human behavior.* New York: Macmillan, 1953.

———. Superstition in the pigeon. *Journal of Experimental Psychology,* 1948, 38, 168–72.

———. *Verbal behavior.* New York: Appleton-Century-Crofts, 1957.

———. *Walden two.* New York: Macmillan, 1948.

Sloane, R. B.; Stapes, F. R.; Cristol, A. H.; Yorkston. N. J.; and Whipple, K. Patient characteristics and outcome in psychotherapy and behavior therapy. *Journal of Consulting and Clinical Psychology,* 1976, 44, 330–39.

———. *Psychotherapy versus behavior therapy.* Cambridge, Mass: Harvard University Press, 1975.

Slotnick, R. S.; Liebert, R. M.; and Hilgard, E. R. The enhancement of muscular performance in hypnosis through exhortation and involving instructions. *Journal of Personality,* 1965, 33, 37–45.

Small, Maurice M., and Hull, Ethel I. Clinical applications of biofeedback technology: A review of the literature and five case histories. *Catalog of Selected Documents in Psychology,* 1975 (Fall), 5, 337.

Smith, J. C. Meditation as psychotherapy: A review of the literature. *Psychological Bulletin,* 1975, 82, 558–64.

Smith, S. M.; Brown, H. O.; Toman, J. E. P.; and Goodman, L. S. The lack of cerebral effects of d-tubocurarine. *Anesthesiology,* 1947, 8, 1–14.

Snyder, I. W., and Pronko, N. H. *Vision with spatial inversion.* Witchita, Ks.: University of Wichita Press, 1952.

Snyder, S. H. Opiate receptors and internal opiates. *Scientific American,* 1977, 236, 44–56.

Sokolov, A. N. Speechmotor afferentiation and the problem of brain mechanisms of thought. *Soviet Psychology,* 1967, 6, 3–15.

Sorensen, R. C. *Adolescent sexuality in contemporary america* (The Sorensen Report). New York: World Publishing, 1973.

Spearman, C. E. *The abilities of man: Their nature and measurement.* New York: Macmillan, 1927.

Spelt, D. K. The conditioning of the human fetus in utero. *Journal of Experimental Psychology,* 1948, 38, 338–46.

Sperling, G. The information available in brief visual presentations. *Psychological Monographs,* 1960, 74, No. 11, (Whole No. 498).

Sperry, R. W. Hemisphere deconnection and unity in conscious awareness. *American Psychologist,* 1968, 23, 723–33.

Spielberger, C. D. *Anxiety: Current trends in theory and research.* New York: Academic Press, 1972.

Spitz, R. Smiling response: A contribution to the ontogenesis of social relations. In J. L. Despert and H. O. Pierce (Eds), *Relations of emotional adjustment to intelligence function.* Provincetown, Mass.: Journal Press, 1946.

Stagner, R. *Psychology of personality.* New York: Mc-Graw-Hill, 1961.

Stampfl, T. G., and Levis, D. J. The essentials of implosive therapy: A learning theory based on psychodynamic behavioral therapy. *Journal of Abnormal Psychology,* 1967, 72, 496–503.

Stern, Curt. *Principles of human genetics.* San Francisco: W. H. Freeman & Co, 1973.

Stern, W. *Differentielle psychologie in ihren methodischen grundlagen.* Leipzig: Barth, 1911.

Sternbach, R. A., and Tursky, B. Ethnic differences among housewives in psychophysical and skin potential responses to electric shock. *Psychophysiology,* 1965, 1, 241.

Stevens, S. S.; Warshafsky, F., and the editors of *Life. Sound and hearing.* New York: Life Science Library, 1965.

Stevenson, H. W. Learning in children. In P. H. Mussen (Ed.), *Carmichael's manual of child psychology, 3rd ed.,* New York: John Wiley, 1970.

Stevenson, R. L. *Strange case of Dr. Jekyll and Mr. Hyde and other stories.* London: Longmans, Green, 1886.

Stogdill, R. M. Personal factors associated with leadership. *Journal of Psychology,* 1948, 23, 36–71.

Stone, L. J.; Smith, H. T.; and Murphy, L. B. (eds.). The competent infant: Research and commentary, New York: Basic Books, 1973.

Stoner, J. A. F. A comparison of individual and group decisions including risk. Unpublished master's thesis, School of Industrial Management, M.I.T., 1961. Cited in R. Brown, *Social Psychology* New York: Macmillan, 1965.

Stratton, G. M. Vision without inversion of the retinal image. *Psychological Review,* 1897, 4, 341–481.

Stricker, L. J., and Ross, J. A description and evaluation of the Myers-Briggs type indicator. *Research Bulletin 62-6.* Princeton, N.J.: Educational Testing Service, 1962.

Strongman, K. T. *The psychology of emotion.* New York: Wiley, 1973.

Strupp, H. H., and Handley, S. W. A tripartite model of mental health and therapeutic outcomes. *American Psychologist,* 1977, 32, 187–96.

Stunkard, A. Obesity and the denial of hunger. *Psychosomatic Medicine,* 1969, 21, 281–89.

Stuart, R. B., and Davis, B. *Slim chance in a fat world: Behavioral control of obesity.* Champaign, Ill.: Research Press, 1972.

Suedfeld, P. The clinical relevance of reduced sensory stimulation. *Canadian Psychological Review,* 1975, 16, 88–103.

————. The benefits of boredom: Sensory deprivation reconsidered. *American Scientist,* 1975, 63, 60–68.

Suedfeld, P., and Buchanan, E. Sensory deprivation and autocontrolled aversive stimulation in the reduction of snake avoidance. *Canadian Journal of Behavior Science,* 1974, 6, 105–11.

Suedfeld, P., and Ikard, E. F. Use of sensory deprivation in facilitating the reduction of cigarette smoking. *Journal of Consulting and Clinical Psychology,* 1974, 42, 888–95.

Swets, J. A. Is there a sensory threshold? *Science,* 1961, 134, 168–77.

Tanner, J. M. Physical Growth. In P. H. Mussen (Ed.), *Carmichael's manual of child psychology,* 3d ed. New York: John Wiley, 1970.

Tart, C. T. *Altered states of consciousness.* New York: Wiley, 1969.

Taub, J. M.; Tanguay, P. E.; and Clarkson, D. Effects of daytime naps on performance and mood in a college student population. *Journal of Abnormal Psychology,* 1976, 85, 210–17.

Tavris, Carol. The end of the IQ slump. *Psychology Today,* April 1976, 9, 69–74.

Tavris, C., and Offir, C. *The Longest War.* Harcourt, Brace, Jovanovich, 1977.

Teevan, R. C., and Birney, R. C. (eds). *Color vision.* New York: Van Nostrand, 1961.

Tepperman, J. *Metabolic and endocrine physiology: An introductory text.* (2d ed.) Chicago: Year Book Medical Publishers, 1969.

Terman, L. M. *The measurement of intelligence.* Boston: Houghton Mifflin, 1916.

Terman, L. M., and Merrill, M. A. *Measuring intelligence.* Boston: Houghton Mifflin, 1937.

————. *Stanford-Binet intelligence scale.* Boston: Houghton Mifflin, 1937 and 1960.

Teuber, M. L. Sources of ambiguity in the prints of Maurits C. Escher. *Scientific American,* 1974, 231, 90–104.

Thigpen, C., and Cleckley, H. M. *The three faces of Eve.* New York: McGraw-Hill, 1957.

Thorndike, E. L. *The elements of psychology.* New York: Seiler, 1905.

————. The psychology of learning. *Educational Psychology.* Vol. 11. New York: Teachers College of Columbia University, 1913.

Thorpe, W. H. *Learning and instinct in animals.* (2d ed.) London: Methuen, 1963.

Thorpe, W. H. The process of song learning in the chaffinch as studied by means of the sound spectrograph. *Nature,* 1954, 173, 465–69.

Thurlow, W(illard) R. Audition. In Kling, J. W., and Riggs, L. A., *Woodworth and Schlosberg's experimental psychology* (3rd ed). New York: Holt, 1971.

Thurstone, L. L., and Chave, E. J. *The measurement of attitude.* Chicago: University of Chicago, 1929.

Thurstone, L. L., and Thurstone, T. G. Factorial studies of intelligence. *Psychometric Monographs, No. 2,* 1941.

Tietze, C., and Lewit, S. Legal abortion. *Scientific American,* 1977, 236, 21–27.

Tiger, Lionel. *Men in groups.* New York: Random House, 1969.

Time, August 21, 1972, 100, 34–40.

Tizard, B., and Ress, J. A comparison of the effects of adoption, restoration to the natural mother, and continued institutionalization. *Child Development,* 1974, 45, 92–99.

Tobias, Jerry V. (Ed.). *Foundations of modern auditory theory.* Vol. 1. Orange, N.J.: Academica, 1970.

Tolman, E. C., and Honzik, C. H. Introduction and removal of reward and maze performance in rats. *University of California Publications in Psychology,* 1930, 4, 257–75.

Triesman, A. M. Strategies and models of selective attention. *Psychological Review,* 1969, 76, 282–99.

Trow, D. Autonomy and job satisfaction in taskoriented groups. *Journal of Abnormal Social Psychology,* 1957, 54, 204–9.

Tryon, R. C. Genetic differences in maze learning in rats. *The thirty-ninth yearbook.* National Society for the Study of Education. Bloomington, Ill.: Public School Publications, 1940.

Tsang, Y. C. Hunger motivation in gastrectomized rats. *Journal of Comparative Psychology.* 1938, 26, 1–17.

Tucker, D., and Smith, J. C. The chemical senses. *Annual Review of Psychology.* Vol. 20. Palo Alto, Calif.: Annual Reviews, 1969.

Tyler, L. E. *The Psychology of Human Differences.* New York: Appleton, 1956.

Twitmeyer, E. B. *A study of the knee-jerk.* Philadelphia: University of Pennsylvania, 1902.

Ulrich, R. E.; Stachnik, T. J., and Stainton, N. R. Student acceptance of Generalized Personality Interpretations. *Psychological Reports,* 1963, 13, 831–34.

Ungar, G. (ed.). *Molecular mechanisms in memory and learning.* New York: Plenum Publishing, 1970.

U.S. Department of Commerce. Bureau of the Census. *Statistical abstract of the United States,* 1976. Washington, D.C.: U.S. Government Printing Office, 1977.

US Bureau of the Census. Marital status and living arrangements: March 1977. Washington DC: US Government printing office, 1977.

Uttal, W. R. *The psychobiology of sensory coding.* New York: Harper & Row, 1973.

Valenstein, E. *Brain control: A critical examination of brain stimulation and psychosurgery.* N.Y.: Wiley, 73.

Valenstein, E.; Cox, V.; and Kakolewski, J. Modification of motivated behavior elicited by electrical stimulation of the hypothalamus. *Science,* 1968a, 159, 1119–21.

Valenstein, E., et al. The motivation underlying eating elicited by lateral hypothalamic stimulation. *Physiology and Behavior,* 1968b, 3, 969–71.

———. Re-examination of the role of the hypothalamus in motivation. *Psychological Review,* 1970, 77, 16–31.

Veda, K.; Hara, T. J.; and Garbman, A. Electroencephalographic studies on olfactory discrimination in adult spawning salmon. *Comparative Biochemistry and Physiology,* 1967, 21, 133–43.

Vogel, G., and Traub, A. REM deprivation—the effects on schizophrenic patients. *Archives of General Psychiatry,* 1969, 18, 287–300.

Von Bekesy, G(eorge). The ear. *Scientific American,* 1957. (August). Reprinted in R. Held and W. Richards (Eds.), *Perception: Mechanisms and models.* San Francisco: Freeman, 1972.

Von Helmholtz, H. L. F. *Physiological optics.* Vol. 2. Tr. by J. P. Southall. New York: Optical Society of America, 1924.

Wade, Nicholas. IQ and heredity: Suspicion of fraud beclouds classic experiment. *Science,* 26 Nov. 1976, 194, 916.

Wahler, R. G. Infant social development: Some experimental analyses of an infant-mother interaction during the first year of life. *Journal of Experimental Child Psychology,* 1969, 7, 101–13.

Wallach, M. A.; Kogan, N.; and Bem, D. J. Group influence on individual risk-taking. *Journal of Abnormal and Social Psychology,* 1962, 65, 75–86.

Walster, E. Review of *Men in groups* by Lionel Tiger, in *Contemporary Psychology,* June 1970, 398 ff.

Warner, W. L.; Meeker, M.; and Eels, K. *Social class in America: A manual of procedure for the measurement of social status.* Chicago: Science Research Associates, 1949.

Washborn, S. L., and DeVore, Irven. The social life of baboons. *Scientific American,* 1961, 204, 62–71.

Watson, J. B., and Rayner, R. Conditioned emotional reactions. *Journal of Experimental Psychology,* 1920, 3, 1–14.

Watson, R. I. *The great psychologists: Aristotle to Freud.* Philadelphia: Lippincott, 1963.

Waugh, N. C., and Norman, D. A. Primary memory. *Psychological Review,* 1965, 72, 89–104.

Weaver, W. *Lady luck: The theory of probability.* New York: Doubleday, 1963.

Webb, E. J.; Campbell, D. T.; Schwartz, R. D.; and Sechrest, L. *Unobtrusive measures: Nonreactive research in the social sciences.* Chicago: Rand McNally, 1966.

Webb, W. B. Sleep behavior as a biorhythm. In P. Coloquohon (Ed.) *Biological Rhythm and Human Performance.* London: Academic Press, 1971

Wechsler, D. *Manual for the Wechsler adult intelligence scale*. New York: Psychological Corporation, 1955.

————. *Measurement of adult intelligence*. Baltimore: Williams and Wilkins, 1939.

Weidenweich, Franz. The human brain in the light of its phylogenetic development. *The Scientific Monthly*, 1948, 67, 103–9.

Weinberg, M. S., and Williams, C. J. *Male homosexuals: Their problems and adaptations*. New York: Oxford University Press, 1974.

Weintraub, D. J. Perception. In M. R. Rosenzweig and L. W. Porter (Eds.), *Annual review of psychology*, Vol. 26. Palo Alto, Calif.: Annual Reviews, Inc., 1976.

Weiss, J. M. Effects of coping responses on stress. *Journal of Comparative and Physiological Psychology*, 1968, 65, 251–60.

Wendt, G. R. Vestibular function. In S. S. Stevens (ed.), *Handbook of experimental psychology*. New York: Wiley, 1951.

Wheeler, H. *Beyond the punitive society: Operant conditioning, social and political aspects*. San Francisco: W. H. Freeman, 1973.

White, P. L. *Human infants. Experience and psychological development*. Englewood Cliffs, N.Y.: Prentice-Hall, 1971.

Whorf, B. L. *Language, thought and reality*. New York: Wiley, 1956.

Williams, C. D. The elimination of tantrum behavior by extinction procedures. *Journal of Abnormal and Social Psychology*, 1959, 59, 269.

Williams, R. J. *Biochemical individuality*. New York: Wiley, 1956.

Williams, R. L. *The drug takers*. New York: Time, 1965.

Williams, R. L.; Agnew, H. W., Jr.; and Webb, W. B. Sleep patterns in young adults. An EEG study. *EEG Clinical Neurophysiology*, 1964, 17, 376–81.

Wilson, E. K. *Sociology: Rules, roles and relationships*. Homewood, Ill.: Dorsey, 1971.

Wilson, Edward O. *Sociobiology: The new synthesis*. Cambridge, Mass.: Harvard U. Press, 1975.

Winterbottom, M. R. The relation of childhood training in independence to achievement motivation. *Dissertation Abstracts*, 1953, 13, 440–41.

————. The relation of need for achievement to learning experiences in independence and mastery. In J. W. Atkinson (Ed), *Motives in fantasy, action, and society*. Princeton, N.J.: Van Nostrand, 1958.

Wohlwill, J. F. *The study of behavioral development*. New York: Academic Press, 1973.

Wolff, P. H. Observations on newborn infants. *Psychosomatic Medicine*, 1959, 21, 110–18.

Wolpe, J. *Psychotherapy by reciprocal inhibition*. Stanford, Calif.: Stanford University, 1958.

Wolpe, J., and Lazarus, A. *Behavior therapy techniques: A guide to the treatment of neuroses*. New York: Pergamon, 1966.

Wynne-Edwards, V. C. *Animal dispersion in relation to social behavior*. Edinburgh and London: Oliver and Boyd, 1962.

Yin, T. C. T., and Mountcastle, V. B. Visual input to the visuomotor mechanisms of the monkey's parietal lobe. *Science*, 1977, *197*, No. 4311, 1381–83.

Yukl, G. Toward a behavioral theory of leadership. *Organizational Behavior and Human Performance*, 1971, 6, 414–40.

Zeigarnik, B. Das Behalten erledigter and uneriedigter Handlungen. (The memory of completed and uncompleted actions). *Psychol. Forsch.*, 1927, 9, 1–85.

Zigler, E.; Levine, J.; and Gould, L. Cognitive challenge as a factor in children's humor appreciations. *Journal of Personality and Social Psychology*, 1967, 6, 332–36.

Zigler, E., and Phillips, L. Psychiatric diagnosis and symptomatalogy. *Journal of Abnormal and Social Psychology*, 1961, 63, 69–75.

Zimbardo, P. G. Shyness: What it is and what to do about it. Menlo Park, Calif.: Addison-Wesley Publishing Company, 1977.

Zimbardo, P. G.; Ebbesen, E. B; and Maslach, C. *Influencing attitudes and changing behavior*. (2nd ed). Reading, Mass: Addison-Wesley Publishing Company, 1977.

Zimbardo, Philip G.; Marshal, Gary; White, Greg; and Maslach, Christina. Objective assessment of hypnotically induced time distortion. *Science*, 1975, 181, 282–84.

Zimmerman, R. R. Analysis of discrimination learning capacities in the infant rhesus monkey. *Journal of Comparative and Physiological Psychology*, 1961, 54, 1–10.

Zotterman, Y., and Schade, J. P. (Eds.). *Sensory mechanisms (Progress in Brain Research)*. Vol. 23. London: Elsevier, 1967.

Zubeck, J. P.; Pushkar, D.; Sansom, W.; and Gowing, J. Perceptual changes after prolonged sensory isolation (darkness and silence). *Canadian Journal of Psychology*, 1961, 15, 83–100.

Zuckerman, M(arvin). Hallucinations, reported sensations, and images. In J. P. Zubek (Ed.). *Sensory deprivation: Fifteen years of research*. New York: Appleton-Century-Crofts, 1969.

Illustration credits

Name index

Maharishi Mahesh Yogi, 321
Mahoney, M. J., 167, 566
Maier, 415
Maincastle, 74
Mainord, Willard, 555
Malinowski, Bronislaw, 41
Malthus, Thomas, 563
Mandler, George, 218
Mann, J., 201
Mann, R. B., 574
Marcuse, Herbert, 618
Mark, V. H., 64, 83, 521
Marks, 161
Marquis, 584
Marshall, J. R., 207, 230
Martella, J. A., 575
Maslach, 230, 604
Maslow, Abraham, 192, 210, 212, 403, 404, 418, 477
Mason, William A., 36
Masters, W. H., 516, 551
Mattern, C. F. T., 107
May, R., 452
Mead, M., 36, 40, 450
Meduna, L. J., 536
Meehl, Paul E., 338, 339, 511
Meglitsch, P., 66
Melhuish, E., 369
Meltzoff, A. N., 364
Melzack, R., 99, 101, 102, 103
Mendel, Gregor, 53
Menninger, K. A., 440
Meredith, H., 362-63
Merrill, M. A., 9
Mesmer, Franz Anton, 304, 308, 543
Metfessel, N., 347
Meyer, Adolph, 7
Milgram, Stanley, 585, 586, 587
Miller, G. A., 149, 280, 455
Miller, J. E., 393
Miller, N. E., 6, 95, 169, 204, 223, 429, 441, 547
Mills, M., 369
Milne, L. J., 104
Milne, M., 104
Milner, P. M., 74, 189, 233, 277
Mischel, W., 408
Moffitt, A. R., 47
Mohr, J. P., 555
Molyneux, William, 127
Money, J., 201, 411
Montagu, A., 36, 50, 58, 67, 158
Mook, D. G., 57
Moore, M. K., 364
Moray, Neville, 93
Morgan, Elaine, 54, 209
Morison, S. E., 40
Morris, D., 36, 57, 157, 221
Morse, S., 455
Moul, M., 349

Mountcastle, V. B., 93, 104, 109
Mower, O. H., 46, 49, 252, 267, 415
Moyer, K. E., 208
Mueller, C. G., 112
Mueller, R. M., 112
Mullins, 368
Munn, N. L., 112
Murphy, G., 6, 185, 399, 449
Murphy, L. B., 363, 366, 368
Mussen, Paul H., 47, 137
Myers, Joseph, 399

N

Naruse, Osake, 163
Nau, S., 302
Neale, J. M., 517, 526
Neugarten, B. L., 379, 380
Newcomb, T. M., 602
Newman, Horatio H., 43
Nievergelt, J., 265
Nisbett, R. E., 195
Norman, D. A., 275, 290
Nye, F. I., 485

O

Offir, C., 410
Ogle, Michael, 307
Olds, J., 189, 233
O'Leary, K. D., 550
O'Neill, G., 487
O'Neill, N., 487
Oriis, J. B., 575
Orne, M. T., 96, 307, 587
Ornstein, Robert E., 76, 299
Orwell, George, 164
Osgood, E. E., 597, 599
Owen, Paul T., 260

P

Pahnke, Walter, 315
Paivio, A., 263, 285
Palyak, S., 114
Paré, Ambroise, 102
Patrick, G. T. W., 301
Paul, L. A., 103, 308
Pavlov, Ivan, 7, 9, 103, 159, 160, 162, 505, 509, 543
Pearlman, J., 552
Pearson, K., 349
Peck, R. C., 83, 362
Pei, M., 253
Penfield, Wilder, 79, 273, 276, 285
Pengelley, Eric T., 37
Pettigrew, T. S., 147, 606
Pfeiffer, J. E., 54, 67, 68
Phares, E. J., 412, 415
Phillips, L., 510
Piaget, Jean, 47, 241, 358, 359, 360, 374, 383
Pinel, Phillippe, 507, 508

Poser, E. G., 102
Postman, L., 147, 290
Potter, Stephen, 552
Premack, David, 50
Pribam, Karl H., 80, 96
Prince, Morton, 514
Proshansky, 10
Proust, Marcel, 289
Purcell, K., 517

R

Ramsay, A. O., 45
Raskin, Evelyn, 403
Raven, B. H., 572
Rayner, R., 224
Redlich, F., 510, 511
Rees, J., 368, 517
Reifler, C. B., 308
Reis, H., 455
Rheingold, H. L., 253, 369
Richards, I. A., 254
Richards, William A., 315
Richardson, A., 244
Rieff, P., 286
Riesen, A. H., 141
Riggs, L. A., 94, 97
Riley, D. A., 290
Rimland, B., 39, 249
Rivlin, 10
Rogers, C., 317, 403, 418, 543, 546
Romer, A., 104
Roosevelt, Franklin, 575
Rorschach, Hermann, 9, 415
Rose, A. M., 608
Rosen, B. C., 489
Rosenberg, S. S., 317, 599
Rosenhan, D., 394, 402, 504, 510, 585
Rosenman, R. F., 220
Rosenthal, Robert, 349
Rosenzweig, M. R., 96, 97, 111, 158
Ross, L., 587
Rotter, Julian, 414, 415
Rousseau, Jean Jacques, 33, 59
Rozelle, R. M., 600
Rozin, P., 107
Rubin, M., 108, 482
Rugg, Harold, 263
Rumbaugh, Duane M., 50
Rush, Benjamin, 507, 508
Russell, Bertrand, 23, 483
Rutter, M., 370

S

Safer, D., 316
Salapatek, P., 131
Sameroff, A. J., 370
Sanford, Fillmore, 12
Sansweet, S. J., 552
Sapir, Edward, 260
Sarbin, T. R., 309, 393

Y–Z

Yin, T. C. T., 93
Yonkston, N. J., 556
Young, 170

Yuille, J. C., 285
Yukly, G., 575
Zamenhoff, Lidovic, 253
Zeigarnik, B., 278
Zigler, E., 230, 510

Zimbardo, P. G., 149, 204, 259, 511, 604
Zimmerman, R. R., 128
Zotterman, Y., 106
Zubek, J. P., 96
Zuckerman, Marvin, 96

Subject index

Eye, structure of, 113–15
  cornea, 113
  iris, 113
  lens, 113, 114
  retina, 113, 114
    fovea, 114–15
    rods, 114–15
Eye/head system, 137–38

F

Facial expression, 111–12
Fact, 16
Family, 564
Fantasy, 435
Fear, 230
Feeble-mindedness, 345
Feedback, 174, 176
Feeling-of-knowing experience, 287, 288
Feelings, 222–23
Feral children, 47
  language learning, 248
Fetishism, 524
Fetus, 362–63
Field method of science, 16–19
Figure-ground organization of perception, 130, 132–33
Figures (data), 635
Finger drumming, 518–19
Fixation, emotional, 515
Flattened effect, 524–25
Flooding (therapy), 554
Foot-in-the-door technique, 605
Forgetting, 288
Formal operations, 360
France, alcoholism, 317
Free association, 303
Freedom, 626
Frequency distribution, 636
Frequency polygon, 638
Friends, Society of, 299
Friendship, 476–80
Frustration, 425–26
Fugue state, 513
Functional disorders, 506, 509
Functional groups, 564

G

Galvanic skin response, 220, 339
Gambling, 23
Gaussian curve, 643
Generalization principle, 161–62
Genetic engineering, 51 n
Genetics, 32, 50–52, 345
Genital stage of development, 358, 400–401
Gestalt psychology, 126, 403
  perception, 132, 135–36
Gestation, 362
Gifted children, 349

Gonorrhea, 464
Grammar, 245–46
Grand mal epilepsy, 527
Graphic presentation, 636
Graphology, 389
Grasping reflex, 363
Group, 567
  behavior, 579
  communication, 577
  inhibition of individual action, 586
  membership categories, 568
  power structure, 572
  reference, 579
Group marriage, 487
Group psychotherapy, 539
Grouping, 130, 134–37
  memory, 280
Guttman Scale, 597

H

Homeostasis, 185–86, 598
Homosexuality, 460, 467–71
Hospital of St. Mary of Bethlehem (London), 506
Hub-threshold stimuli, 72
Hue, 113
Human development, 356
  environmental view, 358
  epigenetic or interaction view, 358
  maturational view, 358
  theories of, 357
Human nature, 34–36
Humanistic theory of personality, 399
Humoral fluids, 394
Hunger, 189, 192–98
  crackerjack effect, 195–96
  physiology of, 192–94
  psychology of, 194–96
Hyperactive children, 316
  drug treatment, 538
Hypermnesia, 306
Hypertension, 517–18
Hypnosis, 299, 304–9
  affect on learning, 306
  conditioning, 163
  mass, 306
  medical uses, 308
  motivation, 307
  physiology control, 307
  psychotherapy, 308
  susceptibility, 309
Hypnotic anesthesia, 308
Hypoanalysis, 308
Hypoglycemia, 193
Hypomania, 524
Hypothalamus, 74, 193–94
Hypothesis, 13, 18
Hysteria, 509
  conversion, 436–37, 512–13

Hysterical neuroses, 512–14
Hysterical personality, 521

I

Id, 432
Idealism, 123
  naive, 123
Idealization, 442
Identification, 408, 441–42
Identity crisis, 401
Ideogram, 332
Ideographic approach to individual differences, 332–34
Idioms, 254
I-E Scale, 415
Illusions, 122, 129, 131
Image retina system, 137–38
Image thinking, 238, 239–44
  visual, 240
Imagery, 239
  aid to verbal thinking, 263
  eidetic, 244
  visual, 240
Imitation, 375
  language, 251
  learning, 171, 173
  social learning theory, 409–10
Implicit learning demands, 372–73
Implosive therapy, 554
Imprinting, 45–46, 369
Impulse-gratification emotions, 233
Inadequate personality, 521
Incentive motivation, 196
  sex, 199
Independent variables, 18
Individual differences, 327
  custom restrictions, 330
  new borns, 364
  politics of, 327
  technology of, 331
Industrial and organizational psychology, 10
Infancy, 359, 363–70; see also Children
  emotional development, 224
  environment, 366–68
  imagery, 241
  individual differences, 364
  language, 250–51
  psychoanalytic theory of development, 400–401
  stress, 367–69
Inference, 22
Information retrieval, 272, 274, 284–92
Information storage, 272, 274–84
Inhibition, 319
  forgetting, 290
Insight, 171
  learning, 176, 239
  thinking, 262

Minnesota Multiphastic Personality Inventory (MMPI), 414, 416
Mode, 20, 639–40
Mongolism, 527
Monogamy, 484
Mood, 456
Moral development, 358, 375
  conventional, 375
  imitation, 375–76
  postconventional, 375
  preconventional, 375
Moral treatment of mental patients, 507
Moro reflex, 363
Morphine, 312–13, 523
Motion parallax, 142
Motivation, 101, 182–211, 429
  antisocial, 208
  deprivation model, 186–87
  hierarchy, 189–92, 210
  hunger, 192–98
  love, 203
  physiology of, 184–92
  sexual, 198–202
  taxonomy, 183–84
Motor neuron, 74
Motor recall, 285
Movement, 125–26, 136, 137–43
  aftereffect, 138
  apparent, 139
  illusion, 137–40
  induced, 138–39
  perception, 125–26, 137–43
  spiral aftereffect, 138
  stroboscopic, 139
Mnemonics, 280–83
Muller-Lyer illusion, 143–44, 145
Multiple personality, 513–14
Multiplexity, 601
Muscular speech, 241
Mutation, 52, 58
Myelin sheath, 69
Myers-Briggs Type Indicator Test, 399
Mystic experience, 404

N

Nailbiting, 518
Names, 564–65
Native American Church, 315
Natural duplicate, 51
Natural language, 254
Natural order, 33
Natural selection, 51–52, 57–58
Nature-nurture controversy, 36–37
Nazis, 33, 36, 586–87
  conditioning, 164
Necker Cube, 132–33
Necking, 463
Needs, 184, 186, 210, 430
Neonate, 363
Neopsychoanalytic stage theory, 401

Neotony, 50
Nerve, 68–69, 71–72
  pressure points, 98–100
Nervous system, 64, 72
Neural impulse, 64
Neurasthenia, 436
Neuron, 69–72
  association, 74
  motor, 74
  sensory, 74
  threshold, 91
Neurosis, 509, 511–17
  hysterical, 512
  traumatic, 516
New brain, 67, 75
Niger-Congo family of languages, 255
Nomethic approach to individual differences, 332, 334
Nominal scaling, 635
Nonsense syllables, 273
Normative approach to individual differences, 332
Nuclear family, 371

O

Observation, 16–18
Observational learning, 171
Obsessions, 439, 514–15
Occipital lobe, 76
Odors, 108
Oedipal complex, 409
Olfaction, 107
Omission behavior, 287
Onanism, 463
Onomatopoeia, 245
Open marriage, 487
Operant conditioning, 158–59, 167–68, 173
  language learning, 253
Operant technology, 167
Opiates, 312
Opinions, 594
Opium, 312
Oral stage of development, 358–59, 400
Ordinal scale, 635
Ordinate, 636
Organic psychiatry, 508
Organismic theory of personality, 399
Orgasm, 201, 463
Overeating, 519–20
Overlearning, 174–75, 283

P

Pain, 101–3
  center in brain, 189
  perception, 121
  psychology of, 102
  psychosomatic, 103
  threshold, 102
  tolerance, 102

Paradoxical thermal sensation, 100
Parameter, 646
Paranoia, 526
Paranoid defenses, 442
Paranoid personality, 521
Paranoid schizophrenia, 525
Parenting, 190, 368
  attachment, 368–69
  caregiving, 368
Paresis, 508, 526
Parietal lobe, 76, 78
Parts of speech, 246
Passive-aggressive people, 521
Passive dependency, 521
Patois, 257
Patterning, 130, 134–36
  memory, 280
Pavlovian conditioning; see Classical conditioning
Pearson product-moment correlation coefficient, 643
Peer culture, 378
Percentile scores, 640, 642
Perception, 10, 120–50
  brain, 91
  evolution of, 122–26
  image, 239
  learning, 126–29
  movement, 125–26, 137–43
  visual, 125–26, 127–28
Perceptual anomalies, 122
Perceptual constancy; see Constancy principle of perception
Perceptual sets, 131–32, 146–47
Perceptual systems
  organization, 128–29, 130, 403
  patterning, 129–30
  stabilizing, 129–30
Personal equation, 335
Personal traits, 406
Personality, 388–418
  definition, 390–92
  dynamics of, 394
  genetic factors, 393
  measurement, 415
  tests, 415–16
  theories of, 392
    dynamic, 399–403
    organic, 394–99
    organismic, 403–5
    trait factor, 405–8
Personality disorders, 509, 520–24
Personality profile, 391
Personnel psychology, 10
Perspective, 142
Petit mal epilepsy, 527
Petting, 463
Peyote, 299
Phallic stage of development, 358, 360, 400

This book has been set in 10 and 9 point Helvetica Light, leaded 2 points. Chapter titles are in 30 point Vanguard Medium and 30 point Vanguard Light. The size of the type page is 37½ by 48 picas.

Perry London was born and raised in Omaha, Nebraska. He attended Yeshiva University in New York for undergraduate studies, and Columbia University for his M.A. and Ph.D. studies, which were completed in 1956. Dr. London served in the U.S. Army Medical Service Corps as a clinical psychologist from 1954 to 1959, and then joined the Psychology faculty at the University of Illinois, Urbana. He has subsequently held appointments at Stanford University and the Hebrew University of Jerusalem, and was a Career Scientist Development Fellow of the National Institute of Mental Health from 1966 to 1971. At present, he is Professor of Psychology and Psychiatry at the University of Southern California and Lecturer in Psychiatry at Harvard University. He has written some 100 theoretical articles and experimental studies on different psychological topics, and several books, including: *The children's hypnotic susceptibility scale* (1963); *The modes and morals of psychotherapy* (1964); *Foundations of abnormal psychology* (with David Rosenhan, 1968); and *Behavior control* (1969; 1977).

The Ponzo illusion The Corinthian columns appear to diminish in size in the distance, but actually the columns in the background are the same size as those in the foreground. Distance perception dominates size perception and develops a misplaced size constancy in our minds.

Color contrast The gray circles are identical in color, but they appear to vary in hue when they are placed on different backgrounds. Your perception of the various hues depends upon how you sense the differences between the colors in contrast to one another.

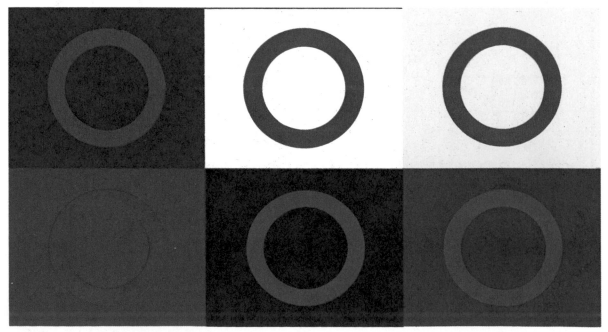